CATALOGUE OF MANUSCRIPTS IN THE INNER TEMPLE

CATALOGUE OF MANUSCRIPTS IN THE LIBRARY OF THE HONOURABLE SOCIETY OF THE INNER TEMPLE

EDITED BY

J. CONWAY DAVIES, M.A., LITT.D.

VOLUME I

The Petyt Collection: MSS. 502–533

PUBLISHED FOR THE MASTERS OF
THE BENCH OF THE INNER TEMPLE
BY
OXFORD UNIVERSITY PRESS
1972

Oxford University Press, Ely House, London W. 1
GLASGOW NEW YORK TORONTO MELBOURNE WELLINGTON
CAPE TOWN IBADAN NAIROBI DAR ES SALAAM LUSAKA ADDIS ABABA
DELHI BOMBAY CALCUTTA MADRAS KARACHI LAHORE DACCA
KUALA LUMPUR SINGAPORE HONG KONG TOKYO

ISBN 0 19 711633 7

PRINTED IN GREAT BRITAIN
AT THE UNIVERSITY PRESS, OXFORD
BY VIVIAN RIDLER
PRINTER TO THE UNIVERSITY

PREFACE

Dr. James Conway Davies died at the age of 79 on 18 July 1971, and it must remain a source of regret that he did not live to see the publication of this catalogue upon which he had been working for the past decade.

Conway Davies was a Master of Arts of the Universities of Wales and Cambridge and a Doctor of Letters of the latter, where he gained the Thelwall Prize in 1917. The greater part of his career was devoted to historical studies and teaching and to the care and publication of original sources for English and Welsh history.

He was for many years honorary archivist to the Church in Wales, the province of Wales and dioceses of St. Davids, Bangor, Llandaff, and St. Asaph, and to the deans and chapters of their cathedral churches, and consulting archivist to the National Library of Wales, the Monmouthshire County Council, and other authorities. In these capacities he did much to encourage the study of the ecclesiastical history of Wales and he was also active in the foundation of the Historical Society of the Church in Wales and honorary editor of its journal.

He held academic posts as Maitland Lecturer at Cambridge and Reader and Head of the Department of Palaeography and Diplomatic in the University of Durham where he was also honorary archivist to the diocese and to the Dean and Chapter of Durham.

Throughout the past fifty years he had contributed several hundred articles to periodicals and the journals of learned societies, including the *English Historical Review*, the *Quarterly Review*, the *Economic Journal*, the *Transactions of the Royal Historical Society*, the *Bulletin of the Institute of Historical Research*, the *Journal of the National Library of Wales*, the *Journal of the Historical Society of the Church in Wales*, and *Y Cymmrodor*.

His published works commenced in 1913 with *The Welsh Revolts of Edward II* and included *Medieval Northumberland* (1918), *The Baronial Opposition to Edward II* (1918), *The First Welsh Assize Roll* (1940), *Records of the Court of Augmentations relating to Wales* (1954), *Welsh Episcopal Acts to 1272*, 2 vols. (1946, 1948), vol. iii in the press, and *Cartae Antiquae* (Pipe Roll Society, 1957). He edited *Studies Presented to Sir Hilary Jenkinson* (1957), to which he was also a contributor.

For some years before and ever since his retirement from academic work he had been an external editor at the Public Record Office, engaged in the classification and cataloguing of the records of the Palatinate of Durham and the Court of Augmentations and the unsorted records of the Prerogative Court of Canterbury in the Principal Probate Registry.

At the time of Dr. Conway Davies's death the introduction, main text, and appendices of the present work were in page proof. These proofs had all been corrected by him, and the typescript of the index had been sent to the printers. It is unfortunate that he was unable to see the index through the press; for an index of this size and complexity needs the knowledge and care of the author from start to finish. Some obvious slips have been corrected, but it must be a matter for regret that the index has not had the benefit of the final careful scrutiny which Dr. Conway Davies would have desired and which only he could give.

As was his custom, Dr. Conway Davies had left the writing of the Preface till the last. Death cut short the completion of this. The full sum of his intentions for the Preface, which he considered to be of importance, cannot now be realized. The following compilation (drawn so far as possible from his own writing) is taken from scraps of draft manuscript, brief notes, his reports to the Bench, and fragments from correspondence, and represents all that is known of what he intended to be included in the Preface. For the omission of material which he intended to insert and the acknowledgements that he wished to make to those who had assisted him on the catalogue no apology is required.

The manuscripts in the Inner Temple Library total 722 volumes, comprising the largest collection in any of the four Inns of Court. They range from the early twelfth to the early twentieth century and are rich in material of historical, legal, and literary interest. The lack hitherto of an adequate catalogue has, however, restricted the use that could be made of the collection by scholars. The present publication is designed to remedy that deficiency.

This catalogue of the manuscripts in the Inner Temple Library has taken a proportion of my time since 1960, when I was invited by the Bench to undertake the work. My instructions were to catalogue all the manuscripts in the Library and to do so in detail. This meant that in such composite volumes as contained hundreds of transcripts of Public Records and in such volumes as contained varying numbers of original documents, ranging from a few to as many as 317, fifty-six volumes have needed 235 pages to fulfil these requirements. It was throughout contemplated that the Catalogue would require three volumes of approximately the number of pages which are here presented.

The following general rules have been followed in the listing of the manuscripts. Each manuscript volume is described in detail with notes on the size, number, and condition of the folios, the material on which it is written, the language used, the handwriting, and an estimated date. In the case of composite volumes each item is prefaced with the number of the folio at which it begins. In addition, an indication is given whether the volume or item is an original document, a draft, or a transcript of an original, and if a transcript whether it is accurate. If other copies are known, their whereabouts are stated, and should the volume or items have been printed before, this is also generally noted and precise references given. In addition, where possible the history and previous ownership of the volume or item has been ascertained.

The work was planned and carried out in four stages. First, the manuscripts were perused and extensive notes made on the content, condition, binding, and other technical matters. Second, the contents which had been printed were keyed with all known printed sources, with references given to the definitive printed text. Third, the notes and printed references were then digested and a draft of what was to appear in the printed catalogue was prepared. Fourth, the draft was revised and typed, and the typed text checked against the draft entries, ready for the press. Fifth, the whole of the printed proofs were checked with the typescript and references, and against a substantial portion of the manuscripts where required.

Introductory notes have been written to each group of manuscripts in the collection. The notes on separate individual volumes contain material on content and technical matters. There is little text in Elizabethan English, in spelling or orthography. The spelling of most extracts has been modernized; less than 1 per cent appears in inverted commas, in the language and spelling of the original. There is some text in Norman French, but apart from the names of writs and processes this is very little. Most of the medieval and Low Latin has been translated. Normally place-names are given in their modern form unless their manuscript form is exceptional or so given in the remainder of the text of the manuscript. As regards personal names, generally the Christian name is given in its modern form; the surname is usually given also in its modern form.

The division of the manuscripts into the five groups was essential and the arrangement within the groups was necessary. The Petyt Collection has borne its press marks for more than 250 years. As is well known, some of the most important Barrington manuscripts were allotted press marks which are associated with the Petyt Collection. It has seemed unnecessary to retransfer them to the Barrington Collection. The Records of the Inner Temple were arranged in classes when the volumes were composed. The Mitford Collection of Legal Manuscripts were listed totally when they arrived in the Library a few years ago. The Miscellaneous Manuscripts have been numbered as they were found in the Library; sometimes a group of manuscripts has been numbered consecutively according to the donor or the subject, and as further manuscripts are discovered, or missing manuscripts retrieved, or additional manuscripts acquired by gift or purchase, they will be added numerically.

Certain of the items in two volumes of the Petyt Collection are calendared or fairly fully summarized in two reports of the Historical Manuscripts Commission: Petyt 538, volumes 46 and 47 in (i) the *2nd Report* (1871), Appendix, and Petyt 538, volume 47 in (ii) the *11th Report* (1888), Appendix IX, Part VII. Where the documents are so dealt with they are treated summarily in this Catalogue, but any additional information which is considered of importance is given, as also the endorsements on the documents. These respective Reports are cited as follows: the *Second Report* as (1), and the *Eleventh Report* as (2). Similarly, many of the items in the Records of the Inner Temple up to the year 1800 are printed or calendared in the *Calendar of the Inner Temple Records.* In fact, most of the items in volumes 1 to 19 of this group are so printed or catalogued. These are referred to briefly only in the text of the Catalogue. In all cases references are given to the printed text. Where there are errors in the transcription or the calendaring or where any essential fact has been omitted, that is stated in the catalogue entry.

It had originally been decided that precise references would be given to all transcripts of Public Records which had been printed or calendared, namely by the Record Commission or in the Calendar series of the Public Record Office. This was done in typescript, but it was found that in order to keep within the limit set it would be necessary to restrict the printed references to such as would be difficult to locate. The problem of giving precise references to printed books for documents and transcripts in the various groups, especially in the Petyt Collection, proved very much more onerous and time-taking that at one time had been supposed. For example, the number of such references in the thirty-eight volumes in Petyt MS. 533 totalled nearly 4,000 items to be looked up and inserted. One volume alone required 227 printed references. The fourteen volumes in Petyt MS. 536, which are also mainly transcripts from the Public Records, required over a thousand references to printed sources from Public Records alone, of which two volumes required 125 and 120 items respectively. The references to printed sources in the following groups of Petyt transcripts from the Public Records, especially from the Chancery Rolls, that is the Charter, Patent, Close, Fine, and Liberate Rolls, and to the records printed by the Record Commission have generally been omitted in the interests of compression and the omission has allowed the purpose of containing the catalogue within the same number of printed pages set:

Petyt MSS.	512	26 volumes
	533	38 volumes
	534/32, 33	2 volumes
	536	14 volumes

In almost all other cases precise references have been given to the sources in which all manuscripts or parts of manuscripts have been printed. These total several hundred volumes dating from the late seventeenth to the mid twentieth century. In the case of Chancery Rolls which have been calendared and the calendars published by the Public Record Office references are given only to the volume of the Calendar. Further references are detailed where the document has been printed in full in other sources, e.g.

Reports on the Dignity of a Peer, *Foedera*, etc., and individual volumes of borough charters. Where Writs of Summons to Parliament are printed in full in *Parliamentary Writs* (entries for Edward I and Edward II) (Record Commission, 1827–34), the references to the *Calendars of Close Rolls* only are given where the references to the *Parliamentary Writs* will be found. Where the references to reign or regnal year or to the record are wrong, they have been corrected in the Catalogue without the fact being specifically stated.

The Introduction contains a general description of the manuscripts and of each of the four main groups into which they have been arranged. It also contains some brief account of the history and provenance of the manuscripts and of the story of their preservation. Additionally, it contains some account of those members of the Society who were the principal benefactors, not only William Petyt and Daines Barrington, the outstanding benefactors, but such benefactors as William Barnsley and Cursitor Baron Maseres.

In view of his importance as a lawyer and as an antiquary, and as keeper of the Public Records, and also of his place as a constitutional historian, it is surprising that no full-length biography of William Petyt has been written. An effort to remedy this deficiency can clearly not be made in the Introduction, but something has been done belatedly to gather together the chief of his attainments and estimate his position in the fields of legal and historical scholarship.

Similarly, a few pages are devoted to Joshua Blew, who served the Society for many years, becoming Chief Butler in 1744 and Librarian for the fifty years from 1713 to 1763. His work on the manuscripts and records of the Inner Temple was outstanding, as the Catalogue will prove conclusively.

The provision of detailed footnotes and references to the Introduction would have inevitably increased the length of a work which is already long; similarly, the provision of a detailed index to it would have added considerably to an Index which is already comprehensive. A considerable part of the Introduction is necessarily based upon material which appears in full in the text and the precise references can be readily established through use of the Index.

It has therefore been thought preferable to indicate briefly here the further chief sources which have been used. For example, references to Acts of Parliament, Bench Table Orders, and Accounts are given by date. The sources of these up to the year 1800 are the five volumes of the *Calendar of Inner Temple Records, 1505–1800* (1896–1937), the first three of which were edited by F. A. Inderwick, Q.C., and the last two by R. A. Roberts, both members of the Society. After 1800, Acts of Parliament and Bench Table Orders have been taken from the original records in the Treasurer's Strong Room. For these precise references would be difficult or impossible to supply as there is as yet no class list of the original records and several of the principal classes were very badly damaged during the last war in 1940–1. Details about Admissions and Calls to the Bar and to the Bench are taken from the same sources for the respective periods, supplemented by the original Admission Books; from the volumes of Admissions in typescript compiled by R. L. Lloyd, a member of the Society, in four volumes with an index covering the whole of the period to 1750, and presented by him; and from *Students Admitted to the Inner Temple, 1547–1660*, edited by W. H. Cooke (1877). The printed works were published by the Masters of the Bench. Material used from other publications of the Bench will be traceable from the section of the Introduction dealing with such publications. Other sources, whether manuscript or printed, are mainly derived from records in the Public Record Office (including Record Commission, Calendar Series, Rolls Series, Calendars of State Papers, Domestic Archives) and manuscripts in the British Museum (including the Additional, Hargrave, Harleian, Lansdowne, and Stowe MSS.) which are generally indicated in the Introduction. When references are to wills, photocopies of the respective wills have been obtained from the Principal Probate Registry, Somerset House, as all these wills were proved in the Prerogative Court of Canterbury.[1] The photocopies have been deposited in the Inner Temple Library. Information has been derived from the standard biographical sources, such as the *Dictionary of National Biography*, Campbell's *Lives of the Lord Chancellors* and *Lives of the Chief Justices*, and Foss's *Judges of England* and *Biographica Juridica*, supplemented by special works, such as, for example, for William Petyt, *The Ancient Free Grammar School of Skipton in Craven* by A. M. Gibbon (1947), as well as material at the Public Record Office and Additional Manuscripts in the British Museum; and for Francis Maseres, Sir F. D. Mackinnon's *Inner Temple Papers* (1948).

It was of the utmost importance for the working use of the Catalogue that the index should be as complete and comprehensive as possible on persons, places, and subjects; and in every case where practicable the words or intention of the manuscript have been reproduced. Where the documents are printed in full elsewhere or fully calendared and nothing valuable is to be gained by inserting the old place-name form, the modern place-name alone is given in the index. Where possible, places have been identified. Every effort has been made to identify and date all persons and find their rank and personal positions, especially those who were members of the Society. The subject index has been made as analytical and comprehensive as possible on all legal and historical matters. In the cases of statutes, when they are described in the manuscript as Statutes, they appear under that head in the index. When they are called Acts of Parliament in the manuscript they appear under that head in the index. In fact, several of the Acts of Parliament are private Acts and a few are Bills which never reached the

[1] The records of the Prerogative Court of Canterbury have since been transferred to the Public Record Office.

Statute Book. Secondly, in the heading Cases, the cases are not all cases in the royal courts; some, for example, are in ecclesiastical courts.

The alphabetical arrangement of the entries in the index follows the principles observed as house rules by the Oxford University Press. That is to say: (1) to decide the order, the keyword is all that comes before the first comma; (2) the order adopted is that of whole words; (3) anything closed up counts as one word; (4) secondary keywords, those between the first and second commas, are listed in strictly alphabetical order, items with none coming before those with any.

Apart from the loose papers of Stuart A. Moore and H. Stuart Moore to which reference is made in the Introduction, mention must be made of certain other manuscripts which are not included in this catalogue, because they were received too late for inclusion. Dr. Conway Davies wrote: 'In my report on the Records of the Prerogative Court of Canterbury made to the Lord Chancellor's Advisory Council on Public Records in 1964 I recommended to the Lord Chancellor that the following manuscripts found among the records of that court should be offered to the Inner Temple Library: "Judge's Note-Books: 40 quarto volumes, Nisi Prius (various circuits), Special Commissions, Crown Court and Central Criminal Court, 1842–1857. Each volume indexed by Sir Cresswell Cresswell when a Judge in the Court of Common Pleas; Note-Books of Reports: about 36 volumes of note-books of cases heard in King's Bench, mainly in the hand of Sir Cresswell Cresswell, made by him, Easter Term 3 George IV to Hilary Term 11 George IV, 1822–1830. These are related to Reports of Cases Argued and Determined in the Court of King's Bench, 1822–1830, R. V. Barnewall and Cresswell Cresswell, 10 volumes." As a result of my recommendation and with the agreement of the Treasurer and Masters of the Bench, the Inner Temple Library was formally appointed an Appointed Repository by the Lord Chancellor on 15 May 1970. Accordingly the above mentioned documents were deposited in the Library on 15 June 1970. Sir Cresswell Cresswell was called to the Bar by the Inner Temple in 1819 and became a Bencher in 1842. He was appointed a Justice of the Court of Common Pleas the same year and continued in that court until 1858, when he became the first Judge Ordinary in the newly established Probate and Divorce Courts, which he organized. He died in 1863. The volumes mentioned above reached Doctors' Commons from his chambers in the Inner Temple between 1858 and 1863, or probably after his death in 1863.'

Upon Sir Cecil Carr's death in 1966 certain manuscripts and papers belonging to and written by him were presented to the Library by his widow. These include: manuscript notes, bound up, of Select Charters of Trading Companies, by C. T. Carr and the original manuscript drafts and notes of the Pension Book of Clement's Inn, by C. T. Carr, both printed subsequently by the Selden Society, together with seventeen large bundles of unsorted manuscript notes, letters, typescript drafts, notes and memoranda relating to legislative drafting, administrative law, and delegated legislation. Sir Cecil Carr was called to the Bar by the Inner Temple in 1902, and became a Bencher in 1942. He was Counsel to the Speaker of the House of Commons 1943–55 and was President of the Selden Society 1958–61. He took a great interest in the preparation of this Catalogue and, it can now be disclosed, generously contributed £2,000 towards the cost of the work. Dr. Conway Davies estimated 'that the addition of the above mentioned papers of Stuart Moore, Sir Cresswell Cresswell and Sir Cecil Carr will add a further hundred volumes to the total of Miscellaneous Manuscripts' for inclusion in a future supplement to this work.

In 1970 Mr. A. N. G. Richards, then Assistant Librarian to the Middle Temple, drew the editor's attention to a manuscript in the Middle Temple Library. He described it as follows: 'The first page is headed "A Diurnall/ Occurrances and proceedeings/ in Parliament houlden at/ westminster 1640 from the/ ffirst beginninge thereof un[to] this present tyme 1641". The period covered is 7th November 1640 to 9th September 1641 and there are 255 numbered leaves, the first carrying the number 2. Before the text are eleven preliminary leaves containing eight Acts of Parliament, written in hands other than those of the text. After the text and comprising leaves 252–255 is a list of the "Committee duringe the recesse", together with a series of Resolutions relating to the prescribed duties and activities of the Committee. There follows—on three leaves—the text of an address delivered by Pym at a meeting of both Houses on 23 June 1641. The leaves measure $11\frac{1}{2}'' \times 7\frac{1}{2}''$. A pencil note inside the front cover shows that the volume was part of a gift made to this Library in June 1846 by the Executors of Paul Treby, of Plympton, Devon, and our donation book—under a date two years later, in 1848—describes the gift as "Judge Treby's Lawbooks". There should be sixteen volumes in this Treby gift (or bequest), but I have only been able to trace thirteen. The present volume is the only one bearing the Petyt arms and the only one with Parliamentary as distinct from more precisely "legal" connections.' Dr. Conway Davies commented as follows: 'It does not seem strange that such a manuscript should be in a collection of Treby manuscripts given or bequeathed to the Middle Temple. . . . Sir George Treby and Petyt would have been well known to each other, and not only from the Middle Temple origin of both. They belonged to the same political persuasion and thought and seem to have been interested in the same political problems and sources. A manuscript relating to Parliament, 1640, 1641, would have been interesting or useful to Treby in his profession in his defence of Sir Patience Ward or of the Seven Bishops and of the City of London in the quo warranto proceedings. In this last cause he and Petyt were associated. The manuscript would also have been interesting or useful to Treby in his official duties as Solicitor-General and Attorney-General and as Chief Justice of the Common Pleas. Treby died in 1700 seven years before Petyt, so if the manuscript was bequeathed by or given by him, the transaction was at least eight years before the Petyt Manuscripts reached the Inner Temple Library. There are at least two series of Petyt parliamentary transcriptions from which it might originally have come, but there seems to have been little doubt that it was lent by Petyt to Treby and never returned. It was probably in Treby's library or chambers when he died.' Dr. Conway Davies had expressed a wish to see this manuscript, but ill health prevented this. However, his intention that it should be mentioned in the Preface is now accomplished.

Finally, acknowledgement is due to the following for their assistance in the construction of this Preface: Mr. H. C. Johnson, C.B., C.B.E., formerly Keeper of Public Records; Mr. A. N. G. Richards, formerly of the Middle Temple Library; Mr. E. W. Denham, Principal Assistant Keeper, Public Record Office; and Miss D. A. Parnham, Sub-Librarian to the Inner Temple.

W. W. S. B.

1 February 1972

INNER TEMPLE LIBRARY

Rules Governing the use of Manuscript Material

1. HOURS OF ADMISSION

Manuscript material may be examined between the following times: 10.30 a.m. to 5.0 p.m. on Mondays to Fridays only, except during official holidays and the Long Vacation; subject to prior arrangement with the Librarian.

2. ADMISSION

Application to consult the manuscript collection must be made in writing to the Librarian. The applicant in addition to stating his full name and permanent address must SPECIFY THE PARTICULAR PURPOSE for which he wishes to consult the MS. material and his application must be supported by a letter of recommendation from a recognized institution (e.g. University, Institute, High Commissioner's Office, Embassy, etc.). Such application must be made at least two days before admission is required. Applicants will be granted admission in the first instance for a period of one month only. Extensions will be granted only upon fresh application. The Librarian's letter of permission must be shown on request.

3. Manuscripts may not be removed from the Library.

4. Manuscripts may not be examined at desks seating more than one reader.

5. One manuscript volume only may be examined at a time.

6. No writing instrument EXCEPT pencils may be used for making notes.

7. Manuscripts must be treated with exemplary care:
   (i) It is forbidden to write or make any mark upon them, to lean on them, to lay notebook or paper on them when making notes, or to make tracings from them.
   (ii) Readers must avoid placing their hand on the open page and must not turn over the leaves with a pencil in their hand.
   (iii) It is forbidden to place books, papers, or other manuscripts upon an open manuscript.

8. Readers who wish to absent themselves from their desk, for whatever purpose, must hand the manuscript volume on which they are working into the care of library staff for the duration of their absence.

9. Readers observing defects or damage in any manuscript are requested to point them out to the Librarian.

10. It would be appreciated if Readers who publish Manuscripts or make extensive references to them in print would notify the Librarian (sending an off-print if possible) so that the facts of publication may be recorded.

11. PHOTOGRAPHING OF MANUSCRIPTS

Manuscripts may be photographed upon application. The Librarian will supply the name of a photographic agency who will perform the work. The applicant must write to the agency stating his requirements. The Librarian will then arrange for the manuscript(s) to be photographed. On the completion of the work the applicant must settle his account directly with the agency concerned. The Librarian does not accept responsibility for mistakes that may arise out of a misinterpretation of the client's instructions to the photographer.

It is a condition of receiving permission to photograph that in each instance the negative shall be given to the Library free of charge. Material thus photographed may not be published without the written consent of the Inner Temple.

12. Infringement of the rules may involve withdrawal of the use of the Library.

GENERAL

1. The staff of the Library are not permitted to engage in research of any kind on behalf of persons making use or wishing to make use of manuscript material in the Library.
2. Readers will save themselves a good deal of time and trouble if upon coming to the Library they supply accurate references to the material that is the subject of their research.

TABLE OF CONTENTS

VOLUME I

VOLUME II

VOLUME III

INTRODUCTION

THE manuscripts in the Library of the Inner Temple arrange themselves into five groups:

1.	The Petyt Collection	386 volumes
2.	The Barrington Collection	57 "
3.	The Records of the Inner Temple	39 "
4.	The Mitford Collection of Legal Manuscripts	79 "
5.	Miscellaneous Manuscripts	211 "

This total of 772 volumes, which total 9,048 separate manuscript items, was almost entirely bequeathed or presented to the Benchers of the Honourable Society of the Inner Temple. Less than half a dozen volumes were acquired by purchase. The earliest donor of manuscripts as manuscripts to be preserved in the Library was Mrs. Anne Sadleir, the eldest daughter of Sir Edward Coke, who made the gift in 1661. Her gift was intended as a tribute to her father and it included manuscripts, printed books, and two pictures. The pictures were her portrait of Sir Edward Coke and his portrait of Sir Thomas Littleton, both of which still ornament the Inn.

The Petyt Collection was largely bequeathed by William Petyt, Keeper of the Records in the Tower of London, Treasurer of the Inner Temple, 1700–1, in 1707. The Barrington Collection was presented by the Honourable Daines Barrington, Treasurer, 1784–5, during his lifetime, or after his death by his brother and executor, Shute Barrington, successively Bishop of Llandaff, Salisbury, and Durham, from 1769 to 1826. The Records of the Inner Temple consist of some 1,500 stray items, mainly from the records of the Inn; other records from the same source appear among the Miscellaneous Manuscripts; there are still further similar items remaining among the records. The Mitford Collection of Legal Manuscripts was presented by Lord Dulverton in 1957. It consists of legal manuscripts once the property of, or composed by, John Mitford, first Lord Redesdale (whose highest judicial office was Lord Chancellor of Ireland), who as Solicitor General was Treasurer, 1795–6. The Miscellaneous Manuscripts contain the few manuscripts purchased by the Inn, but they do not represent 3 per cent of the group.

Coming from such sources the preponderating interest and importance of the manuscripts is primarily legal. More than half of the total number of volumes are of a legal nature, as will appear in the brief analyses of the groups made below. The book-plates of the Inner Temple contain the names of five of its most distinguished members, Littleton, Coke, Selden, Finch, Pratt. The Library contains hardly a manuscript trace of the work of any one of these five. There is no full manuscript example of Littleton's Tenures, nor of the three incunable editions of that work, 'the first great book upon English law not written in Latin and wholly uninfluenced by Roman law'. There is a single manuscript containing some brief part of the works of Sir Edward Coke, with some notes in his own hand, presented in 1898 by a member of the Middle Temple. The rejected Library of John Selden, now divided between the Bodleian Library and the Library of Lincoln's Inn, is still referred to a little uneasily. The Inner Temple Library contains one possible draft of one of his minor works, Touching Judicature in Parliament, naturally in the Petyt Collection. There is a single manuscript annotated by Heneage Finch, first Earl of Nottingham, and for twelve years Treasurer of the Inn, 1661–73. It was presented in 1833, by a Treasurer of the Inn. Of Sir John Pratt, Lord Chief Justice, there is not even a signature, except among the records of the Inn.

Despite the lack of important manuscripts of its most distinguished members, almost the whole of the manuscripts are mainly of a family or domestic nature. They represent the personal and corporate interests of the Inn and its members, from student to Treasurer, who gave them. The effective founder of the Library and its manuscript collection was William Petyt, though there had been a Library and Librarians for some two centuries before his time. The Library had hitherto been a workshop tended by a domestic servant of the Inn and tenuously supported by the Bench. From its institution it had relied largely upon the gifts of its members, who presented copies of their own printed works, as Coke presented copies of his Reports. William Petyt provided a permanent home for the books, enriched it with valuable printed works, and laid a solid foundation for a library rich in legal and historical manuscripts, even if it had missed Selden's rare collection. William Petyt set an example which was followed in a small way by a few of his contemporaries and in a larger way by his successors, especially, for example, by Daines Barrington and Francis Maseres. The list of donors of manuscripts to the Library is impressive and, although most of the volumes came from Treasurers and Benchers and other members of the Inn, the list of foreign donors ranged from a king to an anonymous donor.

The Library has for the last two hundred and fifty years been well tended. The Petyt manuscripts have been in the Library for that period. Notwithstanding the vicissitudes of time and the ravages of two world wars not one of the 254 volumes of manuscripts bequeathed by William Petyt has been lost or mislaid, a truly remarkable record of conservation. The preservation has been mainly due, in spite of the many hazards and difficulties, to the care and consideration of a succession of painstaking Librarians, mainly part-time officers, who continued their chief duties, whether serving in hall, working in the Sub-Treasurer's Office, or assisting at the Temple Church, with that of looking after and cataloguing the books. For that two hundred and fifty years there have been but ten Librarians. For some hundred and forty years the work of the Librarians has been seconded by the interest and activities of a remarkable succession of Masters of the Library.

Yet after the pioneer efforts of Joshua Blew no effort has been made to catalogue the manuscripts, though Bench Table Orders for this purpose have been made since 1816. The list of manuscripts which first appeared in the printed Catalogue of the Library, printed in 1806, was based on the original Catalogue of the Petyt Collection. To this list was added in the printed Catalogue of 1833 a brief description of additional volumes. There the matter rested until 1871, when the Historical Manuscripts Commission published a calendar of two volumes in the Petyt Collection. This occupied a mere five pages. This was supplemented in 1888 by a calendar or brief summary description of 374 volumes of the Petyt Collection, of which less than 30 were calendared, supplemented by a calendar or brief references to a further 19 volumes (of which 4 volumes belonged to the Barrington Collection and 15 volumes are now among the Miscellaneous Manuscripts), also prepared by the Historical Manuscripts Commission. This occupied 82 pages.

It is proposed to deal in the present Introduction with the following matters in the following order: (1) The Inner Temple Library; (2) William Petyt, 1637–1707; (3) The Petyt Collection: (i) The Petyt Manuscripts, (ii) Other Manuscripts in the Petyt Collection; (4) Hon. Daines Barrington, 1727–1800; (5) The Barrington Collection; (6) The Records of the Inner Temple; (7) John Freeman Mitford, Lord Redesdale, 1748–1830; (8) The Mitford Collection of Legal Manuscripts; (9) The Miscellaneous Manuscripts; (10) Some of the Donors of the Miscellaneous Manuscripts: (i) Francis Maseres, 1731–1824, (ii) Mrs. Anne Sadleir and Sir Edward Coke, (iii) Alexander Luders, d. 1819, (iv) Mrs. John Austin, (v) Stuart A. Moore and Hubert Stuart Moore, (vi) Other benefactors; (11) Masters of the Library; (12) Librarians; (13) Joshua Blew, Librarian and Chief Butler; (14) Catalogues of the Library; (15) Publications of the Inner Temple; (16) The use made of the Inner Temple Manuscripts; (17) Preservation and loss of manuscripts; (18) Conclusion: the Inner Temple.

1. THE LIBRARY OF THE INNER TEMPLE

The first official reference to a Library among the official records of the Inner Temple is dated 1506, but this is not surprising as the surviving records do not start before 1505. It is a mere mention of the assignment of a chamber 'newly made under the Library'. It is, however very doubtful whether, as has been claimed, the Inner Temple had a Library 'long before the reign of Henry VII'. It is true that cathedrals and abbeys and priories had had libraries for hundreds of years before this, but the literature of religion was very much more numerous in the middle ages than the literature of the common law. Bibles, commentaries, glosses, the works of the Fathers were very much more numerous and widely dispersed that the Statutes, Year Books, and textbooks of the common law. It would seem likely that there would be no necessity for a library in an Inn of Court until after the introduction of printing into England. Manuscripts written on the Continent could contribute nothing to the student of the common law. There were legal tracts and textbooks written in England from the thirteenth century, but Littleton was available only shortly before the middle of the fifteenth century. It would therefore seem doubtful if there would be any need for a library in an Inn of Court until some time in the reign of Henry VII.

Wat Tyler and his fellow rebels may have destroyed the records of the Temple in 1381, but there is no suggestion that they destroyed any manuscripts. Probably there were none; in any case they would not have been kept in the Temple Church. Apart from Statutes and a few legal tracts, mainly written in the time of Edward I, and some Year Books, there would have been few law books to place in any library. By the time of Thomas Littleton the libraries of the Inns of Court could have had a succession of Year Books, manuscript Statutes, and manuscript legal treatises. By the time of Edward Coke the printed book had almost entirely superseded the manuscript. The first dated Year Book was printed in 1518, the first printed legal tract, 1481, which was Littleton's *Tenures*. The first printed abridgment is Statham's *Epitome*, dated about 1490, which considerably antedates Fitzherbert's *Abridgment* of 1516. Coke's *Institutes* were mainly based upon printed sources, though he had manuscripts as well as printed Year Books and Statutes, and even some Public Records in original or transcript.

Whatever number of manuscripts there may have been in the Inner Temple Library the convenience of the printed book soon ousted them, for speedy reference was essential in law. The Inns of Court were practical not academic institutions. It is doubtful if by the end of the seventeenth century there were many, if any, manuscripts among the working books in the Inner Temple Library. The Petyt Manuscripts contain no reference to any such, though William Petyt mentions several legal manuscripts in private hands and uses them, as well as some of his own.

William Dugdale states that the Library of Lincoln's Inn was finished in the 24th year of Henry VII, but that for a century thereafter it was not furnished with books. So in 1608 it was ordered that a bencher on call should give 20*s.* towards buying books for the Library, and barristers on call to the bar 13*s.* 4*d.*, to spend which a Master of the Library was appointed. He also states that in 1525 the Middle Temple had no Library and that what few books it afterwards possessed were stolen before the Restoration through want of proper protection. On the other hand the Register of Burials at the Temple Church has the following entry: 'William Cox esq., an ancient barrister of the Middle Temple and Keeper of the Library there was buried in the Temple Church . . . the 18th day of April 1655.' William Cox had been admitted to the Middle Temple in 1619 and was described as 'an ancient fellow of this House' when called to the bar in 1642 and designed to be Library Keeper the same year. Gray's Inn, too, had a Library Keeper some decades before the Inner Temple had one. A manuscript in the Harleian Collection, of which Gray's Inn Library has a copy, was compiled by Simon Segar, a descendant of Sir William Segar who was appointed Garter King at Arms in 1603. Simon Segar was called to the bar by Gray's Inn in 1656 and was the author of *Honores Anglicani*. He was appointed Butler and Librarian of Gray's Inn in 1674.

This was more than a generation before a puisne butler was appointed Library Keeper of the Inner Temple Library. The position of a Chief Butler in the administration of the Inns of Court may appear as anomalous. In the sixteenth century and the first part of the seventeenth century he was the senior administrative officer of the Society. The first Under Treasurer in the Inner Temple was not appointed until 1631 and the person then appointed was a barrister of the Inn and was called Deputy Treasurer. Thereafter the Chief Butler continued to be an important and responsible official, with duties far beyond those usually associated with the title. In 1638 a payment had been made to the Chief Butler of the Inner Temple 'for his pains extraordinary in searching records and following the business between Dr. Micklethwaite and the two Societies of the Temple', that prolonged dispute about the powers and remuneration of the Master of the Temple. In 1640 a payment of 19*s*. 6*d*. was made to the Chief Butler for money he had laid out 'for records and copies of deeds in the Chapel of the Rolls', doubtless relating to the same matter. Nor could the Under Butlers have had any difficulties in reading and transcribing, or even writing the script of ancient documents. For a Bench Table Order of 13 June 1673 laid it down that the 3rd, 4th, and puisne butlers 'do by the beginning of Michaelmas term next write a Court Hand and also know the ancient and accustomed way of casting up accounts by counters. And if they should be careless and negligent in attaining thereto then every such butler, so ignorant, should then lose his place and be made incapable of serving the House as butler.'

The dates attributed to the libraries of the other three Inns of Court, Gray's Inn from the reign of Elizabeth I, Middle Temple from 1641, Lincoln's Inn from the time of Sir Matthew Hale, support this suggestion. If there was a Library there would have to be a caretaker and a cleaner. Books and manuscripts would have to be bought and paid for. The end of the fifteenth century would be a safer date to assign to the beginning of a Library in the Inner Temple, unless what is meant is a reading-room, that is a room reserved for reading books, probably one's own books. After 1506 the records contain no reference to a Library in the Inner Temple until 2 November 1530, when it was ordered that Thomas Audley, the Speaker, 'should have a door out of his chamber into the Library of this House, if it be not hereafter to the nuisance of the members of the same House'. In 1534 there is a reference to a building between the Library and other lodgings; in 1553 an Order 'that the Library shall be repaired and the door into Master Beaumont's chamber be closed up, for the safeguard of the books that shall be brought there, and laid for the maintenance of the learning of the laws of the realm'. This suggests that hitherto it may have been used only as a reading-room, without books of its own. During the whole of the sixteenth century these are the only references to the Library as Library found among the records, though the Library as a room used as an overflow dining-room, or for moots, suggests again that it was a room only, and there is no reference to any books bought or given. Library books, however, were being repaired as early as 1608 and in 1609 money was spent on padlocks to 'lock the books upon the iron rods in the new Library', but the first reference to a gift of books made to the Library is also the same year, when Sir Edward Coke gave his Reports to the Library and 18*d.* was paid to a stationer 'for setting the title of my Lord Coke's Reports in golden letters which he gave to the House'. These must have been to Parts 1 to 7 of the Reports, which were all that had been published at that date.

Here only the general history of the Library will be touched upon. The gifts of books and manuscripts, the catalogues compiled of the contents, the use made of it, all these will be mentioned briefly later, as will its custodians. The buildings it occupied at different times, from the late fifteenth century onwards, its furniture and furnishings, its heating and lighting, the perennial problems of hours of opening and dates of opening and the other minutiae of administration, and all other transient matters will be reserved, as they do not come within the immediate purposes of this Introduction, interesting and important as they may be. Of other orders and reports only there must be a strict selection, representative rather than comprehensive.

Thus on 25 November 1670 it was ordered that Benchers consider the setting up of all the Readers' coats of arms in the Library and treat with a herald painter about it. This is the first reference to a part of the Society's tradition which still continues to be effective. This was followed on 10 February 1671 'upon the showing of some coats of arms of the Readers' which were emblazoned by Waker, painter and herald, and adjudged by the Committee to be reasonably done, it was ordered that he paint the same to be fixed in the Library, at 3*s.* an escutcheon, and 5*s.* to be allowed for every new Reader'.

On 15 June 1695 it was ordered that 'a duplicate be made of all the Acts of Parliament and an abridgment of the same and the original books be placed in the Library under lock, the key to be placed with the Treasurer'. On 8 May 1740 it was ordered 'Mr. Peters [the Under Treasurer] to transcribe the Orders of this Table from 23rd day of June 1708 into a book or books to be kept in the Inner Temple Library, and the same rule to be observed as to the Acts of Parliament, and the duplicate of the Chamber Book kept in the Library to be continued to the present time'. Certainly from the late seventeenth century, at least, the Library was considered as the appropriate place to house original records of the Inn as well as transcripts and abridgments of them.

In 1713 it had been ordered that 'the Treasurer for the time being do lay out £20 yearly out of the treasury in purchasing of books for the Library', an annual allowance which was increased in 1728 to £50, but to be spent at the discretion of the Treasurer and four other members of the Bench—the beginning of an effective Library Committee. The original allowance was duly spent in making up deficiencies, for payment was made to a bookseller 'for several books of Reports and others delivered into the Library, £20'. The detailed account is available among the Records of the Inner Temple: Coke's Reports, 11 parts, best edition, £5; Coke's Reports, 3 volumes, best edition, £4-10-0; Dyer's Reports, best edition, folio, 16s.; Leonard's Reports, folio, best edition, £2-10-0; D'Anvers, Abridgment, 2nd edition, folio, £1-5-0; Modern Reports, 5th part, folio, 18s; Modern Cases, folio, 12s.; Gibson's Codex, 2 Volumes, folio, calf, £3; for a set of Acts, 1713, 9s. 6d.; for a set of Acts, 1714, 14-10d.; for binding the volumes above 4s. 8d. In all £20. The increased grant of 1728 was immediately effective. All the 28 volumes of *Tractatus Tractatuum* were bought for £52-10-0; a list of books not in the Library was drawn up; a first payment of £3-3-0 was made for a subscription for a copy of Lord Bacon's Works in 4 Volumes, on large paper.

Within ten years of the delivery of the Petyt manuscripts it was found necessary to safeguard their content from indiscriminate use. For on 18 May 1717 it was ordered 'no copy or transcript of any manuscript books in the Library to be taken and no books to be delivered or taken out of the Library without leave of the Table. This order to be hung up in the Library'. Within half a century:

> Upon the Under Treasurer informing the Table that Mrs. Elizabeth and Mrs. Dorothy Wright, the daughters and executrixes of Sir Martin Wright late one of the Justices of His Majesty's Court of King's Bench, have signified their resolution to present to this Society a valuable collection of his law books and selected by the said Sir Martin Wright agreeable to his intention and declaration before his death, the Under Treasurer to attend Mr. Justice Wright's executrixes and in the name of the Society to return their thankful acknowledgments for such benefaction, and at the same time request that if they have any portrait of Mr. Justice Wright that they will give leave that this Society may take a copy thereof to place up in their public Library.

These manuscripts and books and the portrait are still within the Inner Temple Library.

On 21 November 1783 the Bench referred the duty and salary of the Librarian to a Committee. It worked quickly and reported to the Bench Table on 27 January 1784. After provision for the hours of attendance the Librarian was required to 'enter or cause to be entered in a good writing hand all books brought into the Library and all other proceedings requisite for the care and attention of a Librarian'. If any Bencher or Auditor desired to have a book out of the Library, on application, the Librarian was to deliver such book, entering the name of the borrower in a book kept for such purpose, such book to be returned within a fortnight, and 'no person but a Bencher or Auditor be at liberty to take a book out of the Library'. The Librarian was to be able to inform any member of the Society where any of the books were to be found in the presses and 'permit such member to have the use of such book during the time he stays in the Library and then to replace the same'. He was to supervise the cleaning of the Library and its books; no one but a Bencher or Auditor was to have a key to the Library. He was to 'enter or cause to be entered in the vacation after every term in the respective register books kept in the Library for that purpose the Acts of Parliament and Bench Table Orders and index the same in the Index Book'. It was considered that the annual salary of £20 'without any other emoluments will not be an improper allowance'. The regulations proposed were simple but hardly such as to require a highly qualified Librarian to execute; the salary offered was unlikely to afford one. Two of the signatories of the report were Daines Barrington and Francis Maseres, both of whom had valuable and considerable libraries of their own and who might have been expected to take a broader view on duties and a more generous attitude on remuneration. The report was confirmed by the Bench and a few days after Randal Norris was appointed Librarian.

In 1729 insurance was effected with the Sun Fire Office for £500 on the books and manuscripts in the Inner Temple Library. It would have seemed a low figure except that, at the same time, the figure for the Hall and all its offices with other buildings was but £1,000. In 1812 a Committee was appointed to consider in what sum it be recommended the same should be insured with the same Office. The sum was £3,000 and the Table ordered that the insurance should be effected in the name of the Treasurer for the time being, £2,500 on the printed books and £500 on the manuscripts. When the Sun Fire Office required a catalogue of the manuscripts and a valuation of each of the manuscripts in the Library before insurance was accepted it was ordered that the printed books only should be insured.

With the report considered above on the duties of the Librarian should be considered a report on the same subject requisitioned on 7 June 1825. This is more specific, practical, and detailed as the following extracts show:

> The Librarian should be imperatively responsible for the condition and safety of the books and manuscripts in the Library.
>
> The Librarian should properly class and arrange the several books and manuscripts in the Library.
>
> The Librarian should make an accurate catalogue of the books and manuscripts arranged alphabetically, according to their respective subjects and continue the same as additional books or manuscripts are received into the Library and should also make a shelf catalogue of every book in each shelf.
>
> There should be printed copies of such catalogues, two of which should be interleaved, in which the additions should be made of the new books and manuscripts as they come in, of which each Master of the Bench should have a copy, and there should be six copies kept on the table in the Library, for the use of those frequenting it.

That no person other than the Masters of the Bench and the Librarian be on any occasion, permitted to have access or peruse the manuscripts and the most rare and valuable books (such rare and valuable books to be determined by the Master of the Library for the time being, or by Order of the Bench), without an Order first obtained from the Bench, and then only in the presence of the Librarian.

That no transcript be permitted to be made of any manuscript without an Order first obtained from the Bench for that purpose.

That the Librarian do regularly attend in the Library at the times already fixed for that purpose.

That the Librarian should be furnished by the Sub Treasurer with an alphabetical list of every member of the Society and be continually supplied with the names of new members as soon as the same are admitted for the purpose of the Librarian adding the same to such list.

That no person be admitted into the Library for the purpose of using it other than a member of the Society, without a written order from or being accompanied by a Master of the Bench.

That the Librarian should be provided with a book in which he should require every person, not being a Member of the Bench, coming into the Library to insert his name and address.

That the Librarian do not suffer any book to be taken out of the Library but by the Master of the Bench or by a written order from one of the Masters of the Bench, and that every book so taken to be returned again within fourteen days, or a written statement to be delivered to the Master of the Library for its non production.

That the Librarian do take care that every book after use be immediately returned to its proper place.

That the Librarian do not suffer any person to write in any of the books or to mutilate or abuse the same, and if any person offend in such respect his name to be reported to the Bench or in vacation to the Master of the Library.

That the Librarian do on all occasions report in writing to the Master of the Library all such circumstances as shall occur where the Library may be benefitted or improved, or of any neglect or omission of duty or abuse whereby the same may be injured or affected . . .

It was ordered that these rules be confirmed and the Committee was requested to cause the same to be printed.

It seemed to be only a matter of chance that the Inner Temple did not publish its most valuable manuscript Year Book. On 8 February 1788 Daines Barrington was granted leave 'to procure a copy from a manuscript in the Library which contains the Year Books from the 10th to the 17th of Edward the Third in order that the same may be printed and published at his expense'. The proposal apparently was not proceeded with. Then on 13 February 1827 it was ordered that 'Mr. Treasurer be requested to consult with James Manning esq., barrister at law, respecting the translation and publishing of the manuscript Year Book that is in the Library of this Society'. On 18 May 1827 it was ordered that when translated it was to 'be printed in both languages'. A letter was read from Manning on 3 May 1831 reporting that he had translated into English 1,028 pages (which filled 1,476 pages) and the Bench ordered that he should be paid £200 on account of his services. A Committee was set up on 22 October 1834 to arrange as to the remuneration to be paid for the translation and also as to the expense of printing the same. On 18 February 1835 it was ordered on the report of the Committee that Mr. Manning should be paid a further £300 as a remuneration for his trouble in translating the Year Book and that the consideration of the printing be adjourned *sine die*. It was further ordered that the translation and transcript 'be severally and respectively bound in a manner the most efficacious to preserve the same and that the original also either rebound or rebacked or otherwise repaired as may be done with the least injury . . . most efficacious to preserve it and that the same be restored to and deposited in the Library' and the translation and transcript in another place of safety.

That did not finally dispose of the matter. James Manning, by now a Serjeant, and Queen's Ancient Serjeant, had canvassed the possibility of the four Inns of Court collaborating in the publication, and wrote accordingly to the Bench. He had already offered to prepare and correct a full index to the translation, an offer which had been accepted on 21 April 1835. When he reopened the question of publication in 1849 a report from the Library Committee of the Inner Temple of 8 June was read at the Bench on 12 June. The alternatives suggested were to print the whole, text and translation, or to print the translation only, with notes and reference. Manning had pointed out that this could be done at rather less than half the expense which would be required for text and translation. He would undertake the whole literary labour and proposed that his remuneration should consist of such copies of the work as remained after the Societies had taken as many as they thought right to reserve for themselves. The matter was referred back to the Library Committee. There the matter ended as far as the Inn was concerned until the original manuscript was handed over to L. O. Pike for publication in eight volumes by the Rolls Series, when Manning's work was largely used. Manning's Index still remains among the Miscellaneous Manuscripts.

Throughout its long history the Inner Temple Hall had been used for very few purposes except that for which it was originally built, the most notable being the holding of masques and stage plays in the late sixteenth and first third of the seventeenth century. On the other hand, the Inner Temple Library had been used for purposes as various as it is possible to imagine. It was a natural place for meetings of the Parliament and of the Bench Table whenever required, or its Committees or Audits, or for conferences with the Middle Temple on matters of mutual concern. It was used for moots; certain compulsory moots were called Library Moots. It was used for Christmas festivities, for gambling and dicing by the barristers and students, for drinking by the Benchers, though at one time they were limited to one pint of wine there a head after dinner. It was used as a store room for old glass from the Church, or for furniture. It was used for the reception of the Lord Chancellor and Judges on Grand Night but often for long periods as an additional or subsidiary dining-room, though this was frowned upon by the Bench. In 1606 it was ordered that there should be no further dining or supping in the Library 'in regard it is meant to be kept sweet and cleanly for the exercise of learning and receiving of noble persons at the feasts in the reading time'.

In 1941 Hall, Bench Rooms, and Library ceased to be, after service of more than four and a half centuries. For more than a year previously preparations against destruction had been made. Manuscripts and the rarest books, and later less rare books, pictures, and the Pegasus and plate had been evacuated. All did not reach their refuge. A lorry conveying books to apparent safety was destroyed by fire in collision with an Army lorry. Over three thousand pounds compensation was received but this was no substitute for the books. The loss in records and manuscripts and books was small compared with the loss in buildings and facilities, which for a few brief days ceased entirely. The manuscripts and rare books and the pictures and plate saved most, the records suffered most. The Book of Benefactors which recorded gifts to the Library was destroyed, so it is only with the greatest difficulty that the donors of books and manuscripts can now be discovered. For centuries it had been the custom to record votes of thanks for gifts in the Bench Table Orders, but this had not been done invariably. There is no such order for the whole of the seventeenth century before the Restoration, and after many of the Bench Table Order Books had been damaged, if not destroyed. The records of the Library itself up to 1940 had been burnt. There is now no list of the books given in 1661 by Mrs. Anne Sadleir; or of the books selected from the bequest of Herbert Jacob in 1725. Certain records of the Inn had been considered as manuscripts, the 39 volumes of Records of the Inner Temple, and that valuable series of letters to the Treasurer and Bench of the late sixteenth and early seventeenth centuries, for example. These had been removed to safety with the other manuscripts, but not so the Book of Evidences, which remained among the records of the Inn and was destroyed. But the Pegasus returned and the Phoenix was reincarnated.

2. WILLIAM PETYT, 1637–1707. TREASURER, 1701–1702

William Petyt, the eldest son of William Petyt, was born in 1637 at Storiths, in the parish of Haselwood with Storiths, in the West Riding of Yorkshire. He entered Skipton Grammar School (which had been founded in 1548), as a boarder, the historian of the school presumes, although Storiths is only seven miles distant from Skipton. Thence he proceeded to Barnard's Inn and in 1660 was admitted to Christ's College, Cambridge. The Admission Book of the College has the entry as follows: '1660, April 26, William Petyt, son of William, born at the town of Storiths in the county of York, educated at Skipton under Master Doughty, was admitted, aged 19, lesser pensioner, under Mr. Abney'. There is an error either in the date attributed to his birth, or in his age on admission, or he was a mature undergraduate. If he had studied at Barnard's Inn before going to Cambridge this would, in part, explain the position but not the error. He was admitted to the Middle Temple on 8 June 1660. When he returned to London he was specially admitted to the Inner Temple on 25 November 1664. He obtained a post as one of the Exigenters of the Common Pleas, whose duty it was to make out all writs of exigent and proclamations in cases of outlawry. His duties could not have been very exacting or occupied a great deal of time as he was able to do some amount of historical and legal work and indulge his interests in antiquarian, constitutional, and historical studies.

His association with the Inner Temple was made closer after the riot in 1669 over the bearing erect of the sword of the Lord Mayor of London within the precincts of the Inn, when he prepared the case for the Society when its members were summoned before the Council on the complaint of the city. That very racy letter of Thomas Wroth, who was one of the emissaries from the Inner Temple to the Lord Mayor and Aldermen, before the event, was addressed to him. After the successful conclusion of the case, doubtless on the motion of Sir Heneage Finch, Solicitor General and Treasurer, who had conducted the case before the Council, he was rewarded for his services which must have been highly appreciated. He had already received a fee of £20 for his services in 1669. On 12 February 1671, Parliament ordered that 'William Petyt, Exigenter for London, for his services done in asserting and defending the rights and privileges of the Temple, be called to the bar, and to be an utter barrister'. He took chambers in the Inn which were destroyed in the fire of 1679. He was called to the Bench in 1689, was chosen Reader for Trinity Vacation, 1694, and became Treasurer, 1701–2.

In the meantime his historical and legal researches had extended considerably, and in 1680 the first had reached the point of publication. Almost all his writings dealt with the history of Parliament and were designed to lay the foundations and further the building of the Whig cause, which triumphed in the Great Revolution of 1689, when he got his reward from the government. It will be found more convenient to recount all his published works together in chronological order of publication. They number 5 volumes:

1. Ancient Right of the Commons of England asserted: or Discourse proving that the Commons of England were ever an essential part of Parliament. 1680.
2. Miscellanea Parliamentaria: containing Presidents of Freedom from Arrests, of Censures, 1. upon such as wrote Books to the dishonour of Lords or Commons or to alter the Constitution of the Government; 2. upon Members for Misdemeanours; 3. upon Persons not Members, for Contempts and Misdemeanours; 4. For Misdemeanours in Elections. Besides other Presidents and Orders of a various Nature, both of the House of Lords and Commons, with an Appendix containing several instances wherein the King's of England have consulted and advised with their Parliaments, 1. In Marriages, 2. Peace and War, 3. Leagues, And other weighty affairs of the Kingdom. 1680.

3. Rights of the Commons answered, 1681.
4. Lex Parliamentaria; or Treatise of the Law and Custom of the Parliament of England. By. (G) (P). With Appendix of a case in Parliament between Sir F. Goodwyn and Sir J. Fortescue for the Knight's place for the County of Bucks. From an original French manuscript translated into English. 1690.
5. Jus Parliamentaria: or Ancient Power, Jurisdiction Rights and Liberties of the most High Court of Parliament revived and asserted. 1739.

It was the *Ancient Rights of the Commons of England asserted* which set off the controversy with Dr. Robert Brady and others. Brady replied in 1681 with his *Full and Clear Answer to a book written by William Petyt, printed in 1680, with a historical account of the Colloquium or Parliament, 49 Hen. III, and a glossary*, and also *Animadversions upon a book* [by William Atwood] *called Jani Anglorum facies Nova*; and followed up by his *Introduction to Old English History*, in 3 volumes, 1684, and to a lesser extent in his *Historical Treatise of Cities and Burghs*, 1690. It was also responsible for two books from his friend Thomas Atwood, which were certainly the result of collaboration if not of cunning and conspiracy. His *Jani Anglorum facies Nova: or Several Monuments of Antiquity touching the Great Councils of the Kingdom, and the Court of the King's immediate Tenants and Officers, from the first of William the First to the forty-ninth of Henry the Third, reviv'd and clear'd* was published anonymously in 1680; his *Jus Anglorum ab Antique: or Confutation of an Impotent Libel against the Government by Kings, Lords and Commons, under pretence of answering Mr. Petyt and the author of Jani Anglorum facies Nova* in 1681. *Florilegus, or a Commentary upon some Modern Books*, by W. E., 1705, was not a part of the controversy but an account of it. It is unnecessary to discuss whether *Argumentum Anti Normannicum*, 1680, was written by William Atwood or Edward Coke; it is sufficient to say it was a problem which greatly exercised William Petyt and about which he made transcripts and drafts. On the title-page of his copy of this work was written: 'This is Mr. William Petyt's book, William Prichard'.

The work numbered 4 above requires further notice. The catalogues describe it as 'By G. P. Esq. (George Petyt)'. No George Petyt is otherwise known as an author. The G. P. stands for Gulielmus Petyt and the work is to be correctly assigned to the authorship of William Petyt. The subject is right for him and the material contained in it is to be found among his transcripts. The manuscript now among the Miscellaneous Manuscripts, though purchased by the Society on the assumption that it was the work of William Petyt, is, however, rejected. It is entitled *De Synedriis Britannicis*. The title, the subject-matter, and the material used are not characteristic. Also rejected as the work, though at times fairly authoritatively attributed to him, is *Britannia Languens, or Discourse of Trade, showing the Grounds and Reasons of the Decrease and Decay of Land-Rents, National Wealth and Strength. With Application to the late and present State and Condition of England, France and the United Provinces,* anon., 1680. The preface is signed 'Philanglus'. Again the subject and material are all wrong for him. Lastly, there is another work undoubtedly composed by William Petyt, which, though printed, never seems to have been published. It has on the title-page: '*The Pillars of Parliament struck at by the hands of a Cambridge Doctor, or a Short View of some of the erroneous positions destructive of the Ancient Laws and Government of England. To which is added the true state of the Doctor's error about the Parliament, 49 Henry III.* By William Petyt of the Inner Tenple, Esq., 1681.' This work could not have been intended to be more than a pamphlet; fragments of it have been bound in at the end of several Petyt Manuscripts, doubtless by Joshua Blew, who in one place states that he had never seen a perfect copy. The publication was suppressed by the author and some of the material, at least, used in the work *Rights of the Commons answered*, published in 1681.

Considering William Petyt's indefatigable labours in reading and arranging records, particularly Public Records, and in transcribing them or having them transcribed, his published works are few and the largest, if not the most important of them, was published posthumously. His output was restricted by his heavy legal practice and his official duties. He was also something of a perfectionist and delayed publication in the hope that he would find something more which was relative and important. He could, however, be spurred to action by the heat of controversy, but there was no controversy in the last decade of his life; his views had come to be accepted by the powers that be. He seems to have been conscious of the paucity of his published contribution, though he recognized the value of some of his own drafts and hoped that they would yet be published. Hence the provisions made in his Will for the printing of other works and publications after his death. His research had been painstaking and comprehensive, even allowing that for nearly twenty years his post as Keeper of the Records at the Tower made his facilities for work considerable and convenient. The drafts of his unpublished works are dealt with below.

By 1681 William Petyt must have accumulated many of his volumes of transcripts from the Public Records and must have been a constant searcher himself and through his clerks in the Tower of London. After the Great Revolution of 1689 he was appointed Keeper of the Records there. His tenure of office was not easy. In 1689 there is a document headed 'The State of the Case touching the Office of Keeper of the Records in the Tower of London between Mr. William Petyt now in actual possession of the said records by virtue of his present Majesty's warrant and Sir Algernon May who endeavoured to turn Petyt out by pretence of a patent granted by Charles II'. The following is a summary of Petyt's case. After William III had taken over he was urged by several of his friends to get a warrant to take the records in the Tower out of the hands of Dr. Brady, to whom James II had given the custody at a salary of £300 a year. F. Jephson, Secretary to the King, did so fairly represent Mr. Petyt to him that a warrant was signed directed to all officers and keepers of records to suffer

Mr. Petyt to have free access for the use and service of His Highness and for the public good. After the Convention had met and was resolved into a Parliament Mr. Petyt prepared a warrant, which His Majesty signed, giving him the custody of the records, and Dr. Brady and his deputy were commanded to deliver them over to Mr. Petyt, which the deputy accordingly did. But Petyt wanted a proper patent and said that May's patent was during pleasure and therefore expired on the death of Charles II. A warrant arranged by Sir Algernon May and his counsel to the Master of the Rolls in 1689 to admit Petyt stated that 'by several accidents there had not been for many years anybody bred up to understand the reading of such ancient records and the late deputy is not sufficient for that great trust'. On 18 November 1689 an address was presented to the Lords that William Petyt be employed to methodize the records in the Tower. The patent to William Petyt was certainly issued. Either the two contestants made a gentleman's agreement or an official compromise was arranged. For on 21 July 1702 both names appear as Keepers of the Records, for, on the grant of a pension of £250 to May, Petyt was to have a salary of £250 and to succeed to May's pension.

The main facts appear fairly clear. William Petyt was duly appointed and had his warrant and patents. The memorandum discloses also the following facts. On 5 May 1693 there was a grant to May of £250 per annum in recompense for the Keepership, during pleasure. Petyt had been appointed by sign manual of 25 July 1689, which was confirmed by patent on 5 February 1693, but no salary was mentioned. On 30 July 1689, Sir Henry Powle, Master of the Rolls, by writing granted to William Petyt, for life, the office of Keeper of Records in the Tower, and in 1707 he surrendered the same to Sir John Trevor, Master of the Rolls. The memorandum also contains a significant statement that on the death of William Ryley, the Keeper of the Records, in 1667, his wife and son embezzled and sold several books and calendars which belonged to the office. The memorandum has a later note added: 'these Calendars are now in Mr. Astle's custody'. William Ryley, the younger, had been called to the bar by the Inner Temple in 1665.

So originally William Petyt undertook the office without salary, but apparently with such fees as might arise. These were then quite small. The salary or pension was about all that Sir Algernon May cared about. Eventually Petyt enjoyed office and salary and pension. There still survives at the Public Record Office 'The Book of Account of what searches and copies hath been made in the Office of Records in the Tower, William Petyt Esquire being Keeper'. The Account covers the period 20 March 1690 to 25 June 1705. Under the first date, 20 March 1690, there are the three following entries: (1) Sir Richard Temple for a search for Returns to Parliament for the borough of Buckingham, (2) Sir Humphrey Mackworth for a search for a charter, 10 Edward III, for the monastery of Neath in Wales, (3) Mr. Atwood for a search concerning the Office of Lord High Chamberlain. Peter le Neve was a frequent searcher, and in 1693 Lord Chief Justice John Holt had copies of patents for the Office of Lord Chief Justice in Banco Regis. It is interesting to observe that in 1698 there was a search concerning Cambridge for Silvester Petyt. For he too was interested in history and was a collector. One of the Petyt Manuscripts contains inset a 40-page pamphlet, 'A Record of some notworthy proceedings in the Honourable and Faithful House of Commons in the late Parliament, 1611', which bears his signature. Throughout the period, though the fees received were small, varying between £37 and £72 a year, there was no break in the entries. William Petyt was in effective control throughout.

The Lords Committee of 1704 found many unsorted records in the Tower of London, particularly in Caesar's Chapel, where William Prynne had previously found confusion and unsorted records. They therefore appointed a Sub-committee consisting of Sir Christopher Wren, William Lowndes, Secretary of the Treasury, William Petyt, and John Anstis to prepare a scheme for housing, sorting, and calendaring these documents. The Report was signed 6 September 1704 and was an elaborate effort. The Secretary was George Holmes, a clerk there and a protégé of William Petyt. The Sub-committee had viewed Caesar's Chapel and found there multitudes of records of several reigns lying confusedly, in danger of utterly perishing, unless speedy care were taken for their preservation. Drawers, shelves, and presses should be immediately provided to receive them, as they should be cleaned from the dust. After diligent perusal such as were written on one side and of value (and not writs of course at common law) should be fixed into books, in the same manner as the ancient deeds were in the Cottonian Library, with paste prepared with colliquintida to secure it against worms, by which means the small pieces of parchment would be better preserved than by putting them in bundles. This method could not be expensive since paper fit for the purpose might be had at cheap rates.

They conceived that it would be a labour of too great difficulty to range these instruments according to the exact series of time or their respective subjects. The records of each king's reign should be glued on indiscriminately as they were cleaned, and when a book was finished and bound, an index should be carefully made thereto of subject-matters under their proper heads, according to succession of time, referring to the numbers of the original instruments and not in the dry form wherein the calendars in the Office of Records (which were kept in another part of the Tower) were imperfectly composed, they containing little more than the names of persons and places, being done only for the service of the Court of Wards, to discover tenures and descents. Such bare tables of names would not be of that use to the public as repertories of things would prove, containing abstracts of things digested, according to their various nature under distinct and methodical tables. In this manner the public service seemed also to require that like calendars (whereof there were no abstracts at all in the Office) should be made of the 429 Foreign Rolls as well as to those which should be reduced to order.

The sorting of these records and compiling calendars would be the fruit of great pains and industry and would take a long time. It would not be possible to get a considerable number of clerks conversant with the old French language, the characters and knowledge of those ages, nor was the office convenient for many clerks. They conceived that three would suffice, besides Mr. George Holmes who had been fourteen years in the office and was qualified to be Chief Clerk at £100 yearly. The other three clerks might have £150 among them, to be employed under the direction of the Keeper of the Records, to report yearly to the Treasury.

The work was put in hand immediately, as can be proved by some papers which William Petyt left behind him at the Tower of London and which are still at the Public Record Office. Some of them must have been left in the Tower in error, for they include Petyt transcripts on parliamentary matters, some from the journals of the House of Commons in Ireland, and a catalogue of papers to be found in the Pipe Office, containing 186 pages. So far from subtracting Public Records from the Tower, William Petyt left behind him some of his own manuscripts and papers. There are two further proofs of this. Firstly, the *Catalogue of Manuscripts of England and Ireland*, 1697, volume II, contains a list of the manuscripts in the Tower of London, of sixty titles, recorded by William Petyt. Not one of these sixty titles is to be found among the Petyt Manuscripts. Secondly there are several lists and calendars of records in the Tower of London, compiled by William Petyt, to be found in various manuscript collections in the British Museum. These include the Account of Records in the Tower of London by him among the Hargrave Manuscripts. Among the Lansdowne Manuscripts there are two volumes of A Catalogue of Law, History, Antiquity, Manuscripts and Parliamentary Proceedings of William Petyt, based upon the two volumes in the Petyt Collection, together with the portrait prefaced to each volume. They are marked: 'They were presented to Mr. West by his friend Mr. George Holmes' and in pencil in the margin is added: '28 volumes of these are in the Inner Temple, 11 more are Lansdowne 511 to 521'. These 11 volumes consisted of five volumes of Mr. Petyt's Parliamentary Collections; Mr. Petyt, Treatise De Regno Anglie; Mr. Petyt's Glossary of the various significations of the most general Saxon words. There is added:

> Mr. Umfreville to whom the volume belonged says in a marginal note: of Chapters I and II I can give no account; Mr. Petyt's Monumenta Parliamentarie Anglo Saxonica, in 3 volumes, the 3rd being an Appendix to the others; Mr. Petyt's Treatise on the paraphrase Titulus Parliamentaria in Spelman. N.B. All the preceding collections by Mr. Petyt belonged to Mr. Umfreville and were purchased by him of Mr. George Holmes, Deputy Keeper of the Tower Records.

These eleven volumes must have been given to George Holmes by William Petyt, or left behind by him at the Tower of London, probably the former. There is little doubt that the Mr. West mentioned above is James West, who was Treasurer of the

Inner Temple 1767–8, a great collector of manuscripts and rare books, whom Holmes would have known at the Royal Society and the Society of Antiquaries.

On 30 March 1704, Lord Halifax reported to the House of Lords from the Lords Committee, on Petyt's evidence and the report of a Sub-committee, that the records in the Tower were in good condition and carefully kept; the old calendars of most of the rolls had been fairly transcribed but that there were a great number of rolls from 1 John to the end of Edward IV which had no calendars. By 8 April 1707 he was able to report the very great improvement which had been made in fitting up the office and in sorting and digesting; the records had been transcribed and provided with convenient presses and drawers; the Chancery Proceedings had been made available, whereas before they were laid promiscuously on the floor, covered with dust and rotting. The chapel had been made a great and noble repository. The good work was still being carried on.

Thus the improvements which William Petyt made in the arrangement and accessibility of the records in the Tower of London can be firmly established by a few extracts from official sources. Following the Sub-committee's consultation of 1704, on 29 September 1705 Petyt was able to report on the sorting and digesting of the records in Caesar's Chapel. George Holmes and the other three clerks had collected, cleaned, and reduced into alphabet and calendar great numbers of Depositions which had been dispersed in confused heaps within the chapel in the White Tower and also affixed parchment labels to each bundle for the more easy recourse thereto. On 25 March 1707 his final report was made which enabled Lord Halifax's final approval of 8 April 1707.

George Holmes was a particular protégé of William Petyt. He came from the same area of Yorkshire and had attended his old school, Skipton Grammar School. He had been a clerk of William Petyt at the Tower of London in 1690 and before Petyt's retirement he had been appointed on 28 September 1706 Chief Clerk. Throughout this period he must have lived with William Petyt, for when his Will was made in 1705 he had lived with him more than fourteen years. Throughout the period he certified many records in the Petyt transcripts as correct copies. On Petyt's retirement from the Keepership, Sir John Trevor, Master of the Rolls, on 12 April 1706 made a grant of the office to Richard Topham, of New Windsor, co. Berks., esq., for life, as held by William Petyt. Among the witnesses were Silvester Petyt and George Holmes. Topham on 27 March 1707 appointed Holmes his Deputy; Thomas Madox was one of the witnesses. He became the real head of the office, as after Petyt the Keepership really became a sinecure. He was well known among the scholars of his time and became a Fellow of the Royal Society and of the Society of Antiquaries. Eventually in 1731 he was appointed Keeper of the Records at the Tower. He did much towards a new edition of *Foedera* and compiled a General Calendar of the Records in the Tower which seems to have been a considerable advance on previous lists of such records. When Thomas Carte published his *Catalogues des Rolles Gascons*,

Normans et Francais, 2 volumes, in 1743, he referred in his preface to the work done by Petyt and Holmes and acknowledged his debt to them. Holmes also appears to have done a great deal of the work upon which was based the *Calendars of Ancient Charters* by Sir Joseph Ayloffe, published in 1772. So William Petyt not only rendered great services to the Public Records but provided a successor who was able to continue the work of the master.

The names of others of William Petyt's clerks at the Tower are also known. Two of them were with him to the end, Thomas Jenkinson and William Prichard, who were both remembered in his will. Two others were called in to support him when he was taken to task by Dr. Robert Brady for cutting the text of a record he had used to suit his argument. This was not only a serious accusation against an author but one which Petyt took very much to heart. He therefore got certificates from the clerks then employed by him to transcribe records. The writ in question was transcribed by William Henderson, an Attorney of the Court of Common Pleas at Westminster, as appears by his certificate dated 27 July 1684, when he attested

> that ten or eleven years ago, being ordered by Mr. William Petyt, to whom I was clerk, to transcribe from the Rolls in the Office of Records in the Tower of London, several copies, among others the above mentioned copy, anno 15to Johannis was one, and having now carefully compared it with the very original paper I had at that time writ, which Mr. Petyt hath showed me, do hereby solemnly declare that at the time of transcribing and till this present day, I did believe myself had agreed with the Record.

The certificate of William Towne of Symonds Inn, London, gent., was dated 19 July 1684 and attested

> that I have this day seen and compared the original copy of the above mentioned writ, anno 15to Johannis, and well know it to be in the handwriting of Mr. William Henderson and verily believe it was transcribed by him from the Rolls in the Office of Records in the Tower, about 10 or 11 years since, I, being at that time also employed with Mr. Henderson by Mr. Petyt, to copy out several records in the reigns of King John and Henry the Third, the original papers of some of which Mr. Petyt hath now showed me.

So Petyt was innocent of misrepresentation, except in so far as he had relied upon a faulty transcript.

A few references to records William Petyt discovered, and notes he wrote on records, will be useful as illustrative of the use he made of records in his historical controversies. Though it was as an organizer, or, as in his time and later it was called, a methodizer of Public Records that William Petyt was most effective, it was the discovery of an unknown bundle of writs, especially if they were writs of summons to Parliament, which gave him the greatest satisfaction. He had noted sadly of the Parliament from which came the Statute of Westminster I, 3 Edward I, 'there are no writs of summons, either to the Lords Spiritual or Temporal or Commons yet found to this Parliament, nor any Rolls of Parliament'. He noted 'all the summons to Parliament, either of the Lords or Commons are lost till 49 Henry III and from then till 23 Edward I', citing as his authorities William Dugdale and William Prynne; or alternatively 'all formal writs of summons, both to the Lords and Commons, are lost or perished, as well before 49 Henry III as after, till 23 Edward I, that of 49 Henry II only excepted'.

The elation with which he proclaimed his discovery of the bundle of writs of summons to the Parliament of 23 Edward I is best described in his own words:

> Memorandum. In my searches in the King's Remembrancer's Office in the Exchequer, near 20 years ago, I met with in a great chest several broken bundles of writs of different Kings, huddled together, and amongst them I found an imperfect bundle of writs of summons, with their returns, to a Parliament to be held at Westminster, 23 E. I. The very first precedent of that nature hitherto found by any man that I heard of. This discovery, being thus made by me, I ordered my clerk to take a copy of those writs and returns, which I have, and after acquainted Mr. Halsted [then Deputy to Sir Algernon May, Keeper of Records at the Tower, and after to Dr. Brady] with my discovery, which I believe upon very good reasons Mr. Halsted after told the Doctor of. From this account two observations may arise. The first is that Mr. Prynne had not, in all his searches in the Exchequer, met with the bundle de anno 23 E. I, for if he had, he would undoubtedly have taken notes thereof in his book called *Brevia Parliamentaria Rediviva*, as he did of several of the like nature afterwards. The second is that that bundle was found amongst the records of the Exchequer, and not amongst the records of the Tower, where the generality of the Parliamentary records are kept, from whence it may be presumed that that bundle of 23 E. I. was not the first or only bundle of that kind which was lodged in the Exchequer, but that there may be several others of more ancient time which remain there undiscovered.

In another set of transcripts this bundle is described by Petyt as 'the first formal bundle of writs I have met with in the records for summoning to Parliament 2 knights, 2 citizens, 2 burgesses, with their returns, begin 23 Edward I, years after 49 Henry III', and elsewhere 'in my searches in the Exchequer I discovered a broken bundle of returns of knights of the shire and burgesses to Parliament, 23 Edward I, of which neither he [William Prynne] nor any of his clerks knew anything, witness his books. And it is very probable that if further and free search were made there and in some other offices, more, and more ancient, returns might be found, as well as that of 23 Edward I.'

William Petyt gives the returns made by twenty-four sheriffs from this broken bundle. Later he gives the returns to the writs of summons for the Parliament of 26 Edward I from thirty-five sheriffs. Later in his transcripts he notes that the whole bundle of writs of summons and returns to the Parliament held at Lincoln, 9 Edward II, 'is utterly lost, many more instances of the like nature might be given'. This is repeated in the following form: 'the whole bundle of writs of summons for knights, citizens and burgesses to the Parliament of Lincoln, 1316, is lost'. He also found in the White Tower the bundle of writs of summons to the Parliament of 10 Edward III.

This, however, did not thrill him as much as the discovery of a record which to him seemed to glorify the power of Parliament, which he thus describes: 'a most remarkable record never before found out but myself that I ever heard of, concerning a marriage to be had between Prince Edward and Eleanor, sister of the King of Castille, 38 Henry III, which was assented to by the Common Council of the whole kingdom of England'. As the reference is to the Patent Roll, 38 Henry III, the claim seems a little far-fetched. Elsewhere he reinforces this with the citation that late in the reign of Edward I Parliament assented to the marriage between Prince Edward and the daughter of the King of France, for which his reference is a Miscellaneous Bundle, Henry III to Edward III. On the case John, Earl Marshal, and Richard, Earl of Warwick, on precedence, 3 Henry VI, Petyt enters the note: 'The arguments are entered at large in English in Rot. Parl., 3 H. 6, the first precedent of that kind I ever saw in all my searches and enquiries.'

Sufficient is known of William Petyt as Keeper of the Records in the Tower of London, but very little is known of his legal practice. He had first commended himself to the Inner Temple by his preparation of the case against the city of London in 1669. In the only other well-documented case for which there is information he was acting for the city. When Charles II instituted proceedings against the city of London on quo warranto in 1680–3 William Petyt prepared the city case against the crown. The thoroughness with which this was done is evidenced by the three volumes of Petyt transcripts drawn from the Archives of the city of London. Such specialized work as his would have been very well remunerated; there were comparatively few lawyers who could have undertaken it. Among his private clients was Arthur Capel, Earl of Essex, to whom he had dedicated his *Rights of the Commons asserted*. It is likely that most of his work, however, was of a specialized nature, although he did not die a wealthy man, compared say with his brother, Silvester Petyt, who was more practical in his work, it would seem largely on mortgages and bonds and as a professional money-lender.

His relationship with his Inn seems to have been friendly and fruitful throughout. He served the usual offices and served on the usual committees, but as a Bencher and as Treasurer his work was not exceptional. In 1691 he was one of a committee of three 'to consider an Act of Parliament for the better and more methodical proceedings in drawing and passing Acts of Parliament of this Society', a committee he would have appreciated. In 1695 he was one of a committee of three 'to peruse all the Acts of Parliament and Orders as to the government of the House and have them transcribed into a book to lie at the upper end of the Bench Table when the Bench is in commons and at the upper end of the bar table when the Bench is out of commons'. The coronation of Queen Anne took place during his Treasurership and due celebrations were held at the Fountain Inn. Apart from the Acts of Parliament and the Bench Table Orders a few original documents still survive. There is a petition to the

Treasurer and the Masters of the Bench from the vacation barristers on 12 October 1702. The dissolution of the late and the calling of the present Parliament making it necessary for the petitioners to appear at the elections in their several counties, before the time appointed for their continuance in commons was expired, they requested discharge from further attendance. The petition was signed by twenty-one barristers and was granted and signed by William Petyt. As Treasurer he authorized the payment of the moiety of accounts due by both the Inner Temple and the Middle Temple, including the charge for burying a woman cast up upon the causeway at the Temple stairs, and the pavior's bill for work done in Middle Temple Lane. Other matters with which he had to deal were the repair of the Temple Church and the cleaning and tuning of the organ there by Bernard Smith, jointly, of course, with the Middle Temple. Among the Benchers called were Sir Simon Harcourt, Solicitor General, who followed him as Treasurer and was Lord Keeper and Lord Chancellor, 1710–14. His interest and attendance at the Bench continued as long as he was active. In 1704, for instance, he was one of the Benchers who lent the Society £50 apiece, free of interest, towards the payment of the debts of the House.

Apart from his colleagues in the Inner Temple, it is not easy to discover who were his personal friends, except from his correspondence, very little of which has survived. Thomas Barlow, Bishop of Lincoln, to whom he had sent a copy of his *Commons Rights*, writes thanking him as his cousin. But most of the surviving correspondence is of a scholarly nature. In 1676 there was correspondence with John Mill, The Queen's College, Oxford, a scholar who became Principal of St. Edmund Hall in 1685, in which he thanked Petyt 'for unfolding the mystery of those rude characters I left in your hands' and requested him in vacation to consult Domesday Book, for he could not persuade himself that it had nothing in it of Westmorland and Cumberland. Petyt had written to Mill also about doubts he had about the second edition of Spelman's *Glossarium*. What especially troubled him was the new material under the title Parliamentum. The reply stated that the additions to Spelman's *Glossarium* were made out of loose papers of his study and printed by his grandson, with thousands of errors. In 1676 also he was in correspondence with Sir John Cotton on the origin of the Commons in 49 Henry III. In 1678 he was thanked by Ralph Cudworth, Master of Christ's College, Cambridge, a biblical scholar, for his gift of books, and in 1679 for a gift of Petyt's *Commons Rights*. William Atwood was not only a correspondent but a great admirer of Petyt's work, and though they differed on certain questions their general line was the same. In a letter to Petyt in 1681 Atwood wrote

> by your help I think I have baffled the vulgar error that the tenants in capite made our full representative till 29 Henry III. . . . The difference between the Parliament and the Curia Regis which you first gave the world and me in your learned appendix I heartily thank you for and if ever my collections see the light I shall publish to all men that though you waved the particular proof of everything in your appendix it being enough that you

overthrew the contrary suppositions yet like a master you gave those rules which will interpret and reconcile all the records and all authentic historians.

Obadiah Walker, Master of University College, Oxford, a considerable scholar but wayward in his opinions, was another correspondent. He had been concerned in Petyt's inquiries into the authenticity of the additions to Spelman's *Glossarium* in 1676 and had provided much useful information. He had specialized knowledge as he was a delegate of the Oxford University Press. In 1676 he communicated to Petyt 'the names of such historians as are ready for the press'. It was a formidable list, but he did not know 'when these volumes will be put upon the stocks'. He would acquaint the press with Petyt's kind offer of Gervase of Tilbury. In a postscript he gave the words of the oath of the Anglo-Saxon Kings. He followed this up by giving in another letter the translation of the oath. Petyt had a most useful correspondent in Dublin. Michael Tisdall, writing in 1674, said he was willing but not able to answer Petyt's query, but proceeded to give an account of Irish records. There were few extant in Dublin, none before King John's time, and in his time but one small Pipe Roll. Of succeeding Kings there were some scattered records, mostly Pipe Rolls, some legal proceedings, and some few rolls of enrolments of grants. They were kept in a Tower in the Castle of Dublin and lay open in the late rebellion to soldiers and others: 'whereby many records were embezzled or spoiled and many spoiled and made altogether useless by water falling in there being not so much as care taken to keep the places dry, and of those that remained there is no abstract or directory . . . the choice ancient records of this kingdom (I am informed) are in the Tower of London.' In 1677 Sir John Marsham, the chronologist and Egyptologist, sent William Petyt a collection of all the Parliaments he had met with in the reigns of William I and William II and promised to send him later similar lists of Henry I and Stephen. Lastly James Tyrrell (he had been called to the bar by the Inner Temple in 1666), writing from Oxford in 1681, said that if Petyt thought anything the writer had written in the papers already communicated was of the least use to him, the writer freely offered it (for as far the greatest part of the records he has quoted Petyt may justly challenge them for his own, since he must own himself beholding to him for them). There had lately come to Oxford a new treatise by Sir Robert Filmer called *Patriarcha*, which he was then considering. The result of that consideration was Tyrrell's publication of *Patriarcha non Monacha*.

William Petyt had a house at Chelsea and, according to his obituary, there 'he had erected an edifice for the benefit of the said parish containing a vestry room, a School Room for children and Convenient Chambers for a Schoolmaster'. There he died early in October in 1707 and was buried in the Temple Church on 9 October. He had as a neighbour at Chelsea Francis Atterbury, to whom he must have submitted the manuscript of a work he intended publishing. In returning this on 20 July 1704 Atterbury wrote that it contained 'an account of things very valuable and useful in order to a true knowledge of the state of affairs at that time and consist[s] of particulars which have not been dwelt upon so much as they ought by our historians'. Among the books which he bequeathed to the Inner Temple Library was Atterbury's *Rights, Powers and Priviliges of an English Convocation*, 1701, and inscribed *ex dono Auctoris*. His funeral sermon was preached by Edmund Gibson, then Master of the Temple, afterwards Bishop of London, and himself a historian of distinction. That same obituary which appeared in *The Complete History of Europe—for the year 1707* stated:

> He was very well known and much esteemed by very great and honourable persons and very communicative to all, never denying his labour or advice to any lover of antiquities, as is acknowledged by several learned men in their writings; and was a strenuous asserter of the Ancient Constitution, Laws and Liberties of England. And that his labours might not be lost, he bequeathed all his manuscripts . . . as also his printed books of Law, History and Proceedings of Parliament to several friends whom he made trustees to see them kept entire for public use and service.

Over two and a half centuries a number of myths seem to have gathered around William Petyt. His portraits show that in face and figure he was solid, stolid, as indeed was his performance. It was of the earth earthy. He looked upon the world, full of self-confidence and somewhat complacently, as perhaps indeed he well might.

Great as were his services to the Inner Temple, the Inn does not possess a full copy of his Will; only such extracts as related directly to his benefactions to the Inn. It was made on 12 July 1705 and proved 3 October 1707. On the dorse is a note that he died at Chelsea within a week previously. In his will he described himself as 'late Treasurer of the Inner Temple, London, Esq. and Keeper of Her Majesty's Records in the Tower of London'. Among those to whom he left rings with the inscription 'Wi. Petyt' (his usual signature entered on so many of his manuscripts and printed books) were his cousins, Thomas and William Petyt, of Colkins, Joseph Offley and Humphrey Hetherington, both Benchers of the Middle Temple, and two of the trustees of his will, Richard Webb, a Bencher of the Inner Temple, and John Anstis, a member of the Middle Temple and later Garter King at Arms, also both trustees, and James Tyrrell and William Atwood.

His executor was his brother, Silvester Petyt, sometime Principal of Barnard's Inn, who was to dispose of £200 which William left the Master and Fellows of Christ's College, Cambridge, in augmentation of the maintenance of poor scholars there, with first claim by scholars of his old school, the Free Grammar School of Skipton in Craven 'in remembrance of me in that College of which I was admitted'. He left £50 to the Middle Temple 'to buy books for augmenting their Library and this as a memorial that I was once a member of that Honourable Society'; and similarly £50 to the Inner Temple 'for buying books towards a Library there to be erected'. After a bequest of £50 to the Free Grammar School at Skipton and family bequests came the clause relating to his books and manuscripts.

And as for and concerning my Manuscripts and Printed Books of Law, History, Antiquity and Parliamentary Proceedings which cost me many years pains and study and stood me in much charge in collecting, I give and devise them to Joseph Offley Esq., Richard Webb Esq., Humphrey Hetherington Esq., John Anstis Esq., John Chamberlaine Esq. [a member of the Inner Temple], and my brother Silvester Petyt, my Trustees in trust and to the intent and purpose that they would use their utmost endeavours for preserving and keeping them safe and entire in such place or places as they or the major part of them or the survivors or survivor of them from time to time shall appoint and not to suffer or permit them to be lent embezzled or sold for which purpose I do give one hundred and fifty pounds to buy or build a place and making it convenient for preserving and keeping them which is to be settled upon my Trustees or the survivors or survivor of them or the heirs of the survivor of them in fee simple for the purpose expressed, and for my Trustees pain and care which they may be at I give to each of them five guineas. And to the intent that the said John Chamberlaine may have a more particular care of my said Collections I do give him a further legacy of one hundred pounds.

I give to Mr. George Holmes my Clerk and Deputy at the Tower he having lived with me above fourteen years two hundred pounds.

And I do hereby further earnestly desire my said Trustees that such special care may be taken of my Manuscript Collections by them and Tracts as that they or the major part of them or the survivors or survivor of them would in convenient time after my decease (in justice to truth and my memory) procure such of my manuscripts as I shall appoint under my hand or they may think fit to be printed to remain for public use to posterity. And for that end and purpose I do hereby give devise and consign out of my estate unto my said Trustees four hundred pounds to be laid out by my brother and executor in and about the perusing printing and publishing of them, if less will not do, though I hope they will pay for printing themselves, desiring him to take care of securing the said sum in case of his own death and the benefit of such printing and publishing to go to himself.

In a Codicil of the same date legacies left were £10 to 'Mr. Jenkinson my old Clerk'; £5 to Mr. William Prichard 'my Clerk'; and £1–1–6 to Mr. Silvester, Clerk of the Temple.

There does not appear to have been any appointment made by William Petyt as to what manuscripts were to be printed; the matter was therefore at the discretion of the trustees. This is a problem which has never been determined. The other instructions in the will were not delayed in execution. Silvester Petyt had secured probate immediately. He was prompt in paying the legacies. The £50 for books for the Inner Temple Library was paid in 1708; the £150 for building the Library, on completion, in 1708. On 27 October the Trustees consented, directed and appointed 'that for the preserving and keeping them safe and entire for public use, according to the intent and meaning of the said Will, the same manuscripts and other books shall for ever hereafter be deposited and kept in the late erected Library of the Inner Temple'. On 1 November the Sub-Treasurer gave Silvester Petyt a receipt for William Petyt's 391 volumes of which 209 were manuscripts and 182 printed, 'all of which are placed in the large new room built for a Library'. The details of the Manuscripts were given under the following eight heads: (1) Parliament Rolls, 33; (2) Journals of Parliament, 46; (3) Recorda, 38; (4) De Pardonibus etc., 14; (5) Proceedings in Parliament and Miscellanea, 56; (6) Law Commonplace Books, 6; (7) Charters etc., 7; (8) Placita, 9. This did not complete the delivery of manuscripts, for on 2 May 1709, Sir William Simpson, the Treasurer, gave authority to the Under Treasurer to give a receipt for the remainder of the books and manuscripts lately belonging to the late William Petyt. These must have included the twenty-three volumes of 'Manuscripts in vellum'.

On 28 January 1709 the draft of the Act of Parliament prepared by Silvester Petyt relating to the books, etc., given by William Petyt, his late brother, deceased, was agreed to and was to be put in the paper to pass at the next Parliament. This Act was lengthy and somewhat declamatory. It recited the relative section of the will and the appointment of the trustees, the legacy to build a place to house them. It emphasized that the collection had cost William Petyt many years' pains and study and stood him in much charge in collecting them. The obligation upon the trustees that such of the manuscripts as they should think fit should be printed. It stated that application had been made by several persons to the trustees 'touching the disposing of and placing the said books in several places out of this Society'. But several members of this Society has desired that they should be placed here. William Petyt, when Keeper of the Records in the Tower of London, 'did invite many students in the law to go to the Tower to search and see the records there and take out of them what notes or abstracts they pleased, gratis'. The Society having accepted the necessary conditions had created 'a very spacious and handsome room wherein several of the said books are already placed'. The thanks of the Society to the trustees was expressed. The trustees or any person employed by them were permitted to take copies or make extracts of the manuscripts, in order to be printed. The trustees, on request to the Library Keeper, were permitted to take out at once any one manuscript upon a receipt given, the same to be returned within two months.

Subsequently Silvester Petyt, by his will, 23 May 1719, provided that if the sum of £400 provided by the will of William Petyt was not sufficient for printing and publishing the balance was to be paid out of his personal estate, the transcript to be made at his charge and to be paid for by his executors. The Library was provided, the manuscripts and printed books were placed in it, and the necessary Library Keeper was appointed. The succession of Librarians, the cataloguing of the manuscripts, the facilities granted for search, and the use made of the manuscripts are all subjects which are detailed below, as will be Petyt's sources as a collector of manuscripts. The history of the trustees and their activities it is not possible to trace in detail, but it is clear they functioned sporadically at least until the opening decades of the nineteenth century.

It remains, therefore, but to give a general appreciation of William Petyt and his achievements. Most important of all he was the effective founder, not only of the manuscript collections in the Inner Temple Library but of the Library itself as a building. By his example he stimulated several of his contemporaries and some of his successors as Treasurers to make donations or bequests of manuscripts and books to the Library. The period of his active life covered the Restoration and the Revolution, through the renewed attempts to rule by prerogative and the attempt to return from the Anglican Church to the Roman allegiance. The political and ecclesiastical controversies through which he lived were no less fundamental and acrimonious than the controversies which had produced the Civil Wars and the Commonwealth. Dr. Brady advocated the sovereignty of the Crown; William Petyt advocated the sovereignty of Parliament. The purely political or constitutional aspects cannot be entirely separated from the ecclesiastical aspects. The ecclesiastical aspects were to continue for some years after Petyt's death; the purely political and consitutional aspects had really been resolved by the Revolution of 1689. In the preparation for this Petyt had played his part. It is, however, in his contribution to the story of records that Petyt's influence and work has been most productive. Before William Petyt died Thomas Rymer had published the first volume of his *Foedera* in 1704; Thomas Madox had published his *Formulare Anglicanum* in 1702. Both were indebted to William Petyt, while George Holmes, trained by Petyt, gave still further assistance to both. William Petyt did much to put English Public Records and their searches into a modern atmosphere and by his benefactions to the Inner Temple gave that Society the opportunity to establish a legal library which in manuscripts and books would have met the strict requirements of that master of the use of both, Sir Edward Coke.

3. THE PETYT COLLECTION OF MANUSCRIPTS

The 386 volumes in the Petyt Collection of Manuscripts immediately divide themselves into two distinct and separate sections; first, those manuscripts which were comprised in the bequest of William Petyt and delivered in 1708; and secondly those manuscripts derived from other sources, which during the eighteenth century were added to them to comprise the Petyt Collection, or which have been deemed to be of the Petyt Collection. The pressmarks added to the Petyt Manuscripts were extended to take in other manuscripts as they arrived in the Library. The first pressmark of the Collection, 502, was preceded by the pressmarks of printed books. The last pressmark of the Collection, 538, was followed by the pressmarks of printed books. The gaps between 502 and 538 were also presumably occupied by printed books. Out of the 386 manuscripts in the Petyt Collection 252 volumes were from the Petyt bequest, the remaining 134 from other sources. In Appendix I a full list of these latter manuscripts is given, in so far as they can be established. Of the 252 Petyt Manuscripts 120 volumes are mainly derived from transcripts from the Public Records, 79 comprised in 2 groups are respectively mainly medieval chronicles or other medieval manuscripts which were acquired from various sources by William Petyt, which numbered 23, and 56 were manuscripts or transcripts, many of them composite volumes, many of them made for William Petyt. This group of 56 volumes in all contains 1,227 items separate, the majority of them original documents. The remaining 53 of the Petyt Manuscripts are intermediate between the mainly transcript volumes and the mainly original volumes, as will be made clear below.

i. *The Petyt Manuscripts*

Firstly, as to the volumes which are mainly transcripts from the Public Records. The 120 volumes out of 252 volumes of Petyt Manuscripts which have been described as mainly composed of transcripts from Public Records are arranged into five main groups from the time of the first cataloguing of the Petyt Manuscripts as follows:

512. 'Touching the Government of England'	26 volumes
515. 'Placita de Juratis, Assisis etc.'	9 "
533. 'Recorda'	38 "
534. 'Rolls of Parliament'	33 "
536. 'De Pardonis etc.'	14 "

Of these groups the most complicated is that of Recorda. The Rolls of Parliament can be quickly disposed of, as the thirty-three volumes consist of transcripts from the Parliament Rolls, 5 Edward II to 6 Henry VIII, and contain almost the whole of the period comprised in the printed *Rotuli Parliamentorum*, in seven volumes, but are superior to the printed text, in so far as that was largely taken from transcripts, while Petyt and his clerks used the rolls themselves. Indeed this superiority was officially recognized, for when it was proposed to print a new edition of the Rolls of Parliament the proposed editor sought to use the Petyt set. Of course the Rolls of Parliament are used throughout the Petyt transcripts and drafts of his works and for these references this group of thirty-three volumes was mainly his source-book for these hundreds of other references.

The group of nine volumes of transcripts, extracts, and indexes of the Assize Rolls, Coram Rege Rolls, and Common Plea Rolls, together with a few Curia Regis Rolls, can also be somewhat summarily dismissed, for though they show that the Coram Rege Rolls for the reigns of Edward I to Edward III have been carefully gone through for the selected extracts to be made, many of the other volumes were indebted to Agard's Indexes for their selection and information. The use of the Assize Rolls is restricted to Assizes for three counties during the reign of Edward I. It should be noted also that nowhere in all his transcripts and references does William Petyt borrow from the Exchequer of Pleas Rolls. He did not expect to find anything there which was likely to be particularly relevant to his immediate purposes. In this he was mistaken, but, in his time and since, the Exchequer of Pleas Rolls have been little used for intensive research and comparatively little has been culled from them. Again, throughout the Petyt transcripts there are references to many Coram Rege and Common Plea Rolls not used in this particular group, to late in the reign of Henry VIII, but in this group he seems to have been acquainted with every Curia Regis Roll, as they were known to exist in his time, and with the Coram Rege and Common Plea Rolls in so far as they had been indexed to the reign of Edward III.

This completes what need be said at present about judicial records, for it was the records of the Chancery in particular which William Petyt had transcribed and which he used. For the medieval period the catalogue of Chancery records he used reads like a catalogue of the Chancery Records in the Public Record Office as issued today. There was not a class of that great series of Chancery Enrolments which he did not use. The Charter Rolls he transcribed largely for purposes connected with boroughs and peerage, but he got political history out of them as well. The Patent Rolls he used partly for the same purposes but also for his survey of administration; the Close Rolls for administrative purposes and also especially for summonses to Parliament and writs de expensis which were enrolled on the dorse; what he could not get in taxation from the Patent and Close Rolls he got from the Fine Rolls. The Norman, Gascon, Welsh, Scottish, Roman, and Treaty Rolls (including the Almain and French Rolls) he used for national as well as diplomatic history. The Pardon Rolls, now put amongst the Supplementary Patent Rolls, made their contribution to his accounts of persons and payments out of the Exchequer. He used the Coronation Roll of Edward II for his constitutional studies and the Extract Rolls for the political and other forfeitures they illustrated. He used at least a dozen of the Cartae Antiquae Rolls, not caring whether they were of Chancery or Exchequer origin. He was also indebted to all the Statute Rolls from Edward I to Edward IV, though here he was also well served by his own and other people's manuscript statute books.

Of the Chancery records, next to the enrolments, come the Chancery files or Brevia Regis, a considerable number of which remain unsorted to this day. Those which have been arranged are in classes which would confound William Petyt. Many bundles of what he saw have been dispersed; in his day bundles which had been dispersed were already being reassembled, frequently on a vague chronological basis rather than according to class. Thus for the reigns of Edward I to Richard II he made transcripts from bundles of Brevia Regis and he made transcripts from what he describes as Bundles of Letters and Writs, and Bundles of Letters and Records. He had frequent recourse to what he describes as a New Miscellaneous Bundle *tempore* Henry III, Edward I, Edward II, and Edward III, which must have covered a range of more than a century, and also to a New Miscellaneous Bundle *tempore* Richard II, Henry IV, Henry V, and Henry VI, which probably covered a little less than a century. But he also used a Bundle of Writs, 16 & 17 John, a Miscellaneous

Bundle, 21 Henry III, a Select Bundle of Records *tempore* Richard II, a Bundle of Writs of *scire facias*, 21 Richard II, and even a bundle vaguely described as 'Letters in the Tower'. The main period covered is Henry III to Edward II, and there is nothing after the time of Henry VI. Many of the bundles have been disrupted owing to the activities of William Petyt's predecessor, William Prynne, for a number of them are printed in the third volume of his *Records*. Many of the bundles which were then made up have been dispersed since. Many items and bundles are now lost or untraceable. This can be proved by a check made on the documents printed by Prynne. So in the scores of records transcribed by Petyt his transcripts are now the only source. And besides writs and records there were Bundles of Certificates for 42 Henry III, 49 Henry III, for instance, or a Bundle of Writs of Privy Seals, 25 Edward I.

There were certain classes of records for which William Petyt made special search. They were bundles of Writs of Summons to Parliament and Returns, and Parliamentary Petitions. In his pursuit of the former he was not unsuccessful. Among unknown bundles of Parliamentary Summonses he found in the Tower were those of the Parliaments of 23 Edward I and 10 Edward III, which are to be found amongst his transcripts, but he also made extracts from dozens of Parliamentary Writs and Returns Edward I to Edward III. He made transcripts from some thirty-four Bundles of Parliamentary Petitions, most of which were in regnal years, though sometimes he found a made-up bundle of such records. For instance, he used a bundle of Petitions, *tempore* Edward I, II, and III, uncertain years. He also culled petitions from the K.R. and L.T.R. Memoranda Rolls of the Exchequer. All Parliamentary Petitions have now been placed in a special collection and arranged alphabetically under the name of the petitioner, irrespective of Parliament or date, which is now sometimes almost impossible to establish with accuracy. Hundreds available in Petyt's time have now been lost and of many of these his transcripts provide the only information.

William Petyt's use of Exchequer records is not nearly so comprehensive as his use of Chancery records. The only reference to the Pipe Rolls is to that first surviving Pipe Roll of 31 Henry I, which, in company with his time and later, he dated 5 Stephen. He uses some half dozen Subsidy Rolls, vicariously from 9 Edward II to 2 Henry VI. The Exchequer records he used most, however, were the King's Remembrancer Memoranda Rolls and the Lord Treasurer's Remembrancer Memoranda Rolls, record sources of great importance but little used during his time or before his time, and comparatively little used after his time, except by the great Thomas Madox in his *History of the Exchequer*. Petyt used these rolls, rather indiscriminately, it is true, from 4 Henry III to 17 Edward III, and very exceptionally later. There is one reference to the L.T.R. Memoranda Roll for 2 & 3 Philip and Mary, for example. In all Petyt culled extracts from seventy K.R. Memoranda Rolls and from fifty-four L.T.R. Memoranda Rolls. He utilized almost every section of these many-sided rolls and his selections for transcript were well chosen and illuminating. Even today very few of these rolls have been published in full or calendared, though for some hundreds of years they are a main source of English history. These transcripts of Petyt's, therefore, are of the utmost value still today, for in most cases the contents of the rolls remain unknown and most of them have not even the membranes numbered consecutively.

Of Exchequer records, there are also a few references to Accounts which he describes in such places as Accounts of the 20th granted, 18 Edward II, Book of the 15th and 20th granted, I Edward III, with the Clerk of the Pipe, Account of Aid on marriage of the King's daughter, 17 Edward III. Among the records of the King's Remembrancer he used such cartularies as that of the Abbey of Ramsey and such books of reference as the Red Book of the Exchequer, Testa de Neville or Liber Feodurum, and the Black Book of the Exchequer, just as he had used the Placita Parliamentaria, although it had already been printed by William Riley, and the Memoranda de Parliamento, 1305, which was not edited until 1893 by F. W. Maitland. He used Bundles of K.R. Writs for Henry III and Edward I and even one Bundle of Brevia Emissa pro Rege of 2 Edward I. He used an Original Acquittance from the Lord Treasurer's category and from the Treasury of Receipt including Papal Bulls. Sometimes his references are difficult to trace as the following examples show: Bundle entitled on Flemish merchants etc., Parliament of Westminster, 7 Edward I, in a certain Bag no. 10 in Tower; Miscellanea in a certain box in Tower of London, 1302; and where are now the 'Roll of Superiority of the King of England in the Kingdom of Scotland, 19–23 Edward I' and the 'Roll of Superiority of the sea of England and the office of Admiralty, 26 Edward I'? There are later records which it is difficult to trace today: the Ordinance Roll of the Privy Council, 1–3 Henry VI, and the Roll for Merchants of Newcastle upon Tyne, 29 Henry VI. There are two intriguing records relating to Ireland which cannot be identified, probably because neither exists any longer; 'Roll of the doings of the ministers of Edward II in Ireland' and the White Book of the Exchequer of Ireland.

In addition to the Bundles of Writs of Summons to Parliament which William Petyt found in the Tower of London, and the many Bundles of Parliamentary Petitions which William Petyt transcribed, he found bundles of Clerical Proxies to Parliament, undisturbed, which no longer exist, and from two of them made considerable transcripts, which he describes as Bundle of Proxies of Clergy, 8 Richard II, and Bundle of Procurations in Parliament, which also contained a number of lay proxies. The class of Parliamentary Proxies has now been arranged in a Special Collection but that does not contain all those which William Petyt transcribed.

There is one further group of Public Records from which William Petyt made transcripts, the arrangement of which has been radically altered since his day; they are what he calls Bundles of Escheats or Bundles of Inquisitions. The bundles he uses are mainly of the reigns of Edward III and Henry V, though there are also examples of bundles for 22 Edward I and 2 Edward II. These bundles are now arranged as Inquisitions post mortem, Inquisitions ad quod damnum, and Inquisitions, Miscellaneous, but all Petyt saw and transcribed have not survived.

It will be apparent from the above brief recital that it was not only the Public Records in the Tower of London with which William Petyt was familiar. He also used the records in the Rolls Chapel, in the Chapter House, and at Westminster Hall, as well as the Palace of Westminster. He refers to Acts of Parliament in the Rolls Chapel and to Acts in the custody of the Clerk of Parliament in the House of Lords; to a Docquet of Warrants in the Signet Office, 1686; to Original Bills in the custody of the Clerk of the House of Lords in the Office of the Clerk of Parliament; to Parliament Roll, 27 Henry VIII, in the custody of the Clerk of the House of Lords.

What has been dealt with so far can be contained within the threefold division of Public Records into those of the Chancery, the Exchequer, and the Judicature. But there are among the Petyt Manuscripts one group of forty-six volumes which have always been described as 'Journals of Parliament' and this theme overflows into some dozen volumes of the next group. These forty-six volumes are mainly derived from transcripts which William Petyt caused to be made of the Journals of the House of Lords and the Journals of the House of Commons. Both are used from the beginning of the respective series, those of the House of Lords from 1 Henry VIII to 17 Charles II, those of the House of Commons from 1 Edward VI to 32 Charles II. When the Journals of the House of Commons were to be printed these Petyt Manuscripts were copied to fill in gaps or indecipherable passages which had appeared in the original Journals since the transcription was made. They can still supply deficiencies in the original and the printed versions. The House of Lords Journals as transcribed can similarly supply deficiencies and the House of Lords has sought to remedy its deficiencies by having photostatic copies made of certain of them, as will appear below.

These Petyt Manuscripts, however, do not contain extracts only from the Public Records and the Records of the Houses of Parliament. They also draw lavishly from two other sources, first, the Cotton Manuscripts, which were in Petyt's time still in private ownership, but in a private ownership which was generous in the facilities it gave for inspection and use; secondly, manuscripts in other private possession, including his own, and particularly the Archives of the city of London. The printed sources he used, many of them long published, some of them hot from the contemporary press, and both long published and contemporary well represented by foreign printed books, come only generally within the scope of this Introduction. But it is interesting to note that the printed books most frequently referred to are those of John Selden. Nor is this surprising, as works of his such as his *Titles of Honor*, his *History of Tithes*, his *Eadmer* and *Fleta*, for instance, contained matter essential for Petyt's purpose. The early printed English Chronicles and such authors as William Lambard, Sir Robert Cotton, William Camden, William Prynne, Spelman, Dugdale, and Sir Edward Coke were equally necessary, as were the *Statutes* of Pynson, Rastell, and Totell.

First, as to Petyt's use of the Cotton Manuscripts. In all he makes references to forty-three Cotton Manuscripts besides some very few Cotton Charters. These manuscripts are mainly Ecclesiastical Cartularies and Registers, Chronicles, tracts on specific subjects, and original documents. The Cartularies and Registers include the Register of the Church of Worcester, the Register of the Church of St. Peter's, York, the Great Register of the Abbey of Abingdon, and the History of the Church of Abingdon, the Register of the Monastery of St. Augustine's, Canterbury, the History of the Church of Ely, the Register of the Abbey of St. Benet of Hulme, Charters of the Church of Winchester, the Register of the Abbey of Evesham, the Register of the Church of St. Mary's, Lincoln, the Book on the Site etc. of the Church of St. Martin's, Battle, the Annals of the Monastery of Tewkesbury, and the Register of the Abbey of St. Peter's, Westminster. Among the Chronicles are the Chronicle of Benedict Abbas, the Chronicle of Dunstable, the Annals of Winchelcombe, Abbreviations of Chronicles, Annales Acelphali, 1195–1307, the Chronicle of Roger of Wendover, the Chronicle of Florence of Worcester, the Chronicle of the Church of Winchester, the Chronicle of the Monastery of Hagnaby, the Chronicle of the Monk of Coggeshill, Extracts from Chronicles etc., Liber de Gestis Regum Britonum, Chroniques de London, Annals of the Monastery of Tewkesbury, Annales de Gestis Anglorum ad 1377, and the Cronica de Mailros. On special subjects William Petyt used a volume of Ancient Charters, Papal Bulls, etc., and such items from other volumes as Inquisitions on the Lands of the Church of Ely, Magna Carta, a Charter of King Egbert, sections of Chronicles which he said were in the hand of Matthew Paris, the Order of Coronation, Articles demanded of Edward II by the Earls of Lancaster and Warwick, a Declaration by King Stephen, the Coronation Oath of Richard I, the Modus tenendi Parliamentum, the Officium Senescalii Anglie, the Coronation of Edward II, and the Second Coronation of Henry III.

The original documents are mainly Charters and Papal Bulls. The Charters include several in Anglo-Saxon, and the Papal Bulls number scores, covering several centuries. There is the Barons' Letter to the Pope, 1301, and Writs of Privy Seal. Some of the Papal Bulls have undoubtedly come from the Public Records, as had the Acts of the Privy Council, 10–19 Henry VI. Many of the documents are of the greatest historical importance.

The list of the Cotton Manuscripts used by William Petyt is given in Appendix IV, where those volumes which were destroyed or badly damaged in the fire in the Cotton Library in 1731, or which are otherwise wanting, are indicated. For out of the forty-three manuscripts eight are not now available for use. The brief contents of these eight manuscripts can be obtained from Thomas Smith's *Catalogue of the Manuscripts in the Cotton Library*, which was published in 1697 and so was known to William Petyt. Petyt also had his own manuscript catalogues of the Cotton Manuscripts, two in number, now among the Petyt Manuscripts. These Petyt transcripts have an importance inasmuch as his extracts are arranged chronologically or by subject. Still greater is their importance in so far as they can supply items from or parts of the manuscripts which are no longer available. Thus there are a number of important transcripts from the Annales Acelphali, 1195–1317, some of which are given verbatim in the present catalogue. Among other items in the same category are the Inquisitions on the Lands of the Church of Ely, the Chronicle of Dunstable, and the Chronicle of Florence of Worcester. Every reference to a Cotton Manuscript has been carefully noted in the present catalogue.

Of the other privately owned manuscripts, which William Petyt used extensively in his volumes of transcripts, first place must be given to the Archives of the city of London. Three volumes are almost entirely composed of such extracts and the range of city records which he used is very wide. It included the mysterious Laudes Britannie which must have served as a select city cartulary; the Liber de Antiquis Legibus, the Liber Albus, and the Liber Custumarium, at least twenty-four of the Letter Books, twenty-one volumes of Journals, and fourteen volumes of Repertories. These three volumes were his collections when he was preparing the city's case in the Quo Warranto proceedings of 1683, and he had complete access of its archives. The papers he prepared based on these researches in the city's defence would have been a valuable document, but apart from his raw material in its preparation his manuscripts contain nothing upon the matter. The Laudes Britannie and the Liber de Antiquis Legibus and certain of the Letter Books turn up in many of the other volumes of the Petyt transcripts. As the Letter Books after L (1497) and none of the Journals or Repertories have been printed or calendared, the three volumes, in particular, provide a very valuable approach to certain of the city records designed by an expert in city history and privileges, and selected for a practical purpose.

Of libraries there seemed to be only two to which Petyt was indebted, the Bodleian, for a Laud manuscript on the History of the Church of Ely, and Lincoln's Inn Library, for the Register of the Prior and Chapter of Bath. His debt was indeed considerable to ecclesiastical sources. He made many transcripts from the Old Register in the Archives of the Archbishop of Canterbury, and from the muniments of Christ Church, Canterbury. He acknowledged that he took transcripts from 'certain rolls in the archives of the Arches of London' to Edward I and Edward III 'on the Superiority of the Kingdom of England over Scotland', and he also extracted the text of papal bulls from there. He took from the Great White Register in the possession of the Dean and Chapter of York, and from a manuscript book in the possession of the Dean and Chapter of St. Paul's. He used the Book of the Monastery of Lichfield, and the Register of the Cathedral Church of Chichester in the possession of the Dean and Chapter of Chichester, and original documents in the possession of the Dean and Chapter of Windsor. He got his friend Gilbert Burnet, Bishop of Salisbury, to let him copy the Salisbury Magna Carta, on 21 May 1689, and John Moore,

Bishop of Lincoln, to transcribe from the Register of Old Charters and other Letters Patent and Close of Christ Church, Canterbury, 1285–1327, which was in his possession, 1698. Moore's library was famous throughout Europe, and was bought by George I and presented to Cambridge University.

Petyt transcribed from the Wilton Cartulary in the possession of the Earl of Pembroke; the Red Book of the Church of Bath in the possession of Thomas Guidot, M.D.; the Register of Glastonbury in the possession of Ralph Sheldon, of Beoley, co. Worcester; and he transcribed ten papal bulls from the Register of the Abbey of Winchelcombe in the possession of Sir Ralph Dutton bart. He got his extracts from the Chronicle of Adam Murimuth from the College of Arms, and Peter le Neve, Rouge Croix, not only made available to him the collections of Robert Glover, Somerset, but allowed his own transcripts of charters of Henry I and Stephen to be retranscribed.

He used a manuscript of Sir Ciriac Petyt, in the possession of Thomas Petyt, of Colkins, co. Kent; a Register of Writs in the possession of Lord Holles. His contemporaries and colleagues at the Inner Temple lent him manuscripts from which to transcribe. Thus Sir John Trevor, who was Treasurer, 1674–5, Speaker of the House of Commons twice, and Master of the Rolls, 1685, lent him a manuscript of Sir Roger Owen. Sir Samuel Baldwin, Reader in 1669, and Serjeant at Law the same year, lent him a manuscript of his own. John Peachey, who had been called to the bar the same year as William Petyt, lent him manuscript Statutes which were put to good uses. Sir Nathaniel Powell bart., who was Treasurer, 1691–2, let him transcribe his Magna Carta. Amongst others who contributed manuscript Statutes were Dr. John Lapthorne, Sir Thomas Thynne, and John Cook, one of the Prothonotaries of Common Pleas. Evan Seys, a Serjeant at Law, lent him his Register of the monastery of Malmesbury, and Sir John Maynard, whom he describes as Serjeant at Law to Charles II, his Cases, Edward II, from an ancient manuscript in his hands.

The search of all these manuscripts, if undertaken personally by William Petyt, would not have occasioned him a great deal of travelling, as the great majority of them were in London. On the other hand, time and place make it necessary that he must have taken transcripts from copies rather than the originals of the old manuscript Book which was in the possession of Henry Spelman, 1640, of the Register of Evreux, the Cartulary of St. Denis, and the Register of Charters in the Library of St. Victor. He also used his own manuscript Register of Writs, at least two volumes of Statutes, one of which contained Statutes of Henry VII, one of his own chronicles, that of Roger of Hoveden, and his Register of Charters of the Cathedral Church of Salisbury, and that composite volume of his which contained the Letters and Bulls of Martin V.

The transcripts among the Petyt Manuscripts were, therefore, derived from a large arena of record sources and a very substantial area of private manuscripts. Strictures have been made upon the quality of those transcripts, but such strictures seem to have emanated from one chief source, John Caley, a professional archivist who amassed much work and more money from his undertakings for the Record Commission, most of which work was done by copyists for him, just as much of the transcripts among the Petyt Manuscripts had been done by William Petyt's clerks in the Tower of London. Lord Redesdale's comments on the Petyt transcripts were no doubt inspired by John Caley, who was employed by him in the preparation of the record material for the Reports on the Dignity of a Peer. That there were errors in transcription of both records and manuscripts is certain and inevitable. These do not appear to have been more numerous than one would expect to find in the second half of the seventeenth century when most of them were made. What is more noticeable than errors in the transcripts is the frequent repetition of the same document. This appears, in part, to be deliberate. Some of the groups of transcripts are based upon a chronological order, other groups are based upon a subject classification. This made a certain amount of repetition desirable. Other volumes are drafts of works for publication which used the transcripts. Again repetition was inevitable. But some of the repetition seems to have been entirely unnecessary, though even these enable a comparison for accuracy to be made.

The will of William Petyt had provided for the publication of certain of his transcripts. Not only was publication an obligation imposed on the trustees but the necessary money was made available and subsequently augmented by the will of Silvester Petyt. There is little doubt that it was the intention of the trustees to fulfil their obligations, and there was at least one of the trustees who was more than competent to judge the value of the material and the quality of the transcripts, John Anstis, and in the first few years he would have had available the advice and support of Silvester Petyt, who not only knew his brother's work, but was himself not unacquainted with the problem. Time after time, for more than a century, plans to publish were pursued but nothing eventuated. The value of publication was becoming steadily less as more and more of the originals were published verbatim or in calendar. As transcripts they are still valuable. Owing to losses among the original records and of a few of the Cotton Manuscripts many of the Petyt transcripts are either the only or the most accurate versions which are available. The careful preservation and the complete listing has, therefore, been thought necessary. In many cases the value of the transcripts, even when the originals have survived, remains high. It will, for instance, be several generations before all the K.R. and L.T.R. Memoranda Rolls of the Exchequer will be available in print, even in summary or calendar. Meanwhile the Petyt transcripts of them will continue to supply a deficiency; and, in the case of Parliamentary Petitions which are no more, until the text of the Petyt transcripts has been made available in print, the transcripts will remain an important source of more than Parliamentary History.

Besides the value of Petyt's transcripts of records no longer available through loss, many other Public Records have deteriorated badly since his time and some are now illegible. This gives the Petyt transcripts an added value. The translations of transcripts which he sometimes provides give a further value. For the translations are well done. Special records relating to Scotland are as familiar to him as the general classes of records relating to England and Wales, and he was not unacquainted with special records relating to Ireland.

There remain the rest of the Petyt Manuscripts, 79 out of the 252 volumes, to be described briefly, and some estimate of whence they were derived should be attempted. The remainder of the Petyt Manuscripts have been arranged or have arranged themselves in the following two groups:

511. 'Manuscripts in vellum'	23 volumes
538. 'Proceedings in Parliament and Miscellanies'	56 „

For to the 120 volumes which have been described above as Petyt transcripts there have been added the 46 volumes of Journals of Parliament and the 7 volumes of the group which contains the 3 volumes of transcripts which come from the Archives of the city of London to make the total of Petyt Manuscripts 252 volumes, leaving in the Petyt Collection a further 134 volumes which have been derived from other sources. These two groups, totally 79 manuscripts, are, however, not the only Petyt Manuscripts which remain to be dealt with, for among the group of 9 volumes which contain the Assize and other Judicial Rolls there have been appended 3 volumes which are not transcripts, and to the group which contain the transcripts from the Archives of the city of London 4 volumes which in part only are transcripts from Public Records.

The 23 volumes in the first group consist of 5 volumes of Chronicles, 4 volumes of popular continental works, 9 volumes of legal manuscripts, including Statutes, 4 volumes on ecclesiastical jurisdiction, and 1 volume of historical collections relating to Scotland. Of the Chronicles by far the most important is Roger de Hoveden's Historia, which belonged to Fountains Abbey. It was probably written in the Durham scriptorium about the end of the second decade of the thirteenth century and after it left Fountains had a list of quite distinguished Yorkshire owners. It is well written and has some interesting illuminations. It has never been used for collation purposes, has interesting marginal entries, and it escaped even the great William Stubbs when he prepared his edition of Hoveden for the Rolls Series. In many directions it is an outstanding English medieval manuscript. The other Chronicles are interesting if not specially important, and include Ralph Higden, Robert Manning, and some of the Brute Chronicles. The popular continental works include Vincent de Beauvais's Speculum Historiale, Francis Barbaro's De re Uxoria Liber, and Guido de Columnia's History of the Trojan War. The most important manuscript in this section is the beautifully written and well-illuminated Somnium Scipionis by Macrobius, the earliest manuscript in the Library, dating perhaps to the mid twelfth century.

The legal manuscripts are mainly such as one would have expected William Petyt to acquire, and to acquire for practical use. They include a fifteenth-century Register of Writs, a volume of Statutes, 1 Edward III to 3 Henry VII, with the Modus tenendi Parliamentum prefixed; a volume of Statutes to 25 Edward I, legal tracts and another Register of Writs, of the last years of the thirteenth or the first years of the fourteenth century; a miscellaneous collection of Law Reports and notes on legal cases, Edward III to Elizabeth I, collected by or for Sir James Altham, who became a Baron of the Exchequer in 1605, and a judge of distinction and independence; another special collection of special interest relating to Sir James Dyer, Chief Justice of Common Pleas, 1559–82, which have been edited by John Valliant, a Bencher of the Inner Temple. Another collection of cases, arguments, and notes, 1634–64, were by William Prynne 'and in his handwriting'. Two other volumes contained the only incunabula in the Library, one an Abridgment of the Statutes, printed by Machlinia and Lettou about 1481, another Nova Statuta, 1 Edward III–22 Edward IV, printed by Machlinia in 1484, and Statuta, 1 Richard III, printed by Machlinia in 1485. The first of these volumes had added some 115 folios which the ancient entry described as 'several pleadings and writs in the Reigns of Edward III and Henry VI'.

Of the four volumes on ecclesiastical jurisdiction, two are commonplace; the third is of very great importance. Of the commonplace the first is a collection of treatises, notes, and arguments directed to the dispute with George Abbot, Archbishop of Canterbury, on prohibitions and modus decimandi, in the reign of James I; the second a tract on Consecration of Churches and other matters of ecclesiastical discipline. The third is the earliest known precedent book of English ecclesiastical forms, compiled by Richard de Haute partly out of original documents, and probably first put together about 1300. In form as well as in content it is a volume of the greatest interest and appears to be a formulary for use in the Court of Arches or the Court of Audience of Canterbury and it may well be the source-book on which the Canterbury Cathedral tract on that subject is based. It is of value for investigating not only the judicial ecclesiastical administration of the Province of Canterbury, but also the history of canon law and procedure.

Finally, the group contains the only ecclesiastical cartulary acquired by William Petyt. He was somewhat late for the acquisition of monastic cartularies. The hundreds which had been thrown on the market after the Dissolution of the Monasteries had long been safely bestowed in lay libraries. Unfortunately there is no evidence whence Petyt obtained the cartulary of the Cathedral Church of Salisbury. It contains valuable charters from the time of William II, some of which do not appear in any other Salisbury cartulary. The main part of this cartulary was written in the second half of the thirteenth century and additions were made up to the second half of the fifteenth century. The additions, too, contain material not otherwise available. It was considered important enough by Sir Thomas Phillipps for him to issue privately a two-folio summary of its contents in 1826, but it has never been calendared or collated with other Salisbury cartularies.

The other group generally and vaguely described as 'Proceedings in Parliament and Miscellanies' is more than twice as numerous and more than doubly various in its scope. It opens with some seventeen volumes of Proceedings in Parliament, and naturally, as gathered together by William Petyt, the parliamentary interest persists in many other volumes in the group. Other volumes consist of draft treatises, transcripts of treatises, and collections of precedents. As has been stated many of the volumes are composite and consist of up to 317 items in a single volume. None of the volumes containing Proceedings in Parliament are transcripts of or straight entries from the Journals of the House of Lords or the Journals of the House of Commons, though many of them do contain extracts from them. The Proceedings concerned extend from Henry VIII to Charles II, though the precedents go back to the reign of Edward I. Other volumes contain draft or scribbled notes of proceedings in the House of Lords written by Robert Bowyer or Henry Elsynge, successively Clerks of Parliament. The drafts include three separate drafts of Henry Elsynge's Modus tenendi Parliamentum, one of which is annotated by John Selden. There are two transcripts of John Selden's Touching Jurisdiction in Parliament, and also a draft treatise on The Manner of Proceeding in Parliament.

There are transcripts of William Prynne's Reading on the Petition of Right, 1662, of Sir Robert Cotton's Power of the Crown to raise Money, of A Display of Bastardy, 1552, of Sir John Dodridge's Treatise concerning the Nobility, of Sir Charles Cornwallis's Life and Death of Prince Henry, Treatises on the Court of Chancery and the Court of Star Chamber. There is the author's draft, with corrections, of Sir John Burgh's Sovereignty of the Sea of England, and a Treatise of Ireland, by John Dymoke, probably in the author's hand. Among formularies or precedent books there are two of special importance, Sir George Coppin's, Clerk of the Crown (appointed in 1597), Collection of Commissions under the Great Seal, compiled during the last years of Elizabeth I, and covering almost exclusively 1–45 Elizabeth I, and Francis Alford's Formulary Book of Letters and Petitions. The last mentioned was written by a pushful careerist, long a Member of Parliament, and contains some 250 forms, 1583–91, most of which can be identified and covering a very wide range of curious and important incidents and occurrences. One is interpreted here.

An interesting, if tragic, episode in the domestic history of the Inner Temple is supplied by Francis Alford's Letter Book of forms. In the entry the initials only of the parties concerned are given, but the full names and identities of all of them can be discovered from the Records of the Inn. The entry records the manslaughter of a student by a fellow student in a duel and the protest of the father of the victim against the family and friends of the victor. Richard Blackwell, of Wensley, co. Derby, was admitted to the Inner Temple on 15 June 1586 from Clement's Inn. His pledges were

Nicholas Kynnersley and Ralph Wright. Richard Kynnersley, when he was admitted in 1579, was described as of North Witham, Lincolnshire, and he was called to the bar in 1587. Ralph Wright had been admitted 20 June 1579, when his pledge was Nicholas Kynnersley. He was described as of Snelston, Derbyshire, and of Lyon's Inn, and was called to the bar in 1590, and became a Bencher in 1612. Thomas Hele of Holbeton, co. Devon, was admitted on 7 March 1584, from Lyon's Inn. His pledges were Elize Hele and Warwick Hele. Elize Hele had been admitted in 1580 from Lyon's Inn when he was described as of Brixton, co. Devon. He was called to the bar in 1590. Warwick Hele, of Plymouth, was admitted in 1582 and proceeded no further.

So much for the contestants. The facts as stated by Richard Blackwall Esq., the father of the victim, as put to the Privy Council, are as follows. Richard Blackwall was his eldest son and heir, not passing 19 years old. He had been 'most injuriously beaten and abused' by Thomas Hele, who had unmercifully slain him 'by evil practice, trained into the field, overladen with his weapon and quite out of breath'. Thomas Hele had been apprehended and committed to Newgate. Blackwall senior had come to London to pursue the laws of the realm against Hele, but he was persuaded by Richard Newbold, his own kinsman, Francis Hamond, and Gerard Lowther, to whom he had been specially recommended by Ralph Wright, their true and faithful friend, being godfather to young Blackwall, 'not to follow the rigour of the law'. His son had been slain in the field, Hele was a very young gentleman, and it was not charitable to pursue his death, which was accidental. It would not restore his son's life. Hele had many rich uncles whose heir he was, and many friends. He was therefore more likely to waste his patrimony in the suit than prevail. They exhorted him to a composition by which Henry Hele, an uncle, would pay £300 toward the better education of his other son. The agreement having been made was not kept. What happened to the cause before the Council is not known, but what happened to most of the interested parties can be discovered from the Records of the Society, and the truth of some of the allegations at least can be tested.

Firstly, Thomas Hele would seem to have been about two years older than young Blackwall. The Heles were a large and wealthy family. Between 1565 and 1640 no less than sixteen Devonshire Heles were admitted to the Inner Temple. There is no other Blackwall family that can be identified with Richard Blackwall of Wensley admitted. In the margin opposite the entry in the Admission Book is written 'Mort.'. As to the go-betweens, Richard Newbold of the town of Nottingham had been specially admitted in 1568 at the instance of the Reader, Thomas Marriot, Treasurer, 1577–8. He seems never to have been called to the bar. Francis Hamond of Ockingham, co. Berks., had been specially admitted in 1574, from Clement's Inn, at the instance of Edmund Anderson, the Reader, afterwards Chief Justice of Common Pleas. He, too, seems never to have been called. Gerard Lowther, of Lowther, Westmorland, was admitted in 1581, from Clement's Inn, was called to the bar in 1590 and in 1610 became a Justice of Common Pleas in Ireland.

The lucky duellist, Thomas Hele, was never called to the bar. He became High Sherriff of Devon in 1618 and died at a ripe age in 1634. His pledge Elize Hele became a Bencher in 1603 and was Treasurer, 1614–15, and was buried in Exeter Cathedral in 1635. His other pledge, Warwick Hele, was never called to the bar. Of other members of the numerous family John Hele, the elder, was appointed to the Bench in 1584, was Reader in 1594, and the same year became a Serjeant at Law. John Hele the younger, of Holbeton, became a Bencher in 1601. It would seem that the duel was overweighted in age, wealth, and family connections.

William Petyt's interests as an archivist are substantially represented. There is a list of Acts of Parliament remaining in the Rolls Chapel, 1 Richard III to 7 James I; a Collection of the Records in the Four Treasuries etc. from Arthur Agarde's Compendium; a Description of various classes of records in the Tower of London, arranged alphabetically, including the main series of Chancery Rolls and certain Exchequer and Judicial Records, with notes and comments on certain classes; a Calendar of all the Acts of Parliament in the Office of the Clerk of Parliament, 12 Henry VII to 32 Charles II; a subject index, written in the sixteenth century, to certain matters in the Public Records. The contents of the other volumes range from a Collection of Apparitions 1603–7, to a volume which contains a Brief Summary and Demonstration of the Estate of England and Wales (1574–8); from the In Letter Book of John, Lord Russell, 1549, to the In Letter Book of John Whitgift, Archbishop of Canterbury, 1579–85.

The contents of six volumes consist almost entirely of original documents, and although these cover a wide field and over a century in span, the most important are of the second half of the sixteenth century. They include holograph letters of, or signs manual of Edward VI, as Prince and King, of the Princess Mary and the Princess Elizabeth, and of 'Jane the Queen', and 'Mary the Queen', and signs manual of Elizabeth I and Charles I. The autograph letters, of which there are hundreds in all, include letters of Matthew Parker, Edmund Grindal, and John Whitgift, successively Archbishops of Canterbury, William Juxon, Bishop of London, Matthew Hutton, Dean of York, Richard Cox, Bishop of Ely, Richard Bancroft, Archbishop of Canterbury, William Cecil, Lord Burghley, and his son, Robert, Earl of Salisbury, Sir Edward Coke and Thomas, Lord Ellesmere, Anthony, Earl of Shaftesbury, Lord Chancellor, Arthur Capel, Earl of Essex, and Sir Christopher Wren. This short selection of names, however, gives no real indication of the width or depth of range. On subject the Elizabethan Settlement of Religion struggles for first place with the disputes amongst the recusants between the secular clergy and the Jesuits. The ecclesiastical importance seems to outstrip the legal importance of the material. Tragic happenings demand many documents and much space, such as the careers, trials, and executions of Mary, Queen of Scots, Robert Devereux, Earl of Essex, and Sir

Walter Raleigh, and the less tragic downfall of Francis Bacon. These are all well documented and described.

These two groups, however, do not exhaust the drafts and transcripts of works as many have been included among groups which largely consist of Petyt transcripts from the Public Records. Thus the group generally described as 'Touching the Government of England' contains the draft of part of Petyt's Jus Parliamentaria and drafts of nine others of his published or unpublished works, the contemporary descriptions of the subjects include the Norman Conquest, Successive Governments in England, Parliament and Government of England during the reign of King John, Rights of the Commons, Manner of Succession of the Crown of England, and Anglo-Saxon Parliaments.

Among the nine volumes of the group described as 'Placitis de Juratis et Assisis etc.' the last three volumes are, respectively, the Lord Chamberlain's Entry Book, 1621–2, which contains a mass of most interesting information on plays and players and many other subjects; Annuities or Pensions, Fees and Wages paid at the Exchequer, 1599; and a transcript of Sir Thomas Fanshaw's Practice of the Court of Exchequer. Among the seven volumes described as 'Charters, Privileges etc.' one comprises Statutes, Richard II–1 Richard III; another has transcripts of public and private Acts of Parliament, 1 Richard III–37 Henry VIII; and a third transcripts of certain Acts of Parliament, 4 Henry VIII–17 Charles I, with a lengthy transcript of various matters concerning the town of Calais and its Marches. Another volume has transcripts of public and private Acts of Parliament, 1 Edward VI–8 Elizabeth I, and other extracts and transcripts, particularly concerning Mary, Queen of Scots. Lastly the group of forty-six volumes described as 'Journals of Parliament' has three volumes which are the private journals of Members of Parliament, by Edward Nicholas, 1621, Edward Montagu, 1624, and an unidentified member, 1628. Whatever criticism may be made of the arrangement of these groups of manuscripts the variety and value of their contents cannot be gainsaid.

On the Petyt Manuscripts, one important question only remains for discussion. Whence did William Petyt derive his manuscripts? So far as the transcripts of records are concerned the answer is simple and sure; they were almost entirely the creation of himself and his clerks. The same is obviously true of the drafts of his own published and unpublished works. On the manuscripts other than transcripts the manuscripts themselves give little assistance. But one thing can be established at the outset. It has frequently been suggested that William Petyt took advantage of his position as Keeper of the Records at the Tower to transfer to his own use some of the Public Records. This suggestion is based upon an inaccurate understanding of certain of the original documents which are to be found in certain of the composite volumes of his manuscripts and of certain lists of records which were at the Tower. There is not a single original document anywhere among the Petyt Manuscripts which was wrongfully received by him from official custody. The most interesting and valuable original documents are out documents, and a single item in one of the Petyt Manuscripts, as will be shown below, definitively establishes the source from which Petyt obtained them. On the question of lists or indexes or records at the Tower of London, these lists were the personal property of the individual Keepers of the Records or their clerks, compiled by them for their own use and convenience, and on their departure or death left or sold for the use of their successors.

Entries written in two of the Petyt Manuscripts have some importance in this connection. These two volumes have been added at the end of a group of thirty-three volumes, the remainder of which are extracts from the Rolls of Parliament. They contain Writs of Summons to Parliament, Henry III–Edward III and Richard II–Edward IV, respectively. On the verso of f. 1 in each volume appears the following: 'July the 20th. 1697. Memorandum that this first (or second) volume of Summons to Parliament belongs to my Master, William Petyt Esq., Master of this Office, and is no Official Book. Witness my hand, Geo. Holmes.' Both volumes were written in the late sixteenth century or early seventeenth century, probably by a clerk or other official in the Tower of London. They may have been the property of William or Robert Bowyer when they were Keepers. They look as if they could be private or public indexes or calendars. They had obviously been left by William Petyt, as the owner, for the use or convenience of searchers in the Tower. A caveat was entered lest they might at some time be claimed to be official indexes. They were not indexes at all but transcripts from the dorse of the Close Rolls, 49 Henry III to 23 Edward IV. A similar entry under the same date appears in the Nova Statuta, 1 Edward III–22 Edward IV, printed by W. Machlinia thus: 'Memorandum that this Book is my Master's, William Petyt Esqr., and never was an Office Book. Witness my hand, Geo. Holmes.'

In one of the Petyt Manuscripts which is a composite volume, there is a single folio of which the following is a complete transcript:

'Manuscripts out of John Fox his study'.

1. Regis Henrici 6ti. Miracula.
2. Vita et Mors Regis Edwardi 2di ex Gallico Thomae del A moore aequitis in latinum versa.
3. De Sancto Edwardo nonnulla ex historia Thomae Redborne.
4. Vita Beati Edmundi Cantuariensis Archiepiscopi.
5. Cardinalis Pole de sua ac Card. Moroni suspensione ad papam expostulatio.
6. Solempne othes to Kinge Henry the 8th. against the popes Authority made by the byshops of Wintchester, London, Eborac. Dunelm. etc.
7. Iniunctions geven in the Byshops visitations in the rayge of K. Edward 6th. Anno 1550.
8. Bysshop Bonners Letters to divers, his Petegre.
9. Instructions for Dr. Bonner from the bisshop of Wint. in his office of Ambassage in Fraunce.
10. A Coppy of the Commission for the deprivation of St. Gardner, bisshop of Wint.
11. Dr. Feknams oration at the recantation of Sr. John Cheek.

12. An Alsolution pronounced by Card. Poole to the whole Parliament in the 2 year of Q. Mary. An. 1554.
13. An Instrument of Chichly Archbisshop of Caunt. about the foundation of All Souls College in Oxford.
14. Coppies of King Henry the 8th. his will.
15. Coppies of Edward the 6th will.
16. A coppy of Dr. Storyes will.
17. Divers lers of K. Edward 6, Q. Mary and Jane and other princes and nobles of the realm.
18. The Lord Protectors and divers of the Counsayls lers.
19. Letters of Card. Poole to the pope and other princes.
20. Bulls and Indulgences of Divers popes.
21. Dictata Reverendi patris Aug. Politian.
22. Magistri Wikliff Confessio de Ecclesia.
23. Modus et forma predicandi per Card. Moronum.

This list of twenty-three articles is written in a late sixteenth-century hand. The following notes or references appear in the margin in a hand of about 1700, opposite the following numbers:

3. Vide fo. 389.
4. Vide fo. 481.
5. Vide fo. 391.
8. 1 et vo in principio.
17. Vide fo. 2 ad 14.
18. a fo. 431 ad 471.

The references against nos. 3, 4, 5, 17, and 18 are the correct references to the documents in Petyt MS. 538/46; the reference against no. 8 is the correct reference to this document in Petyt MS. 538/47. The documents nos. 1, 2, 6, 7, 9, 10, 11, 12, 13, 14, 16, 19 are all in Petyt MS. 538/47. So there can be little doubt that William Petyt acquired the documents in this list from whomsoever held certain of John Fox's manuscripts in his time. For John Fox, the martyrologist, died in 1587; his papers were used by John Strype and acquired by Robert Harley, Earl of Oxford, and are in the Harleian Collection at the British Museum, but certainly these never reached Harley. Strype, who ought to have known, wrote: 'Mr. Fox must not go without the recommendation of a most painful searcher into records, archives and repositories of original acts and letters of state and a great collector of manuscripts.' Strype himself has left a reputation of acquiring manuscripts by questionable means. Those royal and other letters, which some have thought William Petyt obtained from the Tower of London, were derived from John Fox.

Another source from which William Petyt derived a considerable number of volumes was Robert Bowyer, the son of William Bowyer, Keeper of the Records in the Tower, 1567–81, who was the first to do any considerable work in sorting and arranging the records. The dwelling-house of the Keeper of the Records in the Tower was called Bowyer's House. Robert Bowyer and his nephew, Henry Elsynge, became Keepers of the Records at the Tower in 1604, but were succeeded by Sir John Borough in 1610. This appeared to be inevitable, as Robert Bowyer had been appointed Clerk of Parliament that year and, although he had retained his Keepership of the Records after he became a member of the House of Commons in 1605 as burgess for Chippenham, he was not allowed to combine the Keepership with his new Clerkship. With his great knowledge of records he was able to bring a trained and alert mind to the Journals of the House of Lords which he perused, criticized, and commented upon from their beginning in the first year of Henry VIII. He was tart but correct on the activities of his predecessors. In 1620 his nephew, Henry Elsynge, was appointed as his deputy, and when Bowyer died in 1621 he was succeeded by Elsynge, who continued as Clerk of Parliament until 1638. His son, the younger Henry Elsynge, became Clerk of the House of Commons, but resigned in 1648. He died in 1654. Robert Bowyer appears to have published nothing. Henry Elsynge the elder wrote or prepared a work on Parliament printed in 1660 as that of his son under the title Ancient Method and Manner of Parliaments in England.

There can be little doubt that the Petyt Manuscript of Roger de Hoveden's Historia was derived from the Bowyers. The last of many names of ownership which appears in it is that of Robert Bowyer, preceded by that of his father, William Bowyer. His signature runs: Robt. Bowyer de Medio Temple, 1595. It is suggested that this and the other Bowyer manuscripts reached Petyt through the Elsynges. For the valuable Hoveden is not characteristic of the Petyt Manuscripts which derived from Robert Bowyer; they were mainly manuscripts relating to the House of Lords, though it is likely that other of the chronicles among the Petyt Manuscripts came from the same source. Thus the Polychronicon of Ralph Higden has a Bowyer entry in it. The manuscript containing the Brute Chronicles has the signature William Bowyer. It is suggested that the volume containing historical notes and records concerning Scotland came from the same source, as the volume was lent to Lord Buckhurst and both Robert Bowyer and Henry Elsynge the elder were accustomed to lend manuscripts and pass information to him.

These four manuscripts are few compared with the seventeen manuscripts relating to the House of Lords, the contents of which can be traced to Robert Bowyer or Henry Elsynge. These open with a run of four volumes of extracts from the Journals of the House of Lords, 1 Henry VIII to 5 & 6 Philip & Mary. These volumes have a number of unnumbered folios added by Robert Bowyer and notes, comments, and corrections by him. A part of the period is covered again by an exceptional volume, in size and contents, which covers the Journals of the House of Lords, 1 Mary to 43 Elizabeth I. It is written in two columns and contains an autograph correction of Bowyer by Sir Simond d'Ewes and a large number of important and valuable notes by Robert Bowyer. The annotations and comments, most of them critical of his predecessors, Clerks of Parliament, have yet useful comments on the entries themselves, on points of law and of procedure, and are of very considerable historical interest. The next volume covers the Journals for 1–12 James I. The same statements and comments, some of which cover matters in Bowyer's personal knowledge as Clerk of Parliament, are of importance, others are within his personal knowledge as a member of the House of Commons. There are many references to his 'rough or scribbled book'. Another, covering the Journals of both Houses, 43–4 Elizabeth I, has annotations by both Robert Bowyer and Henry Elsynge, with extracts from Heyward Townesend's Journal. In another volume there are extracts from and annotations on the Journals of the House of Lords, 1 Henry VIII–4 Charles I. The first part is a transcript of notes by Robert Bowyer; it might have been completed by or from Henry Elsynge. Other volumes contain similar transcripts from Bowyer's notes and composite volumes contain sections which are notes by Bowyer, Elsynge, or both. Thus one contains draft notes and proceedings in the House of Lords, 10 January to 30 March 1621, in which the same volume was continued by the succeeding Clerk. In another massive composite volume of twelve items, all concerned with Parliament, five of the items are almost certainly by Robert Bowyer and the remaining seven by one or other of the Elsynges. There are three drafts of the Elsynge Modus tenendi Parliamentum. In fact, in all, it would seem that not less than twenty-three volumes or parts of volumes were derived from Robert Bowyer or the Elsynges.

It has been difficult to suggest a plausible source for the many hundred original ecclesiastical documents of the reign of Elizabeth I which are among the composite volumes in the Petyt Manuscripts. They seem a little remote from the main fields of Petyt's interests. Mr. W. D. Macray when reporting on the Petyt Manuscripts for the Historical Manuscripts Commission conjectured 'that Petyt acquired the official papers of some one of the law officers of the Court of Arches, possibly those of Dr. Richard Cosin. Some of the papers are stained with damp and injured in the way in which such accumulations of a lawyer's chambers might be expected to suffer.' It may well be so, but Richard Cosin, who was Dean of the Arches and Vicar General of the Province of Canterbury, died in 1597 and many of these papers, especially those relating to recusants, are dated between 1598 and 1603. On the other hand the material concerning disputes between the Official of Canterbury and the Court of Arches and the Vicar General, 1576, the reform of the Prerogative Court of Canterbury, the Court of Audience, the Official of Canterbury, and the validity of grievances in the Probate of Wills and Administrations, as well as some of the correspondence of Matthew Parker, Edmund Grindal, and John Whitgift may well have come from Cosin. In addition to his high ecclesiastical offices he was also a Master in Chancery. There are the other two possibilities that the material or some of it might equally well have come from Doctors' Commons or the Queen's Advocate's Office. There is, however, little purpose in speculating; this material could not have come from the Public Records.

It is clear that William Petyt was not only a transcriber of records but a collector of manuscripts. Those derived from John Fox, Robert Bowyer, and the Elsynges he probably obtained by purchase. Others were similarly obtained, of which no hint of the source is given in his own correspondence or in the manuscript itself. Petyt had friends who were collectors of manuscripts. Some of these or others may have given him manuscripts or documents. One thing is certain, the Petyt Manuscripts do not supply a shred of evidence to support the contention that Petyt, like some of his predecessors and several Record Keepers or Assistant Record Keepers after his time, took what interested him from the records. The scrupulous care with which Petyt's assistant issued certificates that volumes which might have seemed to be indexes to Public Records were not public records but the private property of the Master was a compliment and a caution. If the letters addressed by his sisters, Mary and Elizabeth, to Edward VI and his own holograph drafts had been among the Public Records in his time they would not have escaped the kind attention of Sir Robert Cotton, but perhaps only because they had been pre-empted by John Fox. William Petyt was a controversionalist and had many enemies on account of his historical views. Dr. Robert Brady, who had himself been Keeper of the Records at the Tower, would have spread it abroad if William Petyt had subtracted records from the Tower for his own library as Sir Robert Cotton had done.

ii. *The other Manuscripts in the Petyt Collection*

Of the 134 volumes of manuscripts which did not derive from William Petyt which have become known for approaching two and a half centuries as the Petyt Collection, the following are the main groups:

502.	Journals of the House of Commons, 1604–24, 1660–1708	83 volumes
509.	Judges Papers of Sir Martin Wright	14 ”
516.	Law Reports, Elizabeth–Charles I	6 ”
530.	Sermons and Miscellaneous	6 ”
531.	” ”	7 ”

The remainder are either very small groups or single volumes by individual donors.

The large group of Journals of the House of Commons, 1604–24, 1660–1708, eighty-three volumes, need not detain. They consist of straight transcripts of the Journals, and were presented in 1771 by George III, by the mediation of Henry Bathurst, Lord Apsley, afterwards 2nd Earl of Bathurst, who had been a Bencher of the Inn and was then Lord Chancellor. The Hon. Henry Bathurst had been admitted to the Inner Temple in 1731 and called to the bar in 1736, and on producing his letters patent as King's Counsel called to the Bench in 1746. He was chosen Reader for the

Lent Vacation, 1754. That year he received his gratuity on being appointed Serjeant at Law, upon his elevation as Judge of Common Pleas. On 23 November 1771 a Bench Table Order ran as follows:

The Treasurer to wait on the Lord High Chancellor with the compliments of the Society and desire that he will be pleased to signify to His Majesty, in the most respectful terms, the grateful sense they have of the obligation conferred on them by his gift of the Journals of the Houses of Lords and Commons to this Society, for the use of their Library, through his Lordship's mediation, and at the same time return his Lordship their thanks for the part he has acted on this occasion.

It is difficult to surmise why all the volumes of the Journal of the House of Commons for the reign of Charles I are wanting and why now there are no Journals of the House of Lords. The set is a transcript made several years before 1771 and has its value as containing small sections which were no longer easy to read when the Journals were printed.

The fourteen volumes of Judges Papers presented by the daughters and executrixes of Sir Martin Wright are a far more valuable group. Sir Martin Wright had been specially admitted to the Inner Temple in 1709, at the request of his father, William Wright, whose heir apparent he was. This made him a grandson of Sir Nathan Wright, who was Lord Keeper, 1700–5, who had himself been elected to the Bench in 1682. His father, William Wright, was Treasurer, 1718–19, and his son, Martin, was specially admitted in 1742. His uncle, George Wright, who was Clerk of the Crown, was Treasurer, 1713–14. Sir Martin Wright was called to the bar in 1718 and to the Bench, on his appointment as Serjeant at Law, 1733, when he also received his gratuity on his departure from the Inn. He became a Baron of the Exchequer, 1739–40, was made a Justice, King's Bench, 28 November 1740, and resigned, 1 February 1755. In 1730 he had published his *Introduction to the Law of Tenures*, which ran to four editions, described as 'a learned and perspicuous display of learning on the origin of estates and their legal properties'.

These volumes were the Judge's Papers of a Justice of King's Bench and contain the judgements of the Court of King's Bench, 14–27 George II inclusive. They are the papers or books on cases prepared by the two Clerks assigned to enrol pleas in the King's Bench, who used them during the hearing. In almost every case the judgements, with the date on which they were delivered, were entered upon the papers by Mr. Justice Wright. In many cases the proceedings were recorded, during the hearing, by the Judge and the notes he made and the precedents he collected before hearing the case and his comments upon them were incorporated with the Judge's Papers. In all important cases they are voluminous and in many instances of very great interest and importance. In all there are papers relating to 1,004 cases heard from 1740 to 1754, comprised in 9,256 pages, besides some thousands of unnumbered pages of notes, precedents, and proceedings. As a series of Judge's Papers the group is exceptional, if not unique, in completeness and continuity. They cover the whole of Sir Martin Wright's tenure of office as a Justice of King's Bench. They are important not only on matters of substantive law and procedure, but they throw an invaluable light upon the machinery of justice, detailing private meetings of the Judges in the Lord Chief Justice's Chambers, the discussions which took place there, differences of opinion among the Judges, and interesting personal sidelights.

They were probably presented in 1769, when Sir Martin's daughters presented a collection of his law books. For on 6 June 1769 the Under Treasurer informed the Table that they 'have signified their resolution to present to this Society a valuable collection of law books made and selected by the said Sir Martin Wright agreeable to his intention and declaration before his death'. The Under Treasurer was instructed to attend them 'and in the name of the Society to return their thankful acknowledgment for such benefaction and at the same time request that if they have any portrait of Mr. Justice Wright that they will give leave that this Society may take a copy thereof to place in their public Library'. That portrait now faces all approaching the inner entrance of the Library.

The Catalogue of the books given by Sir Martin Wright is among the Miscellaneous Manuscripts. It includes a Collection of Appeals to the House of Lords, 1701–28, which is in the Petyt Collection. Other valuable books interleaved and with manuscript notes by him are now unhappily missing.

The third of the above groups which consists, at present, of six volumes of Law Reports, Elizabeth I to Charles I, is not complete. Originally the bequest consisted of nine volumes, but the first three volumes are wanting. The donor was William Barnesley, who was Treasurer, 1707–8. So he followed William Petyt as Treasurer and as a donor of manuscripts to the Library. William Barnesley had been admitted in 1670 and was called to the bar in 1675 and to the Bench in 1697. All the nine volumes of Law Reports he gave were straight Law Reports, mainly King's Bench and Common Pleas, though for the reign of James I one volume contained a few cases in the Exchequer of Pleas, Star Chamber, Court of Wards, Duchy of Lancaster and Exchequer Chamber. In addition to this group of Law Reports William Barnesley also presented the Library with two further volumes, one the interesting Instructions for the Master of the Court of Wards and Liveries, 1618, the other the usual kind of volume of notes and arguments in the disputes between the ecclesiastical jurisdiction and the common law Courts, with special reference to Prohibitions in the time of James I.

The fourth and final group of manuscripts consists of a total of thirteen volumes, mainly consisting of small volumes of sermons, the others being of a very miscellaneous nature, but including one volume of very considerable interest and significance. The donor was Mrs. Anne Sadleir, the eldest daughter of Sir Edward Coke, whose gift of books and manuscripts is dealt with below, as a number of her gifts have reached the Miscellaneous Manuscripts. They were given to the Library in 1661, and from each of these two groups one volume is now wanting, as is mentioned below. The volumes of sermons are mainly of a personal or family nature and interest. They were presented to Mrs. Anne Sadleir or were sermons delivered at Sadleir burials, though one volume dedicated to Mrs. Anne Sadleir was by Andrew Marvell, the father of the poet. Of the others one is a devotional work, Philip de Mornay's Meditation on the Lord's Supper; another a student's notebook on logic; a third a tract on the forms of coronations with a collection on the creation of peers, compiled in 1588–9. The really important volume is the author's copy or draft of the History of Scotland, by John Leslie, Bishop of Ross, with corrections and notes. There would seem to be some faint possibility that this manuscript may have come from the possession of Sir Edward Coke, for it would seem to have no Sadleir interest or connection and it does not fall within the special devotional interests of Mrs. Anne Sadleir.

The other non-Petyt manuscripts in the Petyt Collection come from a wide variety of sources and over a long period of time. Thus an early benefaction was the Arms of the Nobility and Gentry, William I to James I, written in the reign of Elizabeth I, with additions to 1605. It was given by John Hales, who was Treasurer, 1705–6. Another early gift was the Proceedings at the Coronation of George I, including the commission on claims, 1714, given by George Wright, who as seen above was Clerk of the Crown and Treasurer the same year. In 1715 Silvester Petyt gave a Catalogue of the Books he presented to the Library. By this time the Petyt Catalogue of Books and Manuscripts, in two volumes, must already have been completed, though notes and additions to it were made for many years after. There were five manuscripts which were certainly given, or it is surmised were given, by Daines Barrington. These are more conveniently dealt with in the next section, where his manuscripts and other gifts are dealt with at length.

This leaves a further eight manuscripts in the Petyt Collection which were not derived from William Petyt or any other known donor. All of these must have been given early, or certainly before the middle of the eighteenth century. The list begins with that well known and much discussed Year Book, 10–17 Edward III. It seems strange that so little is known of a manuscript of this significance; there is a possibility that it was one of the manuscripts which was in the Library before the Petyt bequest, but its pressmark hardly favours this supposition. Another volume is the fifteenth-century Walter de Hilton, Scala Perfectionis, manuscript, which bears the signature of Stephen Gardiner, Bishop of Winchester. It would be interesting to know how this was acquired. The next five volumes, some of them composite, bear consecutive pressmarks and are all transcripts of works of the first half of the seventeenth century, including Sir Francis Vere's Account of the Expedition to Cadiz, 1597, the Letters of John van Barnevelt, a translation of the Treaty of Munster, 1648, and the Treaty of Commerce, 1650, Richard Hakluyt's translation of Grotius' Mare Librum, and the

Life and Death of Prince Henry, by Sir George Cornwallis. The similarity of subject and nearness of period, with the consecutive pressmarks, suggest that they may have come from a single donor. Finally there is a volume of Tracts and Letters in French, also of the first half of the seventeenth century. This also may have come from the same unknown donor.

These manuscripts in the Petyt Collection which were not Petyt Manuscripts, whether the donors are known or unknown, are not generally speaking of the value or importance of the Petyt Manuscripts, though they do include amongst them those valuable legal manuscripts from the second half of the fourteenth century to the eighteenth century and a few isolated manuscripts of some individual interest, an interest which frequently derives from the donor rather than the contents of the volume. Apart from the Judges Papers of Sir Martin Wright they fall well within the scope of the Petyt Manuscripts, though they make no great extension of their dimension. Despite the example shown by William Petyt, followed to some extent by a few of his contemporaries, the complacent eighteenth century had not the urge for the discovery of historical and legal precedents which had been a feature of the seventeenth century. After the opening decades of the eighteenth century there were no great collectors of manuscripts made in England in the Society until the closing decades. Daines Barrington and Francis Maseres belonged to that period of revival of interest in antiquities and origins and things ancient.

In Petyt's time the Inner Temple had a small group of members who were interested in and collectors of legal manuscripts, perhaps to some extent stimulated by his work and example. Just as his benefactions stimulated emulation, witness the gifts of John Hale, William Barnesley, and George Wright, all of whom were Treasurers, Petyt's collection of manuscripts seems to have moved a number of his contemporaries, who made their manuscripts readily available for his use, such as Sir John Trevor, Sir Nathaniel Powell, Sir Samuel Baldwin, and John Peachey.

4. THE HONOURABLE DAINES BARRINGTON, TREASURER, 1784–1785

The Honourable Daines Barrington was the fourth son of John Shute, first Viscount Barrington, described as 'lawyer and polemical and Christian apologist'. As John Shute he had been admitted to the Inner Temple in 1695, but assumed the name of Barrington on inheriting estates in Essex. He was a Whig politician who had been expelled from the House of Commons for his part in a lottery, and had written a *History of the Apostles*. Four of his sons had distinguished careers. His heir William Wildman Barrington, second Viscount Barrington, was a politician who became Chancellor of the Exchequer, Treasurer of the Navy, Secretary at War for nearly 14 years, and Joint Paymaster General. Samual Barrington was an Admiral who, after serving under Hawke, Rodney, and Keppel, became Commander in Chief in the West

Indies and took St. Lucia. The youngest son, Shute Barrington, was successively Bishop of Llandaff, Salisbury, and Durham, a bishop in all for fifty-seven years. The family was well in with the Georges, from the First to the Fourth.

Daines Barrington was born in 1727, was admitted to the Inner Temple in 1745, was called to the bar in 1750, became a K.C., and was consequently called to the Bench in 1777 and was Treasurer in 1784–5. In 1757 he was appointed a Judge of Great Sessions for the counties of Merioneth, Caernarvon, and Anglesey, and from 1778 to 1785 he was second Justice of Chester, Montgomery, Flint, and Denbigh, with Lloyd Kenyon as Chief Justice. In 1764 he was appointed Recorder of Bristol. These were the highest judicial offices he ever held. He had a small private income, which he augmented by the accumulation of valuable sinecure offices. In 1751 he became Marshal of the Court of Admiralty, a post he resigned in 1753 when he became Secretary for the Affairs of Greenwich Hospital. Later he became Commissary General of Stores at Gibraltar, a post worth over £500 a year. In 1785 he resigned all his offices except the last mentioned, which was the most valuable. Naturally, he drew a pension from his Welsh Judgeship.

With an assured income he was able to devote his time and energies to his own interests and pursuits and he was prodigal of both. He had become a Fellow of the Royal Society and of the Society of Antiquaries in 1767. He was a sentimental antiquarian who contributed papers to the journals of both Societies. Some of these he gathered together in his *Miscellanies*, which he published in 1781. Its content was widely diversified. Many were on natural history, the reindeer, the bat, the reremouse, 'the torpidity of the swallow tribe when they disappear', the cuckoo; others were on geography, from the possibility of finding the North Pole to Ohthere's voyage and the geography of the ninth century illustrated; others were potted biographies from Mozart to the Earl of Mornington via Charles Wesley and Samuel Wesley. The whole collection was a bizarre lot and many of his other and later contributions were equally curious.

This, however, was not his first or his most important book, which was his *Observations upon the Statutes chiefly the more ancient from Magna Carta to 21st James the First ch. xxvii, with An Appendix being a proposal for New Modelling the Statutes*, which first appeared without date or name; a second edition was published in 1766 and subsequent editions in 1767, 1769, 1775, and 1796, making six editions in all. His name did not appear on the title-page until the edition of 1769. Today this is not found to be a very readable work, though it contained much original material and was obviously in great if not popular demand. It showed considerable research, not least among the Petyt Manuscripts, a matter which will be dealt with at a little length later in this Introduction. In his Preface he wrote he 'had a view of laying a proposal before the public, with regard to the repealing of such useless Statutes as well as reducing acts which related to the same subject, to one uniform and constituent law'.

This appears to be a commonplace, not a new proposal today, but it must be remembered that Daines Barrington was writing in the middle of the eighteenth century; so he was a pioneer in consolidation and interpretation. His second justification for his study was that in 'the old acts of parliament, as far as they went, the very best materials for an English history; and that they were likewise strongly descriptive of the manners of the time'. His third justification for publication was the comparison he made with other countries, for he had 'looked into the *Ordinances* of most countries of Europe during the thirteenth and three following centuries'. He had therefore consulted the Scottish law, the laws of Denmark, Sweden, and Norway, Normandy and other provinces of France, and even those of Hywel Dda. He seems to have justified his objectives, and it is interesting to note that of the 97 statutes and other documents upon which Daines Barrington makes observations, 65 are dated before 1400, another 17 between 1400 and 1485, and only 15 between 1485 and 1623. The list of printed sources used by him is impressive; it included Mabillon; he had manuscript statutes and legal tracts of his own; and his work contains some sixty-eight references to the Petyt Manuscripts.

Besides his contributions to the journals and transactions of learned Societies, Daines Barrington's separate publications also included *The Naturalists Calendar*, 1767, and an edition of Alfred's *Orosius*, 1773. Nor must his *Letter on the Origins of the Arms of the Inner and Middle Temples*, which appeared in *Archaeologia*, be omitted here.

For Daines Barrington was a devoted member of the Inner Temple, his most special interests being the Library and the Garden. He lived most of his life and died in King's Bench Walk. He was in his lifetime a constant donor of books and other gifts to his Inn. In 1760 his name had been sent to Lyon's Inn as Reader; in 1785 he was Lent Reader of the Inner Temple. On 1 February 1771 he received the thanks of the Bench for the Collection of Private Acts of Parliament and other valuable books presented to the Society and delivered to the Library. An Order of 1778 thanked him for his valuable present of books to the Library; another ordered the gardener 'to purchase gravel and new gravel such part of the King's Bench Walk as Mr. Barrington may think necessary to be done'. On 7 November 1780, the Bench Table referred to him 'to direct a plantation of such trees and shrubs as he shall think proper in the Garden for the purpose of shade and for concealing the path from the dusthole to the Thames'. Thanks were given to him on 4 June 1782 for his valuable present of a book to the Library; on 28 January 1783 for his present of twenty-three volumes of *Philosophical Transactions*, 1753–76; on 13 May 1783 for his present of 'a medal of Domitian with a Pegasus on the reverse'; on 12 May 1784 for his present of books and prints; on 9 November 1784 for his present of eleven volumes of *Irish Statutes* and four volumes of the *Journal of the Irish House of Lords*. That is his last recorded personal gift to the Library. He seldom appears in Parliament or Bench Table after 1790.

Meanwhile, on 13 November 1782, with Arthur Annesley, who had been Treasurer in 1774–5, Daines Barrington had been appointed one of the Superintendents of the Garden, 'they or either of them to give such orders to the gardener or other workmen engaged in the garden as they or either of them may judge proper'. The Superintendents moved quickly. On 7 February 1783 they proposed to the Bench to make a further allowance to the gardener of £5 a year 'for his increase of work in mowing the grass and rolling the gravel in the Garden occasioned by the enlargement of the garden plot and making new gravel walks'. On 13 May 1783 they were empowered 'to remove the ooze from the Thames before the Garden in such a manner as they shall think proper', and that year payments were made to five men for playing the engine in the garden on five days during the summer 'by order of Mr. Barrington'. On 12 February 1785 there was authority for 'fifty loads of loam to be purchased for the use of the Garden, the expense not to exceed £12–10s.'. All his measures concerning the Garden seem to have been practical rather than pedantic.

Daines Barrington died 14 March 1800 in his chambers in King's Bench Walk and he was buried in the vault in the Temple Church on 18 March. The pall bearers were Lord Alvanley, the Master of the Rolls, Sir William Scott, Judge of the High Court of Admiralty, Sir Robert Graham, a Baron of the Exchequer, a Bencher of the Inner Temple, Alexander Popham, a member of the Middle Temple, Sir William Wynne, Judge of the Prerogative Court of Canterbury, Sir John Mitford, Attorney General, Mr. Graves, and Mr. Champion. Among the mourners were three Benchers of the Inner Temple, Robert Aldersley, Richard Stanley, and William Lascelles.

The pall bearers were representative of his interests; the family mourners were few; few of his personal friends and cronies attended. Most of them had predeceased him. There has long been a continuous campaign of denigration of his reputation and achievements. More attention has been paid to the barbed shafts of the wits of his own time, Horace Walpole and Peter Pindar, for example, than to the tributes of his admirers. He was an antiquarian who lived in a romantic, not a scientific age. Among his friends was Thomas Grey. His admirers ranged from Samuel Johnson to Jeremy Bentham, neither of them a fool nor easily deceived. Jeremy Bentham considered him vastly superior to William Blackstone 'in his disposition to improvement; and more impartial in his judgement of men and things—less sycophancy and a higher intellect'. Gilbert White, who was in correspondence with him for nearly twenty years, saw that he was 'a gentleman of great candour, and one that will make allowances; especially where the writer professes to be an out-of-door naturalist, one that takes his observations from the subject itself, and not from the writings of others'. One is content to let the facts speak for themselves. He had few pretensions, but an insatiable curiosity.

It will be noted that in his many gifts to the Inner Temple Library there is no mention of the gift of any manuscript. Yet not only is there a Barrington Collection of Manuscripts, but there are Barrington Manuscripts in the Petyt Collection and among the Miscellaneous Manuscripts. It is extremely difficult to determine when and how these manuscripts reached their respective groups. The difficulty is aggravated by errors. The printed *Catalogue of the Inner Temple Library*, 1833, contains a list of 'Manuscripts sent by the Executors of Bishop Barrington in 1823'. This is not only inaccurate but foolishly inaccurate. Shute Barrington, Bishop of Durham, did not die until 25 March 1826. The manuscripts in this list were received by the Inner Temple in 1817. For on 29 April 1817 'the thanks of the Society were given to the Bishop of Durham for his present of sundry Law Manuscripts'. It is true that Shute Barrington did make a gift to the Society in 1823. For on 22 April 1823 it was ordered that 'the thanks of the Society be given to the Rt. Rev. the Lord Bishop of Durham for his present to this Society of a print of the Hon. Daines Barrington, formerly one of the Masters of the Bench of this Society'. This portrait is still in the possession of the Society.

This single correction does not solve the main problem, but that list which contains eighty-one volumes enables the identification of the majority of the manuscripts in the Barrington Collection to be made. It gives no assistance in identifying all the Daines Barrington Manuscripts in the Petyt collection. Little assistance, too, is given by the holograph will of Daines Barrington which was dated 4 May 1786, or by the seven codicils, the last of which is dated 14 February 1799, most of which merely increase the bequests to his servant who has attended him faithfully during a long lingering illness. There are four main points of interest in the will. As he had frequently been 'troubled by the spasms at the heart I desire my body to be opened to discover what may have been the occasion of them'. He devised to four nephews the remainder of a term in the Opera House and two Playhouses which 'I bought when I began to apprehend I should not be able long to read by candle-light'. Thirdly he appointed his brother, then Bishop of Salisbury, his executor. As Bishop of Durham he had witnessed the last three codicils. Fourthly he left his books to the Society of Antiquaries. The sixth codicil, dated 1 March 1795, read: 'Having disposed of all my books, except a very few, during my illness, I hereby bequeath those few to the Revd. Samuel Gale as a mark of my regard.'

The presumption would seem to be, therefore, that the Society of Antiquaries, of which he was Vice-President, received the books of interest to the Society, that is the books dealing with antiquities and curiosities, during his lifetime, and that the Inner Temple Library received the books and some of the manuscripts of legal interest, during his lifetime. These were put in the presses which housed the Petyt Collection, where they appear to occupy a consecutive series of numbers. The residue of the manuscripts seem to have remained in the custody of his executor until 1817 when, perhaps adding manuscripts which belonged to him, he presented a group to the Inn. These now form the Barrington Collection of Manuscripts. The Revd. Samuel Gale doubtless belonged to that Gale family which produced such antiquarians and scholars as Thomas Gale, Professor of Greek at Cambridge and Dean of York, 1697–1702, and his sons, Roger Gale, who left his manuscripts to Trinity College, Cambridge, and Samuel Gale, the first Treasurer of the revived Society of Antiquaries and the friend and fellow traveller of Andrew Coltee Ducarel. His share of the residue is likely to have been small.

5. THE BARRINGTON COLLECTION OF MANUSCRIPTS

The Barrington Collection of Manuscripts can be most conveniently considered under three heads, first the Barrington Manuscripts in the Petyt Collection, secondly the Barrington Manuscripts among the Miscellaneous Manuscripts, and thirdly the Barrington Collection proper.

The manuscripts associated with Daines Barrington in the Petyt Collection appear to number 504–508. Nos. 505, 506, and 508 bear his signature. Two of them are quite useful Manuscript Statutes, 1 Edward III to 23 Henry VI and 1 Edward III to 29 Henry VI respectively. Both have illuminated capitals and may be dated about the middle of the 15th century. Another volume containing six Law Tracts and a Register of Writs was written early in the reign of Richard II; another containing Statutes, Magna Carta to 14 Edward II, with Legal Tracts and Memoranda belongs to the first quarter of the fourteenth century. The Proceedings in Parliament, 6 February 1626 to 12 May 1626 is less certainly a Barrington Manuscript. Its subject-matter is not characteristic of the main interests of Daines Barrington. It is much more akin to the interests of William Petyt, but it is certainly not a Petyt Manuscript as it does not appear in the Petyt Catalogue. As its pressmark number in the Petyt Collection is preceded and followed by a manuscript with the signature of Daines Barrington, and in the absence of any other possible attribution, it may fairly, at present, be regarded as a Barrington Manuscript. There are other manuscripts in the Barrington Collection proper which are equally outside the general scope of his interests. In books as well as in manuscripts he was somewhat of a magpie.

The Barrington Manuscripts now among the Miscellaneous Manuscripts consist of insets and loose leaves which have been separated from volumes in the Barrington Collection proper. They are not of a great deal of importance, but their nature allows of no doubt of their source. They consist of forty-one items removed from Mickleton Manuscripts in the Barrington Collection, the Mickleton Manuscripts being dealt with below; a second volume contains five items, which were found in a parchment cover marked Barrington 79. They may at one time have formed part of the Barrington Manuscripts as that number is now wanting in the Collection. A third volume, the text of a Reader's lectures on the Statute of Pluralities, 21 Henry VIII, written early in the eighteenth century, admits of no doubt. It bears the signature Daines Barrington.

Coming to the Barrington Collection proper, first the discrepancy in the number of volumes requires some explanation. The list in the 1833 Catalogue consists of 81 volumes; the number of volumes now in the Barrington Collection is 57. The original numbering of these 57 volumes ran 1 to 85. It now starts at 2 and there are gaps throughout the series. On rebinding, the original Barrington Collection pressmarks were retained. This, however, does not provide any explanation for the many gaps in the series. These are mainly accounted for by the dispersion or loss of Commonplace Books, and to a lesser degree by the failure to identify 4 volumes of unspecified Reports in Commons Pleas. The list in the 1833 Catalogue gives three sequences of Commonplace Books of 14, 20, and 5 volumes respectively, in folio, quarto, and duodecimo respectively. There are now but 22 Commonplace Books in the Barrington Collection. It may be that some of the remainder remain unidentified and unidentifiable among the Miscellaneous Manuscripts, where there are 7 volumes of Commonplace Books for which no donor can be traced. On the other hand it must be remembered that there are entered as an addition in the Petyt Catalogue Commonplace Books which likewise, at present, cannot be traced. These and the remainder of the Commonplace Books in the Barrington Collection are probably lost. Many of them were probably quite slim and unimportant volumes.

Of the 57 volumes of manuscripts now in the Barrington Collection there appear to be four main categories, Reports, 17 volumes, Precedents, 12 volumes, Commonplace Books, 22 volumes, and Miscellaneous, 5 volumes, and one volume which may be the volume described in the 1833 Catalogue as 'Year Book, 4to'. Of the Miscellaneous volumes, which generally are the most interesting and valuable, that of by far the greatest importance is probably the early manuscript of Littleton's Tenures. This manuscript is contemporary with Sir Thomas Littleton and is of Worcestershire provenance, and though it may be imaginative to suggest that it was presented to a Colles neighbour by Littleton himself, it is a well-written manuscript, but incomplete. It is doubtful if Sir Thomas Littleton would have given a friend an incomplete manuscript as a present, even if in the first half of the fifteenth-century authors were in the habit of presenting copies of their works to friends. The other manuscript of great interest and value is a kind of cartulary of the Augustinian Priory of Dunstable in the county of Bedford. Its contents are mainly cases in the King's Courts concerning the Priory. The main part of the volume was probably written about 1331, with additions made at later dates from about 1338 to 1437. It contains many interesting particulars not now elsewhere available. Of less importance are the Accounts of William Cecil, Earl of Salisbury, March to May 1648, which are entered in a Law Commonplace Book, though they include a few interesting details. The remaining two volumes of this group are a note- or exercise-book on philosophy and logic, apparently by a Cambridge undergraduate, written in 1655 and 1656, which has an occasional foreign entry, and what the 1833 Catalogue calls 'MS. of Devotion', which is a neatly executed draft translation of a Latin work, Meditations upon the Passion, of little interest or importance.

Of what the 1833 Catalogue list terms Reports and which are adequately listed, there are seventeen volumes, which include Reports by Sir Henry Hobart, Sir Thomas Hetley, Sir Francis Moore, and Sir Edward Coke, all of which have now been printed. There are unprinted Reports by unknown reporters and the whole range covers cases in the House of Lords, Exchequer Chamber, Chancery, King's Bench, Common Pleas, and Exchequer, with many from the Courts of the Palatinate of Durham, some from the Court of Star Chamber, a few from the Court of Wards, and a very few from the Court of the Verge and the Duchy Court of Lancaster, but the great majority are from King's Bench and Common Pleas. The general range of dates is from 4 & 5 Philip & Mary to 30 Charles II, though there are a few cases cited of Henry VI and VII and even of Edward III. There appears to be no special comment called for on these Reports generally, though a word is perhaps necessary on the Reports of the Star Chamber Cases as they are seldom met with in the general run of manuscript reports. This particular volume compares generally with the contents of a Commonplace Book, but because it contains reports of Star Chamber Cases, Hilary 6 James I to Easter 16 James I, it is separately listed in the 1833 list. A little more will be said of the reports which relate to the Palatinate of Durham, as also to Precedents relating to the same, below.

Of the twelve volumes of Precedents, ten volumes relate to Precedents relating to the Palatinate of Durham, or are otherwise associated with that county, by content, signature, or book-plate. The exceptions are a volume of Pleadings and Writs, 22 Elizabeth I to 22 Charles II, of no particular value or consequence; the other consists of two items, the first of pleadings, forms, and notes in a late seventeenth-century court hand, and the second of transcripts of records relating to the manor of Ansty. Of the remaining ten volumes for the present, most of them can be dismissed quickly, so far as their legal content is concerned. One volume contains Precedents of Exchequer Writs, 20–24 Charles II; another Precedents of Issues at Law, 7 Edward IV to 15 Charles I. Both contain the book-plate of James Mickleton, Crook Hall, co. Durham, 1718. Another volume contains Returns of Writs, all relating to the County Palatine; another is a Precedent Book of Bargains and Sales, all between 1652 and 1659. Another volume contains Precedents alphabetically arranged, Abatement to Women, written in the reign of James I; it contains the signature: Ja. Mickleton, 1707. Another volume contains transcripts of Indentures and other documents relating to the County Palatine of Durham etc. of the late sixteenth and the seventeenth century; inset is a red leather label: James Mickleton esq. A volume of precedents, writs, precipes, and original, all relating to the County Palatine, 2–17 Charles I, and a somewhat similar volume, 12 Charles I to 21 Charles II, are both marked: Liber G. Spearman, 1693. There is also a volume of precedents and forms of pleadings in the County Palatine, late Elizabeth I and early James I. With these should be compared entries in the Reports dealt with above. One volume has the entry: J. Mickleton, Hospitii Graiensis, 1716; three other volumes are associated with him in content. One volume of Reports has the entry: Liber G. Spearman de medio Templo Lond.

The last volume of this group of Precedent Books is one of first-rate importance. It is a composite volume of legal tracts and other documents, with a few original items mainly of the sixteenth and seventeenth centuries, eighteen items in all. The seventh section consists of cases and precedents and cases in the County Palatine of Durham, 265 folios of them. It begins with a petition by James Mickleton of the city of Durham about the deposit in his hands in 1668 of various bonds, and the section continues with other bills and documents, mainly of the second half of the seventeenth century relating to proceedings in the Chancery of the Palatinate of Durham. The tenth section, 'Touching the laws for the religion, August 1591', is contemporary and consists of notes and comments on Statutes 5 and 23 Elizabeth I. The eleventh section has on the dorse 'Mr. Solicitor his Breviate on the Queen of Scots' cause, 20 October 1586'. It consists of the original brief of Thomas Egerton (afterwards Lord Ellesmere) as Solicitor General in the proceedings against Mary, Queen of Scots, in the Star Chamber, a document of great historical interest and value. It is followed as the twelfth item by 'A Brief Collection of the Conspiracy made by the Scottish Queen against the person and state of the Queen of England. Translated by Sir Anthony Ashley, 1586.' The Preface is signed by Sir Anthony Ashley, Clerk of the Privy Council, and author of the *Mariner's Mirror of Navigation*, and grandfather of Sir Anthony Ashley Cooper, first Earl of Shaftesbury. The last four items are tracts by 'Richard Robinson, dwelling in Cow Lane, London'. The first is a Breviate concerning the memorable states and conditions of the Queen Majesty's Honourable Courts of Record, 1588; the second is on the same subject, but of different content and arrangement, 1592; the third is A short tract on Attorneys of the Court of Common Pleas, 1592; the fourth and last is A tract on the Spiritual Courts, 1597. All four remain unpublished, but contain interesting information in a very compact form.

Of the twenty-two volumes of Commonplace Books remaining in the Barrington Collection, almost all are of a purely legal nature. Many consist of notes on, or indexes to, reports or legal treatises, some of them printed, some still in manuscript only. Many were compiled as ready aids to reference, some by law students for their own use. Some are almost confined to a single book, for example Sir William Scroggs, *Practice of Courts Leet and Courts Baron*, George Townsend, *Tables to most of the Printed Presidents of Pleadings, Writs and Return of Writs, at the Common Law*, or Christopher St. German, *Doctor and Student*. Others have a greater value. There is a composite volume which contains extracts from Brooke's Novel Cases, Littleton's Tenures, and a large variety of cases from Reports and Year Books. It also contains Moot Cases in Barnard's Inn, 1585, and Furnival's Inn, 1588, and Readings in Gray's

Inn, 1585 and other dates. Another volume contains Ralph Whitfield's Reading at Gray's Inn in 1633 and at Staple Inn in 1628; another Moot Cases, 1624–51, some and possibly all at Clifford's Inn. Three of the volumes contain the book-plate of James Mickleton, 1718, another volume was certainly derived from him. Another volume is marked: Liber G. Spearman, 1692. One of the volumes with the Mickleton book-plate contains very interesting material on 'the case of all the Attorneys of England who are either actually prosecuted, or intended so to be, for negligence and omissions of filing and entering several things upon which stamps ought to be under an Act of Anne', and four other items which were almost certainly compiled by James Mickleton when he was at Furnival's Inn. It also contains a reference to Gilbert Spearman's estate at Taw Law. Another volume has the entry: G. Spearman, 1692.

Two entries in the 1833 list require further investigation. That entry 'Year Book, 4to' has already been mentioned; the other runs equally vaguely 'Tenths Book, folio'. It is conceivable that the so-called Year Book referred to may be a volume of collections from legal notes and definitions from Year Books, Dyer, and other Reports, for the volume does contain miscellaneous extracts from Year Books, 1–14 Henry VII, and otherwise consists of miscellaneous notes arranged alphabetically mainly from Year Books. Otherwise it must be wanting. There is no Tenths Book or anything resembling such a subject in the Barrington Collection now. This, too, is missing and is no longer in the Inner Temple Library.

Of the fifty-seven volumes now in the Barrington Collection of Manuscripts, fourteen volumes have the book-plate or signature of, or by their content associate themselves with James Mickleton; four volumes have the entry: Liber G. Spearman. The Mickletons and Spearmans were Palatinate families who for generations held legal offices under the Bishop of Durham. James Mickleton is described in these manuscripts as of Furnival's Inn and Gray's Inn. A Christopher Mickleton of Clifford's Inn was admitted to the Inner Temple in 1654, but there is no record of his call to the bar. A James Mickleton of Durham was admitted to the Inner Temple in 1656 and called to the bar in 1663. Gilbert Spearman was of the Middle Temple. The entries in these manuscripts relating to the two families are mainly of Palatine interest, Palatine precedents, Palatine cases, and Palatine history, which are comparable with Mickleton and Spearman manuscripts in the University Library, Durham. Sometimes there are notes relating to the family or firm, or personal memoranda written amongst the legal cases or precedents, for instance, a militia warrant and receipts, 1713, a receipt for window cess, 1714, and for Royal Aid, a grant by the Sheriff of Durham to Christopher Mickleton of the office of Steward of all Sheriffs Turns or Views of Frankpledge in the county, 1648, a notarial instrument executed in the house of Christopher Mickleton in Owengate in the city of Durham, 1661, a letter addressed to James Mickleton Esq. at Mr. Peter Taylor's house in Crown Court, Chancery Lane.

Shute Barrington was translated to Durham in 1791, some years after his brother, Daines, had effectively retired from legal work, so it was unlikely that any sinecure post within the Palatinate, of which there were many, would be given him. On the other hand, the Bishop may have fed his brother's interest in manuscripts by sending him, as a gift or on loan, manuscripts from his Chancery or Exchequer. It is possible that Daines Barrington never saw most of the manuscripts now known as the Barrington Collection, but the strong presumption is that he was acquainted with them and that his executor repossessed himself of them and later presented them to the Inner Temple. Those important medieval manuscripts, the Cartulary of Dunstable and the contemporary manuscript of Littleton's Tenures and others, had no connection with Durham and must have been Barrington Manuscripts, that is Daines Barrington Manuscripts.

6. THE RECORDS OF THE INNER TEMPLE

The collection of manuscripts known as Records of the Inner Temple, by its very title, tends to be confused with the five volumes of *Calendars of Inner Temple Records*, 1505–1800. Those are essentially calendars of the Parliament Act Books and the Bench Table Order Books, fortified by extracts from the Account Books of the Inn, though they do include, from 1586 to 1800, some references to this collection of manuscripts, which are grouped under the title Miscellanea. The manuscripts also tend to get confused with the records of the Inn which are kept in the Treasurer's Strong Room and which are dealt with generally and briefly a little later in this section. The great majority of the items in these volumes of manuscripts were drawn from these records and there is at least an equal quantity of similar records still in that Strong Room.

This group of manuscripts mainly consists of miscellaneous loose records of the Inn, including correspondence, accounts and receipts, bonds and other legal instruments, and drafts which have been arranged in broad groups and bound on guards in thirty-nine volumes. There is an original misnumbering of these volumes, Volumes 21 and 21A, and the original numbering has been retained in the catalogue. The thirty-nine volumes contain a total of 1,546 items, of varying interest and importance, the great majority of which relate to the domestic history and affairs of the Inner Temple and its administration, but including a number of documents of considerable value. There are six volumes of Letters and Papers, 1586–1830; four volumes contain Accounts, Estimates, etc., 1673–1780; a single volume contains documents relating to the Library, 1707–1842; another Historical Notes. There is a volume of copies of Public Records etc.; four volumes of Proceedings in Cases, 1630–1741; a single volume of Orders for Burial in the Temple Church, 1771–1851. Two volumes contain documents relating to the Temple Church, its Masters and other clergy, its services, fabric, and music; there are two volumes of Epitaphs in the Church and one of pamphlets relating to the

Church. Another volume contains the draft conveyance between the Inner Temple and the Middle Temple on their respective property, 1731. There are two volumes of Orders relating to Treasurers, Readers, Masters of the Bench, etc., 1660–1774, one of Orders relating to Chambers, 1638–1771, and another on Revels, Foundlings, etc., 1698–1826. Two volumes contain pamphlets on Rules Customs, etc., 1567–1769; one volume contains fifteen Chamber Books, 1709–63. One volume is a Treatise on Officers and Members, written in 1633; another a Treatise on the History and Division of the Temples; and another a Treatise on the Rules and Government of the Inner Temple. One volume is the Butler's Account Book, 1734–5; another the Account and Receipt Book, 1704–9. The last two volumes consist respectively of Miscellaneous Records on Accounts etc., 1708–41, and Bench Table Orders relating to the Inner Temple, 1575–1727. The extreme limits of dates of the whole collection is 1567 to 1851, though the preponderating majority of items come from the eighteenth century.

Though almost all the items in these thirty-nine volumes relate to internal domestic matters of the Inner Temple, many throw a valuable light upon the relationship between the Inner Temple and the Middle Temple, particularly concerning their property and the Temple Church, its Master, and its services. Interesting details are also found about the relationship of the Inner Temple as landlords with their many tenants who were not members of the Inn, on disputes between tenants who were, on the festivities of Bench and Bar, on the humane way in which unwanted children dropped within the precincts of the Inner Temple were dealt with, on its treatment of its servants, and the ways it sought to police its premises and to combat the dangers of fire which were always menacing. Sometimes the issues transcend the boundaries of its immunities and privileges, for example the dispute with the Lord Mayor and city of London following what the city claimed was a riot caused by the Lord Mayor and Aldermen, with their entourage, trying to enter the Inner Temple Hall with the city sword carried erect in 1669, and later disputes with the city on liability to poor law assessment and other rates and duties, including payment for riot damage done without its precincts. Other important items deal with the support and aid given by the Inner Temple to the volunteer movement during the Napoleonic Wars, though it is but seldom that these records show any real awareness of national crises, though the papist scares of the seventeenth century, the Jacobite activities of the first half of the eighteenth century, and the illnesses of George III in the second half of that century are all illustrated.

It is strange to find that the first item in the first volume is a transcript of an entry from the Pension Book of Gray's Inn, dated 10 February 1586, relating to Francis Bacon, who is to that Inn what Sir Edward Coke is to the Inner Temple. This and a slightly later item relating to Francis Bacon have no connection with the ancient amity, but are obviously related to questions of precedency concerning Readers. It is still more surprising to find amongst these records a few entirely extraneous items such as Brief Particulars of the lands of Christopher, Duke of Albemarle, arranged in counties and Ireland, 1678, the note on the Will and Settlement of the same Duke, 1688, and the series of accounts of the estates of Mary, Dowager Duchess of Montagu, at Rotherhithe, New Hall, and elsewhere in Essex, at Norton Disney, co. Lincs., at Cheshunt and Enfield, co. Hertf., and at Grendon, co. Staffs., all dated 1709, or the documents on Sewers, including the Order in Council, 15 July 1624, and the Petition of the owners of the marshes of East Greenwich on the conservation of the marshes and the ancient custom of the town, and decrees from the Commissioners of Sewers, 1573, 1683, and later, an Admittance to land in the manor of Cheshunt, 1710, or the receipt for £80 of a London goldsmith for an indenture of Bargain and Sale to Richard, son of Heneage Finch, Lord Finch, Baron of Coventry, 29 February 1676.

Special attention can be directed only to a very few of the individual internal records. The memorandum of delivery by William Hughes, the last Treasurer, to Doctor Julius Caesar, the then Treasurer, and signed by both of them, on 6 February 1594, of the evidences, writings, plate, and napery, is interesting and important. The evidences and writings were all of the reign of Elizabeth I. Many of them are now among the Miscellaneous Manuscripts. Among them are 'two writings in parchment concerning the Association of the Inner Temple, viz. one touching the bench and the other the bar' and 'three other writings in parchment concerning the several Associations of Clements Inn, Cliffords Inn and Lyons Inn'. These are the Declaration of Loyalty and Oath of Association of 1584. Those of the bar of the Inner Temple and Lyon's Inn are now among the Miscellaneous Manuscripts; the other three are missing. The other items include 'four bundles of letters', now impossible to trace, and a copy of a 'letter from the benchers to the Lords of the Council' which has not been seen.

Passing over the disputes between both the Inner and Middle Temples with Dr. Paul Micklewaite, Master of the Temple, 1627–39, which raged from 1629 onwards, of which there are few records in the Inn, the story of which cannot be written without heavy recourse to records among the State Papers and to printed pamphlets, the most interesting and certainly the best-documented incident of the history of the Inner Temple during the seventeenth century among the Records of the Inner Temple is the dispute with the Lord Mayor and city of London in 1669. The Lent Reader that year was Christopher Goodfellow, who had been called to the Bench in 1660 and been City Pleader since 1666. It was therefore quite natural that he should invite the Lord Mayor and Aldermen to his Reader's dinner which was to be held on 3 March 1669. The persons chiefly involved were notable, and the story can be told in the most minute detail.

It starts before the incident, when two barristers were deputed as an embassy from the Reader to the Lord Mayor. There had been more than murmurings of opposition to the proposed visit. The story of the embassy is told in a humorous and racy letter from Thomas Wroth, who had been called to the bar in 1666, to William Petyt, who seemed as greatly interested in the details as in the implications. The other member of the embassy was George Jeffreys, afterwards Lord Chancellor. His part was one of finesse and diplomacy as against the twinkling eye and staid speeches of Thomas Wroth. It paid George Jeffreys soon, since, though then of only one year's standing at the bar, in 1671 he became Common Serjeant at the age of 23, and in 1678, Recorder of London. Despite warnings the obstinate and imperious Lord Mayor persisted, with the full support of his Aldermen and Sheriffs, in attending the Reader's dinner with sword-bearer and sword still to be carried erect. The Lord Mayor and his sword got no further than the Hall stairs. Their entry was frustrated by utter barristers and students. The city party was forced to retreat and take refuge in the chambers of Francis Phillips, Auditor of the Exchequer, a Bencher since 1649. Meanwhile the Sheriffs and the Recorder, Sir John Nicholls, had been dispatched to Whitehall to seek royal succour and support. Charles II is stated to have advised the Lord Mayor to return to the city. The Recorder came with a message from the King, and the Lord Mayor sent for the Reader and Benchers to hear it. Return to the city was easier said than done. The siege continued, led by John Hodges, a barrister who had been called in 1663 and well acquainted with the city and its ways, for his father, Thomas Hodges, had been an Alderman. After more turmoil the get-away was made.

The city complained to the Council. The Council was in a difficulty. It did not desire to offend either party. The Treasurer was Sir Heneage Finch, who was also Solicitor General. The Benchers included Sir Thomas Foster, whose father, also a Bencher, had died as Chief Justice, King's Bench, in 1663, Sir Edward Thurland, who became a Baron of the Exchequer in 1673, and Sir John Trevor, who became Speaker and Master of the Rolls. James, Duke of York, was a bencher, and of the court, George, Duke of Buckingham, Thomas Sackville, Earl of Dorset, and Sir William Morice, who had resigned as Secretary of State in 1665, were all members. Of the city representatives, Sir William Turner, Lord Mayor, was brother of John Turner, who had been Reader of the Middle Temple in 1665, when Sir John Lawrence was Lord Mayor, who now claimed that when he attended that Reader's dinner his sword had been borne upright all the way, and Sir John Browne, who had promoted the Restoration, had been Lord Mayor. At the Council would be Sir Orlando Bridgeman, Lord Keeper, who had been called to the Bench on 30 May 1660.

The Recorder and two or more of the Aldermen and John Hodges, George Jeffreys, and six other members of the Inner Temple were ordered to appear before the Council on 24 March. This order was issued by Sir Orlando Bridgeman, as Lord Keeper, and was dated 21 March. On the appointed day the Recorder

> and some of the Aldermen and some of the gentlemen of the Temple attending and being called in and heard by Counsel learned and the rights and privileges of bearing up my Lord Mayor's sword within the precincts of the Temple being asserted on behalf of the city and

denied by the gentlemen of the Temple. The same was left to be decided by due proceedings of law in the Courts of Westminster Hall.

On the personal indignities alleged to have been offered to the Lord Mayor, on the same day it was ordered that John Hodges appear at the Board on 31 March, and that as to further allegations of threats a week was given to make out process. It was intimated to the Council that John Hodges being 'On circuit with the Judges could not have notice timely enough to give attendance'. So he, James Munday, and another were ordered to appear on 7 April. On that day they appeared and the case against them, affidavits having been read against them and for them

> to justify their carriage that day, though they could not extenuate the faults of others who in the tumult affronted the Lord Mayor and his officers . . . and the officer of the Lord Mayor who was alleged to have been abused in the tumult did not charge it upon any of these particular persons . . . the matter very much depending on the right and privilege of bearing up the Lord Mayor's sword within the Temple . . . is left to be decided by due proceedings of law in the Courts of Westminster Hall.

The King suspended the declaration of his pleasure until the right and privilege should accordingly be determined at law.

A full account of the proceedings on 24 March is available in the State Papers, although unfortunately not in the Records of the Inner Temple. These are the draft notes or minutes of the proceedings as taken by Sir Joseph Williamson, as Clerk of the Council, as the words were spoken. The proceedings were dominated by the observations of Sir Orlando Bridgeman, Lord Keeper. The other members of the Council present were the King, the Duke of York, James Butler, Duke of Ormond, the Lord Chamberlain, John Egerton, Earl of Bridgwater, William, Earl of Craven, the Bishop of London (Humphrey Henchman), Henry Bennet, Lord Arlington, Anthony Ashley Cooper, Lord Ashley, Francis, Lord Newport, the Treasurer (George Monck, Duke of Albemarle), Mr. Vice Chamberlain, Mr. Secretary (John) Trevor, and Sir John Duncombe. Apart from the Lord Keeper, the only other member who is recorded as having spoken was Lord Ashley, then Chancellor of the Exchequer. After the Lord Keeper had outlined the general line of reference to Westminster Hall and the question of affront was being discussed, the future Lord Chancellor intervened with 'this was in defence of a lawful right and to prevent bringing this into precedence'.

There is another relic of the dispute which is important. Though it is not among the Records of the Inner Temple it is among the Inner Temple manuscripts, in the Petyt Collection. It is the argument of Sir Heneage Finch as to the Temple being without the jurisdiction of the city of London, 1669. It is such a document as one would expect from a Solicitor General who was also Treasurer of his Inn. There is a copy of this document among the State Papers, which was probably left in the Council Office on the eve of the first Council meeting on the matter, as this bears a note upon it, 23 March 1669.

Otherwise the whole story is told in the documents in the Records of the Inner Temple. There is the original letter from Thomas Wroth to William Petyt. There are copies of the three orders to appear before the Council. There are no fewer than twenty-three several depositions on the cause or causes, more on behalf of the Inner Temple than the city. They are dated from 6 March to 7 April 1669. There are also two other related items gathered to support the Inner Temple case for its argument on its behalf of Sir Heneage Finch. For there had been an earlier similar incident concerning the Middle Temple, when the sword of Sir William Gerrard as Lord Mayor had been put down when he went to the Reader's dinner in 1555. Then 'the gentlemen of the younger sort, as well of that House as of the Inner Temple', as well as the Readers of both Houses, 'with all their companies of both Houses were sent for to the Rolls in Chancery Lane, where sat the Marquis of Winchester, Lord Treasurer, assisted with eleven others of the Queen's Privy Council'. They were to deliver the names of the principal doers. This was extracted. There is also a long note 'on the liberties and privileges of the Inner Temple and Middle Temple and the Societies of the students of law therein evidenced and ascertained against the pretended jurisdiction and claims of the Lord Mayor, Sheriffs, Aldermen and Commonalty of the city of London', 18 Henry I to 6 James I. This is by William Petyt.

There the story ends. The city proceeded no further. The Inner Temple and its members in high places had been active from 3 March onwards. The depositions suggest the intense and well-conceived plans to thwart any unpleasant consequences for Inn, junior barristers, or students. Public opinion, or the opinion which counted, was against the city. Its own petty officials ratted on the Lord Mayor. There was undoubtedly much cajolery and probably not a little bribery. The general interest in the episode must have been very great. Pepys witnessed the final meeting of the Council on the matter. His summary of the proceedings recorded in his Diary puts the whole position in a nutshell:

> upon hearing the whole business the city was certainly to blame to charge them in this manner with a riot; but the King and Council did forbear to determine anything in it till the other business of the title and privilege be decided, which is now under dispute between them, whether the Temple be within the liberty of the city or no. But I was sorry to see the city so illadvised as to complain in a thing where their proofs were so weak.

Of the principal actors in the episode, John Hodges was called to the Bench in 1682 and was Treasurer, 1696–7; James Munday was called to the bar in 1678 and to the Bench in 1700, and was the son of Stephen Munday, Secondary of the Prothonotary of Common Pleas, who had been made an associate of the bar in 1648; Thomas Littleton who by the order of 21 March was to attend the Council, had been admitted in 1661, at the request of his father, Sir Thomas Littleton, when he was described as grandchild and heir to Sir Edward Littleton, late Lord Keeper. He was called to the bar in 1671. Of those who made depositions on behalf of the Inn Sir John Tremaine became a Serjeant at Law; Thomas Tutt was called to the bar in 1673 and to the Bench in 1692 and was Reader in 1696. Richard Langhorne, who had been called to the bar in 1654, became engulfed in the accusations of Titus Oates and was executed in 1679. Christopher Goodfellow became Judge of the Sheriff's Court in 1681.

In such matters of privilege, the interest of the Inner Temple and the Middle Temple was the same. In all matters, neither at this time nor earlier and later, was it so. In the Records of the Inner Temple the first major documents relating to differences are those concerning the boundaries of their respective properties. There never seems to have been any major dispute regarding the Temple Church, though on minor matters there were frequently differences of opinion. But there is one whole volume of ten main items relating to proceedings in a Chancery suit which lasted from 1630 to 1633. It arose over buildings built by the Middle Temple which encroached on what the Inner Temple claimed as its property and appears to have started in 1628. The suit is briefly described as 'Sir Julius Caesar, otherwise Adelmare, knight, Master of the Rolls, and one of the Privy Council, Sir John Walter, Lord Chief Baron of the Exchequer, Sir George Croke, one of the Justices of the King's Bench, and other complainants, against Henry, Earl of Manchester and other defendants, 1630'. The others in both cases were the other Benchers of the Inns. If Sir Julius Caesar was still Master of the Rolls, with nearly fifty years of royal service behind him, Admiralty, Chancery, Requests, Exchequer, Henry, Earl of Manchester, was an elder statesman, who had been Recorder of London, Chief Justice of King's Bench and Lord Treasurer, and was still Master of the Court of Wards and Lord Privy Seal. The Lord Keeper was Thomas, Lord Coventry, who had been Treasurer of the Inner Temple, 1617 to 1625, when he was appointed Lord Keeper. The array of Benchers of each Inn was formidable. The parties seemed to be of about equal strength and influence.

Though the volume contains 5 Answers, 22 Depositions, 3 Interrogatories, and 7 Proofs relating to different parts of the properties, the proceedings are by no means complete. There is no Bill, no Replication. These may still repose in the Treasurer's Strong Room. No Decree was ever made. The cause was probably compromised. Disputes on boundaries continued later, until in 1731 the division of the property was agreed and a conveyance drawn up. This determined the disputes. The draft of this agreement is to be found in another volume of the Records of the Inner Temple.

Finally, as an example of interesting and important material among the Records of the Inner Temple, there are a number of very interesting holograph letters of Dr. Christopher Benson, who was Master of the Temple from 1826 to 1845. He was a considerable scholar and an eloquent preacher, who drew crowds to the Temple Church, but a little demanding in his requirements and innovations, on which the two Inns did not always see eye to eye. He desired daily services to be held. He had strong views about music in the Temple Church, about the choir and where it was to be seated, and about the church ornaments and furniture. He could not 'consider the lace embroidered article which is placed on top of what ought to have been a communion table but is an altar to be consistent with the requisition of the rubric'. The pulpit was all wrong, 'the desk or cushion was so small and of such nature as to make the greatest care on the part of the preacher necessary to prevent the sermon slipping through his hands'. In 1832 the Master wrote about allowance to him for a house; the Bench did not think themselves justified to propose a compensation to the Master for the expense of another house. In 1842 a member of the Inner Temple complained that he was one of many the previous morning all but excluded from the service at the Temple Church. 'I had to stand all the time. Should strangers exclude those for whom it was originally intended?' The Master wrote to the Treasurer enclosing this letter and commenting on the 'inconvenience created by the present mode of admitting persons to the seats of the painted church as if it were to a painted theatre'. Troublesome though he had been, when he resigned the Mastership, William Burge, the Treasurer, wrote to him of the 'high respect with which they must ever regard the piety, learning and eloquence by which you continued to the Mastership of the Temple its distinguished rank as the subject of ecclesiastical preferment'. In a somewhat curt acknowledgement Christopher Benson wrote that no consideration with regard to health had had the smallest share in prompting his resignation.

It has been stated above that there is at least an equal quantity of similar material as is contained in the thirty-nine volumes of Records of the Inner Temple still in the Treasurer's Strong Room. In that Strong Room also are the records in volume and bundle form which tell the history of the Inner Temple from 1505 to the present day. Of these, unhappily many of the earlier records were very badly damaged during the last war by enemy action, some irretrievably so. Fortunately of three of the main series of records in volume form, the Acts of Parliament Books have been calendared from 1505 to 1800 and the Bench Table Order Books have been similarly calendared from the date of their commencement in 1668 to 1800. These calendars are in print, but they are calendars only, so recourse must frequently be made to the original records. The Admission Books, which suffered badly, have been extracted in typescript from their beginning in 1547 to 1850. There are, therefore, Calendars of the Acts of Parliament Books, though from quite early in the 19th century these become increasingly less informative, except for formal occasions, and Bench Order Books, which from about the same time become increasingly more informative, to be completed for at least another century. It would also be useful if the extracts from the Admission Books could be extended for another fifty years at least. On Accounts, the General Accounts are briefly summarized in the printed volumes of Calendars from 1605 to 1800, some few being given in full, and there are in addition extracts from other Accounts very occasionally reproduced there, in full or brief abstract. The Account Books require considerably more complete treatment, as will be pointed out below.

It must be stressed very strongly that none of the contents of the Treasurer's Strong Room has been listed. An attempt to draft list the Acts of Parliament Books which total twenty-two volumes, 1505–1962, the Bench Table Order Books which total forty-two volumes, 1668–1962, and the class of Transcripts of Extracts from Acts of Parliament Books and Bench Order Books of which there are seven volumes covering the period 1682–1804, has been frustrated by the condition of certain of the first dozen volumes of the Acts of Parliament Books, the serious damage done to the first nine volumes, and the brittle condition of the next nineteen volumes of the Bench Table Order Books and the whole of the class of Transcripts.

Of the Account Books there are several series or classes, of which the most important are the General Account Books, which are to be found in two series, the first starting in 1605, and covering in three volumes to 1687, and the second which overlaps for a few years, starting in 1682 and running to the present day. Subsidiary to these are General Account Receipt Books also beginning in 1682; Miscellaneous Account Books starting in 1605 as General Account Books and running to 1741; Call Stamp Books, 1695 to the present time; Chamber Account Books, 1759 to the present time. Until these are all listed in detail it will be difficult to determine the completeness of the range, or the ultimate value of any class, but it is quite apparent that the two main series of General Account Books and the General Account Receipt Books must contain a vast amount of information not only essential to the history of the Inn, but of the utmost importance to economic historians.

There are many subsidiary series of Account Books whose span was of short duration, or which have largely disappeared. On Admissions, the use of Admission Stamp Books which run from 1683 to the present day would be useful in filling any gaps or correcting any errors there may be in the Admission Books or other records relating to Admissions. On calls to the bar, the Bar Bonds which start in 1672 and the three volumes of Calls to the Bar which cover the period from 1635 to the present day both antedate by several years the Call Stamp Books, which do not start until 1695 and run to the present day, are the most continuous. There are several series of books relating to Commons and Chambers and the incomplete run of Bench Minutes running from 1706 to 1879, though only drafts would be useful in supplementing or being complementary to the Bench Table Order Books of which so many are now damaged or dilapidated.

The most serious loss of the war, however, was the parchment Book of Evidences which was purchased in 1607 for 14*s.* 8*d.* and which contained registrations of deeds and other documents from 1568 to 1732. Too few of the original evidences have survived and too few entries in this book were transcribed before it was destroyed. It was kept in a safe and on the night when the Inner Temple was fired in 1941 its protection proved a charnel-chamber which shrivelled it to a conglomerate mass. Some of the documents which were registered in it are now to be found among the

Miscellaneous Manuscripts, and others which no doubt still exist should in due course be transferred to the same group of manuscripts and listed. As has been stated above there are amongst the Records of the Inner Temple a series of fifteen Chamber Books, 1709–62, a Butler's Account Book, 1734–5, and an Account and Receipt Book, 1704–9. It would seem logical to transfer to Records of the Inner Temple similar records remaining in the Treasurer's Strong Room, for instance the Buttery Books, 1676–85, 1700–10, and 1721–1800, the Chamber Books, 1709–60 (incomplete), the Accounts of Allowances, 1696–1704, and the Accounts of Commons, 1728–41. Similarly, of course, the hundreds if not thousands of loose papers, which are similar and complementary to the loose papers which have already so successfully been bound up in the thirty-nine volumes of the Records of the Inner Temple.

7. JOHN FREEMAN MITFORD, FIRST LORD REDESDALE, TREASURER, 1795–1796

John Mitford, younger brother of William Mitford, the historian of Greece and the friend of Edward Gibbon, had been admitted to the Inner Temple in 1772, was called to the bar in 1777, became a King's Counsel in 1789, a Bencher in 1791, and Treasurer in 1795–6. After being at school at Cheam he started his career in the Six Clerks Office of the Court of Chancery. He practised at the Chancery bar and had an extensive practice. He became a Welsh Judge in 1789 (for the counties of Carmarthen, Pembroke, and Cardigan), and Chancellor of the County Palatine of Durham in 1791. In 1793 he became Solicitor General and was knighted, and Attorney General in 1799. He had been a member of parliament since 1788 and in 1801 became Speaker of the House of Commons. On 9 February 1802 he was appointed Lord Chancellor of Ireland and was created Lord Redesdale on 15 February the same year. He held the Irish Office until 1806, resigning on account of his unpopularity because of his opposition to Catholic Emancipation. Thereafter he held no judicial office, but was a most active member of the House of Lords and was largely responsible for the preparation, production, and publication of the *Reports on the Dignity of a Peer*, published in five volumes, 1820–9, which he largely drafted. He died in 1830 at Batsford Park, aged 81, and was buried at Batsford.

Such are the salient facts of his career, but in a number of directions there is need for a great deal of filling in, for instance on such matters as his publications, his work as a Law Officer of the Crown, his activities as a Bencher of his Inn, and his valuable work on the Reports on the Dignity of a Peer. Some of these aspects are amply illustrated in the Legal Manuscripts of the Mitford Collection which will be dealt with in the next section. Others are more conveniently dealt with now.

First as to his publications. The most important was *Treatise on the Pleadings in Suits in the Court of Chancery, by English Bill.* First published in 1780, it ran to five editions by 1847, getting progressively more lengthy. His political publications were relatively unimportant. His judgements as Lord Chancellor of Ireland were printed in F. Scholes and T. Lefroy, *Reports of Cases in Court of Chancery of Ireland*, 1802–7, two volumes.

His Treasurership of the Inner Temple was uneventful. The senior Bencher was Lord Thurlow, who put in no appearance at the Bench Table during the year, though he survived until 1806. Francis Maseres and Daines Barrington, both already Treasurers, attended regularly, as did James Mingay, also an ex-Treasurer, who was claimed to be second only to Erskine as an advocate. There was only one distinguished call to the bar, Charles Abbott, afterwards Lord Tenterden and Lord Chief Justice. It was after his retirement from Ireland in 1806 that John Mitford displayed most interest and activity in the Inn. He attended the Bench spasmodically until 1820. He had attended once as Lord Chancellor of Ireland in 1805. His interest in the Library continued. On 8 November he was thanked 'for his trouble and interference in procuring the *Journals of the House of Lords and Commons of Ireland* and the completion of the *Irish Statutes*'; on 14 November 1814 for his *Treatise on the Pleadings in Suits in the Court of Chancery*, 1814 edition, which had many additions; on 6 June 1820 for his present of the *Reports on the Dignity of a Peer*.

He must now have been devoting a great deal of his time to that enterprise. Its full title is very impressive: *Reports from the Lords Committee appointed to search Journals, Rolls and other Records for all matters touching the Dignity of a Peer*. The collection of records was still more impressive. It has been described that 'this important contribution to the stores of constitutional learning was made substantially by the late Lord Redesdale, with, of course, learned and powerful assistance. It consists in fact of a History of the English Legislature traced from the Conquest, through a period of between seven and eight hundred years.' Mitford's interest in Public Records is first noticed when as Attorney General in 1800, he was appointed to carry out the House of Commons resolution on a Record Commission.

A holograph letter written by him from Batsford on 7 December 1816 to Randal Norris as Sub-Treasurer of the Inner Temple is important for a number of reasons. It shows how the information contained in the Reports was collected; it displays Lord Redesdale's continuing interest in the Inn; it forecasts a valuable benefaction.

The copies making by Mr. (John) Caley for the use of a Committee of the House of Lords. Such documents as may appear important will be stated in the report of the Committee to the House and that Report will probably be ordered to be printed, for the use of the House The great use of Mr. Petyt's manuscripts is as an index to the records and copies have been taken only as more convenient than taking copies from the records of original instruments, but the copies will be examined with the records, because the Committee will not rely upon Mr. Petyt's accuracy, and indeed he has in many instances given words at length instead of abbreviations which are in the original and he may have sometimes mistaken the abbreviations.

I intended to move that the Committee should be moved to deposit all the copies of documents which have been made in some public library and one vizt. a complete correction to Dugdale's Summonses to Parliament will be a serious work. The library I had in mind was that of the Inner Temple; the Museum has been mentioned. I confess I think the Temple Library has a superior claim.

Had the transcripts been deposited in the Inner Temple Library they would have formed a logical supplement to the Petyt transcripts and considerably enhanced their use and value. Lord Redesdale must have failed in his intended disposition. They are elsewhere.

8. THE MITFORD COLLECTION OF LEGAL MANUSCRIPTS

The seventy-nine volumes in the Mitford Collection of Legal Manuscripts naturally divide themselves into two sections: first, those manuscripts which derive from the Collection of Sir Thomas Sewell, who was Master of the Rolls from 1764 to 1784, and secondly, the manuscripts which were made by or acquired by John Mitford himself. They are equally divided. Those in the first section total thirty-nine volumes; those in the second section also total thirty-nine volumes. The remaining volume consists partly of transcripts from Sir Thomas Sewell's Collection and partly of Francis Hargrave's Report on that Collection. The total of seventy-nine volumes does not represent the whole of the transcripts which were originally in that collection. At least two volumes of transcripts from Sir Thomas Sewell's Collection which are noted by Francis Hargrave are now missing. Nearly a score of volumes which were in the section made or acquired by John Mitford are now wanting, though fortunately most of these would appear to have been of slight value.

Though Sir Thomas Sewell is not credited with any published works, he was an indefatigable collector of reports and precedents on equity causes which he worked upon, commented upon, and arranged in subjects and sections, doubtless with a view to the production of a major work on equity. For he had had a large and lucrative practice in the Chancery Courts, especially before Lord Hardwicke, and he borrowed the reports of his fellow practitioners Richard Capper, William de Grey, and Richard Perrin. The thirty-nine volumes which came from the Sewell Collection are almost entirely concerned with digests of Chancery causes and decisions. The whole of his collection was taken by his sons and administrators to Francis Hargrave, who wrote a fascinating report upon them in 1785 and had their permission to make copies of them. Most of these Hargrave transcripts are among the manuscripts in the Mitford Legal Collection, but unfortunately not the whole of them, as some had been lost before the Mitford Collection of Legal Manuscripts was presented to the Inner Temple Library. The details of these omissions will appear in this catalogue and will be referred to briefly below.

First, there are thirteen volumes which Francis Hargrave calls Sir Thomas Sewell's Abridgement of Equity Cases and twelve volumes which he calls Sir Thomas Sewell's References to Equity Cases. There is a single volume which is an Index to both these series. There are eight volumes which Francis Hargrave describes as transcript notes of cases in the Chancery in the time of Lord Hardewicke, as Lord Chancellor, of which the reporters were Richard Capper, who was a Bencher of Lincoln's Inn, William de Grey, who became Lord Walsingham and Lord Chief Justice of King's Bench, and Richard Perrin, who became a Baron of the Exchequer. No report of any one of these three has ever been published. This series originally contained ten volumes but nos. 5 and 6 are now wanting. There are two volumes of Notes from Briefs to Cases, in many of which Sir Thomas Sewell himself appeared, and three volumes of Notes found amongst Sir Thomas Sewell's Papers. Both these short series of volumes were collected together or worked upon by Sir Thomas Sewell. The mixed volume contains what Francis Hargrave describes as essays towards a reduction of the equity cases on various subjects into rules and principles in addition to Francis Hargrave's Report on the Sewell Manuscripts. Many of these Sewell volumes have notes, additions, and corrections by John Mitford.

Of the remaining thirty-nine volumes more closely and personally associated with Lord Redesdale, as written by him, annotated by him, collected by him, or concerning his practice and offices, there are four volumes of his Fee Books, eleven volumes of his Notes written in Court as Lord Chancellor of Ireland, and four volumes containing his Opinions as a Law Officer of the Crown. The Fee Books provide complete records of his work as Counsel from 1786 to 1800 and have a substantial value in their continuity and detail. The Notes in Court as Lord Chancellor of Ireland form a record, which must be almost unique, of the day-to-day work of a Lord Chancellor during almost the whole of his period of office. His Opinions as Solicitor and Attorney General, including those of his colleagues John Scott, afterwards Lord Chancellor and Earl of Eldon, and Sir William Grant, afterwards Master of the Rolls, deal with such diverse matters as peerage claims, diplomatic privilege, extradition, denization in British colonies, charters of incorporation, trading with the enemy, whether privilege of Parliament extended to the Isle of Man, the payment for property confiscated in the State of Virginia, the granting of the Peninsular of Sierra Leone.

Another group of volumes collected by John Mitford covered a still wider range of subjects. There is a volume which deals only with the very important case on the right of wreck, Courteney *v.* Bower, 1699. It gives the full judgements of Sir George Treby, Chief Justice of Common Pleas, and his three colleagues, and although these are available in other manuscripts this volume has interesting and important details which are missing in the others. There are two volumes derived from Francis Hargrave by transcript, one containing Reports of Cases in Chancery and King's Bench, 1703–10, the other a Collection of Cases on Debtors and Accountants to the Crown, of the last decades of the eighteenth century, both of which were probably used by John Mitford in writing his *Treatise on the Pleadings in Suits in the Court of Chancery*.

There are three volumes, the only ones remaining, of a series which must have numbered twenty volumes which are so scarce in content that the remnant of the series calls for no immediate comment. Finally there are two volumes described as Miscellaneous Papers, which cover a very wide range of interest and which are transcripts of some very important and valuable papers. These include a short Treatise on the Jurisdiction of the Court of Admiralty of the Cinque Ports, Processes of Appeal from the Cinque Ports to the King in Chancery, and memoranda on other aspects of Admiralty Jurisdiction, Cases on Outlawry, Proclamations on the Currency of Copper Money in Virginia and also in the Island of Bermuda, the Rights of British Merchants resident in Lisbon to be admitted to the meetings of the Factory there, sedition by the Law of Scotland, Appeals to the House of Lords from Criminal Proceedings in the Court of Justiciary, The Laws of the British East Indies Sugar Colonies concerning slaves, Cases of persons removed to other Gaols at instance of the Crown, Duty on Prize Goods condemned as Droits of the Admiralty, a Commission to Cardinal Wolsey in 1526 on the valuation of money in England, and the Opinions of Counsel on a great variety of subjects, Law Officers, such as Sir Fletcher Norton, Attorney General, and several by Serjeant George Hill. Many of these were probably drawn up on John Mitford's instructions for his use as a Law Officer of the Crown.

Though the main content of the Mitford Collection of Legal Manuscripts is, therefore, essentially of a legal character, particularly covering the Court of Chancery, the activities of all the other Courts are represented, and there is scarcely a part of the then known world which is not treated in one or other of the volumes. Even that part of the content of some of the volumes which may appear, at first sight, to be far removed from the legal purview, almost the whole of the memoranda drawn up and the transcripts made were relative to what came within the activities of Chancery Counsel or the Law Officers of the Crown. Though the period preponderantly covered is the whole of the eighteenth century, especially the second half of that century, the seventeenth century also provided its cases and its precedents and facts, and some even go back to the reigns of Henry VI and Henry VIII, and especially to the days of Elizabeth I. In the later, great lawyers represented in the Opinions of Counsel are, for example John Scott, his brother William Scott, afterwards Lord Stowell, Charles Pratt, Attorney General, afterwards Lord Chancellor and Earl Camden, Sir Charles Yorke, Solicitor General, afterwards very briefly for a few days Lord Chancellor, Serjeant George Hill, of Lincoln's Inn, a most prolific and prolix counsel, Charles Fearne, the author of several learned legal works, and Charles Abbott, afterwards Lord Tenterden, Lord Chief Justice.

The Collection throws a great deal of light upon Lord Redesdale's career as Counsel, Solicitor General, Attorney General, and Lord Chancellor of Ireland.

Unfortunately they throw no light upon his time as a Judge of the Court of Great Sessions of Wales, as Chancellor of the Palatinate of Durham, or as Speaker of the House of Commons, or as one of the most active members of the House of Lords from 1806 to 1830. Neither does it throw any light upon his political opinions or his political activities. It is equally silent upon his personal life, interests, and activities.

The Mitford Collection of Legal Manuscripts was presented to the Inner Temple Library by Lord Dulverton, from Batsford Park, Gloucestershire, in 1957, and in 1957–8 was perused, listed, and reported upon by Master George Johnston, who was Treasurer of the Inn in 1963. This list and report have been found most helpful in cataloguing the seventy-nine volumes, and although all his views on certain of the volumes have not been adopted that list and report must be regarded as supplementary and complementary to the catalogue which appears in these volumes.

9. THE MISCELLANEOUS MANUSCRIPTS

The Miscellaneous Manuscripts are not a group or collection. They consist of many individual items without any relationship between them except, occasionally, the source whence they came. But there are several groups among them, according to the interests of the donors. Certain of those groups, albeit small ones, have been dealt with above, when the Petyt and Barrington Collections were treated. Now it is proposed to give a brief general description of the Miscellaneous Manuscripts and then to deal with those whose source and provenance are unknown. Lastly, it is proposed to deal with certain groups under the names of the donors. For the gifts of Francis Maseres represent largely his Canadian and mathematical interests; those of Mrs. Anne Sadleir her devotional and family interests; those of Alexander Luders his literary and legal interests; those of Stuart A. Moore and his son, Hubert Stuart Moore, their specialized legal interests and activities. Then, in appropriate cases, the donors of a single or a few manuscripts will be linked severally with the pursuits and profession of the donors.

Out of the 211 manuscripts which, at present, constitute the Miscellaneous Manuscripts some forty volumes cannot, now, be identified with any person or period of receipt. It seems strange that these should include the first manuscript listed in the Miscellaneous Manuscripts, perhaps the most important of them all. It consists of six sections of a Year Book, Michaelmas term, 26–7 Edward I (1297). These sections have never been bound. It almost shows signs of having been written in Court and it is certainly contemporary. It appears to be unique for three reasons: it is the only known Year Book for the period it covers; its contents have never been printed; it is the only surviving Year Book known which represents the reports of a single term. If so it is the unique survival of one of the 'originals', which were not preserved when they were superseded by larger volumes covering several terms or years.

Of the other manuscripts of which the source is unidentified (and many of them will remain unidentifiable from information in their content), which are of great importance are: an illuminated late fifteenth-century manuscript of Fitzherbert's Digest, that is La Graunde Abridgement; a metrical version of Psalms 1–80, a variation of the Psalms by Matthew Parker, Archbishop of Canterbury, printed by John Day in 1567, which is probably a draft by Matthew Parker; the Letter Book of Arthur Capel, Earl of Essex, as Lord Lieutenant of Ireland, 1677; and six volumes of Henry Rolle's *Abridgment des Plusieurs Cases et Resolutions del Common Ley*, first printed in two volumes in 1668. Sir Henry Rolle was a Bencher and Double Reader of the Inner Temple, Chief Justice of King's Bench and of the Upper Bench, and a member of the Council of State. All these six volumes have been very heavily annotated by Robert Price, a Baron of the Exchequer, 1703–26, with lengthy additions by him. It would seem to have been prepared for a new and very much enlarged edition, which never appeared. The 876 pages of the printed text have been expanded to 4,553 pages (though some of these are blank). The whole contains tens of thousands of notes and references and hundreds of new titles and is a monumental piece of editing.

With this enlarged text for Rolle's Abridgment may be compared Michael Dalton's copy of *L'Office et aucthoritie de Justices de peace*, by Sir Anthony Fitzherbert, enlarged by Richard Crompton, 1606. This volume contains notes and references by Michael Dalton, together with pages of notes in his hand. It was used by him for his works *Countrey Justice*, 1618, and *Officium Vicecomitum*, 1623. Also, a volume of Proclamations, 1–10 James I, and Statutes, 21 James I, which contains 20 additional Proclamations (and the Statutes are annotated in a contemporary hand), appears to belong to the same genre, but neither is derived from William Petyt. The 1652 edition of Robert Burton's *Anatomy of Melancholy* is of the same nature, but here the manuscript additions consist of a biography of the author, with his will, and notes, and the text of *L'Allegro* and *Il Penseroso*. But perhaps the most important of the volumes of this nature are the manuscript additions to Richard Tottell's *Retourna Brevium*, 1581, with many contemporary annotations, to which sixty-five pages of manuscript have been added, which addition is, in effect, a precedent book or formulary for use in the Sheriff's Office, and has been quite appropriately added to Tottell's tract. It is written in a legal hand and the forms were probably collected by an Under Sheriff of Lancashire, not later than 1591. Also interesting is a very heavily annotated volume of Littleton's *Tenures*, which has twenty-three folios added at the beginning, containing brief reports of 121 cases, 17 Elizabeth I to 1 James I, and on sixty folios added at the end, 34 similar cases, 27 Elizabeth I to 11 James I, and a few notes.

So much for a few of the unidentified volumes; next a few words about some of the volumes which may be said to have come into the Inner Temple Library by chance.

On 15 April 1853 'his Grace the Duke of Northumberland having presented to the Library ten volumes of Manuscripts it was ordered that the thanks of the Society be conveyed through and by the Treasurer to his Grace the Duke of Northumberland for his present'. The Duke's librarian was J. E. Martin, then Sub-Librarian of the Inner Temple. He knew the manuscripts and for his purposes there seemed to be no reason to specify them. Today the situation is different; the Library contains no further information concerning the matter. It is fair to make the assumption that they were legal manuscripts. For many generations Dukes of Northumberland have been collectors of many kinds of works of art and antiquity, not excluding manuscripts. If these ten volumes of manuscripts are still in the Inner Temple Library they must now be contained amongst the Miscellaneous Manuscripts. A careful consideration of all those manuscripts which cannot be attributed to a specific donor has forced the conclusion that the ten manuscripts in question consist of two volumes of manuscripts of notes of cases, one at Assizes and other Courts, 1747–92, the other in the House of Lords, King's Bench, Common Pleas, Chancery, and Exchequer, derived from the manuscript notes of Sir Francis Buller, Justice, King's Bench and Common Pleas, and Sir Edward Hyde East, both Benchers of the Inner Temple and the latter Treasurer in 1831, and a distinguished editor of Reports. Sir Francis Buller had been admitted to the Inner Temple in 1763 and was the Lord Chancellor's candidate as Chief Justice of King's Bench in 1788, when Lord Kenyon was appointed. These notes were probably made in preparation for his *Introduction to the Law relative to Trials at Nisi Prius*, first published in 1772, which ran to seven editions. The remaining eight volumes bear the signature of George Courthope, a well-known counsel of the Middle Temple of which he was Treasurer in 1806, and consisting of Notes and Declarations and other Proceedings and Opinions of Counsel, including his own, then of the Alienation Office. The range of dates is from 1760 to 1825, and the volumes contain the opinions of T. Erskine, J. Mingay, Charles Abbott, William Scott, Vicary Gibbs, and George Hill. All the volumes are bound in vellum, the last eight in green vellum. These, too, have notes in faded red ink. So it is not unreasonable to suppose that these are the ten volumes presented in 1853 by the Duke of Northumberland. It is of some appropriate interest to note that nearly six hundred of George Courthope's books were presented to the Society by Lady Courthope, Whiligh, Sussex, to repair some of the damages done to the Library during the war by loss of books.

Of the gifts made by non-members of the Inn perhaps the most important is the original draft of Sir Edward Coke's 12th and 13th Reports, presented by H. D. Greene, Q.C., M.P., of the Middle Temple, in 1898. It contains not only Sir Edward Coke's corrected draft of these Reports but unpublished notes and memoranda by Coke, with the signature of John Bradshaw thrown in for good measure. Sir Edward Coke's notes include his observations on the 'unjust proceedings of him [Egerton] and Bacon, Attorney in my room' and on the seizure of his papers. The whole volume is of the utmost value, for the printed versions of the Reports are quite inadequate, incomplete, and inaccurate versions of Coke's draft. Sir Edward Bulstrode on seeing the text of the 12th Report, published in 1655, declared it to be so faulty as to be unfit for public view. Moreover they were translations of the text. This manuscript contained also several additional cases which were not printed. Serjeant James Manning, of Lincoln's Inn, who had been commissioned by the Benchers of the Inner Temple to edit the Year Book, 10–16 Edward III, in the Petyt Collection, presented his Index to his translation; unhappily the transcript of his text and translation which should have been available are no longer so. Major R. H. Way presented in 1948 a volume containing three indexes to Law Reports, 1635–8, compiled by Roger Hill, who became a Bencher in 1649, Serjeant at Law, 1655, a Baron of the Exchequer in 1657, and a Judge of the Upper Bench in 1660. In addition from the same source is a file of eight items, loose documents associated with Roger Hill as Judge and husband which have considerable interest. His Reports seem never to have been published and it is not known where the manuscript reports now are.

Derived from Elizabeth and Dorothy Wright, who presented their father's legal manuscripts now in the Petyt Collection, is the Catalogue of the Library of Sir Martin Wright, 1769. It contains the list of the books they gave to the Inner Temple Library, many of which with his interleaved manuscript notes were destroyed in the fire of 1941. The Selden Society gave in 1925 a very interesting deed executed in 1631 by John Selden, when he was a prisoner in the Gate House Prison. The witnesses to his signature were William Strode and Sir Miles Hobart, his fellow prisoners. It is interesting to note that it was to Edward Heyward, his friend and colleague for whom Selden acted in this deed, that the *Titles of Honor* was dedicated. Though most of them are mainly of Dutch or French interest there are a number of considerable British interest in a volume of Varia Lettres et Requests, the gift of Francis Turner, when he was Master of the Library in 1860, being Treasurer the following year. Francis Turner presented in fact, and was thanked for, three manuscripts, described as: (1) a manuscript volume of Letters and Requests, (2) a manuscript volume of grants etc. relating to Spanish Flanders, (3) an account of the Household of Mary, Queen of Scots, at Sheffield. These three manuscripts were bound together into a single volume. These include a letter to John Castell, the minister of the Walloon church in Threadneedle Street, 1599, and a unique account of the household of Mary, Queen of Scots in 1573.

Lord Darling, Treasurer in 1915, made two gifts which both illustrate his devotion to the Inn and his artistic sympathies. The first was of four illuminated folios from a mid-fifteenth-century legal manuscript representing the Courts of Chancery, King's Bench, Common Pleas, and Exchequer. These now adorn the walls of the Library. The second is a splendidly produced vellum manuscript of the Roll of Enlistment of members of the Inner Temple who served in H.M.'s Forces from the outbreak of war in 1914 to the end of 1917. It is well illuminated and beautifully written. Also of a domestic nature is the brief of Sir Heneage Finch, then Treasurer and Solicitor General, in the case of the Lord Mayor of London against the Temples for Riot in 1669, presented by Marcus Huish, a barrister of the Inn. In 1932, A. M. B. Bremner, Treasurer in 1921, presented the Inn with an elaborately embellished volume presented to Sir George Bramwell (Lord Bramwell, 1882) on the occasion of his retirement from the Bench as Lord Justice in 1881. The dinner was held in the Inner Temple Hall on 28 December 1881, and this commemoration volume is lavishly illuminated.

The gift by Adam Martin of the two volumes of his Index of Exchequer Records which he presented to the Inn in 1782, and which was published by the Bench, is dealt with below when publications are discussed. Thomas Joshua Platt, a Bencher, who became Baron of the Exchequer in 1845, presented two manuscripts. The first consists of the Account Book of Exhibition Money, King's Bench, 1788–1842, for a part of which period he accounted in succession to his father. The second consists of a file of twenty-three Licences to Plead granted to him, 1838–43, all, of course, under the sign manual of Victoria. A similar licence to plead was presented in 1932 by Sir Thomas Inskip (Viscount Caldecote), Treasurer in 1943. Lastly, in this section is a volume containing a transcript of the Black Book of the Admiralty, acquired by Judge William Willis and given to the Inner Temple Library by his son, William O. Willis, K.C., in 1921. Both were members of the Inn. Apart from its own importance it has a close association with two great Judges of the High Court of Admiralty. It was translated and presented to Sir Leoline Jenkins, who presented it to the Library of Doctors' Commons in 1685, and it was used and annotated by William Scott, Lord Stowell, in whose possession it was.

For reasons which, it is hoped, will be made apparent, there are certain donors of manuscripts now among the Miscellaneous Manuscripts whom it is now proposed to deal with at a little length individually. These are: (i) Francis Maseres; (ii) Mrs. Anne Sadleir; (iii) Alexander Luders; (iv) Mrs. John Austin; (v) Stuart A. Moore and Hubert S. Moore; and finally (vi) certain other benefactors who, for diverse reasons, are given in alphabetical order: J. L. Adolphus, W. H. Cooke, Sir David Dundas, Sir J. G. D. Harding, Sir John Cox Hippisley, Thomas Ley, George Spence, Sir Thomas Edlyne Tomlins, Samuel Warren, and John Wyatt. It will then remain only to consider the items among the Miscellaneous Manuscripts which emanated from the Library itself, from the Records of the Inn, or which were purchased by the Benchers of the Inner Temple.

10. SOME OF THE DONORS OF MISCELLANEOUS MANUSCRIPTS

i. *Francis Maseres, Treasurer, 1781–1782*

The main facts in the long life of Francis Maseres can be told briefly. He was born in London, 15 December 1731. His father, who was a successful physician, and his mother both belonged to Huguenot families which had come to England at the time of the revocation of the Edict of Nantes. He was educated at Kingston upon Thames and in 1748 was admitted to Clare College, Cambridge, as a pensioner. He graduated in 1752 as fourth wrangler and that year also won the first of the Chancellor's Medals for Classics. He proceeded to his Master's degree in 1755 and the following year was elected a Fellow of his College. In 1758 appeared the first of his many books, *A Dissertation on the Negative Sign in Algebra*. He resigned his fellowship in 1759, but was a suppliant for the chair of Mathematics the same year.

He had been admitted to the Inner Temple in 1750, was called to the bar in 1758, and started practising in 1759, going the Western Circuit. He was not particularly successful at the bar but became a common pleader in the city of London, sought a Commissionership in Bankruptcy, and in 1766 was appointed Attorney General of Quebec. After three years in office there he resigned on differences with the Governor and returned to England and resumed practice here. In 1773 he was appointed Cursitor Baron of the Exchequer, a position he retained until his death in 1824. He was elected a Bencher of the Inner Temple in 1774, was Reader in 1781, and Treasurer 1781–2. From 1779 to 1783 he acted as Deputy Recorder of London and in 1780 was elected Senior Judge of its Sheriffs Court, a post he retained until 1822. He died at his house in Reigate, 10 May 1824, in his ninety-third year.

He was a man of very many interests, held a main sinecure post which gave him time to indulge those interests, and was well endowed with wealth, which enabled him to be generous to his Inn and his friends, and to support lavishly the causes in which he believed, particularly promoting publication of his own and their works. Of his interests, the first, certainly from the time at which he became a Bencher in 1774, was the Inner Temple. In the fifty years from 1773 to 1822 no less than twenty-eight Bench Orders of thanks to him for his gifts to the Society were entered in the Bench Order Books. All of these except one were for gifts of books; the exception was a gift of Sir Godfrey Kneller's pictures of King George II and Queen Caroline. One gift of books, in 1817, was accompanied by an engraved portrait of himself. Of the books, twenty-two volumes out of a total of forty-two volumes were books of his own authorship or editing. In addition there were the books and manuscripts which he bequeathed.

He was assiduous in his attendance at the Bench Table and Parliament and to all the many Committees to which he was appointed. During his Treasurership the recurring disputes with the city of London on jurisdiction which arose so frequently took the turn of demanding payment for damage done in the Gordon Riots of 1780. With Lord George Gordon's Protestant Association Maseres would have been in sympathy. It became his duty as Treasurer, acting on the opinions of Lloyd Kenyon and Thomas Dunning, to inform the Recorder of London that the inhabitants of the Inner Temple were not in any degree liable to contribute and were perfectly resolved not to pay any part of the money demanded. Nor would they concur in procuring an Act of Parliament of a retrospective operation that would enable any constables or other officers whatsoever to collect from the inhabitants of the Inner Temple the money claimed by the city . . . or any part thereof. He was active in attendance at the Bench Table almost to the end. Between 1805 and 1823 he appeared as Deputy Treasurer in nine different years. His last attendance at a Bench Table was 20 June 1823; he had first attended on 10 May 1774. Throughout that fifty years he had served on innumerable Committees and unndertaken multifarious duties for the Society, had audited accounts, viewed chambers, conferred with the Middle Temple and the other Inns of Court, signed loyal addresses, and investigated fire insurance and the institution of gas into the Temple, but it was the Library and its welfare that particularly interested him, its contents, its custodians, and its buildings.

Yet it was but grudgingly that he had been elected a Bencher after his appointment as Cursitor Baron. The Bench Table Order of 3 May 1774 set his 'rank at the Table and in all other respects according to the time of his call to the Bench and not otherwise'. Another Order of the same day laid down 'for the future no Baron of the Exchequer, Welsh Judge, Master of Chancery, Master of the Crown or King's Bench Office, Prothonotary or Remembrancer of the Court of Exchequer to be called to the Bench as such'. More than forty-two years after, in 1816, amends were made to an old man of 84. It was then ordered that the Order of 17 November 1697 should be observed; the Order of 3 May 1774 was rescinded and Baron Maseres was to take his place accordingly. This Order of 1697, made on the appointment of William Simpson (who was Treasurer, 1708–9) as a Baron of the Exchequer stated that he was to take his place next the Treasurer, according to his dignity as a Baron.

The Society had become appreciative of his service and generosity. For after his death it was

ordered that the following be entered in the Book of Orders of the Society, viz. On the 10th May 1824 died at his house at Reigate, Surrey, aged ninety-two, Francis Maseres, F.R.S., Cursitor Baron of His Majesty's Exchequer, and during the period of half a century, one of the Masters of the Bench of this Society, to the Library of which he bequeathed a selection of his valuable books. The Treasurer and Masters of the Bench are desirous of recording by this Memorial their grateful sense of his bequest and their veneration of a character so long and eminently distinguished in science and literature.

In politics Maseres was a Whig and a reformer, except on one subject, Roman Catholicism. This may perhaps be attributed to his Huguenot ancestry and Huguenot upbringing. On this subject his attitude was akin to bigotry and it had bedevilled his activities and use in Quebec. Against the asset that he spoke and wrote French like a Frenchman was the debit of his religious intolerance. His time in Quebec has been fully dealt with by Mr. W. Stewart Wallace, who edited *The Maseres Letters*, 1766–8, making Maseres one of the few Treasurers of the Inner Temple whose correspondence has been published. The originals are in the Hardwicke Correspondence in the British Museum, among the papers of the Hon. Charles Yorke, the second son of the first Earl of Hardwicke (who was Attorney General in the Rockingham Administration and died so tragically three days after his appointment as Lord Chancellor), who had been responsible for the appointment of Francis Maseres as Attorney General of Quebec. These letters are readable without being exciting, but are packed full with views and information. They are matter-of-fact without being imaginative. But in so far as Maseres's interest in Canada and its problems and personalities continued long after his hasty departure in 1769, and as several of his manuscripts and printed books are related to Quebec and its welfare, as he saw it, they have a special importance as illustrating another aspect of his many-sided activities.

Francis Maseres never quarrelled with his first love, mathematics, and many of the books and manuscripts which he bequeathed to the Inn were on that subject. Some of these printed books were early and very valuable, and among his own works among the gifts and bequest were almost the whole of his writings on mathematics, including his first published work of 1758 on the *Negative Sign in Algebra*. His last work on mathematics, *Tracts relating to Optics*, was published the year before his death in 1823. In all eleven of his more than forty volumes were on mathematics.

For it is very difficult to determine precisely how many books Maseres wrote or edited, as several were published anonymously and he financed the publication of many more. The *British Museum Catalogue* credits him with 33 titles, containing 12 volumes; the *Dictionary of National Biography* with 33 titles, containing 12 volumes. The first *Catalogue of the Inner Temple Library*, published in 1833 and 1843, gives him 14 titles and 19 volumes under his own name, but to these have to be added a further 10 titles and 11 volumes which it is certain he wrote or edited, making a total of 24 titles and 30 volumes. None of these lists is complete.

Francis Maseres's holograph will was dated in London, 27 August 1820. It was proved 13 May 1824. It was written in a somewhat shaky hand and the signatures to the four codicils, the last of which is dated 9 March 1823, are still more shaky; one is almost a scribble. The second clause left 'to the Society of the Inner Temple all such books contained at Number 5 in the King's Bench Walk in the Inner Temple of which no copies are already contained in the Library of the same Society'. The third clause read: 'I leave to my good and dear friend Mr. William Frend of Bridge Street, Black Friars, all the printed sheets of several books formerly published by me on different subjects, and which are now lying in a garret of my dwelling house in

Rathbone Place, to become his absolute property.' A list of such several books would have been very useful.

William Cobbett, who was a visitor and good acquaintance of Maseres and disliked the Reverend William Fellowes, who was executor and residuary legatee, wrote that Maseres left 'more than a quarter of million of money'; the note made on the will in the Prerogative Court states 'under £100,000'. Friends and servants were well remembered, and the family received about a third of the total; Reigate was not forgotten. It is difficult at this stage to estimate how many of his books reached the Inner Temple Library, though he was accustomed to write his neat signature on the inside cover, the flyleaf, or the title-page of his books. For unhappily many of his books were lost in the Inner Temple fire of 1941, and others have doubtless strayed before and since. A careful perusal of the *Catalogues of the Inner Temple Library*, 1833–43, suggests that the number of his books which reached the Library under this bequest was between 400 and 500 volumes, making him the second biggest benefactor to the Library up to that time, considerably exceeded only by the number of books bequeathed in 1725 by Herbert Jacob, a Bencher, of which 836 volumes were chosen for the Library. Of those bequeathed by Maseres a considerable proportion were works on some branch of mathematics, followed in number by works of French history and literature, many of both categories of which went back to the seventeenth century. Next in number came books relating to Canada and the United States. The law books which he possessed of which the Library would not have copies are likely to have been comparatively few. He had started dispersing his library in 1813, when among the books presented to the Library by him, then or later, had been seven volumes of the works of Sir Isaac Newton, five volumes of *Histoire de l'Edict de Nantes*, 1693, and *Tracts on the Law of Libels*, and *Modern Tables of Interest*, which were probably representative of the general range of his bequest of books.

His gifts or bequests are credited with three manuscripts. The first of these seems foreign to his main interests, and was probably acquired by him by chance, or as a curiosity. It is a List of Leases granted under the Great Seal, 1 Elizabeth I to 5 James I, a useful if not an interesting manuscript. The two others are, respectively, The State of Quebec in 1762, with Extracts from Registers etc., relating to the Province, 1676–1761, and Instructions for Georgia, 1758, with transcripts relating to Virginia, Carolina, and Georgia, 1747–58. The Quebec volume consists of a Report by the Governor of Quebec, 1762, on H.M.'s forces and fortifications, revenues, soil, population, trade, and the character of the people, and certified Extracts from the Registers during French rule on trade and customs, revenue, and a variety of other matters, including 'Paper and Card Money formerly used in Canada'. The Georgia volume contains transcripts of Acts of Parliament relating to Virginia and Carolina and the Instructions to the Governor of Georgia made in 1758, of 108 Articles with twenty-eight Additional Articles. Both these volumes are important and Maseres's interest in the American colonies grew parallel with that in Quebec, as two of his printed works testify: *Considerations on the Expediency of Admitting Representatives from the American Colonies into the British House of Commons*, 1770, and *Papers relative to Massachusets Bay*, 1769.

These three volumes are, however, only a fraction of the Maseres manuscripts now among the Miscellaneous Manuscripts. There are eleven others. Five of them are mathematical manuscripts, and there are three more relating to the affairs of Quebec. One of the mathematical manuscripts is incomplete and consists of sections only of a very much larger one, and comprises some account of William Riddington, Professor of Civil Law at Cambridge, whom Maseres describes as 'one of the most learned and acute mathematicians I ever was acquainted with'. Another consisted of Additions to the *Treatise on the Principles of the Doctrine of Life Annuities* which he had published in 1783. The remaining two consist of problems, solutions, and calculations, with Maseres's observations on the solution of Biquadratic Equations by the method of Lewis Ferrari of Bologna and Professor Edward Waring's extension of that method, on Sir Isaac Newton's Binomial Theorem, Des Cartes, and Professor Pemberton. The third remaining volume which contained entries to 1813 had interesting correspondence with Scottish Professors of Mathematics and others, and important material on the history of mathematics.

The three volumes relating to Canada are all composite volumes and contain in all seventeen items, most of which were printed. Maseres had already published, before his arrival in Quebec in 1766, one book on *Considerations of Providing an Act of Parliament for the Settlement of the Province of Quebec*, 1766. One volume contains printed official papers, 1767–77, of which one item is a draft or proofs with considerable additions by Maseres; another *Things necessary to be settled in the Province of Quebec either by the King's Proclamation or Order in Council or by Act of Parliament*; and other items have manuscript notes by him. The second contains seven items, mainly relating to Quebec and Canada, 1772, but also including a Bill for the Better Support of poor Persons in certain counties by enabling them to grant them Annuities for life, also 1772, all with notes by Maseres. The third contains five similar items, of which three relate to Quebec, 1772, and one to the Province of Massachusets Bay, 1769.

The remaining three manuscripts reflect Maseres's more general interests and editings; firstly *France and Russia*, 1803, which consists of author's corrected proofs which do not seem to have been formally published, but certainly by him; next *La France avant la Révolution*, 1795, with annotations and additions by him, to which he has added five tracts; thirdly Maseres's copy of Blackstone's *Commentaries of the Laws of England*, first edition, volume I, with a considerable number of marginal notes in his hand. The first two are illustrative of the more general works which he wrote or edited, which include *Historiae Anglicanae Selecta Monumenta*, 1807, *May's History of the Parliament begun November 3, 1640*, 1812, *Ludlow's Letters*, 1812, and *Milton's*

History of Britain, 1818. The third illustrates his slender publications on legal subjects, such as *A Short View of the Laws of England relating to Bankrupts*, 1767, *Observations on the Power of Alienation in the Crown before 1 Anne*, 1768, and *Inquiry into the extent of the Power of Juries on Trials of Indictment or information for Publishing seditious or other Criminal Writings*, 1792.

Francis Maseres became a legend in his lifetime. Charles Lamb viewed him at a distance as a relic of a bygone age and wrote of him in 1821 that he walked in the costume of the reign of George II. His obituary in the *Gentleman's Magazine* noted that 'his dress was uniformly plain and neat and he retained to the last the three cornered hat, tye wig and ruffles, and his manners were in correspondence with those of a gentleman of the last age'. To Jeremy Bentham he was a public-spirited Constitutionalist and one 'of the most honest lawyers England ever saw'. He was mathematician, lawyer, and writer, and nearly achieved greatness in three directions, but in none did he reach the height of his powers and ambitions. He was prevented by the diversity of his interests, minor defects in his character, and his private means. His printed works are now largely forgotten; but not all. His *Collection of Several Commissions . . . relating to the Province of Quebec* was reproduced in 1966. It might seem strange that his first official appointment is the one on which most public interest is now focused and that his works on Canadian affairs are now studied and sought after. For nearly a hundred years he retained his record of the length of his service as a Bencher of half a century. When the Earl of Halsbury died in 1921 he had been a Bencher for fifty-six years, and in longevity he was beaten not only by the Earl of Halsbury but also by Sir Harry Poland, who died in 1928. Both were aged 98.

Throughout his long life Maseres's career had been hampered by his self-sufficiency in material resources, his somewhat pedantic attitude and outlook, his prejudices and lack of tact and discretion. He never reached high judicial rank, though he was a competent lawyer. As a draftsman of reports and a collector of information he was painstaking and assiduous, though somewhat blinded by prejudice and misplaced loyalties. Though none of his many works or other activities displayed any great originality, some of his writings can be, and are, read and acted upon today.

ii. *Mrs. Anne Sadleir*

Mr. Anne Sadleir was the eldest daughter of Sir Edward Coke by 'his first and best wife, Bridget Paston'. She had married Ralph Sadleir, of Standon, in the county of Hertford, the heir of a family long established there. Her husband had died in 1660 and in 1661 she determined to make certain dispositions of her household goods. To the Inner Temple she sent certain books and the two portraits which had been commissioned by her father, one of himself and a companion painting of Sir Thomas Littleton. They were gratefully received by the Society. The two portraits adorn the Benchers' Chambers. The contemporary accounts of the Inn contain the entry: 'to the gentleman that brought my Lord Coke's books from the Lady Sadler, £5 . . . given to a man that brought two pictures from my Lady Sadler's, 6s.' The books have been dispersed throughout the Library. Some of the manuscripts now bear pressmarks in the Petyt Collection. Thirteen of these have been dealt with above under the Petyt Collection. They were mostly devotional manuscripts or manuscripts of sermons. A few are now amongst the Miscellaneous Manuscripts. The list of books she presented to the Library was supposed to have been available after the last war, but if so no trace of it can now be found. It is unlikely that it was available in 1945. At some time in the nineteenth century it was determined to affix a small red label to the books she was supposed to have given.

The red label read 'E Lib. Coke'. Such of these books as now survive have been gathered together and an inspection of them has shown that the small red label was scattered indiscriminately among books printed in the seventeenth century, irrespective of their source. Books 'E Lib. Coke' are found to bear dates not only long after the death of Sir Edward Coke in 1634, but years after the death of Mrs. Anne Sadleir late in 1670 or early in 1671. Some of them are dated early in the eighteenth century. Some of them bear the book-plate of Herbert Jacob, whose books did not reach the Library until 1726. The red label is borne by books which have the signature and motto of William Petyt and have his coat of arms upon them. Very few, if any, of them, have any association with Sir Edward Coke. More than half of them are dated after the year of his death. The majority of them are books of devotion or theology or volumes of sermons. There is not a law book among them, except one which belonged, as will be pointed out below, to the Sadleir family. Most of them are books which would in the seventeenth century have been bought by a devout woman, such as Anne Sadleir undoubtedly was. She was a patron of preachers and theological writers. But few of the volumes bear her signature and few of them seem to have been used. A rare volume or two contain a few lines of her handwriting, a couplet, or the note of the donor. For some were books which had been presented to her and bear inscriptions. The great majority of the books with the 'E Lib. Coke' came from her private library. Sir Walter Raleigh's *History of the World* could have belonged to Sir Edward Coke, as it could to Anne Sadleir, but not the 1736 edition.

It would be pleasant to justify a Coke association with Speght's 1602 edition of Chaucer, but there is none, nor with the 1577 edition of Holinshed's *Chronicle*. The latter is noted by Joshua Blew, but there is no suggestion that it belonged to Coke. Of the 157 titles in the list no less than 62 are dated after 1634. True, they contain the 1622 edition of the History of the Reign of Henry VII and the 1557 edition of the Works of Sir Thomas More, but there is nothing to connect either with Coke. On the other hand, Leslie's manuscript History of Scotland, which is in the Petyt Collection, could have reached him as a Law Officer of the Crown, and amongst the Miscellaneous Manuscripts there is one volume which could have been in his possession.

There are, in fact among the Miscellaneous Manuscripts two volumes which bear the 'E Lib. Coke' red label, and a further volume which undoubtedly derived from Mrs. Sadleir. The first of the former is the manuscript cover of a printed text which consists of a late twelfth-century manuscript of a religious work. The printed tract is defective and is a commentary on Psalms 68–82, the kind of work one would expect to be in the library of Mrs. Anne Sadleir. The second consists of two printed tracts. The first is The Copy of a Letter sent out of England to Dom. Bernardin Mendoza, Ambassador in France for the King of Spain, declaring the state of England . . . and losses and distresses suffered to the Spanish Navy. It was printed in London, 1588. The second, also printed in London, 1588, was Certain Advertisements out of Ireland concerning the losses and distresses happened to the Spanish Navy upon the West Coast of Ireland in their intended voyage from the Northern Isles beyond Scotland towards Spain. The first tract has marginal notes and comments in a hand very like that of William Cecil, Lord Burghley, and the annotations are characteristic of Lord Burghley. By the year of the Armada Edward Coke was already very much a coming man, within four years to be Solicitor General. He would have been known to Burghley and it was the kind of work he would have treasured.

The volume which was undoubtedly included in Mrs. Anne Sadleir's gift to the Library was a copy of Pulton's *Abstract of all the Penal Statutes*, printed by Tottell in 1577. It contained the following entry by Francis Sadleir, the grandfather of Ralph Sadleir, Anne's husband: 'Rauf, the first son begotten by the bodies of my son and heir, Thomas, and his wife Gertrude, eldest daughter of Robert Markham, of Cotham, in the county of Nottingham, was born in my house, at Standon, in the county of Hertford, upon Saturday, Saint Mark's Day, being the xxv day of April, at four o'clock in the afternoon . . . 1579. . . .'

It was appropriate that this volume should reach the Inner Temple through Anne Sadleir, for at least two Sadleirs of Standon had been admitted to the Inn, Edward in 1555, and Thomas in 1559. This Thomas could have been Anne's father-in-law. And apart from her father's long association with the Inn, six of her brothers had been admitted. Edward her eldest brother had been admitted in 1600, and in 1610 three other brothers were admitted at the same time, John, Henry, and Clement; in 1606 her brothers Robert and Arthur had been admitted. By 1661 she had four nephews who had been admitted. Only two of her six brothers seem to have been called to the bar, Edward in 1607, and Clement a few years later. Only Clement seems to have practised. He lived in the Inn as did his son, Sir Edward Coke. He was buried in the Temple Church in 1630 and in 1635 his daughter was buried beside him, and in 1645 his nephew, Robert Coke, was buried near him. So in 1661 to Anne Sadleir the Inner Temple, its Church, and its precincts would have seemed almost a holy place.

In Sir Edward Coke's 'Requests to my Executors' written on 27 November 1623, four days after his will, the following appears: 'I heartily desire also mine executors that all my books whatsoever may be safely set up and locked up and preserved for the use of my posterity'. This request appears to have been obeyed implicitly. They have formed the most valuable portion of the Library at Holkham. His legal books certainly went there. His daughter Anne may have received some of his books during his lifetime and certainly received the portrait of himself by Van Somer and the portrait of Sir Thomas Littleton. Coke and his daughter Anne were very close to each other. On his dismissal in 1616 from his post as Chief Justice of King's Bench it was to her house at Standon he retired. But the books labelled 'E Lib. Coke' which had any association with the family were not her father's, with the possible exceptions indicated above.

iii. *Alexander Luders, Treasurer, 1819*

Alexander Luders was admitted in 1770, called to the bar in 1778, nominated as Reader to Clifford's Inn in 1780, called to the Bench in 1811, and appointed Treasurer for 1819–20. When on 19 November 1819 he first took the chair as Treasurer he informed the Bench that he was much indisposed and was empowered to nominate some senior Bencher to officiate on his behalf and to take upon him the duties of the office during the Treasurer's unavoidable absence. His indisposition was mortal. He died three days later, on 24 November. On 25 January 1820 the Masters of the Bench were informed of his death and ordered the election of a new Treasurer.

He was the author of several books, of which the most important were *Reports on Proceedings in Committees, House of Commons (1785–1787) on Controverted Elections*, three volumes, 1785–90, *Essays on the use of the French Language in our ancient Laws and Acts of State*, 1807, *Considerations of the Law of High Treason in the article of levying War*, 1808, *Tracts on various Subjects on the Law and History of England*, 1810, *An Essay on the Character of Henry V as Prince of Wales*, 1813, and *A Treatise on the Constitution of Parliament in the reign of Edward I*, 1818. These cover a fairly wide range of subjects which is extended by the titles of the seven subjects of the tracts included in the volume entitled *Tracts on various Subjects*, which were: (1) On constructive treason; (2) On the judgement in high treason; (3) On the right of succession to the crown in the reign of Elizabeth; (4) On the institution of Parliament in the reign of Henry III; (5) On non obstante; (6) On the use of the French language in our Ancient Laws; (7) An enquiry into the history of the laws of Oleron. His reputation for scholarship may be judged by the fact that he was the first named of the editors of the *Statutes of the Realm* published by the Record Commission.

He took a considerable interest in the administration of the Library and served on the Library Committee and was entrusted with the purchase of books for the Library. He presented his own works as they appeared and was duly thanked by the Bench for his gifts. He bequeathed books to the Library and on 25 April 1820 his son, the Revd. Ale ander Luders, had thanks for transmitting them to the Society. Of his gifts and bequest many were lost in the fire of 1941, but five volumes of his own works survived and these are replete with additions, annotations, and corrections. They have now been transferred to Miscellaneous Manuscripts. These are his works on *Controverted Elections*, on the *Character of the Prince of Wales*, and on the *Parliaments of Edward I*.

For instance, to the first volume of *Controverted Elections*, in additions to preface, printed text, and errata, at the end of the volume have been added thirty-five pages of manuscript which Alexander Luders describes as an Appendix; to the second volume there are also inserted manuscript slips and additions on the flyleaves at the beginning and end. The incorporation of all the additions and corrections to the text of the three volumes would increase quite substantially the length of the work. These additions were used by Henry Hallam in his *Constitutional History of England* and acknowledged to this source. In the *Constitution of Parliament in the reign of Edward I*, in addition to the annotations, additions, references, and corrections, he had added a page of list of contents to each chapter and the annotations relate to foreign comparisons, such as the contemporary laws of Charles II of Sicily and Naples and the Cortes of Arragon, and to the work of his colleague, Francis Maseres, on the Parliament of William I. He has also added an Appendix of five pages. His *Essay on the Character of Henry V as Prince of Wales* is, however, the most heavily annotated. Indeed the volume seems more like an author's very heavily corrected proof but it is useful as illustrating Alexander Luders's critical appreciation of his own work and his comments on early authors' authority, such as Caxton and Holinshed.

iv. *Mrs. John Austin*

John Austin, who was not only a barrister of the Inner Temple but had also lectured to its students on Jurisprudence in 1834, died in 1859. His widow, Sarah Austin, who was a considerable scholar and author herself, wrote on 21 March 1865 to Sir John Shaw Lefevre, then a Bencher and Treasurer in 1868, with whom she had previously discussed the matter, and the letter was read at the Bench Table on 21 April. She desired to leave certain books which had belonged to her husband in a place at once secure and accessible.

They were [she wrote] by no means numerous enough to be called a library, indeed those that I have particularly in view do not amount to more than a hundred volumes. Nor should I have thought of offering them to the Library of the Inner Temple had they not possessed a sort of value peculiar to them. They are some of the books (chiefly Latin or German) which Mr. Austin used in his studies and in preparation of his lectures and the margins of several are covered with his annotations. If you have happened to look into the two volumes of his lectures and other remains I published two years ago you will have seen the frequent recurrence of the words 'Marginal Notes'. All these notes together with several of the Tables which he was in the habit of constituting I extracted from the books in question. Owing to the quality of paper on which German books were formerly printed it was impossible to write on the margin with ink so that several of them are annotated in pencil and must consequently be tackled with great care. I wish, therefore, to leave them where they will be preserved and valued. I wish that they should be kept together and some where marked with the Austin name. As my husband was a member of the Society of the Inner Temple I wish these few and scanty memorials of the ardour and intensity with which he pursued the study of the law should, at my death, be deposited in the Library of that Society. . . . It is my intention to copy all the more important of the notes, volume by volume, and to see whether any of them can be added to any future edition of Mr. Austin's work. But this will require a longer time than probably I have before me; and I am anxious meanwhile to ensure their preservation.

The Treasurer was requested to accept the offer with the thanks of the Bench. In a little more than two years Sarah Austin had died, and her executor, Sir Alexander Duff Gordon, wrote to the Librarian of the Inner Temple, on 1 November 1867, requesting that he should be informed how he had better send the books to the Inner Temple. They were still at Mrs. Austin's house at Weybridge. It was ordered that a letter be written to the executor stating that the Bench highly appreciated the gift and would direct that the conditions would be strictly complied with (as in Mrs. Austin's letter).

The books were duly delivered but no list of the books which arrived is now available. A list has, however, been compiled from the entries in the old typewritten catalogue of the Library. They total 129 volumes of which 30 volumes are noted as having John Austin manuscript notes. When editing her husband's *Lectures on Jurisprudence*, 1863, she wrote a Preface and had drafted an Advertisement, both of which appeared in the 1873 edition. From these the following facts are disclosed: that the volumes totalled 133 in number, that 'many of them were filled with observations and analytical notes in his hand writing', and that in 1873 they were in the Library of the Inner Temple in a separate compartment.

Now there is only one volume of the thirty volumes with the notes available, Jeremy Bentham's *Introduction to Principles of Morals and Legislation*, 1798. Though this, now amongst the Miscellaneous Manuscripts, is an interesting example, with its signatures of Jeremy Bentham and James Mill and a few notes by John Austin, it is not a characteristic volume of the thirty with manuscript notes or of the other 99 or 103, whichever is the correct number, books which were comprised in the gift. Those would be found among the works in Latin and German rather than in English. For instance, *Gaius, Institutionum Commentarii*, edited by J. F. L. Goschen, 1823, which was full of analytical notes by Austin, or the three volumes of *Doctrina Pandectarum*, by C. F. Muhlenbruch, 1827, with manuscript notes by him, would have better deserved survival; it would have been interesting, too, to have seen his manuscript notes of Malthus *On Population* and on Mill's *Essays*.

It seems doubtful whether any of the missing 128 or 132 volumes will ever be found. They were probably destroyed when the Inner Temple Library was destroyed in 1941, or were burnt when the lorry supposed to be carrying books to safety was burnt out shortly before the burning of the Library. In either case it is no consolation that one of the conditions of the gift was observed. They were kept together.

v. *Stuart A. Moore and Hubert Stuart Moore*

Stuart A. Moore was called to the bar by the Inner Temple in 1885; his son, Hubert Stuart Moore in 1893. The father died in 1907; the son in 1951. Yet the manuscripts belonging to both now in the Inner Temple Library range in date from 1863 to 1939. For before Stuart A. Moore became a barrister he had been a member of the firm of Kirk and Moore, which had an extensive practice as Record Agents, largely employed in historical research by solicitors and their lay clients and by many who desired or required the records of the past searched, particularly the Public Records. His work was highly thought of by the officials of the Public Record Office, and Sir William Hardy while Deputy Keeper recommended the employment of his services. Stuart A. Moore wrote the standard work *A History of the Foreshore and the Law relating thereto*, 1888, a vast work of nearly a thousand pages, full of historical learning, record references, and leading cases. To it was added a third edition of R. G. Hall's *Essay on the Rights of the Crown and the Privileges of the Subject in the Sea Shores of the Realm*, first published in 1830, Sir Matthew Hale's unpublished treatise, which was the basis of his *De Jure Maris*, which he reprinted, and a comprehensive Appendix of Several Fisheries around the Coasts and in the Tidal and Non-tidal Rivers of the Kingdom. Moore's Introduction to the volume opened thus: 'The sole purpose of the present treatise is to throw light upon the difficult questions which so often arise between the Crown and the subject with regard to the title to the foreshores of this kingdom.' It is not surprising that the *Times* found that 'he was a thorn in the flesh of the Crown lawyers whose claims to foreshore he opposed with great pertinacity and success'.

In 1903, with his son Hubert, he published the *History and Law of Fisheries*, a work less than half the size of his book on the Foreshore but characterized by the same qualities. The *Law Quarterly Review*'s comment upon it was that 'the amount of information which has been extracted from the records is surprising'. Hubert Stuart Moore also published *Rules of the Road at Sea and Rules in force in Harbours, Rivers and Inland Waters*, 1897, with later editions in 1900 and 1922, and *Salmon and Freshwater Fisheries Act, 1923, and the Rivers Pollution Prevention Acts, 1924*. He also contributed the sections concerning Ferries, Fisheries, etc. to Halsbury's *Laws of England* and was joint editor of the fourteenth edition of Charles Abbott's (Lord Tenterden) *Law relating to Merchant Ships and Seamen*, 1901. The similarity of interest of father and son, makes it difficult at times, to decide what was written by each of them, and as the whole of the manuscripts and books now in the Inner Temple came in after the death of Hubert Stuart Moore, that difficulty is increased, so the gifts are dealt with as a whole, indicating only by date or particular interest what must have been derived from Stuart A. Moore and what from his son. For instance, the father was a very keen yachtsman and greatly interested in Exeter Cathedral; the son was for long the able and energetic Secretary of the Selden Society from 1913. The father had edited and translated in 1863 the *Portion of Domesday Book relating to Northamptonshire*, and in 1872 had edited, for the Camden Society, *The Letters and Papers of John Stillingford, Mayor of Exeter*, 1447–50. The son loaned the whole of his private law library to the Inner Temple during the last war after the destruction of its own law books to enable work to be carried on.

In all the Stuart Moore contribution to the Miscellaneous Manuscripts totals twenty-four numbers, but this constitutes only a portion of the papers which father and son had accumulated over nearly a century. There are, in the possession of the Society, 150 bundles of notes and transcripts from records collected by them which are of local rather than national, and of topographical rather than legal interest. These it is proposed in due course to deposit in Appointed Repositories, that is mainly the repositories of local authorities appointed for the receipt of records by the Lord Chancellor. Those twenty-four numbers represent the main interests and activities of father and son, and as a whole provide a valuable addition to knowledge of foreshore and fisheries and many manorial and other customs.

Such volumes as the Calendar of Records in Lambeth Palace Library, compiled by Stuart A. Moore and R. E. G. Kirk, a draft of a volume still in use at Lambeth and the basis of the new Catalogue shortly to be published; the Yachtman's Log Book, 1832–1841, with its insets; the Additional Supplement to the *Monasticon Exoniensis*, 1844, with its valuable transcripts of additional notes by Dr. George Oliver and the further 24 folios of additional notes and the five folios of Appendix, are all derived from Stuart A. Moore. The last volume mentioned was bought by him, then described as of Greenhithe, for half a guinea in 1867 and the notes are in his hand. Equally clearly the Index to the Collection of Notes relating to Foreshore, Fisheries, Wreck, etc., 1888 and a List of Records and References to places in the East Riding of Yorkshire, from 1100 to 1878 were collected by him for the case of Attorney General *v.* Constable, as was the similar Index to personal names, while the Alphabetical Index of Cases relating to Foreshore, Fisheries, Wrecks, and similar subjects, the dates of which range from 1241 to 1917, though based on his work was a working index used by his son.

The case of Attorney General *v.* Constable was an important one relating to the right of wreck in the Liberty of Holderness on which Stuart A. Moore worked hard and long. His accumulation of evidence included 98 certified transcripts from the Public Records, 8 Edward III to 21 Richard II, all certified in 1892 by L. Owen Pike, as an Assistant Keeper at the Public Record Office, and the subject recurs throughout the volumes of correspondence and reports and opinions. Another case upon which he was concerned was the claim by the Duke of Norfolk to the Earldom of Norfolk. There are two volumes of lithographed copies of translations of documents, mainly Public Records, with corrections, headings, and a few notes in manuscript, ranging in date from Henry II to 1660, but preponderantly before 1483. Inset is a letter from the Duke of Norfolk, 1 January 1907, thanking Stuart Moore for his congratulations and 'for all the excellent work you did for me on preparing the fight. You will have heard of what great service your son has been.' There are two volumes of manuscript and lithographed transcripts of records relating to the case concerning Sutton Pool, Plymouth. The limits of dates are Edward I to 1878. Another volume contains 22 items relating to a case, Merttins *v.* Hill, concerning the manor of Rothley, co. Leicester, mainly translations of Public Records, 1308–1605. Another volume contains a draft opinion on Cockington Foreshore, co. Devon, by Stuart A. Moore, 1887, and a draft opinion on the water of Dartmouth, co. Devon, for the Salcombe Urban District Council, 1937, by H. Stuart Moore.

Two further volumes of Reports and Opinions cover a considerable range. Of these the first contains twelve Reports by Stuart A. Moore 1872–90, mainly on foreshore, fishery, and manorial questions, including the foreshore of the manor of Wilton in Cleveland, on the salt marshes of Kirkleatham, on the Fownhope Fishery in the River Wye, on the North Meols Foreshore, on the Mill Pool Fishery in the River Thames, and on a fishery in the manor of Bray, but among other subjects covered are the Jurisdiction of the Justices of the borough of New Windsor as against the Berkshire Quarter Sessions, the Cumberland Customary Acre, a road in the manor of Arlington and Addle cum Eccup, and common in the manor of Cantred. The second volume contains fifteen similar Reports and Opinions, by Stuart A. Moore on Bromborough Pool Fishery, and again on the North Meols Fishery, and by Hubert S. Moore on foreshore covering fishery in the River Plym, and on the fishery on the River Leven in Lancashire. There are also Reports and Opinions on common in the manor of Cholesbury, the custom of taking gravel and stone from the waste of the manor of Spatchwick, co. Devon, on the manor of Stelling, co. Durham, on the foreshore of the manor of Weston, part of the barony or manor of Halton, co. Lancashire, and on a pew in the church of Masham.

Another number consists of twenty-four miscellaneous items, relating to various cases and matters, covering a wide variety of places, 1283–1914. Again, it is difficult to allocate them precisely between father and son. Holderness and North Meols come in again. There is an explanation of the plan of the country round Wigan showing the various coalfields, 1830; another concerns gavelkind in the manor or part of the manor of Westbere, co. Kent; a note on ancient workings of coal and whether workings made in Elizabeth I's time and say in 1833 can be distinguished; a Report 'on some experiments made to ascertain the effects of the tide in the River Frome, commencing 15 April 1914, and now continuing'; and letters and notes on Exeter Cathedral Glass, some relating to a survey made in 1872 by Stuart A. Moore and others. Most of the contents seem to pertain to him.

Two numbers containing correspondence, 1863–1933 and 1873–1924, seem balanced the same way, the majority of them pertaining to Stuart A. Moore. The first of these contains 148 letters. Some are requests for information on historical matters, the History of Dorset, the Castles of Herefordshire, and even Sacerhill in Stirlingshire. There is an interesting series of letters from the Rt. Hon. James Lowther, M.P., then Under Secretary of the Colonial Office, 1874–5, concerned with the case of Attorney General *v.* Lowther on Tees Foreshore Fisheries, particularly the Yarm Fishery; on markets in manors, with special reference to Market Razen; on search into the muniments of St. Thomas' Hospital; on user of road across Shakeston Common; on the tithe rent charge on the parish of Mounton, co. Pembroke; on the records of the Chamberlain of London, destroyed by fire in 1786; on searches among the records of the Marquis of Bath at Longleat; on the old Winchester bushel and the Imperial bushel; on the Court Rolls of the manor of Widnes; on search of Mrs. Pine Coffin's deeds at Portledge, co. Devon; on the embanking of Canvey by Dutchmen; on the protection of River Works at Thames Haven; on the Beaufort, Glamorgan, and Somerset articles in the *Complete Peerage*; on whether the High Sheriff of Essex 'can claim to attend the Accession Council on the demise of a reigning sovereign'; and on the injustice of the proceedings by the form of English information. The second volume does nothing to readjust the balance. There are in all 134 letters, of which 65 relate to the Holderness case, 7 relate to Caldicot Castle, co. Monmouth, the Earldom of Glamorgan and other rights of the Duke of Beaufort, 12 relate to the collection of material for the history of the Stanley family and the Earl of Derby, 13 are on coronation claims, Chief Butlership of England, and the Duke of Norfolk, 23 are on the Wilton Foreshore.

The remaining five numbers relate to papers and drafts, 1908–32, on cases in which Hubert S. Moore was concerned, mainly on foreshore and fisheries; references to Augmentation Office records at the Public Record Office, on grants of tenements, mills, tithes, manors, and sites of monasteries, and insets which have no relationship to the contents of the volume, including Hubert S. Moore's appointment as a Referee in connection with the recovery of the cost of billeting school children, 1939; an Index to Pier and Harbour Orders, 1922–8, with insets; a foolscap book with insets, of drafts and Opinions of Stuart A. Moore, Hubert S. Moore, and other counsel, 1901–10; and a file of loose papers, 1929–40, mainly correspondence between Hubert S. Moore and the Ministry of Transport. Among the drafts and Opinions are those on an injunction to restrain trespass on strips of land, parcel of the manor of Great and Little Thorp, co. Essex; an injunction to prevent erection of a landing-stage at Newlyn, co. Cornwall; on selling except in the market place of the borough of Woolwich; rights of pasture in the parish of Arlington, co. Sussex; deductions from employees' wages; damaging fishery lines and gear outside exclusive fishing limits of the British Isles; the diversion of the River Ribble; and the ancient market for the sale of cattle in the town of Thirsk.

The details which have been given above are representative of the Stuart Moore papers. They show that father and son were specialists in certain very specialized fields of law; that they had a knowledge of records which few counsel possessed, and that their papers, haphazard as their survival has been, have added a new dimension to the manuscripts in the Inner Temple Library which for nearly a hundred years cannot be surpassed or equalled.

vi. *Other Benefactors*

John Leycester Adolphus, appointed to the Bench in 1851 and himself the editor of twelve volumes of *King's Bench Reports*, 1834–40, and eighteen volumes of *Queen's Bench Reports*, 1841–52, with T. F. Ellis, presented to the Library in 1856 eight volumes of *King's Bench Reports*, 1785–1800, Durnford and East. Each volume has manuscript notes by Sir George Sowley Holroyd, Justice of King's Bench, and bears his book-plate. The notes are of three kinds: first, references to additional cases before and after the case reported; references to previous or subsequent cases reported in the volumes; and annotations or observations upon the judgements reported. The care with which the whole of the text was corrected suggests that the work was being undertaken with a view to the republication of the Reports, the last edition of which appeared in 1817. On Adolphus's death the Library acquired from his widow his collection of pamphlets, after valuation by Sotheby, in 1863.

William Henry Cooke, the compiler of *Members Admitted to the Inner Temple*, 1547–1660, and Treasurer, 1879, presented in 1866 a manuscript entitled A Catalogue of the Nobility of England and a Collection as well of H. M.'s Courts of Records and of his most honourable household, 1616, which contained a certain amount of interesting and out-of-the-way information.

Sir David Dundas, Treasurer in 1853, presented in 1872 a Collection of legal tracts on Prohibition and the Jurisdiction of the Court of Star Chamber and other matters. It is a clear, well-written manuscript with marginal notes and references.

Alfred Joseph Ellison, a barrister of the Inn, who was called in 1921 and died in 1952, was a bibliophile and a lover of bindings. In all he presented at least eight manuscripts to the Library, the contents of which were almost as varied as the bindings he designated for them. He wrote notes on the content of the manuscripts, which, whatever the subject, were well informed and pertinent. One which is well written is a manuscript of Sadler's Parish Fees, full bound in undressed calf. Another consists of the Judgement of Mr. Justice Croke in the Hampden case, 1638, to which have been added family notes and memoranda of the Higgins family. The third consists of two notarial deeds concerning property in Milan, 1591, beautifully written in italic. It contains the armorial book-plate of Joseph Smith, British Consul in Venice, a friend of Canaletto, who bought many Italian pictures for George III, now in the Royal Collection. The volume is bound in stamped vellum. There are two volumes on International Law and Civil Law respectively, both with engravings inset and both bound in part of a parchment indenture relating to property in Cambridge. Another volume on Scottish Legal Forms and compiled by a Committee of the Juridical Society, 1774, is decorated by the addition of portraits of contemporary Scottish Judges and bound in brown morocco. The last of his gifts is a collection of essays on Visits, by Arthur Highmore, whom he describes as 'a well known author and barrister', written in 1827. It has tinted illustrations added from *La Belle Assemblee* and bound in blue calf and buckram. Finally, there is a manuscript on Advowsons by Sir John Dodridge, 1627, consisting of sixteen lectures on the subject, with other miscellaneous matter, 1559–60, added.

Sir John G. Dorney Harding was a Bencher and Queen's Advocate. In 1856 a question arose on the precedence of the Attorney General, the Solicitor General, and the Queen's Advocate. The question was referred to the Lord Chancellor, Lord Cranworth, who decided in favour of Harding. The Attorney General was Sir Alexander Cockburn, afterwards Lord Chief Justice of England; the Solicitor General was Sir Richard Bethell, afterwards Lord Westbury, Lord Chancellor. In 1857 Harding presented the correspondence, in which all four figured, to the Inner Temple Library.

Sir John Cox Hippisley, bart., Treasurer, 1813–14, was a politician and diplomatist. He prepared for publication the Letters from Cardinal Borgia and the Cardinal of York, 1800. These were never published. They were addressed to himself in 1799–1800. To them he added an extract of a letter from Pius VII to himself, with manuscript notes by himself and facsimiles of certain of the letters and correspondence between Lord Minto, British Minister in Vienna, and the Cardinal of York in 1800. These, full bound in leather with gold tooling, he presented to the Inner Temple Library in 1800. This appears to be a very rare item.

Thomas Ley was a barrister of the Inner Temple who was invited to the Bench in 1791. When he died in 1796 he bequeathed to the Library 'my manuscript Law Notes in one folio volume and the index of principal matters and names of cases, both marked A and my manuscript cases in Chancery in two volumes, B & B., Vol. 1–2'. These three volumes are almost sufficiently dealt with in the will. It remains only to add that the volume containing cases and notes in King's Bench, 1750–65, also includes a few in the Court of Common Pleas, and that the second volume of the Cases in Chancery, 1763–5, includes forty pages of notes on testamentary matters. All three volumes have notes by Thomas Ley.

E. R. G. Robertson, a barrister of the Inn, presented in 1867 a manuscript of Observations on the Eyre of Pickering, 1592, by William Fleetwood, Serjeant at

Law and Recorder of London, to which are appended seven documents concerning the House of Commons, 1621. The volume was formerly in the libraries of Lord Somers and Sir Joseph Jekyll.

George Spence, Treasurer 1846, was a pioneer in Chancery reform and greatly interested in legal education. He wrote *Equitable Jurisdiction of the Court of Chancery*, a standard work on the origin of English equity, which appeared in two volumes, 1846–9, and which he presented to the Library. It was but natural that the two manuscripts he gave the Library should be concerned with the Chancery. The first was a collection of precedents and Actions on the Case which he received as a present in 1807. The second was a foolscap printed Report on the Masters' Office, with a long note by the author on the printing of the Report. The Report was not published. The title page described it as a summary of Documents and Propositions relating to the Six Clerks' Office and the Registrars' Office submitted to Lord Langdale, M.R., in answer to Lord Langdale's letter, 24 December 1841, by George Spence, 8 March 1842. Though there was an assurance that it would be printed, it was in fact printed at the expense of the author, and Lord Langdale received the whole print, excepting six copies, for distribution among the Masters and Clerks in Court. To add insult to injury, when Spence applied to Lord Cranworth, the Lord Chancellor, for payment he replied that 'I had been very unwise in putting myself to any expense in such a subject and for such a purpose considering I had refused to take any payment for preparing the Chancery Legislation Bill for Lord Brougham. I thought this refusal rather ungracious.'

Sir Thomas Edlyne Tomlins, Treasurer, 1827–8, and his many publications are dealt with elsewhere in this Introduction. Here the concern is only with two manuscripts for which his association with the Inn was responsible. The first is a volume containing the manuscript notes of his nephew, also named Thomas Edlyne Tomlins, in Cowel's *Interpreter*. The nephew describes himself as 'Attorney at Law and Record Solicitor'. The whole volume is replete with interesting notes and references, most of which are initialled T.E.T., which go far beyond the scope of his purpose and provide a mine of curious and interesting information. The second is a somewhat similar interleaved volume of Adam Martin's *Index of Exchequer Records*, with scores of notes and observations and several thousand additional entries of references to Exchequer Records, some two hundred under the letter A alone. This compilation, too, was probably by the nephew.

Samuel Warren, Treasurer, 1866, probably better known in his own time as a novelist than as a lawyer, presented the autograph manuscript of his Ten Thousand a Year, in three volumes, in 1841, the only strict work of fiction in the Inner Temple Library, among the manuscripts at least.

John Wyatt, Treasurer, 1833, was the donor of a manuscript of first-rate importance, that is the volume on the Chancery and its Rules annotated by Heneage Finch, Earl of Nottingham, Lord Chancellor. When Wyatt was preparing his *Practical Register in Chancery*, 1800, for the press he was lent the manuscript which was afterwards given to him by a descendant of Finch's. It is sufficient attestation of its importance to state that in 1965 it was published by the Cambridge University Press, edited by D. E. C. Yale, as *Lord Nottingham's Manual of Chancery Practice*.

Of the items relating to the Inner Temple Library both volumes consist of Catalogues of the Library, which are dealt with at some length below. The first contains the Carter Catalogue of 1713 and the Blew Catalogues of 1715, 1726, and 1733; the second the Jeff Catalogue of 1773, with later additions to 1791. The latter, in fact, contains two catalogues bound together, the one being the draft, the other the fair copy. These are the only manuscript catalogues of the Library which now survive, apart from those in current use. And before 1941 there is barely a surviving vestige of the correspondence, files, accounts, minutes, or lists of additions to the Library or any memoranda or reports, except those which had long before been bound into the group of manuscripts known as Records of the Inner Temple. They were all consumed in the conflagration of 1941. The Librarian's desk and cupboards were in the most vulnerable part of the Library.

Of the Records of the Society now among the Miscellaneous Manuscripts the most ancient and curious is the Old Grace Book which was presented to the Inn by John Roper. It was written in 1505 and it remained in daily use in term time until 1830. It was re-bound in 1656, 1671, 1723, 1765, 1799, 1824, and again repaired in 1929. Constant use for over three centuries and the frequent rebindings have taken their toll of the manuscript. The parchment, although originally of good quality, has been seriously worn and discoloured and its margins have been mutilated. Folios have been lost. The manuscript consists of Calendars, Historical and Biblical Notes, as well as Graces. It was superseded by the second Grace Book, which was in use only from 1830 to 1932, when a dummy book of blank leaves was substituted. Only a small proportion of the contents of the Old Grace Book were entered into the second.

John Roper, who came from Linsted, co. Kent, was of a family of lawyers, members of the Inner Temple. He married a daughter of Sir John Fineux, Lord Chief Justice of King's Bench, and was for a few years Attorney General to Henry VIII. His eldest son, William, married the eldest daughter of Sir Thomas More and was his biographer. John Nethersole, for whose soul the manuscript was written, was of Lincoln's Inn and made a gift for the building of a Library in that Inn. His will was proved by John Roper, one of his executors and residuary legatees, 11 February 1505. It was from John Roper's family that the Inner and Middle Temple purchased the Master's House.

There are also representative manuscripts relating to each of the three Inns of Chancery belonging to the Inner Temple. For Clement's Inn there is the Pension Book, 1714–50, edited, in 1960, for the Selden Society by Sir Cecil Carr, Bencher. For Clifford's Inn there are three vellum panels containing the Statutes of Clifford's

Inn, made in the reign of Henry VII and newly rewritten in 1528–9. The statutes or ordinances number forty-seven and the middle panel has an illuminated coat of arms. The three panels seem to have been written and framed for hanging in the Hall of the Inn for the information of the students, and probably hung there for centuries, perhaps until the end of this Inn of Chancery. Lyon's Inn is represented by the Declaration of Loyalty to Queen Elizabeth I and the Oath of Association, 4 November 1584, by the Treasurer and members of Lyon's Inn, duly signed and sealed.

Interesting as the last item is it cannot be compared in importance with the similar Declaration and Oath signed and sealed by the barristers of the Inner Temple. This document has the signatures of sixty barristers. The Declaration was started by Robert Dudley, Earl of Leicester, a very effective patron of the Inn, after the discovery of conspiracies against the Queen. Of the signatories, seven, from Sir Edward Coke, subsequently became Treasurers of the Inn, twenty became Benchers. Of those who afterwards held high judicial office Sir Edward Coke was afterwards Solicitor General and Attorney General, Chief Justice of Common Pleas and Chief Justice of King's Bench, Sir Lawrence Tanfield became Chief Baron of the Exchequer, Sir John Croke, a Justice of King's Bench, his brother Sir George Croke, a Justice of Common Pleas and afterwards of King's Bench, Sir Thomas Coventry, a Justice of Common Pleas. Sir Edward Coke and Sir John Croke were also Speakers of the House of Commons. Eight of the sixty became Serjeants at Law. Similar Declarations of the Benchers of the Inner Temple and for Clement's Inn and Clifford's Inn were formerly among the Records of the Society.

Of remaining Records of the Society now among the Miscellaneous Manuscripts are five volumes of signatures of those attending Communion in the Temple Church, 1668–1771, a volume of List of Admissions, Calls, Benchers, and Miscellaneous Notes, Inner Temple, 1520–1684, probably a Butler's reference book, a volume of Reports, Acts of Parliament, and Bench Orders, arranged under subjects, 1667–1800, eleven title-deeds, 1582–1640, some relating to the Master's Lodgings and some to Lyon's Inn, and three volumes of Admissions, 1660–1750. A volume of eighty-four original letters, mostly holograph and mainly from distinguished personages to the Treasurer and Benchers, 1570–1679, made up in 1867 from the Society's correspondence, contains holograph letterst from Robert Dudley, Earl of Leicester, Sir Roger Manwood, Sir Christopher H aton, Sir Francis Walsingham, Sir John Puckering, William, Lord Wentworth, afterwards Earl of Strafford, as well as signed orders from the Council and letters under the sign manual of Charles I. Many are of great importance on the domestic history of the House. A transcript of the volume was made under the superintendence of J. E. Martin, then Librarian, in 1867–8. These two volumes were made as a result of a Bench Table Order of 26 March 1867, which ordered 'that the ancient documents relating to Chambers produced by the Treasurer be bound and copies made under the superintendence of the Librarian'.

There is an interesting Report of 2 December 1891 by G. E. L. Pickering, the Librarian, on the custody of the manuscripts, and pointing out that the Librarian should not be responsible for books located in a room outside his jurisdiction. This was a timely warning. The Catalogue of 1833 lists among the manuscripts in the Library 'Acts of Parliament and Bench Table Orders of the Honourable Society of the Inner Temple, 5 volumes, folio', and states they were in the Treasurer's Office. The Catalogue of 1806 placed them in the Library. These were the volumes which on Orders of the Bench it was the duty of the Librarian to compile. They were still in the Treasurer's Office in 1941. Their charred remains are in the Treasurer's Strong Room today. Had they remained in the Library they would have been dispatched to a place of safety with the manuscripts and would be available today as a handy means of reference to the Parliament Act Books and the Bench Table Order Books.

Lastly there are among the Miscellaneous Manuscripts ten volumes which have been acquired by the Benchers. The earliest of these is a Treatise in English entitled Synedriis Britannicis, an unpublished work of the late seventeenth century. Thorp's Catalogue ascribes it to William Petyt. By the corrections and alterations, with additions, in a hand other than that of the transcriber, it is suggested that this might be the author's copy, but it is unlikely that the author is William Petyt, as neither the style nor the material suggests his authorship. The second is a manuscript on the Antiquities of the Inner and Middle Temples, which was written in the seventeenth century. Much of the information contained in it concerns the reign of James I but there is some material of the Restoration period, but it contains no exclusive information. The third is a somewhat indifferent manuscript of Bracton's De Legibus Angliae. It is a manuscript of the fourteenth century but is incomplete, a chapter being missing and there are omissions in other chapters. The text contains nothing new by way of gloss nor is it worthy of collation. The most interesting feature about it are twenty-one fragments or folios of manuscript which appear to have come out of the old binding. These include four pages of Ovid's Metamorphoses, of the late twelfth or early thirteenth centuries, containing more than a hundred lines from Book I. This appears to have been acquired in 1886.

The only other manuscripts which seem to have been acquired are eight volumes which are described as Wetherell Manuscripts. They are all legal manuscripts; one containis Declarations, 3–21 George II, five are Reports, mainly King's Bench and Common Pleas, Elizabeth I to Anne, another has Chancery Reports, 1748–72, and the eighth Chancery Reports, 1795–9. They are all quite straightforward, useful rather than exciting, the most important of which is the first volume of Chancery Reports, 1748–72, which may be the original of Serjeant Kemp's Reports, and contains many of his notes. Kemp's Reports were never published. The manuscripts come from the library of Sir Charles Wetherell, Treasurer, 1824–5, Solicitor General and Attorney General, who was very unpopular as a politician and the cause of the Bristol riots in

1831. On his death in 1846 his library was sold and these of his manuscripts were acquired for the Inn.

Many of the manuscripts among the Miscellaneous Manuscripts have not been mentioned above. These will appear in the Catalogue and in Appendix V. But enough has been written to indicate the very wide range of subjects. The majority were contributed by the Inn itself and members of the Inn, especially Treasurers and Benchers, though a few barristers also appear as donors. With these as the main source it is not surprising to find that out of 211 manuscripts no less than 177 are legal manuscripts or relate to the Inner Temple.

II. THE MASTERS OF THE LIBRARY, 1825–1969

The appointment of a Master of the Library had its germ in the Report of a Committee which reported to the Bench on 6 February 1818. It reported that the members had been

> actuated by the feeling which appeared so generally to prevail among the Masters of The Bench . . . that a system which operates practically almost to the exclusion of the members of the Society from the advantages which such a collection of books ought to afford and also frequently occasions unfavourable comparison with Lincoln's Inn, ought not to continue in a Society possessed of such ample pecuniary resources as to obviate all objections to incurring any expenses which may be necessary to place the establishment of so important a property upon a reasonable and proper policy.

The Committee, therefore, obtained from Lincoln's Inn the regulations governing that Library. The reply showed that one of the Benchers was chosen annually as Master of The Library. The Deputy Master of the Library, or Librarian, had a salary of £60 a year, corrected the catalogue, and arranged the Library, but his attendance was but seldom. The Library Keeper was also second butler, attended the Library daily, and had no salary but was allowed a chamber and coals in virtue of both offices.

The Inner Temple Committee considered that these regulations 'although completely effective as to the important object of affording free and continuous access to the Library are very objectionable in other respects'. It was considered that the

> valuable collection of books and manuscripts constituting the Library of this Society ought not to be entrusted to the custody of a person in the station of life of a butler or under butler and that the daily and regular attendance of a Librarian, competent from his education and station to the trust imposed in him, would combine advantages of higher responsibility, more effective cooperation and in the gradual improvement of the collection and once extended assistance in the information he might occasionally afford to those who resort to the Library than the arrangement of Lincoln's Inn can afford.

It submitted the propriety of appointing a Librarian with a salary of £100 per annum who should be required to arrange the Library, make out and keep a catalogue, and attend regularly every day. . . . The Committee further submitted that one of the Masters of the Bench should be appointed annually Master of the Library and that he be allowed to expend fifty pounds in the purchase of books in addition to the fifty pounds which is at the disposal of the Treasurer for the same purpose. This report was confirmed and a day set for the choice of a Librarian.

On 14 April 1818 it was ordered that the following Friday should be appointed for the choice of a Master of the Library. On 17 April this meeting was postponed until the following Tuesday. On 21 April it was ordered that the matter be reconsidered on 1 May, and the same day the Reverend William Henry Rowlatt was appointed Librarian. On 1 May the part of the report which related to the appointment of a Master of the Library was rescinded. There had clearly been a fortnight of considerable disagreement among the Masters of the Bench. Had the proposal been accepted then Francis Maseres might have been honoured by being appointed the first Master of the Library of the Inner Temple. It was several years before the matter was raised again. On 13 May 1825 it was resolved that the Bench Table Orders of 6 February and 1 May 1818 be reconsidered on 7 June 1825. On that day it was ordered that one of the Masters of the Bench should be annually elected Master of the Library and that he be authorized to expend £50 on the purchase of books for the Library in addition to the Treasurer's £50 and that the election thereof should be on the same day as the Treasurer was elected in Michaelmas term.

John Gurney was to be Master of the Library until the last day of Michaelmas term. On 25 June 1825, when the Report of the Committee on the duties of the Librarian was considered, it was laid down that 'the Librarian do on all occasions report in writing to the Master of the Library all such circumstances as shall occur wherein the Library may be benefitted as of any neglect or omission of duty or abuse whereby the same may be injured or affected'. John Gurney, who had been elected to the Bench in 1816, was re-elected for the following year and succeeded as Treasurer in 1826–7. In 1832 he became a Baron of the Exchequer. In 1835 he presented to the Library a volume *The Vindication of the Proceedings of the Gentlemen of the Inner Temple*. He had defended Horne Tooke and John Thelwall and also Arthur O'Connor, the Irish rebel, and procured the conviction of two of the Cato Street conspirators.

On 24 January 1826 the first standing Library Committee was appointed. It was a strong powered but representative body. Out of its nine members, including John Gurney, the Master of the Library, were eight who had been or were to be Treasurers: William Welch, 1818–19, William Harrison, 1825–6, James Scarlett, 1823–4, Sir Charles Wetherell, 1824–5, Sir Edward Hyde East, 1831, Sir Robert Baker, 1832, and John Wyatt, 1833. The only exception was John Vaillant, editor of Dyer's *Reports*.

John Gurney was succeeded in 1826 as Master of the Library by Robert Ray and so the appointment went on annually until 1932; the occupant succeeded to the Treasurership in almost every case. The names of the Masters of the Library for over a hundred years are virtually the names of the Treasurers and that long catalogue contains scores of illustrious names, the complete list of which appears in Appendix III, i. The creation of the office was caused by dissatisfaction with the state of the Library and the status of its officers. It was wisely proposed that the first appointment of a Librarian who was not a servant of the Inn and of the first Master of the Library should be made on the same day. This was thwarted by opposition, but within seven years the status of the Library had been completely upgraded. Among those who figure in the list of Masters of the Library from 1825 to 1932 are many donors of books and manuscripts and other valuable presents to the Library. These will be given elsewhere, but of others who are not otherwise mentioned in this Introduction are Lord Langdale, Lord Chancellor Chelmsford, Lord Cross, Lord Knutsford, the Earl of Loreburn, the Earl of Desart, Lord Atkinson, Lord Sumner, and Sir John Simon.

On 15 April 1932 a change was made in the Order for election. It was then proposed that the following Order should be substituted: 'A Master of the Library shall be elected from among the Masters of the Bench and shall remain in office for three years from the date of election and shall be eligible for re-election. The Election of the Master of the Library shall be held on the first business day in Trinity term or in the case of vacancy on the first day of the term next after the occurrence of the vacancy'; and he was to be authorized to spend £50 a year on books in addition to the Treasurer's £50. The general principle of the new rule was adopted but it was left to the Treasurer to settle the final draft which he read on 19 April 1932, the only variation being the addition after Master of the Bench 'and shall be a member of the Library Committee'. On 24 May it was unanimously agreed that Master Bucknill should be Master of the Library. When he became a High Court Judge in 1935, C. T. le Quesne succeeded him on 5 July 1935 and remained Master of the Library until 1955, when he was succeeded by Neville Laski, who held office until his death in 1969. He was succeeded by George Squibb, who had been Deputy Master of the Library since 1961.

12. THE LIBRARIANS

Though there was a Library, or at least a room used for reading books from the late fifteenth century, and though such a room had its caretaker and cleaner drawn from the domestic officers of the Society, the caretaker, no doubt, from the butlers or waiters, and the cleaner from the lower domestic ranks, there was no one called Librarian until the appointment of Samuel Carter in 1709, and it was another hundred and fifty years before another full-time Librarian was employed, the part-time duties being undertaken in the meantime by officers of the Society, from puisne butler or clerk to the Sub-Treasurer to Reader of the Temple Church or Sub-Treasurer.

On 26 October 1709 'Orders were made that Samuel Carter, the Library Keeper give two securities in the penalty of £1,000 for the true performance of his office;

that the Library Keeper attend in the Library from Lady Day to Michaelmas from 9 a.m. to 12, and from 3 p.m. to 6 p.m., and from Michaelmas to Lady Day, from 10 a.m. till 12, and from 3 p.m. till 5 p.m.'. His salary was to commence from Michaelmas, when he had the key of the Library delivered to him. Samuel Carter was a somewhat aged and impecunious barrister of the Inn who had been called in 1673. His salary was to be £20 a year. His son, Thomas Carter, was accepted as a sufficient security and 'the question being put whether the Masters of the Bench should have keys of the Library or not, it was ordered that every Master have a key of the new Library'. There can be no doubt that the appointment was prompted by the opening of the new Library to house the Petyt bequest and that the first work on Petyt's books and manuscripts was done by Samuel Carter. He also produced a catalogue of the books in the Library, dated 1713, which still survives, and seems to have justified his salary for the few years he held the post. For he was buried in the round of the Temple Church on 8 March 1713.

His successor was Joshua Blew, a puisne butler, whose long career and services to the Library cannot be condensed into a few sentences. His fifty years as Librarian deserve separate treatment which is postponed to the next section without interrupting the continuity of the story of the Librarians of the Inner Temple. For he was the greatest Librarian of a line of eleven who have served the Society to the present day and served the Society notably in many capacities.

On the resignation of Joshua Blew in 1763 as Librarian he was succeeded by Charles Chambers, who was clerk in the Sub-Treasurer's office, a position he continued to occupy. He too had served the Inn well in many ways. In 1756 he had received a gratuity of £3–19–0 for apprehending two persons who had dropped a child in the Inner Temple. Besides his salary as clerk, he received extra allowances for winding up the clocks (£3) and for keeping the office book of commons (£5–5–0). Upon his appointment as Librarian with the usual salary, that is £20 a year, he continued to care for the clocks and received his other perquisites, and in 1769, on the appointment of a new Sub-Treasurer, he had a reward of 10 guineas 'as a gratuity for his extraordinary trouble and labour in assisting the Committee to whom it was referred to consider and report the several duties, services and salaries of all the officers and servants of the House'. In 1768 the Bench Table had ordered that 'the entries on the Register Books in the Library of Acts of Parliament and Bench Table Orders to be completed, and an index made by Mr. Chas. Chambers, the Librarian', a work which Joshua Blew had commenced. For this additional service which he had carried from Trinity term 1740 for the Acts of Parliament and from Hilary term 1741 for Bench Table Orders, to the end of the last Trinity term, on 1 February he was paid £16–9–4 and also ten guineas as a gratuity for his trouble and pains. The entries were in two large Register Books 'now by him produced and made an index thereto . . . and the said Registers to be deposited in the Library'. The Order added ominously 'the

Librarian for the time being as part of the duty of his office in the vacation after every term to enter in the respective Register Books (to be kept in the Library for that purpose) all future Acts of Parliament and Bench Table Orders and Index the same in the Index Books'. He died on 21 February 1777 after a long and expensive illness and was buried in the Inner Temple side of the churchyard. The Burial Register adds: 'Ground given. No fees paid.' The Society was generous to his widow, to whom a gratuity of £30 was given and to his daughter, Charles Lamb's schoolmistress, to whom in her old age and affliction they paid an annuity of £10 from 1807.

On his death another experiment was made on the appointment of his successor. The Reverend William Jeffs, Reader of the Temple Church since 1767, was appointed Librarian. He had already been employed in 1772 when it was ordered that

> the Librarian with the assistance and direction of the Rev. Mr. Jeffs to make a complete Catalogue of all the books in the Library and to range the books relating to the several subjects they treat upon in distinct presses so as to compose a separate Library of Law and Equity, Civil Law and Parliamentary proceedings, Classics, General and Biographical History, Theology, Heraldry, Physic, Miscellaneous Books or others relating to any particular science or subject and manuscripts; that in the Catalogue to be made there be one column to signify the number of the press, another the shelves, another the name of the book, another the name of the printer and another the date of the year, and that the books may follow in an alphabetical manner, as much as may be, and that all duplicates may be placed together in two or three presses, and that the same may be completed by the first full week in Michaelmas term, and for which this Society do desire his acceptance of ten guineas.

Mr Jeffs had clearly been asked in as an expert to direct and assist the Librarian. Certain members of the Bench had very clear views as to how cataloguing should be done and the instructions were meticulously detailed. The Reader of the Temple Church was paid a fee of £21. His catalogue is to be found among the Miscellaneous Manuscripts.

On 29 April 1777 he was 'unanimously appointed Librarian to the Society in the room of Mr. Charles Chambers, deceased, with the same salary and allowance in lieu of Commons'. In the interregnum John Spinks, clerk to the Sub-Treasurer, who had made a transcript of the Jeff's Catalogue and been paid £8–17–6 for this, and became Sub-Treasurer in 1780, attended to the duties of Librarian and was paid the 'profits of the Librarian's place from the date of Chambers's death to that of his successors appointment' which amounted to £9. Jeff's appointment had been an experiment which had not been successful. When his death was reported to the Bench Table on 11 November 1783 (he had died on 4 November and been buried in the churchyard 8 November) it was ordered 'it shall be taken into consideration . . . whether there shall be any Librarian in future'.

It was obviously decided that there should be and the appointment reverted to a Sub-Treasurer's clerk. For on 31 January 1784 Randal Norris was appointed Librarian at a salary of £20 'without any other emolument'. This presumably means that he was not entitled to payment in lieu of Commons. In 1801 he was appointed Sub-Treasurer, and on 16 May 1806 it was ordered that he be paid £100 for the five years he had acted as Librarian since his appointment as Sub-Treasurer and £20 a year until a Librarian was chosen. On 27 November 1818 an additional allowance was made to the Sub-Treasurer into which this payment of £20 was merged. It was during his time that the first printed Catalogue of the Library was published, so he or his clerk must have revised and added to the Jeffs Catalogue. There can be little else said of achievement during his term of office. The replies he sent to Charles Abbot, the Speaker and a member of the Inn, as Chairman of the Committee upon the Public Records in 1800 were most unsatisfactory and entirely support the views on his intelligence and knowledge expressed by Charles Lamb, who knew him well but probably exaggerated his foibles.

His successor, the Reverend William Henry Rowlatt, M.A., was a Librarian of an entirely different stamp. He had been called to the bar by the Inn in 1804, having been admitted in 1795. On 6 May 1814 his bond was discharged; he was then described as 'late a barrister of this Society entered into Holy Orders'. He had already been appointed Reader of the Temple Church when on 21 April 1818 it was ordered that 'Rev. William Henry Rowlatt be Librarian of the Society and be paid a salary of £100 per annum, to commence Michaelmas next'. On 10 November 1818 the thanks of the Bench were conveyed to him for the present of two volumes of his sermons. These had been published in 1816. In 1824 he published his *Sermon to the Grocers Company* and in 1830 his *Sermons at the Temple Church*. A letter was considered by the Bench on 27 June 1856 resigning his office and the Treasurer moved a retiring allowance to the full amount of his present salary. This was approved on 11 November, so he received a pension of £150 a year. On 13 January 1863 a letter was received from his son announcing his death the previous day.

It was during his Librarianship that the Catalogues of the Inner Temple, 1833, 1843, were published. The first catalogue was entirely his work. Though it was based upon the catalogue of 1806 it was an entirely different piece of work, with many additions, well organized and arranged, upon which all later catalogues have been founded. On 5 February 1819 it had been ordered that 'Mr. James Gardner, on the recommendation of Mr. Treasurer be clerk to Mr. Norris, the Sub Treasurer'. He was to have a salary of £100 a year in that capacity, 'and for his assistance and attendance upon the Librarian whenever they may be required so as his services in that respect do not interfere with the duties which may be required of him by Mr. Norris'. A report of a Committee of the Bench in 1825 directed that the Librarian should make an accurate catalogue of the books and manuscripts alphabetically according to their respective subjects and continue the same as additional books and manuscripts are received into the Library and shall also make a shelf catalogue of every book in each shelf. There should be printed copies of such catalogue, two of which should be interleaved in which the additions should be made of the new books and manuscripts as they came in, of which each member of the Bench should have a copy and there should be six copies kept on the table of the Library, for the use of those frequenting it.

The work must have proceeded slowly, despite the assistance in Library duties he was to receive from Gardner, for the Order to print five hundred copies of the catalogue was not made until 6 June 1832, which enabled the Librarian to draw the attention of the Bench to his salary. On 16 November 1838 in consideration of his services and other circumstances his salary was increased to £150 a year. On 6 May 1842 a report was received upon the subject of preparing an alphabetical catalogue and the option of preparing this was given to Mr. Rowlatt, it being left to the Treasurer to make what communication he should think proper. It may be that the Librarian and Treasurer could not agree terms on the constitution of the new catalogue, for its preparation was undertaken by Mr. C. Ellis, who also received payment for his work. The new catalogue was little more than a continuous alphabetical arrangement of the classified catalogue of 1833, with additional entries between that date and its date of composition added, not many more than 350 in all. The making of this new catalogue did not please the Librarian. He wrote a protest that 'making a catalogue which must be based upon mine comes strictly within my province as Librarian'.

The Revd. William Henry Rowlatt's successor was the first full-time Librarian of the Inn. On 16 April 1850 Mr. J. E. Martin had been appointed by the Treasurer as Sub-Librarian. He was already Librarian to the Duke of Northumberland, presumably at Sion House, and it had been through his influence that the Duke of Northumberland had presented ten volumes of legal manuscripts to the Society for which he had been thanked on 15 April 1853. On the resignation of Rowlatt a letter was received from Martin on 11 November 1856 requesting appointment as Librarian and the same day he was appointed, subject to any arrangements the Bench might make. The Library Committee recommended that a salary of £250 should be paid him and this was confirmed by the Bench Table on 21 December 1856. On 27 January 1860 he wrote a letter to the Bench on the want of accommodation at the Library and in due course a Committee was appointed to consider the matter. It was to consider the best means of providing adequate accommodation in the present Library for the proper arrangement of the books and the convenience of those who resort to the Library. On 25 May 1860 his salary was increased to £350. While Committees considered and reconsidered measures the accommodation problem was getting worse. On 12 January 1862 the Librarian submitted a memorandum 'as to the admission of members of other Inns to read in the Library'. On 26 February 1862 the Committee reported that it was 'undesirable except under special circumstances to grant the habitual use to any person not being members of the Inn, unless tenants of the Society'. Still the Committees considered accommodation and meanwhile a Sub-Librarian was authorized at a salary of £100, within a few years increased to £150 and then to £225, and a messenger at 30*s*. a week.

On 26 October 1867 it was ordered that transcripts of the ancient letters which had been recovered by the Treasurer should be made under the superintendence of the Librarian. On 16 November 1880 his salary was increased to £600 and on 4 November 1881 he was given six months' leave of absence. He was obviously already failing in health and increased work was being placed upon the Sub-Librarian. When on 3 November 1882 a letter from Mrs. Martin on her husband's health was read the Treasurer was required to obtain a medical certificate. On 21 November 1882 the Library Committee recommended that the Librarian should be asked to resign and that he should be granted a pension of £300 a year. On a letter from him, on 19 December 1882 the office was declared vacant on the ground of the medical certificate and a Committee was instructed to draw up a scheme for the appointment of a Librarian, the salary to be paid, and the best means of obtaining a successor.

So Mr. J. E. Martin disappeared from the scene. He was to that time easily the most professional Librarian the Inn had had. As Sub-Librarian he had been thanked by Lord Campbell for his assistance on his *Lives of the Lord Chief Justices*. He had been Librarian when the Historical Manuscripts Commission compiled its first *Report on the Manuscripts of the Inner Temple*. He had procured manuscripts for the Library and his last main service to the Inn had been his compilation of the *Masters of the Bench of the Inner Temple*, which was printed in 1883.

His successor J. E. L. Pickering had been Sub-Librarian since 1869 and was appointed Librarian on 12 January 1883, at a salary of £300 a year, to increase by £50 a year until it reached £500. The initial salary meant an increase to him of only £75 a year. There were a few extras. In 1892 it was ordered that £50 should be allowed him 'in consideration of his extra labour in the preparation of the new catalogue'. Writing to the Bench on the publication of the first volume of the Calendar of the Records of the Inner Temple on 17 November 1896, the editor, F. A. Inderwick, stated that he 'wished to bring definitively before the Committee, at this, the earliest opportunity I have of so doing, . . . the great assistance and cordial co-operation which I have received from Mr. Pickering, our Librarian, both in the literary and the mechanical production and publication of the records, to whom for his services in this matter I think the Society is under considerable obligation', and he continued that on very many different subjects such as the early history of the Soceity his 'assiduity, his knowledge of the Library, of the valuable manuscripts belonging to the Inn, and of contemporary historians have been most valuable and placed unreservedly at the disposal of the Society'. On this high commendation the Bench thanked Mr. Pickering for his great services in the preparation of Volume I. In 1915 on the completion of the Catalogue of Pictures, Plate, etc. he was thanked by the Bench and presented 'with a piece of plate costing not more than £20'.

The excellent memorandum he wrote in 1891 on the custody of the Inner Temple manuscripts, short and salient, shows his quality as a Librarian. He saw the first three volumes of the Calendar of Records published, but his health was failing. On 23 May 1924 twenty guineas were given to the Sub-Librarian for 'his services in connection with the Librarian's absence'. On 8 May 1925 a gratuity of £300 and a pension of £300 a year were granted Pickering on his retirement, and a further gratuity of £50 to the Sub-Librarian.

That Sub-Librarian was F. J. Snell, who had been appointed Assistant Sub-Librarian in 1892 and Sub-Librarian in 1911. He was appointed Librarian on 9 June 1925 and resigned 22 November 1939. His successor was E. A. P. Hart, who was appointed Assistant Sub-Librarian in 1925, and Sub-Librarian in 1931. He was appointed Librarian on 22 November 1939 and retired 3 November 1964. The present Librarian had been Sub-Librarian from 1950 and was appointed Librarian on 21 January 1965. For convenience a list of Librarians from 1709 to the present day appears in Appendix III, ii.

13. JOSHUA BLEW, CHIEF BUTLER AND LIBRARIAN

The first appearance of Joshua Blew in the official records of the Inner Temple is 28 November 1713, when he was appointed 'to attend and keep the library open at library hours till further order'. He was then described as fourth butler, that is the junior. There can be little doubt that he had held that post for at least four years for he himself times his service at the Inn from 1709. He continued as Librarian until 1763, after a tenure of fifty years. By 1744 he had advanced in the hierarchy to the post of Chief Butler, a position he kept until his death in 1765. Thus he had served the Inn for at least 56 years.

Joshua Blew must have been one of the most extraordinary servants that any English institution ever had. The length of his service is overshadowed by the variety of his achievements, the multiplicity of his duties, and the surviving remains of his work. His duties can be most usefully considered under the two following main heads, firstly his services to the Library and secondly his services as the general adviser and researcher of the Bench in all that pertained to the detailed administration and the privileges and precedence of the House.

First as to his services to the Library. When he succeeded Samuel Carter as Librarian, the Petyt manuscripts and printed books had only recently been transferred to the new Library which had been built to contain them. Samuel Carter had been Librarian for but four years, for he had been appointed on 4 June 1709 and was not given charge of the Library until the following Michaelmas. So Blew's first task was to organize the new Library, and in this work he appears to have been very successful in the next few years. His initial salary as Librarian was £10 as against the £20 belonging to his predecessors, but in less than ten years it had been increased to £15 and the Bench's satisfaction with his services had already been expressed tangibly in other ways. By 1715 he had already catalogued the Library and he was given a gratuity of £5 for his catalogue; and thenceforth an annual fee of £2 was given him for writing the buttery book and the weekly rolls of commons, in addition to his emoluments as a puisne butler. This £2 a year he continued to draw for fifty years. In 1727 his salary as Librarian was increased to £20. The next year he was allotted the chamber of the late Chief Butler at 8 Fig Tree Court, in place of the chamber which had formerly been occupied by Samuel Carter in Hare Court which he had had since 1718.

As Librarian Joshua Blew was directly responsible to the Treasurer. There was no Master of the Library in his day. The order of 28 November 1713 appointing him had as an appendage 'That the Treasurer for the time being do lay out £20 yearly out of the Treasury in purchasing books for the Library'. The Librarian was responsible for the purchase of books and for their binding and even for the publication of some of the manuscripts. Thus on 27 May 1728 he was given permission to 'give a copy of such part of the manuscript book in the Library of this Society as relates to Lord Bacon's Treatise about the Alienation Office'. It was also ordered that 'subscription be made on behalf of this Society for the whole book of Lord Bacon's now about printing wherein that aforesaid to be part'. For non-legal books his choice of purchases was discriminating: in 1723, for example, *Le Grand Coutumier de Normandie*; in 1742 the six volumes of *The Religious Ceremonies of all Nations*.

It was for his work on the catalogues of the Library that he was most useful. Four catalogues of the Library wholly or mainly in his hand survive. The first is one part of the contents of which he inherited from his predecessor. For it contains a signed receipt, 19 July 1710, for a Petyt manuscript borrowed by John Anstis, with Samuel Carter's acknowledgement of its safe return. The second appears to be that which Blew completed in 1715. This does not seem to be complete. The third is a detailed catalogue of books and manuscripts compiled by him in 1726, the descriptions of the manuscripts being a tabloid version of the entries in the two-volume catalogue of the Petyt Books and Manuscripts which has so many entries in his hand. This third Blew catalogue contains characteristic notes by him. The entry 'Robert of Gloucester' is struck through and the following added: 'The learned Jno. Anstis esq. informs me that this book is only a translation of Peter Langtoft's History in French by Robert de Mannyng as appears in several places.' The fourth catalogue was compiled by Blew in 1733, but like the third contains later additions. It also contains the only known list of the manuscripts of reports presented to the Library by William Barnesley, the first three of the nine volumes of which are now missing, and thanks to this entry by Blew can now be identified. They are as follows:

Reports in tempore Eliz. in Com. Banc.
" " the 2nd.
" " in King's Bench, Common Pleas, Exchequer.

This catalogue must have remained the one in use until that of 1773 was produced.

On 29 June 1759 the following Order was made: 'Mr. Blew with such assistance as he shall think necessary, before the next term, to clean the books and shelves in the Library and make a general catalogue out of the three Catalogues now in the Library, under the direction of the Treasurer [Joseph Brand] and Mr. [Thomas] Tower.' The cleaning was doubtless duly done; there is now no trace of such a Catalogue. Perhaps it has been worn out by age.

For his method and care as a Librarian consider the following three characteristic entries made by him in manuscripts in the Petyt Collection. In Walter de Hilton's Scala Perfectionis he wrote: 'Since printed by Wynkyn de Worde in Wm. Caxton's press. See Thorsby's Catalogue of Ancient Printed Books, 1484. J. B. 1730.' In a volume of Transcripts or Extracts from the Journals of the House of Lords, 1–25 Elizabeth, he wrote: 'This Book I found thus imperfect and believe it to have been so delivered into the Library by reason of the note on the back of the volume does not mention the 14th year, which is the Session which has been cut out, as appears by Sir Sim. d'Ewes Journal from whence this may be perfected. J. B.' In a volume of Transcripts from printed works of antiquarians on Parliament he wrote: 'Thus found by me J. Blew and seems to have been so by my predecessor Saml. Carter Esqr. by his reference under the title of Parliament.' Here wrote the true Librarian.

It is not surprising that, when he retired from the Librarianship in 1763, the Bench Table ordered that 'Mr. Blew be allowed £20 a year during his lifetime in consideration of his long and faithful service'. It was not as Librarian, however, that the Society prized his services most. A multiplicity of duties, extending far beyond any which pertained to any of the offices he held, were placed upon him, all of which seem to have won him the complete confidence of the Bench. A list of the papers of Nicholas Courtney (who was Treasurer in 1694), which he drew up in 1718, had considerable value, particularly upon the vexed question of precedency. On 18 November 1726 he was ordered 'to make an index of all the Acts of Parliament and Orders of this House from the year 1600 to this day'. On 19 June 1740 it was ordered 'an index to be made by Mr. Blew of all the Orders of this House under the proper heads'. So highly valued was this compilation that on 5 May 1741 it was ordered that 'the sum of 25 guineas be paid to Mr. Blew, Library Keeper, for his extraordinary services collecting together and making an extract of the Rules and Orders of this Society and in reducing them under proper heads for the use of this House, and the same Extract when bound, to be placed in one of the cases in the Library to which every Master of the Bench have a key, but no copy of the Extract to be taken, nor the said Extract itself carried from the Library, or to this Table, or to the parliament chamber, without special order of the Table and the instructions given to the managers concerning the precedency of this Society to be added to the said Extract'. The payment ordered was duly made and all these compilations still survive.

Other duties imposed upon him were sometimes trivial but at other times important and onerous. Thus on 14 June 1729 he was ordered 'to draw out the duties of the Steward as settled by the Committee and lay it before the Table'. This document was made an Order of the Table on 29 January 1730 and confirmed by Parliament the following 6 February. The fourth of the duties was that the Steward should 'daily take an account from the butlers what bread and beer is spent, and the same account for candles, coals etc., and to buy coals and candles at the best hand, and to see to the disposal of them, and keep an account thereof, and deliver Mr. Blew from time to time a particular of the quantity and prices, with the days and the tradesmen's names'. By Act of Parliament, 6 February 1730, the day the above order was confirmed, Joshua Blew was to be paid 'the sum of £20 per annum for his care in inspecting the weight and quantity of provisions and examining the tradesmen's bills of provisions for this Society, pursuant to the agreement of the Committee of 2nd May 1729, as it has been since done'. In 1747 the payment of this salary was determined.

In 1730 with a Bencher and the Chief Butler, Blew was 'to overlook the workmen and see how many are employed and for how many days' in the setting of the new gates fronting the Hall stairs; in 1737, with the Chief Butler he was to view a building then being erected and report to the Table how far other chambers would be affected by it; in 1740 to take an inventory of the effects of a deceased member of the Inn; in 1750 he was to attend Court with a lease on the trial of a cause, at the expense of the parties; in 1759 rings were left with him to be distributed to Masters of the Bench; in 1758 he reaped the reward of the assignment to chambers which had been granted to him gratis in 1753 'in consideration of his diligent and faithful services to this Society for upwards of forty years'.

With all the many reports, drafts, notes, and annotations made by him over the many years, only one letter written by him has been seen and that to an unknown correspondent, though it was certainly written to a member of the Inn, probably to one who had been rendered homeless by the fire of 1737. This letter of 10 January 1738 informs the recipient of the dispatch of some oysters, according to directions, and answers questions addressed on the work done on the Temple Church and the rebuilding of chambers burnt in the fire. It duly reported that 'the kitchin and offices being already built and finished by the House workmen in a very handsome and magnificent manner'. In reply to personal inquiries Blew reported himself to be in good health, but his wife had been ill and under Dr. Douglas for a long time as a result of the great fright she had at the time of the fire, which was a great trouble to him, as well as the loss of all his goods and 'valuable collection of curiosities'. That he had strong antiquarian interests is certain and those were largely centred on the Inner Temple and its properties though they were not entirely so concentrated.

The original of this letter will be found in the collection of Records of the Inner Temple, where also have been placed scores of compilations, memoranda, and drafts by him on the administration of the Inn. Of these the following are representative. There is a memorandum on Acts of Parliament relating to the Temple Church, 1631–1716; one on the call of Serjeants, twelve in number, of which seven were from the Inner Temple, on 30 April 1724, when the procession met in the Inner Temple Hall; one on Imparlances, 12 June 1735. He contributes an account of the proceedings on the call of Serjeants, 4 June 1736, which raised the vexed question of the precedency of the Inner Temple on such occasions. There is a memorandum on exercises to be performed by the students before they are called to the bar, 11 March 1738; a note of 1741 on the 'inscription round the great bell [erected 1686] hanging in the round tower of the Temple Church'; his draft, 1744, on the office of Sub-Treasurer, 1682–1739; an account of the 'ancient doors and windows discovered on scraping off of plaster work on the outside of the north wall of the old rooms formerly belonging to the house of the Knights Templars now called the butteries, fronting to the now cloisters', with sketch, 8 March 1756. He wrote a note of evidences relating to the soil, buildings, and boundaries of the Inner Temple, from 6 James I, and a lengthy compilation on the rules, customs, and administration of the Inner Temple, 1660–1723. Another compilation of his was the Table of General Heads contained in his Abstract, under twenty sections. The Chamber Books survive for almost the whole of the time he was employed by the Inn, 1709–62, in fifteen volumes.

Of wider interest are the brief notes concerning the Temples, from Henry II to the death of Queen Catherine, Queen Dowager of Charles II (1705), on which he wrote on the dorse 'My own account of the Temple drawn up by myself, Jos. Blew, for my own use only'. As a collector he procured 'The Clerk of the Temple Church, his Book, 1653', on which he wrote: 'This book was procured by me from Old Sylvester, the Clerk. Henry Clark was Chief Butler of the Middle Temple when I was admitted to my office in 1709.' He wrote a note on the Law of Sewers, 1573–1744, in which he must have been indulging a personal interest. His acumen is shown by his note on John Wilde's Treatise on the Duties of the Officers and Members, 1633: 'This is a copy of a manuscript belonging to Lord Somers and sold after the death of Sir Joseph Jekyl, kt., late Master of the Rolls, to Mr. John Nicholls, a curious antiquary, near the Bear Key, London, and by him lent to me, J. Blew, 19 January 1745. . . . It appears to be written by a member of the Inner Temple.'

Joshua Blew's executor was Andrew Coltee Ducarel, a member of the Inn, admitted in 1735, and who had had a chamber there from that year to 1756. Ducarel was a distinguished civilian and antiquary, a Doctor of Civil Law of Oxford in 1742, as Advocate of Doctors' Commons in 1743, a Fellow of the Royal Society and the

Society of Antiquaries, and from 1757 Keeper of the Library at Lambeth, after holding many other posts under the Archbishop of Canterbury. He was a prolific author and an archivist and although many years younger than Blew, the two would have had many interests and pursuits in common, not the least libraries, records, and antiquities.

The process of proving Joshua Blew's will provides a number of very interesting details. He had the large sum of £202–1–0 in his chambers. The remainder of his term in his chambers was sold for £143–10–0. His household goods were sold by public auction for £162–10–5. There was owing to his estate £7–15–2 for board wages due to him as Butler and Librarian and a quarter's salary of £7–10–0 as Butler and £5 as Librarian. He had various bonds due to him, one for as much as £105 and another from carpenters of the Whitefriars of £21 and interest. The latter he had apparently given, shortly before his death, to Sarah Fulford, his servant. He owned £2,000 old South Sea Annuities on which one year's dividend of £60 was due. His gold striking watch, with a gold chain, hook, and seal he left to his niece, Hannah Blew. These details were sworn on 26 August 1765 by his executor.

The same day the executor's account was sworn. Joshua Blew's assets, apart from the South Sea Annuities, totalled £696–9–7. Among the debts due from his estate were £19–18–3 to the undertaker, £3–2–0 to an apothecary for medicines, £12–12–0 to a jeweller for rings for distribution, £1–19–0 to a mason for inscribing his name on his tombstone. He owed the Society of the Inner Temple £7–6–6 and the Society of Antiquaries £2–2–0 for two years' subscription; and his servant £12–4–4 for wages. He bequeathed his servant £5–5–0 for mourning and a legacy of £10. There was a legacy of £21 to his executor and an annuity of £20 to his nephew, Henry Blew, or £500 of South Sea Stock in satisfaction, together with one half year's payment of £10. The residue was equally divided between William Blew and Hannah Blew, obviously a nephew and niece, and Eleanor Moxham, wife of Thomas Moxham, probably another niece, each to receive £156–10–8. The remainder of the South Sea Annuities was also divided equally between the same three, £500 each.

There was no bequest of his curiosities. He had probably distributed these before his death. There is no mention of the Inner Temple except of the sums owing on both sides. His legacy to the Society had been paid during his lifetime in devoted, painstaking, and valuable services rendered. His name or initials appear in many of the manuscripts and in more of the records. His research for the Inn was thorough and accurate. His comments on manuscripts were shrewd and generally well informed. He was not too proud of his knowledge to consult the experts. It was not many Butlers, even Chief Butlers, who ever became Fellows of the Society of Antiquarians. When he was buried in the round of the Temple Church on 28 January 1765, he had served his Inn for nearly 56 years, and was probably an octogenarian. As Sir Frank MacKinnon has written, 'Mr. Blew was evidently an unusual Butler. . . . If I may play the role of Posterity I indeed commend his sedulity.'

14. CATALOGUES OF THE LIBRARY

In the last two sections some reference has been made to the Carter Catalogue of 1713, the Blew Catalogues of 1715, 1726, and 1733, and the Jeff Catalogue of 1773. All these are in manuscript. The earliest printed Catalogue is that of 1806, printed during the librarianship of Randal Norris. A few words must be said about this catalogue. As early as 1750 a Committee had been appointed to 'consider the present state of the Library and what books may be proper to be added thereto and examine the catalogue and put the same in order for printing in case the Table shall judge proper, and the Masters of the Bench now present and such others as shall choose to attend, or any three of them, to be of the Committee and to report next term'. Nothing further was heard of this proposal for a printed catalogue. On 9 June 1795 it was ordered 'that the catalogue of the books in the Library to be properly arranged and classed and printed under the direction and inspection of Mr. Treasurer and 300 copies to be struck off, and such law books of which there are no editions in the Library and such other books as are wanting to complete the works already therein to be purchased'. Thereafter again there is silence.

The catalogue of 1806 cannot be the work of Randal Norris, who had been Sub-Treasurer since 1801 and pretty fully occupied with the duties of that office. It is most probably a rehash, with additions, of a manuscript catalogue prepared under the Order of 1795. Its full title is *A Catalogue of the Printed Books and Manuscripts in the Library of the Inner Temple alphabetically arranged.* It is important to stress that a catalogue of manuscripts is included, for up to this time there had been no mention of a catalogue of manuscripts. The printed books occupied 103 octavo pages, the manuscripts 22 octavo pages. It is interesting to note that the volumes of pamphlets and tracts are detailed. Among the manuscripts after the end of the catalogue of the Petyt Collection appear four entries only. They relate to the five volumes of Acts of Parliament and Bench Table Orders, the two volumes of Martin's Index of Exchequer Records, the three volumes of Thomas Ley's Reports in Law and Equity and the Reading on the Statute of Pluralities, now all among the Miscellaneous Manuscripts, except the first mentioned.

On 14 November 1806 it was ordered that the thanks of the Society be given to Benjamin Way Esq., one of the Masters of the Bench, for 'his care, trouble and attention to the reprinting of the Catalogue of the Library'. So he, rather than the Librarian, was responsible for the production, though it is difficult to explain the word 'reprinting', as no earlier printed catalogue has been seen or heard of, and the Inn itself has no copy of the catalogue of 1806. Taken with the generous distribution which was made to high-powered persons, it would seem that the publication of a printed catalogue was a very auspicious occasion and publicized, as indeed it would have been if it had been the first. For the recipients included the Lord Chancellor and the Master of the Rolls, the Lord Chief Justice and the rest of the Judges, Sir William Wynne, Judge of the Prerogative Court of Canterbury, Sir William Scott, Judge of the High Court of Admiralty, the Archbishop of Canterbury, and the Master of the Temple.

Something has already been said about the preparation of the Catalogue of 1833. Its full title was *A Catalogue of the Printed Books and Manuscripts in the Library of the Inner Temple arranged in Classes*. The printed books occupied 262 pages, the manuscripts 27 pages. The manuscripts in the Petyt Collection are slightly more fully described than in the 1806 catalogue, though not nearly as fully as in the original catalogue of that collection, which of course relates only to the Petyt Manuscripts in the Collection. They are followed by the four entries which have been mentioned above. There are three additions: (1) what is described as 'Manuscripts sent by the Executors of Bishop of Barrington in 1823' (as has been pointed out above a false description), which total 81 volumes; (2) 'Manuscripts received from the Executor of Baron Maseres in 1825'; (3) 'Manuscripts purchased', two volumes, which are described as Letters from Henry Coventry and others, 1676–7, and Curious Petitions bought at Southgate's sale, May 1830.

As has been pointed out above, the Catalogue of 1843 was based on that of 1833. It is entitled, *Alphabetical Catalogue of the Printed Books in the Library of the Inner Temple with an Index to the Law Treatises and Reports*. The Advertisement states: 'This Catalogue is a Supplement to the Catalogue formerly compiled which is arranged in classes. The Manuscripts are not included in this Catalogue.' The circulation of this Catalogue was very limited. By an Order of 31 January 1843, 60 copies were to be printed for the use of the members of the Bench.

The three Catalogues of 1806, 1833, and 1843 are the only three catalogues of the Inner Temple Library which ever seem to have been printed and they are less numerous than the catalogues in manuscript. which survive for the eighteenth century. For general purposes of consultation a manuscript catalogue, if available, is as useful as a printed catalogue. From 1843 onwards Order followed Order for the compilation of a catalogue. It was explicitly stated in the Orders on the duties of a Librarian that a primary duty of his was the keeping of a catalogue and there was little doubt that this duty was faithfully discharged.

On 6 February 1849 it was ordered that the subject of the Catalogue of the Library should be referred to the Library Committee, with powers to carry out the proposals verbally submitted to the Bench by George Spence, who had been Treasurer in 1846. This Order must have been carried out, for on 1 May 1857 it was resolved that the Catalogue of the Library be printed; two years previously the Library Committee had recommended the completion of the catalogue by Hilary term 1856. The Treasurer was requested to carry this resolution into effect. There is no evidence that any publication was ever made, nor is there any further reference to the matter. In 1889 it was ordered that a new Catalogue of the Library be prepared and 'written by type-writer' and in 1892 £50 was granted to J. G. L. Pickering, the then Librarian, for his extra pains in preparation of the new catalogue. That ends the chronicle of catalogues of the printed books in the Library, but the current catalogue was kept up to date, revised, retyped, and added to until books and Library records were destroyed in 1941. Then not only a new library had to be gathered together and a new building built but a new catalogue had to be compiled. The old typewritten catalogue was not destroyed, but many of the books contained in it were. That old catalogue records in twenty-one volumes what was in the Library in 1939. The new typewritten catalogue which is in progress contains, at present, all the law books in the main Library and is in seven volumes. It is supplemented by a card index of thousands of other books and both versions are in progress towards completion but it will take some time before all the books in the Library and storage rooms are included.

The story of the catalogue of the manuscripts is very different from that of the printed books. No printed catalogue of the manuscripts has ever been produced. As far as can be ascertained no manuscripts in the Library, if there were any such, before the Petyt bequest, have survived in custody. The Petyt Manuscripts arrived with their own catalogue, which has since been quite heavily annotated, especially by Josiah Blew during his librarianship. To some of the items he added further information in his catalogues of the Library of 1715, 1727, and 1733. There were few manuscripts in the Library other than the Petyt Manuscripts and such as came in were put in the presses with the Petyt Manuscripts and this practice continued until the opening decades of the nineteenth century. Thereafter the accumulation of manuscripts has been steady if not a stream. But already it was felt by the Bench that the available means of reference to the manuscripts were insufficient. The failure to comply with the request of the Sun Fire Office in 1812 to supply a catalogue of the manuscripts and a valuation of each individual manuscript is to be regretted, but it may have drawn attention to a regrettable deficiency. For on 24 May 1816 the Bench Table 'resolved that it is expedient that a catalogue should be formed of the Petyt Manuscripts in the Library of this Society and that the means of carrying the same into execution be taken into consideration in the next term'. The matter is not referred to again.

On 15 June 1832 the Bench considered a Report of the Library Committee which stated that it had considered the Catalogue and was of opinion that the Librarian had discharged his duty well in ascertaining the contents of the Library, although they strongly recommended that the Librarian should be required to direct his earliest attention to the manuscripts to afford by means of the Catalogue (ordered to be printed) 'such further information of their nature and content'. On 2 November 1832 the Bench ordered 'that 150 copies of the Catalogue of Manuscripts in the Library be printed'. It was clearly then contemplated that there should be a separate catalogue of the manuscripts. It never eventuated, though the list of manuscripts in the printed catalogue of 1833, as has been stated above, did contain a slightly extended version of some of the manuscripts in the Petyt Collection and of other manuscripts which had been acquired up to 1825. The *Reports of the Historical Manuscript Commission* of 1871 and 1888 did not stimulate any proposal to prepare a complete catalogue of all the manuscripts in the Inner Temple Library. There the matter rested until 1961.

Throughout, the Bench Table has generally been particularly anxious for over a hundred and fifty years to promote the compilation and publication of printed catalogues of books in the Inner Temple Library, and that for purely practical reasons of convenience. It is difficult to ascertain the reason for the failure to implement the various Orders which had been made. It would seem that the Bench was, particularly in the nineteenth century, still more insistent that a catalogue of the manuscripts should be published. Here it is more easy to suggest reasons why the Orders were not implemented. The Librarian and his staff were not qualified to catalogue manuscripts which ran from the twelfth century onwards. They were not so qualified nor could they have been expected to be so qualified. The result has been that these manuscripts have remained uncatalogued until the present day.

15. PUBLICATIONS OF THE INNER TEMPLE

The publications of the Inner Temple appear to number fifteen titles and nineteen volumes, ranging in date from 1806 to 1939. All but one may be fairly said to relate to the affairs and interests of the Inn. Three are Library Catalogues, of 1806, 1833, and 1843, which have already been dealt with. The *Facts and Observations relating to the Temple Church and the monuments contained in it* was published in 1811. By a Bench Table Order of 1 February 1811, 250 copies were to be printed. Though issued anonymously it was known to be the work of Joseph Jekyll, better known as a wit and politician and friend of the Prince Regent than as a lawyer and serious writer. He was elected a Bencher in 1805 and was Treasurer 1815–16. When he died in 1837 he was senior K.C. and senior Bencher. Lord Eldon claimed that he was tricked by the Prince Regent into appointing him a Master in Chancery in 1815. Joseph Jekyll was, however, genuinely interested in the Temple Church and was present at the opening of the stone coffin there which contained 'the effigy of a person in episcopal habit, mitre and crozier, cut in granite, with a degree of sculptural merit unusual in ancient times'. Drafts and proofs of this work are among the Records of the Inner Temple.

The first full-scale publication was made in 1819, of Adam Martin's *Index to Exchequer Records*. Adam Martin was a barrister of the Inn, called in 1761, who in 1782 had given his index to the Library and duly received the thanks of the Bench on 15 June, and it was in demand for search there in 1799. For it was a very useful work of reference. Adam Martin was of the Exchequer Office and the Exchequer Office was in the precincts of the Inner Temple. He was one of the Six Clerks of the King's Remembrancer's Office. He was in fact a hardworking official who had produced an excellent index to a wide range of Exchequer records which has never been superseded. On 14 May 1819 it was ordered that 'five hundred copies of the book called "Index Locorum" sometime since presented to the Library by Adam Martin esq. be printed for the use of the Society'. Copies of the work were presented to the Masters of the Bench, the Lord Chancellor, the Master of the Rolls, the Vice Chancellor, the Judges, and the Libraries of the Inns of Court.

On 12 May 1820 it was ordered that James Gardner, the Sub-Treasurer's clerk, 'be paid fifty guineas for preparing for and correcting the proofs of Mr. Martin's Index to Exchequer Records and half a guinea for making thereof in sheets be charged to the booksellers and they are to charge fifteen shillings in boards and whatever the sale produces after defraying all expenses to the Society, including the said fifty guineas to be received by Mr. Gardner for his own benefit'. The publication seems to have been inspired by Gardner for his own financial benefit rather than as a commercial enterprise on behalf of the Inn. The manuscript is now among the Miscellaneous Manuscripts, in two volumes, as is a bowdlerized version of the printed text, by Thomas Edlyne Tomlins, both of which would be very useful for another edition of a much-used work.

Mr. James Gardner was very active in 1819, for on 23 November it was ordered that the pamphlet to be called '*The Student's Guide to the Inner Temple*, compiled by James Gardner (clerk to Mr. Norris, the Sub-Treasurer) be printed at the expense of the Society and that he be allowed to sell the same at the price of one shilling each for his own benefit'.

On 23 November 1877 an entry in the Bench Table Order Book stated: 'Mr. Cooke thanked in his place for preparing and editing the *List of Members admitted to the Inner Temple*, 1547–1660.' W. H. Cooke had been elected to the Bench in 1863 and became Treasurer in 1879. The book had been published, with a preface dated March 1877, and without the name of the compiler, who stated that 'the Masters of the Bench of the Inner Temple a few years since assented to a proposal that a list should be printed containing the names and a brief account of the members of the Inn from the earliest date of which any records have been preserved' and said that the labour required for such an investigation had been greater than might be supposed. 'It has been necessary to search county histories, family records and a variety of sources of information, in order to obtain accurate information.' The result was a very useful and necessary compilation of 410 pages, which despite certain inaccuracies and other disadvantages, still remains the most easy and accessible means of reference for the period which it covers. It seems never to have got into general circulation and is now a very rare work.

The next work also related solely to the Inner Temple. It was a list of the *Masters of the Bench of the Hon. Society of the Inner Temple*, 1450–1883, *and Masters of the Temple*, 1540–1883, compiled by J. E. Martin, then Librarian, and issued in 1883. This, too, is an invaluable publication, which contains short notes about most of the Benchers, often with a few biographical details, and though there are omissions, may usually be regarded as a work of accuracy. Its circulation also must have been very limited and it is now impossible to obtain a copy from any source, and the copy which is in the Inner Temple Library is incomplete in index. It has been followed by two supplements. The first was issued in 1901 (32 pages) and was entitled *Masters of the Bench of the Hon. Society of the Inner Temple, Supplement*, 1883–1900, *to which* is *Appended a List of Treasurers*, 1505–1901; the *Second Supplement*, 1901–18 (24 pages), printed in 1918, contained also Addenda to the Previous Supplement, Masters of the Temple from 1894, and an index to both supplements. In neither case was the name of the compiler given; he was probably the Librarian at the time of issue. On the title-page of both appeared the words 'not published'.

The Catalogue of the Paintings, Engravings, Serjeants' Rings, Plate, Stained Glass etc. belonging to the Honourable Society of the Inner Temple was printed in 1915 by Order of the Masters of the Bench. The introductory note dated April 1915 by J. E. L. Pickering, the Librarian, stated that it superseded a List of Portraits and Prints which was made in 1891. 'The first part containing a list of Portraits has had the advantage of the revision of Mr. A. M. Bremner, and the fourth part giving the list of Plate that of Mr. E. Marshall Hall K.C., both Benchers of the Inn.' The List of Portraits and Prints of 1891 and the present catalogue are both documented in the Bench Table Orders.

In 1933, at the request of the Bench, J. E. Singleton K.C. (later Lord Justice Singleton and Treasurer in 1952) delivered two lectures at the Niblett Hall on *Conduct at the Bar and Some Methods of Advocacy* and the Bench desired that they should be published by the Society, the proceeds to go to the Barristers' Benevolent Association. They were published in 1933 and reprinted in 1937. On the occasion of the *Tercentenary Celebrations of Sir Edward Coke* held on 17 December 1934 important speeches were made. On 11 January 1935 the Treasurer reported to the Bench that he proposed to circulate the speeches made at the dinner to Benchers and other guests. This was duly done and on 21 April 1936. Master Schiller was thanked by the Bench for his binding of the Proceedings of the Coke Centenary Dinner.

On 13 May 1938 the Bench gave the Library Committee permission to spend up to £200 on printing the autobiography of Sir John Rolt. In 1939 *The Memoirs of the Right Honourable Sir John Rolt, Lord Justice of the Court of Appeal in Chancery*, 1804–71, was published, edited by C. T. le Quesne, the Master of the Library. Sir John Rolt, after his apprenticeship to a woollen draper and a period as clerk in Doctors' Commons, joined the Inner Temple and was called to the bar in 1837, was elected a

Bencher in 1846, became Attorney General in 1866 and a Lord Justice of Appeal in 1867. He had been very active in the affairs of the Society and took a particular interest in the Library and served on the Library Committee. His Memoirs have charm and historical value for a social historian of the first seven decades of the nineteenth century.

Of course the most solid, substantial, and expensive publication sponsored by the Society has been the five volumes of the *Calendar of Records of the Inner Temple*, published between 1896 and 1937, and edited, the first three volumes by F. A. Inderwick, a Bencher and Treasurer in 1898, and the last two volumes by R. A. Roberts, a barrister of the Inn who had been for many years Secretary of the Historical Manuscripts Commission. These monumental volumes have already been dealt with several times above and there is no occasion for further mention at present.

Besides all the above publications which have been seen there appear to be a number of works which were ordered to be prepared and printed but which have not been traced, if ever they were issued. It is possible that, like Catalogues of the Manuscripts which never eventuated, they were never completed and put in a form to be printed and published. Two examples must suffice. On 16 April 1901 it was ordered that the 'lectures by Mr. Baylis entitled Treasure Trove and The Moot should be published'. No such publication appears in the law catalogues. On 18 March 1892 it was ordered that 100 copies of a Digested Index of the Law Treatises in the Library to be printed at a cost not exceeding £75. There is no trace of such a work.

16. THE USE MADE OF THE INNER TEMPLE MANUSCRIPTS

The Inner Temple appears always to have been generous in the use it has permitted of its manuscripts, although essentially a private Library and frequently suffering from insufficient accommodation for its own necessary purposes. Though the permission of the Bench was required for search of them that permission was seldom refused and never without appropriate cause. The only persons with free access to the manuscripts were the Benchers and the Librarian. Apart from the manuscripts mentioned in the *7th Report of the Historical Manuscripts Commission* (1888) which totalled 387, of which 369 were in the Petyt Collection, 4 in the Barrington Collection, and 14 were Miscellaneous Manuscripts, and the 496 manuscripts mentioned in the *Catalogue of the Inner Temple Library*, 1833, of which 395 were in the Petyt Collection, 81 in the Barrington Collection, and 20 were Miscellaneous Manuscripts (the figures have to be adjusted by losses) there has been no means of knowing what manuscripts were contained in the Inner Temple Library. It will be noted that the manuscripts are described as mentioned in these two sources. For neither is a catalogue of manuscripts and in many cases it would be a serious exaggeration to describe them as lists even. They also left 325 manuscripts entirely unknown and many of the remainder virtually unknown. The lack of a catalogue has been the only restriction imposed upon the use of the Inner Temple manuscripts.

The means of knowing what use has been made of the Inner Temple manuscripts, therefore, refer almost exclusively to the manuscripts in the Petyt Collection. These are few and unsatisfactory. After a certain date applications to search were normally placed before the Bench Table and permission was generally entered in its Order Books. No Registers of Users appears to have been kept until the present century. So generally it is not possible to know how frequently or when a manuscript was worked upon, or for what purpose. Apart from the records of the grant of permission to search the only means of discovering use is by reference to printed works which contained transcripts of material or information derived exclusively from them. Over two hundred and fifty years, considering the variety of subjects covered by the manuscripts, this is a very considerable task, particularly as few users appear to have repaid permission with a gift of the printed work which resulted.

In the present catalogue, in most cases, when material in any manuscript is to be found in print that fact is stated. That, however, does not mean that the particular manuscript was used in the printed work, or whether other manuscripts were compared, corrected, or collated with the manuscript in question. All authors or editors have not had the grace to acknowledge their sources. As has been suggested above, the Bench of the Inner Temple has itself undertaken the publication of only one of its own manuscripts, Adam Martin's *Index to Exchequer Records*, though it seriously contemplated the publication, under the editorship of Serjeant James Manning, of the Year Book, 10–17 Edward III, full text and translation, which would have been a very large undertaking, as it took nine volumes in the Rolls Series when eventually published.

The difficulties of stating briefly the use which has been made of Inner Temple manuscripts, which in this connection means a comparatively few volumes of the Petyt Manuscripts, can be illustrated by the use made by one of the earliest, if not the earliest user, after the manuscripts were in custody of the Inn. This was John Strype, the ecclesiastical historian and biographer, who wrote the lives of three successive Archbishops of Canterbury, Matthew Parker, Edmund Grindal, and John Whitgift. His *Life of Matthew Parker* was first published in 1711, his *Life of Edmund Grindal* in 1710, his *Life of John Whitgift* in 1718. In each case he was substantially indebted to manuscripts in the Petyt Collection, which he duly acknowledged in his books. He not only derived exclusive information from them but also transcribed and printed exclusive documents from them. Yet there is no trace of any Bench Table Order giving him permission to use the manuscripts. The dates of the publications suggest that he probably started work upon them before the death of William Petyt and continued his work upon them after their removal to the Inner Temple Library. For his later published works, *Annals of the Reformation*, four volumes, 1725, and *Ecclesiastical*

Memorials, seven volumes, were also substantially indebted to the same Petyt Manuscripts and equally acknowledged indebtedness. Of course, it is possible that all his notes and transcripts were made during the life time of William Petyt, but for his later publications, at least, this would not seem likely, and in any case, before publication he would have required further sight for verification and checking.

Another early user who, probably next to William Petyt himself and his clerk, George Holmes, knew the contents of the Petyt Manuscripts better than anyone else, was John Anstis, who was a Trustee of William Petyt's Will. He received exceptional treatment from the Bench. Not only was his son admitted specially gratis to the Inner Temple in 1710 (though for some reason the actual admission did not take place until 1724, but with seniority from 1710) and presented, the same year, with 'the two first volumes of Her Majesty's books, given to this Society, there being in the Library duplicates thereof', but he was allowed to borrow manuscripts from the Petyt Collection for his researches into heraldry. He was himself of the Middle Temple. After he became Garter King at Arms in 1714 his first major publication, the *Register of the Garter*, two volumes, was not made until 1724, and his *Knighthood of the Bath* until 1725. In 1729 he was thanked by the Bench for his present of the latter work.

As the evidence for use before 1800 is different from that after that date, the use before 1800 will be considered separately—and that in effect means the use of manuscripts in the Petyt Collection, with the addition of a few further manuscripts entered in the list of manuscripts in the first printed Catalogue of the Library, 1806. Once the Library had been built to house the Petyt books and others and a catalogue had been made, it was ordered, 18 May 1718, that 'no copy or transcript to be taken by any person of any manuscript book in the Library and no books to be delivered or taken out of the Library without leave of the Table'. This order was to be hung up in the Library. The first Order to be issued accordingly was an auspicious one. It was dated 19 May 1732, when the Clerk of the House of Commons was given 'the liberty of inspecting the books given to this Society by Mr. Petyt and now in the Library and take copies of such parts thereof as may be of use or service towards completing the Journals of the House of Commons, the Library Keeper to lay before the Table tomorrow such directions as can be made as shall be expedient'. But by an earlier order Joshua Blew, as Librarian, had been given permission to give 'a copy of such part of the manuscript book in the Library of the Society as related to Lord Bacon's Treatise about the Alienation Office'. The fact that Spedding rejected this treatise as of Francis Bacon's authorship and attributed it to William Lambard is irrevelant to the fact of permission to transcribe. It was required for the edition of Bacon's *Works* in four volumes which appeared in 1728 and for which the Society subscribed.

Though there is no proof of any permission to inspect manuscripts ever having been given to Thomas Hearne, a complete collection of whose fifty-one volumes was purchased for the Library by subscription as they were issued, 1715–45, yet he used the Petyt Manuscripts, especially the Chronicle of Robert le Brunne, published by him in 1725 as *Peter Langtoft's Chronicle*, and acknowledged his source. He had a friend among the members of the Inn, Philip Harcourt, who probably obtained access for him.

The next order does not appear in the Bench Order Book until 1 February 1773 and runs thus: 'on reading a letter from Francis Hargrave esq., of Lincoln's Inn . . . requesting leave to make an extract from a manuscript in the Inner Temple Library entitled "Reports of Several Cases and Arguments in Law" all of Mr. William Prynne's own handwriting leave granted to him to make it in the Library'. Daines Barrington, although already a Bencher and an ex-Treasurer, on 8 February 1788 was 'granted leave to procure a copy from a manuscript which contained the Year Books for the 10th to the 17th of Edward the Third in order that the same may be printed and published at his expense'. His application must have been made on grounds of publication because for several years he had used the Petyt Manuscripts in the preparation of the various editions of his *Observations upon the Statutes*, which contained, as has been stated above, a total of sixty-eight references to them. The Petyt Manuscripts which he had put under tribute were some thirty in number, but there is not one reference to Petyt's printed works, though there are references to those of his opponent Dr. Robert Brady.

The next Order for inspection was also made in favour of a member of the Inn. It was dated 16 November 1792 and ran: 'upon application of John Vaillant esq., a barrister, to make inspection of a manuscript in the Library containing certain cases collected by Lord Chief Justice Dyer, marked 13, in order to the preparing of a new edition of Lord Chief Justice Dyer's *Reports*, Mr. Vaillant given leave to have copies, and the Librarian to attend him to collect the same'. Mr. Vaillant who became a Bencher in 1825, and was senior Judge of the Sheriffs' Court, used admirably the Dyer material contained in this volume, which was not available anywhere else. His edition of *Dyer's Reports* was published in three volumes in 1794. They were entitled *Sir John Dyer's Reports (Ascun Nouel Cases), translated into English, with additional references, marginal notes and a new index, with a life of the author prefixed.* They were a great advance on all previous editions and contained new cases, additions to old cases and notes about Dyer and the judgements and about his life.

Thus for the whole of the eighteenth century there were only four Bench Orders giving access to the manuscripts recorded and there was no impressive increase in the demand in the opening years of the nineteenth century, but interest was speeded up by the publication in 1801 of the *First Report of the Record Commissioners*. It contained a return on the Inner Temple manuscripts from Randal Norris, the Librarian, which Charles Abbot, Speaker of the House of Commons and Chairman of the Commission, although a member of the Inner Temple, had some difficulty in extracting. To the circular letter of 25 February 1800, signed by the Chairman, no reply was forthcoming, so on 6 March Charles Abbot followed with a personal letter. He said he was sorry that the Inner Temple had not made a return, 'so as to share the valuable MSS. which they really possess—as I have myself seen them—I mean particularly Petyt's valuable and voluminous collection of Transcripts from the Public Records and the Year Books'. He added that Lincoln's Inn had employed John Caley of Gray's Inn to draw up their return and suggested that the Inner Temple might consider doing the same. Again there was no reply, so it was ordered by the Select Committee 'that the Benchers of the Inner Temple do without further delay make a return to the Order of this Committee dated the 25th of February last'. This produced a brief return dated 7 May, from Norris, intimating in the covering letter that the Inner Temple Library would 'be open at all times for your inspection or that of any member of the Committee or to such gentleman as you or the Committee may think proper to appoint to make such inspection'.

This return stated that there were not in the custody of the Inner Temple 'any original Records, Rolls, Instruments, Registers or Manuscript Books and Papers containing any Acts or Proceedings by Royal, Parliamentary, Judicial or other Public Authority, or any authentic Manuscript copies of any such Original Manuscripts, Records, Rolls, Instruments, Books or Papers of Public Authority enquired after'. Neither was there 'in the custody of the Society any Manuscript Catalogues or Indexes of any Manuscript in any other public Repository except an Index to some Records in the Court of Exchequer'. If these remarks applied to documents which should have been in public custody the return was correct. It was strictly accurate as far as official documents were concerned but not entirely so regarding transcripts, but it would be true to say that there was not in the Inner Temple Library any Public Records or official indexes to such. But the Record Commission had got its foot in and employed as assistants, experts who knew their duty, and the Commission proceeded on its course.

Thomas Edlyne Tomlins, who was, as has been seen, a member of the Inn, later to become a Bencher and Treasurer, was one of the Sub-Commissioners of the Record Commission. As early as 20 November 1801, at his request, he was permitted to consult, collate, and copy some part of certain manuscripts. These are fortunately clearly specified in the Order and were all volumes of Statutes, namely Petyt MSS. 505, 506, 508, 511/6, 511/8, 511/9, the last three being Petyt Manuscripts, the first three Barrington Manuscripts. These he required as one of the editors of the *Statutes of the Realm*, of which Alexander Luders was the first named of the editors, who included also John Caley. The first volume was published in 1810, but Tomlins' original inspection could not have been completed beyond the end of the reign of Edward III, for on 26 November 1813, again at his request, it was ordered that he should be permitted to copy the French text of the Statutes of 1 and 3 Henry VII, that is Petyt 511/6.

This Petyt Manuscript had been referred to in the Record Commission Report for 1812.

Thereafter there is silence as far as the Record Commission is concerned until 9 May 1822, when a memorial came from Francis Cohen, a member of the Society (afterwards Sir Francis Palgrave, first Deputy Keeper of the Records, 1838), who had been appointed a Sub-Commissioner for the purpose of preparing a new edition of the *Rolls of Parliament*. The memorial pointed out that the transcripts collected by Silvester (*sic*) Petyt would greatly assist him in the execution of his task by referring him to the original records, and he requested that he might be allowed to read in the Library at extra hours. Whether because of the gratuitous error or because of the somewhat unreasonable request the memorial was not well received. It was not complied with. Upon a second request by letter, it was ordered, 22 April 1823, that 'leave be given at the usual hours of attendance'. The new edition of the Rolls of Parliament did not appear and recourse must still be made to the old edition compiled largely from transcripts or to the Petyt transcripts compiled directly from the original rolls.

Meanwhile other official searches were being made to which there is no reference in the Bench Order Books. Permission to search must have been arranged by Lord Redesdale with the Treasurer or with the Bench unofficially. The details of these searches are obtainable only from correspondence among the Records of the Inner Temple. Reference has already been made to Lord Redesdale's letter to the Librarian on 7 December 1816 about copies of Petyt's transcripts taken by John Caley for the Committee of the House of Lords on the Dignity of a Peer, of which he was Chairman. A few days later, 19 December 1816, John Caley himself wrote to Randal Norris:

> In answer to your question whether I mean to cause the Extracts from Petyt MSS. in the Inner Temple Library to be printed I have no hesitation in saying that I have no such intention, as the Extracts have not been made for my use nor are they my property. I will add that the MSS. of Mr. Petyt's cannot with propriety be printed by any person because they are not exact or correct copies from the originals which exist in the Tower and other Public Repositories of Records and from whence alone they ought to be given to the public. I shall probably recommend that some of these originals should be printed but Mr. Petyt's Extracts will be of no service in this respect.

A draft or copy of a letter from Norris to Lord Redesdale dated December 1816 adds a few further details. Caley had been permitted by an amanuensis to make Extracts and copies in consequence of Lord Redesdale's application. The Order was that he was to take copies 'of such parts as your lordship pointed out'. The person employed had been engaged 'not only in Trinity term and vacation but also the last term and had not yet completed his Extracts'. The Librarian desired to be informed if it was intended to print the same. 'If so', he continued, 'the Society must be consulted for several gentlemen who style themselves Trustees under Mr. Petyt's Will have lately made application about the manuscripts.' They had lately agreed about printing and publishing them but till lately had not discovered where they were deposited. The *Reports on the Dignity of a Peer* do not, however, indicate the extent to which the Petyt transcripts were used for that work. There is only one reference to a specific Petyt Manuscript throughout the Reports, with a few further to his printed works, but there can be no question that the Petyt Manuscripts were used for more than the index which Lord Redesdale suggests.

John Caley apparently altered his opinion to suit his own purposes. For in his contribution to the *Report of the Select Committee on Public Records*, 1800, he had written: 'I am convinced that they [the Petyt Manuscripts] contain an abundant fund of information of the highest importance evidently evincing the skill and judgement of the collector and may be consulted with advantage by the lawyer, the historian and the antiquary.'

A private application was not the subject of a recorded Order until 13 November 1821, when Saxe Bannister, a barrister of Lincoln's Inn, requested admission to the Library for the purpose of examining and making extracts from the manuscripts preserved there and he was permitted to do so in the presence of the Librarian. This was the first of three applications from him. Further Orders were made on 25 November 1829 and 29 January 1830, both granting permission, but neither grant was specific. Of the many published works of Saxe Bannister which covered a wide range of subjects, perhaps his searches among the Inner Temple manuscripts were best reflected in his *The Use of Historical Manuscripts during the last 174 years*, published in 1863.

On 21 June 1825, as has been mentioned above, the Report of the Committee was accepted which recommended that no person other than Masters of the Bench and the Librarian be, on any occasion, permitted to have access to or peruse the manuscripts and the most rare and valuable books, without an Order first obtained from the Bench and then only in the presence of the Librarian; and that no transcript be permitted to be made of any manuscript without an Order first obtained from the Bench for that purpose. Twelve years later Sir George Rose and Mr. Burge reported to the Bench on 15 December 1857, concerning the manuscripts, that subject to the discretion of the Bench upon any particular application there was no reason why any persons applying to make copies or extracts from the same should not have such indulgence. It was realized that manuscripts are not treasures to be buried in a vault. They were for use and that use had a practical purpose.

Even before the Rolls Series was established Sir Frederic Madden, then Assistant Keeper of Manuscripts at the British Museum, received permission, on 3 June 1834, 'to borrow one of the Petyt Manuscripts containing a translation of Wace's Chronicle made by Robert of Brunne . . . provided the Trustees of the late Mr. Petyt's Will give their consent'. Two Benchers undertook to deliver it to him and to be responsible for its return by the first day of Michaelmas term next. This did not lead to publication, but on 18 April 1865 F. J. Furnivall was granted permission to send a copyist into the Library to copy the manuscript of the Chronicle of Robert of Brunne. When, however, he later asked for the use of the manuscript during a long vacation he was informed, 24 July 1869, that the Bench would grant the request upon receiving application from the Master of the Rolls. This was duly forthcoming and Lord Romilly's letter produced the necessary Order on 14 July 1869. It was not, however, until 1887 that *Chronicles of Robert Manning of Brunne*, edited by F. J. Furnivall, edited from MSS. at Lambeth Palace and the Inner Temple, two parts, was published in the Rolls Series.

The name or letter of the Master of the Rolls was one which obtained additional privileges speedily from the Masters of the Bench. On 14 November 1862 a letter from the Master of the Rolls requesting the loan of four volumes of the Petyt MSS. (unspecified) was complied with for six months. On 31 January 1879 the application of the Master of the Rolls for the loan of the Year Book, 10–17 Edward III, was granted. This was a follow-up of the permission which had been given on 14 November 1871 for L. O. Pike to examine the Petyt MSS. in the presence of the Librarian. The result was the loan of the Year Book to L. O. Pike, together with the Manning volumes of text and translation for more than 14 years, and the publication in the Rolls Series of *Year Books, 11–17, Edward III*, 1883–1903, and continued later.

But already the almost exclusive publication of historical records and historical material by official sources at national expense, such as the Journals of the House of Lords, the Journals of the House of Commons, the publications of the Record Commission, the Reports on the Dignity of a Peer, and the Rolls Series, were being challenged from two main directions, the publications of learned societies and the independent work of individuals. The societies especially concerned are the Camden Society, the Parker Society, the Roxburghe Club, and the Selden Society, in which the Bench of the Inner Temple has always been greatly interested, subscribing generously, and whose Benchers have throughout its history served as members of the Council. The Camden Society published its first volume in 1838; the Parker Society in 1841.

On 12 May 1840 John Bruce, the Treasurer of the Camden Society, received permission to inspect the Petyt Manuscripts, and on 4 November 1843 to make extracts from the Petyt Manuscripts. The results can be seen in many publications of the Camden Society, including *Correspondence of Robert Dudley, Earl of Leicester . . . Government of the Low Countries, 1585–6*, 1844, *Verney Papers, Notes of Proceedings in the Long Parliament*, 1845, and several other works, such as the *Correspondence of Matthew Parker, Archbishop of Canterbury*, 1853, for which he duly expressed his gratitude. Permission was given on 17 April 1866 to Samuel Rawson Gardiner to consult certain manuscripts in the Library. The result was *Notes of the Debates in the House of Lords officially taken by Henry Elsing, Clerk of the Parliaments, 1621,*

1870, and other works, such as *Debates in the House of Commons in 1625*, 1873. The use of the Petyt Manuscripts made by the Camden Society is continued with the publication of *Notes of Debates in the House of Lords officially taken by Robert Bowyer and Henry Elsing*, 1929, and of a Miscellaneous Manuscript in *Selections from the Correspondence of Arthur Capel, Earl of Essex, 1675–7*, 1913. The last volume of the Camden Society which contained a contribution from the Petyt Manuscripts was contained in *Camden Miscellany*, xx, in 1953, of a *Brief Collection of the Queen's Majesty's High and Honourable Courts of Record*, by Richard Robinson. Previously other Miscellanies had included *The Earl of Bristol's Defence of his Negotiations in Spain*, 1624, edited by S. R. Gardiner, and other contributions by the same editor; *The Œconomy of the Fleet*, printed in 1879, drew on Petyt Manuscripts, while *The Archpriest Controversy: Documents relating to the dissensions of the Roman Catholic Clergy, 1597–1603*, was 'edited from the Petyt MSS. in the Inner Temple', two volumes, 1896, 1898.

The Parker Society is represented by *The Works of John Whitgift . . . Archbishop of Canterbury*, 3 volumes, edited by John Ayre, 1851–1853, and the *Correspondence of Matthew Parker, Archbishop of Canterbury*, 1853, and the *Remains of Edmund Grindal . . . Archbishop of Canterbury*, 1843. The Revd. John Arye was given permission to collate copies of letters of Archbishop Whitgift. Of the Roxburghe Club the representative is the *Literary Remains of Edward VI*, edited by J. G. Nichols, a copy of which was presented to the Inn in 1859.

The close link with the Selden Society continues. As far as publication is concerned it does not begin until Sir Cecil Carr edited the Miscellaneous Manuscript *The Pension Book of Clements Inn*, 1960, though as early as 1913 Sir Cecil Carr had edited *Select Charters of Trading Companies, 1530–1707*. Also on 13 November permission had been given for one of the Petyt Manuscripts to be taken to the Public Record Office and on 24 November 1936 permission was given to the Selden Society to borrow and print one of the Petyt Manuscripts. Both these Orders referred to the early Ecclesiastical Precedent Book which it was proposed should be edited by Professor H. D. Hazeltine, Downing Professor of Law in the University of Cambridge, and a member of the Inn, and Sir Hilary Jenkinson, who became deputy Keeper of the Public Records. Physical reasons prevented the proposal and this very important manuscript still awaits publication.

Before proceeding to deal with individual writers there is one Order which does not come within any of the categories which have been suggested. On 18 November 1851 the Duke of Bedford was given permission to make extracts from a manuscript in the Library. After this search an application was received from the Librarian to the Duke of Bedford to have copies of certain manuscripts in the Library relating to the Russell family. On 28 April 1854 permission was granted to make extracts, the expense to be borne by the Society. On 13 June 1854 a letter was put before the

Bench from the Librarian to the Duke of Bedford conveying thanks for copies of the Russell Papers. This Duke of Bedford was the 7th Duke, brother of Lord John Russell, afterwards Prime Minister and Earl Russell; the Russell Papers were doubtless the Letter Book of John Russell, first Earl of Bedford, in the Petyt Manuscripts.

Of the individual writers there must be a still stricter selection of those who deserve special notice, for the number of those who were seeking permission to search was progressively increasing during the last two thirds of the nineteenth century. Of those who must be mentioned because of the great time they spent upon the manuscripts were two members of the Inn, Serjeant Henry Alworth Merewether and Edward Foss. There is that vast collector of historical material, John Gough Nichols, who searched everywhere and published about everything he found, and there are those fugitive figures, foreigners as well as denizens, who sought a fleeting acquaintance with a manuscript or group of manuscripts without any result eventuating. But James Spedding, W. J. Christie, W. T. Ellacombe, F. A. Carrington, and R. Simpson cannot be numbered among these.

Of individuals who were working on major projects of their own a special place is occupied by Serjeant H. A. Merewether, who was admitted in 1802. While he was working on his History of Boroughs no less than ten Bench Table Orders were made in his favour, beginning on 13 February 1827 and ending on 9 November 1833. On 13 February 1827 he was given permission to make extracts 'from such of Mr. Petyt's MSS. in the Library of the Inner Temple of all such charters and public documents that are to be met with in the Tower or other public offices'. On 10 June Serjeant Merewether was allowed to have the two volumes of transcribed charters of Mr. Petyt's during the long vacation upon his producing authority from the surviving Trustees under Mr. Petyt's Will and giving a receipt and undertaking to return the books without injury on the first day of Michaelmas term. The remaining Orders related to the extension of the time of borrowing and the loan of further Petyt Manuscripts. The work was published as *History of the Boroughs and Municipal Corporations of the United Kingdom*, 3 volumes, 1835. Serjeant Henry Alworth Merewether was Town Clerk of London, 1842–57, and his son and namesake was Treasurer of the Inner Temple in 1868.

On 23 November 1849 Mr. Edward Foss was permitted to consult works in the Library 'with a view to the History of Lives of the Judges'. He had made his application to Sir Frederick Thesiger, who had been Treasurer in 1843, and who had already been Solicitor General and Attorney General. On 1 February 1850 on his requesting permission to inspect numerous books and documents of the House, as a member of the Inn he was informed that the Sub-Treasurer had orders to answer any question with regard to Lives of Judges, members of the Society. Thus he had permission not only to inspect the manuscripts in the Library but also the records of the Society. The use which he made of these facilities can be seen in his *Judges of England*, *with sketches of their lives and notices connected with the Courts at Westminster, 1066–1864*, nine volumes, 1848–64. He had already published an *Abridgment of Blackstone* in 1820 and had written on the *Origin of the title and office of Cursitor Baron of the Exchequer* in 1855. In 1865 he presented a copy of his very useful *Tabulae Curialis* to the Library. His *Biographia Juridica, or Biographical Dictionary of the Judges of England to the year 1870*, was prepared by him and published shortly before his death in 1870. This in now probably the most used of his many very valuable works.

Meanwhile James Spedding was preparing for his great edition of the *Works of Lord Bacon* which was published in seven volumes, 1857–9, and his *Life and Letters of Lord Bacon*, also in seven volumes, 1861–74. There was sufficient Bacon material among the Inner Temple Manuscripts to require perusal and he accordingly sought permission through Frederick Pollock, a Bencher, 'to have access to manuscripts in the Library with a view to possible publication'. This was granted on 5 December 1845. On 17 April 1868 a letter was read from him requesting permission to publish extracts from certain manuscripts in the Library and his request was complied with. On the very same day on which his first application was considered the application of William Dougal Christie to copy manuscripts in the Library was granted. W. D. Christie was equally well known as a diplomatist as he was as a writer. What he required from the manuscripts it is difficult to discover, for his publications, which came considerably later and which included his edition of Dryden's Works, his vindication of John Stuart Mill, and his Life of Shaftesbury, could derive little from them.

John Gough Nichols's application to consult the Petyt MSS. was acceded to on 6 November 1845. He probably used his permission for many purposes in his many intended works. It is known that he used the exclusive material from them for his *Progresses of Queen Elizabeth* and *Progresses of King James I*. It is seldom that the applicants are specific in their requirements, but on 26 November 1850, permission was given to John Brett, of the Chapter House, to extract from the manuscript treatise on the Nature of the Court of Wards and Liveries. F. A. Carrington's permission in 1858 was doubtless given for his search of legal manuscripts in continuation of the several volumes of *Nisi Prius Reports* he had already published, and Richard Simpson's in 1873 for researches into Roman Catholicism. Yet there is no record of any permission having been granted to M. A. Tierney, who edited Charles Dodds's *Church History of England*, 1839–43, though he drew quite lavishly on at least three of the Petyt Manuscripts. Sometimes it is difficult to identify those to whom permission to search was granted if they were natives. It is interesting, however, to find that as early as 1851 permission was sought and given to inspect Ley's MSS. Reports. For foreigners the description in the Orders is more precise. They obviously had to have the personal backing of a Bencher or other authority. One is described as 'a Danish historian of eminence'; another as 'a distinguished German writer on jurisprudence'; a third as a

'Doctor of Jurisprudence of Heidelberg University'; while for a Russian applicant reference was made to the Russian Embassy. As long as Orders on inspection were entered in the Bench Order Books there is no Order giving permission to any United States citizen.

For some time in the 1870s the Orders of such permission ceased to be entered. What new arrangements were set up to give leave it is not now possible to be certain. It would seem that the authority to grant permission must have been deputed to the Library Committee, or to the Master of the Library, perhaps in consultation with the Treasurer. There is no reference to the matter in the Bench Order Books. The Library Committee Minute Books before 1941 have been destroyed and almost all the other records relating to the Library. There is, therefore, a considerable gap in knowledge of the use made of the manuscripts of the Inner Temple extending from about 1873 to 1945, for between 1940 and 1945 the manuscripts had been evacuated and were no longer available for search and for a few years after 1945 Library conditions would have made facilities for search difficult if not impossible. For this period, therefore, the only proof of search is to be found the publication of the results.

During this long interval of over seventy years the conditions under which historical and legal research was pursued were changing radically. Legal research was broadening from Henry Spelman to F. W. Maitland; legal historical research from John Reeve to Sir William Holdsworth; constitutional historical research from Henry Hallam to Sir William Anson; historical research from Thomas Babington Macaulay to George Macaulay Trevelyan. There was similar progress in literary research. The demand for unused manuscript sources was becoming insatiable. Following German practice a Doctorate of Philosophy had been introduced into British and American Universities, for the award of which original research on some detailed subject, however unimportant, was the only passport. Seminars took the place of lectures and wide reading. The progress of these trends it is not possible to follow in detail from the records concerning the manuscripts in the Inner Temple Library.

From 1947, however, a Register has been kept of the names of those who have had access to the manuscripts in the Library. Now the procedure was that on written application the Librarian, after consultation with the Master of the Library, and where necessary the Library Committee, gave permission to inspect, and even to have photographs taken, under certain conditions. Publication might still be referred to the Bench Table. It still required a Bench Table Order to remove a manuscript from the Library. The new procedure had been growing up gradually over some time. Thus on 13 November 1936 permission was given 'for one of the Petyt Manuscripts in the Muniment Room, no. 51, with a reputed signature of Sir Francis Bacon to be taken to the Public Record Office to be compared with a known signature there'. On 11 May 1954, upon application by Columbia University, New York, permission to photograph and publish copies of Four Illuminations of the Courts of Chancery, King's Bench, Common Pleas, and Exchequer, in the time of Henry VI, was granted 'on condition that the publication should be "by permission of the Masters of the Bench of the Inner Temple" and that copies should be supplied for the records of the Inn'.

It is, however, clear that since 1900, and especially since 1920, with the greater number of persons from home and abroad working on historical, legal, and literary research, the use of the manuscripts in the Petyt and other Collections has been continuous and widespread. The records relating to searchers are, unfortunately, available only from 1947. By that time the difficulties for search occasioned by the war and its consequences had been overcome and all the Inner Temple manuscripts left were again available for search. An examination of the relative books establishes that the pre-war trend had been confirmed and extended. The searchers were mainly writing theses for minor doctorates of British and overseas Universities, particularly Universities in the United States, and those working at the Institute of Historical Research.

The range of subjects for which search was made was very wide and diverse. As might be expected, historical and legal subjects were the most prominent. History was represented in all its facets. Parliamentary History and Proceedings in the House of Commons were especially sought, subjects in which the Petyt Manuscripts were particularly rich. It was equally rich on the Proceedings of the House of Lords, including unique Bowyer and Elsyng manuscripts. In 1961 and 1962 a total of 30 volumes of these were photographed for the House of Lords to fill in gaps in the records of that House. Work was done on certain parliaments of Elizabeth I, but more particularly on certain parliaments of James I and Charles I. Some searchers were concerned with parliamentary procedure. Ecclesiastical History, especially Roman Catholic History in the reign of Elizabeth I, the History of the Church of England and the Puritans for the same period, attracted many searchers. Ecclesiastical precedents and ecclesiastical courts, the Court of Arches, for instance, and ecclesiastical administration, were almost as popular. The range of those interested in Legal History was more restricted and specialized, for example, such subjects as the Order of Serjeants at Law, or the History of the Inns of Court during the Renaissance, or Year Books and Early Reporters. Manuscript Reports, too, were in some demand, but more especially of such courts as the Court of Star Chamber and the Court of Wards and Liveries, which had few printed reports. Economic History, Local History, and even Military History produced searchers. Next to history the demand was perhaps greatest by those concerned with biography and the lives extended from the middle ages to modern times. Cardinal Reginald Pole, for example, had many would-be biographers. Medieval Chronicles, particularly the later ones in English, were popular and English medieval texts in general also drew searchers; the Making and Circulation of English Books in the later Middle Ages and Middle English Dialects were amongst the subjects. Finally several searches were concerned with the more technical aspects of manuscripts and records, palaeography and diplomatic and even illumination and heraldry.

For the later searches it would be invidious to mention names, but in so far as certain searchers founded schools, the members of which still follow the work of their masters, it is justifiable to mention three names: Professor A. Notestein of Yale on Parliamentary Debates in the reign of James I, Professor J. M. Neale of London on the reign of Elizabeth I and her parliaments, and Dr. Neil Ker of Oxford on the location of Medieval Manuscripts and on English Medieval Manuscripts.

On this topic it remains merely to sum up on the uses which have been made, from the beginning of the eighteenth century to the present day, of the manuscripts in the five main groups, or rather four main groups, for the Mitford Collection of Legal Manuscripts do not come into the picture, as they have not yet been in custody for ten years and it is not known to potential searchers that they are in the Inner Temple Library. Naturally for three reasons the Petyt Collection has been the most sought after group, for they are the most numerous (being more in number than all the other four groups put together); they were the foundation manuscripts of the Library; and thirdly because of the general importance of the contents, whether in original or in transcript. The Records of the Inner Temple, though freely used in the preparation of the *Calendars of Records of the Inner Temple*, are largely unknown, as no printed source refers to them. Though there has been some use made of the Barrington Manuscripts in the Petyt Collection, only three volumes in the Barrington Collection seem to have been sought after. Of the volumes among the Miscellaneous Manuscripts the great majority of them are not known to exist, though many of them are of the utmost importance. Yet some have already achieved publication.

Of the 252 Petyt Manuscripts there are few that have not been seen at some time or another. Since 1947, a period for which reasonable statistics are available, 105 of the total have been used by searchers. Of the group of Petyt Manuscripts the fifty-six volumes which have always been described as 'Proceedings in Parliament and Miscellanies' and on account of the valuable original documents amongst them are easily the most important group of Petyt Manuscripts, forty-seven were consulted. To go through the use made of their contents would almost necessitate a repetition of their catalogue. But on the use from the beginning of the eighteenth century onwards certain general propositions present themselves. First, the most important of the manuscripts have not always been those which have been consulted or published. Secondly, there seem to have been sometimes a very considerable lag between consultation and publication: in the case of the Year Book, 10–17 Edward III, over a hundred years. The Ecclesiastical Precedent Book may even take as long. Thirdly, though there has been at times intensive use of that portion of the Petyt Manuscripts which are his own transcripts, mainly of Public Records, the use made of the original documents which he collected and got bound into volumes has been infinitely greater. This is due, in part, to the greater historical value of the original documents, but it is due also, in part, to the diminishing value of the transcripts as many of them have been printed or calendared in the publications of the Record Commission and of the Public Record Office. The Calendar Series, for example, has restricted the use of these transcripts, even as indexes to the Public Records. There is, however, a large proportion of the transcripts of Public Records which have been lost since the time of Prynne and Petyt. Two classes, one of great importance and the other of some interest, come to mind. The Petyt Manuscripts contain scores of Parliamentary Petitions which are no longer available in original or other transcripts; similarly they contain Ecclesiastical Proxies not otherwise available. Though the value of the transcripts will continue to diminish as publication of the originals takes place, and therefore their use for search will be less, their presence will continue to have an insurance value until all the originals are published in full or duplicate copies of them are taken and kept elsewhere than the repository of the originals.

Finally, it has been calculated that in 1843 the Inner Temple Library possessed of printed books 5,500 titles and over 12,000 volumes. Today it contains 26,000 titles and over 76,000 volumes. The comparative number of manuscripts are 492 volumes in 1843 and 765 volumes today. Naturally the increase in printed books has been very much greater. Papers written by hand are very much more durable than typescript or photograph, than photostat or microfilm, if slower to produce. But there is a sufficient reservoir of manuscripts, especially of legal manuscripts, which have a peculiarly British attraction and value, in many places, unknown or little regarded, which need succour and shelter. Of a printed book there are always duplicates, sometimes hundreds if not thousands of them; of a manuscript there is only one copy. Preservation is for use, but preservation must be coupled with availability before use can be made effective. The experience of the war of 1939–45 should have proved the danger for the sources of scholarship, whether books or manuscripts, but books are dispersed, manuscripts are not. Thence the necessity of having them in proper custody, as Sir Edward Coke and William Petyt wrote in their wills, for posterity, in a library devoted to preservation and use.

17. PRESERVATION AND LOSS OF MANUSCRIPTS

The preservation of the manuscripts in the Inner Temple Library has been most meticulously regarded as a primary objective. Preservation postulates conditions of safety against fire and theft, against moisture and microbes; proper handling and use and care for parchment, paper, and binding. The great majority of the manuscripts in the Library have been re-bound and carefully and expensively re-bound, mainly in morocco. For example on 2 May 1851 the Bench passed a resolution that the Treasurer 'be requested to have bound such manuscripts as he shall think proper and require it', which as far as the manuscripts in the Petyt Collection are concerned seems to have been completed by 1871. In the rebinding such special features of the old binding as were worthy of it were incorporated into the new binding: for instance, such Petyt manuscripts as had the Petyt coat of arms embossed upon the covers had those coats of arms inserted in the new binding. Similarly all such flyleaves as contained anything of interest or importance have also been incorporated into the volumes. During the last hundred years, if not before, the necessary care has been taken to see that excessive cutting has not been done. In a few cases where essential repairs to parchment or paper have been made they have been carried out generally skilfully. The manuscripts have been kept in dry and secure conditions. Their use for search has not been very great and permission to see them has not been given indiscriminately, though properly supported applications have always been granted. In the case of composite manuscripts containing a considerable number of documents the placing on guards has been carefully done, though there has been a tendency to allow some of the most important and rare original documents to be over-inspected and handled.

The result of the care in custodianship has been that of the 252 manuscripts among the Petyt Manuscripts, which have been in custody for over two hundred and fifty years, not a single one has been lost or injured. In fact they are now in better general condition than when they first entered the Library in 1708 and 1709. Of the remaining 132 manuscripts which were given pressmarks in the Petyt Collection there have been slight losses which have already been noted, three volumes of the Law Reports presented by William Barnesley and two from the manuscripts presented by Mrs. Ann Sadleir, and these must have disappeared during the eighteenth century. Apart from these the only manuscripts listed in the Catalogue of 1833 which are no longer available are the following:

513. Law Manuscripts with an alphabetical index of Cases, 3 vols., folio.
514. Pine's engraved Magna Carta, with the Arms of the Barons emblasoned, folio.
521. Catalogue of Benefactors to the Library of this Society, from the reign of Queen Anne to the year 1742, folio.
522. Law Commonplace Books (French), 6 vols, folio.

These eleven volumes have not been seen or identified. Exhaustive search for the Catalogue of Benefactors has produced no result. It has disappeared completely, and all trace and recovery of it and its contents have been lost. The description of the three volumes of Law Manuscripts is so vague that they would, in any case, be difficult to identify, but it is possible that one or more of them may lurk among the Miscellaneous Manuscripts, as may some of the Law Commonplace Books, as has been suggested above. On the other hand, there does not seem to be any volume among the Miscellaneous Manuscripts, the donor of which is not known, which seems to fit with the description. Pine's engraved Magna Carta can hardly be called a manuscript, but whatever may be its status it is no longer available. It should be pointed out that the present Petyt Collection pressmarks include one manuscript with a different pressmark from that in the 1833 Catalogue. This is due to the repetition in the latter of the same pressmark for two different manuscripts.

Fewer of the Barrington Collection required rebinding but such as did have been re-bound on the same scale as manuscripts in the Petyt Collection. On the question of missing manuscripts, however, the position is more complicated. As has already been stated, the volumes in the Barrington Collection bear an original enumeration which runs from 1 to 85. The possible no. 79 has also been indicated. There are, therefore, some 24 volumes which appear to be missing, as the number given in the 1833 Catalogue is 81; the number at present in the Barrington Collection is 57 volumes. It has also been suggested that most of the volumes missing in the Barrington Collection are probably Law Commonplace Books and where some of these may now be found has been indicated. It is difficult on the present information available to go further than this. It is unlikely that there was any miscount in the number of volumes which arrived at the Library. It also seems unlikely that it is possible that any of these were destroyed in the fires of 1940–1. The Barrington Collection was removed to a place of safety, with the Petyt Collection, before the fires took place. So the matter must remain a mystery.

The Records of the Inner Temple, thirty-nine volumes, have never been re-bound. They were not composed until the middle of the nineteenth century. The placing of the individual documents on guards had been carefully done and not one item seems to have escaped. The binding is serviceable and will remain adequate for many years to come. They, too, were removed during the war with the Petyt and Barrington Collections. So there has been no loss. This is, however, a group which could be conveniently extended by adding similar loose documents which have come to light since their original composition.

The Mitford Collection of Legal Manuscripts are all in their original binding, and as none of them are earlier than the last decade of the eighteenth century, when they arrived in the Inner Temple Library in 1957 they were in almost as good a condition as when bound, and the text as when they were written. Though there had been losses, as has been pointed out above, since they were in Lord Redesdale's Library, little can now be done towards recovery. The seventy-nine volumes received are intact. It is, of course, possible that the missing volumes may yet turn up in some strange place, perhaps in Gloucestershire.

As far as the Miscellaneous Manuscripts are concerned, as they had been acquired, often as individual items, over two centuries and more, their bindings vary greatly in quality and condition. Some of the larger groups within Miscellaneous Manuscripts have been strongly bound since they came in, the six volumes of Rolle's

Abridgment, the 8 volumes of Wetherell Manuscripts, and the seven volumes of *Reports*, Durnford and East, for example. Many had been re-bound before they were presented, and of the volumes presented by Alfred J. Ellison the binding is often as interesting as the content. De Synedriis Britannicis has been re-bound in red morocco, doubtless because it was taken to be a work by William Petyt. The two volumes of Library Catalogues have been re-bound but not so sumptuously. The binding of the much re-bound Old Grace Book merely required slight repair. The original 12th and 13th Reports of Sir Edward Coke have been reverently placed in a wooden box with a leather label. The original letters to the Treasurer and Benchers, 1570–1679, have been bound in red morocco, as has the volume containing the transcripts of them. The illuminated Fitzherbert Abridgment is in the white vellum cover in which it was received. The Pension Book of Clement's Inn has been re-bound in dark blue morocco and placed in a cloth case. The transcript of the Black Book of the Admiralty has its original Doctors' Commons binding but the spine has been repaired. The Bracton De Legibus Angliae has been bound in brown morocco; the Barrington Manuscript on the Statute of Pluralities, 21 Henry VIII, in the same. The binding and rebinding, in fact, seem to have been determined, in part, by the status of the author and the importance of the content of the manuscript, but throughout, the work has been done with care and consideration, and at considerable cost. Ownership has been maintained by stamping the front or both covers with the Inner Temple coat of arms.

But repair work is still required on the bindings of a number of manuscripts. Strangely only one of the many manuscripts given by Francis Maseres has been re-bound appropriately, the volume of Leases under the Great Seal, Elizabeth I to James I, in red morocco. Several of his other manuscripts require repair and attention. A few other manuscripts also require repair and rebinding. The volume containing three Tottell tracts 1576, 1583, is without a cover. Apart from the Stuart Moore manuscripts only two other volumes show deterioration through damp. These are the manuscripts from the Treasurer's Strong Room, the List of Admissions etc., 1520–1684, and Reports, Acts of Parliament, and Bench Orders, 1667–1800. The bindings of both also require attention. Of the last considerable gift of manuscripts, the papers of Stuart A. Moore and Hubert Stuart Moore have been in the Library less than fifteen years. Many of the volumes and papers had been seriously damaged by damp, before they were received, so much so that some require treatment and may require decontamination. Almost all the twenty-four volumes require a certain amount of cleaning, and almost all require binding or placing in appropriate boxes.

Of equal interest and importance with the Miscellaneous Manuscripts are the manuscripts which should have been in that group, which either never reached it, or which having reached it have been dispersed or lost. A list has been compiled of manuscripts which should appear among the Miscellaneous Manuscripts. They fall into two different categories, manuscripts of which there is evidence of the gift to the Library or Inn, and books which are recorded in catalogues to be interleaved or to possess many manuscript notes and annotations. The latter include some from the bequests of William Petyt and Sir Martin Wright. The twenty-nine out of the thirty such volumes given by Mrs. John Austin have already been mentioned. Others are so recorded in the 1833 and 1843 Catalogues, including works by Francis Maseres and Alexander Luders.

In the 1833 Catalogue is the following entry among the 'Manuscripts Purchased': 'Curious Petitions bought at Southgate's Sale, May 1830'. There is no manuscript among the Miscellaneous Manuscripts which can possibly fit this description. It must have been lost, for it cannot be in any other group of manuscripts.

Next as to the manuscripts which are recorded as having been given to the Library or Inn. It has already been stated that the Bench commissioned Serjeant James Manning to transcribe and translate for publication the Year Book 10–17 Edward III, and that he presented an index to the same which is now amongst the Miscellaneous Manuscripts. There can be no doubt that he placed his transcript of the text and his translation in the Library. Indeed it was the property of the Inn. When the original manuscript of the Year Book was lent to the Master of the Rolls to enable L. Owen Pike to edit it for the Rolls Series these volumes of text and translation were also lent to him. On 10 October 1893 he returned to J. C. L. Pickering, the Librarian, the seven volumes of transcripts and translations of the Year Book 'so kindly lent to me by the Benchers of the Inner Temple . . . some of the side notes made by Serjeant Manning in the earlier volumes were of considerable use to me in preparing one of my indexes and I am greatly obliged for the loan.' These volumes have not been seen to be catalogued.

A manuscript entitled 'Three Sermons by Dr. Winiffe' appears in the manuscript catalogue of 1776, but is not in any later catalogue. The presumption is that it had disappeared before 1833 so it must be given up as lost. These sermons must have been written by William Winniffe, who became Bishop of Lincoln in 1642; they do not seem to have been printed. They appear to have been the kind of work which may have come from Mrs. Anne Sadleir. In 1871 the Hon. G. Pepys presented a volume of Cases, House of Lords; in 1874 A. Raynyard presented a volume of Cases, 1739. Neither has been seen. G. Pepys was a son of the first Earl of Cottenham who became Master of the Rolls in 1834 and was Lord Chancellor, 1836–41 and 1846–50. In 1857 the Bench Table Orders records the loan of a manuscript entitled 'Father Smith and his Organs' to the then Organist of the Temple Church. It could never have been returned. It would have been interesting to see an account of the work of Bernard Smith, the renowned organ builder, who built organs for Westminster Abbey and St. Paul's Cathedral, for Durham Cathedral and the Bishop's Chapel at Auckland Castle, and for the Sheldonian Theatre, Oxford, and the Temple Church, London.

Dr. Edward J. Hopkins, the Organist, was given permission to copy the manuscript and contributed learned papers on early church organs in the *Archaeological Journal* and some of his papers have very recently been given to the Inner Temple Library by a descendant. A programme or pamphlet by him was issued at the performance on 24 June 1858 in celebration of the bicentenary of the completion of this organ, which contains a succinct account of the history of that organ over two centuries. Further material by Dr. Hopkins appears in Grove's, *Dictionary of Music*.

There are also a number of single items which should be among the Miscellaneous Manuscripts. For instance, in 1934, Lord Hanworth, Treasurer, 1936, presented a receipt to the Inner Temple by his grandfather, Sir Frederick Pollock, Chief Baron of the Exchequer, dated 1836, for a fine of £50 paid by him to the Inn for not serving the office of Reader. Sir Frederick was Treasurer in 1837. In 1936 another grandson, Sir John Pollock, bart., presented the grant of an annuity to Lord Chief Baron Pollock dated 1866. In 1932 Lord Hanworth had presented a Commission of Bankruptcy under the Great Seal and signed by Lord Thurlow. These could have been lost in the fires of 1940–1. In 1935 Sir Frank MacKinnon presented a field postcard sent to him during the 1914–18 war by Master Greene. This could have been lost in the 1939–45 war. In 1897 Mr. Wentworth Sturges had presented a deed dated 20 April 1703, which provided for payment of rent 'at the font stone in the Temple Church'. This is no longer available.

After the destruction of the Temple in the 1939–45 war Sir Frank MacKinnon produced an elaborate memorandum on The Ravages of the War in the Inner Temple. While it was true that much of the material contained in this memorandum is printed in his *Inner Temple Papers* in the article on The Ravages of War 1939–45, and part in his article in the *Law Quarterly Review* in 1942, it would have been interesting to have seen the whole story. This cannot now be produced. In 1962 Viscountess Simonds presented an Album of Legal Cartoons. The fires of 1940–1 cannot be blamed for the absence of this.

Next, as to the printed books containing a mass of manuscript notes and annotations and corrections. Many of these additions and annotations were made by lawyers of the greatest distinction, others by their authors, whose corrections were as important as their notes and annotations. Among the books presented by his executrixes the Catalogue of Books of Sir Martin Wright contained the two following entries:

Doctrina Placitandi, interleaved with manuscript notes.

Finch, H, Law or Discourse thereof, written in French, done into English by the author, 1627, two volumes, interleaved with manuscript notes.

The former work by Serjeant Sampson Euer was a work of great importance and any manuscript notes on it would have been valuable, especially if written by Sir Martin Wright. The latter by Sir Heneage Finch, Serjeant at Law, Recorder of London, called to the Bench of the Inner Temple in 1621, Speaker of the House of Commons and father of Heneage Finch, first Earl of Nottingham, has been described as 'till the publication of Blackstone's Commentaries the best elementary book to be placed in the hands of students'. Again, the manuscript notes, especially if by Sir Martin Wright, would have been invaluable. There is now no trace of either work.

The Catalogues of 1806, 1833, and 1834, which contain the former but not the latter books, add to the list of important books interleaved and with manuscript notes. These include the following entries:

Law, Directions for the Study of, W.P., 1662.
Law Commonplaced, with MS. notes, 1583.
Finch's Law, French, 1613.
City Law, with MS. notes, 1647.

William Phillips' *Directions for the Study of Law* calls for no special comment. Heneage Finch's *Description del Common Leys D'Angleterre* was a forerunner of his *Law or Discourse thereof. Law Commonplaced* is taken to be Arthur Gregory's *De Legibus Angliae Municipalibus Liber, Ordine locorum communium depositus*, 1583. In that case it was derived from William Petyt's bequest and is duly catalogued as such among the Miscellaneous Manuscripts. *City Law, or Course and Practice in Judicial Proceedings in the Hustings in Guildhall London* 'had been Englished out of an ancient French manuscript'. It also contained a list of the offices disposed of by the Lord Mayor of London and concerned the customs and franchises of the city and the proceedings of its courts. The subjects fall within William Petyt's special interests and its disappearance is a real loss, as is that of the other volumes.

Style's *Reports*, with manuscript notes, was presented by S. L. Wilkinson in 1843. Though the Library possesses a copy of this work it is not annotated and is among the books bequeathed by William Petyt. The annotated copy has disappeared. In 1866 Dr. Stephen Lushington, a Bencher, presented his judgement in the well-known Banda and Kirwee Booty Case. Though among the Miscellaneous Manuscripts there is a volume on this case it is not this one. It consists of the Papers presented to Parliament concerning the case and was presented by R. S. Rothery, the Admiralty Registrar, in 1867. Dr Lushington's judgement with notes by him would have been a valuable volume, as he was a civilian of eminence who was Judge of the Consistory Court of London as well as of the High Court of Admiralty and Dean of the Arches, 1858–1867. To these must be added some score of volumes of the works of Francis Maseres, an inveterate annotator, four volumes of the works of Alexander Luders, and some more of the works bequeathed by William Petyt. For both Petyt and Luders also had a habit of writing notes and additions in their books.

There can be no doubt that many of these missing manuscripts and annotated printed books were destroyed in the fires of 1940–1, when about half of the original content of the Library was destroyed, despite a large evacuation of manuscripts and books, carefully organized fire precautions, and long and devoted preservation service by members and staff of the Inn. Some which were not destroyed were so badly damaged that it has not been possible to list them without extensive and expensive repairs. These include the four volumes of extracts from the Parliament Act Books and the Bench Table Act Books which in the last printed Catalogue of the Library were noted as T.O., meaning that they had been taken to the Treasurer's Office for conference and consultation. Unfortunately they were not returned to the Library. But all those now missing cannot be condemned to the fire. There were occasionally before the fires, and very occasionally since, minor lapses on gifts which had been made. The volumes which have been mentioned do not comprise all the gifts made to the Library or the Inn. References have been seen to only one Book of Benefactors and that covered but a comparatively short period and has been lost for many years. The Bench Table Orders on votes of thanks cannot be regarded as a complete record of all the gifts made, and in any case after 1895 the gifts, unless made by Benchers, were not recorded in the Bench Table Order Books. The Bench Table Order ran that thanks were given to benefactors 'as entered in the Register under this date'; in other words the Sub-Treasurer wrote the letters of thanks on a list supplied by the Librarian. These Registers, too, perished in 1940–1, so for nearly half a century, unless the benefactor was a Bencher, no record remains. There may be manuscripts missing or mislaid. Yet despite the dangers of weather and war, of damp and disturbance, on the whole the physical condition of the manuscripts is excellent. None have been worn by searchers nor show any signs of mishandling.

The greatest loss which the Library of the Inner Temple ever sustained, or can sustain, was the failure of the Bench to accept the manuscripts and printed books of John Selden in 1654. In due course, some of these manuscripts and printed books reached the Bodleian Library, Oxford, and later still, a few manuscripts reached the Library of Lincoln's Inn, through Sir Matthew Hale. The lists of these Libraries, however, give but little indication of the grandeur of Selden's Library. For five chests of his manuscripts perished by fire before they were removed from his residence. This would not have occurred had the Inner Temple accepted the benefaction and its conditions. Selden's residence was in Whitefriars and not more than a stone's throw from his chambers in what are now called Paper Buildings and the Library of his Inn.

There is, however, little doubt that a comprehensive list of benefactions to the Library since the beginning of the eighteenth century to the present day could be compiled. It might not be possible to make this a complete record, but it could be added to as information came along or was discovered. Taking this as a temporary basis the Book of Benefactors could be kept for the future, which would augment the dignity of the Library, increase its efficiency, and be a slight tribute of gratitude for the generosity of its members and friends.

18. CONCLUSION: THE INNER TEMPLE

The records of the Inner Temple span over four hundred and sixty years; the manuscripts in the Inner Temple Library cover from the late twelfth century to the middle of the twentieth century, over three hundred years longer. Yet there is a close relationship between the records and the manuscripts. The records all concern the domestic history of the Inn; most of the manuscripts reflect the interests and generosity of the members. The perusal of the records and manuscripts suggests a number of firm conclusions. Firstly, the Inn was a very closely knit corporation. Secondly, the legal profession and the Inns of Court tended to run in families, sometimes for centuries or often for several generations. Thirdly, apart from their knowledge of law and of legal literature, the members had a wide variety of interest or hobbies, which made the Bench Table particularly almost as diverse a fellowship as the senior common-room of an Oxford or Cambridge College, from which Universities so many of the members have always come. Fourthly, in response to their individual specialized knowledge of the law and to their special interests, members presented to the Library of their Inn copies of their works and of the material which had gone towards the composition of those works. Lastly, the most valuable benefactions to the Library were made by gift or bequest of members of the Inn, especially by Treasurers and Benchers. It is now proposed to particularize on these five points.

First, the closeness of the corporation of the Inner Temple can be emphasized by a number of examples. In the earlier days this was evidenced by the insistence on precedence and privilege. This was expressed mainly by the question of precedence against the Middle Temple, as, for example, on the question of the position of members of the Inn in the processions on the making of Serjeants. Except as against each other there would be a united front on the part of both Inns on privilege against all other bodies. This would have been especially so against the Lord Mayor, Aldermen, and city of London. This was a problem which did not affect Lincoln's Inn or Gray's Inn, as both were sufficiently far removed from the boundaries of the city to prevent any claims by London. Incidents concerning the bearing erect of the city sword within the precinct of the Temple were equally resisted by both the Inner and the Middle Temple. On other privileges which were challenged by other civil authorities the four Inns of Court almost invariably consulted and acted together. All had user on their side, but on the whole the legal position of the Inner Temple and the Middle Temple, as the inheritors of some, at least, of the privileges of the Knights Templar and the Knights Hospitaller, seemed to be the better founded. As against the crown the position was more difficult. Until the grant of James I in 1608 the title of the Inner Temple and the Middle Temple seemed to be a little precarious. Thereafter it was very much more certain. That grant was purchased by the present of very expensive plate but it was worth it. But the crown was still the fount of all honour and almost every judicial post throughout the realm was filled by its appointment. Not only were the judges so appointed but also all King's or Queen's Counsel and Serjeants at Law.

This could be a strength as well as a weakness, for all persons in positions of legal power or influence were members, or had been members, of one or other of the four Inns of Court. They were entrenched where they could protect the interests of their former colleagues and their profession, and in inter-Inn disputes could perhaps tilt the balance slightly in favour of a particular Society, witness the lobbying and intrigue when the Middle Temple tried to filch one of the Inns of Chancery belonging to the Inner Temple in 1561. The final arbiter was to be Sir Nicholas Bacon, who was of Gray's Inn, as Lord Keeper. The Middle Temple was relying upon the influence of Sir Robert Catlin, Chief Justice of England, and Sir James Dyer, Chief Justice of Common Pleas, their former colleagues. The Inner Temple 'did by our common assent make our humble suit to the Right Honourable the Lord Robert Dudley, Knight of the most noble Order of the Garter and Master of the Queen's Majesty's Horse, as our chief refuge, to be a means to the Queen's Highness', though they did not ignore the fact that the 'Lord Keeper, who hath been of the company and fellowship of Grays Inn, which have been of ancient amity, familiarity and friendship with this our House'. It is hardly necessary to add that the Inner Temple retained their Inn of Chancery.

For there was also a subtle form of flattery, if not bribery, which an Inn could offer, by making the heirs or entourage of the sovereign and notables with great influence at court members or Benchers of the Inn. Robert Dudley, Earl of Leicester, was no doubt flattered by the deference which the Inner Temple always showed him. His ancestors had been members. His father, John Dudley, Duke of Northumberland, had been a member. In 1562 there was a special admission to the Inner Temple, which included Lord Robert Dudley, his elder brother Lord Ambrose Dudley, afterwards Earl of Warwick, Henry, Lord Hunsdon, a first cousin of the Queen, and William, Lord Howard of Effingham, Lord High Admiral. There was another mass special admission in 1605, which included Thomas Howard, Earl of Arundel, Henry de Vere, Earl of Oxford, Robert Devereux, Earl of Essex, Henry Howard, Earl of Northampton, Thomas West, Lord Delawarr, Richard Vaughan, Bishop of London, Sir Robert Rich, knight, and even one of the Prince's Bedchamber, an attendant upon the Prince and a Gentleman of the Prince's Horse.

In 1588 there had been a special admission of Robert Devereux, Earl of Essex, K.G. and Master of the Horse; in 1622 of George Villiers, Marquis of Buckingham. The Inner Temple was following the favourite. In 1632, Francis, Lord Cottington, afterwards Lord Treasurer, was specially admitted. The long lists of members and Benchers specially admitted on a number of occasions after the Restoration certainly bought friends at Court. For instance, in 1661, Charles, Duke of Richmond, was specially admitted. The same year James, Duke of York, the Duke of Buckingham, the Earl of Dorset, and Sir William Morice, Secretary of State, were specially admitted, the heir apparent being also admitted to bar and bench. This cost little but was very rewarding. William Stanhope, Lord Harrington, was invited to the Bench in 1734, when Secretary of State.

Doubtless there was a financial loss in the facilities which the Inner Temple offered to certain legal departments in premises within the precincts. The Alienation Office was established within the Inner Temple. King's Bench Walk and Crown Office Row are suggestive. Several other offices were within the precincts also, the Office of the Prothonotary of Common Pleas, of the Prothonotary of the Marshal's Court, the Fines Office, the Offices of the Filacers. Also, having these offices in the Inn was a convenience to members which easily outweighed any financial loss to the Inn.

There are many instances of the Bench showing justifiable pride in the achievements of its members, past and present. The tercentenary of the death of Sir Edward Coke was commemorated by a ceremonial dinner in the Inner Temple Hall on 17 December 1934, attended by some of his descendants. Though John Selden was buried in the Temple Church, when it was proposed that a monument to his memory should be placed in West Tarring Church in the county of Sussex, it was ordered on 25 May 1880 that a sum not exceeding £20 should be applied for that purpose.

On 23 November 1939 a Committee was appointed to consider the most appropriate mode of commemorating the unique position of the Inner Temple with reference to high judicial office held by the members during the Treasurership of Lord Roche in 1939. The commemoration Committee reported on 24 January 1940 that Lord Roche, Treasurer, H.M. King George VI, the Lord Chancellor (Viscount Caldecote), the Lord Chief Justice (Lord Hewart), the Master of the Rolls (Sir Wilfred Greene), the President of the Probate, Divorce, and Admiralty Division (Sir Boyd Merriman), the Chancellor of the Exchequer (Sir John Simon), the Chief Justice of India (Sir Maurice Gwyer), the Attorney General (Sir Donald Somervell), and the Solicitor General (Sir Terence O'Connor) were Benchers of the Inner Temple, and of the other forty-two English lawyers at that time in the House of Lords, the Court of Appeal, and the High Court of Justice, twenty-one were Benchers of the Society. It might be interesting to compare this list with the formidable list of twenty-eight Benchers which appeared in 1678 in the Bill against the Middle Temple on the bounds and jurisdiction of the Inns. The Bill was addressed to Heneage Finch, Lord Finch, Lord Chancellor, who had been Treasurer of the Inner Temple, 1661–72, longer than any other Treasurer had held the office. The twenty-eight Benchers included Sir George Jeffreys, afterwards Lord Chancellor, Sir Thomas Foster, afterwards Chief Justice of King's Bench, Sir John Trevor, afterwards Speaker of the House of Commons and Master of the Rolls, Sir Robert Sawyer, afterwards Attorney General, Christopher Milton, afterwards a Baron of the Exchequer and a Justice of Common Pleas, and five who afterwards became Serjeants at Law.

On 19 June 1936 the attention of the Bench was called to the pictures of Lord Chancellor Talbot and Sir Thomas Littleton (ancestors of the Treasurer) appearing on the menus of Grand Day in the Treasurership of Master Talbot and the suggestion was made that some permanent means should be made in memory of this unique incident. The result was the setting up of the inscription. The then Treasurer was Sir George Talbot, Justice of King's Bench. The inscription set up in the Parliament Chamber recorded that he was on his father's side 6th in descent from Charles, Lord Talbot, Lord Chancellor, 1733–7, and Treasurer, 1727; and on his mother's side 13th in descent from Sir Thomas Littleton; and that he was also, on his mother's side, 9th in descent from Sir Thomas Bromley, Lord Chancellor, 1579–87, and Treasurer, 1574.

On 22 January 1897 the Treasurer was empowered 'to receive for the Hall if he can portraits of the Lord Chancellor (Lord Halsbury) and the Speaker of the House of Commons (J. W. Gully) and to expend therefor a sum not exceeding £700 in order that the House may commemorate the fact that both Houses of Parliament are presided over by members of the Inn in the year 1897'. The portraits were duly commissioned and delivered to be hung up in the Hall.

Secondly, on Inner Temple families, something has already been said about the families of Hele, Coke, Wilde, Hampden, and Sackville, but compared with others their close associations with the Inn were short-lived. Families of equal distinction had associations with the Inn which extended over centuries. The examples which will be briefly considered at present will be the families of Littleton, Croke, and Finch, in that order of the first known date when a member joined the Inn. There are other families equally distinguished who could have been taken, for example, the Hares and the Coventrys, perhaps the Caesars, and in later times the Pollocks and the Thesigers.

As is well known, the first name which can be identified as belonging to the Inner Temple was Sir Thomas Littleton. His is the first Reader's shield; his name appears first in the accredited list of members which has been compiled. The second name on that list is that of John Paston, of the Paston letters, who appears as a student in 1443. In his long litigation on the doubtful will of Sir John Fastolf his counsel was Humphrey Starkey, a member of the Inn who became a Serjeant at Law in 1478 and was Chief Baron of the Exchequer, 1483–6. The Paston name disappears from the records of the Inn but the family connection was long continued, for Sir Edward Coke's first wife was Bridget Paston. On his known dates (he was Sheriff of Worcestershire in 1447, Serjeant at Law, 1453, and a Judge, 1466), it is not unreasonable to suppose that Sir Thomas Littleton joined the Inn in the third decade of the fifteenth century, or slightly before, and was Reader before 1448. After Sir Thomas Littleton the next Littleton who appears in the records of the Inn was Richard Littleton, who was Lent Reader in 1493 and was appointed Governor in 1505. He was probably a grandson of the Judge. Edward Littleton was admitted in 1518 and was 'assigned the chamber where his father lay', and Richard Littleton, his son and heir apparent was admitted in 1533. George Littleton, of Grovely, co. Worcester, the son of Roger Littleton, was admitted in 1575 and called to the bar on the recommendation of Sir Thomas Bromley, Lord Chancellor in 1583, 'his sufficiency for that place being testified by the greater part of the Bench and bar'. He became a Serjeant at Law. Edward Littleton, of Munslow, co. Salop, was admitted in 1576 and was called in 1584. John Littleton, of Frankley, co. Worcester, was specially admitted, 1580, at the instance of Sir Thomas Bromley, Lord Chancellor. Thomas Littleton was specially admitted, at the instance of the Reader, in 1598. Thus before 1600 at least seven Littletons had been admitted to the Inner Temple.

To return to Edward Littleton of Munslow. He was the second son of the Revd. John Littleton, rector of that parish. He became Chief Justice of North Wales in 1621. His son and heir apparent, Edward Littleton, described as of Henley, co. Salop, was admitted in 1609, and in 1617 'in respect of the sufficiency and good deserts as well of Edward Littleton himself as of his father and other his friends' was called to the bar. He was called to the Bench in 1629 and was Treasurer, 1634–8. He became Recorder of London in 1631, Solicitor General in 1634, Chief Justice of Common Pleas in 1640, and in 1641 he became Lord Keeper and was created Baron Littleton of Munslow. On 26 May 1639 there was a special admission of 'James Littleton D.C.L., Chancellor of Worcester and Master of the High Court of Chancery, brother of Sir Edward Littleton, and he is also called to be an associate of the bar, and shall take place and sit uppermost at the ancient bar table'. On 30 June 1639 he was called to the Bench 'and he shall have place and voice there with all other privileges as an absolute Bencher notwithstanding the Act of 7 June 5 James I'. On 22 May 1642 'upon the request of Edward, Lord Littleton, Lord Keeper of the Great Seal of England, . . . Thomas Littleton, fellow of this House, who has married the daughter and heir apparent of the said Lord Keeper, is called to the bar'. This was Thomas Littleton of Stoke Milborough, co. Salop, son and heir of Sir Adam Littleton, bart., who had married his cousin, Anne, and who was admitted in 1637. On 27 May 1661 there was a special admission of 'Thomas Littleton, grandson and heir to Sir Edward Littleton, late Lord Keeper, at the request of his father, Sir Thomas Littleton'.

Meanwhile William Littleton, of Henley, co. Salop, second son of Edward Littleton, of Munslow, had been admitted in 1612. He was called to the bar in 1620 and to the Bench in 1638. His brother Timothy, the seventh son, was admitted in 1626, called to the bar in 1635, and to the Bench in 1640, 'having obtained the King's writ to receive the degree of Serjeant at Law . . . that he may take his place this night at supper'. He became a Baron of the Exchequer in 1670. He and his widow were buried in the Temple Church. Thomas Littleton, eldest son of John Littleton, was admitted in 1612, his brother John in 1616, at the request of Edward Bromley, Baron of the Exchequer. William Littleton, of Naunton Beauchamp, co. Worcester, son of Francis

Littleton, was admitted in 1604, called to the bar in 1620, and to the Bench in 1638. A Fisher Littleton was admitted in 1620, and a James Littleton in 1639. A Philip Littleton appears as Auditor of the Steward's Account in 1663. Walter Littleton, of Sandon, co. Stafford, eldest son of Sir Walter Littleton, was admitted in 1657. He was called in 1663 and became a Master in Chancery. Thereafter there does not appear to have been an active Littleton practising law until the last quarter of the nineteenth century.

Besides these twelve Littletons who were admitted between 1600 and 1657, another member of the family during this period became Master of the Temple. He was John Littleton, D.D., who was appointed in 1639. Though members of his family remained in the Inner Temple during the Civil War and Commonwealth he was superseded in 1646 by a Master more conformable, but when he died in 1658 he was buried in the Temple Church.

There remains Sir Thomas Littleton who succeeded his father as 3rd baronet in 1681. He was admitted in 1671. He was Speaker of the House of Commons, 1698–1700, and Treasurer of the Navy, 1701–10. He was the first distinguished member of a very distinguished legal family, who became prominent as a politician rather than as a lawyer or churchman. Although many of his predecessors had been members of the House of Commons, none had distinguished themselves in politics. He set a new trend in the family in the Houses of Parliament, both in the House of Commons and the House of Lords.

In the eighteenth-century records of the Inn there is only one Bench Table Order and there is no Act of Parliament which relates to the Littletons. On 5 June 1758 it was ordered that Lord Lyttleton could appoint any painter who was at liberty, to take a copy of the picture of Judge Littleton. The devotion of the Inn and the family to the memory of Sir Thomas Littleton and his Tenures remained. A signal expression of the Inn's regard was made in October 1633, when the family was at, or about to reach, the height of its power and position. Sir Thomas Littleton, bart., had enquired of the Bench what fine he had to pay on admittance to certain chambers.

> It was thereupon, by the whole company of the Bench now present, without voice, granted and desired that the said admittance should be freely, without any fine, and that it might be accepted and expressed as a testimony of that great respect the whole Society doth owe to the name and family of Littleton and therefore not to be drawn into example or precedent for the future.

In 1878 the Hon. Alfred Lyttleton, the eighth son of the 4th Baron Lyttleton, was admitted to the Inner Temple. He was called to the bar in 1881, became a Bencher in 1899, and a Q.C. in 1900. After he had been appointed Recorder of Hereford in 1890 and of Oxford in 1894 he entered the House of Commons in 1895. He was Secretary of the Colonies, 1903–5, but died in 1913. Since his time other members of the family have been admitted to the Inner Temple and are still members of the Inn.

With the twenty-one admissions of the Littletons before 1900 may be compared the thirty-three admissions before 1800 of members of the Croke family. Though the Crokes could not claim a Lord Keeper, they produced a number of very distinguished Judges, law reporters, and writers of miscellaneous works. As with the Littletons there is a long hiatus in their membership of the Inn, extending from about the same time in the late seventeenth century to somewhat earlier, indeed a century earlier, in the late eighteenth century.

The first Croke who appears in the records of the Inner Temple is John Croke, who was admitted in 1515. Between 1515 and 1655 no less than 25 of his descendants had been admitted to the Society. He himself became a Serjeant at Law and a Master in Chancery and wrote Ordinances upon Estate of the Chancery Court. He died in 1554; his son John had been admitted in 1547. John Croke, who was knighted in 1575, does not seem to have practised. He died in 1608. His son, John Croke the younger, had been admitted in 1570, became a Bencher in 1592, and Treasurer in 1597–8, having been made Recorder of London in 1595. He was Speaker in 1601, became a Serjeant at Law in 1603, and a Justice of King's Bench in 1607. His two brothers George and Henry were admitted in 1573 and a younger brother Paul Ambrose in 1581. Both Henry and George were called to the bar in 1584; Paul Ambrose in 1590. Henry's son Henry was admitted, after his father's death, at the request of his uncle George. George had been made a Bencher in 1597, was Treasurer in 1609–1610 (as Treasurer his name is inscribed on an Inner Temple chalice dated 1610), became a Serjeant at Law in 1623, Justice of Common Pleas in 1625, and a Justice of King's Bench in 1628. He was the first reporter in the family and his *Reports of Cases in King's Bench and Common Pleas, 1582–1641*, were first published 1658–61. Paul Ambrose Croke had been called to the Bench in 1605.

John Croke, the eldest son of Sir John Croke, the Judge, was admitted in 1607, Henry, his second son in 1607, Charles Croke, his third son, in 1610, Edward, his fifth son, in 1618, as was his fourth son, Unton, the same year. When Henry was called to the bar in 1617 he was already a knight and Master of the Pipe Office. He became an associate of the Bench in 1638. Unton was called to the bar in 1616 and to the Bench in 1635. He was Lent Reader in 1639 and became a Serjeant at Law in 1654. His son Unton was admitted in 1647 and called to the bar in 1653; his sons Charles and George were admitted in 1653; and his son John in 1654.

So the roll continues, with Henry Croke, son of Henry Croke and grandson of Sir John, the Judge, being admitted, at the request of George Croke, Treasurer, his uncle, in 1610; Francis Croke in 1621; Robert, the son and heir of Sir Henry Croke, admitted in 1627 and called to the bar in 1635; and Robert, his grandson, admitted in 1655. Thomas, the son of Sir George Croke was admitted in 1627 and called to the bar in 1635. His cousin, Daniel Croke, the son of Paul Ambrose Croke was admitted in 1629. His cousin John Croke, described as son of Sir John and grandson of Sir

John, was admitted in 1634. Richard Croke, son and heir apparent of Unton Croke, a Bencher, was admitted in 1636. Thomas Croke, eldest son and heir of Sir George Croke, the Judge, was admitted in 1627 and called to the bar in 1635. Richard Croke, son and heir of Alexander Croke, was admitted in 1636 at the request of Justice Croke, his uncle. John Croke, a younger son of Unton Croke, the Bencher, was admitted in 1654 and called to the bar in 1662. Robert Croke, described as Clerk of the Pipe, was admitted in 1655 and called to the bar in 1661.

This completes the admissions of Crokes to 1655. Of the twenty-five admissions seven became Benchers and two were Treasurers. Three became Serjeants at Law, two Judges, and one a Master in Chancery. But the story does not end there. During the Civil Wars, the descendants of that first John Croke were divided in their allegiance. Sir Robert Croke, Clerk of the Pipe, sat in the Parliament at Oxford and had to compound for his estates; John Croke, son and heir of Sir John Croke and grandson of Sir John Croke, the Judge, raised a troop of horse at his own cost but at such a charge that he had to sell his estates later. Unton Croke, son of Unton Croke, Serjeant at Law, was a very successful Colonel in the Parliamentary army and was awarded £200 a year by Cromwell for his services; his brother Charles Croke left Oxford to accompany his cousin Bulstrode Whitelocke on his embassy to Sweden in 1653–4 and held a commission in his brother's troop. Their father was a Commissioner for Treason Trials in 1656. The Croke family was intimately connected with the heads of the Parliamentary party 'the Lord Commissioner Whitlocke, Ingoldsby, St. John, Hampden, Waller the poet, Mayne, Grimstone, Sir Hardres Waller, and even the Protector were related by blood or affinity'.

After 1655 the family was not as prolific in members of the Inner Temple. Richard Croke, Unton Croke's eldest son who had been called to the Bench in 1662, was Reader in 1670. Of others mentioned above Robert Croke was called to the bar in 1661, John Croke in 1663, and George Croke in 1665. Between 1660 and 1681 there were seven further Croke admissions: Henry, son of Sir Robert Croke, in 1660; Richard, eldest son of Richard Croke, Bencher, in 1661; Unton Croke, at the request of Unton Croke, Serjeant at Law, his grandfather, in 1669; Wright, son of Richard Croke, and Charles, his brother, in 1672; Sir George Croke, 1673; and Richard, eldests on of George Croke, 'an utter barrister, brother of Serjeant Croke, at the request of the Serjeant', in 1681. Wright Croke was called to the bar in 1679; Charles Croke in 1682.

Thereafter there is silence until 1776 when Alexander Croke was admitted; he was called in 1786, and became a member of the College of Advocates in 1797. He was called to the Bench in 1823 and was Treasurer in 1830. He had been knighted in 1816 for his services as Judge in the Vice Admiralty Court of Nova Scotia, 1801–15. His law publications include *Argument in the High Court of Admiralty, Nov. 27, 1799, in the case of the Hendrick and Maria*, 1800; *Report of the Case of Horner against*

Liddiard . . . with an essay upon the laws relating to Illegitimate Children, also 1800; and *Remarks on Mr. Schlegel's 'Vindication of Neutrals under Convoy'*, 1801. This last was a defence of the High Court of Admiralty against Schlegel's virulent attacks. *Reports of Cases argued and determined in the Court of Vice Admiralty at Halifax in Nova Scotia 1802–1813, in the time of Alexander Croke*, was published in 1814, edited by James Stewart. His legal works, however, were small compared with his other publications. His *History of the Croke Family*, 2 volumes, 1823, was a massive quarto, containing 1,686 pages besides numerous plates and tables. It contains a worthy history of the Croke family, though marred by an effort to identify the Crokes 'originally named Le Blount'. Among his other works were *On Rhyming Latin Verse*; 1828, *Case of Otmoor*, 1831; *Patriot Queen*, 1838; and *Poems*, 2 volumes, 1841, a sufficiently wide variety of subjects. He was not the last Croke to be admitted. His son, Alexander, was admitted in 1816, while an undergraduate at Oxford, but he died in 1818.

Sir Heneage Finch has already been met as the author of two law textbooks. He is the first Finch to be found in the Bench Table Order Books or the Acts of Parliament Books, but by no means the first Finch to be admitted to the Inner Temple. A Richard Finch, of Faversham, had been admitted in 1556; an Anthony Finch, of Lewes, in 1584. Thomas Finch, of Eastwell, Kent, the second son of Sir Moyle Finch, bart., was admitted in 1596. His two brothers, John Finch and Heneage Finch, respectively the 3rd and 4th sons of Moyle Finch, were both admitted in 1598 and both were called to the bar in 1606. Their eldest brother succeeded his father as 3rd baronet and his mother in the Earldom of Winchilsea. Heneage Finch was Summer Vacation Reader in 1622, having been called to the Bench in 1621. He had been Recorder of London since 1620, became a Serjeant at Law in 1623, and was Speaker of the House of Commons in 1626. Another brother, Francis Finch, Moyle Finch's 6th son, was admitted in 1605 and was called to the bar in 1614, and to be an associate of the Bench 'saving the antiquity of such as be his ancients' in 1628. Robert Finch, a younger son of Sir Thomas Finch, was admitted in 1613. John Finch, of Rushock, Worcester, the son and heir of Francis Finch, was admitted in 1641, and Windsor Finch, of the same place, in 1659; he was called to the bar in 1682. It does not seem that John Finch of London, admitted in 1632, and John Finch, described as of The Queen's College, Oxford, belonged to the same family.

Three of the sons of Sir Heneage Finch were admitted to the Inn: Heneage Finch, his son and heir, in 1639, and Francis and John, his second and third sons, in 1643. Francis was called to the bar in 1650; John became a physician and a diplomatist, was knighted, and was Ambassador at Constantinople, 1672–82. The progress of Heneage Finch was impeded by the Civil Wars and the Commonwealth, for the Finches were a Royalist family. He was not called to the bar until 1646 and had to wait until the Restoration to establish himself, though he was about the Temple in the meantime and in 1658 obtained a special admission for his eldest son, Daniel, as 'son of

Heneage Finch of the bar'. Thereafter his promotion was rapid. He had not co-operated with the Parliamentary Party or with the Commonwealth. On 29 June 1660 Sir Heneage Finch, Solicitor General, was called to the Bench and duly attended the next Parliament on 10 July 1660. He was made a baronet the same year. He was Treasurer from 1661 to 1673, only relinquishing his post on his appointment as Lord Keeper on 9 November 1673. He was created Lord Chancellor, 19 December 1675. He had been created Lord Finch in 1674 and was made Earl of Nottingham in 1681. He rendered signal service to his Inn not only during his long Treasurership but also as Lord Keeper and Lord Chancellor. He defended the Inn before the Council on the riot of 1669; his three sons, Daniel, Heneage, and William, were the trustees of the Inn in the acquisition of the £10 fee farm rent due to the crown on the Inner Temple in 1676. His judgements were published in 1725 as *Reports, Court of Chancery (1673–1681) during the time Finch was Lord Chancellor*, and his *King's Power of granting Pardons in Cases of Impeachment* in 1791. His draft on the Rules of the Court of Chancery, now among the Miscellaneous Manuscripts, has been published recently. Perhaps his greatest gift to the nation and the Inn was his sons.

Daniel Finch, his eldest son, as has been mentioned above was admitted in 1658 but was never called to the bar. He became a Privy Councillor in 1680 and as 2nd Earl of Nottingham was First Lord of the Admiralty, 1681–84, Secretary at War, 1688–93, Secretary of State, 1702–4, and President of the Council, 1714–16. His second son, Heneage Finch, and his third son, William Finch, were both specially admitted at the request of their father, already Treasurer, in 1662, and both were called to the bar in 1673. Heneage Finch became a K.C. and a Bencher in 1677, was Reader in 1682, and Solicitor General, 1679–86. After his dismissal by James II he was leading counsel for the Seven Bishops. He was created Baron Guernsey and made a Privy Councillor in 1703 and created first Earl of Aylesford in 1714. William Finch was called to the Bench in 1696 and was Reader in 1697. The fifth son, the Hon. Edward Finch, was specially admitted in 1685 at his own request. He was a clergyman and a musician and composer who was never called to the bar. Heneage Finch, the eldest son of the Hon. Heneage Finch, Master of the Bench, was specially admitted at the request of his father in 1703, and the second son, John Finch, similarly in 1710. He was called to the bar in 1719, became a K.C. in 1729, and was consequently called to the Bench 'but not to have any privilege of election of Bench chambers or being chosen Treasurer but by his seniority of being called to the Bench'. He was Reader in the Summer and Lent Vacations, 1736–7, and Treasurer, 1738–9.

This was the heyday of the family of Finch as lawyers or politicians or statesmen. The family had collected three earldoms, those of Winchilsea, Nottingham, and Aylesford. The earldoms of Winchilsea and Nottingham were united in Daniel Finch, who was 6th Earl of Winchilsea and 2nd Earl of Nottingham. His son, Edward, assumed the name of Hatton under the Will of an aunt, and henceforth that branch became Finch-Hattons. The subservient support of the prerogative of the first Sir Heneage Finch had been modified to a less firm support and absolute independence in judgements by the first Earl of Nottingham. The second Earl of Nottingham and the first Earl of Aylesford had remained royalists and tories, but both were a moderating influence in politics; both supported Dutch William and German George. The remainder of the legal history, as of the political history of the family, is comparatively humdrum.

In addition to the admissions of Heneage Finch in 1703 and of John Finch in 1710 there are further Finch admissions in the eighteenth century. Edward Finch was admitted in 1724; Savile Finch in 1714; Roger Finch in 1750; Henry Finch in 1769; John Finch in 1770; the Hon. Edward Finch in 1776. Thomas Finch was admitted in 1776 and was called in 1781. Finally, in 1776, John Emilius Daniel Edward Finch-Hatton was admitted. He was called to the Bench in 1816, was Treasurer in 1823, and was senior Bencher when he died in 1841. So for the period 1556 to 1776 a total of twenty-six persons admitted to the Inner Temple were named Finch. In view of the number of admissions and the outstanding performances of so many of them in law and politics it would seem that less than justice has been done by the Inn to the Finch family and its contribution to the history of the kingdom and of the Society.

Thirdly, something must be said of the wide variety of professional as well as personal interests, hobbies, and activities of members of the Inn. Many, from the sixteenth century onwards, were specialists in their own chosen fields and in their diversions. Some wrote or edited legal textbooks, some reports, commentaries, abridgments, law dictionaries, produced definitive editions of the statutes, or even wrote law books for the layman. Others were dramatists or wrote masques, poems, or essays; others were antiquarians (there were many of them), mathematicians, philanthropists. There were patriots, parliamentary leaders, and politicians; patrons of learning and founders of colleges and professorships; profligates and misers. History, as a close ally of the law, attracted many: national history, local history, family history. There were archivists and hewers of wood and drawers of water for the archivists. There were soldiers and sailors, puritans and papists who suffered for their cause. There were notabilities and nobodies.

The Inner Temple legal authors picked out by William Dugdale for special mention were, perhaps naturally, Christopher St. Germain for his *Doctor and Student*, Robert Keilwey for his *Reports*, William West for his *Symboleography*, Edward Bulstrode for his *Reports*, Thomas Blount for his *Law Dictionary*, John Perkins for his *Treatise* or *Profitable Book*.

The names of Sir Thomas Littleton and Sir Edward Coke will ever be linked together, not only in the Inner Temple, where their twin portraits hang on the same wall, but also wherever English law is known and its history studied. For Littleton's *Tenures*, first printed by Lettou and Maclinia about 1481, ran to 51 editions in Norman

French, by 1839, with a further 43 editions in English, from Redman's first edition early in the sixteenth century to 1903. H. Cary had written a *Commentary* upon it, but this was not published until 1829. Coke's *First Institute, or Commentary upon Littleton* first appeared in 1628. It has been accorded 19 editions in the lists but there are twenty-nine impressions in all up to 1832. These two great works were the text-books of English lawyers for nearly five and three centuries respectively. On the death of Sir Edward Coke his old friend and colleague, Sir Julius Caesar, Master of the Rolls, wrote: 'of famous memory, a general good scholar, and the most skilful in the common law of England of any of his time, or before him for the space of three hundred years, at least, as may appear by his Book of Reports and his Commentaries upon Littleton'. The Inner Temple also provided one of the earliest law reporters. The printed *Year Books*, as their manuscript predecessors had been, were anonymous compilations, distinguished only by the name of the printer, Pynson, Redman, Tottel, for instance. While these were still being printed Robert Keilwey was collecting his *Relationes quorundam Casuum Selectorum*, which was first published by John Croke, in 1602, covering King's Bench and Common Plea Cases, 1496–1531. Robert Keilwey was Autumn Reader in 1547, and Treasurer, 1558–9. He was Surveyor of the Court of Wards. Sir John Croke has been dealt with above. Sir Julius Caesar, Treasurer, 1593–4, wrote *State, Authority and Proceedings of the Court of Requests*, 1596, of which he was Master, as well as Judge of the High Court of Admiralty.

Thomas, Lord Coventry, a protégé of Coke's, was Treasurer, 1617–25, and Lord Keeper, 1625–40. He wrote the *Ordinance of the Chancery*. Sir Robert Heath, who followed him as Treasurer, 1625–8, and was Chief Justice of King's Bench, 1642–5, wrote *Maxims and Rules of Pleading in Actions, Real, Personal and Mixt, Popular and Penal*, published posthumously. Sir Heneage Finch, Autumn Reader 1623, Speaker of the House of Commons, and Recorder of London, had two books to his credit: *Un Description del Common Leys d'Angleterre selonque les rules del art Parallelee sove les prerogatives le Roy*, published in 1613, and the more popular *Law, or Discourse thereof. Written in French: done into English by the author*, first published in 1627. This latter work has been described as 'till the publication of Blackstone's *Commentaries* . . . the best elementary book to be placed in the hands of law students'. Edward Bulstrode, who was Autumn Reader in 1632 and a Bencher since 1629, was a reporter and wrote *Reports in King's Bench, 1609–26*, published in three parts in 1657–9; Sir Henry Rolle, called to the Bench the same time as John Selden, in 1633, was Lent Reader in 1637. Besides his two-volume *Abridgment*, he wrote *Les Reports de divers Cases, Banke le Roy, 1614–16*, with a continuation, *1618–25*.

Robert Moyle, who wrote *Exact Book of Entries of the most select judicial Writs used in the Common Law*, was called to the Bench in 1635. Sir Orlando Bridgeman, who was called to the Bench in 1660 and was Chief Baron of the Exchequer, 1660,

Chief Justice of Common Pleas, 1660–7, and Lord Keeper, 1667–72, wrote a two-volume work *Conveyances; Precedents of Deeds and Instruments concerning the most considerable Estates in England*, and the *Reports of Judgements delivered . . . when Chief Justice of the Common Pleas, 1660–7*, were published in 1823. Sir John Kelyng, who was called to the Bench on the same occasion, wrote *Reports of divers Cases in Pleas of the Crown, 1662–9*. He was Chief Justice of King's Bench 1665–71. Sir John Vaughan, also called on the same occasion, Chief Justice of Common Pleas, 1668–74, and one of Selden's executors, had his judgements published by his son, *Reports and Arguments in the Common Pleas, being all of them special Cases, 1665–74*. Sir Simon Degge's contribution was slighter, *Parson's Counsellor with the Law of Tithes or Tithing*, first published in 1682, which ran to seven editions. He was called to the Bench in 1669 and became a Welsh Judge in 1682. Sir Thomas Robinson, Treasurer, 1680–3, wrote *Book of Special Entries, Declarations, Pleadings, Issues, Verdicts, Judgements and Judicial Processes, with Notes*, which was published posthumously in 1684. He was Chief Prothonotary of Common Pleas and was buried in the Temple Church, having perished in a fire on his staircase in 1683.

Sir John Fortescue Aland, 1st. Baron Fortescue, who was Treasurer in 1716–7, and himself descended from Sir John Fortescue, was responsible for *Reports of Select Cases in all the Courts of Westminster Hall, 1695–1738*. He was successively a Baron of the Exchequer, a Justice of King's Bench, and a Justice of Common Pleas. Sir George Cooke, Treasurer, 1728–9, claimed one major work and two minor ones. The major work was *Reports and Cases of Practice, Court of Common Pleas, 1706–41*. The minor works were *Rules, Orders and Notices in the Court of Common Pleas, 1457–1740*, and *Rules, Orders and Notices in the Court of King's Bench, 1604–1740*. He was Chief Prothonotary of Common Pleas. Richard West, called to the Bench in 1718, wrote *Discourse concerning Treasons and Bills of Attainder*, 1716, and *Inquiry into the manner of creating Peers*, 1719.

Charles Talbot was Treasurer in 1726–7, when he was already Solicitor General. In 1703, as Lord Talbot of Hensol, he became Lord Chancellor and as such was responsible for *Cases in Equity during the time of Chancellor Talbot, 1730–7*. Henry Bathurst, Lord Apsley, later Earl Bathurst, had been called to the Bench as the Hon. Henry Bathurst on presenting his patent as K.C. in 1746. After being Solicitor General and Attorney General to Frederick, Prince of Wales, he became a Justice of Common Pleas in 1754, was Lord Chancellor, 1771–8, and Lord President of the Council, 1779–82. He is credited with three works. The first, *Institute of the Law relative to Trials at Nisi Prius*, was originally published in 1760 and a second edition came in 1789. Then it was incorporated in Sir Francis Buller's (himself a member, a Justice of King's Bench from 1778 and of Common Pleas from 1794), which ran to seven editions. The others were *Theory of Evidence*, 1761, and *Introduction of the Law relative to Trials at Nisi Prius*, 1767.

Sir James Burrow, who was Treasurer, 1764–5, was Master of the Crown Office, and a voluminous reporter. His *Reports, King's Bench, 1756–72*, occupied 5 volumes. His *Decisions, King's Bench, upon Settlement Cases, 1736–68*, had two continuations, *1768–72* and *1772–6*. His slightest work was *Question concerning Literary Property determined by the Court of King's Bench, April 20, 1769*. Among other volumes of his were the *Use of Pointing* and *Anecdotes and Observations relating to Oliver Cromwell.* Sir Thomas Edlyne Tomlins, who was Treasurer, 1827–8, was a still more voluminous writer. His best-known work was his *Law Dictionary*, which was, in fact, an enlargement of Jacob's *Law Dictionary*, which had already run to ten editions by 1782. Tomlins enlarged it to two volumes and published his first edition in 1797. There were further editions in 1800, 1820, 1835, and 1836. His *Repertorium Juridicum; a General Index to the Cases and Pleadings in Law and Equity in the Reports, Year Books etc.* was an extension and revision of K. Freeman's book of the same name published in 1742. Only the first part of Tomlins' work appeared, in 1786–7. He had done his digest and his dictionary. He had already published his *Familiar Explanation of the Law of Wills and Codicils*, described as his chief work, in 1785. This ran to several editions. His next work was a *Digested Index to the Term Reports, 1785–98*, first issued in 1799 and which the next year he extended to 1800 and subsequently, by stages, to 1811. In 1796 he had turned reporter, following the current interest, with his *Cases explanatory of the Rules of Evidence before Committees of Election in the House of Commons, 1689–1795, compiled from the Reports of the Trials of Controverted Elections before such committees*. In 1810 appeared his *Law Dictionary abridged*; in 1838 his *Popular Law Dictionary*. In 1829 he published *Index to Acts in force, passed in the Parliaments of Great Britain and Ireland, 1801–29*, and in 1838 *Plain Directions for Proceedings under the Act for the Abolition of Imprisonment for Debt*. With Raithby he edited *Statutes at Large, Magna Carta to the Union*, 1800, in 20 volumes. He also found time to edit the *St. James Chronicle*. His output was greater than his originality.

The next great reporter of the Inn was Sir Edward Hyde East who was Treasurer in 1831. There are four other reporters who must be mentioned: Richard Vaughan Barnewall, who does not seem to have joined the Inner Temple until 1827; Sir Edward Hall Alderson, who after a brilliant career at Cambridge, where he was Browne's medallist, senior wrangler, first Smith's prizeman and first Chancellor's medallist, was admitted in 1806, and called in 1811, became a Justice, Common Pleas, 1830, and a Baron of the Exchequer, 1834; Sir Cresswell Cresswell, who became a Bencher in 1834, a Justice, Common Pleas, 1842, and in 1858 became the first Judge of the newly created Court of Probate and Divorce; and John Leycester Adolphus, already noted as called to the Bench in 1851.

Sir Edward Hyde East became Chief Justice of Bombay and Calcutta and a member of the Judicial Committee of the Privy Council. He was responsible for *Reports, Kings Bench, 1800–12*, in sixteen volumes, 1801–14. He also wrote *Pleas of the Crown, or Principles and Practice of Criminal Law*, two volumes, 1803. Barnewall and Alderson edited Kings Bench Reports, 1817–22, in five volumes, 1818–22; Barnewall and Cresswell edited King's Bench Reports, 1822–30, in ten volumes, 1823–32; Barnewall and Adolphus edited King's Bench Reports, 1830–4, in five volumes, 1831–5; Adolphus and T. F. Ellis, of Lincoln's Inn, edited King's Bench Reports, 1834–40, in twelve volumes, 1835–42, and Queen's Bench Reports, 1841–52, in 18 volumes, 1843–56. Thereafter the series was continued by Ellis to 1861. The Inner Temple team of four was therefore responsible for fifty volumes of reports, 1817–52, and Adolphus had found time also for literary criticism and was the first to assign the authorship of the Waverley novels to Sir Walter Scott. After 1865 the reports of Chancery, King's Bench, Common Pleas, and Exchequer became anonymous again as in the days of the manuscript and printed Year Books.

Though Sir Edward Coke must lead the procession of Inner Temple lawyers, of all the members of the Inn Selden was probably the most noteworthy of its writers. The range of his output, though very wide, was not as great as his learning, or skill as a writer. His *Titles of Honor*, *History of Tithes*, *Eadmer*, *Fleta*, and *Judicature in Parliament* have already been mentioned. His *Eadmer* and *Fleta* are as carefully edited as if they had been done in the most modern times. His *Mare Clausum*, *De Jure Naturali et Gentium*, *Jani Anglorum Facies Altera*, *Duello*, *De Synedriis*, *De Diis Syris*, are all models of this kind. The posthumously published *Table Talk* is almost a bedside book. There were many other expert works as diversified in subject and content as can be imagined and there were many speeches, memoranda, and notes. He was lawyer, historian, orientalist, Hebraist, antiquarian, and almost universal scholar, far more deserving of that title than Francis Bacon. John Milton styled him the chief of learned men of the land. He was also a practical man of affairs, a practising lawyer, a parliamentarian, a politician, and a patriot. His funeral sermon in the Temple Church was preached by the learned Archbishop Ussher of Armagh. The burial register describes him as a 'learned and judicious antiquary'.

It has already been pointed out that, although more than half of the total number of manuscripts in the Inner Temple Library are works of a legal nature, the most eminent of its members are barely represented among them. It will therefore not appear strange that its most eminent members who were famous in other fields than that of law are equally deficiently represented in the five collections. The bestowal of Geoffrey Chaucer upon the Inn is due to a misunderstanding. His works suggest a better acquaintance with Doctors' Commons than the Inns of Court, but Doctors' Commons was created long after his time. There seems to be no more ground for claiming John Gower. When it comes to the Elizabethan and Jacobean dramatists there is a very certain foundation for pre-eminence. Thomas Norton, the author of more than half of *Gorboduc*, the first tragedy written in English in blank verse, was a practising member of the Inn who became Remembrancer of the city of London. Thomas

Sackville, who became the first Earl of Dorset, came of a legal family, which before his time had been for generations an Inner Temple family, and he had many other literary claims to fame besides his collaboration with Norton in the writing of *Gorboduc*. Francis Beaumont, of the Beaumont and Fletcher partnership, was the son of a Judge and the friend of Ben Jonson and Michael Drayton, and the brother of Sir John Beaumont, another member of the Inn, who wrote *Metamorphosis of Tobacco*. William Browne, the author of the Inner Temple Masque, was the friend of John Selden, resided in the Inn, and wrote most of his poems there. *Gorboduc* was performed in the Inner Temple Hall in 1561; the *Inner Temple Masque* was performed there in 1615. Here the dramatists cease until the Restoration dramatist, William Wycherley, the son of Daniel Wycherley, a barrister of the Inn, who was himself admitted in 1659, one at least of whose plays was performed in the Inner Temple Hall.

If Samuel Johnson and Oliver Goldsmith were residents whose names were honoured by having buildings named after them, James Boswell was a member of the Inn, and William Cowper was invited to the Bench. Charles Lamb was born and bred in the Inner Temple and had chambers there. He was admitted in 1795. He is commemorated by the name of a building and his whimsy by a monument in the Temple Gardens. The manuscripts possess no trace of the work of these great names and the printed books no sufficient remembrance.

Nor was it in the world of letters alone that Treasurers and Benchers and members of the Inner Temple made themselves famous on a wider continent than the law. Daines Barrington was probably a better antiquarian than lawyer. The highest judicial office he held was a Welsh judgeship. Francis Maseres was probably a better mathematician than lawyer. The highest judicial office he held was as a Cursitor Baron of the Exchequer. John Howard was unknown as a lawyer but was known throughout Europe and beyond as a reformer. He presented a copy of his *State of Prisons in England and Wales* to his Inn in 1784. In jurisprudence and constitutional law the Inn's contribution extended from John Austin to Sir William Anson, a Bencher. Austin's widow presented his books to the Inn. Of constitutional and political historians it contributed Henry Hallam, a Bencher, and Sir Francis Palgrave, and of legal historians a long succession to Professor P. H. Winfield and Professor H. G. Hanbury. Though the Inn is indebted by gifts of manuscripts and books to many of these, of none of them does it possess an important personal manuscript. Of the 30 of John Austin's books with his voluminous manuscript notes only one now remains.

If Samuel Johnson, Oliver Goldsmith, and Charles Lamb are commemorated in masonry, even if Geoffrey Chaucer and John Gower are not so remembered, probably for very good reason, John Hampden has no place in any memorial in the Inn, physical or pictorial. Yet he was the fourth member of his family to be a member and his cousins and contemporaries Arthur Goodwin, Edwin Goodwin, and Robert

Waller, his maternal uncle, were all members. Yet this did not betoken any lack of sympathy for the Parliamentary cause. The Parliamentary General, Robert Devereux, Earl of Essex, and the Parliamentary Admiral, Robert Rich, Earl of Warwick, were both members of the Inn. Edmund Prideaux, Attorney General to the Commonwealth, was Treasurer of the Inner Temple, 1648–59, nearly as long as Heneage Finch held that office on the Restoration. Henry Rolle was Chief Justice Upper Bench from 1648 to his retirement in 1655. Ten of the Regicides were members of the Inn. The Bulstrodes were an Inner Temple family and related to the Crokes. Richard Aske, counsel against the King, had been a Bencher since 1633.

Sir Brian Tuke, who was Secretary successively to Wolsey and Henry VIII and a patron of learning, was admitted a member of the Society in 1523. His colleague, Sir Richard Sutton, who died in 1524, was the first lay founder of a college, being joint founder of Brasenose College, Oxford. Nicholas Wadham, admitted in 1553, was the founder of Wadham College, Oxford. Sir Richard Grenvile was admitted in 1560; Sir Francis Drake in 1582, after his voyage round the world, it would seem rather grudgingly, 'upon a fine at the discretion of the Treasurer'. Henry Bradshaw, the historian of Cheshire, was Treasurer, 1544–6: he had been Solicitor General 1540, Attorney General 1545, and became Chief Baron of the Exchequer. Sir William Pole, the historian of Devon, was Treasurer, 1564–5. William Camden, a national as well as a local historian, was admitted in 1571. Sir Henry Savile, Warden of Merton and Provost of Eton, founder of the Savile professorships at Oxford, was admitted in 1578. There were, too, members who were eccentrics. Hugh Audley, who was considered fabulously wealthy and a miser, was a money lender who was a Chief Clerk in the Court of Wards and Liveries. He was admitted in 1604, called to the bar in 1611, and was called an assistant to the Bench in 1638. John Clendon was admitted in 1660, called to the bar in 1668, to the Bench 1689, and was Treasurer, 1700–1. On complaint made to the House of Commons of a book entitled *Treatise of the word Person etc.*, by him, it was ordered to be burnt by the common hang-man and an address to the Queen to prosecute the author, on 25 March 1710. He was found guilty of writing the same.

William Petyt was not the first or the last Keeper of the Records in the Tower to belong to the Inner Temple. John Selden had held the post before him. He was appointed in 1643. Samuel Lysons was appointed Keeper in 1803. He was admitted in 1782 and called to the bar in 1799. Like Petyt he was an author as well as an archivist. With his brother, Daniel Lysons, he compiled *Magna Britannia*. Sir Francis Palgrave, the first Deputy Keeper of the Public Records in 1838, was also a member of the Inn. There were also those who were members whose work aided the archivist. Thomas Blount, whose *Law Dictionary* was first published in 1670, 'which interpreted difficult and obscure words and terms in Common or Statute, Ancient or Modern Laws', was a friend of Selden, Dugdale, and Anthony Wood. He was admitted to the Inner Temple in 1640 and called to the bar in 1648. His *Fragmenta Antiquitatis; Ancient Tenures of Land and Jocular Customs of some Manors*, first published in 1679, reaching seven editions, was also useful to searchers and users of records. Andrew Wright, who wrote that best-seller *Court Hand Restored*, was admitted in 1772 and in 1776 presented a copy of his work to the Library. It ran to ten editions and described itself as a 'Student's Assistant in reading Old Deeds, Charters etc., with appendix containing the ancient names of places in Great Britain and Ireland; also table of ancient surnames'. It was upon Wright's work that Trice Martin's *The Record Interpreter*, which the author described as an amplification of the appendix to the 9th edition of Wright's *Court Hand Restored*, was based. Adam Martin's *Index to Exchequer Records* has already been mentioned.

Francis Throckmorton, who was executed in 1584 for treason against Queen Elizabeth, was admitted in 1577. William Tresham, who was arrested for complicity in the Gunpowder Plot, had been admitted in 1599. Thomas, William, John, and Robert Wentworth, sons of Sir William Wentworth, bart., of Wentworth Woodhouse, were all admitted to the Inn, the first two in 1608, the third in 1612, and the fourth in 1616. The family had chambers in the Inner Temple. Thomas Wentworth became Earl of Strafford in 1640 and was executed in 1641. Richard Langhorne, one of Titus Oates's victims, was executed in 1679. He had been admitted in 1647 and called to the bar in 1654 and acquired an extensive practice.

Sir William Blackstone, 'having been called to the bar in the Society of the Middle Temple, November 1746, as by certificate appears, and being now a member of this Society, requests to be admitted ad eundem gradum', was on 29 June 1759 granted accordingly. In 1785 and 1793 respectively, two members of the Middle Temple with the same Christian name and similar surnames, applied for membership of the Inner Temple. They were Charles Abbot, afterwards Lord Colchester, and Charles Abbott, afterwards Lord Tenterden. The likeness of names has caused much confusion but their careers were very different. Charles Abbot had been called to the bar by the Middle Temple on 9 May 1783 and was admitted ad eundem, at his own request, on 29 April 1785. In 1794 he became Clerk of the Fines in the Court of King's Bench. He entered the House of Commons in 1795, became Chief Secretary for Ireland in 1801, and Speaker of the House of Commons in 1802, retiring to become Lord Colchester in 1816. Charles Abbott became a special pleader and applied for membership of the Inner Temple in 1793. He had been admitted to chambers there on 8 May 1793 and was called to the bar in 1796. He became junior counsel to the Treasury and in 1801 Recorder of Oxford, a Judge in the Court of Common Pleas in 1816, moved to the King's Bench the same year, and became Lord Chief Justice in 1818 and was created Lord Tenterden in 1827. Charles Abbot was Chairman of the Committee on Public Records and afterwards of the Record Commission and directed its affairs with vigour and vigilance. He was the author of *Jurisdiction and Practice of the Court of Great Sessions of Wales upon the Chester Circuit*, 1795, and *Rules and Orders of the King's Bench, 1731–95*, 1795. Charles Abbott was the author of *Law relating to Merchant Ships and Seamen*, 1802. This ran to fifteen editions.

The wide range of members, their activities and interests, from the early fifteenth century to the present time, can be gauged by a brief recital of names and publications, or posts held, of a very further few. Sir Robert Brudenell, the founder of a family, who became Chief Justice of Common Pleas in 1521, had been a Bencher. The brothers Sir Thomas Gawdy and Sir Francis Gawdy, Treasurers respectively in 1562–4 and 1570–1, were respectively a Justice, King's Bench, and Chief Justice, Common Pleas. John Ferne, the writer on heraldry and author of the *Blazon of Gentrie*, was called in 1587. To jump two centuries, Thomas Creevey was admitted in 1789. Thomas Ruggles, who was Treasurer 1811–12, was the author of the *History of the Poor and the Law relating to them*, 1797, and *The Barrister, or Strictures on the Education proper to the Bar*, two volumes, first published in 1818. John Arthur Roebuck, a distinguished back-bench Member of Parliament and reformer, was Treasurer in 1857. Sir Cecil Carr, already mentioned as editor of the *Pension Book of Clement's Inn*, had published his *Delegated Legislation* in 1921. He is the latest Bencher benefactor to the Library, for when he died in 1966 he bequeathed manuscripts and books.

Fourthly, some space must be devoted to authors and their gifts to the Library. The first recorded gift of books to the Library is appropriately that made by Sir Edward Coke in 1608 of his *Reports*. Of other gifts of books only a selection will be given, though there are few recorded until the second half of the eighteenth century, and those donors or donations which have already been mentioned will not be repeated. The unevenness in the information available is due to the same causes as have been given above on the donation of manuscripts to the Library. It is strange that in only two instances is there evidence of a legacy to buy books for the Library. In 1723 Charles Pulteny, who became a Bencher in 1713 and was Reader in 1719 and 1720, bequeathed £10; in 1731 John Smith, who had been called to the bar in 1721, bequeathed £5. That insatiable reporter Sir James Burrow was thanked in 1773 for the gift of *Question concerning Literary Property determined by the Court of King's Bench, April 20 1760*, which had been published that year, and in 1778 for his *Decisions of King's Bench upon Settlement Cases*. In 1776 the Right Hon. Sir Thomas Parker, who having received his writ to be called Serjeant at Law was called to the Bench on 28 May 1733 and only made a single appearance at the Bench, and who had been Chief Baron of the Exchequer until 1772, was thanked for his *Reports concerning the Revenue, Court of Exchequer, 1743–67*, which had been published that year. In 1778, 1780, and 1783 Josiah Brown, who had been called in 1770, had presented the volumes of his *Reports, Court of Parliament, 1701–79* as the seven volumes came out.

These gifts are all law reports. These were to continue for some time further, but the age of such reporters was drawing to a close. In 1807 Robert Henry Peckwell was thanked for his Reports on *Cases of Controverted Elections in the Second Parliament, 1802–1806*, 2 volumes. Lawyers were now writing more treatises and studies on particular legal problems. Thus, in 1806 Edward Hyde East presented his *Pleas of the Crown; or Principles and Practice of Criminal Law*, two volumes; in 1811 George Rose his *Law of Vendors and Purchasers of Personal Property*; in 1830 F. Page his *Essay on the Poor Laws*; in 1829 George Crabb, a voluminous compiler, his *History of the English Law*; in 1833 Henry Chance his *Treatise on Powers*, two volumes. Other members presented abridgements or summaries, or new editions of old works. In 1811 Barron Field, a poet and friend of Charles Lamb, presented his *Analysis of Blackstone's Commentaries*; in 1827 Richard James Greening his edition of J. Perkin's *Profitable Book relating to the Laws of England*, which had been first published in 1528, and which contained easily the best translation; in 1810 William Selwyn his *Abridgment of the Law of Nisi Prius*, two volumes. Treatises continued to be produced in considerable numbers: in 1832 John Nares, a Bencher, presented his *Summary of the Law on Penal Convictions*; in 1832 William Tidd his *Supplement to Practice in Courts of King's Bench, Common Pleas and Exchequer of Pleas*; James Ram his *Law of Assets, Debts and Incumbrances including Executors' Accounts* and his *Act for Uniformity of Process in Personal Actions*; and John Tidd Pratt his *Historical Tables of the Saving Banks*. The next year William Theobald presented *What is Special Pleading?*.

Some members combined legal treatises with other more general works they had written. Thus John Jones, who had presented his *De Libellis Famosis, or Law of Libels* in 1812, followed up in 1818 with his *Translation of the Gospels into Welsh* and in 1824 with his *History of Wales*. Others confined their gifts to their purely literary works. Thus in 1819 James Caldecote presented his *Specimen of a new edition of Shakespeare;* in 1848 Henry Hallam his *Supplemental Notes to the View of England during the Middle Ages*. On 12 May 1866 the Treasurer was thanked for his gift of literary books in five volumes. The Treasurer was Samuel Warren, who was a novelist, though he had published legal textbooks and literary tracts. There can be little doubt that these literary books included his novels, the best known of which was, perhaps, *Ten Thousand a Year*.

Charles Abbot, as Speaker of the House of Commons, was thanked in 1806 for ordering the completion of the *Journals of the House of Commons* in the Library and in 1807, as Chairman of the Record Commission, for 'his order to supply the Library of this Society with a copy of each book published under the authority of the Commission on Public Records'. In return he was to be presented with a copy of the 1806 Catalogue of the Library. In 1896 J. W. Gully, Speaker, was thanked at his place at the Bench 'for directing that Parliamentary Papers and Blue Books as delivered to Members be delivered to the Library'.

Other Benchers and former Treasurers were less generous in their gifts. Some seemed almost to use the Library as a dump for unwanted books. Thus Joseph Jekyll in 1816 presented a *Catalogue of the Books and Manuscripts of the London Society of Antiquaries*; though Catalogues could be acceptable, as when in 1818 the Trustees of the British Museum were thanked for their gift of the *Catalogue of the Hargrave Collection of Manuscripts*. In 1833 Sir George Rose, Treasurer in 1835, who has been mentioned as one of the editors of the *Statutes of the Realm* and was joint editor of *Abbrevatio Placitorum* for the Record Commission, on behalf of the bar in America, presented some books to the Library. C. P. Cooper, who had been Secretary of the Second Record Commission in 1843, presented in 1843 a number of publications relating to the Public Records. One ex-Treasurer and one future Treasurer made gifts of personal interest to the Inn. John Gurney, when a Baron of the Exchequer in 1835, presented *A Vindication of the Proceedings of the Gentlemen of the Inner Temple*, and William Burge, in 1843, *The Temple Church; an Account of its Restoration*. Masters of the Temple, lecturers, and preachers at the Temple Church presented volumes of their sermons preached there or elsewhere, sometimes of more than local or passing interest. Thus the Revd. John Lonsdale presented in 1819 the sermon he had preached at the Temple Church on 2 December 1818, the day of the funeral of Her late Majesty Queen Charlotte.

Lastly there were the presentations to the Library of their works by grateful searchers who had been permitted to search the manuscripts in the Library. Some such examples have already been given. Some were grateful for other facilities granted. Thus G. C. Addison, in 1841, presented his *History of the Knights Templar, the Temple Church and the Temple*; John Bruce, Treasurer of the Camden Society, presented his *History of the Arrival of Edward IV in England* and his *Annals of the First Four Years of the Reign of Queen Elizabeth by Sir John Hayward*, both published by the Camden Society; in 1855, the Parker Society *The Correspondence of Matthew Parker, Archbishop of Canterbury*, which it published; in 1859, the Roxburghe Club its publication of *The Literary Remains of Edward VI*; in 1864, Saxe Bannister a copy of his *Address to the Barristers of England, Ireland and Scotland*. This seems a somewhat meagre return for favours received; most of the recipients of the favours seem to have failed to reciprocate.

The gift of books to the Library by members of the Inner Temple, or by its friends, and by those who owed the Library a debt of gratitude is, however, far less substantial that the gifts of manuscripts it received, though it far outnumbered them. But there came a time when sentiments of sympathy produced by a calamity provided almost a flood of accessions or rather replacements. The losses of 1940–1 due to enemy action were very largely replaced within a little more than a decade, so far as the working books were concerned, by the generosity of many members and a still greater number of friends. Sir Frank MacKinnon's appeal produced a flow of offers of help. Those who earliest responded were in many ways the most helpful. Only the bare mention of the names of some of the greatest benefactors can be made here. They included Sir Frank MacKinnon, Sir William Holdsworth, Sir John Simon, Mr. Hubert Stuart Moore, Master Neville Laski, the executors of Lord Schuster, and the House of Commons Library.

Fifthly and finally, the benefactions to the Inner Temple Library in manuscripts and books must be briefly summarized generally. In both manuscripts and books the most lavish benefactors have been Treasurers and Benchers of the Inn, with members, including an occasional student, coming second. Important manuscripts and rare books have been given by friends, but these are but a small proportion of the whole. William Petyt, the virtual founder of the Library, stimulated several of his contemporaries to emulate him and give in their way and according to the means at their disposal by presenting books as well as manuscripts. Daines Barrington presented many books and a few manuscripts in his lifetime as did a number of his contemporaries, Francis Maseres, for example. Many more Barrington manuscripts were to follow through his executor and brother, Shute Barrington, Bishop of Durham. In the meantime Herbert Jacob had presented his massive collection of books. John Mitford gave a few books during his lifetime; his manuscripts accrued to the Inn through his association with it. But there were many who gave one manuscript or more and hundreds who gave one volume or more.

Of the manuscripts given or bequeathed the great majority were law books; of the books given again the great majority were law books. This was natural and appropriate, for the law and its practice was the profession for which the Inn had been established. The stock-in-trade of the profession varies but slightly throughout the centuries and the principles remain the same. The early law books are more usefully in national or university libraries than in the libraries of the four Inns of Court. For they reveal facets which extend far beyond the domain of law. They are packed with information which illustrates political and social history and occasionally economic history, which has no relevance to the law as it exists today. Lawyers are allowed diversions and these have always taken many forms, but have most usually been associated with antiquarian pursuits, particularly, perhaps, the curiosities of their profession, of which there are many. If they are not factual they can be reduced to fact within the legal discipline. Antiquarianism from the sixteenth century to the nineteenth century was not the antiquarianism of the twentieth century, with its new scientific techniques. There was then no aid to excavation but digging and hard work. Information was based on tradition, often unreliably established. These antiquarian interests must be read in the light of those days and not in that of today.

Next to the antiquarian interests must be placed the purely historical interests. The donors would probably not have recognized any differences between historical and antiquarian interests, except, perhaps, in so far as records were concerned, but the attitude to records was not that of today. Biography, too, would not have been differentiated from history. It is not fair to stress mathematical interests any more than it would be fair to stress medical interests; both were exceptional. The more imaginative arts, the writing of masques or plays, of poems or novels, were adequately represented among the interests. There were those who were interested in privilege, pedigree, and peerage, as well as in prerogative and precedence. Interest in the classics and modern languages, other than English, was scanty. Pictorial art is scarcely represented, except portraits, and that mainly of famous members or of officers of the Inn. A slight interest in church music is disclosed, but not in music as an art or craft. Sermons are now seldom printed, but that is a twentieth-century fact. Apart from Masters of the Temple few showed any interest in theology and apart from periods in the seventeenth century Masters of the Temple were more regarded for their rhetoric than theology.

If manuscripts, particularly medieval manuscripts and the most modern holograph manuscripts of popular works, have appreciated and are appreciating in value with speed owing to an unsatisfied demand in the New World, previous ages had little interest in autographs, the collection of which is a comparatively modern cult. Holograph letters among the manuscripts are comparatively few; most of the most important appear to be derived from the records of the House, which are very rich in autographs. They should contain at least one autograph for every member of the Inn from the middle of the sixteenth century. Otherwise they are not many and few are of great interest and importance.

Transcripts, even medieval transcripts, were normally written not by craftsmen, but by copyists of varying skill and education. The result was that foolish mistakes were often made. On the other hand knowledge of medieval and later scripts was very much more widespread than it is today, despite its adventitious aids and the means of technical instruction available. Translations were, on the whole, better done. Every lawyer and lawyer's clerk up to the 1730s knew that strange kind of jargon into which Norman French had deteriorated and could render it into intelligible English. The translation of the Norman French of such documents as petitions, letters under privy seal, and letters under signet or sign manual, was not so well done. The medieval Latin of other Public Records had long been reduced into common form and its translation, if it appeared to be somewhat stilted, presented no difficulties. The manuscripts have a few fragments of Anglo-Saxon, and there are complete manuscripts of medieval English, though late. Other languages are hardly represented.

The manuscripts include, on the legal side, Year Books from the time of Edward I, Reports from the early sixteenth century, Treatises from the time of Bracton onwards. There are precedent books, commonplace books, and formularies. The Reports and Treatises cover the Chancery, King's Bench, and Exchequer of Pleas, the Prerogative Courts of Star Chamber and Wards and Liveries, the Court of Augmentations, and the Courts of the Palatinate of Durham and the Duchy of Lancaster. Ecclesiastical Courts, such as the Court of Arches and the Prerogative Court of Canterbury, are well represented. Many Advocates were also members of the Inner Temple. There are volumes of Statutes and even of Private Acts of Parliament. There are hundreds of opinions of Law Officers of the Crown as well as of other leading Counsel. There are drafts of historical and legal Treatises, some still unpublished. There is even one incunable bound in with a manuscript Year Book. There are unique Judges' Papers.

On the historical side undoubtedly the most numerous and valuable section are the manuscripts relating to Parliamentary History, with transcripts of all the Rolls of Parliament to the reign of Henry VIII and the Journals of the House of Lords and the House of Commons and diaries kept by members of the House of Commons. There are Cartularies of the churches of Salisbury and Dunstable. Ecclesiastical History is well covered, especially for the reign of Elizabeth I, with much original material for the Archiepiscopates of Matthew Parker, Edmund Grindal, and John Whitgift, and for the disputes among the English Catholic clergy during the last decade of Elizabeth I. There are interesting and valuable items on local history. There is unique material on the history of the Navy and the Army and on the Universities of Oxford and Cambridge and their Colleges. There are medieval chronicles from Roger of Hoveden to Ralph Higden. The law and history of Scotland and Ireland are embraced, including the Irish Chancery Court. There is much on the early history of the Province of Quebec and on some of the United States. Other Colonies are also represented, especially in the West Indies, from the first half of the seventeenth century, and the East Indies comes in through the East India Company. There is new material on the history of countries in Western Europe, especially the Low Countries, but France, Spain, Switzerland, Germany, and Italy are not ignored and there is even material relating to Russia and Turkey.

There are many original documents of state, including holograph letters of Edward VI, Mary, and Elizabeth I and one sign manual of 'Jane the Queen'. Naturally there are many original documents relating to the Inner Temple and a few relating to its three Inns of Chancery, Clement's Inn, Clifford's Inn, and Lyon's Inn. The records relating to the Society start early in the sixteenth century and the history of the site can be traced back from the reign of Henry II. The history of the Temple Church is well documented, as well as the domestic history of the Inner Temple. Some of this domestic material is of great importance to national and literary history.

For the importance of the manuscripts is national not domestic. Though they are a part of the inheritance of the Society, mainly derived from the bequests and free-will offerings of its Treasurers, Benchers, barristers, and other members, they have a much wider significance. Though the foundations of the collection of printed books was similarly laid they have been mainly derived from purchase. The manuscripts and books are, therefore, mainly of a legal or historical importance and value, though some of both still represent the personal interest and specialized knowledge of the donors, entirely outside professional practice and activities. They have, therefore, an essential unity and symbolize the history of the Inn over at least four hundred and fifty years. Those few which have been transferred from the records of the Society emphasize that essential unity.

The law has for centuries been closely associated with politics, national and local. If more of the Treasurers and Benchers had left or given to their Inn some remembrance of their association with it, what a wonderful Library it would now be. For they have held almost every position of importance in the Palace of Westminster and in Whitehall, in Westminster Hall and the Law Courts, in the city of London and in the counties and cities and boroughs of England and Wales; and as Britain spread overseas they have followed to spread English law and equity throughout the Commonwealth and beyond. For, besides the Assizes, there were the Courts of the Great Sessions of Wales and besides the Chancellors and Judges of the Palatinate of Durham and the Duchy of Lancaster, Ely had its Chief Justice and the Duchy of Cornwall its Law Officers. Scotland had its own legal hierarchy, including a Chief Baron of the Exchequer. Ireland had its Chancellor, Judges, and Law Officers parallel with those of England. The Church had its many Courts; every Bishop and every Archdeacon had his Consistory Court. Quebec, Bombay, Calcutta, and eventually India had their judiciaries. There were dozens of local courts with peculiar names which had to be manned. Even the great Sir Edward Coke had to serve as a High Sheriff. All produced records; most produced reports.

Only a few examples can be given of the contribution of the Inner Temple to the filling of these multifarious offices. Only two members of the Inn have become Prime Ministers, George Grenville, 1763–5, and Clement Attlee, 1945–51. From the time the offices became held by laymen and lawyers, that is from the time of Sir Thomas More, out of sixty-seven who have held the office of Lord Chancellor or Lord Keeper, twenty-nine have come from the Inner Temple. The first was Sir Thomas Audley, who succeeded Sir Thomas More in 1532; Lord Gardiner, who became Lord Chancellor in 1964, has been a Bencher since 1955. Three recent predecessors were Lord Caldecote, Lord Simon, and Lord Dilhorne, all Benchers of the Inn. Of the fifty-seven Chief Justices of King's Bench there have been since 1500, sixteen have been of the Inner Temple, from Sir Thomas Bromley to Lord Goddard. Of the eighty-two speakers of the House of Commons there have been since 1500, twenty-one have been of the Inner Temple. The first was Sir Robert Sheffield in 1510. He is the first mentioned of those who were Governors in 1511. The last was Sir Henry Hylton-Foster, who was Speaker, 1959–65. He was appointed a Master of the Bench in 1954. The proportion remains about the same for other legal posts, such as Master of the Rolls, Chief Justice of Common Pleas, Chief Baron of the Exchequer, and Attorney General and Solicitor General. From 1621 to 1640 there were five successive Solicitors General from the Inner Temple, Thomas Coventry, Robert Heath, Richard Shilton, Edward Littleton, and Edward Herbert. Three became Lord Keepers, and one Chief Justice of King's Bench.

I

THE PETYT COLLECTION OF MANUSCRIPTS

PETYT MS. 502

This group consists of 83 volumes of transcripts of the Journals of the House of Commons, 1604–24, 1660–1708, numbered according to the reigns, 11 volumes for that of James I, 22 for that of Charles II, 2 for that of James II, 34 for William and Mary and William III, and 14 for that of Anne. They are uniformly bound in full calf, with the Inner Temple coat of arms on both covers. The size of the volumes has but slight variations, the largest being $12\frac{1}{2}'' \times 8''$, the smallest $12\frac{1}{8}'' \times 7\frac{1}{2}''$, except for an abnormal volume, $12\frac{3}{8}'' \times 6\frac{3}{4}''$. The condition of the volumes is tolerably good, though many are foxed and some have been stained by damp. Volumes three to fourteen for the reign of Anne are in mint condition. All the volumes, except the last for the reign of Anne, are alphabetically indexed. The first volume for the reign of James I followed the original numbering of the Journals themselves, by numbers in the margin. For all the 83 volumes the following list gives references to the folio version of the *Journals of the House of Commons*: Volumes I, VIII–XV.

James I, 11 volumes

1. 19 March 1 James I (1604)–2 May 1604 — 318 ff.
(*H. of C. J.*, I, pp. 139–97.)

2. Pt. I, 3 May 1604–7 July 1604 — 550 pp.
(Ibid., pp. 197–256.)

2. Pt. II, 5 November 1605–27 May 1606 — 554 pp.
(Ibid., pp. 256–314.)

3. 18 November 1605–24 March 1606/7 — pp. 1–375
(Ibid., pp. 314–54.) (Index in succeeding volume.)

4. 26 March 1607–4 July 1607 — pp. 376–731
(Ibid., pp. 354–392.)

5. 9 February 1609/10–2 May 1610 — pp. 1–300
(Ibid., pp. 392–424.) (Index in succeeding volume.)

6. 3 May 1610–23 July 1610 — pp. 301–596
(Ibid., pp. 424–54.)

7. 5 April 12 James I (1614)–6 June 12 James I (1614) — 544 pp.
(Ibid., pp. 455–506.)

8. 18 January 18 James I (1621)–17 March 18 James I (1621) — 524 pp.
(Ibid., pp. 507–561.)

There is a volume missing here, covering 19 March 1621–12 May 1621 (Cf. *H. of C. J.*, I, pp. 562–619.)

9. 14 May 18 James I (1621)–18 December 18 James I (1621) — 509 pp.
The following note appears on p. 239: The remainder of this book so torn and worn away as not to make anything of it being about 5 or 6 sheets. (Ibid., pp. 619–69.)

10. 12 February 21 James I (1624)–29 May James I (1624) — 481 pp.
(Ibid., pp. 670–715.)

CHARLES II, 22 volumes

1. 25 April 1660–9 July 1660 — 820 pp.
(*H. of C. J.*, VIII, pp. 1–85.)

2. 10 July 1660–13 September 1660 — 825 pp.
(Ibid., pp. 85–175.)

3. 6 November 1660–29 December 1660 — 660 pp.
(Ibid., pp. 175–244.)

4. 8 May 1661–30 July 1661 — 746 pp.
(Ibid., pp. 245–316.)

5. 20 November 1661–11 March 1661/2 — 651 pp.
(Ibid., pp. 316–384.)

6. 12 March 1661/2–18 May 1662 — 489 pp.
(Ibid., pp. 384–436.)

7. 18 February 1662/3–12 June 1663 — 595 pp.
(Ibid., pp. 436–501.)

8. 13 June 1663–20 August 1664 — 607 pp.
(Ibid., pp. 501–66.)

9. 24 November 1664–11 August 1665 — 434 pp.
(Ibid., pp. 567–613.)

10. 9 October 1665–15 November 1666 — 350 pp.
(Ibid., pp. 613–50.)

11. 16 November 1666–10 October 1667 — 409 pp.
(Ibid., pp. 650–92; IX, p. 1.)

12. 14 October 1667–7 March 1667/8 — 587 pp.
(Ibid., IX, pp. 1–63.)

13. 9 March 1667/8–11 December 1669 — 575 pp.
(Ibid., pp. 63–121.)

14. 14 February 1669/70–5 January 1670/1 — 618 pp.
(Ibid., pp. 121–88.)

15. 9 January 1670/1–30 October 1672 — 542 pp.
(Ibid., pp. 188–245.)

16. 4 February 1672/3–10 November 1674 — 599 pp.
(Ibid., pp. 245–314.)

17. 13 April 1675–22 November 1675 — 580 pp.
(Ibid., pp. 314–82.)

18. 15 February 1676/7–4 May 1678 — 812 pp.
(Ibid., pp. 382–476.)

19. 6 May 1678–30 December 1678 — 742 pp.
(Ibid., pp. 476–566.)

20. 6 March 1678/9–27 May 1679 — 599 pp.
(Ibid., pp. 567–634.)
The printed Journal, p. 567 does not begin until 18 March 1678/9. By the asterisks there should be eight or nine days' proceedings missing.

21. 17 October 1679–10 January 1680/1 — 650 pp.
(Ibid., pp. 635–704.)

22. 1 March 1680/1–28 March 1681 — 69 pp.
(Ibid., pp. 705–12.)

JAMES II, 2 volumes

1. 19 May 1 James II (1685)–28 April 1687 — 361 pp.
(Ibid., pp. 713–62.)

2. The Prince of Orange's Declaration: Assembly Book, 26–8 December 1688: — 63 pp.
pp. 1–22. Declaration, The Hague, 16 October 1688.
p. 33. Additional Declaration, St. James, 23 December 1688.
p. 46. The Association, Exeter, 19 December 1688.
pp. 48–63. 26–8 December 1688.
(Ibid., x, pp. 1–8.)

WILLIAM AND MARY AND WILLIAM III, 34 volumes

1. 22 January 1688/9–9 April 1689 — 519 pp.
(*H. of C. J.*, x, pp. 9–85.)

2. 12 April 1689–14 May 1689 — 432 pp.
(Ibid., pp. 85–132.)

3. 15 May 1689–17 June 1689 — 463 pp.
(Ibid., pp. 133–83.)

4. 18 June 1689–20 July 1689 — 394 pp.
(Ibid., pp. 183–230.)

5. 22 July 1689–21 October 1689 390 pp.
(*H. of C. J.*, x, pp. 230–72.)

6. 23 October 1689–31 December 1689 403 pp.
(Ibid., pp. 273–321.)

7. 2 January 1689/90–27 January 1690 240 pp.
(Ibid., pp. 321–45.)

8. 20 March 1689/90–12 September 1690 690 pp.
(Ibid., pp. 347–424.)

9. 2 October 1690–5 October 1691 1,088 pp.
(Ibid., pp. 425–538.)

10. 22 October 1691–9 January 1691/2 894 pp.
(Ibid., pp. 538–619.)

11. 11 January 1691/2–26 September 1692 691 pp.
(Ibid., pp. 619–95.)

12. 4 November 1692–31 December 1692 653 pp.
(Ibid., pp. 696–767.)

13. 2 January 1692/3–26 October 1693 842 pp.
(Ibid., pp. 767–851.)

14. 7 November 1693–14 February 1693/4 902 pp.
(Ibid., XI, pp. 1–95.)

15. 15 February 1693/4–6 November 1694 729 pp.
(Ibid., pp. 95–171.)

16. 12 November 1694–28 February 1694/5 778 pp.
(Ibid., pp. 171–253.)

17. 1 March 1694/5–8 October 1695 774 pp.
(Ibid., pp. 253–333.)

18. 22 November 1695–12 February 1695/6 881 pp.
(Ibid., pp. 334–445.)

19. 13 February 1695/6–1 September 1696 1,000 pp.
(Ibid., pp. 445–566.)

20. 20 October 1696–29 January 1696/7 988 pp.
(Ibid., pp. 566–684.)

21. 1 February 1696/7–23 November 1697 930 pp.
(Ibid., pp. 684–791.)

22. 3 December 1697–16 February 1697/8 903 pp.
(Ibid., XII, pp. 1–116.)

23. 17 February 1697/8–30 April 1698 1,049 pp.
(Ibid., pp. 116–248.)

24. 2 May 1698–5 July 1698 839 pp.
(Ibid., pp. 249–344.)

25. 24 August 1698–31 January 1698/9 911 pp.
(Ibid., pp. 345–467.)

26. 1 February 1698/9–9 March 1698/9 751 pp.
(Ibid., pp. 467–558.)

27. 10 March 1698/9–24 October 1699 992 pp.
(Ibid., pp. 558–688.)

28. 16 November 1699–21 December 1699 648 pp.
(Ibid., XIII, pp. 1–91.)

29. 22 December 1699–3 February 1699/1700 576 pp.
(Ibid., pp. 91–173.)

30. 5 February 1700–21 November 1700 999 pp.
(Ibid., pp. 173–323.)

31. 6 February 1700/1–24 March 1700/1 700 pp.
(Ibid., pp. 324–426.)

32. 25 March 1701–8 May 1701 719 pp.
(Ibid., pp. 426–522.)

33. 9 May 1701–6 November 1701 959 pp.
(Ibid., pp. 522–642.)

34. 30 December 1701–7 March 1701/2 906 pp.
(Ibid., pp. 644–782.)

ANNE, 14 volumes

1. 8 March 1701/2–23 April 1702 pp. 1–365
(*H. of C. J.*, XIII, pp. 782–858.)

2. 24 April 1702–25 May 1702 pp. 366–604
(Ibid., pp. 858–908.)

3. 22 October 1702–4 January 1702/3 pp. 1–482
(Ibid., XIV, pp. 2–101.)

4. 5 January 1702/3–29 January 1702/3 pp. 483–815
(Ibid., pp. 101–168.)

5. 1 February 1702/3–15 December 1703 pp. 817–1025
(Ibid., pp. 168–249.) ff. 1–155

6. 16 December 1703–10 February 1703/4 ff. 157–512
(Ibid., pp. 249–331.)

7. 11 February 1703/4–16 November 1704 ff. 513–692
(Ibid., pp. 331–425.) pp. 1–400

8. 17 November 1704–3 February 1704/5 pp. 401–1204
(*H. of C. J.*, XIII, pp. 425–514.)

9. 5 February 1704/5–14 March 1704/5 pp. 1205–1661
(Ibid., pp. 514–578.)

10. 14 June 1705–19 January 1705/6 pp. 1–834
(Ibid., XV, pp. 2–100.)

11. 21 January 1705/6–21 November 1706 pp. 835–1629
(Ibid., pp. 101–200.)

12. 3 December 1706–20 February 1706/7 pp. 1–738, then unnumbered
(Ibid., pp. 200–304.)

13. 21 February 1706/7–24 April 1707 pp. 739–796, 1–626
(Ibid., pp. 304–390.)

14. 23 October 1707–21 February 1707/8 pp. 1x–3x, 1–793
(Ibid., pp. 392–559.)

PETYT MS. 503

A slim volume, full bound in light-brown calf, with the coat of arms of the Inner Temple on both covers. Given by George Wright Esq., Clerk of the Crown in the Court of Chancery, Bencher of the Inner Temple. 12″×7¾″. 38 ff.

The Proceedings at the Coronation of George I, 20 October 1714, with the writ appointing the Commission on Claims, Westminster, 2 October 1 George I (1714); the proclamation on claims, 4 October 1714; the petitions on claims and their results; the list of those who did fealty.

PETYT MS. 504

A volume in parchment containing 6 Law Tracts and a Register of Writs. Full bound in red morocco, with the Inner Temple coat of arms on both covers. 11″×7⅞″. 59 pp., 213 ff.

The volume is foliated i to cciiii and 205 to 213. The manuscript is well written, probably in the early years of Richard II, certainly in the last third of the fourteenth century. The dating of the Register of Writs is discussed below; the first section is of the same date, perhaps a few years earlier. The Law Tracts at the beginning are really no part of the Register, but this section has been added to it on resemblance of subject. The foliation of the volume is a little vicarious and there appears to have been some confusion in rebinding the manuscript at some time. Throughout both sections of the manuscript there are illuminated capitals in red and blue, and paragraph marks in the same colours in the text, running headings and marginal entries. On a new paper flyleaf is written 'Presented by W. Barnesley' and on the old flyleaf of parchment at the beginning, 'W. Barnesley'. The owners of the manuscript up to its presentation to the Inner Temple Library appear on the last end flyleaf (see below, f. 218^{v}). There are additional entries made on the flyleaves at the beginning and at the end. From the additional writs added to the text, the margin and other notes, and the entries on the flyleaves, it is clear that the Register was in constant use during the time of

Richard II, continued to be well used until well into the reign of Henry VI, and was consulted until late in the second half of the seventeenth century at least.

1. p. 5. Natura Brevium. Incipit: Bref de novell disseisin. Explicit: ou les heirs avoir recouerir.

2. p. 16. Extenta manerii. Incipit: Inquirendum est de castris. Explicit: et omnia alia per annum. (*Stat. of Realm*, I, pp. 242–3.)

3. p. 18. Notabilia Statuta. Incipit: Dampna in triplico. Explicit: in eodem statuto c. xliii.

4. p. 20. Calumpnia Essoniarum. Incipit: Hic demonstratur quot modo. Explicit: per omnes terras et catalla. (Ibid., pp. 217–18.)

5. p. 21. Magnum Hengham. Incipit: Licet ordo placitandi. Explicit: sic peremptor distenditur actio actoris. (Cf. in John Selden's edition of Fortescue, *De Laudibus*, 1616, 1660.)

6. p. 42. Parvum Hengham. Incipit: Notandum quod quinque sunt essonia. Explicit: si compertus fuisset tenens. (Cf. Ibid.)

p. 50. The form of homage done to the King as Duke of Lancaster. (French.)

p. 51. Brief definitions of Rent sec, Suit Service, Service real, Intrusion, Prefixation, Usurpation, Spoliation, Prescription, Agistment, Waif, Stray, Burgage, Messuage, Tenement, Place, Charter, Condition, Quitclaim, Obligation, Acquittance.

7. Registrum Brevium.

p. 53. Preceding the Register is an index or tabula, alphabetically arranged, in two columns, of the contents of the Register, the references being to the original foliation of the next section, ff. i–cciiii, which occupies 6 pp. At the end of p. 57, under the heading alia brevia, eight new writs are added, preceded by the signature: R. Fytt.

p. 59. The Register of Writs starts with an illuminated E(dwardus) in gold, blue, and purple. The first writ is the usual writ of right with which Registers of Writs invariably start. Throughout, most of the writs are of the time of Edward III, and occasionally the regnal year of the writ is entered in the margin. At the entry at the end of f. 39 referring to a decision before the King's Council at the Parliament of Salisbury, 1384 was the date of Richard II's parliament held at Salisbury, and the undated writ of Richard II, in the original text (f. 129), is probably before this date. The Register was, therefore, probably written early in the reign of Richard II. After each section of the Register, a substantial space was left for the insertion of additional writs, with a similar smaller space for similar insertions at the end of each such section. In these spaces additional writs have been inserted, of which the eight writs inserted at the end of the tabula are probably the earliest insertions. There are also additional notes inserted in the margin, of two main periods, firstly, those almost contemporary with the writing of the manuscript, and secondly, those of later date. In many cases the additional writs and marginal notes have a substantial importance. For example:

f. 21. Fait assavoir qe nul bref datteint poet grauntes forsqe par le Roy mesmes horspris attaint de novel disseisyn et de mort dauncester et ceux poet le Chanceller grauntier de sa grace et auxint atteynitz de trespas.

f. 60. Nota hoc breve fundatur de Statuto de anno H. VIII.

Other additional writs and entries range from the time of Henry IV (f. 56) to that of Henry VIII (f. 60). Of special significance are three writs which are dated: to John (Buckingham), Bishop of Lincoln 26 May 17 Richard II (1394) (f. 191v); to W(illiam Courtney), Archbishop of Canterbury, (1392) (f. 191v); and to Richard (Mitford), Bishop of Chichester, 2 October (1393) (f. 192). These two folios contain three other writs of about the same period. The Register is divided and subdivided into the usual subject sections and sub-sections and should be compared with the printed *Register of Writs* (1687).

The additional entries on flyleaves are as follows:

p. 1. Articles granted for the liberties of the church in the Parliament at York, Letters Patent, York, 24 November 10 Edward II (1316). (*Stat. of Realm*, I, pp. 175–6.)

f. 4v. Letters Patent, incomplete and undated, referring to the grant of Edward I, in his Parliament at Westminster, 14 Edward III, at the special request of the clergy, on the liberty of the goods and chattels of the clergy. (Ibid., pp. 292–4.)

ff. 208v–210v. Additional writs, all undated: De supersedacione in breve de excommunicate: Dedimus potestatem recipere recognicionem in speciali assisa: Supersede priviligium pro clericis in Cancellaria.

f. 211v. Capto gallo armata Italia aucti Imperio.
Capta vrbe obsesse Pontifice hoc cineres.
Marmor habet.
In a different hand: En le Chauncerie fuist touche par le Chaunceller qe en la Chauncerie home ne serra prejudice par myspleder ou par defaulte de forme mez selonqe devers del mater, etc.

f. 212. Writ of capias, tested William Montague, Westminster, 12 February, 29 Charles II (1677), addressed to Sheriff of Pembroke, in a hand of the late seventeenth century.

f. 212v. Writ to Treasurer and Barons of the Exchequer, tested John, Duke of Bedford, Keeper of England, Westminster, 26 October 7 Henry V (1419), about the translation of Benedict (Nicholls), Bishop of Bangor, to be Bishop of St. Davids, on the translation of Stephen Patrington, Bishop of that see, to the see of Chichester. Enrolled among the Brevia directa Baronibus, Mich. term, 7 Henry V, rot. 15, K.R. Mem. Roll. In the margin appears the signature: Ellys Williams. Writ to the Chancellor of the County Palatine of Lancaster on the record and process of outlawry of John de B(   ) in that county. n.d.

f. 213. A note referring to Humphrey, Duke of Gloucester, as Protector of England, followed by a parody of a writ, dated in nostro domo exteriori Templi feste et noctis instantis exordia.

f. 213v. Liber Ricardi Welles olim et nunc Willelmi Savage ac postea datus eundem Willelmum Savage Roberto Gayer nunc possessori vero et ad presens Ricardi Fytt ex dono Petri Marker et postremo Will. Barnesly. In margin: 1582.
The original hand ends after possessori: from vero to Marker is in another hand: the last four words are in a third hand.
At the top of the folio in a large hand: Welles. At foot: Ry Fytt.

PETYT MS. 505

A volume in parchment containing the Statutes, 1 Edward III to 29 Henry VI, re-bound in full green morocco, with the Inner Temple coat of arms on both covers. $10\frac{7}{8}'' \times 8''$. 262 ff. Though listed as a Petyt MS., it is, in fact a Barrington MS. The signature Daines Barrington appears on the third front flyleaf. The manuscript may be dated shortly after the middle of the fifteenth century. The hands are not so attractive as those in Petyt MS. 506 below, though it is a well-written manuscript. The parchment, though fairly good, is not so good as the latter. There are a few errors and on f. 44 there are two blank spaces as if the transcriber could not read a word in the manuscript which he was copying. The manuscript has been little used. There are but five marginal additions throughout (ff. 53 (*bis*), 56, 64, 214), two of which link up with an amendment in the Table of Contents. It has five illuminated capitals (ff. 41, 104, 152v, 100v, 200) at the beginning of the Statutes for the five reigns, Edward III, Richard II, Henry IV, Henry V, and Henry VI. The colours are gold, blue, pink, green, etc. There are capitals and marks in red and blue throughout the manuscript, as also running headings. The running headings begin on f. 41v with the regnal year of the king on one side and his name on the other.

f. 1. The following appears at the top of the folio: Liber Ricardi Birkheued ex dono Willelmi Massy Interioris Templi generosi.

Then begins the Table of Contents, alphabetically arranged, beginning with Accusaciuns and ending (f. 38) with Wursted, the references being to the regnal year and chapter. The Table of Contents has illuminated capitals and marks in red and blue.

f. 41.	Statute, 7 March	1	Edward III,	Westminster. (*Stat. of Realm*, I, pp. 251–4.)
f. 42v.	Statute,	1	Edward III,	Westminster. (Ibid., pp. 255–7.)
f. 43v.	„	1	„	„
f. 44v.	„	1	„	„ (Cf. *C.P.R.*, 1327–30, pp. 98–9.)
f. 45.	„	2	„	„ (*Stat. of Realm*, I, pp. 257–61.)
	„	2	„	Northampton. (Ibid.)
f. 47.	„	4	„	Westminster. (Ibid., pp. 261–5.)
f. 49.	„	5	„	„ (Ibid., pp. 265–9.)
f. 51.	„	9	„	York. (Ibid., pp. 273–4.)
f. 51v.	„	9	„	„ (Ibid., pp. 269–72.)
f. 53.	„	10	„	Westminster. (Ibid., p. 275.)
f. 53v.	„	10	„	„ (Ibid., pp. 276–8.)
f. 54v.	„	10	„	„ (Ibid., pp. 278–80).
f. 54v.	„	11	„	„ (Ibid., pp. 280–1.)
f. 55.	„	14	„	„ (Ibid., pp. 281–9.)
f. 60.	„	14	„	De Prerogativa Regis, 14 Edward III (1340.)
	„	14	„	Westminster. (Ibid., pp. 289–92.)
f. 61v.	„	14	„	„ (Ibid., pp. 292–4.)
f. 62v.	„	17	„	Statuta de Hibernia. (Ibid., pp. 193–4.)
f. 63.	„	18	„	Westminster. (Ibid., pp. 300–1.)
f. 64.	Declaration on Exigends,	18	Edward III.	(Ibid., p. 299.)
	Statute,	18	Edward III,	Westminster. (Ibid., pp. 300–1.)
f. 65.	„	18	„	„ (Ibid., pp. 302–3.)
f. 65v.	„	20	„	„ (Ibid., pp. 303–6.)
f. 66v.	„	23	„	„ (Ibid., pp. 307–9.)
f. 67v.	„	25	„	„ (Ibid., pp. 311–13.)
f. 69.	„	25	„	„ (Ibid., pp. 327–8.)
f. 70.	„	25	„	„ (Ibid., pp. 324–6.)
f. 71.	„	25	„	„ (Ibid., pp. 314–16.)
f. 72.	„	25	„	„ (Ibid., pp. 319–24.)
f. 75.	„	25	„	„ (Ibid., p. 310.)

f. 75v.	Statute,	25	Edward III,	Westminster	(*Stat. of Realm*, I, pp. 316–18.)
f. 77.	”	27	”	”	(Ibid., pp. 329–31.)
f. 78v.	”	27	”	”	(Ibid., pp. 332–43.)
f. 84.	”	27	”	”	(Ibid., pp. 343–4.)
f. 84v.	”	28	”	”	(Ibid., pp. 345–9.)
f. 87.	”	31	”	”	(Ibid., pp. 349–53.)
f. 88v.	”	31	”	”	(Ibid., pp. 353–5.)
f. 89v.	”	34	”	”	(Ibid., pp. 364–9.)
f. 92v.	”	35	”	”	(Ibid., pp. 369–70.)
f. 93.	”	36	”	”	(Ibid., pp. 371–6.)
f. 96.	”	36	”	”	(Ibid., pp. 376–8.)
f. 96v.	”	37	”	”	(Ibid., pp. 378–83.)
f. 97v.	”	38	”	”	(Ibid., pp. 383–5.)
f. 98v.	”	38	”	”	(Ibid., pp. 385–7.)
f. 99v.	”	42	”	”	(Ibid., pp. 388–90.)
f. 100v.	”	43	”	”	(Ibid., pp. 390–2.)
f. 102.	”	45	”	”	(Ibid., p. 393.)
f. 102v.	”	47	”	”	(Ibid., p. 395.)
f. 102v.	”	50	”	”	(Ibid., pp. 396–8.)
f. 104.	”	1	Richard II,	”	(*Stat. of Realm*, II, pp. 1–5.)
f. 106.	”	2	”	Gloucester.	(Ibid., pp. 6–11.)
f. 108v.	”	2	”	Westminster.	(Ibid., p. 12.)
f. 109.	”	3	”	”	(Ibid., pp. 13–15.)
f. 110.	”	4	”	Northampton.	(Ibid., p. 16.)
f. 110v.	”	5	”	Westminster.	(Ibid., pp. 17–23.)
f. 114.	”	5	”	”	(Ibid., pp. 23–6.)
f. 115v.	”	6	”	”	(Ibid., pp. 26–30.)
f. 117v.	”	6	”	”	(Ibid., pp. 30–1.)
f. 118v.	”	7	”	”	(Ibid., pp. 32–6.)
f. 121.	”	8	”	”	(Ibid., pp. 36–7.)
f. 121v.	”	9	”	”	(Ibid., pp. 38–9.)
f. 122v.	”	10	”	”	(Ibid., pp. 39–43.)
f. 124v.	”	11	”	”	(Ibid., pp. 43–55.)
f. 129v.	”	12	”	”	(Ibid., pp. 55–60.)
f. 132v.	”	13	”	”	(Ibid., pp. 61–8.)
f. 136.	”	13	”	”	(Ibid., pp. 68–74.)
f. 137v.	”	14	”	”	(Ibid., pp. 76–7.)
f. 138v.	”	15	”	”	(Ibid., pp. 78–82.)
f. 140v.	”	16	”	Winchester.	(Ibid., pp. 82–7.)
f. 143.	”	17	”	Westminster.	(Ibid., pp. 87–92.)
f. 145.	”	20	”	”	(Ibid., pp. 92–4.)
f. 146.	”	21	”	”	(Ibid., pp. 94–110.)
f. 152v.	”	1	Henry IV,	”	(Ibid., pp. 111–19.)
f. 156v.	”	2	”	”	(Ibid., pp. 120–31.)
f. 162v.	”	4	”	”	(Ibid., pp. 132–43.)
f. 168.	”	5	”	”	(Ibid., pp. 143–8.)
f. 170v.	”	6	”	Coventry.	(Ibid., pp. 148–50.)

f. 171.	Statute,	7	Henry IV,	Westminster. (Ibid., pp. 150–8.)
f. 175.	,,	9	,,	Gloucester. (Ibid., pp. 159–61.)
f. 176v.	,,	11	,,	Westminster. (Ibid., pp. 162–6.)
f. 178v.	,,	13	,,	,, (Ibid., pp. 166–9.)
f. 180.	,,	1	Henry V,	,, (Ibid., pp. 170–4.)
f. 182v.	,,	2	,,	Leicester. (Ibid., pp. 175–87.)
f. 188v.	,,	2	,,	Westminster. (Ibid., pp. 187–90.)
f. 190v.	,,	3	,,	,, (Ibid., p. 191).
f. 191.	,,	3	,,	,, (Ibid., pp. 191–6.)
f. 193.	,,	4	,,	,, (Ibid., pp. 196–200.)
f. 195.	Ordinance,	5	Henry V,	16 January (1418). (Ibid., p. 200.)
f. 195.	Statute,	7	,,	Westminster. (Ibid., pp. 201–2.)
f. 195v.	,,	8	,,	,, (Ibid., p. 203.)
f. 196.	,,	9	,,	,, (Ibid., pp. 204–9.)
f. 198v.	,,	9	,,	,, (Ibid., pp. 209–12.)
f. 200.	,,	1	Henry VI,	,, (Ibid., pp. 213–16.)
f. 201.	,,	2	,,	,, (Ibid., pp. 216–27).
f. 204v.	,,	3	,,	,, (Ibid., pp. 227–8.)
f. 205v.	,,	4	,,	Leicester. (Ibid , pp. 229–32.)
f. 207.	,,	6	,,	Westminster. (Ibid., pp. 232–8.)
f. 209v.	,,	8	,,	,, (Ibid., pp. 238–62.)
f. 220v.	,,	9	,,	,, (Ibid., pp. 263–72.)
f. 224v.	,,	10	,,	,, (Ibid., pp. 272–6.)
f. 226v.	,,	11	,,	,, (Ibid., pp. 278–88.)
f. 231v.	,,	14	,,	,, (Ibid., pp. 289–94.)
f. 234.	,,	15	,,	,, (Ibid., pp. 294–300.)
f. 236.	,,	18	,,	,, (Ibid., pp. 301–15.)
f. 242v.	,,	20	,,	,, (Ibid., pp. 315–25.)
f. 247.	,,	23	,,	,, (Ibid., pp. 326–43.)
f. 255.	,,	25	,,	Bury St. Edmunds. (Ibid., p. 344.)
f. 259.	,,	28	,,	Westminster. (Ibid., pp. 353–7.)
f. 261.	,,	29	,,	,, (Ibid., pp. 357–9.)

On flyleaf at end: Wright, Robert, del Temple In.

PETYT MS. 506

A similar volume of parchment, but not of the parentage of no. 505, containing the Statutes from 1 Edward III to 23 Henry VI, which has been re-bound in full red morocco, with the Inner Temple coat of arms on both covers. Inset on flyleaf, the old label: 'MSS. Edwardi III, Ricardi II, Henrici IV, V, VI'. On another flyleaf: Statutes from the 1st of Edward the 3rd to 23rd of Henry the 6th. Though listed as a Petyt MS., it is, in fact, a Barrington MS. The signature Daines Barrington appears on a front flyleaf. $10\frac{5}{8}'' \times 7\frac{3}{8}''$. 345 ff.

f. 1. A Table of Contents, alphabetically arranged, Accusementz to Wursted (f. 43).

f. 45. Begins in the middle of the Statute of 7 March 1 Edward III (1327), the first folio of the Statutes proper being missing. The manuscript follows generally the order of the Statutes in no. 505, to 23 Henry VI, but the entry in this manuscript is not complete for that year, ending abruptly. The following are the main divergences, especially in order and omission:

Statutes 1 Edward III are omitted. (They should appear at f. 49.)

Statutes 10 Edward III are omitted. (They should appear at f. 63v.)

f. 75v. Statute 15 Edward III (not in no. 505) has after the title: but it was revoked.

f. 77. Has the writ to the Sheriff of Lincoln, 1 October 15 Edward III (1341), revoking the abôve Statute. (Not in no. 505.)

f. 77v. Has another Statute of 15 Edward III which is not in no. 505. (*Stat. of Realm*, 1, pp. 297–8.)

f. 78v. Has a correction in the margin: et nemy dens autres to des autres, probably made by Daines Barrington.

f. 81v. Oath of Justices made 18 Edward III. (Not in no. 505.)

f. 82. Oath of Clerks of Chancery made 18 Edward III. (Not in no. 505.)

f. 117v. Statute 31 Edward III. (Not in no. 505.)

Statute 20 Henry VI is omitted. (It should appear at f. 335.)

The references to *Stat. of Realm* naturally follow those given for no. 505.

The manuscript may be dated about the middle of the fifteenth century. The writing is done with care, although occasionally the chapter numbers are missing, yet the red and blue marks have been put in. The parchment is of good quality. The first folio is missing and another put between the present foliation 34 and 35. The former has probably been torn out for its illumination; the latter has just been torn away. The beginning of the Statutes of each successive reign has an illuminated capital the full length of the folio, in gold, blue, red, green, purple, etc. (R, f. 144v; H, ff. 213v, 251, 277v). There are some red and blue capitals throughout the text, also paragraph marks, and in the margins for the chapter numbers, and the running headings, which have the regnal year one side and the name of the king on the other. The Table of Contents has some additions in the margins. There are few marginal notes to the text and the whole appearance suggests that the manuscript has been little used.

PETYT MS. 507

Proceedings in Parliament, 6 February 1626–12 May 1626. The volume is full bound in red morocco, with the Inner Temple coat of arms on both covers. Inset in a flyleaf is the old label: 'Proceedings in Parliament, 1625'. On a flyleaf: 'Proceedings in the Parliament begun Anno 1625'. Inset are 3 ff. folded in, comprising a List of Contents. $7\frac{1}{4}'' \times 5\frac{3}{4}''$. 517 ff.

f. 1. H.M.'s speech on Monday, 6 February 1625/6, being the first day of Parliament.

f. 7v. Mr. Speaker's speech, 8 February. In margin: 'When the Speaker was presented he made a speech disabling himself.'

f. 9. The Lord Keeper's answer. In margin: 'The Speaker is approved of by the King as by the Lord Keeper's speech.'

f. 10v. The Speaker's second speech. 'The Speaker's speech after his being approved of and confirmed.'

f. 21. Lord Keeper. In margin: 'The Lord Keeper's speech after the Speaker had made his and is inter alia about the affairs of Spain etc.'

f. 29. The Lord Chamberlain's speech delivered at a Committee of both Houses on 7 March. In margin: 'The Lord Chamberlain's speech, 7 March, in Parliament, touching the general estate of the affairs of Christendom.'

f. 34. Dr. Turner's queries. In margin: '11 March, about the evils which the Commonwealth labours under.'

f. 37. Dr. Turner's letter to the Speaker, 16 March. To Sir Hennage Finch, Speaker of the House of Commons.

f. 39. The heads of H.M.'s message sent to the House of Commons, by Sir Richard Weston, Chancellor of the Exchequer, 10 March, touching supply.

f. 39. Dr. Turner's letter in defence of his queries.

f. 43. The answer of the House of Commons to Sir R. Weston's message and presented by the Speaker at Whitehall, 15 March 1625/6. In margin: 'An answer of the House of Commons to the King's message, wherein they desire the King that he will be pleased to accept the faithful and necessary information and advice of his Parliament, which can have no end but the service of H.M.'

f. 44v. H.M.'s answer the same day.

f. 46v. Mr. Secretary Coke, on Monday, 20 March, was appointed to give an account unto the House of the King's occasions of money.

f. 48v. The King's letter to the Speaker of the Commons House of Parliament, sent on Monday, 20 March. In margin: '. . . about a supply with respect to the estate of Christendom and the common cause.'

f. 52. On Monday afternoon, 20 March. In margin: 'The causes of grievances and advice to the King how to remedy them by the Parliament advising the King to take unto him assistants, noble men, not upstarts and of a night's growth.'

f. 54. Sir John Eliott's speech, 27 March. In margin: '. . . about the nation being weakened in strength and safety and many men and ships lost.'

f. 58v. H.M.'s speech at Whitehall, 27 March. In margin: '. . . to both Houses . . . wherein he shows the Commons their errors and unparliamentary proceedings in Parliament.'

f. 59v. The Lord Keeper's speech the same day. In margin: '. . . to the same purpose, wherein he mentioned the insolvency of Dr. Turner and commendations of the Duke of Buckingham.'

f. 69. H.M.'s second speech. In margin: '. . . about the war in the Palatinate.'

f. 70v. To the King's Most Excellent Majesty. The Humble Remonstrance of the Commons now assembled in Parliament, 5 April. In margin: 'Delivered by Committee of 30 of House of Commons.'

f. 78. 13 April 1626. Mr. Chancellor of the Exchequer's message from the King to the House of Commons on Thursday.

f. 80. An explanation from the King delivered by the Duke of Buckingham at a Conference of both Houses in the Painted Chamber, 30 March 1626.

f. 96v. Lord Conway. In margin: 'speech against the jealousies raised in the House that the monies have been expended unusefully and without counsel, wherein is taken notice of the charge of the Palatinate war.'

f. 100v. The Duke of Buckingham. In margin: '. . . account of the business of Rochelle.'

f. 103. The Lord Chamberlain. In margin: '. . . about the same matter.'

f. 104v. The Duke of Buckingham. In margin: 'justification of himself against the accusations of him of selling Bishoprics, Judge's places, honours etc.'

f. 110. The Lord Keeper's letter to the Earl of Bristol. In margin: 'with his writ of summons to the Parliament, yet his lordship by the Lord Keeper's letter was not to appear in Parliament.'

f. 111. The Earl of Bristol's answer to the former letter, 12 April 1626.

f. 115. The Earl of Bristol's petition to the Lords, 18 April, 'presented to the Committee by his Countess.'

f. 117v. My Lord Keeper's message from the King to the House of Peers.

f. 119. Concerning the Duke's not answering the House of Commons.

f. 122v. Sir John Eliott's speech.

f. 140. The humble remonstrance and petition of the Peers, 18 April. In margin: 'about their privileges and in particular about the absence of the Earl of Arundel.'

f. 143. The speech of Sir Dudley Carleton, Mr. Vice-Chamberlain, the next day, after the commitment of Sir Dudley Digges and Sir John Eliott, delivered to the Commons House of Parliament, 12 May 1626.

f. 151. Wednesday, 17 May 1626. The Peers second petition to H.M. concerning the Earl of Arundel, 20 May 1626.

f. 155. Grants and gifts to the Duke himself or to his mediate use.

f. 160. Divers grants to the Duke's brothers and others of his kindred.

f. 162. The answer of the Duke to these grants and gifts contained in the schedule, which either were or are affirmed to have been to him or to his mediate use.

f. 174. Articles preferred and charged to the Earl of Bristol against the Duke of Buckingham.

f. 179. Articles of the Earl of Bristol concerning the Lord Conway, presented to the Lords of the Higher House of Parliament, 1 May 1626.

f. 189. 1 May 1626. Order of proceedings.

f. 190. Reasons why the Lords should not give way of judgement against the Earl of Bristol till the cause be examined in the House of Peers and found to be a consequent fit for such manner of proceeding.

f. 194. The protestation of the Lower House of Parliament, 13 May 1626. In margin: 'touching Sir Dudley Digges being charged in the article of the plaster applied to King James.'

f. 195. To our trusty and most well beloved Sir Hennage Finch, kt., Speaker of our Commons House of Parliament.

f. 196v. The message to the Lords agreed upon, 9 May 1626, to be delivered to the Lords House at the bar, 11 May, by Sir Nathaniel Rich, touching the commitment of the Duke.

f. 198. Articles of several high treasons and other great, enormous crimes, offences and contempts committed by John, Earl of Bristol, against our late Sovereign Lord King James of blessed memory, deceased, and our Sovereign Lord the King's Majesty that now is, charged by H.M.'s Attorney General, on H.M.'s behalf in the most Ancient Honourable Court of Parliament, 1 May 1626, before the King and his Lords there.

f. 212v. The answer of Lord Conway to the eleven articles delivered against him in the Upper House of Parliament by the Earl of Bristol, 1 May 1626. In margin: 'heard in the House, 13 June 1626.'

f. 258. The Earl of Bristol's speech, 6 May 1626. In margin: 'and Mr. Attorney's reply.'

f. 277. The answer of John, Earl of Bristol, to the articles of several high treasons (as f. 198 above). Eleven articles.

f. 361. The Commons declaration and impeachment against the Duke of Buckingham. Thirteen points.

f. 395. The eight speeches presented by the House of Commons against the Duke of Buckingham to both Houses of Parliament, in the Painted Chamber, by the Committees and persons following in order as they were delivered, vizt. Sir Dudley Digges, being the first of the eight.

f. 399v. The 2nd and 3rd articles of the Commons' complaint against the Duke of Buckingham were presented to the Lords and opened by Mr. Herbert in this manner.

f. 408. Mr. Selden against the Duke for his not guarding the seas, and for stay of the ship called the St. Peter after sentence.

f. 423v. The substance of the Commons' evidence against the Duke of Buckingham touching the £10,000 by him unlawfully exacted and extorted of the East India Company, by colour of his office of Lord Admiral of England. Delivered by Mr. John Glanvill.

f. 470v. Mr. Sherland's speech, being one of the eight that presented grievances of the Kingdom to both Houses of Parliament against the Duke for selling honours, delivered in the Painted Chamber, 10 May 1626.

f. 488. Mr. Pym against the Duke of Buckingham for his procuring honours for his poor kindred.

f. 503. Mr. Wansford's speech against the Duke delivered before both Houses of Parliament, in the Painted Chamber, 10 May 1626, for his presumption in giving physic to the King.

f. 508. Sir John Eliott's speech, being the last of the eight that presented the grievances of the kingdom to both Houses of Parliament, in the Painted Chamber.

The above Proceedings are very much fuller than the account in the *Journal of the House of Commons* and are clearly a compilation by a member of the House of Commons. They should be compared with the Diary of the Parliament of 1626, in a manuscript in the Cambridge University Library, February to March 1626, part of which is printed in the *English Historical Review*, XVII (1902), pp. 705–7, where it is suggested that this diary is possibly the work of Bulstrode Whitlocke, and with the Lonsdale MS. noted in *Hist. MSS. Com., Thirteenth Report*, App. Pt. VII, pp. 1–33.

PETYT MS. 508

A volume on parchment containing the Statutes from Magna Carta to 14 Edward II, with miscellaneous Legal Tracts and Memoranda, re-bound in full red morocco, with Inner Temple coat of arms on both covers. Though listed as a Petyt MS. it is, in fact, a Barrington MS. The signature Daines Barrington appears on a flyleaf and on f. 12v, and a brief description of the manuscript, apparently by him, follows the signature. The manuscript is fairly well written in several hands. There is a little illumination in red and blue, paragraphing in the text and in the margins, and a few illuminated capitals in the same colours. The parchment is not of good quality and is somewhat stained by damp. It appears to be a somewhat mediocre manuscript, to be dated about the first quarter of the fourteenth century, with a few later additions. $5\frac{5}{8}'' \times 4''$. 220 ff.

On the preliminary parchment leaves are various notes, including f. 3, the length of the reigns of English kings, William I to Henry V; f. 4, a recipe for staunching of blood and some verses beginning: Gode that was born in Bedleam; ff. 5–9 contain the capitula of the Statutes, Magna Carta to Westminster II; ff. 9v–10, a list of the Statutes contained in the volume, numbered 1–50. The Statutes proper begin f. 13.

f. 13. Magna Carta, 11 February 9 Henry III (1225), taken from the confirmation of 12 October 25 Edward I (1297). (*Stat. of Realm*, I, Chart. of Liberties, pp. 22–5.)

f. 20v. Charter of the Forests, 11 February 9 Henry III (1225), again taken from the confirmation of 12 October 25 Edward I (1297). (Ibid., p. 27.)

f. 24v. Sentence and the Pope's confirmation of the above charters, Ides of May (15 May) 1253. French. (Ibid., pp. 6–7.)

f. 25. Provisions of Merton, Morrow of St. Vincent 20 Henry III (23 January 1236). (Ibid., I, pp. 1–4.)

f. 29. Statute of Marlborough, Octave of St. Martin 52 Henry III (18 November 1267). (Ibid., pp. 19–25.)

f. 38v. Statute of Westminster I, Morrow of Close of Easter 3 Edward I (12 April 1275). (Ibid., pp. 26–39.)

f. 59v. Statute de Bigamis, 4 Edward I. (Ibid., pp. 43–4.)

f. 62. Statute on appointment of Justices (Ragman), 4 Edward I. (Ibid., f. 44.)

f. 63v. Statute of Gloucester, Quindene of St. John the Baptist 6 Edward I (8 July 1278). (Ibid., pp. 45–50.)

f. 69v. Explanations of Statute of Gloucester, Sunday after the Feast of St. Peter ad Vincula (7 August 1278). (Ibid., p. 50.)

f. 74. Statute de Religiosis, 7 Edward I. (Ibid., p. 51.)

f. 75v. Statute of Merchants, 12 October 13 Edward I (1285). (Ibid., pp. 53–4.)

f. 80. Statute of Westminster II, Quindene of St. John the Baptist 13 Edward I (8 July 1285). (Ibid., pp. 71–95.)

f. 119v. Statute of Winchester, Octave of Michaelmas, 13 Edward I (4 October 1285). (Ibid., pp. 96–8.)

f. 123v. Statute de Prerogativa Regis, 13 Edward I. (Ibid., pp. 226–7.)

f. 128. Statute of Exeter, 13 Edward I. (Ibid., pp. 210–12.)

f. 134v. Statute of Quo Warranto, 21 Edward I. (Ibid., p. 107.)

f. 135v. Statute of Quo Warranto (New), Third Day of Whitsun, 18 Edward I (23 May 1290), recited and confirmed, 6 February 20 Edward I (1292). (Ibid.)

f. 140. New Addition to Statute of Quo Warranto, 21 Edward I. (Ibid.)

f. 140v. Writ sent to Justices according to the constitution, 12 July 21 Edward I (1293).

f. 141. Statute of Westminster III, Quindene of St. John the Baptist, 18 Edward I (8 July 1290). (Ibid., p. 106.) (Quia Emptores.)

f. 142. Statute on liberties purchased, 1 April 19 Edward I (1291). (Ibid., p. 131.)

f. 143v. Statute of Champarty, 20 Edward I. (Ibid., p. 139.)

f. 144. Statute for defence of right, 20 Edward I. (Ibid., p. 110.)

f. 145. Statute of vouching to warranty, Feast of St. Hilary, 20 Edward I (13 January 1292). (Ibid., pp. 108–9.)

f. 146. Statute of Waste, 20 Edward I. (Ibid., p. 109.)

f. 148. Statute of evil-doers in parks, 21 Edward I. (Ibid., pp. 111–12.)

f. 148v. Statute of Conspirators, 6 November 21 Edward I (1293). (Ibid., p. 216.)

f. 149. Statute on putting on Assizes, 22 Edward I. (Ibid., p. 113.)

f. 150v. Statute of Conspirators, 22 Edward I.

f. 152v. Confirmation of Magna Carta and Charter of the Forests, 2 April 27 Edward I (1299). (Ibid., pp. 114–19.)

f. 154. Statute of Fines, 2 April 27 Edward I (1299). (Ibid., pp. 126–30.)

f. 157v. Articuli super Cartas, 28 Edward I. (Ibid., pp. 136–41.)

f. 166. Statute of Escheators, called the Statute of Lincoln, Octave of St. Hilary, 29 Edward I (20 January 1301). (Ibid., pp. 142–3.)

f. 167v. Statute on taking inquisitions, Sunday after Michaelmas, 33 Edward I (3 October 1305). (Ibid., p. 143.)

f. 168v. Statute of Protections, 18 November 34 Edward I (1306). (Ibid., p. 131.)

Statute of the Forests called Additions to the Statute of the Forests, 34 Edward I. (Ibid., pp. 147–9.)

f. 169v. Statute of Joint Feoffees, 27 May 28 Edward I (1300). (Ibid., pp. 145–7.)

f. 172. Statute of Carlisle, Octave of St. Hilary, 35 Edward I (20 January 1307). (Ibid., pp. 150–2.)

f. 175. Statute of Attorneys and receiving Fines, called Carlisle II. (Ibid., p. 215.)

f. 179. Statute Circumspecte Agatis, 13 Edward I. (Ibid., p. 101.)

f. 179v. Statute called Consultations, 18 Edward I. (Ibid., p. 108.)

f. 180v. Statute of Lincoln on Sheriffs, 9 Edward II. (Ibid., pp. 174–5.)

f. 181v. Statute on foreigners vouched to warranty, 9 Edward II.

f. 182v. Articles for the clergy, 10 Edward II. (Ibid., pp. 171–6.)

f. 189. Statute of York, 12 Edward II. (Ibid., pp. 177–9.)

f. 194. Statute de Scaccario, 14 Edward II. (Ibid., pp. 197–8.)

f. 198. Distraints of the Exchequer. (Ibid., pp. 197–8.)

f. 199v. Glossary of Words (Expositio Vocabulorum).

f. 202. Statute of Articles of View of Frankpledge. (*Stat. of Realm*, I pp. 246–7.)

f. 203v. Assize of Bread and Ale. (Ibid., pp. 199–200.)

f. 205. Assize of Weights. (Ibid., p. 204.)

f. 205v. Agreement of money and measures. (Ibid., p. 219.)

f. 206. Agreement made on punishing those who break that assize and on forestallers and bad victuallers. (Ibid., pp. 201–2.)

f. 207v. The Manner of extending a Manor. (Ibid., pp. 242–3.)

f. 208v. Manual of Calculating (a later addition of about 1400), being rules for calculating the Golden Numbers, Leap Year, etc., based on Latin mnemonic verses.

PETYT MS. 509

14 volumes

This group of manuscripts consists of 14 composite folio volumes, uniformly bound in full light-brown dressed calf, with the Inner Temple coat of arms on both covers. They are of almost uniform size, none varying more than $\frac{1}{8}''$ from the standard $16\frac{3}{8}'' \times 10\frac{3}{8}''$. They are not, of course, Petyt manuscripts. All the volumes, except 2, 5, and 13, which are foliated, are paged. The totals of pages or folios numbered are given below. Besides these numbered pages or folios, the volumes contain a substantial number of unnumbered pages or folios, which consist of notes on paper of varying sizes. Volumes 5 to 12 have alphabetical indexes of parties at the end. All the volumes are entitled 'Adjudicata B. R.'. They are, in fact, the judge's papers of a Justice of King's Bench, and contain the judgements of the Court of King's Bench, covering the period 14 to 27 George II, inclusive. They belonged to Sir Martin Wright, who after being a Baron of the Exchequer, 1739–40, was made a Justice of King's Bench on 28 November 1740, and resigned on 1 February 1755. They were the papers or books on cases prepared by the two Clerks assigned to enrol pleas in the King's Bench, given to the judge, who perused them before the case reached the Court and used them during the hearing. They were probably presented to the Inner Temple in 1769, when Sir Martin's daughters and executrixes, Elizabeth and Dorothy Wright, presented a collection of his law books. (*Cal. of Inner Temple Records*, v, 1751–1800, p. 232, 6 June 1769.) In almost every case, the judgements, with the date on which they were delivered, were entered upon the papers by Mr. Justice Wright. In many cases the proceedings of the case were recorded during the hearing by the judge, and the notes and precedents which he collected before hearing the case and his comments upon them were incorporated with the judge's papers. In all important cases these are voluminous and in many instances of very great interest and importance. In all, there are papers relating to 1,004 cases heard from 1740–54, comprised in 9,256 pages, besides some thousands of unnumbered pages of notes, precedents, and proceedings. The 1,004 cases consisted of 384 cases on writs of error. Of these, 339 cases came from the Court of Common Bench, 2 from the Court of Exchequer, 16 from the Court of the Palace of Westminster, 2 from the Palatinate of Durham, 1 from the Palatinate of Lancaster, 2 from the Court of Great Sessions, Wales, 2 from Assizes, 14 from Courts of Quarter Sessions, 11 from Borough Courts of Record etc., 4 from Justices of the Peace, 1 from the Hundred Court of Penryn, and 1 from a Court of Sewers, 7 from the Court of King's Bench, Ireland, and 1 from the Court of Exchequer, Ireland. There are 38 cases on writs of mandamus, 20 on quo warranto and 18 cases for the opinion of the Court. After cases in error the most numerous were cases on debt for goods, services, rent, or loans, or on bonds or writings obligatory, which totalled 301. There were 68 cases on Promissory Notes, 10 on Bills of Exchange, 7 on Policies of Insurance, 13 on ejectment, and 15 on covenant. The remainder of the cases are of a miscellaneous nature, including treason, sedition, assault, forgery, retaining goods found, charterparty, bill of sale, lotteries, impounding, defamatory words of a Justice of the Peace, withdrawing from employment and riot, bribery at elections, return of a knight of the shire, taking game, and obscene libel.

As a series of judge's papers this group is exceptional, if not unique, in completeness and continuity. They cover the whole period of Sir Martin Wright's tenure of office as a Justice of King's Bench. They are important, not only on matters of substantive law and of procedure, but they throw an invaluable light upon the machinery of justice, detailing private meetings of the judges in the Lord Chief Justice's Chambers, the discussions which took place there, differences of opinion among the judges, and interesting personal sidelights. Representative examples of their interest and importance are given below in the account of each volume. These must be regarded as representative only, and as an indication of the material which can be found in few other sources for the history and practice of law in the middle decades of the eighteenth century.

Many of the cases covered in these 14 volumes are found in the following reports: Strange, *K.B.*, ed. Nolan, 2 vols., 1716–49; Wilson, *K.B. & C.B.*, 3 vols., 1742–74; Blackstone, *K.B.*, 2 vols., 1746–79; Sayer, *K.B.*, 1751–6; Kenyon, *K.B.*, ed. Hanmer, 2 vols., 1753–9; *English Reports*, vols. 94, 95, 96.

VOLUME I

Judgements of the Court of King's Bench, 14 George II, 1740–41. 538 pp.

Of the 67 cases for which there are papers in this volume, 24 are on writs of error, 21 from the Court of Common Bench, 2 from King's Bench, Ireland; 9 are on writs of mandamus, 1 on quo warranto, 1 for Opinion of the Court; 26 are on debt for goods, services, rent, or on bonds or writings obligatory, 1 on a promissory note, 1 on a bill of exchange; 1 each on forging an affidavit and certificate, regulating cloth in the West Riding, ejectment, and on a plea by the Board of Admiralty on Woolwich dockyard.

The following cases are of some interest or importance:

Error Common Bench: Samuel Worrall *v.* Mary Hoff. Objection upon certiorari return. No original, rather judgement by default and not on verdict, but in the book certiorari is not returned but in book delivered to L.C.J. Return the p.c. is no original. Query how it is. The Court was afterwards moved for a certiorari ad informandam conscientiam and was granted. (pp. 325–34.)

The plaintiff in error returned a certiorari that no original was filed with the Custos Brevium of the Common Pleas. And the defendant in error has obtained a rule to return a certiorari to inform the Court of the original sued out by him. 8 June 1741. Judgement affirmed. (pp. 413–16.)

Mandamus: King *v.* Hasswell. John Hasswell of town of Cambridge exercised office of one of Common Council. 2 May 1741. Judgement for King. (pp. 131–4.)

King *v.* Sir Henry Penrice, kt., Doctor of Laws, Official of Archdeacon of Middlesex. Moses Tucker and William Kendale, in Easter vestry elected Churchwardens of parish of St. Martins in the Fields, co. Midd. Refused to swear them. 9 May 1741. Return allowed.

King *v*. Sir Henry Penrice (as above). Edward Shepherd and William Campbell elected Churchwardens of parish of St. Georges, Hanover Square. Refused to swear them. 9 May 1741. Return allowed. (pp. 161–4.)

King *v*. Charles Pinfold the Younger, Doctor of Laws, Commissary, co. Surr. William Trehearne and Thomas Webb elected Churchwardens of parish of St. Thomas, Southwark. Refusal to swear them. 9 May 1741. Return allowed. (Trehearne not elected.) (pp. 165–6.)
King *v*. Charles Pinfold (as above). Edward Davis and Thomas Webb elected Churchwardens of parish of St. Thomas, Southwark. Refusal to swear them. 9 May 1741. Return allowed. (Webb not elected.) (pp. 167–8.)

King *v*. Richard Tucker, of borough and town of Weymouth and Melcombe Regis, co. Dorset, esq. Exercised office of Mayor. 4 May 1741. Judgement absolute for King. Writ of error was brought upon the judgement in the House of Lords and the judgement affirmed 1 December 1741, L. C. J. Willes, Carter, Reynolds and Abney, Barons, and Burnet and Denison, Justices, being present and giving their opinions seriatim for affirmance of the judgement. Note, L. C. J. Lee, bro. Chapple and I did not attend, it being our judgement. Ld. C. B. Parker was accidentally absent, and bro. Fortescue not in health to attend. The Lords upon searching precedents gave no costs, the statute not extending to affirmance of judgement in quo warranto. Note that all the justices agreed that an Alderman was a burgess, but not a burgess qualified to be Mayor, upon which some of the Lords disliked the notion being a burgess and not a burgess, upon which Ld. C. J. Willes, to show the reasonableness of his being a burgess and yet not qualified to be Mayor, put the case that if an Act of Parliament was made that all the members of the House of Commons should be chosen out of freeholders, their lordships were freeholders and yet would not be qualified to be chosen members of the House of Commons. (pp. 169–98.)

King *v*. Nance. James Nance, of borough of Grandpond, otherwise Grandpound, co. Cornwall, gent., exercised office of Mayor. 23 November 1741. Opinion of Court delivered by L. C. J. Lee. Judgement for King. (pp. 425–442x.)

Martin Wardell, citizen of London, elected to Common Council for ward of Vintry. Writ to Sir William Rous, kt., Alderman for Ward of Vintry, refused to swear him. To hold wardmote on precept of Lord Mayor. Question of right of 35 persons to vote. No judgement was given at this time bro. Chapple doubting but on Monday, 15 June 1741, L. C. J. Lee declared that bro. Chapple had further considered this matter and concurred in opinion with the rest of the court and gave judgement for plaintiff. Note that when Rule is given upon the Postea for Judgement, a Peremptory Mandamus will issue of course. (pp. 515–28.)

King *v*. William Bryan, John Ashton, and William Blackshaw, Churchwardens of parish of St. Mary Matfallen, otherwise Whitechapel, co. Midd. Inhabitants and parishioners have been accustomed to choose a parish clerk. Vacant. Churchwardens ought to call a vestry. Have neglected to do so. Defendants deny the ancient custom. 9 February 1741. Return allowed. (pp. 7–10.)

Quo warranto: King *v*. Samuel Hollester, of King's town and parish of Maidstone, co. Kent. Exercised office of one of Jurats of town. To be tried at the bar on Wednesday, 29 April. Tried accordingly and verdict for King on all counts. (pp. 135–56.)

Justices of Peace, co. Surr. King *v*. John Avenel, dwelling in hamlet of Newdigate, in parish of Newdigate, co. Surr., convicted of having sold beer there without being duly licenced, 17 June 1741. Conviction confirmed. (pp. 423–4.)

Opinion: Assizes, New Sarum, 15 July 1738. Zachary Talbot, plaintiff, *v.* George Hubble and 6 others, Officers of Excise and Justices of the Peace and Constables for the city. Talbot, a public-house keeper, concealing in his house a quantity of run tea, £6 being treble value. Goods seized. Judgement by Court 9 June 1741. (pp. 505–14.)

Debt etc.: John Baker esq. *v.* Gyles. Geo. Agar moved for leave to withdraw demurrer and had leave to withdraw it (Mr. Denison, on the other side, not opposing it), upon payment. Pleadings are issuable and taking note of trial the first sitting of next term. (pp. 75–86.)

James Bowyer *v.* Samuel Bampton. Money advanced on notes to game and play at dice and other games. The single question is whether the defendant who gave these notes is chargeable with the payment of the several sums of money therein mentioned to the plaintiff or not. Argued 12 June 1741 and by the opinion of the whole Court the defendant was not chargeable. Judgement for the defendant and plaintiff to pay the costs of a nonsuit. (pp. 359–90.)

Forging an affidavit and certificate: King *v.* William O'Brien. Copy Record for forging an affidavit and certificate by which he received the bounty money of Ann Pearce. Defendant had judgement the last day of Michaelmas term, 14 George II, 1740. On the said conviction to go to all the Courts, with a paper on his forehead importing his crime. Imprisonment for 1 year and to find £1,000 security for his good behaviour for 7 years. On 2nd. conviction to stand in the pillory at Charing Cross for 1 hour with the like paper importing his offence, to pay a fine of £5 and to be imprisoned till paid. (pp. 17–22.)

Regulating cloth in West Riding of Yorkshire: King against John Charlesworth, of Gomersal, clothdresser, on information by John Waller, cloth searcher. Conviction on St. 11 Geo. I for regulating cloths in West Riding of York. 1. Objection that Act relates only to cloth made in West Riding of York. 2. Act relates only to cloth made, not dressed, and also that it had not seals after it was penseved, not after it was dressed. Quashed 7 February 1741. £20. moiety to be paid to informer, moiety to Overseers of parish of Gomersal. (pp. 27–8.)

Withdrawing from employment in dockyard and riot; King *v.* William Reeve and 5 others. Dudley Ryder esq., Attorney General stated offence while at war with King Philip of Spain. For national defence ships being built in the dockyard at Woolwich. Defendants and others to number of 100 and upwards, unknown, to prevent public service of kingdom, 3 November 1740, withdrew from employment in dockyard and created riot. The defendant is to be called upon his recognizance on the morning, Tuesday, 10 February 1741 in order to receive final judgement. The defendant stands convicted by his own default. Defendant was brought up the last day of Easter term to receive judgement, but the Court not having considered what judgement to give, committed him, and in Trinity term gave judgement that he should be imprisoned for 6 months and be bound in his own recognizance of £100 for his good behaviour for 7 years, defendant having made affidavit that he was worth nothing and had a large family. (pp. 453–8.)

Notes: Notes on the case of the Earl of Montague against the Lord Preston, for office of Master of King's Wardrobe. Grant 23 Charles II, to plaintiff for life, reciting a former grant to the Earl of Sandwich. Defendant claimed office by virtue of a grant of 1 James II. Objected that an excommunication is a spiritual judgement and therefore the temporal judges shall not dispute upon the manner of it. Note. Judges of the common law may adjudge upon the manner and also upon the matter of the Certificate. Abuse or misuses is cause of forfeiture. On case of Sir John Bennett *v.* Doctor Estdale. Men excommunicated by the bishop not criminal persons, cannot be judges. (pp. 207–14.)

VOLUME 2

Judgements of the Court of King's Bench, 15 George II, 1741–1742. 482 ff.

Of the 110 cases for which there are papers in this volume, 53 are on writs of error, 46 from the Court of Common Bench, 1 from the Court of the Palace of Westminster, and 1 each from the Court of Record of the Borough of Boston, co. Lincs., Quarter Sessions, co. Surr., Justices of the Peace, Saxmundham, co. Suff., Court of Guildhall, Worcester, Justices of the Peace, co. Midd., and Court of City of Norwich; 2 are for the Opinion of the Court, 8 on writs of mandamus, 2 on quo warranto; 32 are cases on debt for goods, services, rent, or on bonds or writings obligatory, 8 on promissory notes, 1 on charterparty, 2 on setting up lotteries, and one each on impounding geldings and defamatory words of a Justice of the Peace.

The following cases are of some interest or importance:

Error Common Bench; Christina Heaseman, widow, *v.* Robert Moore, gent. Ejectment. 2 8 October 1741. Agreed at Ld. C. J.'s chambers to affirm judgement. (pp. 85–91.)

Surrey Quarter Sessions: King *v.* Inhabitants of Putney. Appeal to Quarter Sessions by Churchwardens and Overseers of parish of Wandsworth in settlement case. (p. 98.)

Justices of Peace, Saxmundham, co. Suff.: King *v.* George Lindup of Saxmundham. Thomas Mason of Little Glemham. co. Suff. on information of Lindup, conviction poaching partridge. Objection that informer is witness. Informer is not a good witness. 28 November, 1741. Quashed. (ff. 99–100.)

Justices of Peace, co. Midd.: King *v.* Keene. At parish of St. Mary's, Islington, before 2 Justices of the Peace. Copy of Conviction. 30 June 1742. Affirmed that Justices of the Peace having signed the conviction since it was filed, which Mr. Lacy objected to and desired time to enquire how he came to sign it, but the original conviction being signed by both Justices, and there being no other objection to it the Court affirmed it. Edward Turner, citizen and draper of London, for the poor of the parish of St. Andrews, Holborn, and himself, that David Keene, of parish of St. Clement Danes, a retailer of coals, since 6 March 1664, sold to William Bennett, of parish of St. Andrews, Holborn, surgeon, 78 bushels of sea coals, being 10 bushels less than 3 chaldron, equals 108 bushels, forfeited cases and broke value, £9–12s. (ff. 315–17.)

Mandamus: King against William Leonard, of borough of Leominster, co. Hereford, innholder, claim to be capital burgess. 11 November 1741. Judgement for King. (ff. 103–4.)

King *v.* Samuel Shenton, rector of parish of St. Johns, Wapping, co. Midd., to appoint a lecturer or curate at £30 p.a. to assist him. Return has appointed Richard Nagle. 18 November 1741. Return allowed. (ff. 105–7.)

King *v.* Mayor, Sheriffs and Commonalty of Lincoln. Indenture of apprenticeship to be enrolled and freedom. No such custom. 10 February 1742. Return allowed. (ff. 209–10.)

King *v.* Inhabitants of parish of St. Michael's near Winchester, in Hampshire. Settlement. Churchwardens and Overseers of poor of parish of Godalming, co. Surr., and the same parish of St. Michael's. (ff. 320–5.)

King *v.* Thomas Taylor, clerk, curate of parish of Clifton. Office of parish clerk. 25 May 1742. Return allowed. (ff. 339–40.)

Bosworth esq., Chamberlain of London *v.* Blegden. Return by Lord Mayor and Sheriffs to Sir William Lee, kt., C.J.K.B. Custom that no person, being free of city, shall set to work in any manual occupation or handicraft any foreigner. Blegden taken into custody by original bill on Act of Common Council and prosecuted at suit of John Bosworth, Chamberlain of city of London, plaintiff, in a plea of debt, £5, for breach of Act. (ff. 397–400.)

King *v.* Thomas Towle, Doctor of Laws, Commissary of peculiar jurisdiction of Dean and Chapter of Norwich. Churchwardens of parish of St. Pauls, in city of Norwich, 7 July 1742. Return allowed. (f. 432.)

Quo warranto: King *v.* Francis Woodhouse, of borough of Leominster, co. Hereford, esq. Office of capital burgesses. 11 November 1741. Judgement for King. (ff. 109–109x.)

Opinion: King *v.* Thomas Fletcher. Argued 25 May 1742. Plaintiff desired till Monday to consider the case. Defendant was brought again to the bar on Monday 31 May 1742 but the Attorney General did not appear to support the indictment. Judgement was then instantly given for the defendant. Sessions of oyer and terminer etc. at Thetford, smuggling tea. 31 May 1742. Ld. C. J. Lee delivered judgement of Court. (ff. 309–14.)

King *v.* John Robins, of borough of Bossinney and Trevena in Tintagel, co. Cornwall, yeoman. Used office of Mayor. 12 May 1742, Bro. Broke for King. Mr. Robinson for defendant consented that judgement be given for King, and judgement was given accordingly without argument. (ff. 326–38.)

Setting up lottery: King *v.* Francis Gregg, of parish of St. Paul's, Covent Garden, co. Midd., set up lottery of 13 chances for disposal of clock by dice. Copy indictment. Judgement arrested. 23 June 1742, it having hung long and no one appearing to oppose the arresting of judgement. (ff. 421–2.)

King *v.* Henry Bond, of Thames Street, London, yeoman and others. Lottery at Hampstead. (f. 423.)

VOLUME 3

Judgements of the Court of King's Bench, 16 George II, 1742–3. 846 pp.

Of the 82 cases for which there are papers in this volume, 46 are on writs of error, 34 from the Court of Common Bench, 1 from the Court of King's Bench, Ireland, 1 from the Court of the Palace of Westminster, 1 from the Court of Pleas, Palatinate of Durham, 1 from Assizes, co. Northampton, 1 Assizes, co. Southampton, 1 Assizes, co. Cumberland, 1 Quarter Sessions, co. Westmorland, 1 Court of Record of Portmote, Rochester, 1 Court of Hundred of Penryn, co. Cornwall, 1 Pleas, Borough of Harwich, and 1 Justices of Peace, co. Oxford; 2 for Opinion of the Court, 3 on writs of mandamus, 20 are cases for debt or goods, services, rent, or on bonds or writings obligatory; 5 on promissory notes; and 1 each on covenant, impounding a cow, ejectment, retaining goods found, assault and imprisonment, accused of having French pox.

The following cases are of some interest or importance:

Error of Outlawry: Elizabeth Sericold *v.* Sir George Hampson, late of London, bart., 29 November 1742. Rule upon bro. Draper's motion to show cause why the outlawry should not be reversed upon filing common bail. 21 April 1743. Outlawry was reversed. (pp. 533–44.)

Northampton Assizes. Ball *v.* Hundred of Wynnersley. Occupier of farm at Weston at yearly rent of £140, going with a waggon of cheese to Daventry fair robbed of sum of £130. 15s. in Preston Lane, about a mile from his house, which Preston Lane in Hundred of Wynnersley. Notice given of robbery. Notice given to inhabitants of villages he rode through. Hue and cry. 12 November 1742 argued again and whole Court of opinion for plaintiff. Rule to stay if postea is discharged. (pp. 25–8.)

Cumberland Assizes: King *v.* William Grave of Glencoyne in parish of Barton, co. Westmorland, yeoman, on information of Richard Brown of Greystoke. Conviction for killing deer. Conviction confirmed. (pp. 603–6.)

Quarter Sessions, Westmorland: Elizabeth Richardson went to Justice of Peace and confessed with child. 'Sessions case referred to bro. Parker and me in the York circuit and our opinion thereon'. 'This case is darkly stated etc.,' signed J. Parker, M. Wright. Durham Quarter Sessions. Appeal by Thomas Bellys and 5 other officers of H.M. Customs in the port of Sunderland. Rateable for relief of poor. 'Upon hearing counsel on both sides we are of opinion that Thomas Bellys and the other officers of the customs are not liable towards the relief of the poor of the parish of Sunderland in respect of their salary. 29 December 1741. J. Parker, M. Wright. Westmorland Quarter Sessions. Opinion competent witness to W. being bound as an apprentice. Signed as above. Other opinions Durham Quarter Sessions, settlement at Haswell, settlement Hesleton: Case of the Inhabitants of Walkridge *v.* the Inhabitants of Chester. (pp. 825–46).

J.P.s. Oxfordshire. Giles Harris of parish of Asthall, yeoman, in parish of Shipton under Wychwood, in Wychwood Forest, killed a deer. Copy Record of Conviction. 29 November 1742. Conviction confirmed. (pp. 143–8.)

Mandamus: King *v.* John Adlam, Mayor of borough of Westbury. Patrick Marky elected mayor. Return allowed, no objection being made to it. (pp. 135–8.)

King *v.* Ralph Bridesale, clerk, Archdeacon of Winchester. Churchwardens of parish of Bentworth, co. Southampton. 24 November 1742. Return allowed, no objection being made to it though liable to exception as prevailed in Q. *v.* Guise. (pp. 139–42.)

King *v.* Robert Lacy and William Richardson, Justices of the Peace, co. Surr., fraudulent removal of goods. 18 June 1743. Return allowed. (pp. 741–6.)

Ejectment: John Martin *v.* John Strachan the younger, late of Milton Abbas, esq., and Luke Harrison, late of same, yeoman. The cause will be in the paper Tuesday, 3 February 1740/1. To next term, Mr. Gundry being absent. Argued 5 June 1741. For further argument. 21 May argued again. Stands for judgement. 6 November 1742, on motion at side bar appointed for judgement in Hilary term next. (pp. 302x–372.)

Retaining goods found: Sir John Hartopp, bart., *v.* Henry Hoare, Benjamin Hoare, Richard Hoare etc. Hartopp in possession of a pair of single stone brilliant diamond earrings with large single drops; casually lost; found by defendants; refused to deliver; disposed to their own use. 18 December 1742. L.C.J. Lee, bro. Chapple, Denison and I met at Ld. C. J. Lee's chambers and agreed that the property of the jewels remained in the plaintiff and that the action lies against the defendants and that judgement ought to be given for the plaintiff upon the merits. We agreed likewise that pawns are not to be considered as sales in market overt. 10 May 1743, Judgement for plaintiff. (pp. 548x–558.)

VOLUME 4

Judgements of Court of King's Bench, 17 George II, 1743–4. 571 pp.

Of the 62 cases for which there are papers in this volume, 31 are on writs of error, 23 from the Court of Common Bench, 3 from the Court of the Palace of Westminster, 1 from Quarter Sessions, co. Middlesex, 4 from Court of town of Kingston upon Thames; 3 are for the Opinion of the Court, 3 on writs of mandamus; 13 cases are for debt for goods, services, rent, or on bonds or writings obligatory, 5 on promissory notes; 2 on covenant, and 1 each on entering manor etc., ejectment, sedition, return of knight of the shire, bribery at election.

The following cases are of some interest or importance:

Error Common Bench: Richard Newdegate, Esq., executor of John Newdegate dec., late one of the Sworn Clerks of the Six Clerks Office, in the division of Isaac Whittington, Esq., *v.* William Goostrey, gent., Attorney of Common Bench. 22 November 1743. Judgement affirmed. (pp. 45–54.)

Quarter Sessions, Delivery of Newgate. King *v.* William Chetwynd, aged 15, for death of Thomas Ricketts, aged 19. Special Verdict and plea of pardon for murder. 11 February 1744. Pardon allowed with bail or surety for good behaviour, the both were strongly insisted upon (pp. 241–94.)

Opinion: Dorothea Gwynn, Priscilla Gwynn and Elizabeth Gwynn, by their next friend *v.* John Hooke, Esq., 18 November 1743. Argued again for opinion of Court. Plaintiff not entitled to estate (Angle, co. Pembroke) by will 14 November 1693. (pp. 231–4.)

Watkin Wynne and Jane, his wife *v.* Sir Watkin Williams Wynne, bart. Shropshire manors. Argued, 25 May 1742; argued, 23 November 1742; argued again, 8 November 1743; stands for judgement; judgement, 9 February 1744. (pp. 346–83.)

Mandamus: King *v.* Henry Norris, Samuel Tyssen and Stephen Ram, Esqs. Repair of highway, parish of Enfield. Parish of Hackney to pay £100 p.a. Refusal to make assessment. 16 November 1743. Whether return good or not. Writ quashed. (pp. 67–72.)

King *v.* Robert Eden, Archdeacon of Winchester. Churchwardens of Bentworth co. Southampton. 4 February 1744. Return allowed no objection being made to it though bad. (pp. 294x–296.)

King *v.* Vicar and Churchwardens of parish of Frome Selwood. Office of Sexton. 6 June 1744. Return allowed.

Sedition: Attorney General *v.* Richard Marlborne, late of parish of All Saints in town of Derby, labourer, supporter of Young Pretender. 28 November 1743. Judgement to be kept imprisoned for 3 months and to enter into recognizance of £100 for good behaviour for 1 year from this time. Note the defendant had already lain in prison near six months and was a drunken noisy fellow and at Derby called Crazy Dick. (pp. 59–66.)

Debt: 13 May 1743. Judgement for plaintiff unless conge before end of term, but the rule was discharged last day of term upon the importunity of brother Willes, he agreeing to argue the case as it now stands on 1st paper day in the next term. 7 June 1743, argues the case being imperfect to be amended. (pp. 1–2.)

Return of knight of shire: Sir Watkin Williams Wynne bart., *v.* William Middleton, esq., late Sheriff of co. Denbigh. John Middleton returned. This cause was tried at bar 4 November 1743 and a verdict given for plaintiff of £1,400. (pp. 129–44.)

Ferry Boat over River Avon: Richard Davy *v.* James Collett and Henry Langford. Plaintiff has a lease of the ferry from the Corporation of the city of Bristol. Defendants kept a ferry boat. 27 January 1744. But nobody appearing for defendants and the Court thinking there was nothing in case postea was ordered to be delivered to plaintiff. (pp. 215–20.)

Promissory note: Elizabeth Hull *v.* Charles Pitfield. Guildhall, London. Argued and determined. 7 February 1744, whole Court on this point of opinion for defendant that the note was discharged. The Court gave no opinion upon the point of usury. (pp. 235–40.)

Bribery at election: Samuel Mead esq., *v.* Luke Robinson, late of parish of St. Clement Danes, co. Midd., esq. £4,000. Bribery at election Heydon, co. Yorks. 8 counts £500 each. 9 February 1744. Ld. C. J. Willes declared in Com. B. that the opinion of the majority of the judges was against a new trial and that as he had great regard for the opinion of the judges which was taken late last night he should give no opinion but discharged the rule to show cause why there should not be a new trial. (pp. 297–318.)

VOLUME 5

Judgements of the Court of King's Bench, 18 George II, 1744–1745. 415 ff.

Of the 83 cases for which there are papers in this volume, 49 are on writs of error, 43 from the Court of Common Bench, 3 from the Court of the Palace of Westminster, 2 from the Court of Exchequer, 1 from the Mayor and Justices of the Peace of the City of Chichester; 2 are for the Opinion of the Court, 1 on a writ of mandamus and 1 on quo warranto; 17 cases are for debt for goods, services, rent, or on writings obligatory, 2 on covenant; and 1 each on detention of goods found, taking away cattle and goods, assault, assault and imprisonment, taking game, and forgery.

The following cases are of some interest or importance:

Error Common Bench: On Thursday, 13 December 1744 Ld. C. J. Lee, J. Denison and I met at Ld. C. J.'s chamber and agreed to affirm the judgement, the custom insisted upon by the defendant being void and the judgement well entered, it appearing upon the whole record that the plaintiff was entitled to recover. Note J. Chapple was ill and had absented all Michaelmas term. (ff. 337–48.)

Opinion: Hand *v.* Dineley, widow. 8 February 1745. Payment into Court. (f. 164.)

On Thursday, 13 December 1744. Ld. C. J. Lee, J. Denison and I met at Ld. C. J.'s chambers and agreed that the licence granted . . . was not a good licence under the Stat. 5 & 6 Ed. 6 c. 25 . . . Note J. Chapple was ill and had absented all Michaelmas term. (ff. 250–4.)

Mandamus: King *v.* Sir Henry Penrice, Doctor of Laws, Official of Archdeaconry of Middlesex, churchwarden of parish of Heston. 3 July 1745. Return allowed. (ff. 390–1.)

Quo Warranto: King *v.* Charles Colborne, of borough of Lymington, co. Southampton. Exercised office of mayor. 8 May 1745. Judgement for King. (ff. 279–86.)

Assault: 6 November 1744. Argued, further consultation, at importunity of Mr. Ley but at length consented that defendant should have judgement and judgement was given for defendant accordingly. (ff. 81–3.)

Assault and imprisonment: 26 November 1744. Judgement to enter over. Note Sergt. Draper did not attempt to support the demurrer, the replication being agreeable to Luke 24. (ff. 131–2.

Taking game. Trevor Webber for himself and poor of parish of Oldbury on the Hill, co. Glouc., and for King *v.* Richard Gowen, £5, used one purse net and one gate net to destroy the game. 20 November 1744. Judgement for plaintiff without argument. (ff. 155–6.)

Treason: King *v.* James Dougan, otherwise James O'Daniel, late of City of Chester, gent., treason, Spain. Tried at bar B.R. Verdict guilty but recommended him to mercy. (ff. 165–9.)

Forgery. King *v.* Hugh Morgan. To plead his pardon. Pleaded 9 February 1745. Pauper.

VOLUME 6

Judgements of the Court of King's Bench, 19 George II, 1745–6. 612 pp.

Of the 71 cases for which there are papers in this volume, 31 were on writs of error, 27 from the Court of Common Bench, 1 from the Court of Great Sessions, cos. Carmarthen, Pembroke and Cardigan, 1 from Quarter Sessions, city of London, 1 from Quarter Sessions, co. Yorks., 1 from the County Palatine of Lancaster: 2 on writs of mandamus; 23 cases were for debt for goods, services, rent, or on bonds or writings obligatory, 5 on promissory notes, 4 on policies of insurance; 2 on ejectment, and 1 each on covenant, entering cellar of mansion house, putting up a stall, and setting a barn on fire.

The following cases are of some interest or importance:

Court of Great Sessions. Error on Common Recovery. 15 January 1746, L. C. J., Denison and Foster JJ. and I met at Ld. C. J.'s chambers and agreed that the plaintiff's replication was not good, for that the recovery had been suffered above 20 years, he as heir was barred by the Stat. 10 & 11 W. 3, and he had not shown such access brought him within the proviso. (pp. 534–56.)

Mandamus: Burgesses of Wigan *v.* Rector of parish. Attendance at Court Leet. Return allowed. (pp. 102–29.)

King *v.* Master and Wardens of Skinners Company of London. Election of Assistants. 13 July 1745. All the Js. B.R. met at Ld. C. J. Lee's chamber on this case and agreed that the words of the proviso were words of limitation and not of condition but differed as to the manner of establishing the further devises . . . Ld. C. J. and J. Denison thinking that they might be established as contingent . . . but J. Foster and I thought they must be made good . . . they not being concurrent. (pp. 84–93.)

15 January 1746. L. C. J., Denison and Foster Js. and I met at L.C.J.'s chambers and agreed that Haile was interested and he not a creditable witness and that 2 witnesses must be credible at the time of the execution of the will and that the will was not well executed, there not being 3 credible witnesses to the execution thereof. (pp. 338–51.)

Putting up a stall. Mayor etc. of Northampton *v.* Thomas Ward the younger, for putting up a stall in Butchers Row. (pp. 148–59.)

VOLUME 7

Judgements of the Court of King's Bench, 20 George II, 1746–7. 638 pp.

Of the 72 cases for which there are papers in this volume, 26 were on writs of error, 21 from the Court of Common Bench, 3 from the Court of the Palace of Westminster, 1 from the Court of the Palatinate of Durham, 1 from the Court of Sewers, Doncaster; 1 writ of mittimus; 27 cases were for debt for goods, services, rent or on bonds or writings obligatory,

8 on promissory notes, 2 on bills of exchange; 3 were on covenant, including one on charter party, 2 on high treason, and 1 each on ejectment, assault, and a building lease.

The following cases are of some interest or importance:

Court of Sewers. Held at Doncaster. To repair foreshore in Reedmere. King *v.* Stephenson and Thompson. Copy Order of Sewers, Level of Hatfield Chase and parts adjoining cos. Yorks., Lincs., and Notts. 20 November 1746 Quashed. (pp. 133–6.)

Mittimus. King *v.* John Murray esq. Writ of mittimus to Sir William Lee, L.C.J. Act of Parliament. Writ of certiorari to Ashley Cowper, Clerk of Parliament. Act to attaint Alexander, Earl of Kellie etc. 12 February 1747. Copy of record of attaint. (pp. 508–22.)

Debt: 25 June 1747. Judgement for defendant and conge on Monday, 30 June 1747. Serjeant Belfield moved to amend. 8 July 1747 Conge not shown against the amendment that defendant must lie in prison until superseded and thereupon Sergt. Belfield moved for leave to discontinue on payment of costs and obtained a rule for that purpose. (pp. 423–6.)

26 June 1747, argued, judgement for plaintiff and conge before the end of term. 8 July, being last day of term, Sir Tho. Bootle mentioned the case and offered to argue it next term, but the Court being satisfied that the plea is not to be maintained, the Court pronounced judgement for plaintiff. (pp. 555–76.)

Treason: King *v.* Charles Ratcliff and others. Saturday, 22 November 1746, Sir Dudley Ryder, Attorney General, acquainted the Court that Charles Ratcliff, a prisoner, was in the Hall and desired that he might be brought to bar, and he being brought to the bar, the Attorney General prayed that the return of the Hab. Corp. might be read, which was read accordingly, but before it was read the prisoner asked the gent. at the bar who sat next to him who were his judges, and he was told the Ld. C. J., bro. Wright, etc., were the judges, upon which he said he thought it proper to acquaint the gent., that he had a commission from the K. of France and that he acknowledged no other master.

Then the return of the certiorari was read, which being read, he was called upon by the name of Charles Ratcliff to hold up his hand, which he refused to do, saying he was Lord Derwentwater and protested against any proceedings against him, he being a French officer and insisted also that he was not the person called Charles Ratcliff, but did not plead it.

Then Mr Ford, as counsel for the prisoner, prayed time, admitting that if he should plead that he is not the same person, that a jury, it being an inquest of office, only ad informandum conscientiam curie might be returned instanter, but doubted whether in case he pleaded any other matter a jury ought not to be returned, according to the course of the Court in other cases, and said that he had never seen his client before and that he heard nothing from him till that night before and he prayed time to consider of his plea, and that the Court gave him until Monday. Then he prayed a copy of the Record which was denied him but the Court said it should be read over again if he desired it, and it was accordingly read a second time. Then the Attorney General prayed that the Pet. of Hab. Corp. and certiorari be filed, which was ruled and then the prisoner was remanded to the Tower by rule, and was ordered to be brought up again by rule on Monday.

24 November 1746. 'Mr Herd prayed a copy of Record but it was denied as a thing never done, yet he prayed that it might be read to him by the Clerk at any time out of Ct., but that was refused likewise but it was read again in Court at his instance'. (pp. 87–104.)

Gaol Delivery, co. Surr., at Southwark. King *v.* Sir James Kinloch, late of Murrayshire, bart., Alexander Kinloch, late of same place, merchant, Charles Kinloch, late of same place, gent., and Nicholas Glascoe, late of same place, gent. High Treason. All Guilty. (pp. 621–38.)

VOLUME 8

Judgements of the Court of King's Bench, 21 George II, 1747–8 692 pp.

Of the 68 cases for which there are papers in this volume 30 were on writs of error, 23 from the Court of Common Bench, 2 from the Court of the Palace of Westminster, 1 from King's Bench, Ireland, 1 from the Court of Great Sessions, co. Denbigh, 1 from Justices of the Peace, co. Staffs., 1 from Justices of the Peace, co. Midd., 1 from manor of Stepney and Hackney; 1 for Opinion of Court; 1 mandamus; 6 quo warranto; 13 were for debt for goods, services, rent or on bonds or writings obligatory, 7 on promissory notes, 2 on policy of insurance; 1 each on measure of corn, water course over land, impounding cattle, pulling down a stone footbridge, and 3 on ejectment.

The following cases are of some interest or importance:

Error, King's Bench, Ireland: 23 June 1748. Sir Thomas Bootle moved for the judgement of the Court, upon which L. C. J. Lee, Just. Denison and I declared that we had delivered our opinion and saw no reason to alter them. Just. Foster declared that he saw no reason to alter his, but as the Court was of different opinion he did not oppose judgement and therefore judgement was affirmed. (pp. 551–90.)

Case for Opinion: In Chancery. Thomas Snelson and other creditors of Sir Brian Delves dec., *v.* Sir William Corbet bart., and other executors of Sir Brian Delves. 3 November 1747. To stand. Opinion to be certified to Ld. Chancellor. (pp. 373–84.)

Mandamus: King *v.* Mayor etc. of Newcastle upon Tyne. On removal of Matthew Featherstonhagh from office of alderman. 11 November 1747. 'Mr Luke Robinson for the prosecution put the Ch. Just. in mind of this case, whereupon the Ch. Justice declared that the Court would not award a peremptory mandamus upon this return for it appearing that Matthew Featherston Haugh had for many years deserted the town and now lived at a great distance from it. He had no right to be restored and that the Court would then do as was done in the case of K. *v* Tidderley, 1 Sid, 14, where noted the insufficiency of the return it appearing that the party had no right to be restored the court would not restore him. Note this declaration was made upon a prior consultation with me and my brothers and we severally declared ourselves to be of the same opinion'. (pp. 123–42.)

Quo warranto: County Borough of Carmarthen. King *v.* William Johnson, Sheriff. Judgement for king. 11 November, 1747. (pp. 143–56.)

Like *v.* Woodford Rice, Sheriff, gent., 11 November 1747. Judgement for king. (pp. 171–84.)

Like *v.* William Thomas, Mayor, clothier, 11 November 1747. Judgement for king. (pp. 157–70.)

Like *v.* John Williams, Sheriff, mercer, 11 November 1747. Judgement for king. (pp. 185–204.)

Like *v.* Richard Williams, Sheriff, ironmonger, 11 November 1747. Judgement for king. (pp. 205–20.)

King *v.* Master and Wardens etc. of Skinners of London, on election of freemen. 10 February 1748. Return allowed. (pp. 290–9.)

Promissory note: 26 November 1747. Judgement that defendant answer over. Note there was no attempt to support the plea. (pp. 7–12.)

Measure of corn: George Hogge, merchant *v.* Charles Turner, Esq. 'Ld. C.J. asking why they did not go to Parliament to have this matter resolved as on the salt duties'. (pp. 439–48.)

Pulling down foot bridge: King *v.* Jerome Dyke, of parish of Stanton, co. Wilts., pulling down stone foot bridge on footway in parish of Beaching. 11 November 1747. Rule to show cause why judgement should not be accepted was discharged. (pp. 121–2.)

Taking 40 bushels of barley: Hilary 1748. Mr. Pratt on the last day of term moved for the opinion of the Court upon which Lee C. J. said 'We have considered of it and are of opinion that the plea should be allowed and that there must be judgement for defendant'. (pp. 309–2.)

Court of Record. Manor of Stepney and Hackney. Richard Duplex *v.* Walter Port. Defamation. 3 May 1748. Judgement affirmed. (pp. 467–78.)

Smuggling: King *v.* John Harvey of Pond Hall, co. Suff., 'This cause being the first of its kind was tried at the bar B.R., 22 June 1747. It was a proceeding against the defendant as a person attainted of felony by Stat. 19 Geo. II, in order to have execution accorded against him according to the Stat., he not having surrendered himself according to H.M.'s order in Privy Council, but as the Stat. requires that the order be transmitted to the sheriff of the co. where the offence was committed, who shall cause the same to be proclaimed in the market places, upon the respective market days of two market towns in the same co. near to the place where such offence was committed. It appears upon the evidence that the order was proclaimed at Ipswich, where the prisoner was known, and not at Hadleigh, near Pont Hall, where the prisoner lived, and at Laystock, but that Ipswich was 30 miles and Hadleigh 43 or 44 miles distant from Bonacre where the offence was committed, and that there were other market towns nearer than either of them, the Court (Lee C. J. and I absent) was of opinion that they could not be said to be near within the meaning of the Act, there being other market towns near the place where the offence was committed, yet though they need not be the next, yet they must be as near in estimation and computation of miles as any and that within a reasonable sense of the word near, that the letter of the Act must be adhered to, as in the case of the K. *v.* Fletcher and that in a capital case no discretion could be left to the sheriff, upon which the jury of consent and direction found all the issues for the king, except that proclamation was made in two market towns near the place where the offence was committed and that they found for the prisoner. Whereupon the prisoner was remanded to Newgate in order to be tried for smuggling etc.'. (pp. 643–52.)

VOLUME 9

Judgements of the Court of King's Bench, 22 George II, 1748–9. 729 pp.

Of the 67 cases for which there are papers in this volume, 32 were on writs of error, 29 from the Court of Common Bench, 2 from King's Bench, Ireland, and 1 from the Court of the Borough of Devizes; 1, mandamus, 5 quo warranto; 15 were for debt for goods, services, rent or on bonds or writings obligatory, 6 on promissory notes; there were five cases of sedition and one each of forgery of will, charterparty, and refusal to allow bread to be weighed.

The following cases are of some interest or importance:

Error, King's Bench, Ireland: William Reynolds, of city of London, Esq. *v.* Thomas Kennedy, of city of Cork, gent. Seizure in hold of ship called the Unity of Newcastle,

John Thistlewaite, master, 61 hogshead of brandy, put in Kingston, and exhibited an information before the Sub Commissioners of Excise and New Impost for port and district of Cork without payment of excise. 22 November 1748. Judgement affirmed. (pp. 169–80.)

Mandamus: King *v.* John Turner of London, linen draper, and others. Master and 4 Wardens, Company of Skinners. Charters of company of 1327, 1393, 1438, 1557, 1560, 1561, 1606, and 1667 given or quoted. False return. (pp. 419–64.)

Quo warranto: King *v.* William Bromley, of city of Worcester, Esq. exercised office of burgess of borough of Wych, otherwise Droitwich, co. Worcs. (pp. 91–103.)

King *v.* John Brough of Rowleston, co. Yorks., Esq., exercised office of mayor of town of Hedon, co. Yorks. (pp. 235–58.)

King *v.* John Farbridge, of town of Hedon, co. Yorks., gent., exercised office of one of bailiffs of town of Hedon. (pp. 239–41.)

King *v.* Francis Moore, of town of Hedon, co. Yorks., gent., exercised office of one of bailiffs of town of Hedon. (pp. 243–8.)

King *v.* John Phillips, the younger, of county borough of Carmarthen, exercised office of mayor. 10 February 1749. Agreed there should be a rule by consent of prosecutor and defendant that if the Court shall be of opinion that the bye-law is good there shall be judgement for the king and that if the Court shall be of opinion that the bye-law is not good there shall be judgement for the defendant. And this was agreed upon, a proposal from the Court as the most expeditious way of determining the question and putting the corporation upon a proper foot. 27 May, 1749 Serjeant Poole moved to make the rule absolute for judgement for defendant. Rule made absolute in the following words: '1. The bye-law is bad because it takes away the capacity of burgesses to be elected mayor and has confined it to a select number,' etc. (pp. 587–648.)

Sedition: Sir Dudley Ryder, kt., Attorney General, information against James Dawes, of St. Mary's Hall, of city of Oxford, gent., as a wicked, seditious, malicious and ill disposed person (supporter of Young Pretender). Defendant found guilty. 28 November, 1748. Judgement of the Court: to pay a fine of 5 nobles; to be imprisoned for 2 years, at the end of 2 years to be bound with 2 sureties for his good behaviour for 7 years, himself in £500 and his sureties in £250 each, and to remain in prison until the fine be paid and sureties found, and to be immediately led by the marshal of this Court to the several courts now sitting at Westminster, with a paper on his forehead denoting his offence and the judgement of the Court thereupon. (pp. 104–10.)

Sir Dudley Ryder (as above) *v.* John Whitmore, of city of Oxford, gent., as above. Defendant found guilty. Judgement of Court: verbatim as above. (pp. 119–38.)

Sir Dudley Ryder (as above) *v.* John Purnell, of city of Oxford, DD., John Whitmore of city of Oxford, gent., James Dawes, of same place, gent., and Charles Luxmore, of same place, gent., and divers other malefactors and disturbers of the peace to the number of 40 and upwards, made great riot, pretended Prince of Wales. John Purnell, being Vice Chancellor and one of the Justices of the Peace, on a complaint by Richard Blower on his request to take depositions neglected and refused to do so. Copy issue. To be tried at the bar, Monday 21 November 1748. 'Countermanded and never tried'. (pp. 629–48.)

King *v.* John Purnell. Copy of issue. To be tried at the bar, Thursday, 8 June 1749. 'On the second information appointed for trial at the bar, 8 June 1749, but countermanded and nolle prosequi entered'. (pp. 650–70.)

Forgery of will: 'This cause was tried at the bar, Easter term, 22 George II, 1749. It began on Sat. 29 April and lasted till Sat. 6 May inclusive, when the jury gave a verdict for the plaintiff on both issues on the fact of forgery. Note Ascension Day intervened upon which the Court could not sit but the Court sat every other day from 10 in the morning till between 11 and 12 o'clock at night'. (pp. 292–302.)

Charterparty. George Fryer of good ship called the Havannah, James Anderson, master, 250 tons *v.* Commissioners for Victualling H.M.'s Navy, in a plea of breach of covenant. Copy of issue: To be heard on Friday next, being 18 November, instant on the matters mentioned in the annexed rule against a new trial. Moved 21 November 1748. Rule enlarged to next term. Mentioned 11 February, and rule enlarged to next term. To come on at the beginning of term. 14 April 1748. The Court agreed with the jury. Verdict to stand. 'Verdict to stand as given by jury, the rule discharged and the postea delivered'. (pp. 333–56.)

Refusal to allow bread to be weighed: John, Duke of Bedford *v.* John Allcock. Aleconners or Aletasters of Court Leet of manor of St. Giles in the Fields with Bloomsbury, went to shop of defendant to weigh small bread, to wit, 2d. and 3d. loaves. Refusal. Fined 100s. 14 June 1749, Judgement for plaintiff. (pp. 551–66.)

VOLUME 10

Judgements of the Court of King's Bench, 23 George II, 1749–50. 650 pp.

Of the 65 cases for which there are papers in this volume, 27 were on writs of error, 20 from the Court of Common Bench, 1 from Justices of Palatinate of Durham, 1 from Court of Palace of Westminster, 1 from Barons of Exchequer, Ireland, 4 Quarter Sessions etc.; Opinion of Court, 4; 19 were for debt for goods, services, rent or on bonds or writings obligatory, 5 on promissory notes, 2 on bills of exchange; and one each on a policy of insurance, assault, trover and conversion, breaking and entering close, covenant, taking away goods and ejectment.

The following cases are of some interest or importance:

Opinion of Court: The case of Abraham Eves, receiving one silk handkerchief, value 12d., feloniously stolen, from person of Sir Gillies Payne bart., by John Avery. Guilty. Old Bailey, May Sessions, 1749. Convicted of receiving stolen goods where the principal was convicted only of petty larceny. 24 November 1749. Ld. C. J. Lee and Js. Willes, Porter, Wright, Abney, Denison, Clerk, etc. Agreed that judgement must be arrested, the principal being indicted of petit larceny to which there can be no accepting. Note Burnet and Foster Js. were absent being indisposed. 14 years transportation. (pp. 53–6.)

At General Sessions of oyer and terminer at Old Bailey, 11 October 1749. Thomas Yelden was indicted for feloniously forging a deed with intent to defraud, and for feloniously uttering a forged deed as true with like intent. The deed related to prize money for taking St. Domingo ships. 19 November 1749. The Judges agreed to meet at Serjeants Inn on Friday next to consider the special verdict. 24 November 1749. At Serjeants Inn Ld. C. J. Lee and Willes, Ld. C. Baron Parker, Wright, Abney, Denison, Clerke, Clive, Birch, and Legh agreed that at the next Sessions at the Old Bailey should declare their opinion that judgement must be for the defendant. He being indicted for forging a deed and the special verdict has found no deed, it not being executed but that it was intended that defendant should go before the Mayor to execute it. Note Burnet and Foster Js. were absent being indisposed. (pp. 79–82.)

J.P.s co. Middlesex. Edward Clarke, late of parish of St. Georges, Hanover Square, indicted for murder with pistol, in liberty of Dean and Chapter of Collegiate Church of St. Peters, Westminster. Defendant convicted of murder pleaded a pardon which was conditional; that he should transport himself within 6 months and that he was discharged without bail. 'Memorandum. Upon sight of the St. of 3 H. VII c. 1., it appeared that the St. extends only where persons are indicted for murder and are acquitted, then they are to be committed or bailed till year and day past that if anyone will bring an appeal he may be forthcoming. But extends not to persons who being indicted for murder are found guilty of manslaughter or se defendendo or by mischance.' 30 June 1750. Plea of pardon allowed. (pp. 601–16.)

Mandamus. King *v.* Mayor and Burgesses of town of Northampton. Office of Common Council of Junior Council of 6 persons vacant. Return; Not bound to elect. The return allowed. (pp. 329–34.)

Insurance: £1,000 journey to Jamaica, 12 months, Privateer Goodfellow, Peter Joyce, Master. 15 May 1750. Judgement for plaintiff, 22 May 1750 in 7 other causes in like insurances and special verdicts. Note these special verdicts were all found against the opinion of Ld. C. J. Lee who tried the causes at the instance of the counsel (urged as was said by Sir John Bernard) in order to carry the question to the House of Lords. (pp. 311–22.)

Trover and conversion. 'gold Moores' to value of £248. 12s. 6d. (pp. 27–36.)

Covenant: Articles of agreement, 8,000 seamen's beds at 8s. 9d. each to Commissioners of H.M.'s Navy, Store House, Deptford in River Thames for use of the several regiments going to Gibraltar. (pp. 141–6.)

VOLUME II

Judgements in the Court of King's Bench, 24 George II, 1750–51. 414 pp.

Of the 52 cases for which there are papers in this volume, 14 were on writs of error, 11 from the Court of Common Bench, 1 from King's Bench, Ireland, 1 from Sessions of Chester, 1 from Court of Palace of Westminster; 20 were for debt for goods, services, rent or on bonds or writings obligatory, 3 on promissory notes, 1 on a bill of exchange; and one each of mandamus, quo warranto, ejectment, on rights in River Medway, breaking close, assault, treason, and obscene libel, 3 on taking goods in house and 2 on retaining goods found.

The following cases are of some interest or importance:

Debt etc. 3 May 1751. Judgement for plaintiff on writing obligatory. Charles Salkeld *v.* William Loveday, Chaplain to the Factory in St. Helena. (pp. 269–74.)

Mandamus. To William Hole B.D., Archdeacon of Barnstaple, on election of church warden of South Molton, co. Devon. (pp. 307–10.)

Quo warranto: King *v.* Dr. Isaac Madox, Bishop of Worcester, exercising office of a burgess, borough of Wych, otherwise Droitwich. 'Ld. C. J. Lee declared that it is the opinion of all the judges that the challenge for want of knights was a good challenge and that the counter-plea was bad and that the arraignment was quashed. But note this challenge is now taken by St. 24 Geo. II'. (pp. 359–75.)

On rights in River Medway: Mayor and Citizens of Rochester and others *v.* William Baker and others. Issue, concerning the River Medway, co. Kent, and the creeks and indraughts adjoining the River and the right of fishing and dredging oysters in the same between Hashwood and Sheerness and the right claimed by the freemen of the Corporation to fish and dredge for oysters without serving apprenticeship to a free dredgerman of the oyster fishery there'. (pp. 239–44.)

Breaking close. 'Lord C. J. Lee delivered the opinion of the Court that the verdict for the plaintiff is right that there was acceptance for a new assignment because the trespass was sufficiently ascertained and the defendant plea is applied to that trespass. Rule that the postea be delivered to plaintiff'. (pp. 303–6.)

Treason: Sir Dudley Ryder, kt., Attorney General. Information against Thomas Jones the elder, of borough of Walsall, co. Staffs., engraver of buckles and others, supporters of the Young Pretender. Gallows with effigy of king. 'Makes this nation stink of turnips'. Defendant Thomas Jones and others found guilty on all counts: 2 defendants acquitted. 'The defendants were brought into court in order to receive judgement but it being an extraordinary case and the C. J. not in court they were remanded to be brought up next term'. (pp. 311–34.)

Obscene libel: Sir Dudley Ryder, kt., Attorney General. Information against John Purser, printer. In parish of St. Brides in ward of Farringdon without. Obscene libel entitled Ancient and Modern Pederasty Investigated and Exemplified. 'The defendant will be called on his recognizance on Monday, 11 February to receive the judgement of the Court. N.B. He pleads not guilty in Easter term last and in Michaelmas term following. Now he withdrew his said plea and confessed the information.' 20 May 1751. 'Defendant was brought up to receive judgement but it being an extraordinary case and an exemplary judgement proper the Court (the C. J. being absent) remanded him and he is to be brought up next term'. (pp. 335–58.)

VOLUME 12

Judgements in the Court of King's Bench, 25 George II, 1751–2. 464 pp.

Of the 61 cases for which there are papers in this volume, 18 were on writs of error, 16 from the Court of Common Bench, 1 from King's Bench, Ireland, 1 from Quarter Sessions; 2 were cases for the opinion of King's Bench; 6 were on writs of mandamus; 23 were debt for goods, services, rent or on bonds or writings obligatory, 5 on promissory notes, 3 on covenants, 1 on a bill of exchange; and 1 each on money received and not paid, lost gun and dog found in possession of defendant, and assault.

The following cases are of some interest or importance:

Quarter Sessions: at Shaftesbury, co. Dorset. Appointment of Nathaniel Bestland as Overseer of the Poor for the parish of Woodyates, otherwise Westwood Yates. Sir Martin Wright's note: 'I met Ld. C. J. Lee at his Chambers and agreed that the Stat. 43 Elizabeth, being introductory of a new law relating to the poor and the authority of J.P.s to appoint overseers also new, and the overseers themselves new officers, that an authority given to the justices must be executed in the manner prescribed by the Stat. and in no other manner and that they could not appoint one overseer only. This being the case that concerned many parishes in the West of England it might in its determination have bad consequences, the court from time to time declined giving any opinion and hinted that it might be proper to set it right in another place, meaning parliament, but 1 May 1752 Mr Gould moved for the judgement of the court in this case but the Ld. C. J. Lee told him that the Court had intimated that it was a matter of great consequence to the western part of the kingdom it would have been set right in another place, upon which Mr Kirton, who was counsel on the other side said he was surprised at the application for judgement and asked Mr Gould who was his client and added that the court would soon be delivered of this case, and in 11 May, being the last day of term, he moved that the defendant Bestland's recognizance be discharged and upon a suggestion that Mr Gould, who was then absent, did not oppose it, the recognizance was discharged'. (pp. 235–40.)

Opinion: Henry Perkins, merchant *v.* John Smith, chapman, taking goods of a bankrupt in the city of Chester. Judgement for plaintiff. (pp. 377–94.)

Mandamus: To Thomas Lediard esq., J.P., Liberty of Dean and Chapter of Westminster, conviction, forfeiture of a black mare etc. King *v.* Ralph Rutter, one of constables of parish of St. James, Westminster, and William Newman. Held that certiorari does not lie and therefore quashed. (pp. 37–40.)

To Thomas Lediard (as above). Breach of assize of bread and ale. King *v.* Thomas Bye, otherwise Boy. Conviction quashed. (pp. 135–40.)

To Charles Carlesse esq., J.P., Liberty of Dean and Chapter of Westminster. Breach of assize of bread and ale. Conviction quashed. Note by Sir Martin Wright: 'Note the same objections were taken to this conviction as in the case of King *v.* Bye, otherwise Boy, on the same day'. (pp. 141–4.)

To Waring Ashley esq., J.P., co. Leics., killing game. King *v.* George Allen and others. Conviction quashed by consent, defendants having agreed to bring no action and that by agreement made part of Rule. (pp. 227–34.)

To Mayor, Alderman and Burgesses of Doncaster, removal of John Beal from office of Alderman. 9 May 1752. 'Called but being last day but one of term, it seemed too long to come on and it went over to next term. 3 June 1752, argued. Return held insufficient and the peremptory mandamus accorded'. (pp. 315–30.)

To Mayor and Burgesses of Nottingham. Places and office of Common Council vacant. 2 June 1752. 'The objection to the writ of mandamus was over-ruled upon view of the following precedents and the Return allowed', 4 precedents Devizes. Mich. 7 Anne to Taunton, East. 5 Geo. II. (pp. 331–50.)

VOLUME 13

Judgements in the Court of King's Bench, 26 George II, 1752–3. 287 pp.

Of the 58 cases for which there are papers in this volume, 14 were on writs of error, 12 from the Court of Common Pleas, 1 from the Court of the Palace of Westminster, 1 from Quarter Sessions; 1 was a case for the opinion of King's Bench; 1 was in the nature of quo warranto; 1 on a writ of mittimus; 24 were on debt for goods, services, rent, or on bonds or writings obligatory, 7 on promissory notes, 4 on ejectment, 3 on covenant, 1 on assumpsit; and 1 each on breaking and entering and taking goods, on money received and not paid, on assault and imprisonment, for exercising the trade of a worsted weaver not having served an apprenticeship, and against the Sheriff of co. Radnor for not serving a summons of sci. fa. before the Barons of the Exchequer.

The following cases are of some interest or importance:

Quarter Sessions, co. Cumberland by a woman against four men as disturbers of the peace and entering her dwelling house. Serjeant Poole pressed to have the case restored to the paper and upon his undertaking to argue it, it was restored. The conviction was quashed. (ff. 258–258v.)

Quo warranto: Robert Alberry, of the borough of Midhurst, co. Suss., yeoman, for exercising the office of bailiff. (ff. 54–5v.)

Case for opinion: Case of trover. Navy Bill made payable to the plaintiff for £1,229. 4s. 1d., for freight of the Happy Jennett to the Commissioners of the Navy was lost. (ff. 109–10.)

Mittimus: King *v.* Archibald Cameron. The writ, together with a writ directed to the Clerk of Parliaments and the return to the same and also the record of the Act of Parliament, the Act to attaint Alexander, Earl of Kellie and others (a long list). On 17 May 1753 the Court awarded execution. The Lord Chief Justice pronounced the sentence of high treason from the precedent of Lord Lovat's case. (ff. 163–8.)

Assumpsit: Arthur Young LL.D. *v.* John Lynch D.D. The defendant was Dean of Christ Church, Canterbury. (ff. 196–207v.)

In the case of the worsted weaver plaintiff's counsel said that he 'could not maintain that this is a public law, of which the Court is bound to take notice, it having been held in 2 Keb., to be a private act . . .' he said that wherever penalty was given to the crown it shall be considered a public act and this according to a statute of P. & M. and upon looking into the act it appears to be a public law and that he gave no opinion to such dictum. Judgement was for defendant. (ff. 1–5.)

VOLUME 14

Judgements in the Court of King's Bench, 27 George II, 1753–4. 734 pp.

Of the 76 cases for which there are papers in this volume, 20 were on writs of error, 13 from the Court of Common Pleas, 3 from the Court of the Palace of Westminster, 3 from Quarter Sessions, 1 from King's Bench, Ireland; 3 were in the nature of quo warranto and 3 on writs of mandamus; 29 on debt for goods, services, rent, on bonds or writings obligatory, 11 on promissory notes, 3 on breach of covenant and 1 on a bill of exchange; and 1 each on assault, arrest and imprisonment in a civil plea, trespass arrest and imprisonment, and on a chapman offering hares for sale when not qualified, the plaintiff acting for himself and the poor of the parish of St. Peters Cornhill; 2 for opinion of King's Bench.

The following cases are of some interest or importance:

Error, Common Bench. On a seaman's ticket for the wages of a seaman, dec., on H.M.'s ship Winchester. (pp. 243–50.)

For opinion of King's Bench, case stated for opinion pursuant to the order made upon hearing the case in Chancery. (Land in the manor of Lechlade, co. Glouc.). A lengthy and complicated case during which the Lord Chief Justice died and among the papers is a certificate signed by Wright, J., Denison, J., and Foster, J., 'that the late Lord Chief Justice Lee concurred with us in this opinion'. (pp. 307–42.)

From Quarter Sessions: At the Castle of Leicester for the co. of Leics., digging a pit 6′×5′ 6″×2′ 6″ in the common highway leading from the village of Great Sheepy to Leicester. (pp. 195–200.)

At Wells for co. Somerset, conviction of a victualler for selling beer without licence. (pp. 475–6.)

Borough and Liberty of St. Albans, by Rev. John Boys, vicar of Redbourn in that liberty against a rate for relief of the poor confirmed. (pp. 575–84.)

Quo warranto: Shirley Cotes, clerk, holding a Court Leet and View of Frankpledge in the borough of Wigan, co. Lancs. (pp. 89–92.)

Roger Holt Esq., of borough of Wigan, constituting a jury to serve at a Court Leet or View of Frankpledge. (pp. 93–6.)

John Luffe, of borough of Haslemere, co. Surr., exercising the office of constable. (pp. 97–100.)

Mandamus: Justices of the Peace for the borough and foreign of Walsall co. Staffs., no Overseers of Poor appointed. (pp. 101–8.)

Justices of Peace for borough of Wootton Bassett, co. Wilts., for refusal to confirm rate for poor of Churchwardens and Overseers. (pp. 585–90.)

Steward of Court Leet and View of Frankpledge of manor or lordship and borough of Michscholl, otherwise Mitchell, co. Cornw., on election as Portreeve of one of five mesne lords and return of Burgesses by him. (pp. 625–36.)

PETYT MS. 510

Year Book, 10–17 Edward III, full bound in dark green morocco, with Inner Temple coat of arms on both covers. Inset in flyleaf 2 old red leather labels: 1. Year Books xxi, xii, xiii, xiv, xv, xvi. 2. Edward the 3d. never printed. $13\frac{3}{4}'' \times 8\frac{1}{8}''$. 129 ff.

A well-written manuscript of the Year Books, 10–17 Edward III, contemporary, probably written in sections. There is some slight mutilation of certain folios in the margin. At times there is a dual foliation. The running headings are general, with the legal term on the left and regnal year on the right. Inset in the volume is a letter to Mr J. G. L. Pickering, the Librarian of the Inner Temple from L. Owen Pike, from Fleetwood House, 201 Maida Vale, 10 October 1893, returning the seven volumes of transcripts and translations of Year Books 'so kindly lent to me by the Benchers of the Inner Temple. Some of the side notes made by Serjeant Manning in the earlier volumes were of considerable use to me in preparing one of my indexes and I am greatly obliged for the loan. With your permission, I am retaining, for the present, the original manuscript of Year Books of the reign of Edward III, which is of inestimable value and which I have found most useful. I have had a cover put on the volume to preserve the binding and I keep it locked up in an iron fire-proof safe when not in use.'

The text has been printed, edited by L. O. Pike, in *Year Books*, 11–12, 12–13, 13–14, 14, 14–15, 16, 17 Edward III, 9 volumes, in the Rolls Series (1883–1901), and this volume is fully described by Mr Pike in his introduction to volume 1, *Year Book*, 11–12 Edward III, pp. x–xii.

f. 1. at top of folio: Fr. Cranley his Book, in a hand of the seventeenth century.

f. 129. is the old flyleaf or cover of the volume which is fully written on, on both sides, some of the writing being very faint on account of wear.

The manuscript is written in a considerable variety of hands and the additions contain recipes and scribblings. The marginal notes of the manuscript are of two main periods, the contemporary and the key words or phrases which indicate the nature of the case reported; the more important later marginal notes vary from a cross reference to a brief description of the case or point of law.

PETYT MS. 511

This group consists of 23 volumes, of which volume 15 is a printed text, the remaining 22 volumes being a variety of medieval manuscripts, many of them chronicles, the others covering a wide range of subjects. All are bound in full morocco, volumes 1–3, 10, 19–23 in dark blue morocco, volumes 4–9, 11–13, 16–18 in black morocco, and volume 14 in red morocco. All have the Inner Temple coat of arms on both covers, except volumes 4, 11, and 23, which have the Petyt coat of arms on both covers. There is considerable variation in size, the details of which are given below for each volume.

Volume 1 is the Speculum Historiale, by Vincent of Beauvais; volume 2, Historia Anglorum, by Roger de Hoveden; volume 3, Ecclesiastical Court Precedents; volume 4, a Register of Writs; volume 5, the Polychronica of Ralph de Higden; volume 6, Modus tenendi Parliamentum, with Statutes, 1 Edward III to 3 Henry VII; volume 7, Historia Britanniae, by Robert Manning, and Gesta Anglorum, by Peter Langtoft; volume 8, Statutes, 1 Edward III to 29 Henry VI; volume 9 consists of Statutes, Legal Tracts, and a Register of Writs; volume 10, Macrobius' Somnium Scipionis; volume 11 is a composite volume of Lydgate's Life of St. Alban and Chronicles; volume 12, Miscellaneous Law Reports, Edward VI to Elizabeth I; volume 13, Legal Collections of the time of Elizabeth I; volume 14, a Year Book, 38–42 Edward III; volume 16, Collections on Ecclesiastical Jurisdiction concerning Prohibitions, etc., in the time of James I; volume 17, Transcripts of Records relating to Scotland; volume 18, Cartulary of Cathedral Church of Salisbury; volume 19, another composite volume mainly of Chronicles in French: volume 20, De re Uxoris Liber, by Francis Barbari; volume 21, Tract on Consecration of Churches; volume 22, History of the Trojan War, by Guido de Columna; volume 23, a Collection of Legal Cases and Arguments, in the hand of William Prynne.

VOLUME I

The Speculum Historiale, by Vincent de Beauvais. On flyleaf: Vincentius Speculum Historiale de Origine Regnorum, etc., $16\frac{7}{8}'' \times 11\frac{5}{8}''$. 343 ff.

ff. 1–343. The Speculum Historiale, by Vincent de Beauvais.

Begins: Ab anno Gratiani qui fuit ab incarnacione domini cclxxi.

At foot. Johannes Armorer vicarius de Sutton Valaunce Hedecroncforde modo rector de Pensehurst.

f. 343. Ends: Expliceat ludere scriptor eat.

The manuscript, which is written in two columns, has decorated capitals in red and blue. It appears to be of the second half of the fourteenth century, and it may be of foreign provenance, though the annotations, glosses, etc., appear to be made in England. It was written by a very ignorant or careless scribe, particularly in the omission of words, phrases, and even paragraphs. The marginal notes, which are in several hands, were written in ink or crayon. There are figures and pointer marks in the margins of hands, heads, and grotesque figures. Some are quite well drawn and are in a better ink than the text and the marginal notes are generally written in a more pleasant hand than that of the text. Many of the marginal notes are amplifications or corrections of the text. The parchment is of good quality but has in part been damaged or stained by damp, especially in the lower left-hand corner. The ink of the text is of a greenish brownish colour.

VOLUME 2

The Historia Anglorum of Roger de Hoveden. On flyleaf: Annales Rogeri de Hoveden. $14\frac{3}{8}'' \times 10\frac{3}{8}''$. 132 ff.

ff. 1–132. The Historia Anglorum by Roger de Hoveden (cf. *Chronica Rogeri de Hoveden*, ed. W. Stubbs, (R.S.), vols. I–III).

f. 1. Incipit Historia Anglorum sive Saxonum post Bedam edita a Magistro Rogero de Hoveden.
In exordio huius operis Genealogiam.
At top of f.: Liber sancte Marie Ryevallis (in an early thirteenth-century hand).
Liber monasterii Reuallis (in a sixteenth-century hand).
Signatures: William Bowyer; Robt. Bowyer de Medio Templo, 1595.

f. 111. At top of f.: Liber monasterii gloriose virginis Marie Revallis (in a thirteenth-century hand).

f. 131v. At end of folio: Robert Constable.

f. 132. Explicit: Nisi forte aliquando urgente necessitate pro bono pacis conuincto talis toleretur.
After end of text: Iste liber pertinet Roberto Constable.
Johannes Williams is my (blank).
Jesus est amor.
Signature: Thomas Beverlay.
John Williams est verus huius libri.
Johannes Williams is my (blank).

This manuscript was clearly in the possession of the Abbey of Rievaulx early in the thirteenth century. It seems subsequently to have been in the possession of Sir Robert Constable, Thomas Beverlay, and John Williams, then of William Bowyer and his son, Robert Bowyer, so many of whose manuscripts reached the Petyt Collection. It is natural that a Yorkshire monastic house should have a manuscript by a Yorkshire author, who took his name from Howden, which was but 35 miles from Rievaulx. As Rievaulx was not dissolved until 1538 and Sir Robert Constable was executed in 1537 for his part in the Pilgrimage of Grace, the manuscript had obviously reached him or his family some years before the dissolution. William Bowyer, Keeper of the Records in the Tower of London, 1567–81, was a Yorkshire man and a collector of manuscripts, most of which became the property of his son, Robert Bowyer, who was Clerk of the House of Lords 1610–21. The manuscript may have been written in the Durham scriptorium, for Howden and Howdenshire belonged to that house, and in hand and illumination it has close resemblances to more than one manuscript in the Dean and Chapter Library, Durham. Therefore, the manuscript seems to have had none but Yorkshire associations until after the death of Robert Bowyer in 1621. From him it may have descended to his nephew and successor as Clerk of the House of Lords, Henry Elsyng.

Though this manuscript was not used by William Stubbs for his edition of Hoveden for the Rolls Series, probably because he was not aware of its existence, it is one of the most important and earliest surviving manuscripts of Hoveden's Historia. The most important additions and variations are detailed below, as are also descriptions of some of the most important special features (variations in spellings of place and proper names and slight variations in the text are not noted):

f. 5. c. 1. Hic contexitur genealogia Elfredi Regis Anglorum et postea Athelwlfi patris eius et sequentium Regum. (cf. vol. I, p. 19.)

f. 5v. c. 2. De Rege Kynwlfo et Offa strenuissimo. (cf. p. 22.)

ff. 7x. c. 2, 7v. c. 1 & 2, 9. c. 1 & 2, 9v. c. 2 have captions missing in printed text.

f. 15. c. 2. Edwardus Rex Anglie senior obiit. (p. 53, Anglorum in printed text.)

f. 18v. c. 2. Rex Edwardus iniuste occiditur. (p. 65, iniuste omitted.)

f. 25. c. 1. De Edmundo Rege. (omitted.)

f. 26. c. 1. De expulsione Olaui regis. (omitted.)

f. 27v. c. 1. De Haroldo Rege. (omitted.)

f. 26v. c. 2. Sanctus Edwardus Rex efficitur. (last word omitted.)

f. 34v. c. 1. Quare de causa Willelmus Dux Normannorum angliam bello petiit.

f. 39v. c. 2. De Turgoto monacho post episcopo facto.

f. 40. c. 2. De coniuratione quorundam contra Willelmum.

f. 40v. c. 2. Decretum Gregorii Pape qui et Hildebrand de presbiteris ux(o)ratis.

f. 46v. c. 1. Sanctus Wlstanus obiit.

f. 53v. c. 2. Controversia inter Ricardum Cantuarensem archiepiscopum et Turstinum Eboracensem electum (cf. p. 170). The Ricardum is an error of the illuminator. Rad. in the text. (f. 53v. c. 1.)

f. 54. c. 2. Concilium Calixti pape. (p. 172. In both cases the word pape has been crossed out in black ink.)

f. 60v. c. 1. There is a whole section left out in this MS. here beginning in printed text (p. 191) Concordiam cum rege to vel nichili pendebat, including the caption: Tertius annus regni regis Stephani.

f. 64v. c. 1. De cruce signatis.

f. 65v. c. 2. Obiit Beatus Bernardus abbas.

f. 66v. c. 1. v annus eiusdem.

f. 72. c. 1. De perfectione Regis in Gualliam.

f. 82v. c. 1. De adventu legatorum domini pape in Normannia.

f. 83v. c. 1. Annus xvi Regni regis Henrici II. (regni omitted vol. II, p. 3.)

f. 86v. c. 1. Epistola Lodowici Regis Francorum ad Alexandrum summum pontificem de morte beati thome martiris et archiepiscopi Cantuariensis.

f. 93. c. 2. De proditoribus Regis.

f. 98. c. 2. Calumpnia clericorum Eboracensis ecclesie.

f. 99v. c. 1. De captione et interfectione Walteri de Fontanis.

f. 100v. c. 2. De aduentu Regis Scocie ad consilium.

f. 104v. c. 1. iiiitum capitulum agit de verbis domini in cena.

f. 124v. c. 1. Epistola ad canonicos.

This section does not contain the whole of the letter to Richard, Archbishop of Canterbury, legate, from Geoffrey, son of the King of England and Chancellor (elect of Lincoln), as given in the printed text (p. 176). It ends titulo pignoris obligare (as does the Bodleian Laud MS., cf. p. 207, n. 2). This MS. has: Bene vale. Thereafter the captions agree almost verbatim with those of the printed version and there are no omissions or additions in either. (cf. II, pp. 226 seq., III, pp. 1–77.)

In this MS. the word pape has been struck through in black ink, in addition to the cases already given, on ff. 111. c. 1, 111v. c. 1, 113v. c. 1, 118v. c. 2, 123. c. 1, 123v. c. 1, 124v. c. 1, 126v. c. 1 (bis), 126v. c. 2, 127. c. 1, 127v. c. 1, 127v. c. 2 (bis), 128. c. 1, 128v. c. 2, 129. c. 1 (bis), 129v. c. 2, (bis), 130. c. 1, 131. c. 2, 131v. c. 2, 131v. c. 2 (three times), 132. c. 1.

Throughout there are verbal differences and differences in spellings of place and proper names and other minor differences, e.g. f. 1. c. 1, Husco for Husso (p. 3), viiitam, octo (ibid.), Egfridus, Ecfridus (p. 4), annotantes, notantes (ibid.), f. 1. c. 2, Thatwine, Tatwine (ibid.), Alwin, Alwig (ibid.), Brichwaldus, Berchwaldus (ibid.), Fridbertus, Frithebertus (p. 5), ordinatus, confirmatus (ibid.).

Where the MSS. used in the printed version (II, p. 89) the Constitutions of Clarendon are given, the following note appears instead (f. 100v. c. 2), which is apparently not in any other MS: Si quis tamen eas videre aut legere desiderat in libro qui dicitur Curialis querat et ibi plenarie eas inveniet.

The text of the Historia (in which Glanvill's De Legibus Anglie is omitted) ends f. 125, c. 1: titulo pignoris obligare Vale. Hic incipit quedam sentencia Willelmi Bastard Regis anglie quam de Regis nomine pippino et Karolo eius filio sciscitantibus scripsit nondum Regibus nec non et alia quedam gesta atque statuta eiusdem.

f. 126v. c. 1. Quo defuncto Johannes frater eius successit eum regno Anglie. Et regnauit annis xiiii.

Explicit pars prima hystorie anglorum post venerabilem bedam illius gentes hystoriographum. Incipit decreta Alexandri pape tercii sicut superius promisi.

The decreta begin:

f. 126v. c. 1. Primum igitur de electione Romani pontificis agit.

f. 126v. c. 2. Decretum Alexandri pape iiicii Qualiter prelati debeant subiectos sentenciam preferre.

Decretum Alexandri pape tercii. Qualiter prelati debeant cum subiectos hospitari.

f. 127. c. 1. Decretum Alexandri pape iii. Prohibetur ne aliquid exigatur pro sacramentis ecclesiasticis non noui census imponantur ecclesiis veteres augeantur. (pp. 74–5.)

The marginalia are of varying dates up to the sixteenth century, if not to the seventeenth century. Some are in ink, others in crayon. There are head markers. The following are characteristic:

f. 6. apud (required in text, written in margin) contemporary.

f. 18. Basilius idem quod Rex R.

f. 23. Eadmundus filius Regis cognominatus ferreum latus. In margin Irenside.

f. 31v. Sanctus Wlfstanus.

f. 86. Passio beate (Thome) beate Godrico die reuelata.

f. 110. Nota de Neuille (16th century).

The margins are very wide and on the whole the marginalia are very few. The proper names are in small capitals and Ead is always found for Ed in Edwardus, Edmundus etc.

f. 132v. The following additions have been made on this blank last page:

1. Writ to the Abbot and Convent of Rievaulx containing a transcript (in French) of letters in the King's Treasury of the acknowledgement by the Scottish Lords of the sovereignty of Edward I, 1291. Tested by Master William Marsh, Treasurer, 19 Edward I.
2. In a different and later hand. Memorandum of a decree in a General Chapter of the Cistercian Order, 1301, in a dispute between the Abbey (of Savigny) and the Abbot of Buildwas, on the patronage of St. Mary's Abbey, Dublin. (cf. *Chart. of St. Mary's Abbey* (R.S.), vol. 1, p. 381.)

This is a very well-written manuscript written in two columns, on good-quality parchment, in a good-quality black ink and in an even hand. The illumination is well done. It has illuminated capitals in red and green, some of them well formed and executed. The captions which are numerous are in red. The following, also in red, call for special notice: f. 60. Where the account of the Battle of the Standard is given there is a drawing of a standard on a waggon (four wheels) surmounted by a cross with the pennon flying from it and at the side, in red, the words: de Standardo.

f. 102. In red: Signum Willelmi Regis Magni Scicilie.

The following marginalia are important on provenance and date:

f. 58. Eodem uero anno iiii N. Marcii fundata fuit abathia Ryeuall a nobili uiro Waltero Espeek (in a book-hand of the thirteenth century).

Et anno domini MoCCCo xvii Scoti Dilapidauerunt et destruxerunt atque asportauerunt libros calices et sacra ornamenta monasterii de Ryevall in festo Sancto Kalixti pape et martiris (fourteenth century, in a contemporary hand or slightly later).

The date of the manuscript can be fairly accurately determined by the reference to the reign of King John on f. 126v. The number of John's regnal years is, of course, incorrect, but the manuscript could not have been written before the end of 1216. The manuscript is, therefore, one of the earliest and most valuable of the manuscripts of Roger de Hoveden's Historia and though not used for the latest printed edition will certainly have to be used for any future edition.

VOLUME 3

A Precedent Book of Proceedings in Ecclesiastical Courts. The manuscript is in various sections of different sizes, a collection of precedents and notes rather than a formal compilation. The sizes of what may fairly be called folios varies from $11\frac{3}{4}'' \times 8\frac{5}{8}''$ (of which there are 8 ff.) to $15\frac{5}{8}'' \times 9\frac{5}{8}''$ (47 ff.). The rest may be regarded as insets of different shapes and sizes. The back cover is not bound in. Label inset in flyleaf: Book of Instruments and Proceedings in the Ecclesiastical Courts. The following note is attached at the end: MS. I. 8 in the Dean and Chapter Library at Canterbury is a Formulary of Ecclesiastical Courts containing treatises on procedure in the Court of Arches. The manuscript is contemporary with Petyt No. 511/3. 511/3 may be notes for the treatise at Canterbury. Fol. 178 of 511/3 may be an early form of written customs of the Court of Arches and is similar to Ashmole 114, f. 114 (approx.) and Camb., St. John's, E. 3. 511/3 dated about 1312–30. Information from Revd. F. D. Logan, work for dissertation on Medieval Court of Arches. E. A. P. Hart, 20. vi. 61. 188 ff.

f. 1 is the early parchment cover which has been bound in the volume. It is mutilated.

f. 1v. Transcripts of four documents in a fourteenth-century hand:

1. On the church of 'Quartermilr', diocese of London. (mutilated.)
2. Letter to Dean of Dengie, Prior and Convent of Horton, diocese of Canterbury. In church of St. Paul's, London. Thomas, Rector of church of Purleigh, diocese of London.
3. Proctor of Prior and Convent of Horton, of Cluniac Order, diocese of Canterbury. Thomas, Rector of church of Purleigh.
4. Letter to Dean of Dengie. Bartholomew de London, proctor of Prior and Convent of Horton.

f. 2. Notes on exceptions; among the names mentioned are Stephen, rector of Cowden and Richard, rector of Westerham. (a slip only, 6″×4″.)

ff. 3–8 (except f. 7). A kind of index to the precedents in the volume, being lists of Suggestiones, Exceptiones, Libelli, Articuli, Querele, Litere, Excusatoria, Obligationes, Suspensiones, Petitiones, Recuperaciones, Revocationes, Concessiones, Communicationes, Constitutiones, Replicationes, Privilegia, Offensa, Manifesta, Allegationes, Appellaciones, Procurationes, Relaxaciones, Citationes. (14″×9″.)

f. 7. Richard de Haute, Auditor of the Court of Audience of the Prior and Convent of Christ Church, Canterbury, sede vacante, John de Gatton and James, his brother, executors of Will of Dame Joan de Gatton, their mother, at procuration of Alice de Gatton, daughter of Joan. (a slip, $6\frac{1}{4}$″×$9\frac{5}{8}$″, inserted.)

f. 16. Transcripts of two documents, both dated 4 December 1285.

f. 17. Richard de Haute, Auditor of Court of Audience of the Prior and Convent of Christ Church, Canterbury, sede vacante, on Hamo de Beracre, executor of Dionisia de Beracre, his mother.

f. 19. Writing indented between John de Silveston, clerk, and John Boye of Eastry, on digging of ditch in prejudice.

f. 21. 1323. Master Robert, rector of St. Martin's in suburbs of city of Canterbury, and Ralph, Master of the Scholars of the Grammar School of the city, priest.

f. 29v. This may be the end of the first original volume, corresponding to f. 1.

f. 37. Official of Bishop of Rochester on cause of certain tithes which Master Richard de Haute, rector of church of Westerham, diocese of Rochester, had against Stephen, rector of Cowden, same diocese.

f. 40. Richard de Haute, Auditor of Prior and Convent of Christ Church, Canterbury, sede vacante, on James de Gatton, executor of Will of Joan de Gatton, his mother, at instance of Alice, daughter of Joan. (see above, f. 7.)

f. 43. Suit concerning Master (Edmund) de Meopham, rector of church of Brasted, diocese of Rochester.

f. 45. 1294, 3 Ides December (11 December). Philip de Pontefracto, chaplain, proctor, against proctor of Hospital of St. Anthony, diocese of Vienne, on church of All Saints, Hereford, R(ichard Bromfield), Bishop of Hereford.

f. 48. A slip cut from Estreats. See others especially f. 47, Amerciaments before J(ohn) de Cobham, 2 Edward II (1308–9). Cf. also ff. 92, 156.

f. 62. Memorandum. Prior and Convent of Christ Church, Canterbury, parish church of Halstow, diocese of Canterbury; Abbot and Convent of St. Augustines, Canterbury, parish church of Middleton.

f. 69. Official of Archdeacon of London to all in the Archdeaconry. London, Thursday after Feast of St. Peter ad Vincula (6 August) 1294. This is an original document.

f. 72. (William) de Montfort, Dean of St. Paul's, London, to the Archdeacon of London and his Official. Eve of Trinity (12 June) 1294. Also an original document.

f. 74. Letter from Commissary of Canterbury to Robert (Winchelsey), Archbishop of Canterbury, acknowledging his letter to Master Martin (de Hampton), his Commissary of Canterbury, concerning John de Monsdun, on the expenses of Alice, his wife. Chatham, 8 Kal. May (24 April) 1297, with reply, Ickham, 5 Ides May (11 May) 1297. Also an original document.

f. 75. Clemencia, late wife of Stephen Petit, of Canterbury, granting William de Heigham and Isabella, his wife, the manor of Besaltre. Canterbury, Monday before Nativity of St. Mary (16 September) 1294.

f. 80/1. E(rnald) de Stok, Commissary General of R(ichard Gravesend), Bishop of London, to the Archdeacon of London, his Official. Master John de Silveston, Vicar General of Bishop of London. Stebonheath, 2 Ides May (13 May) 1294, with reply, London, Ides of May (15 May) 1294. An original document.

f. 80/2. R(ichard Gravesend), Bishop of London, to Archdeacon of London. Harringay, 3 Kal. March 14 Pont. (27 February 1294). An original document with mark of green wax seal on dorse.

f. 80/3. Official of Salisbury to Dean of Abingdon. Watford, Thursday after Assumption (21 August) 1278.

f. 83. Clement V to Walter de Maidstone, Canon of Socoa diocese of Auch. Lyons, 7 Ides February (7 February) 1 Pont. (1306). Executed 23 March.

f. 84. Archdeacon of Oxford in church of Lincoln, to Master Henry de Nassington, Canon of Lincoln. and John de St. Clare, Canon of church of St. Paul's, London, in cause of appeal. London, 6 Ides October (10 October) 1297. (draft.)

f. 87. Henry, Prior of Christ Church, Canterbury, to Master Hugh de Forsham, his Commissary. Margaret de Greyli against Sir Stephen de Tidmarsh, kt., before Master Richard de Haute. (draft.)

f. 93. Official of Bishop of Rochester to Official of Archdeacon of Rochester. Lately Master Thomas de Northwood, rector of church of Cowden and John de Ferring, priest of that church, against Master Richard de Haute, rector of church of Westerham. Thursday after Sunday on which the office of quasi modo geniti (6 April) 1309. Before us in the parish church of Malling.

f. 97. Before Judge. Master Richard de Haute, rector of parish church of Westerham, diocese of Rochester. Mary, former wife of Ralph de Bode, and John, his son, executor of his Will. (draft.)

f. 97v. Before Judge. Master Richard de Haute, rector of church of Westerham. Against Felicia, former wife of Richard Rodding, of Westerham, dec. (draft.)

f. 98. Before Judge. Master Richard de Haute, rector of Westerham. Against Luke, called le Bedel of Codham. (draft.)

f. 99. To Official of Rochester. Richard de Haute.

f. 100/1. Before Master R(ichard) de Ros, Canon of St. Paul's, Commissary of R(obert Winchelsey), Archbishop of Canterbury, Agnes le Panur, of Nottingham, diocese of Lincoln, against John Spit, of Leicester.

f. 110/2. Before Judge. William de Cleydon, clerk, diocese of Coventry and Lichfield. Against Master John de Dalby, diocese of Lichfield.

f. 118. Dean of St. Mary of the Arches, London, called Court of Canterbury, Commissary, to Official of Archdeacon of London. London, 8 Ides June (6 June) 1288.

f. 125. To Official of Court of Canterbury and his Commissary, from Official of Bishop of Chichester. Order Dean of Arches in these words: Dean of church of St. Mary of the Arches, Office of Court of Canterbury, Commissary. Prior of La Sale, diocese of Chichester, proctor. Master Richard de Haute, clerk of diocese of Canterbury, at instance of Thomas Forte, diocese of Canterbury, cause on church of St. Mary of Southwark, diocese of Winchester, near London. London, 12 Kal. July (20 June) 1299. Return, London, 4 Ides July (12 July) 1299. Executed Yeldham, 12 Kal. August (21 July) 1299.

f. 133. Writ to Sheriff of Salisbury. John, the son of Adam, of Welton, complains of Richard de Haute, Henry Crewe, Robert Kethal and Henry de Haute, of disseisin of a free tenement. Tested John (Droxford), Bishop of Bath and Wells, Westminster, 16 June 6 Edward II (1313). Writ tested by Roger le Brabazon, Westminster, 23 May 4 Edward II (1311). William de Haute in King's Court, 22 Edward I (1294), before J(ohn) de Metingham and his fellows, Justices of the Bench, against Roger de Grastet and Roberta, his wife, recovered a message, 16 a. etc. Like writ tested by R(oger) le Brabazon, Westminster, 5 July 5 Edward II (1312).

f. 143. John (Dalderby), Bishop of Lincoln, one of executors in underwritten business, to Dean of Oxford. Binbrook, 16 Kal. December (16 November) 1300.

f. 151/1. Dean of church of St. Mary of the Arches, London, Commissary of Office of Court of Canterbury, to Official of Lincoln and Dean of Nassington. Appeal. London, 8 Ides July (8 July) 1290.

f. 155. Letters Patent by Richard de Haute, rector of church of Westerham, diocese of Rochester, to John de St. Lawrence, chaplain, 'to which I have put my accustomed seal'. Westerham, 8 Ides April (6 April) 1312.

f. 162/1. Dean of church of St. Mary of the Arches, London, to Abbot of Abingdon, on pensions from the church of Chilton.

f. 178. 'The way of proceeding in historical matters is this': ($18\frac{3}{4}'' \times 6\frac{1}{2}''$.)

f. 180. Replication of Peter de Leicester. In execution of the decree of the Court of Canterbury, appellant on the church of Cliff, diocese of Worcester, against G(odfrey Giffard), Bishop of Worcester, and Master Robert de Wythie. (draft.)

f. 182. Ex parte Thomas de Barton on the church of St Edmunds, Salisbury.

f. 183. To Official of Court of Canterbury. John de Sutton, on church of St. Patrick. Bishop of Lincoln.

f. 184. John de Sutton, Clerk of King's Customs, and church of North Mimms, and church of Westhall, diocese of Norwich.

f. 185. To Official of Court of Canterbury, J(ohn of Pontoise), Bishop of Winchester. William de Saham.

f. 186. To Official of Court of Canterbury. Philip de Guildford, church of Mileham, diocese of Norwich, presented by Theobald de Verdun.

f. 187. Master Peter de Den, Clerk of King of England, to church of Billingshurst, diocese of Chichester. G(ilbert of St. Leonards), Bishop of Chichester.

f. 188. In a later hand: Pro incumbente contra presentatum. James de Dover, rector of the church of St. Peter in the Bailey, Oxford, diocese of Lincoln.

The importance of this manuscript, as probably the earliest surviving precedent book of ecclesiastical courts, demands detailed investigation on two main points, first its date of compilation and secondly its compiler. The range of dates of the documents which are dated or can be dated approximately is from 1278 to 1323. The earliest and latest dates are exceptional, the greatest number of dated documents being between 1285 and 1300. There are more for the year 1294 than for any other year. The date of compilation would therefore appear to be about 1300 or a little later.

It will be noted that many of the precedents refer to Master Richard de Haute, rector of Westerham, in the diocese of Rochester. He is three times described as Auditor of the Court of Audience of the Prior and Convent of Christ Church, Canterbury, sede vacante (ff. 7, 17, 40). Master Richard de Haute was certainly Auditor for the Prior and Convent during the vacancies, 1313–14 and 1333–4 (Churchill, *Canterbury Administration*, I, p. 563a; II, pp. 224–5, 243). When the see of Canterbury was vacant the Prior and Convent exercised the ordinary ecclesiastical jurisdiction of the Archbishop, as, after the Reformation, the Dean and Chapter did. They generally took over, under their commissions, the late Archbishop's officers, so there is a strong presumption that Richard de Haute was the Archbishop's Auditor of his Court of Audience. Unfortunately none of the documents is dated, but some appear to relate to the vacancy of 1292–4. Of the documents which are dated which refer to him one is dated 20 June 1299 (f. 125), in which he is described as Master Richard de Haute, clerk, of the diocese of Canterbury, and appears to have been concerned with the Court of Arches with a cause appealed from in the diocese of Chichester. In 1309 he was himself party as rector of Westerham in a cause of tithes against the rector and priest of Cowden (f. 93), as he had been previously against a former rector (f. 39). About the same time he was party to civil as well as ecclesiastical causes, as is witnessed by transcripts of writs tested by the Chief Justices of Common Pleas to the Sheriff of Salisbury, dated 23 May 1311, 5 July 1312, and 16 June 1313 respectively (f. 133), in which a Richard de Haute with others, among whom was a Henry de Haute, were sued on disseisin. The case seemed to hark back to a successful action by one William de Haute, possibly the father of Richard and Henry, in 1294. The appearance of these three writs in what are otherwise all ecclesiastical precedents is strange, unless Richard de Haute was the compiler of the collection, or it was his commonplace book, both personal and ecclesiastical. The only other dated document relating to him is one of 6 April 1312. It takes the form of letters patent by him in which he describes himself as rector of the church of Westerham, diocese of Rochester, to which he had put his accustomed seal, at Westerham (f. 155). There are three documents which are all undated which relate to his activities as Judge. Of these one is addressed to the Official of Rochester (f. 97); another relates to a Westerham woman; and the third to a Codham man (ff. 97v, 98). All three are drafts. They may relate to the Court of Audience or the Court of Arches, and one cause at least related to a cause which later would have come before the Prerogative Court of Canterbury.

Two further points deserve some attempt at elucidation; to what Courts do the precedents relate? The precedents given relate to notifications, replications, revocations, exceptions, citations, libels, commissions, agreements, appeals, sentences, petitions, presentations, certificates, and so on, of which the documents given above are characteristic. Many of these precedents would be applicable to any ecclesiastical court, of bishop or archdeacon; some of them appear to be applicable only to the Court of Arches or the Court of Audience of the metropolitan. The manuscript should therefore be regarded as primarily a precedent book for these two Courts.

Secondly on foliation. The manuscript has four different foliations: first the latest which is followed above, ff. 1–188; the second seems to start on f. 8v, which is f. 1, which seems to have been misbound, and continues to f. 178, which is f. 105 (though this is not continuous); the third starts at f. 109 as f. i and runs to f. 143, which is f. xxvi; at f. 135 the remains of another foliation appears, f. v, f. 136 is f. vi, f. 139 f. vii, f. 141 f. viii, and then ff. 145–160 ff. i–viii, and ff. 161–176 ff. i–xii. These last were obviously made before the present book was made up to anything like its present form. Lastly too a word should be said about the great variation in the sizes of the folios of the manuscript. These alter so frequently that the volume naturally presents an irregular and untidy appearance. The sizes of what may fairly be called folios varies from $11\frac{3}{4}'' \times 8\frac{5}{8}''$, of which there are 6 ff., to $15\frac{3}{8}'' \times 9\frac{5}{8}''$, of which there are 47 ff. The remainder may be regarded as insets of different shapes and sizes. Most of the items or precedents are in contemporary cursive hands and naturally in a considerable variety of styles. The irregularity is further increased by the emendations and corrections inevitable in drafts. Throughout the parchment is serviceable, the hands easily read, and the general condition in all the circumstances very good. The value of the contents is very great. It is probably the earliest authentic volume of precedents of ecclesiastical forms which has survived in England, the greater part of them for the last decade of the 13th century. It is earlier than the manuscript in the Dean and Chapter Library at Canterbury which is noted above. Indeed the last mentioned is probably based upon it. Its importance has been realized by the Selden Society, who proposed to publish it in full, but the proposed editors, the late Professor H. D. Hazeltine and the late Sir Hilary Jenkinson, did not find it possible to continue the work. It was their opinion that the volume was a draft treatise on procedure in ecclesiastical courts.

VOLUME 4

Register of Writs. On flyleaf: Registrum Brevium. $11\frac{5}{8}'' \times 8''$. 120 ff.

This volume follows the usual pattern of the Register of Writs. It is incomplete at the end, at least one folio being missing and as the last existing folio is worn it has been the last for a long time. It was probably written about the middle of the fifteenth century, though most of the writs are of the time of Edward III and Richard II. The Regula are in Latin or Norman French and there are marginal notes in addition to the description of the Writs and the

Regula. There are a few additional writs added in the usual spaces left at the ends of the sections. There is a certain amount of duplication of foliation. The manuscript is slightly stained by damp throughout, the first ff. and the last being those most affected. There is no illumination and space has been left for the entry of main capital letters. There are running captions to the various sections of the Register.

VOLUME 5

The Polychronicon of Ralph Higden, full bound in black morocco with Inner Temple coat of arms on both covers. On flyleaf: Higden. Radulphus Higden, Historia Polychronicon. $11\frac{3}{4}'' \times 8''$. 267 ff.

ff. 1–9. Contains an alphabetical index written in a hand different from that of the Chronicle. Each section A to Z begins with an illuminated capital, decorated with foliage. The colours are green, yellow, purple, and gold.

At top of f. 1, in a seventeenth-century hand: Radulphus Cestrensis.

At foot of f.: Edmund Parkinson.

At foot of f. 6: Dew the xx day of March and askyd at the visitacion.

At foot of f. 9v: Signature: Franciscus Babington, 1559; followed by a line in Greek characters: Richard Babington is a knave as he saith himself who best doth knowe.

The references in the index are to folio and chapter.

ff. 10–267. The Polychronicon in seven books, ending in 1377 (*Polychon R. Higden* (R.S.), vols. I–VIII).

The first leaf of the Chronicle is missing and it begins: per omnia teneri non poterit certitudo nam diuina miracula secundum Augustinum.

At the top of f. 10: Signature: F. Babington.

The books 1–4 have an incipit and explicit, book 5 has an incipit only, book 6 has an explicit only and there is nothing to mark the beginning of chapter 1 of this book. Book 7 has an incipit and explicit. At f. 256 there is a complete change of hand and the running captions cease. The chapter numbers too are different.

f. 264. Explicit liber septimus qui est ultimus historie policronicae.

ff. 264v–267v. These folios have no illumination or paragraph marks and the capital letters of sections have not been inserted.

f. 264v. Begins: unus igitur cum ad plagam. The subsequent sections all begin with a date, the first, f. 264v, being 843 and ending with 1377, the coronation of Richard II, 17 Kal. August (16 July), followed by a list of popes corresponding to English King Alfred, Leo.

f. 267v. At foot of folio: To the Right Worshipful Mr. Bowyer at his house in Hand Alley without Temple Bar, give these in Fleet Streete.

There are on most folios a few marginal notes of no particular significance. There are drawings in or related to the text on ff. 49v, 80v, 182v, and inconsequent scribblings on ff. 51v, 52, 104, 105, 116, 122, 144, 150. The following are worthy of note or comment:

f. 150. In margin: Thomas Wood.

At foot: Thomas Wode, God make him a good man.

ff. 151v. 152. Some religious verses at foot and in margin of f. 152 some drawings of heads and the following: Yermouthe natus est bte. Leonard. Simachus papa.

f. 157. A proverb or witty saying.

ff. 223v. 224. A long section apparently omitted in the text has been added at the end of the ff.

The paragraph marks are in red and blue, the capitals of the chapters are illuminated in blue, purple, green, and gold, with a floral design. The captions of the chapters are in red. Some of the chapter capitals are damaged. The margin has chapter numbers. At the beginning of Books 2, 3, 4, 5, and 7, at ff. 45, 74, 115v, 148, 214, there are more elaborate capitals, illuminated in the same colours as the capitals of the chapters but extending the length and width of the columns. The volume is written in two columns throughout. The hand is moderate, the parchment reasonable, and the ink satisfactory for its period. The manuscript may be safely dated to the first decades of the fifteenth century.

All that can be said of the provenance of the manuscript is that it was sometime in the possession of a Thomas Wood and of an Edmund Parkinson, and that in 1559 it was certainly in the possession of Francis Babington, from whom it perhaps passed on to Richard Babington. It then reached William Bowyer and so passed on to his son, Robert Bowyer, and reached William Petyt with the other Bowyer manuscripts.

VOLUME 6

Statutes, 1 Edward III to 3 Henry VII, with the Modus tenendi Parliamentum prefixed. On an additional flyleaf added on rebinding is the following note: This copy of the Statutes is mentioned in the Appendix (R) to the *Report of the Record Commissioners*, 1812, p. 181. The first two original flyleaves have now been foliated, but the original manuscript now begins at f. 3. On f. 1 is a list of the sovereigns of England from Edward the Martyr, with the length of their reigns, except that Henry VIII, Edward VI, and Mary are left blank; f. 1v has further notes on the reigns of Richard III and Henry VII; f. 2 has a note of the murder of Richard Tracy, gentleman, his master, by James Grave, late of London, yeoman, 9 February 11 Henry VII (1496), at Brentwood, co. Essex. $9\frac{7}{8}'' \times 7''$. 446 ff.

ff. 3–7v. Modus tenendi Parliamentum. (cf. *Mod. Ten. Parl.* (R.C.), 1846.)

ff. 8–9v. Notes of Kings, with length of their reigns, from Edward the Confessor to Edward V.

ff. 10–446. Statutes, 1 Edward III to 3 Henry VII, beginning with the Statutes at Westminster, 1 Edward III (*Stat. of Realm*, I, pp. 251–398); and ending with the Statute of 3 Henry VII (ibid. II, pp. 1–523).

ff. 10–343v. The Statutes follow the run of those which appear in MSS. 505, and 506 above, up to 29 Henry VI (see pp. 176–80 above).

f. 344x.	Statute,	31	Henry VI,	Reading.	(*Stat. of Realm*, II, pp. 360–369.)
f. 350v.	”	33	”	Westminster.	(Ibid., pp. 369–78.)
f. 356v.	”	39	”	”	(Ibid., pp. 378–9.)
f. 361.	”	1	Edward IV,	”	(Ibid., pp. 380–91.)
f. 369.	”	2	”	”	(Ibid., pp. 392–402.)
f. 376.	”	4	”	”	(Ibid., pp. 403–18.)

f. 386.	Statute,	7 Edward IV,	Westminster		(*Stat. of Realm*, II, pp. 418–23.)
f. 389.	„	7 & 8	„	„	(Ibid., pp. 424–30.)
f. 394.	„	12	„	„	(Ibid., pp. 431–44.)
f. 401.	„	14	„	„	(Ibid., pp. 445–51.)
f. 404v.	„	17	„	„	(Ibid., pp. 452–67.)
f. 413.	„	22	„	„	(Ibid., pp. 468–76.)
f. 418v.	„	1 Richard III		„	(Ibid., pp. 477–98.)
f. 432.	„	1 Henry VII		„	(Ibid., pp. 499–508.)
f. 437.	„	3	„	„	(Ibid., pp. 509–23.)

f. 446. Explicit statuta de anno iiitio Henrici Septimi. Ro. Fulwode.

From f. 10, where the statutes begin, there is red illumination of the margin and text by way of marks to f. 125. Up to f. 289, where the Statute 7 & 8 Edward IV begins, each Statute has an illuminated capital in red and blue. Throughout the beginning of each chapter has a space left for an illuminated capital. At the beginning of the Statutes for each reign, Edward III to Edward IV, there is an illuminated capital of gold and faint other colours, f. 10 C(ome), the first word of the Statute, and in the other cases the first letter of the king's name, f. 112 R, f. 182, 225, 282v H, f. 361 E. Where the Statutes for the reigns of Richard III and Henry VII respectively begin there is a blank space left for the insertion of R f. 418v. and H f. 432. There are very full marginal notes, contemporary or later. The modern foliation is careless, e.g. ff. 50x, 62x, 181x (bis), 344x. On f. 109v there appears to be a gloss on Stat. West., 47 Edward III with a reference to Hil. term, 7 Henry VII. The Statutes have numbers and summaries of the caps. The parchment is not good and is uneven. The various hands are adequate; the ink is characteristic of the period. The Statutes up to the end of Edward IV were probably written in a volume about 1485, those for Richard III and Henry VII were added. The date of the additions is probably about 1488.

VOLUME 7

A volume on parchment containing: 1. Historia Britannie by Robert Manning of Brune; 2. Gesta Anglorum by Peter de Langtoft. On flyleaf: Robert de Gloucester, which is struck through and replaced by Petrus de Langtoft. The text is preceded by four parchment flyleaves on the first of which are 42 lines of verse, the verso is blank; on the second is the signature: Robert Haxe, and on the verso: Iste liber pertinet Edmundo Pymond vicario de Laghton. The other two ff. are blank, except for some scribbling of the first. $11\frac{3}{8}'' \times 8\frac{1}{8}''$. 195 ff.

1. ff. 1–95. The Chronicle of Robert Manning of Brune (*Chron. of Robt. Manning of Brune*, ed. F. J. Furnivall, (R.S.), 2 parts; cf. also Appendix to T. Hearne's Preface to *Peter de Langtoft* (1725), pp. xcvi–ci, clxxxviii–cxcvi).

f. 1. Incipit Prologus de Historia Britannie scripta per Robertum in materna lingua.

lordlynges that be now here
if ye will listen and lere
Al the story of Inglande
als Robert Mannyng wryten it fand.

f. 95v. Explicit Historia Britannie transposita in linguam maternam per Robertum.
Incipiunt Gesta Anglorum per Petrum de Langtoft transposita per eundem R(obertum) Mannyng.

Up to this point the manuscript is written in two columns and column 2 begins:

Now haf I told of the Bretons
Of kynges and some barons.

Hereafter the volume continues in one column only.

2. ff. 95v–195. The Gesta Anglorum by Peter de Langtoft (*Chron. of Pierre de Langtoft in French verse* . . . ed. T. Wright, (R.S.), 2 vols.; cf. also Appendix to T. Hearne's Preface to *Peter de Langtoft* (1725), pp. cv–cvii (prologue only).)

f. 195. Expliciunt Gesta Anglorum Britonum et in lingua materna per Robertum Mannyng transcripta anno Christi Millmo CCCmo tricesimo viii Idus Maii litera dominicale D prima et tempore Regis Edwardi tercii a conquestu xio.

This is followed by six parchment leaves on the 2nd of which appears: Sir Jhon Chume; on the 3rd: drawing of an animal, geometric figures, and scribbling; on 4th: v, geometric figures and: This book to be delivered at the sign of the Bell in Foucestre to be sent to John Wyre dwelling at the parsonage at Leghton, anno 1522, vo die Maii mccccxxii.

f. 4v. the drawings of a leaf, a dog, and a tree trunk and the signature: John Turner; f. 6v: Sell this book for 5s. if you can.

This manuscript, written on moderately good parchment, really contains two entirely separate translated works which have been combined together, the second part, written slightly later than the first, being coalesced into it. The hands are fair, as is the ink, and the manuscript may safely be dated about the middle of the fourteenth century. The date 1338, which is the year of Robert Manning's death, may be accepted as correct for the second part. The only other manuscript of this work is Lambeth MS. 131 and from that and the present manuscript F. J. Furnivall published his edition.

VOLUME 8

Statutes, 1 Edward III to 29 Henry VI, full bound in black morocco, with Inner Temple coat of arms on both covers. On flyleaf: 'Statuta ab anno 10 Ed. III ad annum 30 Hen. 6'. Signature: John Leveson. $11'' \times 7\frac{7}{8}''$. 247 ff.

ff. 1–31. A Table of Contents, alphabetically arranged, the references being to the regnal year and the chapter. It has illuminated capitals in red and blue, with paragraph marks throughout. There are no notes or additions.

ff. 33–246. Statutes, 1 Edward III to 29 Henry VI (*Stat. of Realm*, I, pp. 251–398; II, pp. 1–359.)

There are running headings throughout, the regnal year on one side and the name of the king on the other, with paragraph marks, red and blue. On ff. 33, 98v, 136, 165, 194 there are illuminated capitals in gold, red, blue, and green. The manuscript is well written, but there are signs of carelessness in the transcription. It has been little used. There are but twelve marginal notes throughout, of which eight are references to previous statutes, all in the same hand; three are notes concerning labourers, as follows:

f. 59v. Labourers to serve in Somerset: where they served in Somerset under penalty of imprisonment; f. 159. Labourers to be sworn any time in the year for every lete to serve after the ordinance of the statute; f. 236v. Nota Bene how servants shall depart from their masters. The twelfth addition is a note on penalty on sheriffs, under-sheriffs, and sheriffs' clerks.

There is also a contemporary addition at the bottom of f. 129v: 'ix quaternie hic immediate sequentes sunt liberari Tho. Shipton ad copia inde'.

The foliation has been very carelessly done, there being no less than twelve duplicate folios. The manuscript may be dated shortly after the middle of the fifteenth century.

The Statutes follow the run of those which appear in MSS. nos. 505, 506 above. (See pp. 176–80.)

On a flyleaf appears the signature of John Leveson. On f. 246, which is really a flyleaf, there is scribbling and the name John Croxton, and on the verso more scribbling and the following note: Memorandum that John Watkynson before Thomas Brown and other Justices of the Common Bench recovered his seisin against Joan Illingworth, widow, of 12 acres of land etc. in Sutton in the month of February 4 Henry VII. On f. 247, which is the last flyleaf, appears a little scribbling and the names: William Petyt: Est liber Johannis Croxton.

VOLUME 9

This volume contains Early Statutes, Legal Tracts, and a Register of Writs. On flyleaf: The Statutes, Magna Carta, Carta de Foresta, Merton, Marlborough, West. 1, Gloucester, West. 2. It consists of two separate sections, (1) Statutes and Legal Tracts, (2) Register of Writs, though it would appear that the two sections have always been bound together. $10'' \times 6\frac{3}{4}''$. 136 ff.

ff. 1–3v. At top of f. appears: Liber John Byrche, written in a hand of the late 16th or early 17th century, followed by a table of the chapters of Magna Carta and of other Statutes, ending with Westminster II.

ff. 4–6v. Magna Carta (2 Henry III). (*Stat. of Realm*, 1, pp. 17–19.)

ff. 6v–8. Charter of the Forests (2 Henry III). (Ibid., pp. 20–1.)

ff. 8–9v. Provisions of Merton (20 Henry III). (Ibid., pp. 1–4.)

ff. 9v–13v. Provisions of Marlborough (52 Henry III). (Ibid., pp. 19–25.)

ff. 13v–23. Statute of Westminster I (3 Edward I). (Ibid., pp. 26–39.)

ff. 23–25v. Statute of Gloucester (6 Edward I). (Ibid., pp. 45–50.)

ff. 25v–26. Explanations of the same. (Ibid., p. 50.)

ff. 26–42v. Statute of Westminster II (13 Edward I). (Ibid., pp. 71–95.)

ff. 42v–43. Statute de Medio (18 Edward I). (Ibid., p. 106.)

ff. 43–43v. Statute de Religiosis (7 Edward I). (Ibid., p. 51.)

ff. 43v–45v. Statute de Mercatoribus (13 Edward I). (Ibid., pp. 53–4.)

ff. 45v–47v. Statute of Winchester (13 Edward I). (Ibid., pp. 96–8.)

ff. 47v–50. Statute de Scaccario. (Ibid., pp. 197–8.)

ff. 50–50v. Statute de Militibus. (Ibid., pp. 198–212.)

ff. 50v–51. Statute de Transgressionibus. (Ibid., p. 111.)

f. 51v. Statute Monete et Mesure. (Ibid., pp. 218–19.)

ff. 51v–52. Statute de Bigamis (4 Edward I). (Ibid., pp. 42–3.)

ff. 52–52v. Statute de Juratoribus.

f. 52v. Statute de Anno et Die Bisextili (40 Henry III). (Ibid., p. 7.)

ff. 52v–53. Statute de habentibus Redditus in Civitate Lond. (Ibid., p. 222.)

ff. 53–53v. Statute de sentencia lata in transgressores libertatum, 25 Edward I. (Ibid., pp. 114–19.)

ff. 53v–54v. Capitula de Foresta (25 Edward I). (Ibid., pp. 120–2.)

f. 54v. Statute de Conspiratoribus et Breve (33 Edward I). (Ibid., p. 145.)
ff. 54v–55. Extenta Manerii. (Ibid., pp. 242–3.)
ff. 55–55v. Modus faciendi homagii. (Ibid., pp. 227–8.)
ff. 56–56v. Districtiones Scaccarii. (Ibid., pp. 197–8.)
ff. 56v–60v. Summa Iudicium Essonionum (12 Edward I.)
f. 61. Statute Quo Warranto (cancelled) (18 Edward I). (Ibid., p. 107.)
ff. 61–62v. Statuta Nova de Scaccario.
ff. 62v–63v. Statute of Exeter. (Ibid., pp. 210–12.)
ff. 63–64v. Articles of Statute of Exeter. (Ibid., p. 210.)
ff. 64v–70v. Summa Cadit Assisa.
ff. 70v–77. Summa Parva Hengham. (Cf. Fortescue, *De Laud.*, 1616 edn., edited by John Selden.)
ff. 77–81. Tractus or Summa Bastardie.
ff. 81–85v. Exceptiones contra Brevia.
ff. 85v–88v. Summa pro Brevibus Cassandis.
f. 88v. Quot Modis Essonia sunt calumpnianda. (*Stat. of Realm*, I, pp. 217–18.)

ff. 89–136. Registrum de Cancellaria. This ends abruptly as at least one f. has been lost at the end. The Register opens with the writ of right and ends with the writ of attorney by letters patent. Throughout there are marginal captions, illuminated in red and blue, of which there are 397. In no case where a writ is addressed to a Sheriff is a county mentioned. After the writs there are glosses in Latin or Norman French which are underlined in red. There are only two marginal notes, one of which is a cross reference and the other a reference to Bracton. In the first section (Statutes and Tracts) the regnal year of the Statute is put in the margin in a much later hand, as shown in brackets above. In no case is there a Statute later than 25 Edward I. This section also has a number of drawings in the margin, of grotesque men's heads, fifteen in all. They appear only at the beginning of Statutes and Tracts. Thereafter there are two such heads at the foot of f. 89, where the Register starts. This first section also has marginal notes. On illumination the capitula have captions in red, paragraph marks in blue and red, and paragraph marks in the text in the same colours. On f. 5 there is an illuminated capital H (ic), with the King seated with a sword of state in his hand, in gold and blue; ff. 82–8 are not illuminated. These ff. were left blank and filled in later; the hand is different and the capital letters are in blue and red. The whole manuscript may be safely dated as of the last years of the thirteenth century or the opening years of the fourteenth.

VOLUME 10

Somnium Scipionis, a commentary by Ambrosius Theodosius Macrobius on the Somnium Scipionis narrated by Cicero in his De Republica. On flyleaf: Scipionis Afr. Somnium. In pencil: Pagination of last four folios is incorrect. On first parchment flyleaf: Macrobius (in an early hand) followed by same in a later hand. D. viii G. ix primo. $9\frac{7}{8}'' \times 6\frac{5}{8}''$. 67 ff.

f. 4. Publii Africani Scipionis Somnium in Africa. Incipit (all in red). Cum in Africam venissem.

f. 66. Explicit Liber Macrobii (the last three words in red rustic capitals). (edited by L. von Jan (1848–52) and F. Eyssenhardt (1893).)

This is a beautiful manuscript, on good parchment, well written and well illuminated. The first line on f. 4 is in red rustic capitals, and on f. 7 there are three lines in blue rustic capitals and three in red rustic capitals. There are marginal captions in red on most pages, several on some. On f. 4 there is an illuminated C for Cum, in red, green, purple, blue, and yellow, the main motif of which is grotesque heads. It is very pleasantly drawn. The other figure subject is f. 7, a man playing a viola, in the same colours. There are two further coloured capitals, f. 44, the S of Superiore, in red and blue only, and f. 54, a small purple L for Locus, in the middle of the text. In addition to the above illumination there are 27 geometrical drawings, of which three circles have not been filled in with colours, writing, or figures. These are on ff. 12v, 14v (2), 15v, 16v (3), 17, 17v, 21, 29v (2), 33, 33v (not filled in), 34v, 35 (not filled in), 38 (2), 38v (not filled in), 39, 39v, 40, 40v, 43v, 50, 52v, 54v. Some or all of the following colours are used in these figures: red, blue, green, purple, and yellow. Some have human figures in them, others geometrical designs, some writing. ff. 4–43 appear to be in the same hand, but where Liber 2 begins on f. 44, which is also the beginning of a new quire, and has the capital S referred to above, a new scribe appears to begin. There are a few interlineal glosses and a few words have been inserted interlineally. There are also notes in the margin, the hands of all of which are early, not later than the first decades of the thirteenth century. The tailed 'e' is used throughout and a number of the abbreviation marks used suggest a date for the manuscript of perhaps the mid twelfth century.

VOLUME II

A composite volume containing four items: (1) Lydgate's Life of St. Alban, (2) The Brute Chronicle, (3) The Story of Walter Brute, (4) Transcript of Ailred of Rievaulx. On first flyleaf: The Martyr St. Albon, of England being first called Albion, and by Brute Bretayne etc. On original flyleaf: Touching the Life of St. Albon, How England was first called Albion, of London, of Kings and how made etc. $11\frac{5}{8}'' \times 8\frac{3}{8}''$. 247 ff.

1. ff. 1–65v. The Life of St. Alban, by John Lydgate, in English verse.

f. 1. Begins: 'To call Clio my dulnesse to redresse'.

In margin in a seventeenth-century hand: 'The prologue and first book of the glorious martyr Albon'.

f. 2. At end: Explicit Prologus.

f. 2v. First line: 'Tyme Remembered of old Antiquity'.

f. 14. Here endeth the first book.
And here beginneth the Prologue of the Second Book of the conversion and convertynse of the blessed Martyr Seynt Albon.

f. 15. Here endeth the Prologue of the Second Book.
And here beginneth the Second Book of the glorious Martyr Albon. How he was made governor of the famous city of Verolamye.

f. 65v. Here endeth the glorious life and passion of the blessed Martyr Seynt Albon and Seynt Amphiball which glorious lives were translated out of French and Latin by Dan John Lydgate, monk of Bury, at the request and prayer of Master John Whethamstede, the year of our Lord MCCCC and XXXIX and of the said Master John Whethamstede of his abbacy XIX year. (Cf. *Cat. of Materials* (R.S.), I, p. 23.)

This section is a curious alternation of parchment and paper, the following ff. being parchment, 1, 6, 7, 12, 13, 18, 19, 24, 25, 30, 31, 36, 37, 41, 42, 47, 48, 53, 54, 58, 59, 62, 63, the remaining ff. paper. It is illuminated in red and blue, with decorated capitals, and some words underlined in red.

2. ff. 66–169v. The Brute Chronicle of England, to the beginning of the reign of Henry VI, in English.

f. 66. (which is mutilated). Begins: 'Here men may know how England was first called Albion and through whom it had the name of Albion'. 'In the noble land of Surrye there was a noble king and a mighty and a man of great renown'.

f. 67 (at top). Signature: William Bowyer.

f. 80. Richardus Watkyns . . . Per me Richard Watkyns.

f. 93v. In reverse at foot of f. (which is mutilated): Be it known to all men to whom this present writing shall come that I, Gruff. ap John ap Davyth, of Carnarvonshire, of the commote of Tynllayen, of the town of Abereche (   ) hath received of my uncle, Sir Robert Dauyth, curate of Clehidon in Devonshire the sum of £4–16s. of lawful money of England to be paid to him or his sectores (of his signes of the said) Gruff. at the Feast of St. Peter and St. Paul (next coming) or within vi days after and this is my writing of my own hand (and my own schele for it is my Warrant. Written at Cleyhdon the 23 day of May anno sup(radicto per me) Galfridus Johannes juniorem, generosum.

f. 114v. At top of f.: Richard.

f. 116. In reverse at foot of f.: Be it known to all men to whom this present writing shall come that I Gruff. ap John ap Dauyth, of Carnarvonshire, of the commote of Tynllayen, in the town of Abereche, the year of our Lord 1555, hath received of my uncle, Sir Robert Dauyth, curate of Clehidon in Devonshire, the sum of £4–16–0 of lawful money of England, to be paid to him or his sectores or his signes of said Gruff. or his sectores or his signes at the Feast of St. Peter and St. Paul next coming or within vi days after and this is in my writing and my own schele for it is my warrant. Written the 23 day of May anno supradicto per me Galfridus Johannes juniorem, generosum.

f. 118. At end of f.: John Brodforde.

f. 138. At top of f.: John ap Dauyd.

f. 154. At foot of f.: John Brodford of Devonshire.

f. 155. At foot of f.: John Wyller.

Ends f. 169v, which has a good deal of scribbling which does not appear to be of much consequence. It is followed f. 170 with a few notes about Edward Balliol with references to records.

This section is also separately foliated 1 to 110. This section, too, is a curious alternation of parchment and paper, the following ff. being parchment, 70, 73, 74, 79, 80, 86x, 87, 93, 100, 101, 115, 116, 122, 123, 130, 131, 138, 139, 146, 147, 154, 155, 162, 163, the remaining ff. paper. There is some scribbling. There appears to be an addition at the foot of f. 98 beginning: 'The whole history of Cadwaladr is not here written'. $10\frac{1}{2}'' \times 7\frac{3}{4}''$.

3. ff. 172–208. 'The Story of Walter Brute in English'.

Begins: 'The Protestation of Walter Brute, sinner, layman, husbandman and a Christian, exhibited to the Bishop of Hereford for his defence'. I, Walter Brute, . . . (having my offspring of the Britons, both by my father and mother's side) of the Britons have been accused to the Bishop of Hereford that I did err in many matters concerning the Catholic Christian faith, by whom I am required that I should write an answer in Latin'. With references to many Books of the Bible. (Fox's *Acts*, vol. III, pt. I, pp. 131–88.)

This section is an early seventeenth-century transcript written on paper. $11\frac{7}{8}'' \times 7\frac{1}{2}''$.

4. ff. 221–247v. A transcript of Ailred of Rievaulx. Latin.

Begins: 'Illustrissimus huius Rogerus Houenden historiographus splendidissimus hanc de Regibus Angliae historiam contulit'.

f. 222. 'Liber Magistri Willelmi Reed Episcopi Cicestren. quem emit a venerabili patre domino Thoma Trilleck Episcopo Roffensi. Oretis igitur pro utroque continens historiam de quibusdam Regibus Angliae inventam in celeberrima bibliotheca monasterii de Merton'.

This interesting entry must have been written between 1369 and 1372.

f. 247v. Ends: 'de te ad postero transmittimus'. (Twysden, *Script. Decem*, pp. 347–69.)

This section is a sixteenth-century transcript on paper. $11\frac{3}{4}'' \times 8''$.

This manuscript also appears to have reached William Petyt through William and Robert Bowyer.

VOLUME 12

Transcripts of miscellaneous Reports of Cases, Edward III to Elizabeth I. Collected by or for Sir James Altham, Baron of the Exchequer (1607). On flyleaf: 'Reports of Law Cases argued, collected and reported temporibus E. 3, H. 6, Phil. and Mary and Elizabeth Regine'. $11\frac{3}{4}'' \times 7\frac{7}{8}''$. 8 ff. 405 ff.

f. 1. Notes and observations on a case in which husband and wife were seised of lands to them and the heirs of the body of the husband, with remainder to the heirs of the wife, by conveyance of the husband. n.d.

f. 2. Pedigree from Charles, Duke of Suffolk, to his grandchildren by 2 wives. Note that Charles, Duke of Suffolk, was seised of divers manors etc. Whether the fee simple lands shall come to the sisters of the half blood or to the collateral heirs of the whole blood, is the question. Cases cited of 1, 5, and 24 Edward III and 3 Henry VII.

f. 3v. Process in co. Southampton against William Carecter, concealment of £52–4–8. Trin. term, 31 Edward III.

f. 4. Note on a case, East. term, 3 Henry IV, that when a man was indicted before the Commissioners of oyer and terminer, in the time of the insurrection of Owen Glyndwr against Henry IV, the King judged that the town of Shrewsbury was on the frontiers of Wales and sent his letters under the privy seal to the Bailiffs and all the men of that town.

f. 5. A note on Scandalum Magnatum. Lord Beauchamp, Mich. term, 13 Henry VII, with references to Kelway, *Reports* and Dyer, *Reports*, 12 Elizabeth I.

These eight folios seem to have been added as a section to the volume, and its foliation 1 to 8 is in lead pencil. A new foliation begins thereafter in ink. The paper, too, is different.

ff. 1–328. Brief reports and notes of cases, 18, 29 Henry VI, 1 Henry VII, 3–37 Henry VIII, 1–7 Edward VI, 1 Mary, 1 & 2–5 & 6 Philip & Mary, 1–24 Elizabeth I, all the cases generally in Common Pleas, with the following exceptional entries:

ff. 151–158v. The Report of a case depending in the Star Chamber between Lord Cromwell and James Tavener, a copy holder of Lord Cromwell in the manor of North Ellington, co. Norf. Trin, term. 14 Elizabeth I.

ff. 263–264v. The Dean of St. Paul's Case. Hil. term, 18 Elizabeth I.

ff. 269–74. The Report of a case argued in Common Pleas on a quare impedit by John Gylez against the Bishop of Exeter and John Colshill. Trin. term, 18 Elizabeth I.

ff. 318–319v. A decree of the Court of Wards and Liveries from the Book of Decrees of that Court. Trin. term, 23 Elizabeth I.

f. 328–329v. Order by Sir Thomas Bromley, kt., Lord Chancellor, on the cause between Hawle, compt., and Digby, deft. 31 May 24 Elizabeth I (1582).

ff. 330–405. This section contains a collection of cases and notes (as detailed below), which appears to have been added to the main part of the volume, making it a kind of Common Place Book. The range of cases covered by this section is 15–33 Elizabeth I. It would appear that the main portion, ff. 1–328, was written not much later than 24 Elizabeth I and that the two added sections, that is the first 8 ff. and ff. 330–405, were added before 1600. The whole manuscript may therefore be fairly dated as late sixteenth century and was probably a working book of James Altham.

f. 330. A case in Common Pleas, 25 Elizabeth I.

f. 330v. A case in King's Bench, Mich. term, 25 & 26 Elizabeth I.

f. 331. On 24 April 1539, Henry VIII, by letters patent, granted to Sir William Sidney and Dame Agnes, his wife, the manor of Robertsbridge, which letters patent were surrendered and cancelled. Sir Robert Sidney, as son and heir, has prayed for an exemplification. Reasons against the exemplification, beginning: 1. The record is cancelled and not resealed and therefore the constat or exemplification etc.

ff. 331–3. Various miscellaneous brief notes, some with references.

f. 334. Arguments and references in the case of Thomas Keare, junior, plt., Julian Jeffreys, Thomas Clerk and Henry Jeffreys, defts., on ejection from a messuage etc. in Childerditch and Littel Warley, co. Essex.

ff. 336–344v. Serjeant Gawdy, for plts., in case of Anthony Mildmay and Grace, his wife, plts., *v.* Roger Standish, deft., on manors of Lacock and Besoken. 20 August 15 Elizabeth I (1573), with Serjeant Puckering's reply.

ff. 347–55. Various miscellaneous brief notes and cases, some with references.

f. 353. Arguments on grant for life by Elizabeth I of office of Clerk or Baron of Exchequer. The question is (1). Whether grantee may make a deputy by himself and so whether he may make several deputations to several persons, (2). Whether he be within the danger of the Statute of 5 Edward VI, cap. 16.

f. 355v. The case of Dame Agnes Bulkley, widow, for a reasonable part of the goods of Richard Bulkley, her husband, under the Statute of 13 Elizabeth I, cap. 5, on fraudulent gifts. East. term, 16 Elizabeth I.

f. 356. On the conveyance of Prestbury, 2 June 16 Elizabeth I (1574).

f. 357–63. Notes and reports of cases.

f. 365. Case in Star Chamber, 14 February 28 Elizabeth I (1586).

f. 366. Case in Court of Wards and Liveries, 14 May 28 Elizabeth I (1586).

ff. 367–9. Monstrans de droit by the Wardens and Commonalty of the Saddlers of London in the Chancery. n.d.

f. 370x (slip inset). 'Upon a thorough examination of the Book the name of the Reporter nowhere appears, but upon examining 371b with leaf 134 it is to be conjectured that these cases are of the late James Altham who afterwards died a Baron of the Exchequer. E. Ll.'

f. 371. Case in trespass in King's Bench between John Grendon, plt., and Thomas Albarne, deft., Hil. Term, 28 Elizabeth I.

f. 371v. 'Mon argument pur le Plaintif'.

f. 373. 'After my argument Edward Coke that argued on the other side prayed to amend the pleading of the Indenture'.

ff. 377–86. Miscellaneous notes and cases.

f. 388. 'May it please your good lordship that the cases in law between the Rt. Hon. the Earl of Huntingdon and the Lord Mountjoy of the other agreed upon before us by the counsel of both sides we think as hereafter is mentioned'. Signed, 6 names.

ff. 389–97. Miscellaneous notes and cases.

ff. 397–404. Case depending in Court of Wards, on Sir Thomas Cheyney, kt., argued at Serjeants Inn, Trin. term, 33 Elizabeth I.

ff. 404v–405. A brief scrappy index.

VOLUME 13

A miscellaneous collection of law reports and notes, with some legal tracts, as detailed below. On flyleaf: 'A Manuscript Book of Law, being a Collection of Law Cases etc.' There is much confusion in the foliation in certain sections, $11\frac{5}{8}'' \times 7\frac{5}{8}''$. 379 ff.

ff. 1–33. Notes on legal matters. The first f. or ff. are missing and many of the remaining. ff. seriously mutilated. On some ff. the notes have been cancelled by scoring through ff. 19x–29v contain the notes of the Reading of Thomas Nicholls, of the Middle Temple, on the Statute of 11 Henry VII, cap. 20. Thomas Nicholls was Reader in 1566.

ff. 34–47. 'Here follow certain cases which are probably thought to be of Lord Dyer's Collection in his circuits but they were gathered by some Judge it doth appear'. The cases are of the time of Philip and Mary and Elizabeth I.

ff. 49–70. 'Here follow certain cases of Lord Dyer's Collection which for some private reason he thought not fit to make them vulgar'. This section has county captions and names of cases, with some references to the rolls. This section has some special material relating to Dyer, as follows:

f. 66v. 'A supplication exhibited to the Lords of the Council, at Hampton Court, 28 November 1579, against Justice Dier by 8 or 9 of the Justices of the Peace of co. Warwick'.

f. 67. 'A particular declaration of certain speeches uttered by the Lord Dier openly, at the Assizes holden at Warwick, 30 July 16 Elizabeth (1574), wherein the Justices of the Peace of that County were touched both in credit and honesty'.

f. 68. 'The true state of the title by Dier'.

f. 68v. 'The answer of the said Justice Dier to the articles contained in the aforesaid supplication'.

f. 71. Cases collected and reported in the time of Elizabeth I, arranged alphabetically. A and B only.

f. 73. 'Out of the Star Chamber'.

f. 74. 'Certain observations upon the Court of Star Chamber'.

ff. 75–93. Notes arranged alphabetically from Condition to Waste.

ff. 94–102. Similar notes, but not arranged alphabetically, Reversion to Extinguishment.

ff. 102–113v. Miscellaneous notes including notes on the charges for a fine etc.

ff. 114–151v. Cases in Star Chamber, the latest dated 44 Elizabeth I.

ff. 152–159v. 'A method or ready way to the better understanding of the Statute laws of England'.

ff. 160–78. 'The second volume containing matter for the better understanding of the Statute laws of England'.

ff. 179–220v. 'The nature of a justicies, the general and special parts of it, the difference and other accident of it and precedents and declarations and pleadings and other legal notes on pleading'.

ff. 221–231v. The Customs of the city of London. (French.)

ff. 232–260v. Transcripts of parts of the Statutes of Merton, Marlborough, Gloucester, and Westminster II (some caps. of some Statutes omitted).

ff. 261–73. 'A Treatise of the Masters of the Chancery'. (Ptd. in Hargrave's *Tracts*, pp. 291–319.)

f. 274. 'Notes out of a Book in Chancery about proceedings there'.

ff. 279–379v. Notes, alphabetically arranged, Abatement to Quo Warranto. Some of Dyer's material in this volume is printed in *Report of Cases in the reigns of Hen. VIII, Edw. VI, Q. Mary and Q. Elizabeth taken and collected by Sir James Dyer, kt., sometime Chief Justice of the Common Pleas*, first translated . . . , John Vaillant (3 parts, 1794). 'To this edition . . . from an original manuscript in the Library of the Inner Temple several new cases of his are introduced in the notes'.

VOLUME 14

A printed Abridgment of the Statutes, with manuscript Year Books, 3, 14, 19 Henry VI, 4 Henry IV, 38, 40, 41, 42 Edward III. On flyleaf: A common law Common Place Book of very ancient print; several pleadings and writs in the Reigns of Edward III and Henry VI, in court-hand. The volume consists of two distinct sections, as detailed below. $11\frac{1}{2}'' \times 8\frac{3}{4}''$.

224 ff.

1. ff. 1–108. A printed text by Lettou and W. de Machlinia, circa 1481.

f. 1. Incipit Tabula hoc libri. Alphabetically arranged from Abjuration to Utlagarie.

ff. 5–108v. Abjuration to Outlawry. There is no colophon or title-page. Hand-decorated in red with lines and paragraph marks for all titles of text. The first word in section on Abjuration has a crudely illuminated Q (for Que), red and blue. The last Statute referred to is 33 Henry VI, c. 13 (f. 54v).

2. ff. 109–41. Year Book, Mich. to Trin. terms 3 Henry VI.

f. 109. At top of f.: de termino Michaelis anno tercio H. VIti.

At foot of page: Lyber Francysci Stradlynge.

This section has a separate original foliation for each term. It has two classes of notes in the margin: (1) written contemporaneously, of nature of case, e.g. repleg., quare impedit, scire fac., cessavit; (2) subsequent notes on the cases, with references to other earlier and later cases.

f. 112v. 19 Henry VI, Mich. term.

f. 113v. 34 Henry VI, Hil. term, East. term, 44, East. term, 43 Edward III.

f. 130. Mich. term, 4 Henry IV.

There are red paragraph marks on ff. 129–133.

ff. 142–72. Year Book, Hil. to Mich. terms, 38 Edward III.

f. 142. At top of f.: De termino Hil, anno regni Regis Edwardi tercii 38o.

At foot of f.: Lyber Francisi Stradlyng.

This section has two classes of marginal notes: (1) contemporary description of cases; (2) a few unimportant later notes.

ff. 173–94. Year Book, Hil. to Mich. terms, 40 Edward III.

This section has two classes of marginal notes as above, but 2 has a great number.

ff. 195–209. Year Book, Hil. to Mich. terms, 41 Edward III.

This section has marginal notes similar to ff. 142–72 above.

ff. 210–224v. Year Book, Hil. to Mich. terms, 42 Edward III.

This section has marginal notes, but they are few in number.

VOLUME 15

Nova Statuta, 1 Edward III to 22 Edward IV, printed by W. Machlinia, c. 1484, and Statuta, 1 Richard III, also printed by W. Machlinia, 1485, with manuscript notes, full bound in brown morocco, with Petyt coat of arms on both covers. Inset label: An Old Statute Book of very Ancient Print with large Table to it. It begins 1 E. 3 and ends 1 R. 3. On flyleaf; the same in hand of late seventeenth or early eighteenth century. Added in pencil: The Statutes Ric. 3 are not included in the table and are by a different printer from the rest of the book. J.E.T., $10'' \times 7\frac{7}{8}''$.

1. f. A i. At top: Petyt motto and signature Wi. Petyt.

The Nova Statuta, 1 Edward III–22 Edward IV, printed by W. Machlinia, *c.* 1484. (Beale, *Bibliography of Early English Law Books* dates this volume *c.* 1485.)

f. A. iiiiiv. July the 20th. 97. Memorandum that this Book is my Master's Wm. Petyt Esqr. and never was an Office Book, witness my hand Geo. Holmes. In the Table of Contents, f. A. iiiv quarto is struck out and quarto decimo substituted in a contemporary hand.

f. a. iiiv. In the margin opposite the Statute of Northampton: Inter Communia de termino Pasche 2 E. e penes Rememorator. Domini Thes. in Sccario remanen. Transcriptum Statutor. apud Northt. editor. in Parliamento ibidem convocato ad tres septimanas Pasche Anno Regni Regis E. tertio post conquestum. Anno sedo. (Inserted by William Petyt.) The printed text of the Statute is corrected and cap. numbers inserted in the margin.

f. c. vi. In margin (in same hand): Ex Libro Statut. MS. penes Johannem Peachy de Inter. Templo Ar. (with corrections in printed text).

f. d. viii. In margin: noblez MS. penes J. Peachy substituted for Counts Barons et autres of printed text.

f. f. iii. At top of margin: De Enervantibus Iudicalia Regis MS. Peachy (at beginning of Statute of Provisors).

f. nn. i. Running caption anno duodecimo anno duodecimo altered to septimo.

Each Statute in the printed text starts with a red capital put in by hand. The Statutes for each reign, Edward III to Edward IV, begin with a capital in red and black put in by hand. There are marginal captions on many of the folios, inserted in a variety of hands.

2. Statuta apud Westmonasterium edita Anno primo Regis Ricardi tercii.

This section is also printed by W. Machlinia but is printed in a different font from section 1 above and contains caps. 1–xv. 1485. Space has been left for the insertion of (R)icardi.

At the top of the last folio: By comparing this Act with the type used by Wm. Machlinia I find it the same. D. Ames, 20 Feby. 1747. See Speculum Christian.

This section, with a blank folio at the beginning of 16 folios, is of different paper as well as font from section 1 above. It has contemporary MS. captions in the margin. (This copy had not been seen by Beale, ibid., who says the book probably had a blank at the beginning.)

VOLUME 16

A collection of treatises, notes, and arguments relating to ecclesiastical jurisdiction and the dispute with George Abbott, Archbishop of Canterbury, on prohibitions and modus decimandi, in the reign of James I. The volume may be conveniently divided into the 26 items following. On flyleaf: 'Jurisdiction of the clergy'. $8\frac{5}{8}'' \times 6\frac{5}{8}''$. 232 ff.

ff. 1–2. Table of Contents.

f. 4. Title Page: 'A collection showing what Jurisdiction the Clergy hath heretofore lawfully used in the Realm of England, as also the exaction of oaths by Ordinaries and Ecclesiastical Judges, with the Arguments between the Lord Archbishop of Canterbury, the chief of the High Commissioners, and all the Judges of England concerning prohibitions and modus decimandi, in the time of our late Sovereign Lord King James'.

1. f. 4v. 'A collection showing what Jurisdiction the Clergy hath heretofore lawfully used in the Realm of England, wherein is manifestly proved that the Prelates or Ecclesiastical Judges never had any authority to compel the subject of the land to an oath, unless it were in causes testamentary or matrimonial, or thereunto appertaining, with a confutation of such frivilous, unlearned surmises as have been made for the maintenance of the Clergy's unlawful proceedings, whereby they have sundry ways incurred the penalties of provision and premuniri'.

2. ff. 26v–51v. 'A Brief Treatise of oaths exacted by Ordinary and Ecclesiastical Judges to answer generally all such Articles or Interrogatories as pleaseth them to propound of their forced and constrained oaths ex officio, wherein is found the same are unlawful'.

3. ff. 51v–55. 'Of oaths in Ecclesiastical Courts'.

4. ff. 55–7. 'The question is whether the Ecclesiastical Judges may hold plea and minister an oath in any cause other than in causes testamentary or matrimonial or no'.

5. ff. 57v–63. 'A Preface to the Answer of the Judges of the Court of Common Pleas unto the objections and arguments made on the behalf of the Lord Archbishop of Canterbury against the Prohibitions'. The long Preface, 6 & 7 July 1609, at Whitehall.

6. ff. 63–5. 'The grounds of the Prohibitions to the High Commission and the answers unto them'.

7. f. 66. 'A Declaration of the True Grounds of the Prohibitions to the High Commission and the authorities and reasons approving the same'.

8. f. 73v. 'Propositions grounded upon this proposition that the interpretation of all Statutes belong to the Judges of the Temporal Courts'.

9. f. 75. 'The Second Question propounded on the behalf of the Lord Archbishop of Canterbury touching the exposition of Statutes concerning Ecclesiastical Causes, whether the same belong to the Judges of the Realm or to the interpretation of the Civilians and Canonists. A question never made in any of our books nor moved by anyone in time before'.

10. f. 81. 'The third Question that hath been made on the behalf of the Lord Archbishop of Canterbury is whether if tithes in kind be not divided and set forth an action may be brought in any of the King's Courts at Westminster by the party aggrieved for treble damages grounded upon the Statute of 2 E. 6, cap. 13'.

11. f. 85. 'A Breviate of the chief proofs touching the recovery of treble value in the Spiritual Courts'.

12. f. 87. 'A Breviate of the chief proofs selected touching the modus decimandi'.

13. f. 91v. 'An answer to the chief proofs selected touching the modus decimandi'.

14. f. 98. 'Authorities in law approving the point in question and the reason first set down'.

15. f. 102. 'Concerning the three Acts of Parliament of 27 H. 8, 32 H. 8, and 2 E. 6; we have set down the causes of making of them, their coherence and the true interpretation of them concerning the matter in question'.

16. f. 115. 'A Conference by the King's special appointment held before the Lords of the Council, touching prohibitions, on 23 May 1611, where were present both the chief of the High Commission and all the Judges of the Realm, the Lords of the Council, Ellesmere, Chancellor, Northampton, Zouch, Stanhope, Parry, Salisbury, Worcester, Wotton, Caesar, Ecclesiastics, Archbishop of Canterbury, Bishop of Ely, Bishop of Bath and Wells, Dean of Westminster, Doctor Bennett, Doctor Martyn, Doctor Byrd, Judges, Sir Thomas Fleming, Lord Chief Justice of England, Sir Edward Coke, Lord Chief Justice of the Common Pleas, Sir Laurence Tanfield, Lord Chief Baron, Sir Thomas Walmesley, Sir Peter Warburton, Sir David Williams, Sir James Altham, Sir John Crook, Sir John Foster and Baron Brownlow'.

17. ff. 118v–133v. 'A Breviate of the selected proofs of prohibitions out of the Common Pleas, no record being before them'. (The Table of contents, ff. 1–2, ends here.)

18. f. 135. Miscellaneous historical notes on tithe (from 14 John).

19. f. 137. Ordinance on vicars of St. Mary's, Wells, 1322.

20. f. 141. Petition of the Clergy in Parliament, 1 Richard II.

21. ff. 142–153v. Notes (from 12 Edward I) against the usurpations and provisions of Popes and Bishops.

22. f. 160. Prohibitions of the Pope and Bishops (from 4 Henry III).

23. f. 164. Prohibitions of Archbishops, Bishops and Kings (from 29 Henry III).

24. f. 173. Wills, Administrations, etc.

25. f. 191. On the cause of the translation of the episcopal see of Somerset from Congresbury to Wells.

From here the volume is reversed.

26 ff. 232–220v. Extracts from Journals of the House of Commons, 8 February 1575/6.

f. 231v. The third Session of the Fourth Parliament of Elizabeth I, held at Westminster, after sundry prorogations, upon Monday, 16 January 1581 (to 23 January 1581.)

f. 226. Wednesday afternoon, Saturday, 18 March.

f. 216v. Whether the Sabbath be moral or no or else whether Christians now in the times of the Gospel are bound in conscience by the word of God to observe any particular day or days which they cannot alter as more Holy or to be kept more Holy than others. Negat.

VOLUME 17

A collection of historical notes and records concerning Scotland, from the time of Edward I to 1594. On flyleaf: Collections of several records and other matters in history concerning Scotland and the subordination thereof to England. The whole manuscript has been damaged by damp and many of the ff. are badly mutilated. It has been repaired. The volume probably belonged to Robert Bowyer and Henry Elsyng, both of whom were accustomed to pass on information to Lord Buckhurst. $8\frac{1}{4}'' \times 6\frac{3}{8}''$. 152 ff.

f. 1. 'Commissions taken out of an ancient written book of the time of Edward IV, found in the Study of Mr. Rigby, Master of Requests, and lent to me by Serjeant Harris, and by me to my Lord Buckhurst'.

Commission to George, Archbishop of York, Chancellor of England, Richard, Earl of Warwick and Salisbury, John, Earl of Northumberland, Thomas, Abbot of St. Mary's, York, John Scrope, kt., of Bolton, and Robert de Ogle, kt., Master Richard Andrew, Dean of the Cathedral Church of York, Master John Shirwood, Archdeacon of Richmond, James Strangeways, kt., and Roger Thornton, esq., appointing them commissioners to treat with the Scots at Newcastle upon Tyne, 4 December (1464), Westminster, 20 November 1464. (*Rot. Scot.*, II, p. 418.)

f. 1v. Inspeximus and confirmation, 1 June 5 (Edward IV) (1465), of arrangements made by the above, at Newcastle upon Tyne, 12 December 1464. (Ibid., pp. 419–20.)

f. 2. Commission to Richard, Earl of Warwick and Salisbury, Keeper of West March against Scotland, and John, Earl of Northumberland, Keeper of East March, and Ralph Greystoke, of Greystoke, kt., Henry Fitzhugh, of Fitzhugh, kt., John Scrope of Bolton, kt., Thomas Lumley of Lumley, kt., Robert Ogle of Ogle, kt., Henry Nevill, kt., James Strangeways, kt., Robert Constable, kt., John Conyers, kt., Robert Claxton, kt., and Robert Thornton appointing them commissioners, 10 October (1466). (Ibid., p. 420.)

f. 8. Commission to Laurence, Bishop of Durham, Henry, Earl of Northumberland, Thomas, Abbot of St. Mary's, York, Richard, Prior of Durham, Ralph Greystoke of Greystoke, kt., William Parr, kt., Masters John Lilford, Doctor of Laws, and Richard Langford, clerk,

King's Councillors, appointing them commissioners at a place to be chosen, 6 August next, 18 July (1470). (*Rot. Scot.*, II., pp. 422–3.)

f. 9. Commission to Master John Alcock, Keeper of the Rolls of Chancery, Doctor of Laws, Master William Hatteclyff, Secretary and Master of Requests, and William Parr, kt., appointing them ambassadors and commissioners to treat with James, King of Scotland. 26 August 11 (Edward IV) (1471). (Ibid., p. 429.)

f. 11. Commission to William, Bishop of Ely, Laurence, Bishop of Durham, Edward, Bishop of Carlisle, John, Earl of Wiltshire, Richard, Prior of Durham, Ralph Greystoke of Greystoke, kt., Humfrey Dacre of Dacre, kt., Master John Alcock, Keeper of the Rolls of Chancery, Doctor of Laws, Master William Hatteclyff, Secretary, Richard Martin, Doctor of Laws, and James Strangeways, kt., appointing them commissioners. 26 August (1471). (Ibid., p. 430.)

f. 15. Commission to William, Bishop of Ely, Laurence, Bishop of Durham, Edward, Bishop of Carlisle, Henry, Earl of Northumberland, John, Earl of Shrewsbury, John, Earl of Wiltshire, Richard, Prior of Durham, Ralph Greystoke, of Greystoke, kt., Humfrey Dacre of Dacre, kt., Master Henry Sharp, Archdeacon of Bedford, William Parr, King's Councillor, and James Strangeways, kts., appointing them commissioners. 26 August (1471). (Ibid.)

f. 26. The Pope sent an injunction to Edward I, with references to Walsingham, Camden, *Remains*, Crompton, *Jurisdict.*, and Fitzherbert, Statute 34 Edward III, cap. 12, and petition F. 2.

ff. 29–32. Chapters of treaty of friendship between Elizabeth I and James VI, 5 July 1586. (Latin.)

f. 35v. Cause between Mary, Queen of Scots, and her subjects, 8 October 10 Elizabeth I (1568), with reference to Camden, *Elizabeth*.

ff. 35–51. A Journal of Scottish accidents, 1581–1594.

f. 53. Writs of summons to Scottish war, 16 December 1295. List. (*C.C.R.*, 1288–96, pp. 501–2.)

f. 60. In the Tower among the records is a roll entitled (the Scrope Roll).

f. 61. Miscellaneous extracts and notes from Hoveden, French Roll, 21 Richard II, Scottish Roll, 34 Henry VI (*Rot. Scot.*, II, pp. 375–6), Act, 2 & 3 Edward VI (Scotland part of England), Knighton, Camden, *Remains*, Patent Roll, 4 Edward IV (*C.P.R.*, 1461–7, p. 391) (at f. 64v there is a reference to a Patent of Edward II. It is, in fact, a reference to a grant by Edward I, as superior lord of the kingdom of Scotland, granting Gilbert de Clare, Earl of Gloucester and Hertford, of the marriage of Duncan, son and heir of Duncan, formerly Earl of Fife, tested at Berwick on Tweed, 25 June 20 Edward I (1292). The entry has the following memorandum: the deed above mentioned hath a seal pendant, cut like the seal of an obligation, in the one side is the image of Christ, standing upright, his legs and arms in salter. On the reverse is the arms of Scotland. On each side the edge of the seal is broken so as the writing cannot be read. The deed or patent aforesaid I borrowed of Sir Robert Cotton, to whom also I restored it. This patent was made by Edward II), Holingshed, Register of Writs, Stow, Fitzherbert, Fortescue, Froissart, Fox, *Acts*, Littleton, Walsingham, Patent Roll, 22 Richard II (*C.P.R.*, 1396–9, pp. 39, 267), Patent Roll, 28–9 Elizabeth I.

f. 78v. There is a printed book entitled: A Treatise concerning the defence of the honour of the right, high, mighty and noble Prince, Mary, Queen of Scotland and Dowager of

France, with a declaration as well of her right, title and interest to the succession of the crown of England, as that the regiment of women is conformable to the law of God and nature, made by Morgan Phillips, Bachelor of Divinity, An. 1570. Leodis, Apud Gualterum Moberini, 1571.

There is a printed book entitled: Ane detectioun of the duinge of Marie, Quen of Scottes, touchand the murder of hir hisband and hir conspaci, adultrie and pretended mariage with the Earle of Bothwell And ane defence of the trew lordis mainteineris of the kingis graces actioun and authoritie. Translated out of the Latine quileke was wrytten by G.B.

Historia Belgica A. E. Materan belgam folio 411 doth set down exactly Vitam et mortem Marie Scottorum Regine.

f. 80. There is a book of this title: A treatise touching the right, title and interest of the most excellent princess Mary, Queen of Scotland, and of the most noble King James, her grace's son, to the succession of the crown of England . . . compiled and published before in Latin and after in English by the reverend father in God, John Lesley, Bishop of Ross. An. 1584.

f. 83. Ra. Brooke, York Herald, in his carping pamphlet entitled: A discovery or error prejudicing noble descents.

References to Hoveden and Camden, *Brit.*

f. 91v. Writ of privy seal, 20 October 1601, to Treasurer and Chamberlains of the Exchequer, to pay £2,000 to messenger of James VI.

Mr. Skynner: Make an order for payment hereof, 29 October 1601. T. Buckhurst.

f. 97. Of the Parliament, Easter, 21 Edward I.

f. 110. Letters Patent sealed with the seal deputed for kingdom of Scotland, Berwick on Tweed, 25 June 20 Edward I (1292). Description of seal 'showed unto me and lent me by Robert Cotton', 19 January 1606/7.

f. 112v. Commission to William, Marquis of Winchester, Sir Richard Sakevill, Under Treasurer, Sir Walter Mildmay, Chancellor of Exchequer, reciting Act, 2 & 3 Philip & Mary, for castles cos. Northumberland, Cumberland, Westmorland and bishopric of Durham, from Patent Roll, 4 Elizabeth I, 8 July 1562 (*C.P.R.*, 1560–3, pp. 274–6).

This section appears to end at f. 139. It contains hundreds of references to records, especially to Patent, Close, and Scottish Rolls, and is followed at f. 141 (which is a dilapidated folio) with a treatise concerning Scotland, 1617, which begins: (1) Laws, making and abrogating, and ends f. 152: the King and Commonalty is ever moving and fleeting, like a boat on the sea, tossed to and fro, vento nobilitatis vulgi fluctibus.

VOLUME 18

Cartulary of Cathedral Church of Salisbury. On flyleaf: Registrum Cartarum Ecclesie Sarum. $8\frac{1}{8}'' \times 5\frac{5}{8}''$. 126 ff.

f. 1. At top of folio the signature: Wi. Petyt.

Charter of St. Osmund, Bishop of Salisbury, 'who gave many things to that church'. Signa. n.d. (1091). (*Reg. S. Osm.* (R.S.), 1, pp. 198–200.)

Scriptum est autem hoc carta et confirmata Anno incarnacionis domini MXCI indiccione xiiii Willelmo Rege Monarchiam tociius Anglie strenue gubernante Anno iiii Regni eiusdem apud Hastynges.

f. 2. Protestation of Stephen, King of England, on the dignities and privileges of the church of Salisbury, Witnesses. At Oxford, 1136, 1 Stephen. (*Reg. S. Osm.* I, pp. 209–10.)

f. 2v. Charter given to the church of Salisbury, by Stephen, King of England, quitclaiming all secular customs, granting and confirming all churches which Roger, Bishop of Salisbury, had acquired, and giving protection. Witnesses. Christmas Day (1139). (*Charters and Documents of Salisbury* (R.S.), p. 10, n. 1).

f. 3. Charter given to church of Salisbury, by same, of perpetual acquittance of all lands belonging to the church of Salisbury and all other secular customs and all churches which Roger, its Bishop, had purchased, and especially of the church of All Cannings, and granting and confirming the same. Christmas Day (1139). (Ibid., pp. 10–11.)

f. 3v. Charter given to Roger, Bishop of Salisbury, by same, granting land in Lavington, and other liberties and free customs. Witnesses. Cirencester. n.d. (1136). (Ibid., p. 8.)

Charter given to Roger, Bishop of Salisbury, by same, granting the borough of Malmesbury and adjoining lands. Witnesses. Oxford. n.d. (1136). (Ibid., pp. 7–8.)

Charter of Stephen, King of England, notifying the grant to the church of Salisbury of the churches of Hurstborne (Tarrant) and Burley. Witnesses. At Salisbury. n.d. (1139+). (Ibid., p. 9.)

f. 4. Charter of same granting the liberties and free customs of the church of Salisbury in markets and fairs throughout England. Witnesses. Clarendon. n.d. (1139). (Ibid., pp. 9–10.)

Charter of Henry I to Roger, Bishop of Salisbury, confirming the acquisition by Roger of churches and of the tithes of the forest of Salisbury and of timber to maintain the church of Salisbury and of certain lands and liberties. Witnesses. n.d. (1115). (Cf. *Reg. S. Osm.* I, pp. 200–2.)

f. 4v. Charter of same granting the church of Salisbury the churches of Heytesbury and Godalming. Witnesses. Marlborough. n.d. (1106, May ?). (Cf. *Regesta, Henry I*, p. 53. no. 751.)

f. 5. Charter of same granting the church of Salisbury certain churches. Witnesses. Winchester. n.d. (1110–1122). (*Reg. S. Osm.* I, p. 208.)

Charter of same to church of Salisbury of the church of Hurstborne (Tarrant). Witnesses. Cricklade. n.d. (1107, June ?). (*Reg. Hen. I.*, p. 67, no. 824).

f. 5v. Charter of same granting the church of Salisbury all the tithes of the New Forest and of Wiltshire, Dorset, and Berkshire etc. Northampton. Witnesses. n.d. (1107, 16 April). (Ibid., p, 138, no. 1162.)

Charter of the same granting the church of Salisbury liberties and especially from tolls and other duties in markets throughout England. Clarendon. n.d. (1121, April ?). (Ibid., p. 160, no. 1273.)

Charter of same granting the church of Salisbury certain lands, tolls, and other free customs. Witnesses. Westminster. n.d. (1121). (*Chart. & Docs.*, p. 4.)

f. 6. Charter of same granting the church of Salisbury the chapel of Woodcote. Witnesses. Odiham. n.d. (1117).

Charter of Henry II granting the church of Salisbury the churches of Heytesbury and

Godalming, with their lands and tithes, and other lands. Witnesses. Gloucester. n.d. (1156). (*Reg. S. Osm.* I, pp. 238–9.)

f. 6v. Charter of Henry, son of the Duke of Normandy and Count of Anjou, granting the church of Salisbury and Jocelin, Bishop of Salisbury, the manor of All Cannings, with its hundred, as in the time of Roger, Bishop of Salisbury, with certain specific exceptions. Witnesses. 1149, Ides of April (13 April). (*Chart. & Docs.*, pp. 15–16.)

Charter of Henry II granting the church of Salisbury the churches of Heytesbury and Godalming, tithes and lands, and the churches of the New Forest etc., and fairs and other lands, liberties and free customs. Witnesses. Salisbury. n.d. (1158). (*Reg. S. Osm.* I, pp. 203–6.)

f. 7v. Agreement between Henry, Duke of Normandy, and Jocelin, Bishop of Salisbury, on the conditional restitution of the castle of Denys and of the park. Witnesses. At the Ford of Stockbridge. 1152, 5 Ides April (9 April). (*Chart. & Docs.*, pp. 22–3.)

f. 8. Charter of Henry II granting the liberties and free customs of the church of Salisbury throughout England. Witnesses. Salisbury. n.d. (1158). (*Reg. S. Osm.* I, pp. 203–6.)

f. 8v. Charter of same granting the ancient customs and liberties to the churches of Heytesbury and Godalming. Witnesses. Winchester. n.d. (1156). (Ibid., pp. 238–9.)

Charter of same granting liberties and free customs to the burgesses of the church of Salisbury dwelling in Guildford. Witnesses. Winchester. n.d. (1156). (Ibid., p. 238.)

Charter of same on the grant and gift of the manor of Chardstock made to Gilbert de Percy, as reasonably pleaded in the court of the Bishop of Salisbury. Witnesses. Westminster. n.d. (1155). (*Chart. & Docs.*, pp. 25–6.)

f. 9. Charter of same granting liberty to Jocelin, Bishop of Salisbury, that no tenant of his answer any royal bailiff, except coram Rege. Witness. Malmesbury. n.d. (1155). (Ibid., pp. 24–5.)

Charter of Richard I to the church of Salisbury and Hubert, Bishop of Salisbury, granting them power to enclose their wood at Lodden and make a park therein. Witnesses. Les Andelys. 1 October 10 Richard I (1198). (Ibid., p. 47.)

f. 9v. Charter of King John on the custody and protection of the lands, men, things, rents and possessions of the men of the Bishop and church of Salisbury. Caen. 3 June 1200. (*Rot. Chart.*, p. 66.)

Charter of same on the maintenance, protection and defence of all belonging to the church of Salisbury. Molinell. 31 March (1203).

f. 10. Charter of same on restitution of the lands and rents of the church of Salisbury. 18 July 15 John (1213). (*Rot. Litt. Pat.*, p. 101.)

Charter of same confirming the gifts and grants of Henry I and Henry II to church of Salisbury. Witnesses. Falaise. 4 June 2 John (1200). (*Rot. Chart.*, p. 67.)

f. 10v. Charter of Henry III inspecting the charter to the church of Salisbury confirming the gifts and grants of Henry I, Henry II and Stephen. Witnesses. Westminster. 22 March II Henry III (1227). (*C. Ch. R.* I, p. 24.)

f. 11. Charter of same to church of Salisbury granting the amercements of the men, lands and fees of the Bishop, Dean and Canons. Witnesses. 23 March 11 Henry III (1227). (Ibid., pp. 24–5.)

f. 12. Charter of same to church of Salisbury on the grant and ratification of the translation of the church of Salisbury and confirmation of all liberties granted by his predecessors and granting liberties to the citizens of New Salisbury as the citizens of Winchester had in their lands. Witnesses. Westminster. 30 January 11 Henry III (1227). (*C. Ch. R.* I, p. 1.)

f. 13. Charter of same granting amercements (as f. 11). Witnesses. Marlborough. 18 February 20 Henry III (1236). (Ibid., p. 218.)

f. 14. Charter of same confirming the tithes received from the forests of Pancet and Buckholt etc. and of the other forests of Wiltshire, Dorset, Berkshire and elsewhere. Clarendon. 21 December 23 Henry III (1238). (*Chart. & Docs.*, pp. 249–50.)

Charter of same to Bishop of Salisbury granting a yearly fair for three days at Ramsbury. Witnesses. Westminster. 1 August 24 Henry III (1240). (*C. Ch. R.* I, p. 252.)

f. 14v. Charter of same granting Bishop of Salisbury a yearly fair for four days at Southbury without the town of Denis. Witnesses. Westminster. 16 July 11 Henry III (1227). (Ibid., p. 51.)

f. 15. Charter of same on the church of Hurstborne (Tarrant) on an agreement between the King and the Bishop and Chapter of Salisbury and on the admission of a King's clerk. Witnesses. Worcester. 21 May 16 Henry III (1232). (Ibid., p. 155.)

f. 15v. Charter of same to Bishops of Salisbury granting them free disposition of their Wills before death and of their things moveable and immoveable. Witnesses. Westminster. 27 March 18 Henry III (1234). (*Chart. & Docs.*, pp. 231–2.)

f. 16. Letters Patent of same granting that the grant of a twentieth part of the benefices of the clergy of England should not be drawn into a custom. 20 October 10 Henry III (1226). (*C.P.R., 1225–1232*, p. 64.)

f. 16v. Charter of Jocelin, Bishop of Salisbury, restoring the church of Chardstock to Gilbert de Percy. Witnesses. n.d. (1155). (*Chart. & Docs.*, pp. 18–19.)

f. 17. Charter of same on the judgement on the church of Chardstock. n.d. (1160). (Ibid., pp. 19–20.)

f. 17v. Charter of same on the exchange of land at Potterne. n.d. (1173). (Ibid., pp. 37–8.)
Charter of same to William de Erleg of land in the manor of Sonning in exchange for land he claimed in the park of Sonning. Witnesses. n.d. (1160). (*Reg. S. Osm.* I, pp. 248–9.)

f. 18. Charter of Henry II on the quitclaim of the castle of Devizes made by the Bishop of Salisbury and of 30 librates of land which the King gave in exchange for the castle. Witnesses. Morrow of St. Luke the Evangelist (19 October) 1157. (*Chart. & Docs.*, pp. 29–30.)

Charter of the Abbot and Convent of Sherborne to Jocelin, Bishop of Salisbury, on quittance made of the church of Sherborne of the castle of Sherborne and the island. Witnesses. n.d. (1160). (*Reg. S. Osm.* I, pp. 235–6.)

Charter of Hubert, Bishop of Salisbury, on the acknowledgment of certain lands as free assart and not of the Bishop's Lordship and ratification of the gift of the same. n.d. (1190–3).

f. 19. Charter of confirmation by John to Hubert, Bishop of Salisbury, and confirmation of all gifts of Henry I, Henry II and Stephen made to the church of Salisbury and especially of the church of Melksham. Witnesses. n.d. (4 June 1200). (*Rot. Litt. Cart*, p. 67.)

Charter on the confirmation of the patronage of the church of Winsford and Manningford by

R(ichard), Bishop of Salisbury. Chardstock. 2 Ides November 2 Pont. (12 November 1218). (*Chart. & Docs.*, p. 84.)

f. 19v. Charter of Richard, Bishop of Durham, on the grant of Hugh de Sanford, kt., of half of all the profits of Chilton made to the Bishop of Salisbury, giving the text of the charter of Hugh de Sanford. Given at Charent. 14 Kal. May (18 April) 1233. (Ibid., pp. 228–9.)

f. 20. Charter of Richard, Bishop of Salisbury, on the Bishop's prebend as a canon to be admitted to the secrets of the Chapter and of what that prebend is constituted. n.d. (1219). (Ibid., p. 95.)

f. 20v. Charter of William, Dean, and the Chapter of Salisbury, confirming the gift of Richard, Bishop of Salisbury, of certain land in Lavington, to William Paas, the Bishop's servant. n.d. (1228). (*Reg. S. Osm.* I, p. 321.)

Agreement between Master Elias de Derham, Canon of Salisbury, and John de Ymmere on the tithes of a tenement in Imber. Salisbury. Morrow of Assumption (16 August) 1228. (*Chart. & Docs.*, pp. 246–8.)

f. 21v. Agreement between Master Elias de Derham, Canon of Salisbury, and the Prior and Convent of two parts of certain tithes in his parish of Lavington. Salisbury. Morrow of St. Laurence (11 August) 1239. (Ibid., pp. 250–1.)

f. 22. Agreement between Richard, Bishop of Salisbury, and Hugh de Sanford, on the advowsons of the churches of Blewbury and Marlborough. 17 Kal. May (15 April) 1223. (Ibid., pp. 123–4.)

f. 22v. Charter of direction of a charter confirmed by the Pope on certain lands in the soke of Potterne, by R(oger), Bishop of Worcester, and G(eoffrey), Dean of Hereford. Bath. 17 Kal. September (16 August) 1173. (Ibid., p. 37.)

f. 23. Agreement between Jocelin, Bishop of Salisbury, and William, son of Alexander, on certain land in the soke of Potterne. Bath. 17 Kal. November (16 October) 1173. (Ibid., pp. 37–8.)

f. 23v. Charter of protestation by B(enedict), Bishop of Rochester, on the dignities of the church of Salisbury in the consecration of Bishops will not be prejudiced by him. n.d. (1221). (Ibid., p. 109.)

f. 24. Agreement made by Jocelin, Bishop of Bath and Wells, and Hugh, Bishop of Lincoln, between Richard, Bishop of Salisbury, and the Chapter, and Adam de Brompton, kt., on the collation of the churches of Shipton and Brickworth. n.d. (1220–8). (Ibid., pp. 102–5.)

f. 25v. Charter of A(dam), Dean, and the Chapter of Salisbury granting the prebend of Horton to Richard, Bishop of Salisbury. 3 April 2 Pont. (1219). (Ibid., p. 95.)

Ordinance of the Chapter between Master Henry and Martin de Summis and the Bishop of Salisbury on the dispute between them. In Chapter of Salisbury. Translation of St. Swithin (15 July) 1237.

f. 26v. Charter of the ordinance of the churches of Inglesham and Coxwell which are in the use of the Abbot and Convent of Beaulieu, at the instance of the King of England, changed by papal authority. 4 Ides February (10 February) 1244. (Ibid., pp. 255–7.)

f. 28. Agreement as f. 21v.

f. 28v. Agreement as f. 22.

f. 29v. Confirmation of Robert, Dean, and the Chapter of Salisbury on the agreement on f. 20v. 16 August 1228.

f. 30v. Charter by Hugh, Archbishop of Rouen, to A(zo), Dean, and Chapter of Salisbury confirming the restitution made by the Empress Matilda of lands in All Cannings and Potterne. Falaise. Month of June 1148. (*Chart. & Docs.*, pp. 14–15.)

Agreement between Robert, Bishop of Salisbury, and Henry, Abbot, and the Convent of Sherborne, on the amercement of the same and the rent of the church of Salisbury. 16 Kal. September (17 August) 1238. (Ibid., pp. 245–6.)

f. 31. Ordinance on certain churches. Robert, Bishop of Salisbury, and the Chapter, on one side, and the Abbot and Convent of Sherborne, on the other on the churches of Lyme and Halstock. In Chapter of Sherborne. 9 Kal. September (24 August) 1238. (Ibid., pp. 248–9.)

f. 31v. Charter by William, Abbot of Sherborne, and the Convent, to Hubert, Bishop of Salisbury, and the church of that place, of Lyme and Halstock. 5 Ides June (6 June 1193). In Chapter of Salisbury. (Cf. *Reg. S. Osm.* I, p. 247.)

f. 32. Charter by William, Abbot of Sherborne, and the Convent, to Hubert, Bishop of Salisbury, and that church of their right in the churches of Poulshot and Deverell. n.d. (1191). (*Chart. & Docs.*, pp. 50, 248–9.)

Charter of Henry, Abbot of Bec, and the Convent to Robert, Bishop of Salisbury, and the Chapter on ordinance of Richard, formerly Bishop of Salisbury, and Reginald, then Prior of St. Neots, on the church of Boscombe, Month of April 1230. (Ibid., p. 282.)

f. 32v. Charter on tenements in St. Brides, London, granted to Bishops of Salisbury by the Abbot and Convent of Westminster, confirmed by William, Abbot of Westminster. n.d. (1223). (*Reg. S. Osm.* I, pp. 229–30.)

Charter of obligation by H(enry), Abbot of Reading, and the Convent granting Hubert, Bishop of Salisbury, that 13 poor persons in their Hospital at Reading should be clothed and fed for the souls of Hubert and all his ancestors and successors and of Ranulf Glanvill etc. and Geoffrey, Archdeacon of Berkshire. n.d. (1190–3). (*Chart. & Docs.*, p. 46.)

f. 33. Charter by Adam, Abbot of Reading, and the Convent granting to the church of Salisbury, and Richard, Bishop, and the Dean and Chapter, that they and their men who hold in chief of them shall be quit of toll and all other customs in the town of Reading. Witnesses. n.d. (1230). (Ibid., p. 204.)

Charter by the Abbot of Waverley and the Convent, at instance of Richard, Bishop of Salisbury, and the Chapter and the Convent of Malmesbury deputing to them the custody of the manor of Huish and the advowson of the church of Bremhill. n.d. (1219). (Ibid., pp. 93–4.)

f. 33v. Charter by Richard, Archbishop of Canterbury, confirming to Walter, son of Swein, the whole land of Wootton and the lands of Sherborne to hold of the Archbishop of Canterbury by a quarter part of a knight's fee as Jocelin, Bishop of Salisbury gave it. n.d. (1180). (Ibid., p. 43.)

f. 34. Charter of obedience made by Walter, Prior, and the Brothers of the Hospital of St. John of Marlborough for indulgence to their house by R(ichard), Bishop of Salisbury, A(dam), Dean, and the Chapter and the Canon Prebend of Westbury. n.d. (1220). (Ibid., p. 100.)

Charter of ratification of the charter by the Prior of Noyon and the Convent to Richard, Bishop of Salisbury, on the ordinance on the church of Hendred. n.d. (1228). (Ibid., pp. 199–200.)

Charter on hindrance of the business of Nicholas, Prior of Noyon, on Andelys because their seal is unknown to Master R(obert), Chancellor of Salisbury, and Master W(illiam), Archdeacon of Berkshire. n.d. (1228). (Ibid., p. 199.)

f. 34v. Charter of obligation by R(eginald), Prior of St. Neots, and the Convent on the ordinance on the church of Boscombe made by R(ichard), Bishop of Salisbury. n.d. (1218–28). (Ibid., p. 85.)

Charter to Herbert, Archdeacon of Canterbury, by the infirm brothers of the Hospital of St. Giles, their Keeper, and Ralph, son of Adam, of the lands they have in the parish of St. Brides, 15s. 3d. p.a., n.d. (1188). (Ibid., p. 45.)

f. 35. 'Then follow the charters of Abbots of which the first is the charter of Walter, Abbot, and the Convent of Malmesbury, of peace between them and Richard, Bishop of Salisbury, on the manor of Highway and the advowson of the church of Bremhill'.

f. 35v. Charter of confirmation of the previous perpetual ordinance between the church of Salisbury and the Abbot and Convent of Malmesbury. n.d. (1219). (Ibid., pp. 92–3.)

Agreement between the Bishop of Salisbury and the Abbot and Convent of Malmesbury that they are absolutely free from episcopal subjection for the manor of Highway and the advowson of the church of Bremhill. n.d. (1219). (Ibid., pp. 91–2.)

f. 37. Charter on the manor of Highway and the adowson of the church of Bremhill, Walter, Abbot of Malmesbury, and the Convent, n.d. (1219). (Ibid., pp. 92–3.)

Charter of deposition by Adam and Jordan, Abbots of Waverley and Durford, with the assent of Richard, Bishop of Salisbury, and the proctor of the Chapter, Master Abraham, Treasurer of Salisbury, on one side, and John Walensis, proctor of the Abbot and Convent of Malmesbury, on the other, on instruments on the subjection of the monastery of Malmesbury to the church of Cirencester, n.d. (1219). (Ibid., pp. 93–4.)

f. 37v. Charter of Walter, Abbot, and the Convent of Cirencester, on acknowledgement of the instruments of the church of Salisbury. n.d. (1219). (Ibid., pp. 94–5.)

f. 38. 'Here begin the charters of Earls of which the first is the charter of Reginald, Earl (Consul) of Cornwall, son of King Henry, to Robert, Dean of Salisbury, on preservation of the lands and men of the Bishop of Salisbury and correction of trespasses done.' Potterne. 11 Kal. July (21 June) 1152. (Ibid., pp. 23–4.)

Charter given to the church of Salisbury by Ralph Patrick addressed to John, Bishop of Exeter, who has restored to the church of Salisbury and Lewis Canon the prebend of Allington. n.d. (1150). (Ibid., p. 22.)

Charter given by Baldwin, Earl of Exeter, to the Chapter of Salisbury, on restitution of all possessions of the church of Salisbury (named). n.d. (1150). (Ibid., pp. 20–1.)

f. 38v. Charter by the Empress Matilda to the church and Jocelin, Bishop of Salisbury, of full restitution of lands in Cannings and Potterne. Witnesses. Falaise, n.d. (1148). (Ibid., p. 14.)

Charter of Matilda, Countess of Gloucester, and William, her son, Consul of Gloucester, to Jocelin, Bishop of Salisbury, of restitution of hundred of Sherborne, hundred of Yetminster, and their markets and other free customs. n.d. (1160). (Ibid., pp. 32–3.)

f. 39. Confirmation of the charter of the advowson of the church of Stapleford made to the church of Salisbury by Gundreda de Warenne. Witnesses. n.d. (1220). (*Chart. & Docs.*, pp. 100–1.)

f. 39v. Charter to the church of Salisbury and Robert, Bishop, by Margery, late wife of Nicholas de Gloucester, in widowhood, of the meadow at Spray in the manor of Potterne. Witnesses. n.d. (1240–1244). (Ibid., p. 274.)

f. 40. Charter of provision of Alan de Bayeux of the advowson of the church of Upwey to the church of Salisbury. n.d. (1201). Another charter is within in which is expressed the same gift. (Ibid., pp. 64–5.)

Charter of Robert, Treasurer of the Brothers of the Hospital of St. John of Jerusalem in England, with the assent of his chapter, of their house in the parish of St. Brides near Fleet Bridge at London, and in neighbouring parishes of all buildings etc. which Richard, formerly Bishop of Winchester, held and after him the Bishop of Salisbury, n.d. (1206). (Ibid., pp. 71–2.)

f. 40v. Charter of Adam de Brompton, kt., to Richard, Bishop of Salisbury, on the ordinance and disposition of the churches of Shipton and Brickworth. n.d. (1226–1228). (Ibid., pp. 173–4.)

Charter of Hugh de Sanford to the church of Salisbury and R(ichard), Bishop of Salisbury, of half the church of Chilton. n.d. (16 May 1223). (Ibid., pp. 125–6.)

f. 41. Charter of Hugh de Sanford quitclaiming the churches of St. Mary and SS. Peter and Paul in Marlborough to the church of Salisbury and R(ichard), Bishop of Salisbury. n.d. (1223). (Ibid., pp. 126–7.)

Charter of Hugh de Sanford of quitclaim of right of advowson of the churches of St. Mary and St. Peter in Marlborough to Richard, Bishop of Salisbury. n.d. (1223).

f. 41v. Charter of Walter Dispenser of Wootton of the rents of the salt works near Keyhaven which Nigel de Kylhaven holds to Philip, his son. n.d. (1200). (Ibid., pp. 63–4.)

f. 42. Charter of Baldwin, son of Walter Dispenser, the younger, to Richard, Bishop of Salisbury, of his right in the land of Wootton, for which the Bishop gives him what he had in H[ ]lington, for which he pays the Bishop 20s. p.a. n.d. (1228). (Ibid., pp. 194–5.)

Charter of the exchange of lands between Philip, son of Walter Dispenser, and Richard, Bishop of Salisbury, of his right in the land of Wootton for 2½ virgates of land in Sherborne etc. Witnesses. n.d. (1228). (Ibid., pp. 196–7.)

f. 42v. Charter of remission and quit claim of all right which Ralph de Vallibus has in the manor of Chardstock, to the church of Salisbury and Richard, Bishop. n.d. (1226–8). (Ibid., p. 174.)

Agreement between Herbert, Bishop of Salisbury, and Stephen de Tyrell, of all the land of Chardstock and of Compton for which the Bishop gives him 1 hide of land called Millhall for service of half a knight's fee. n.d. (1201). (Ibid., pp. 66–7.)

f. 43. Charter of quitclaim of the right which John, son of John, of Woolmington, has in rents in Chardstock, which he holds in demesne of the Bishop of Salisbury. Witnesses. n.d. (1201). (Ibid., p. 67.)

Charter of certain lands in the manor of Potterne given by Ralph de Page, with the consent of Edith, his wife, to the church of Salisbury, and Robert, Bishop, at Spray in manor of Potterne. Witnesses. n.d. (1240–5). (Ibid., p. 275.)

f. 43v. Charter of Peter de Camera of his tenement at Baydon, of the Bishop's manor of Ramsbury, given and confirmed by R(ichard), Bishop of Salisbury, for service to his ancestor H(erbert), Bishop of Salisbury. n.d. (1228). (*Reg. S. Osm.* I, pp. 317–18.)

Agreement between Richard, Bishop of Salisbury, and James de Potterne of 2 crofts in Potterne. Salisbury. Thursday in Easter Week (6 April) 1222.

f. 44. Charter of exchange of a meadow in the park of Sonning and of arable land between Jocelin, Bishop of Salisbury, and John de Erleg, John quitclaiming what he had in the park of Sonning and the Bishop giving him 2 virgates of land in Potterne. Witness, the hundred of Sonning. n.d. (1160). (*Reg. S. Osm.* I, pp. 248–9.)

Charter between Richard, Bishop of Salisbury, and A(dam), Dean of Salisbury, of exchange of a messuage etc. in vill of Potterne. n.d. (1217). (*Chart. & Docs.*, p. 81.)

f. 44v. Charter of Alan de Bayeux to the church of Salisbury of the advowson of the church of Wey in alms. Witnesses. n.d. (1201). (Ibid., p. 64.)

Charter of John Wanci, son of William Wanci, to the church of Salisbury quitclaiming certain lands to the office of carpenter to the church of Salisbury. Witnesses. n.d. (1219). (Ibid., p. 96.)

f. 45. Charter of Nicholas de Bruer to the church of Salisbury acknowledging its right to certain lands in Winterbourne which is in the parish of Chieveley. n.d. (1210). (Ibid., pp. 75–6.)

Ordinance on the church of West Kington. William, Bishop of Salisbury, and John, Abbot of St. Peters of Foyeres, of Order of St. Augustine. Witnesses. Salisbury. Saturday before Ash Wednesday (13 February) 1249. (Ibid., pp. 317–18.)

f. 45v. Composition between Hubert, Bishop of Salisbury, and the church and William, Abbot, and Convent of Sherborne, of certain land in Kingston and the residence made in the church of Salisbury, in name of prebend of Sherborne. n.d. (1191). (Ibid., pp. 50–1.)

f. 46v. Charter of William, Abbot of Sherborne, to Hubert, Bishop of Salisbury, of collation of churches of Lyme and Halstock. 8 June 1191. Chapter of Salisbury. Witnesses. (Ibid., p. 48.)

Charter of ordinance and disposition of Richard, Bishop of Salisbury, about the church of Caundle, W(illiam), Prior, and Convent of Breamore, 5 marks p.a. Salisbury. 1225. (Ibid., pp. 166–7.)

f. 47. Charter of Robert, Bishop of Salisbury, of ordinance made on church of Breamore, church of Ebbesborne Wake, with assent of Prior and Convent of Breamore. Witnesses. Salisbury. 17 Kal. May. (15 April) 1233. (Ibid., pp. 164–5.)

f. 47v. Charter of Jocelin, Bishop of Salisbury on land granted to W(illiam), son of A(lexander), of Potterne, Cannings and Wootton, in presence of R(oger), Bishop of Worcester, and G(eoffrey), Dean of Hereford. Witnesses. n.d. (1173). (Ibid., pp. 57–8.)

f. 48. Charter of Jocelin, Bishop of Salisbury, of collation of prebend of Sherborne to Henry, Abbot, and Convent of Sherborne, and of the vicarage, n.d. (1165). (Ibid., pp. 249–50.)

f. 48v. Composition between H(erbert), Bishop of Salisbury, and Reginald de Leye and Roger de Breng'. Witnesses. n.d. (1200+).

Final Concord between Herbert, Bishop of Salisbury, pet., and Roger, son of Everard, on certain lands in Ramsbury, 2 hides in manor of Lavington, 1 hide, 5 hides in manor of All Cannings, 1 hide in la Hurst etc. In King's Court at Westminster. Monday after Ascension, 7 Richard I (3 June 1196), before (Hubert), Archbishop of Canterbury, R(ichard), Bishop of London, (Gilbert), Bishop of Rochester, Wiliam of St. Marychurch, Dean of St. Martins, London, Henry of Canterbury, Ralph of Hereford, Richard of Ely, Archdeacons, G(eoffrey) fitz Peter, William de Warenne, Richard de Heriet, Osbert de Emey, Simon de Pateshull, Master Thomas de Hussebur'. (*Chart. & Docs.*, pp. 57–8.)

f. 49. Final Concord between H(erbert), Bishop of Salisbury, pet., and Jocelin and Walter Leuric, ten., on 2 virgates of land in manor of Old Salisbury, in King's Court at Westminster, Thursday after St. Martin, 7 Richard I (16 November 1195), before H(ubert), Archbishop of Canterbury, Richard, Bishop of London, G(ilbert), Bishop of Rochester, William of St. Marychurch, Master William de Cuvill, Ralph of Hereford, Richard of Ely, Archdeacons, William de Warenne, Osbert, son of Hervy, Richard de Heriet, Simon de Pateshull, Master Thomas de Hussebur'. (Ibid., pp. 55–6.)

f. 49v. Final Concord. between Herbert, Bishop of Salisbury, pet., and William Nigel, ten., on 1 virgate of land, 1 meadow, 1 mill in Potterne. Date as above f. 49. (Ibid.)

f. 50. Final Concord between William de Percy, pet., and Herbert, Bishop of Salisbury, ten., on whole vill of Chardstock, in King's Court at Westminster, Day of St. Edward the King, 7 Richard I (18 March 1196), before H(ubert), Archbishop of Canterbury, R(alph), Archdeacon of Hereford, Osbert, son of Hervy, Simon de Pateshull, Master Thomas de Husseburn, Richard de Heriet. (Ibid., p. 57.)

Final Concord between Herbert, Bishop of Salisbury, pet., and Hamelin, son of John, ten., on 1 virgate of land in Tisted and of Bishop's Court in same vill, in King's Court at Westminster, morrow of Holy Trinity 4 John (10 June 1202), before G(eoffrey) fitz Peter, Richard de Heriet, Godfrey de Insula, William de Crepyng. (Ibid., p. 59.)

Final Concord between Nicholas de Winterburn, pet., and Herbert, Bishop of Salisbury, ten., on ½ a knight's fee in vill of Winterbourne, Thursday after Octave of SS. Peter and Paul 4 John (11 July 1202), in King's Court at Westminster, before G(eoffrey) fitz Peter, Earl of Essex, Richard de Heriet, Master Ralph de Stokes, Jordan de Turri. (Ibid., p. 70.)

f. 50v. Final Concord between Herbert, Bishop of Salisbury, pet., and Elias, clerk, and his brother Roger, sons of Stephen Tyrell, ten., on 1 hide of land at Alwoolston and 1 hide in Millhall, in King's Court at Westminster, Three weeks after Michaelmas 4 John (20 October 1202), before G(eoffrey) fitz Peter, Richard de Heriet, Master Godfrey de Insula, William de Crepyng. (Ibid., pp. 70–1.)

Final Concord between Roger, son of Everard, pet., and Herbert Bishop of Salisbury, ten., on ½ hide of land in Potterne claimed by writ of mort d'ancestor, and a stank in Lavington, made to damage of free tenants of Roger, 15 days after Easter 4 John (28 April 1202), before G(eoffrey) fitz Peter, Richard de Heriet, Simon de Pateshull, Eustace de Fauconberg, John de Gostlyng, Godfrey de Insula, Walter de Crepyng.

f. 51. Final Concord between William, son of Robert, pet., and Herbert, Bishop of Salisbury, on 1½ hides of land in Chardstock. Date as last on f. 50v. (Ibid., p. 68.)

f. 51v. Final Concord between Bernard de Ymesfeld, pet., and Herbert Bishop of Salisbury, ten., on ½ a knight's fee in Winterbourne near Chieveley, in King's Court at Westminster, Octave of Hilary (20 January) 4 John (1203), before G(eoffrey) fitz Peter, Richard de Heriet,

Simon de Pateshull, John Gostling, Eustace de Fauconberg, G(odfrey) de Insula, Walter de Crepyng. (Ibid., pp. 67–8.)

Final Concord between Stephen Tyrell, pet., and Herbert, Bishop of Salisbury, ten., on whole manor of Chardstock and 5 hides of land in Childscompton, in King's Court at Westminster, 15 days after Hilary 2 John (27 January 1201), before Geoffrey fitz Peter, R(ichard) de Herford, John de Gestling, Henry de Wycheton, Godfrey de Insula, Walter de Crepyng. (Ibid., pp. 65–6.)

f. 52. Final Concord between Richard, Bishop of Salisbury, pet., and William, son of Alan, ten., on 4 virgates of land in Potterne, before King's Court at Wilton, Morrow of Ascension 3 Henry III (17 May 1219), before Richard, Bishop of Salisbury, Matthew, son of Herbert, Richard Havering, Walter Foliot, James de Potterne, Walter de Ripariis, Maurice Cheirevill, John de Wykenholt.

Final Concord between Thomas de Banelyngham, and Mabel, his wife, pet., and Richard, Bishop of Salisbury, ten., on the hundred of Godalming, in King's Court at Westminster, Morrow of Ascension 8 Henry III (24 May 1224), before Martin de Pateshull, Thomas de Multon, Stephen de Segrave, Thomas de Heyden, Robert de Lexington, Geoffrey le Sauvage. (Ibid., p. 165.)

f. 52v. Final Concord between Thomas Cosyn and Juliana, his wife, pet., and Richard, Bishop of Salisbury, ten., on ½ hide of land in Old Salisbury, before King's Court at Wilton, Morrow of Ascension 11 Henry III (21 May 1227), before Thomas de Molton, Robert de Lexington, William Schorwell, Jordan Oliver, Warin, son of Ivel. (Ibid., pp. 182–3.)

Final Concord between Richard, Bishop of Salisbury, quer., and Agnes de Candel, deforc., on vill of Caundle in King's Court at Westminster, 15 days after Easter 12 Henry III (16 April 1228), before Martin de Pateshull, Archdeacon of Norfolk, Stephen de Seagrave, William, son of Warin, W(illiam) de Insula. (Ibid., p. 193.)

f. 53. Final Concord between Richard, Bishop of Salisbury, quer., and Richard de Rammesbury, deforc., on 8 virgates of land in Ramsbury, as last entry f. 52v.

f. 53v. Final Concord between Richard, Bishop of Salisbury, quer., and Philip de Wootton, deforc., on 2 carucates of land in Wootton, as f. 53. (Ibid., pp. 195–6.)

f. 54. Final Concord between Richard, Bishop of Salisbury, quer., and Geoffrey de Dunesden, deforc., on 5 virgates of land in Sonning, as f. 53. (Ibid., pp. 197–8.)

f. 54v. Final Concord between Richard, Bishop of Salisbury, quer., and Baldwin, son of Dispenser, deforc., on 2 carucates of land in Wootton, as f. 53. (Ibid., pp. 193–4.)

f. 55. Final Concord between Gregory de la Dune, pet., and Robert, Bishop of Salisbury, ten., on 1½ virgates of land in Lillington, in King's Court at Westminster, Octave of St. Martin 14 Henry III (19 November 1229), before Thomas de Multon, Stephen de Seagrave, William de Ralegh, Robert de Lexington, William de Insula, William de London, Master Robert de Scherdelawe.

Final Concord between John Bayeux, quer., and Robert, Bishop of Salisbury, deforc., on church of Wey, in King's Court at Westminster, 15 days after St. John the Baptist, 21 Henry III (8 July 1237), before Robert de Lexinton, William de Ebor, Adam, son of William, William de Culworth. (Ibid., pp. 242–3.)

f. 55v. Final Concord between William de Harleweston, quer., and Robert, Bishop of Salisbury, deforc., on advowson of church of Wey in King's Court at Lincoln, Morrow of Close of Easter, 14 Henry III (15 April 1230), before Robert de Lexington, Robert de Haya, Warin Engayne, Justices Itinerant.

Final Concord between John de St. George, pet., and Robert, Bishop of Salisbury, ten. on ½ hide of land except 8 a. in Kingston in King's Court at Reading, 3 weeks after Michaelmas, 25 Henry III (20 October 1240), before William de Ebor., Provost of Beverley, John, Abbot of Abingdon, Roger de Curkelly, William de Paston.

f. 56. Final Concord between Miles Basset, pet., and William, Bishop of Salisbury, ten., on 3 a. of land in a messuage in Northmorton and advowson of that vill, in King's Court at Reading, Octave of St. John the Baptist 32 Henry III (1 July 1248), before Roger de Torkesby, Gilbert de Preston, Master Simon de Wauteton, John de Cobham, Justices Itinerant.

f. 56v. Charter of Peter de Pymbyr' kt., of sale of tenement in vill of Lavington. Witnesses. n.d. (1295). (Cf. *Chart. & Docs.*, p. 57.)

Charter of Baldwin de Clopton of rent sold to William, Bishop of Salisbury, in vill of Lillington, homage and service of Thomas le Breton. Witnesses. n.d. (1246–56).

f. 57. Charter of Walter de Whytfeld to William, Bishop of Salisbury, of croft at Whitefield called Biencroft and 6½ a. of another croft called Hundcroft. n.d. (1246–56).

Charter of same to same of croft at Whitefield, 7 a., with vachery. Witnesses. n.d. (1246–57).

f. 57v. Charter of Walter, Bishop of Salisbury, to John de Southeye of land which he held of him at Southey, in p. of Wokingham, in villeinage. n.d. (1263–71).

f. 58. Ordinance of Walter, Bishop of Salisbury, on hospice of Wootton Bassett. Sir Philip Basset and Walter de Gay, rector of church of Wootton Bassett on foundation. Salisbury. 6 Ides June (13 June) 1266.

f. 59v. Confirmation by Walter, Bishop of Salisbury, of land which William de Domerham, vicar of church of Potterne, gave to church of Potterne; inspecting grant. Salisbury. Month of December 5 Pont. (1267).

f. 60v. Letters of Giles, Bishop of Salisbury, on gift of church of Laverstock and ordinance. £10 from fruits of church of Laverstock. n.d. (1256–62).

Composition between Alan Basset and Prior and Convent of Bicester on advowson of church of Compton, by Hugh, Bishop of Lincoln, and Jocelin, Bishop of Bath. n.d. (1220–8). (Ibid., pp. 100–5.)

f. 61v. The form and hand changes here and documents now have no captions. Heading: Carta de Kylhaven. 1252. Tuesday in Easter week (2 April). Questions moved between W(illiam), Bishop of Salisbury, and William, son of Nigel Kye, and Nigel de Boccland, on concealment of a mill at Bassleslegh or rent of men of Bassleslegh, Ebbesford and Alketon. Witnesses.

f. 62. Letters Patent of licence in mortmain for fine paid by S(imon), Bishop of Salisbury, for rent of a cellar under a hall in the town of New Salisbury, in a place called Fysshechamals by him newly built, with shops to Dean and Chapter of Salisbury. 6 May 7 Edward II (1314).

f. 62v. Heading in later hand: Wynterburn. Charter (in later hand) by Richard, Bishop of Salisbury, to William Giffard, all land of Winterbourne at annual rent of £4 p.a. Witnesses. n.d. (1211–28).

f. 65. Heading in another hand: Carta Episcopi Sar. pro redditu in civitate Sar. Charter by R(obert), Bishop of Salisbury, to free citizens of New Salisbury of free tenement in New

Salisbury. n.d. (1228–46). Heading in yet another hand: Wambergh pro sustentacione unius presbyteri. Indenture between Adam Fitzwilliam of Wanborough to Robert de la Mare of all his lands in Up Lambourne and Chipping Lambourne for a priest daily in church of Wanborough. Witnesses. Friday after Feast of St. Scolastica 23 Edward III (10 February 1349).

f. 66. In another hand: Articuli statum Civitatis Sar. contingentes viz. Episcopum et civitatem Sar. cum pena adiecta. Reginald de Todeworth, Mayor of city of Salisbury, and community of said place, Simon, Bishop of Salisbury. Appointment of attorneys coram Rege, New Salisbury, 24 March 33 Edward I (1305). 28 articles follow. S(imon), Bishop of Salisbury, to Master Walter Hervy, Canon of Salisbury, to go to Salisbury, Sonning, 6 June 1306; S(imon), Bishop of Salisbury to citizens of New Salisbury on above appointment, Sonning, 6 June 1306; Agreement in testimony of which common seal and seal of mayoralty of city of New Salisbury affixed. Witnesses. Thursday morrow of St. Bartholomew, 25 August 1306, 34 Edward I.

f. 74v. Aldermanry of New Street. List of names.

f. 75. Aldermanry of the market. Like.

f. 75v. Aldermanry of St. Martin. Like.

f. 76. Aldermanry of the meadow. Like.

Hec ordinaciones sic nominantur de verbo ad verbum per litteras regis Edwardi tercii post conquestum que sic incipiunt. Letters Patent, 5 May 30 Edward III (1357), inspecting letters patent of Mayor and community of city of New Salisbury. (*C.P.R. 1354–8*, p. 535.)

f. 77. Heading: Licencia concessa maiori et civibus pro emendis terris ad summam etc. Robert, Bishop, and Dean and Chapter of Salisbury. New Salisbury, Tuesday after Feast of Easter 13 Henry IV (5 April 1412). Letters Patents, two parts in hands of Spirituals and outsiders and scarcely a third part in hands of citizens of Salisbury and citizens charges, collections and subsidies in city, licence to Mayor and community to acquire lands, tenements and rents to value of 100 marks p.a. within city, by grant of Bishop and Dean and Chapter. 1 June 7 Henry IV (1406). (*C.P.R. 1405–8*, p. 185.)

f. 78. Grant by Nicholas Bildeston. Dean, and Chapter of Salisbury, that as Edward III, by charter, gave Robert, Bishop, the canons and citizens of New Salisbury licence to ditch the city, and Robert, Bishop of Salisbury, confirmed the same, if not done to be of harm to Bishop and church. Chapter House, Salisbury, 26 August 1440.

f. 78v. Grant by Reginald de Tuddeworth, Mayor, and community of city of New Salisbury, that as Simon, Bishop of Salisbury, at their request, has granted on ditch that, land remains property of the Bishop. Salisbury, Monday after Feast of St. John ante Portam Latinam, 1 Edward II (13 May 1308).

f. 79. Heading: Sentencia lata contra Canonicos Sar. pro Episcopo. On visitation by John, Bishop of Salisbury. n.d. (1392).

f. 80v. Grant by Jocelin, Bishop of Salisbury, to Segar, his servant, of ½ hide of land in Wanborough, which was the land of the Bedel. Witnesses. n.d. (1180). (*Reg. S. Osm.* I, pp. 226–7.)

f. 81. Charter to R(ichard), Bishop of Salisbury, confirming liberties etc. and on Justices of the Peace in city of Salisbury etc. 20 February 1 Edward IV (1462). (*C. Ch. R.* VI, p. 180.)

f. 82v. Charter granting a market and fair at Chardstock. 20 February 1 Edward IV (1462). Witnesses. (Ibid.)

f. 84. Letters Patent, 5 December 12 Edward IV (1472). (*C.P.R. 1467–77*, p. 371.)

At top of f.: Ista Carta scribitur in registrum Johannis Machon fo. cxxx iiii.

At foot of f. 86v.: Irrotulatur in Memor. Scacc. vide inter Recorda de termino Sancti Michaelis 13 Regis Edwardi 4, Rot. 5, ex parte Rememor. Regis.

f. 88. Letters under great seal of Richard, Bishop of Salisbury, to Henry Lange esq., his Steward, John Inguler, Mayor of city of New Salisbury, John Whettokes, Richard Jay, Morgan Kydwelly and John Humpton, appointing them justices to deliver his gaol in said city. 7 May 19 Edward IV (1479). Edward IV (1479). Precept thereon to Bailiff of Salisbury, same date, addressed to John Cheyne esq.

f. 94. Grant by Richard, Bishop of Salisbury, to his free citizens of New Salisbury of free tenement in the city. 3 Non. April 9 Henry III, 8 Pont. (3 April 1225.)

f. 95. In Memoranda of the Parliament summoned at Westminster, first Sunday in Lent 33 Edward I (7 March 1305), and King's writ to Sheriff of Wilts. on inspection of charter of Henry III to Bishop of Salisbury on tallage, 5 March 33 Edward I (1305) and return and writ to Master Richard de Abyndon and Henry de Cobham, 8 April 33 Edward I (1305).

f. 99. Writ to Sheriff of Wilts. on tallage of citizens of Salisbury, 27 May 33 Edward I (1305).

f. 99v. Letters of Reginald de Tudeworth, Robert de Basyng, John le Scut etc. of New Salisbury, to Simon, Bishop of Salisbury, Monday after Feast of St. John ante Portam Latinam 1 Edward II (13 May 1308).

f. 104v. Charter on rents, lands and liberties of the citizens, 28 May 34 Edward I (1306). (*C. Ch. R.* III, p. 67.)

f. 106. Letters of Reginald de Tudworth, Mayor, and community of city of New Salisbury to Simon, Bishop of Salisbury, Monday after Feast of St. John ante portam Latinam 1 Edward II (13 May 1308).

f. 106v. Letters of Simon, Bishop of Salisbury, to Master Walter Hervy, Archdeacon of Salisbury, Sir Henry Pentlane, kt., Sir Alexander de Hemyngby, Canon of Salisbury, and John de Cherleton, to assess tallage of citizens of city of Salisbury, London, 10 April 33 Edward I (1305).

f. 107. Letters of Robert, Bishop of Salisbury, on charter of Henry III, that Salisbury should be a free city etc, on the walling of the city. Manor of Woodford, 10 June 1367, 41 Edward III.

f. 108. Letters Patent on inquisition taken by Escheator, co. Wilts., ex officio, that Robert, Bishop of Salisbury, by charter granted Mayor and citizens of New Salisbury that they might purchase land in city, rent 1d. per perch. 20 October 44 Edward III (1370). (Cf. *C.P.R. 1370–4*, p. 220.)

f. 109. Confirmation by Thomas Montagu, Dean, and Chapter of Salisbury of grant of Richard, Bishop of Salisbury, to free citizens of place 7 perches in length and 3 perches in breadth, 12d. p.a. Chapter of Salisbury, 2 Kal. October (30 September) 1366.

f. 110. Letters Patent to Dean and Chapter of Salisbury to elect Bishop on death of Roger, Bishop, on request of letters patent of Master Robert de Ayleston, Archdeacon of Wilts., and Master Ralph de Euerendon, Sub Dean. 16 March 4 Edward (III) (1330). (*C.P.R. 1327–30*, p. 498.)

f. 110v. View of the lands, tenements and churches belonging in common to the Canons of the Cathedral Church of Salisbury made by Mr. Nicholas Upton, Precentor of the church, and John Cranborn, Canon, 7 February 1451/2.

f. 112. Composition of the vicar of Stourpaine. William, Dean, and Chapter of Salisbury, to William de Polden, priest, the manse of their church of Stourpaine which was accustomed to be the rector's. Salisbury. 2 Kal. October (30 September) 1278.

f. 113. Hilton. The rectory of Hilton is appropriated to the Canons by Robert, Bishop of Salisbury.

f. 114v. Powerstock. This church is appropriated to the Dean and Chapter by Robert, Bishop of Salisbury.

f. 116v. Composition of the vicar of Powerstock. R(obert), Dean, and Chapter of Salisbury to Roger de Mera, chaplain, vicarage of Powerstock, Salisbury, Morrow of St. Thomas the Martyr (30 December) 1255. (*Chart. & Docs.*, pp. 324–5.)

f. 117v. Composition of vicarage of Alton. This was granted to Warin, vicar of Alton. Jocelin, Bishop of Salisbury, granted this church to the church of Salisbury.

R(obert), Dean, and Chapter of Salisbury, grant to William Bond, for homage and service, of land in manor of Whitchurch, 40d. p.a. n.d. (*c.* 1225).

f. 121. Powerstock. Grant by Roger Arundell, in alms, to church of St. Mary of Salisbury of Powerstock and the parson there, of liberties and free customs which he had in time of his ancestors. Witnesses. n.d. (1160+). (Cf. ibid., pp. 26–31.)

f. 121v. Bishop's Cannings. List of lands. Gift of the vicarage of Bishop's Cannings. William de Abyndon, Archdeacon of Wilts., Thomas de Bridport and Robert de Strode, Canons of the church of Salisbury, church of Cannings to be a perpetual vicarage. Ordinance by Nicholas, Bishop of Salisbury, addressed to the above 3 (incomplete). n.d. (1297).

ff. 122–5. Table of Contents covering ff. 1–50 only (the remainder apparently lost).

f. 126. Rental of certain lands belonging to the Chapter.

Omnia qua in isto tomo decimo quinto continentur ad novem capitula referri possunt viz. ad: Cartas Regis Anglie; Cartas aliorum; Finales Concordie; Compositiones; Indenturas; Appropriationes; Observationes; Rentale. Ad aliquid in isto tomo decimo quinto investigandis ille numerus est accipiendus qui in medio superius partis cuiusque foliis continetur.

The main part of this manuscript was written in the second half of the thirteenth century and additions were made up to the second half of the fifteenth century.

First as to foliation and pagination: (1) there is a neat pagination in ink beginning at 15 to 251 (present f. 121), the index pp. not being included in this pagination, for f. 122 has 3, as if 2 pp. are missing, f. 123, 5, f. 124, 7, f. 125, 9, 362, 179. This pagination is all in the corner. The first, p. 15, cannot mean that 14 pp. of the text are missing as the first entry is of a charter of St. Osmund. The first 14 pp. may have been of a table of contents which has been lost. (2) in the centre of the pages there is a second pagination, running 1 to 239 (f. 122) which is then discontinued. (3) there is a later foliation, 1 to 84, which then ceases but this has for convenience of reference now been continued in pencil, ff. 85 to 126. The documents are also numbered 1 to 160 (which ends on f. 64). The entries on these ff. appear to have been the original cartulary, running 1 to 154 (f. 61). The contents of ff. 61v to 66 seem to have been added to the original cartulary, as have all the following quires. It will be noted that up to f. 61 there is no document entered later than Henry III. The Edward I documents are later additions. It may therefore be stated safely that the original entries were all made before 1272, that those on ff. 62–3 were added in the late thirteenth or early fourteenth century, and that all entries after f. 64 were made in the fourteenth or fifteenth centuries. This includes the index or calendar.

Throughout, from f. 1 to f. 60v, the initial letter of each document has been omitted for illumination or rubrication, which was never done. However, from f. 1 to f. 12 the captions have been underlined in red and there are red capitals to the captions and on f. 1 further red added to capital letters. The parchment is ordinary, the hands vary from ordinary to bad. The transcriber of the original cartulary was careless and ignorant; having but slight knowledge of Latin and not being an expert reader he makes many simple errors. At most ff. throughout there are marginal notes, frequently at the top or foot of the page. The manuscript was a reference book in frequent use.

There is a brief list of the contents of this manuscript printed privately by Sir Thomas Phillips in 1822 (2 folio sheets) and it is briefly described in G. R. Davis, *Medieval Cartularies* (1958), p. 93.

VOLUME 19

A composite volume containing the following 5 items. On flyleaf: The History of England by the name of Albion. $8\frac{3}{4}'' \times 5\frac{1}{2}''$. 149 ff.

1. f. 1. This appears to be an old flyleaf, at the top of which is written: Veritas post quam latebris latuit tandem emergitur.

Begins: (   ) orbamus magni adiurati Machameti filii Attinii cum fratribus eius Kedibergi etc. f. 1v. Ends: Dat. anno Machametis viiC. xliO die xviiiO mensis Kalen.

Explicit litera a Sarazenis quibusdam in litera prescriptis domino Clementi pape nuper transmissa.

This is written in a hand of the late fourteenth or early fifteenth century.

2. ff. 2–6. A short chronicle written in rhyming Latin hexameters, with a genealogical table, of Kings of England, William I to Edward III.

f. 2. Begins: Dux Normannorum Willelmus vi validorum. Rex est anglorum bello conquestor eorum.

f. 6v. Ends: Princeps Edwarde non sit tua lancea tarde. In Scotis mota per te sit cambria nota.

Edwardus filius Regis Edwardi filii Regis Henrici genuit.

Edwardum Regem qui vivit

Johannem de Eltham

Johannam de Tours.

Of the same date as no. 1 above.

3. f. 7. Four riddles in French with answers, translated into English.

About the same date as no. 1 above.

4. f. 7v. A prologue or introductory note to the main section which follows running thus: En ceste livre est contenu coment les xxix soers viendrent en Engleterre des queux les geantz furent engendre par les mauveis espiretz demorauntz en leir dount liegne soer appelle

Albine apres qui noun ceste terre feust appelle Albion. Et comment Brutus vient en Engleterre et conquist la terre sur les geantz et oustra le noun de Albion et lappelle Bretaigne aforces son noun sememe. Et coment les Saxons vindrent de Germanie en ceste terre et la conquistrent et engetterent les Bretons et ousterent le noun de Bretaigne et lappellerent Engistlonde apres le noun Engist qe feust le mestre et le sustre des Seissons. Et coment William Bastard conquist ceste terre ensemblement oue totes les auentures et Batailes qe ount este en ceste terre du temps Bruyt oesque (a la bataile de Halidon Hill). The last six words in brackets are in a different hand.

En ceste volum sounte contenuz xxix quaiers. Et chescun Quaier de perchemin 1d. Et pur les alumpner vd. Et pur lescrive de chescun quaier iiid. La somme de tut (erased).

ff. 8–12v. A Brute Chronicle in French.

Ci Commence lestorie des geant (written in red ink).

Begins: Ci poet home sauer coment quant et de quele gent les grauntz geantz vindrent Re Engleterre.

Ends: Ke en escripture les mettrent. Amen.

Then follows in the same hand a note in Latin beginning De potissimi Regis greue nullis, ending vero Englistlond nominavit.

In a later hand in a black ink: beginns: Albina senes soror; ends: cum omnibus actibus usque Halydon hill inferius aperte patet.

5. ff. 13–147v. The Romance of Brute.

Ci comence la Romaunce de Bruyt (in red ink).

Begins: En la noble citie de graunt Troie ily avoit un noble chiualer.

Ends: totes les bestes et biens ce illoques furent et ent firent lour volente (referring to the battle of Halidon Hill).

The ms. proper, that is ff. 13–148, has illuminated capitals in red, blue, and purple, with a few paragraph marks in red. There are a few marginal notes of no particular consequence. The parchment is fair, the hand fairly good for the period, late fourteenth or early fifteenth century, and the ink is the light brown characteristic of the period. In the preliminary folios (ff. 2–12) there are a few headings and markings in red only.

f. 147v. The Romance is followed by Latin hexameters on Sanguineus, Colericus, Melencolicus, and Flammaticus (8 in all), followed by definitions of these four words and some more hexameters.

f. 148. (which is really a flyleaf 1): Respons assez couenables par comune assent de Countes et Barons de clers ensement a Nichol sur Wyhame.

A translation into French of a letter from Pope Boniface (VIII) to the English Barons at Lincoln (1301).

f. 149. From old binding, being a fragment of a theological work.

VOLUME 20

Francis Barbaro's De re Uxoria Liber, full bound in dark blue morocco, with Inner Temple coat of arms on both covers. On flyleaf: Francisci Barbari De Re Uxoria Liber. On another flyleaf: Sum Henrici Giuleingbini (in an Italic hand) with fine writing in red on both sides of the folio. $7\frac{5}{8}'' \times 5\frac{3}{8}''$. 87 ff.

ff. 1–87. FRANCISCI BARBARI DE RE UXORIA LIBER (in red square capitals).
Begins: Maiores nostri Laurenti carissime benivolentia vel necessitudine.

Ends: Que cum dicta essent surreximus
Optimus est homini linguae thesaurus et ingens
Gratia quae fascis mensurat singula verbis
followed by a number of short extracts or quotations.

This manuscript is of foreign origin, probably Italian. It is written in a good italic hand, probably of the Renaissance period. The parchment is good uterine and the ink a good black. The illumination is almost restricted to the first folio, which has the title in red. The initial M of Maiores is illuminated in red, blue, green, purple, and gold. There is a design in red, blue, green, purple, and yellow at the foot of the folio. There are a number of capitals in the text in red, blue, or green, having been inserted or intruded later in a later hand, also foreign, in a faded red ink similar to the ink used on the flyleaf. The dates of Francis Barbaro are 1398–1454. The manuscript is of about the middle of the fifteenth century.

VOLUME 21

A tract on Consecration of Churches and other matters of ecclesiastical discipline, defective at beginning and end. Inset label: A Civil and Canon Law Book touching Consecration of Churches. $6\frac{5}{8}'' \times 4\frac{1}{4}''$. 180 ff.

f. 1. At top: A Civil and Canon Law Book touching Consecration of Churches etc. The first f. or ff. must be missing, as it starts abruptly: novent quociens in carcare positos tardius.

The following headings appear in the text:
f. 9. De consecratione ecclesie uel altaris.
f. 12. De usuris.
f. 25. De pinetencia et confessione.
f. 34v. (at top of f.) Qualiter se debet habere sacerdos audiendo confessionem.
f. 42. Pro quibus peccatis est peccator ad episcopum mittendus.
f. 47v. Pro quibus peccatis est peccator ad papam mittendus.
f. 51. Iste sunt penitencie in canonibus diffinite.
f. 63. De indulgenciis remissionibus et satis factionibus.
f. 67v. De caritate et elemosinis.
f. 69. De furto.
f. 72. De sepulturis et iuris funerandi.
f. 78v. De sacramentis iterandis uel non iterandis et de sacramento confirmacionis.
f. 81. De sacra unctione.
f. 85. De baptismo et eius effectu.
f. 92. De cognacione spirituali.
f. 94. De eo qui cognouit consanguinam uxoris sue.
f. 95v. De coniugio leperosorum.
f. 96v. De eo qui duxit in matrimoniam quam prius poluit per adulterium.
f. 101. Qui clerici uel noventes matrimoniam contrahere possunt.
f. 102. De clandestina desponsacione.
f. 104. Incipit liber iiii de sponsalibus et matrimoniis.
f. 114. De purificacione post partum.

f. 115. De homicidiis.
f. 116. Item de sponsalibus et matrimoniis.
f. 117. Explicit de sponsalibus et matrimoniis.
f. 118. De divorciis.
f. 124v. De frigidis et maleficiatis.
f. 130v. De matrimonio contracto contra interdictum ecclesie.
f. 131. De secundis nupciis.
f. 132v. Qui sunt filii legitimi.
f. 134. De adulteriis et stupro et de incestuoso coitu.
f. 138v. De monialibus et aliis mulieribus religiosis.
f. 141v. De raptoribus.
f. 144v. De solucionibus et obligacionibus.
f. 145. De sentencia excommunicationis et suspencionis.
f. 178v. Casus in quibus est aliquis ipso iure excommunicatus.
f. 180v. Ends: with continuing words as key. Therefore incomplete.

The manuscript has red paragraph marks throughout. The running headings, which are also red, do not begin until f. 9v, but then continue throughout. The section headings in the text are red. There are marginal notes and also additions at the end of the ff., but neither appear to be of much consequence. Parts of the manuscript are stained by damp. The hand is tolerable, the parchment not of good quality, the ink light brown. The manuscript is probably of the late fourteenth century.

VOLUME 22

Guido de Columna, History of the Trojan War. On flyleaf: Historia de Bello Trojano. $6\frac{3}{4}'' \times 4\frac{1}{4}''$. 156 ff.

The following appears on the original flyleaf: Guido de Columpna predictum opus compositur A.D. 1287. Tho. Leventhorpe de Alnebery me possidet 1571.

1657
1287
0370

f. 1. Hic incipit tabula super Bello Trajano.
f. 8 Explicit Tabula super bello Traoiano.
Deo gracias quod J. de W.
f. 8v. Tabula super epistolas Pharnaombr.
Explicit Tabula quod J. de W.
ff. 10–156v. Historia de Bello Trojano.
Begins: Licet cotidie vetera recentibus obuiant.
Ends: Deo gratias quod J. de W. Amen.
The contents of the second Tabula (f. 8v.) are not in this volume.

The manuscript, which is divided into 36 books, is not an exciting volume. It is not well written, the parchment is not good, the ink a brownish grey, its date late fourteenth or early fifteenth century. It has illuminated capitals in red and blue and paragraph marks in the same colours. The chapter headings are underlined in red.

VOLUME 23

A Collection of cases, arguments, and notes by William Prynne and in his handwriting, 1634–66. Label on flyleaf is not easily decipherable but probably ran: Reports of several Cases and Arguments in Law all of Mr. William Prynne's handwriting. $11\frac{3}{4}'' \times 3\frac{7}{8}''$. 136 ff.

f. 1. The case of the borough of Tewkesbury about Mr. Edward Stephens's election. Mich. term, 1 Charles I.

f. 8v. The case of Barking parish. Mr. Alderman Fowler and other sequestrators of the vicarage of All Hallows, Barking in London, by an ordinance of Parliament, 3 February 1642/3.

f. 14. The case of 17 Charles I, before the Committee for Printing. The printers of London have exhibited a petition to this Committee for the better regulating of the art of printing and the calling in of 4 several patents concerning printing, which they conceive to be monopolies. The 4 patents are detailed. These patents were all ordered to be brought in before you this day, the last session on Monday past, and I conceive and put to you are all monopolies. The original of printing. Against the patent for Bibles. List of printed Bibles.

f. 26. St. Giles, Cripplegate case, concerning their vestry men and vestry. n.d.

f. 31. King *v.* John Wood. John Chambers on return of habeas corpus. Hil. term, 21 Charles I, King's Bench.

f. 41. Stannaries in Cornwall, a note citing Fine and Patent Rolls, 4 Henry III.

ff. 42–60v. Miscellaneous notes on a great variety of legal points.

f. 136v. (MS. reversed). The case of Thomas Worsley, esq., in H.M.'s Court of Exchequer, Hil. term, 17 Charles I. Thomas Worsley, of Manchester, co. Lancs. esq., was indicted and convicted or recusancy in co. Yorks, whereupon by an inquisition taken at the Castle of York, 25 September 5 Charles I (1629) all the land in Hoveringham and Sutton, co. Yorks, then and late before in his occupation were found by inquisition and extended and two parts of them seized into the King's hands.

f. 131v. Prynne *v.* Wharton, at Worcester House, 20 August 18 Charles II (1666); Question: Whether the house and rooms in the Tower of London, wherein Captain Wharton, Clerk to Col. Legge, Lieutenant of the Ordnance, belongs to the Lieutenant of the Ordnance and his Clerk, or to the Keeper of H.M.'s Records at the Tower.

f. 126v. John Reynolds, clerk, plt., William Court, dft. East. term, 18 Charles I, King's Bench.

f. 123v. Hawell *v.* Birrell, East term, 18 Charles I.

f. 120v. The case of Cornelius Maguire, Baron of Enniskillen, in the realm of Ireland. He was apprehended at Dublin in Ireland, 23 October 1641, as a conspirator and actor in the late rebellion. Mich. term, 20 Charles I.

f. 114v. Le Gay and Fairfax *v.* Johns. Mr. Johns, in Lent vacation 1635, libelled, in the Court of Admiralty, for 26,000 weight of Barbados tobacco, sold to him at St. Malo, in France, within the jurisdiction of the English Admiralty. East. term, 20 Charles I, in Parliament before the Judges.

f. 111v. John Body *v.* Arnot. (Admiralty case). East. term, 22 Charles I, King's Bench.

ff. 110v–80v. The same case. Mich. term, 23 Charles I, King's Bench.

f. 79v. The Wardens and Commonalty of the Grocers of London, in Parliament against Francis Welles, of London, grocer, deft. East term, 1657, King's Bench.

ff. 74v–66v. Miscellaneous notes on a variety of legal points.

PETYT MS. 512

26 Volumes

This pressmark consists of 26 volumes, lettered A to Z and AA and BB. All are uniformly bound in dark blue morocco. All except volumes C, D, E, U have the Inner Temple coat of arms on both covers; these four volumes have the Petyt coat of arms on both covers. All the volumes are fractionally near the standard size $12\frac{3}{4}'' \times 8\frac{1}{8}''$, the slight variations being due to cutting on rebinding. The volumes consist of transcripts made by or for William Petyt from the Public Records or other manuscript sources and from English and continental printed books in his researches into English history, especially parliamentary history, mainly for his controversies with Dr. Brady, or of drafts of his in such controversies. Thus volumes A, AA, B, BB, C, D, E, G, O, Q, T, Y, Z are such transcripts covering the period from the Anglo Saxons to the sixteenth century; volumes U and W are such transcripts relating to Scotland; volume X such transcripts relating to Ireland; volume F is a draft work by William Petyt concerning the Norman Conquest; volume H a draft work by him concerning successive Governments in England; volume I a draft work by him on Parliament and the Government of England after John; volume K is a draft or transcript of part of his *Jus Parliamentaria*; volume L is a draft work by him on the Rights of the Commons; volume M on the Rights of the Commons of England; volume N a draft by him on Errors of English historians on Parliament; volume P a draft work by him on the Several Governments of England; volume Q drafts and transcripts on the Norman Conquest of England; volumes R and S drafts by him on English Saxon Parliaments.

VOLUME A

A volume of transcripts and extracts, mainly from printed sources, with a few from the Public Records and manuscripts, on the coming of the Saxons to Britain. On flyleaf: 'The Britons call the Saxons to assist them against the Picts and Scots'. $12\frac{3}{4}'' \times 8\frac{1}{8}''$. 123 ff.

ff. 1–2. Elenchus Sectionum Introductionis (4 Sections).

ff. 4–123. The transcripts and extracts come mainly from the following standard English printed sources: Camden, *Brit.*, Bede, *Eccles. Hist.*, Spelman, *Gloss.* and *Conc.*, Lambard, *Archion* and *De Priscis*, Selden, *Jani Angl.* and *History of Tithes*, Somner, *Gloss.*, Crompton, *Jurisdiction of Courts*, Godwin, *De Presul.*, *Books of Statutes*, Dugdale, *Mon. Angl.*, Smith, *De Republ. Angl.*, *Plac. Parl.*, and the rarer *Law of Tithes affirmed against all oppressors*, Hubbard, *Exact Collections of all Remembrances*, and *A Method for Travel shewn by taking the View of France as it stood in the year 1608*, published by Robert Dallington; and from many more printed sources from the continent such as Grotius, *De Republ. Holl.*, *De Jure Belli*, *De Antiq. Republ. Batav.*, Lindenborg, *Legum Antiq.*, Bodin, *De Republ.*, du Fresne, *Gloss.*, *Chron. Sigeberti*, and Reyner, *De Antiq. Mon. S. Bened.* The following English chroniclers are used: Huntingdon, Symeon of Durham, Florence of Worcester, Matt. of Westminster, Matt. Paris, Knighton, Walsingham, and Brompton. The only manuscripts used are Claudius

D. 10. (Register of St. Augustine's, Canterbury) and Domitian A. 13 (Annal. Winton.). There are a few references to Parliament Rolls, Close Rolls, and Charter Rolls and a single reference each to L.T.R. Memoranda Rolls, Patent Rolls, the Journal of the House of Commons, and an Act of Parliament described as in the Rolls Chapel.

VOLUME AA

A volume of transcripts, extracts and notes, from the Public Records and other sources, printed and manuscript, William I to Henry I. On flyleaf: 'Grants, Charters, Elections of Bishops etc.'. On another flyleaf: 'Touching Grants, Charters, Elections of Bishops, Causes, Coronations, Marriages'. 331 ff.

f. 1. Charter of William I of possessions and privileges to monastery of St. Peters, Westminster, 1068, from Cart. Antiq, CC. no. 2, and inspeximus 1 Henry VI, on Patent Roll.

f. 15. Extract from Hoveden on the laws of England and the Statutes of William I, with reference on tithes to Lambard's *De Prisc*.

f. 17. Charter of William I to St. Martins without the walls of London, 2 William I, from inspeximus of 1 Richard II, on Charter Roll, with reference to Patent Roll, 1 Henry VI.

f. 18. Extract from Odericus Vitalis on peace in England, 1070.

f. 19. Extract from Matt. Paris on the third oath which William I made to the English at Berkhampsted for observation of laws of the Saxons.

f. 20. Extract from Gervase of Canterbury on the election of Lanfranc as Archbishop of Canterbury, 1070.

f. 21. Extract relating to William I from an Anonymous Author t. Henry I at end of Taylor *Treatise on Gavelkind*.

f. 23. Extract from Gervase of Canterbury on election and consecration of Lanfranc, with some notes.

f. 24. Charter of William I to St. Martins of Bec, from Selden. *Ad Eadmer*, with note from Abbrev. Chron. Angl. in Claudius D. 6 ('in Matthew Paris' own hand').

f. 27. Extract from William of Poitou.

f. 29. Extract concerning Lanfranc from Gervase of Canterbury etc.

f. 31. Second Charter of William I to St. Peter's, Westminster, 9 William I, from Faustina A. 3.

f. 36. Third Charter to St. Peter's, Westminster, 14 William I, from same, with notes from Spelman, *Gloss.* and Somner, *Gloss.*

f. 47. Fourth Charter to St. Peters, Westminster, 15 William I, from same.

f. 54. Charter of Thomas I, Archbishop of York, to St. Cuthbert of Durham, with notes from Hoveden and Godwin, *De Presul.*

f. 59. Charter of 17 or 18 William I to Dean and Chapter of Lincoln, from inspeximus, 2 Richard II, on Charter Roll. With note from Selden, *De Synodiis*.

f. 61. Excerpt from William I's Great Charter, from Lambard, *De Prisc*.

f. 63. Collection of charters and writs of the reign of William I in which he ordered equal distribution and administration of justice and law to all his subjects, Norman and English, with notes from Eadmer and Spelman, *Gloss.*

f. 65. From Register of Charters of Abbey of Evesham in Vespasian B. 24, writ, with note from Cart. Antiq., X. no. 9; another writ.

f. 66. Three charters of St. Paul's, London, From Cart. Antiq., A. nos. 1–3 (*Cart. Antiq., Rolls 1–10*, pp. 1–2) and by inspeximus on Charter Roll, 9 Edward II.

f. 67v. Six charters to St. Peters, Westminster, from Faustina A. 3, (1) of Stratford, (2) of Aldenham, (3) of land in Worcestershire, (4) of Battersea and Wandsworth, (5) of the same, (6) of Ash.

f. 69xv. Charters concerning the Archdeaconry of Durham and to Ranulf Flambard, Bishop of Durham, from *Mon. Angl.*

f. 70. Two charters for St. Augustine's, Canterbury, from Cart. Antiq., I. no. 3. (*Cart. Antiq., Rolls 1–10*, p. 129.)

f. 70v. Charter for Abbey of Ely, from Cart. Antiq., B. no. 13. (Ibid., p. 28.)

f. 71. Charter for St. Andrew's, Rochester, from *Angl. Sacra.*

Charter for St. Mary's, Thorney, from Cart. Antiq., EE. no. 7.

f. 75. Extracts from William of Poitou, on coming of William, Duke of Normandy, to England, 1066.

f. 84. Writ of William I to Lanfranc, Archbishop of Canterbury, on restoration of Bishoprics and Abbeys, from Cleopatra E. 1.

f. 85. Extract from Ordericus Vitalis.

f. 88. Plea between Gundulf, Bishop of Rochester, and Viscount de Grandebrugg, from *Angl. Sacra.*

f. 92. Extract from William of Poitou.

f. 107. Brief Relation of William I, from Anonymous Author in Taylor, *Treat. on Gavel.*

f. 141. On site, institution, privileges, gifts and other matters of St. Martins of Battle, from Domitian 2.

f. 178. Charter of Osmund, Bishop of Salisbury, under seal of William I, from inspeximus, Patent Roll, 5 Richard II.

f. 183. Promise made by William II to Lanfranc, Archbishop of Canterbury, from Eadmer, with notes from Saxon Chron., Hoveden, and Ann. of Waverley.

f. 184, 196. Charter for Dean and Chapter of Lincoln by William II, from inspeximus, Charter Roll, 2 Richard II.

f. 185. Extracts from Eadmer, Saxon Chron., Malmesbury and Alan de Insulis in Prophes. of Merlin, on life and character of William II.

f. 198. Charter for St. Mary's, York, from inspeximus, Charter Roll, 4 Edward III.

f. 214. An account of the reign of Henry I, with references to Matt. Paris, Saxon Chron., Florence of Worcester, Hemingford, Symeon of Durham, Hoveden, Contin. of Florence of Worcester, Gervase of Canterbury, Huntingdon, du Fresne, *Gloss.* etc.

f. 238. Order of coronation, from Claudius A. 3.

f. 248. On the Great Charter of Henry I, with notes from Lambard, *De Prisc.*, and a transcript in French from an ancient transcript in poss. of Peter le Neve, Rouge Croix.

f. 257. Of the gathering of the whole kingdom of England, Windsor, 14 Henry I, from Eadmer.

f. 259. 'That no one can give, dispose of or sell the hereditary right of crown or kingdom', from Malmesbury, Camden, *Brit.* and Selden, *Ad Fletam.*

f. 263. General Council, St. Peter's, Westminster, 13 May 1127, from Contin. of Florence of Worcester.

f. 268. On marriage and coronation of Matilda, daughter of Malcolm, King of Scotland, wife of Henry I, from Eadmer, Contin. of Florence of Worcester, with Dr. Brady's account in his *Compl. Hist. of Engl.* and William Petyt's answer thereto.

f. 277. Election of Ralph d'Escures, Bishop of Rochester, as Archbishop of Canterbury, from Eadmer and Contin. of Florence of Worcester.

f. 283. Great Meeting, Whitsun, (blank) Henry I, from Eadmer and Matt. Paris.

f. 288. Council held at London, 7 Henry I, on the investiture of churches and the election of prelates, from Hemingford and Spelman, *Gloss.*

f. 289. Three charters for St. Paul's, London, from Cart. Antiq. (as f. 66v above, but a very corrupt transcript) and a fourth charter from the same source (no. 4). (*Cart. Antiq., Rolls 1–10*, p. 2.)

f. 291. Another collection of charters and writs of the time of Henry I.

f. 292v. Writ to Samson, Bishop of Worcester, and Urse d'Abetot etc. of Worcestershire on plea, from Claudius D. 2.

f. 293. Charter for Abbot of Hyde, from Charter Roll by inspeximus, 4 Edward III.

f. 294. Charter for St. Andrew's, Rochester, from Cart. Antiq., F. no. 2 (*Cart. Antiq., Rolls 1–10*, p. 96.)

f. 295. Charter for Abbey of Abingdon, from Register of Abingdon, Claudius, C. 9.

Charter for Bishop of Lincoln of fair at Newark, from Vespasian E. 16.

f. 295v. Charters for Lincoln (1) Of church of St. Benedict of Wickford, (2) of toll of Eston, (3) of forfeitures in wapentakes, from same source.

f. 297. Charter for Abbey of Abingdon, from Register of Abingdon, in Claudius B. 6.

f. 297v. Charter for Lincoln of Ashby, from *Mon. Angl.*

f. 298. Charter for Abbey of Abingdon, from Register of Abingdon in Claudius B. 6.

f. 298v. Charter for Christchurch, London, on rights of burial, from Cart. Antiq., N. no. 18. (*Cart. Antiq., Rolls 11–20*, p. 68.)

f. 299. Charter for Lincoln of church of Sutton etc., from *Mon. Angl.*

f. 300. Charter for Abbey of Abingdon, from Register of Abingdon, in Claudius B. 6.

Charter for Abbey of Ramsey, of Over, from Register of Ramsey, in Vespasian E. 2.

f. 300v. Charter for Lincoln of manor of Biggleswade, from Vespasian, E. 16.

f. 301. Two charters for Abbey of Abingdon of land in London, from Reg. of Abingdon in Claudius C. 9.

f. 302. Three charters for Holy Trinity, London, from Cart. Antiq., N. nos. 3, 4 & 9 (*Cart. Antiq., Rolls 11–20*, pp. 62–3, 64–5.)

f. 304. Charter for Christ Church, Canterbury. (No reference.)

f. 304v. Charter to Hugh de Bocland, followed by charter to same in Anglo Saxon, from *Antiq. Brit.*

f. 305. Charter to St. Paul's, London, from Cart. Antiq., A. no. 4 (*Cart. Antiq., Rolls 1–10*, p. 2.)

f. 306. Writs of Henry I, from charters and privileges of Kings, Popes and Bishops, to monastery of Ely, from Tiberius A. 6.

Charter to Hervey, Bishop of Ely of castle of Helgot, co. Salop.

f. 307. Letter of Henry I on bishopric of Ely.

Charter to church of Ely.

f. 308. Charter for St. Peter's, Newminster, (Hyde) from Charter Roll, by inspeximus, 4 Edward III.

f. 312. Extract from Eadmer on sending of Peter, monk of Cluny, by Calixtus II, with note from Matt. Paris and Plea, Coram Rege, Trin. term, 12 Edward II.

f. 316. Synod at London, 26 Henry I, from Contin. of Florence of Worcester, Walter of Coventry, with notes from Spelman, *Gloss.*, and Brompton.

f. 325. Extract 3 Henry I from Spelman's *Conc.*

f. 326. Extract from Lambard, *De Prisc.*, on general pleas of counties among the Anglo Saxons.

f. 328. Extract from Malmesbury.

f. 331. Extract from Appendix of *Reflections upon the Opinions of some Modern Divines concerning the nature of Government*, 1689.

VOLUME B

A volume of miscellaneous transcripts, extracts, and notes, mainly from English printed and manuscript sources and from the Public Records. On flyleaf: Touching the Britannic Church, Deposition of King Sigebert, Treaties, Pope, De expensis Militum, Summoning of Parliaments. 299 ff.

f. 1. Touching the government of the Britannic Church, 1180, with references to Spelman, *Concil.*

f. 6. 754. Deposition of Sigebert, with references to Malmesbury and Huntingdon.

f. 8. The Council of Calchuch. From Spelman, *Conc.*, with references to Selden, *Hist. of Tithes*, etc.

f. 14. General Council, Ingelheim, 788. From Goldast, *Constit. Imper.*, with note.

f. 18. Coronation of Egbert as King of all Britain, 800. From Ann. of Church of Winchester in Domitian A. 13, Ausonius, *De Diff. Verb.*, the Register of St. Leo of Evereux, *Mon. Angl.*, with reference to Malmesbury.

f. 20. Great Gathering, 911. From Ann. of Winchcombe in Tiberius E. 4.

f. 24. Council, Synod or Parliament, Clovesho, 822. From Claudius D. 2 with references to Spelman, *Conc.*, and note from Adam Littleton, *Dict.*

f. 32., 824. Papal and Synodical Council at Clovesho. From Reg. of Church of Worcester, *Mon. Angl.*, and reference to Tiberius A. 13.

f. 37. Council of Winchester, 5 Non. November (9 November) 865. From Spelman, *Conc.*

f. 41. 855. Election and consecration of Edward as King of East English. From Matt. of Westminster.

f. 44. 971. Edgar's grant to Glastonbury. From Usher, *De Brit. Eccles. Primor.*, Malmesbury and Reg. of Church of Glastonbury.

f. 45. Concerning a plea. October 996. Grant to Wolverhampton. From autograph in possession of Dean and Chapter of Windsor, with reference to *Mon. Angl.*

f. 48. On the plea before Ethelred, with note from du Freyne, *Gloss.*

f. 50. On the General Plea held at Hertford, Alfwold, land at Streatham. From Ethelwold, Bishop of Ely, in Vespasian A. 19.

f. 52. c. 1009. The General Council at Elmham. From Claudius A. 3 (cf. Wilkins, *Concil.* 1, ff. 285–94), with references to Lambard, *De Prisc.*, Valea, *Elegant. Ling. Lat.*, Close Roll, 24 Edward I, Junius, *Nomenclat.*

f. 80. On the designation, election, and consecration of Henry, Duke of Saxony, as Emperor of Germany. From Witchind, *Gest. Saxon.*, with references to Chron. Regionis.

f. 88. On the inauguration of King Edgar. From *Anglia Sacra*, Eadmer, Life of St. Dunstan.

f. 94. The letter sent by King Canute from Rome to the orders of the kingdom of England, 1031. From Malmesbury.

f. 98. The Will of King Alfred. From the *Life of Alfred the Great*.

f. 105. On the coming of the monk of Cluny to England in the time of Henry I to perform the office of Legate. From Eadmer.

f. 107. Of the office of King as between Kings, Edward the Confessor. From Lambard, *De Prisc.*, with notes from Spelman, *Concil.*, and the letter of John (Peckham), Archbishop of Canterbury, on the liberties of the English Church.

f. 109. Edward the Confessor sent a letter to Pope Leo IX to absolve him from a vow, which the Pope did on certain terms. (No reference.)

f. 117. On the making of laws under the Anglo Saxon power, From Selden, *Jani Angl.*, and Reyner, *De Antiq. Ord. S. Bened.*

f. 119. The preambles to the Anglo Saxon laws of Alfred the Great, Athelstan, Edward the Elder, Edmund, Ethelred, and Canute. From Lambard, *De Prisc.*, Spelman, *Conc.*, and Brompton.

f. 137. On the election and coronation of Harold, son of Godwin. From Malmesbury, Camden, *Brit.*, Parliament Roll, 40 Edward III, with references to Selden, *Ad Fletam* and the *Life of Alfred the Great*.

f. 141. Coronation of Edward I and his oath. From Close Roll, 2 Edward I.

f. 144. On the nobility and ornament of the coronation of Edward I, with references to Lib. de Antiq. Leg. in archives of city of London, Patent Roll, 2 Edward I, Ann. of Ireland, Camden, *Brit.*, Hist. Angl. Script. Quinque.

f. 148. Of the Parliament at Westminster, 3 Edward I, with references to Statute of Westminster I, Coke, *2nd Inst.*, Patent Roll, 3 Edward I, Close Roll, 13 Edward I (*C.C.R. 1279–1288*, p. 367), Close Roll, 9 Edward III, Various Statutes and Constitutions of the kingdom of England from Henry III in Vespasian B. 7.

f. 157. Letter of Edward I to the Pope about the power of Parliament in refusing what the Pope desired, 19 January 1275, with references to T. Smith, *De Republ. Angl.*

f. 159. Oath of Edward I, 3 Edward I. From Ann. of Ireland in Camden, *Brit.*

f. 160. Statute of Gloucester, 6 Edward I, from Statute Roll, 6 Edward I, with translation (extract only).

f. 162. Provision on petitions in Parliament. From Close Roll, 8 Edward I (French).

f. 163. From Bundle of Letters and Writs, 10 Edward I.

f. 164. 11 Edward I. Parliament at Shrewsbury, condemnation of David ap Gruffydd. Writs of summons, with references to Walsingham, Welsh Roll, 11 Edward I, 28 June 1283.

f. 174. Letters to Sheriffs etc. on rebellion of Welsh, from Welsh Roll, 24 November 1282.

f. 177. Writs of summons to Parliament to Sheriffs, 14 June 1290, from Bundle of Summons to Parliament, 18 Edward I.

f. 179. Ordinance on petitions (French), from Close Rolls, 21 Edward I.

f. 180. Writs of summons to Council to Sheriffs, 8, 9 October 1294, Close Roll, 22 Edward I.

f. 182. 'The first formal writs I have met with in the records for summoning to Parliament 2 knights, 2 citizens, 2 burgesses, with their returns, begin 23 Edward I, years after 49 Henry III. From a certain Bundle of Writs of Summons, with Returns, to Parliament, 23 Edward I, 3 October 1295'. References to Close Roll, 23 Edward I, on prorogation of Parliament, 2 November 1295. Returns to writs given.

f. 192. 25 Edward I. Confirmation of Magna Carta and Charter of Forests from Statute Roll, 25 Edward I, with notes from Coke, *2nd. Inst.*, and Close Roll, 25 Edward I.

f. 199. Letters Patent on King's passage to Flanders (French).

f. 200. Writs of summons to Parliament to Sheriffs, 29 December 1299.

f. 202. 28 Edward I. The King, from Berwick, sent to John de Langton, Chancellor, a privy seal, to cause to be elected for Parliament, London. From New Misc. Bundle, t. Henry III, Edwards I, II, III, 29 December 1299 (French), with translation and note from Close Roll, 28 Edward I.

f. 206. 29 Edward I. Truce between English and French Kings. From Prynne, *Records*, III, p. 874 (extract only).

f. 207. Mandates on observance of Statute of Winchester, 22 June 1306.

f. 211. Memorandum on death of William de Hamilton, Chancellor, 35 Edward I.

f. 213. Writs de expensis, knights and burgesses, 13 May 1309.

f. 214. Mandates to cause those who left Parliament to return, 1 October 1311.

f. 215. Writs of summons to Parliament to Sheriffs, 4 March 1309.

f. 216. Like, 16 June 1311.

f. 217. Letters Patent sent to prelates for 12d. the mark, 14 April 1311.

f. 219. Edward II. Roll of Ordinances touching the state of the kingdom which were afterwards confirmed in Parliament at London the same year. 41 articles (French). Reference to the Archives in the Tower.

f. 243. 'These are the chapters of the Ordinances', 5 Edward II, from the MS. Laudes Britanniae in the Archives of the city of London (French). 44 heads.

f. 245. Extract from the Liber de Antiq. Leg. in same. 5 Edward II. (French).

f. 247. 'This is the writ which was sent to publish the Ordinances', 5 October 1311 (French). From Laudes Brit.

f. 248. Mandates to take castles etc. of Peter Gaveston into the King's hands, 20 January 1312.

f. 249. Writ to Sheriff of Herts. on burgesses from St. Albans, 20 January 1312, with return. From Brevia Regis, 5 Edward II.

f. 253. Section from Roll of Ordinances, 5 Edward II, about annual Parliaments (French), with translation.

f. 254. Writ de expensis to Bailiffs of St. Albans, 18 December 1311.

f. 255. The like to same, 11 October 1311.

f. 256. As f. 249 above, with translation.

f. 260. Writs of summons to Parliament to Sheriffs, 19 December 1311, with reference to writ to Sheriff of Cornwall in New Misc. Bundle, t. Henry III, etc.

f. 261. Mandates to Richard, Bishop of Durham etc. not to leave because of summons to Parliament, 20 February 1313.

f. 263. Letters Patent to come without force and arms, 30 October 1313 (French). with translation.

f. 266. Extract from Parliament Roll, 8 Edward II, for burgesses of St. Albans.

f. 268. Plea Coram Rege, Trin. term, 17 Edward II.

f. 270. Writs of summons to Parliament to Sheriffs, 24 October 1314.

f. 271. Writ of summons to Keeper of Spiritualities, York, 17 January 1316.

f. 273. Writs of summons to Council, 16 December 1315 (French).

f. 274. Mandates to Master Gilbert de Middleton etc. to come, 20 January 1317.

f. 276. Writs on recall of Parliament to Thomas, Earl of Lancaster etc. 8 June 1318.

f. 278. Writs de expensis, 9 December 1318.

f. 280. Writs of summons to Parliament to Sheriffs, 15 May 1321.

f. 281. Writs de expensis, 25 May 1319.

f. 283. Writs of summons to Parliament to Sheriffs, 20 March 1319.

f. 284. The like, 25 August 1318.

f. 285. The like, 5 August 1320.

f. 286. The like, 18 September 1321.

f. 287. The like, 26 December 1323.

f. 289. Writs de expensis, burgesses, 18 March 1324.

f. 290. The like, knights, 18 March 1324.

f. 291. Mandate to Archbishop of York concerning Archbishop of Canterbury, 8 October 1324.

f. 293. Writ that men of ancient demesne are not to contribute to expenses of knights, 19 Edward II, from Register of Writs, with notes from Close Roll, 15 Edward II, and Roman Roll, 3 Edward III, both for William de Herlaston.

f. 294. Petition of William de Herlaston to Parliament (French), t. Edward II. From New Misc. Bundle, t. Henry III, etc.

f. 295. Extracts from Fitzherbert, *La Second Part du Graund Abridg.*, Mich. term, 11 Henry IV, on replevin, avowry and deliverance.

f. 297. Writs de expensis, knights, 5 December 1325.

f. 298. On exoneration from tallage of men of Chippenham. From L.T.R., Mem. Roll, Comm. Rec. Trin. term, 19 Edward II, 28 April 1326.

VOLUME BB

A volume of transcripts, extracts, and notes from the Public Records and other sources, printed and manuscript, John to Henry III. On flyleaf: Coronations, Marriages, Parliaments etc. On another flyleaf: Touching Coronations, Marriages, Parliaments, de expensis militum, pardons, safe conducts. 218 ff.

Last flyleaf (f. 2). On the election and coronation of John, Count of Mortain, as King of England, from Matt. Paris.

f. 3v. Charter made, 1 John, on lessening the fees for the great seal, from Register in Archives of Archbishop of Canterbury.

f. 4. On the coronation of Isabella, wife of King John, giving the charter of her dower, 5 May 1203, with late enrolment, from Charter Roll.

f. 10. On the pact at Runymead, 17 John, from Close Roll, Matt. Paris, Close Roll, 28 Henry III. Agreement between King and Barons, with notes from Matt. Paris and Walter of Coventry.

f. 15. Letter from Louis, eldest son of King of France, to Abbot of St. Augustine's, Canterbury, from. Chron. W. Thorne, 1216.

f. 20. Letters Patent to men of Seaford, to men of Hastings, Sandwich etc. 2, 3 September 1216.

f. 22. Capitula between King John and the Barons and Articles of Magna Carta etc. from Matt. Paris.

f. 36. The Common Council held at St. Paul's, 11 Henry III, from MS. Stat. in poss. of William Petyt, with notes from Close Roll, 2 Henry III, Patent Roll, 3 Henry III.

f. 38. On the Common Council of the whole realm, or Parliament, Westminster, 9 Henry III, from Matt. Paris, Vitellius E. 13, with reference to certiorari of trespass, between Bishop of Winchester and John Giffard, 3 Richard II, about afforestation, in Tower of London, Stat. Roll, 25 Edward I, Magna Carta, and 25 Edward I, Confirmatio Cartarum.

f. 43. Diatribe of the Barons, two Councils, Westminster, 29 & 30 Henry III, Camden, *Brit.*, *Mon.*, Selden, *Tit. of Hon.*, Spelman, *Gloss.*, Close Roll, 4 Henry III.

f. 51. Extract from Bracton.

f. 52. Extract from Matt. Paris 'of a most general Parliament at Westminster, 30 Henry III, in which letters of grievance were sent to the Pope'.

f. 55. Effect of a sentence of excommunication in the Great Hall at Westminster, 37 Henry III, against transgressors of the liberties of the church etc., with references to Matt. Paris, Patent Roll, 37 Henry III, Fleta, Rastell, *Stat.*, Lib. de Antiq. Leg. in Archives of city of London.

f. 67. 'A most remarkable record never before found out but myself that I ever heard of, concerning a marriage to be had between Prince Edward and Eleanor, sister to the King of Castile, 38 Henry III, which marriage was assented to by the Common Council of the whole Kingdom of England', with references to Patent Roll, 38 Henry III, and note from Patent Roll, 48 Edward III.

f. 72. On the Mad Parliament held at Oxford, 42 Henry III, from Patent Roll, with notes from Parl. Roll, 45 Edward III, Lib. de Antiq. Leg.

f. 83. General Proclamation, 5 August 1261, from Patent Roll.

f. 89. Mandate on knights coming to King, 18 February 1261, with reference to Patent Roll, 18 February 1261.

f. 97. Letters Patent for community of prelates of England, 18 October 1264.

f. 99. Letters Patent on form of peace between King and Barons, June 1264.

f. 105. Letters Patent concerning Robert de Clifford and others who despised the commands, 3 July 1264.

f. 108. Letters Patent, 6 July 1264 etc., with note from Lib. de Antiq. Leg.

f. 111. Letters Patent on proclamation against undue tallage, 20 December 1263.

f. 115. Extract from Chron. of Melrose on battle of Lewes, 1264.

f. 122. Form of writs of summons to Parliament, 14 December 1264, from Close Roll, and writs de expensis, 15 February 1265.

f. 134. Extract from Chron. of Melrose on battle of Evesham, 1265.

f. 141. On the escape of Prince Edward with references to Patent Roll, 49 Henry III, and extracts, 45–49 Henry III.

f. 143. Letters Patent on ecclesiastical persons robbed in disturbance of realm, 8 December 1264.

f. 144. Mandates to Sheriffs, 23 February 1265.

f. 145. Writs de expensis, 15 February 1265.

f. 146. Writs of summons to Parliament, 14 December 1264, 20 January 1265.

f. 156. Mandate to Dean and Chapter of Salisbury, 15 May 1265.

f. 157. Mandate to Sheriff of York, 3 May 1266.

f. 159. Letters Patent of pardon to Gilbert de Clare, Earl of Gloucester and Hertford, 15 June 1267 (French).

f. 163. References to Patent Rolls, 7 Edward II, 12 Edward II, Statute, from MS. Stat. in poss. of William Petyt, Close Roll, 1 Edward III.

f. 168. Letters Patent of general pardon for city of London, 5 June 1267 (French), with notes from Close Roll, 51 Henry III, Patent Roll, 7 Edward I, Plea Coram Rege, Trin. term, 12 Edward II.

f. 171. Letter to King of France, 20 September 1268, with note from du Fresne, *Gloss.*

f. 173. Statute of Marlborough, 52 Henry III, from Coke, *2nd Inst.*, with notes from Patent Roll, 7 Edward II, 11 Edward III, Year Book, East. term 39 Edward III, Close Roll, 1 Richard II.

f. 178. Preamble to Statute of Marlborough, 52 Henry III, from Coke, *2nd Inst.*, with notes from Patent Roll, 11 Edward III, Close Roll, 1 Richard II, du Fresne, *Gloss.*

f. 183. Grant of 20th., 54 Henry III, translation of relics of Edward the Confessor, from Chron. Thomas Wykes.

f. 188. Mandate on general proclamation on absolution of Henry III from oath on Provisions of Oxford, 2 May 1262, with references to Bulls of Alexander IV, 13 April 1261, from Cleopatra E. 1, and Urban IV, 24 March 1264.

f. 196. Letter to Urban IV, 11 December 1261, from Close Roll.

f. 198. Extract from Brady, *Compl. Hist. of Engl.*, on scutage or aid imposed by Common Council of Realm.

f. 203. Letters of protection and safe conduct for Henry de Boreham, 2 May 1270.

f. 208. Extracts from Matt. of West. and Annals of Waverley on excess of Henry III, departure of Prince Edward overseas and on death of Henry III.

f. 213. Letters Patent on preservation of peace in Ireland, 7 December 1272.

f. 215. Mandate on proclamation of King's peace, 23 November 1272.

f. 217. Extracts from Matt. of West. and Ann. of Wav. on great meeting held at Westminster after death of Henry III.

VOLUME C

A volume of transcripts, extracts, and notes from English and continental printed and English manuscript sources, with a very few references to the Public Records. On flyleaf: Touching the Saxon Kings, their Coronation, Oaths, Government, Laws etc. Vol. I. $12\frac{3}{4}'' \times 8\frac{1}{8}''$. 246 ff.

f. 1. Gildas, touching the ancient British Church. From Stillingfleet, *Orig. Brit.*, Epistola Gild.

f. 2. Of the time the Danes came to England. From Spelman, *Conc.*

f. 4. Monumenta Parliamentaria Anglo Saxonica.

f. 5. The Anglo Saxon alphabet.

f. 8. The glory of Rome left the island of Britain. From Bede, *Eccles. Hist.*, Claverius, *Germ. Antiq.*, with note from Grotius, *De Repl. Holl.*

f. 13. The Heptarchy of the Anglo Saxons and their successors in Britain. From Spelman, *Conc.*

f. 19. The Common Council of Canterbury, held 5 Ides January (9 January) 605. From the same, with note from Bede, *Eccles. Hist.*

f. 21. Ethelbert's charter to the monks of St. Augustine's, Canterbury. From Cart. Antiq., I. no. 18 (*Hist. Mon. St. August., Canterbury* (R.S.), p. 116), with references to Charter Roll, 20 Edward II, 36 Edward III.

f. 25. Charter of Wulfhere, King of Mercia and the South English. From Gunton, *Hist. of Church of Peterborough.*

f. 29. The Council at Rome under Pope Agatho, 680, on matters concerning the British Church. From Spelman, *Conc.*

f. 33. 688. Baldred, King of Kent, from Malmesbury.

f. 34. 692. Charter of Nothelm, King of the South Saxons. From *Mon. Angl.*

f. 35. On the Provincial Parliament of Kent held at Bearstead, 694. From Spelman, *Conc.*, with notes from *Germ. Antiq.*, and Saxon Chron.

f. 40. Charter of Wihtred. King of Kent. From Spelman, *Conc.*, with note from Somner, *Antiq. of Canterbury.*

f. 44. 705. Synod by Archbishop Beorhtweald. From Hody, *Hist. of Engl. Coun. and Convoc.*

f. 48. 709. Letter from Pope Constantine I to Beorhtweald. From Malmesbury, *Mon. Angl.*, with note from Stillingfleet, *Orig. Brit.*

f. 52. Charter of Coelred, King of Mercia. From Reg. of Abbey of Evesham in Vespasian B. 24.

f. 55. Preamble to the Laws of Ini. From Lambard, *De Prisc.* (Anglo Saxon and Latin in parallel columns), Brompton, with notes from Spelman, *Gloss.*, and du Freyne, *Gloss.*

f. 57. Charter of Ini to Glastonbury, 724. From *Mon. Angl.*

f. 59. 725. The Common Council of Ini. From the MS. Hist. of Glastonbury, with reference to *Mon. Angl.* and note from Stillingfleet, *Orig. Brit.*

f. 65. 747. Charter of Eadbert, King of Kent. From W. Thorne from the muniments of Christ Church, Canterbury.

f. 66. More of the Councils of the ancient Germans or the administration of the Teutonic Empire under Charlemagne, 768. From Hincmar, Archbishop of Rheims and Congringius, with notes from Spelman, *Gloss.*, Lambard, *Archion.*, Selden, *Jani Angl.*, Spelman, *Conc.*, Brady, *Compl. Hist.*

f. 74. 773. Charter of Egbert. From Augustus A. 2.

f. 76. 799. Charter of Ethelbald. From Spelman, *Conc.*

f. 79. The expulsion of Sigeberht, King of the West Saxons, and the election of Cynewulf in his place. From Malmesbury, Huntingdon, Brompton.

f. 81. 758. The deposition of Beonred, King of Mercia. From Matt. of Westminster.

f. 82. 3 August 773. Charter of Ceadwalla to Chichester. From the Reg. of the Cathedral Church of Chichester in poss. of the Dean and Chapter.

f. 84. 787. The appointment of the Anglo Saxon Kings of the Council of Celchyth (Chelsea). From Spelman, *Conc.*, with note from Alexander Scott, *Vocabulary*.

f. 86. Decree of the Council of Celchyth. From Selden, *Hist. of Tithes* etc.

f. 89. 788. On the General Council of Ingelheim under Charlemagne. From Goldhast, *Constit. Imperial.*, with various notes from foreign printed sources.

f. 93. Charter donated by King Offa. From Tiberius A. 13.

f. 95. Gathering Synod or Parliament celebrated at Celchyth, 793. From Matt. Paris, Addit., and charter of inspeximus and confirmation in Charter Roll, 8 Edward II, for Abbot and Convent of St. Albans.

f. 101. The Council of St. Albans under Offa, 794. From Spelman, *Conc.*

f. 102. 796. Egfrid's charter to St. Albans. From Matt. Paris, Addit.

f. 105. 798. The Great Council at Clovesho. From Spelman, *Conc.*

f. 107. 799. Cenwulf's charter to Christ Church, Canterbury. From Thorne.

f. 108. Cenwulf's charter to Wells. From Godwin, *De Presul.*

f. 109. 800. Coronation of Egbert. From Ann. of Church of Winchester in Domitian A. 13, Ausonius, *De Diff. Verb.*, *Mon. Angl.*, with notes from Malmesbury and *Anglia Sacra*.

f. 114. 801. The dispute between King Cenwulf and Bishop Whihthun. From Reg. of Cath. Church of Chichester, *Mon. Angl.*, with reference to Spelman, *Conc.*

f. 111. The Provincial Synod at Clovesho, 801. From Spelman, *Conc.*

f. 116. 804. At a certain Parliamentary Synod at Clovesho, charter, from *Mon. Angl.*

f. 119. 805. Charter of Cuthred, King of Kent, to Christ Church, Canterbury. From Thorne.

f. 120. 811. Great Gathering. From Ann. of Winchcombe in Tiberius E. 4.

f. 124. 816. Great Synod at Celchyth. From Spelman, *Conc.*

f. 125. 817. Cenwulf's charter to Worcester. From Tiberius A. 13.

f. 127. 821. Cenwulf's charter to Abingdon. From Charter Roll, 10 Edward III.

f. 129. On the Annual Gathering or Parliament at Shewsham, al. Clovesho, 822. From Camden, *Brit.*, with notes from Somner, *Dict.*, Bede, *Eccles. Hist.*, Spelman, *Conc.*

f. 131. 822. On the Great Synod, Council or Parliament at Clovesho on injuries to Archbishop Wulfred by King Cenwulf. From Claudius D. 2., with reference to Spelman, *Conc.*, and note from A. Littleton, *Dict.*

f. 135. 824. Pontifical Synod at Clovesho. From Tiberius A. 13, with reference to Spelman, *Conc.*

f. 139. 825. Synod at Clovesho, charter of Archbishop Wulfred restoring Denton to the church of Selsey. From Reg. of Cath. Church of Chichester, with reference to *Mon. Angl.*

f. 141. 833. King Wigtaf and the monastery of Heanbury. From Reg. of Church of Worcester in Tiberius A. 13.

f. 143. 833. The Pan Anglican Council of London, monastery of Crowland. From *Mon. Angl.*, with reference to Spelman, *Conc.*

f. 150. 835. Charter of Egbert to Abingdon. From the Reg. of the monastery of Abingdon in Claudius C. 9.

f. 152. 838. The Pan Anglican Council at Kingston, charter of Egbert to Christ Church, Canterbury. From Claudius D. 2, Augustus A. 2, with reference to Spelman, *Conc.*

f. 154. 844. Council at Canterbury, the manner and form of causes judicially decided among the Anglo Saxons is described. From Somner, *Antiq. of Canterbury.*

f. 160. 845. At Christmas in royal place called Tamworth, King Beothwulf's grant to Bishop Heaberthtt. From Tiberius A. 13.

f. 163. 854. King Beothwulf's grant to Bredon. From Gunton, *Hist. of Church of Peterborough.*

f. 167. 855. Election of Edmund as King of Province of East England. From Matt. of Westminster.

f. 168. 5 Non. November (9 November) 855. The Pan Anglican Council at Winchester. From Spelman, *Conc.*, two parallel texts from Ingulf and Malmesbury, with notes from Florence of Worcester, the *Life of King Alfred.*

f. 172. 855. Grant of King Ethelwulf, King of West Saxons, to Alher, his prince. From Charter Roll, 36 Edward III.

f. 174. 856. Grant by Edwig to Chichester. From *Mon. Angl.*

f. 176. 864. Grant by King Burgred to Bishop Eahlhun. From Tiberius A. 13.

f. 178. 869. Grant by King Burgred to Wulflafe, with Anglo Saxon boundaries. From Augustus A. 2.

f. 180. 876. Peace between King Alfred and Guthrum, King of East Anglia. From *Life of King Alfred.*

f. 182. 881–900. Will of King Alfred the Great. From Life of *Alfred the Great*, with notes from Coke, *2nd Inst.*, Camden, *Brit.*, and Casney, *Catal. Glor. Mundi.*

f. 190. 904. Charter of Ethelfrid to Glastonbury. From Reg. of Glastonbury in poss. of Ralph Sheldon, of Beoley, co. Worcs., with reference to *Mon. Angl.* for charter of Edred of Wrighton, co. Somerset.

f. 192. Great Council or Synod. 905. The Bishops of Winchester and Sherborne divided possessions. From Antiq. Brit. Eccles., Symeon of Durham, Roff. Hist., *Mon. Angl.*, Godwin, *De Presul.*, Spelman, *Conc.*

f. 195. 920. On the coronation of Henry, Duke of Saxony, as Emperor in Germany. From Witichind, *De Gest. Saxon.*, with reference to Chron. Reg.

f. 202. 924. On the election and coronation of Athelstan at Kingston. From Malmesbury, with notes from Fasc. Temp. and Matt. of Westminster.

f. 204. 943. Grant by King Athelstan to Abbey of Middleton. From Reg. of Abbey of Middleton in K.R. Exch., with reference to *Mon. Angl.*

f. 209. 928. Council celebrated at Grateley, Laws of Athelstan. From Lambard, *De Prisc.*, with references to Spelman, *Conc.*, Grotius, *De Antiq. Republ. Batav.*

f. 212. 929. Grant by King Athelstan to Church of St. Mary's in city of Worcester. From Tiberius A. 13.

f. 214. 930. Grant by King Athelstan to Archbishop of York. From the Reg. of Church of St. Peter's, York, in Claudius B. 3.

f. 217. King Athelstan to Lulling Minster. From *Mon. Angl.* 930.

f. 220. 936. On the coronation of Odo, son of Henry, Duke of Saxony, as Emperor of Germany. From Witchind, *De Gest. Saxon.*

f. 226. Grant of King Edmund to Glastonbury. From *Mon. Angl.*

f. 228. 948. King Edred concerning the monastery of Crowland. From Ingulf, with reference to Patent Roll, 17 Richard II.

f. 238. 945. Grant of King Edred to Abingdon. From Brief Reg. in Claudius C. 9.

f. 240. 955. The like. From the same, with note from Matt. of Westminster.

f. 242. 957. Grant of privileges by King Brithelm to Bishopric of Selsey. From *Mon. Angl.*

f. 244. 958. Grant by King Edwy to Bishop Oscytel. From Great White Reg. in possession of Dean and Chapter of York, with reference to *Mon. Angl.*

f. 246. 959. King Edmund. From Florence of Worcester, with note from Grotius, *De Republ. Holl.*

VOLUME D

A volume of transcripts, extracts, and notes from English and continental printed and English manuscript sources, with a few references to the Public Records.

On flyleaf: Touching the Saxon Kings, their Coronation, Oaths, Laws, Government etc. On first original flyleaf: Monument. Parl. Anglo Saxon. Vol. II. 241 ff.

f. 1. The death of King Edmund. From Florence of Worcester, with note from Grotius, *De Republ. Holl.*

f. 2. 959. The inauguration of Edgar. From *Anglia Sacra*, with notes from Florence of Worcester and Ingulf.

f. 8. 959. The Council of the Realm called by Edgar at Brandenford. From Spelman, *Conc.*, and Antiq. Brit.

f. 9. 960. King Edgar to minister Wulfri. From Augustus A. 2.

f. 12. 963. King Edgar grants Sherborne to Aslac. From *Mon. Angl.*, with note from Spelman, *Gloss.*

f. 15. 964. King Edgar's charter of Oswaldeslaw. From Patent Roll, 4 Edward IV.

f. 21. Extract from Vespasian A. 8.

f. 24. 970. Promise or oath of King Edward or Ethelred on the day of his coronation at Kingston to Dunstan, Archbishop of Canterbury. From *Life of Alfred the Great.*

f. 26. Form of oath which the Saxon Kings took on the day of their coronation. From the same. 'About the year 970'. Anglo Saxon and Latin in parallel columns.

f. 28. 970. Charter of King Edgar to St. Peters, Ely. From Cart. Antiq., B. no. 11. (*Cart. Antiq., Rolls 1–10* (P.R.S.), pp. 24–6.)

f. 32. 971. Charter of King Edgar to Glastonbury. From Usher, *De Brit. Eccl. Primor.*, with notes from Malmesbury and Antiq. Eccl. Glaston.

f. 34. 973. Charter of King Edgar to Glastonbury. From Reg. of Glastonbury in poss. of Ralph Sheldon, with note from Addit. to *Mon. Angl.*

f. 35. 974. Charter of King Edgar to monastery of Ramsey. From Charter Roll, 8 Edward III.

f. 42. Foundation of Abbey of Ramsey. From the Reg. of Ramsey in K.R. Misc. Books (*Cart. Mon. de Rams.* (R.S.), II, pp. 51–9), with references to Charter Roll, 8 Edward III, Reyner, *De Antiq. Mon. S. Bened.*

f. 44. 977. Controversy on celibacy between Edward the Martyr and Archbishop Dunstan. From Antiq. Brit.

f. 47. On the general plea held at Hertford. Adelwold bought 7 hides in Streatham. From the Life of Athelwold in Vespasian A. 19.

f. 50. 979. On the election, coronation, promise or oath of Ethelred, King of the Anglo Saxons. From Claudius A. 3, with notes from Ausonius, *De Diff. Verb. etc.*

f. 64. 994. Charter of King Ethelred to Wilton. From Cart. of Wilton in poss. of Earl of Pembroke, with reference to *Mon. Angl.*, Anglo Saxon boundaries, with note from *Anglia Sacra.*

f. 66. 994. Charter of Ethelred to Aelfweald, Bishop of Exeter, of St. Petroc. From Charter Roll, 36 Edward III.

f. 69. 996. On the plea or public gathering, October, 12 Ethelred. From the original in poss. of Dean and Chapter of Windsor, with reference to *Mon. Angl.*, and note from du Freyne, *Gloss.*

f. 75. 1001. Charter of Ethelred of immunities to Bradford. From *Mon. Angl.*

f. 80. 1009. The Great Council of Elmham, at Whitsun, Decree. From Spelman, *Conc.*, with note from the same and from Lambard, *De Prisc.*, Valla, *Elegant. Lat. Ling.*, Close Roll, 24 Edward I.

f. 92. 1016. On election and coronation of Edmund Ironside. From *Anglia Sacra*, with note from Thomas Rudborne.

f. 94. 1017. Confirmation of Canute in the kindgom of England. From Florence of Worcester and Brompton.

f. 95. King Canute sends a letter to Rome. From Malmesbury.

f. 97. King Canute's charter to monastery of Bury St. Edmunds. From Charter Roll, 5 Edward II.

f. 101. 1019. King Canute's charter to Exeter, destroyed by pagans. From Charter Roll, 36 Edward III.

f. 105. 1022. Council or Parliament at Winchester, held by Canute. From letter of Coke, then Chief Justice of Bench, *9th Rep.*

f. 108. The great plea held at Oxford after the death of Canute on the succession to the kingdom. From Brompton, with note from Florence of Worcester.

f. 112. 1054. Election and coronation of Edward the Confessor. From the Annals of Winchester in Domitian A. 13, with reference to *Mon. Angl.*

f. 117. More of the appointment of Edward the Confessor to the kingdom of England. From Huntingdon and Matt. of Westminster.

f. 118. 1054. Charter of Edward the Confessor to St. Peter's of Ghent in Flanders. From Cart. Antiq., T. no. 10. (*Cart. Antiq., Rolls 10–20*, pp. 175–8.)

f. 123. 1055. The Decree of Edward the Confessor. The Second Charter to St. Peter's, Westminster. From the charter in the Cotton Collection.

f. 127. 1052. The Witanagemot or Parliament of London. From Brompton.

f. 132. 'What was old and new in the Dukes and Kings of the Saxons and English'. With references to Shaftnaburg, *Hist. Germ.*, and *Chron. Sigebert.*

f. 134. 1056. Abbot Elfric sent to Pope Leo. From Reyner, *De Antiq. mon. S. Bened.*

f. 135. 1059. Letters Patent of Edward the Confessor to the Abbey of St. Denis, Paris. From the Cart. of St. Denis, with reference to *Mon. Angl.*

f. 140. 1059. Charter of Edward the Confessor to the church of Rouen. From Patent Roll, 4 Richard II.

f. 140. 1065. Charter of Edward the Confessor to Malmesbury. From Patent Roll, 1 Henry IV.

f. 143. 1066. Large privileges granted by Papal Bull to St. Peter's, Westminster, confirmed by Edward the Confessor. From Cart. of Westminster in the Cotton Library.

f. 153. Coronation of Harold, son of Earl Godwin. From Malmesbury, Camden, *Brit.*, Parliament Roll, 40 Edward III, with reference to Selden, *Ad Fletam*, *Life of King Alfred.*

f. 160. Appendix to the Memorials of Anglo Saxon Parliaments. Of the jurisdiction of the Parliament of the Anglo Saxons. From Selden, *Titles of Honor*, Brompton, Bede, *Eccles. Hist.* etc.

f. 168. The manner, time and business of the Folkmoot among the Anglo Saxons as shown in the laws of Edward the Confessor. From Spelman, *Gloss.*

f. 170. Of the officials and magistrates of the lesser orders in the time of the Anglo Saxons and later. From Lambard, *Duties of Constables.*

f. 176. On the ancient forms of Wills in the times of the Anglo Saxons. A definition of words. From Lambard, *Perambul. of Kent*, Selden, *Titles of Honor*, with reference to Milles, *Cat. of Honor and Nobility*.

f. 188. Collections from Camden, *Brit.*, Hotoman, *Juriscons. Franco Gallia*, Somner, *Gloss.*, Lambard, *Archion*, Spelman, *Gloss.*

f. 193. The Modus tenendi Parliamentum, From Vespasian B. 7. Certified by George Holmes and William Prichard, with note from Selden, *Titles of Honor*.

f. 208. On the making of laws under the Anglo Saxon rule. From Selden, *Jani Angl.*, Reyner, *De Antiq. mon. S. Bened.*

f. 210. In what manner St. Edward the Confessor was elected King of England. From Ailred, Abbot of Rievaulx.

f. 212. On the office of the King of England as found among the laws of Edward the Confessor. From Lambard, *De Prisc.*, with note from Spelman, *Conc.* On the letter of John Peckham, Archbishop of Canterbury, to Edward I, on the liberties of the English Church.

f. 214. The General Pleas of Counties among the Anglo Saxons. From Lambard, *De Prisc.*

f. 217. Two Records which belong to the time of Edward the Confessor, William I, and William II, with many notable reasons especially against the Norman Conquest. From Cart. Antiq., EE. no. 1.

f. 224. An old memorandum on the promotion and dignity of the orders and grades of the Anglo Saxons. From Milles, *Cat. of Honor*, with references to Spelman, *Gloss.*, du Freyne, *Gloss.*, Somner, *Gloss.*, Lambard, *De Prisc.*, Somner, *Dict.*, Pipe Roll, 5 Stephen (r. 31 Henry I). Fleta, Funger, *Lex. Phil.*, and A. Littleton, *Dict.*

f. 231. On the Gemotes of the Anglo Saxons. From Spelman, *Gloss.*, with notes from Goldast, *Almann.*, *Chron. of Sigebert.*, Claudius D. 2 etc., with reference to Spelman, *Conc.*

f. 238. On the tribute of Danegeld first imposed in the time of King Ethelred. From Spelman, *Gloss.*, and the Black Book of the Exchequer, with Brompton and Florence of Worcester.

VOLUME E

A volume of miscellaneous transcripts and extracts, almost entirely from English printed and manuscript sources, with some references to the Public Records. On flyleaf: 'Concerning William the First, his oath, government, consecration, coronation'. On another flyleaf: 'Monumenta Parliamentaria Anglo Normannica tempore Willelmi 1mi'. 247 ff.

f. 1. 'Mr. Prynne's Opinion how the Parliamentary Records of Ancient Times came to be embezzled, lost and destroyed. I will use his own words', from Prynne's Preface to Cotton's *Exact Abridgement of the Records in the Tower of London*, with notes from Prynne's *Register of Parliamentary Writs* and Parliament Roll, 1 Henry IV.

f. 3. On the election and coronation of William, Duke of Normandy, to the kingdom of England, with the oath made to the English, according to the custom of the Saxon Kings, from the Brief Relation concerning King William, by Sylvanus Taylor, at the end of the *Treat. on Gavel.* References to Malmesbury, William of Poitou, Hoveden, Florence of Worcester, Symeon of Durham, Roger of Wendover in Otto B. 5, Ordericus Vitalis and Rerum Brit. Script.

f. 7. Restoration of lands to St. Paul's by William I at his coronation, from a MS. Book in the poss. of the Dean and Chapter of St. Paul's.

f. 9. On the deeds of King William I after his coronation, from 'the Gesta of William, Duke of Normandy and King of England, by William of Poitou, written contemporaneously'.

f. 14. The Great Charter of William I which he himself made for the benefit of the English, from Lambard, *De Prisc.*

f. 20x. The Second Oath William I made at Hastings that he would inviolably observe the laws of Edward the Confessor, from the Brief Chronicle of England in Claudius D. 6 'and written as it seems by Matthew Paris', with reference to Selden, *Ad Eadmer*.

f. 21x. The Charter of William I enriching the monastery of St. Peter's, Westminster, from Cartae Antiquae CC, no. 2, with reference to Patent Roll, 1 Henry VI.

f. 32x. The gift of a Saxon, Ingelric, to St. Martin's, London, 2 William I, from Charter Roll, 19 Henry VI, with references to Charter Roll, 1 Richard II, and Patent Roll, 1 Henry VI.

f. 38. The laws of Edward which William the Bastard afterwards confirmed. From Lambard, *De Prisc.*, with a note from the relation of D. Vaughan in the case of Thomas *v.* Birch, in Exchequer Chamber in the time of Charles II.

f. 49. 1070. None to be denied justice and right, from Ordericus Vitalis.

f. 51. Charter of William I confirming to the Abbey of Fecamp the land of Steyning etc., co. Southampton, from Cartae Antiq., S. no. 1. (*Cart. Antiq., Rolls 11–20*, pp. 147–8.)

f. 53. Writ of William I to Lanfranc etc. from Cleopatra E. 1.

f. 54. Plea at Pinnenden between Lanfranc, Archbishop of Canterbury, and Odo, Bishop of Bayeux, from Selden, *Ad Eadmer*.

f. 61. Extract from above from Dr. Brady's *Compl. Hist. of Engl.*, Preface.

f. 63. Plea in the time of William I between the Bishop of Rochester and Picot, Viscount of Grandbrigge, with note from Preface to first edition of *Anglia Sacra*.

f. 67. Confirmation on the agreement on certain lands between Bishop Wulfstan and Walter, Abbot of Evesham, in the time of William I, from Tiberius A. 13.

f. 71. Confirmation of the land of St. Edward by William I, 4 William I, from Lambard *De Prisc.*, with notes from Selden, *Ad Eadmer* and Huntingdon.

f. 74. Election of Lanfranc as Archbishop of Canterbury, from Gervase of Canterbury, with notes from Relation of William I in Taylor, *Treat. on Gavel.*, *Antiq. Brit.*, Roger of Chester, Joraval, *Hist. Chron. Sax. Cont.*

f. 78. 1071. The Great Gathering at Pedreda. Quarrel, Lanfranc,Archbishop of Canterbury, and Bishop of Worcester, from Ralph de Diceto.

f. 80. The Third Oath of William I made to the English at Berkhamsted on the relics of St. Alban, from Selden, *Ad Eadmer*, Matt. Paris and Malmesbury.

f. 84. 1075. Council at Westminster, 9 William I. The Third Charter of William I to Westminster, from Faustina A. 3.

f. 89. 13 or 14 William I. Two Pleas held at Kentford, from the charter to the monastery of Ely in Tiberius A. 6.

f. 97. c. 14 William I. The Universal Synod called at Westminster. The Third Charter to Westminster, from the Cart. of Westminster in Faustina A. 3., with notes from Somner, *Gloss.*

f. 106. 1081. The case between Anfalt, Bishop, and Baldwin, Abbot of St. Edmund's, at Winchester, 15 William I, from *Mon. Angl.*, with note from L.T.R. Mem. Roll, Comm. Recorda, Trin. term, 7 Edward II.

f. 113. 15 William I granted liberties of the church. Fourth Charter from Cart. of Westminster in Faustina A. 3.

f. 120. 1083. 16 William I. Charter of Thomas, Archbishop of York, to St. Cuthbert, from Hoveden, with note from Godwin, *De Presul.*

f. 125. 17 or 18 William I. General law for Dean and Chapter of Lincoln, from Charter Roll, 2 Richard II, with note from Selden, *De Synod.*

f. 128. Charter of William I to Durham, 18 William I, from Cart. Antiq., B. no. 4 (*Cart. Antiq., Rolls 1–10*, p. 21) with note from *Mon. Angl.*

f. 133. 1085, 19 or 20 William I. Great Council of the kingdom of England, from Saxon Chron.

f. 134. On the gathering of all orders of the kingdom at Salisbury, 20 William I, to swear fealty, from Ann. of Waverley, Camden, *Brit.* Saxon Chron., with note from Brief Relation of William I in Taylor, *Treat. on Gavel.*

f. 136. Consecration of Matilda, wife of William I, from Charter Roll, 19 Henry VI, for Dean of St. Martins, with references to Charter Roll, 1 Richard II, and Patent Roll, 1 Henry VI.

f. 143. Excerpt from the Great Charter of William I on rights of clients and fees, from Lambard, *De Prisc.*

f. 144. Exclamation of the kingdom of England, William I, from Matt. Paris, with note from Malmesbury.

f. 150. Certain Positions against the theory of the absolute conquest of England by William I, in a pamphlet by Robert Brady. *A Full and Clear Answer to a Book written by William Petyt, esq.*, printed in 1680, with notes from Huntingdon and Gale, Hist. Brit. in *Scriptores XV.*

f. 157. Evidence from the charters of William I, William II, and Henry I against a full conquest of England, from Cart. Antiq., CC. no. 2, Patent Roll, 1 Henry VI, Charter Roll, 1 Richard II, Patent Roll, 1 Henry VI, Cart. Antiq., B. no. 4 (*Cart. Antiq., Rolls 1–10*, p. 21) and note from Alan de Insulis, *Prophet. Merlini.*

f. 160. Charter of Matilda, Queen of William I, to Malmesbury, from Patent Roll, 5 Edward IV.

f. 162. Charter of William II to Dean and Chapter of Lincoln, from Charter Roll, 2 Richard II and from Chron. of Abingdon in Claudius B. 6.

f. 162v. Charters of Henry I, from *Mon. Angl.* and MS. of Roger Owen esq. in poss. of John Trevor, Master of the Rolls.

f. 163. 'Not called Conqueror in any of his letters patent or charters, nor by histories, Malmesbury, Newburgh, Hoveden, Chron. of Melrose'.

f. 165. Evidence from Camden, Spelman, and John Davies, Attorney General of Ireland, James I, in the case of the household of Sherborne, t. William I.

f. 166. The general law William I promulgated for the restoration of the English to the land from which they were ejected. Examples from a certain old MS. Book, which was in the possession of Henry Spelman, 1640, with references to Spelman, *Gloss.*, *Le Primer Report des Cases collect et digest.* per Sir John Davys, kt., and Camden, *Brit.*

f. 170. Evidence by Daniel that William I never claimed any power of conquest, from Daniel, *Hist.*

f. 172. Evidence of Edward, Earl of Clarendon, Chancellor, against the Norman Conquest of England. 'The Earl of Clarendon's Survey of Mr. Hobbes' *Leviathan*, with reference to Dr. Brady's like lewd principles concerning our English constitution and government published to the world in several volumes in the last two reigns'.

f. 180. 'Further evidence of John Davis de Laudibus legum Anglie against the Norman Conquest, from Sir J. Davis' Reports in the preface dedicatory to Thomas, Lord Ellesmere, Chancellor'.

f. 185. 'Evidence of Selden against the conquest of England by the Normans', from his *Hist. of Tithes*, with references.

f. 189. 'Evidence of Sylvanus Taylor that William I did not abrogate the Saxon laws but confirmed them from his *Hist. of Gavel.*'.

f. 191. 'Evidence of Roger Twysden that William I disposed of all lands of all English in the way of absolute domination, Lambard, *De Prisc.* in Preface of Roger Twysden'. With references to Camden, Spelman, *Gloss.*, Selden, Malmesbury, and Florence of Worcester.

f. 193. Evidence from Sylvanus Taylor, Matt. Paris, Judge Shardelow, and Spelman on the significance of the words conquest and conqueror.

f. 197x. Evidence of Thomas Gale against the pretended conquest.

f. 202. 'The elaborate oration of Bulstrode Whitlock and in *Archivis Historiis*, 1650'.

f. 203. The Lord Protector from *Memorials of English Affairs*.

f. 222. Recapitulation of the Positions Anti Anglicanarum of Dr. Brady on the Norman Conquest.

f. 227. 'On the origin and use namely Post Conquestorem and Post Conquestum as appears in the records of the kingdom', with references to Close Roll, 1 Edward III, from the petitions of those who were of the quarrel of Thomas, Earl of Lancaster and the titles of the Rolls in the times of Henry III, Edwards I, II, and III.

f. 234. 'Two Treatises of Government, in the former the false principles and foundation of Sir Robert Filmer and his followers are overthrown; the latter is an *Essay concerning the true original extent and end of Civil Government*'.

VOLUME F

A volume written by a clerk of William Petyt, with additions and corrections by Petyt and clearly written by him. On flyleaf: Concerning the Conquest per W. P. 173 ff.

f. 1. Preface. Begins: I conceive it to be a presumptuous thing for private persons to interest the Government in their disputes, where they cannot manifestly show that it is concerned in them.

f. 3. 'A Supplement to Dr. Brady's Introduction to the Old English History. By the author of Jani Anglorum, facies nova Jus Anglorum ab Antiquo, and Reflections upon Mr. Hunt's Book and Postscript, with a vindication of those Treatises'. Then follow 10 Chapters. References and notes are given throughout, these being mainly the printed and manuscript sources of which transcripts, extracts, references, and notes are to be found in Volumes D and E above, which appear to be the material collected for this work. There are, however, a number of additional sources cited: including some Public Records, such as a Plea, East. term, 11 John, Testa de Nevill (cf. *Book of Fees*, pt. I, pp. 74, 349; II, pp. 198, etc.) and Close Roll, 6 John.

VOLUME G

A volume of transcripts and extracts from manuscript and printed sources, including the Public Records, to which references are not always given. On flyleaf: De Regimine Angliae temporibus diversorum Regum. 281 ff.

f. 1. What was done in the Council of Clovesho under Beornwulf, King of the Mercians, with notes.

f. 7. The Oath of the Saxon Kings on the day of their coronation, from the Life of Alfred the Great, with notes.

f. 11. The Reign of Alfred the Great.

f. 17. The Reign of Athelstan, son of Edward the Elder, from Malmesbury.

f. 21. On King Canute, from Spelman, *Conc.*

f. 26. The Reign of Edward the Confessor.

f. 33. On Earl Godwin and Harold and Sweyn, his sons, from Malmesbury.

f. 39. On guilty fleeing to the church etc.

f. 47. The Laws of William I, from Lambard, *De Prisc.*

f. 51. The Great Charter of William I, from certain Statutes.

f. 61. 'These are the laws and customs which King William granted to all the people of England after the land was taken, the same which King Edward, his relation, observed before him'. In parallel columns in Latin and French, numbered I to L.

f. 79. On Odo, Bishop of Bayeux and Earl of Kent, from Ordericus Vitalis.

f. 85. 1088. Among the chiefs of England, from Hoveden.

f. 90. The Reign of William II.

f. 94. On Ranulf Flambard.

f. 108. On Anselm, Archbishop of Canterbury, from Eadmer.

f. 126. On the coronation of Henry I, from Matt. Paris.

f. 127. The Great Charter of Henry I, from the same.

f. 135. After the Feast of Whitsun the coming of Earl Robert.

f. 139. On Robert, Duke of Normandy, from the same, Knighton etc.

f. 145. On various French Abbots and crimes, from Hoveden.

f. 146. The Council of London.

f. 151. On the Reign of Stephen, from Gesta Stephani.

f. 155. The General Confirmation of Stephen of the dignities and privileges of ecclesiastical persons.

f. 159. The Great Charter of Stephen, from Laudes Brit. in Archives of city of London.

f. 161. How Nigel, Bishop of Ely, was elected at Rome, from Chron. of Ely.

f. 161v. The Common Council of the Realm celebrated at London, 3 Stephen, from Gesta Stephani.

f. 165. The Great Charter of Henry II made to the community of the Realm, from Laudes Brit.

f. 167. On Thomas, Archbishop of Canterbury, from Hoveden.

f. 183. On the reign of Richard I, the Council of Pipewell, 1189, from Hoveden.

f. 187. On William Longchamp, Bishop of Ely, from the same, Brompton, Matt. Paris and William of Newburgh.

f. 213. On John, Count of Mortain, brother of King Richard, from Hoveden

f. 233. On King John.

f. 238. The charter moderating the fees of the Great Seal made 1 John, from the Ancient Reg. in the Archives of the Archbishop of Canterbury.

f. 243. The Agreement between King John and the Barons, from the Close Roll, 17 John.

f. 245. Magna Carta granted by King John, 43 caps., from Matt. Paris.

f. 259. The Charter of the Forest.

f. 265. For the amendment of the Realm, Barons to choose 25, 15 June 1215.

f. 269. Letters Patent on peace with the Barons, 19 June 1215, from Patent Roll, 17 John.

f. 270. Letters Patent to the Sheriff of Warw., and the 12 knights chosen, 27 June 1215.

f. 271. Letters Patent to Stephen, Archbishop of Canterbury, 9 August 1215.

f. 272. Mandate to Sheriff of Southampton, 28 June 1215.

f. 273. Letters of King John to the Pope for aid against the Barons, 13 September 1215.

f. 273v. Another letter to the Pope.

f. 275. The election of Louis by the Barons, 1216, from Matt. Paris and W. Thorne.

VOLUME H

Draft of a work by William Petyt in his historical controversies with Dr. Robert Brady, on the successive governments in England. On flyleaf: Touching the Several Governments in England. $12\frac{3}{4}'' \times 8\frac{1}{2}''$. 290 ff.

f. 1. The Norman Government, with references to Selden, *Titles of Honor*, *Ad Eadmer*, Lambard, *De Priscis*, Ingulf, Gervase of Canterbury, Brief Relation of William I at end of S. Taylor, *Tract on Gavelkind*, Somner, *Gloss.*, Brady, *Compleat Hist.*, Hoveden, Malmesbury, *Hist. Norm. Script. Antiq.*, Ordericus Vitalis, Bracton.

f. 13. Ends: I shall now proceed to William Rufus.

f. 13v. An incomplete note without beginning or end.

f. 14 Begins: It is demonstrable by the course and practice in the time of William I.

f. 15v. Objection the 4th (with solution).

f. 27. Objection the 2nd (ditto). (3rd altered to 2nd.)

f. 29. Objection the 3rd (ditto). (This contains the first reference in this section, to Pulton, *Stat.*)

f. 30. Reference to MS. in possession of Sir Roger Owen.

f. 33. 2. Observation. (This seems to be a jumble. It may have been misbound.)

f. 38. The Rights of the Commons under the Norman Government. King William the First, with references to *Platonic Theology*, Brady, *Compl. Hist.*, Spelman, *Gloss.*

f. 44. Argument 1. The judgement of learned men that William the First did not claim by the sword nor make an absolute Conquest in the Doctor's sense. References to Selden, *Hist. of Tithes*, *Ad Eadmer*, Quintilian, Calvin's Case, Hoveden, Book of Abingdon, Preface to Coke's *Reports*, Fortescue, *De Laud.*, Charter to Church of Westminster, Camden, *Brit.*, Malmesbury, Matthew Paris, Lambard, *De Prisc.*, Ingulph, Patent Roll, 3 Edward III,

Pleas uncertain t. John, Spelman, L.T.R. Mem. Roll, Mich., Comm. 35 Henry III, Coram Rege Roll, Hil. term, 14 Richard II, Bracton, *Fleta*, and foreign printed sources.

f. 85. Argument the 6th. From Domesday Book with the contradictory evidence that Dr. Brady did err when he asserted an absolute Conquest in King William when he came in and that the English had neither estates nor fortunes left and therefore it would have been no great matter to them by what law, right, or property other men held their estates.

f. 86. The oath of King Edward or King Ethelred for Dunstan crowned them both at Kingston about the year 970. Translation. References to *Exact Collection*, Bracton, Close Rolls, 9 Henry III, 9 Edward I, Statute Roll, 25 Edward III.

f. 88. Argument the 3rd. References to Cart. Antiqu., Roll D (*Cart. Antiq., Rolls 1–10*, p. 61), Charter Rolls, 4 Edward IV, Charter of Westminster, Hist. Elien. Eccles. in Laud MSS. in Bodleian, MS. of Sir Roger Owen.

f. 90v. Argument the 4th. From the general direction of King William's writs and charters it is demonstrated the Dr. was much mistaken when he writ that William the Conqueror divided all the lands of England among the great followers to hold of him. References to *Mon.*, Fuller, *Church Hist.*

f. 92v. Argument the 5th. The confirmation of the Saxon Laws by William the First plainly proved against the Dr. that the English had estates and fortunes left after the Norman Conquest. References to Malmesbury, Lambard, *De Prisc.*, Selden, *Spicil.*, Parliament Roll, 15 Richard II, *The Anonymous Author against Mr. Petyt*, Rastell, *Stat.*, Parliament Roll, 16 Richard II, Sir Winston Churchill, *Divi Brit.*

f. 97v. Argument the 2nd. References to Taylor, *Tract on Gavel.*, Camden, *Brit.*, Symeon of Durham, Selden, *Ad Fletam*, *Hist. of Tithes.*

f. 109v. Charter of 784, from *Mon.* References to Spelman, *Conc.*, Lambard, *De Prisc.*, William of Poitou, Malmesbury, Hoveden.

f. 115. Chap. (blank). The Right of the Commons in the Saxon times to be part of their Witanagemot or Parliament. References to Camden, *Brit.*, *Tract. de Moribus German.*, Lambard, *Arch.*, L.T.R. Mem. Roll, Comm. Mich., 18 Edward I, ibid., 19 Edward I, Patent Roll, 9 Henry III, ibid., 19 Edward I.

f. 126. Argument the 7th. (Chapter heading only.) From the general observation that the General Courts of Justice in the Saxon times continued after the Conquest and remain to this day.

f. 130. Argument the 8th. The Answer. That the Sovereign Court of the Kingdom The Saxon Witanagemot, Council or Parliament was not abolished and destroyed by William the First but survived the Conquest and notwithstanding the professed assertion of Dr. Brady and others to the contrary the Commons now called and distinguished from the Great Lords were an essential and constituent part thereof.

f. 132. 3. Observation. (Chapter heading only.) That several cities etc. used and enjoyed the same customs under the Conqueror as under King Edward.

f. 134. 4. Observation. (Chapter heading only.) From instances of grants made by William I.

f. 136. Argument the 9th. (Chapter heading only.) From comparing the general law and custom of the Saxons.

f. 138. Starts in the middle of a sentence. The section has references to Parliament Roll, 2 Henry V, the Author of the Grand Question, Fleta, and foreign printed works. Note. This remarkable record amongst several others is entirely left out in the *Exact Abridg. of the Rolls of Parliament* published under the name of Sir Robert Cotton by Mr. Prynne.

f. 151. An Answer to Dr. Brady's Argument of the general alteration of the Ancient Constitution of Parliament anno 49 Henry III. Reference to Patent Roll, 37 Henry III.

f. 159. References to Matthew Paris, Patent Roll, 17 John, Like, 42 Henry III, Camden, *Brit.*, Coke, *2nd Inst.*, Bundle of Certificates, 42 Henry III, Close Roll, 43 Henry III, Patent Roll, 42 Henry III, Close Roll, 45 Henry III, Patent Roll, 48 Henry III, Extracts, 45–48 Henry III, Matthew of Westminster, Patent Roll, 51 Henry III, Rastell, *Stat.*, Patent Roll, 54 Henry III, Selden, *Hist. of Tithes.*

f. 175. The Recapitulation. References to Patent Roll, 51 Henry III, Pulton, *Stat.*, Coke, *2nd Inst.*, Patent Roll, 54 Henry III.

f. 185. Marginal note on Parliament, 3 Edward I (Stat. of West. I). 'There are no writs of summons either to the Lords Spiritual or Temporal or Commons yet found to this Parliament nor any Rolls of Parliament'. Reference to Statute Roll, 3 Edward I, Close Roll, 9 Edward I, Matt. of West., Register of Writs, Spelman, *Gloss.*

f. 189. On expenses. References to Close Roll, 28 Edward I, Like, 33 Edward I, Coke, *2nd Inst.*, MS. Statutes in poss. of John Peachey, of Inner Temple, Esq., Parliament Roll, 2 Henry V (Note verbatim as f. 138 above), Stat. Roll, 25 Henry VIII, cap. 2.

f. 196. The True State of the Dr. and his Authors' error about the Parliament of 49 Henry III.

f. 198. General Council, Westminster, 9 Henry III. References to Matt. Paris, Stat. Roll, 25 Edward I, Coke, *2nd Inst.*, Register of Writs, Parl. Roll, 15 Edward III, Stat. Roll, 15 Edward III, K.R. Mem. Roll, Comm. Hil. 17 Edward III, Bracton, Patent Roll, 37 Henry III., Stat. Roll, 25 Edward I, Broke, tit. Parl., Jones, *Reports*, Totell, *Stat.*, Stat. Roll, 28 Edward I, MS. in poss. of William Petyt, Parl. Roll, 2 Henry V, Plowden, *Comm.*, Rastell, *Stat.*, Close Roll, 2 Henry III, Patent Roll, 3 Henry III, Like, 9 Henry III, Cotton, *Records.*

f. 251. Dr. Brady's Fifth Argument. In margin: 'An Answer to Dr. Brady's Argument for the general alteration of the Ancient Constitution of Parliament anno 49 H. 3 drawn from several records of writs in the Reigns of E. 1, E. 2 and E. 3 for summoning sometimes one sometimes more knights, citizens and burgesses to Parliament'. References to Patent Roll, 33 Edward I, Like, 21 Edward I, Coke, *2nd Inst.*, *Grand Question*, Close Roll, 26 Edward III, Bundle of Writs, 18 Edward I, Close Roll, 22 Edward I, Like, 10 Edward II, Like, 16 Edward II, Like, 18 Edward II, Like, 10 Edward III, Like, 26 Edward III, 27 Edward III, Like, 6 Richard II, Rastell, *Stat.*, MS. in poss. of William Petyt. Parl. Roll, 15 Edward III.

f. 269v. Marginal note: 'Inference may be drawn from the Dr's record. All the summons to Parliament either of the Lords or Commons are lost till 49 Henry III and from then till 22 Edward I. Sir William Dugdale and Mr. Prynne'.

f. 270. References to Parl. Roll, 1 Henry IV, Walsingham, Close Roll, 11 Richard II, Rastell, *Stat.*, Burnet, *Hist. of Reform*, and foreign printed sources.

f. 281. Recorda. Form of assessing and collecting 15th, from Patent Roll, 9 Henry III, 15 February 1225.

f. 284v. Like, from Patent Roll, 42 Henry III (French).

f. 286. References to Patent Roll, 42 Henry III, L.T.R. Mem. Roll, Comm. Mich. 18 Edward I, Stat. Roll, 25 Edward I, Close Roll, 28 Edward I.
There are corrections and additions to the text and references and notes in the margin.

VOLUME I

Another draft of a work by William Petyt in his historical controversies with Dr. Robert Brady on the Parliaments and Government of England after the reign of King John. On flyleaf: Touching the Parliaments and Governments of England after the Reign of King John. $12\frac{3}{4}'' \times 8\frac{1}{8}''$. 296 ff.

ff. 1–41. Chapters 1, 2, 3, 4, and 5 of the work, with the characteristic references to Matt. Paris, Hoveden, Matt. of Westminster, Eadmer, Malmesbury, Walsingham and Flores Hist., the Mirror of Justice, the Charter, Patent, Close and Welsh Rolls, Parliament Rolls, Statutes and more unusually in this series Journal of the House of Lords, Selden, *Titles of Honor*, *Notes on Fortescue*, Spelman, *Concilia*, *Gloss.*, Rastell, *Stat.*, Pulton, *Stat.*, *Plac. Parl.*, Coke, *2nd Inst.*, Plowden, *Comment.*, Davis, *Reports*, Camden, *Brit.*, and single references to Herbert of Chirbury, *Life of Henry VIII*, Powel, *Repertory of Records*, Fox, *Eccles. Hist. of England*, King, *Vale Royal of England*, Prynne, *Plea for House of Lords*, John Skene, dedicated to James I. Exceptional references are to Subsidy Rolls, 5 Edward III, 1 Richard II, 6 Richard II, and 2 Henry VI.

ff. 42–61. Chapter 6, with like references to Matt. Paris, Hoveden, Knighton, Patent, Close and Norman Rolls, Parliament Rolls, Spelman, *Conc.*, *Plac. Parl.*, Pulton, *Stat.*, Rastell, *Stat.*, Coke, *4th Inst.*, Kelway, *Reports*, Fox, *Eccles. Hist. of Eng.*, Crompton, *Jurisdiction*, Fortescue, *De Laud.*, and unusually in this series Journals of House of Commons, and single references to Twysden, *Hist. Vindication of Church of Engl.*, *Basilika or Coll. of Declarations* etc., King James I, *Works*.

ff. 61v–93. Chapter 8, with like references to Matt. Paris, Brompton, Matthew of Westminster, Walsingham, Knighton, Fleta, Murimuth, Patent, Close, Liberate and Gascon Rolls, Parliament Rolls, Spelman, *Gloss.*, Somner, *Dict.*, *Gloss.*, Pulton, *Stat.*, Rastell, *Stat.*, *Plac. Parl.*, Dugdale, *Orig. Jurid.*, Hobart, *Reports*, *Antiq. Brit.*, Heylin, *Stumbling Block*, Prynne, *Records*, Preface to *Exact Abridg. of Parl. Rolls*. Exceptional references to Subsidy Rolls, 9 Edward II, 12 Edward II, 10 Edward III, 13 Edward III, Laud MS. X. 84 in Bodleian, Cleopatra E. 7, Cleopatra A. 16, MS. in poss. of Sir Thomas Thynne, Book of Exceptions of Sir John Trevor.

f. 72. 'To this the ensuing record may be properly connexed'. Agreement between John and Barons from Close Roll, 17 John.

ff. 94–101. Chapter 9, with like references to Matt. Paris, Knighton, Walsingham, Matt. of Westminster, W. Thorne, Patent Roll.

ff. 103–30. Positions, with like references to Matt. Paris, Gervase of Canterbury, Matt. of Westminster, Fleta, Charter, Patent, Close, Oblate Rolls, Parliament Rolls, Statute Rolls, Spelman, *Gloss.*, Dugdale, *Orig. Jurid.*, Prynne, *Brief Register of Parl. Writs*, *Truth Triumphant over Falsehood*, *Records*, Preface to *Exact Abridge*, Somner, *Gloss.*, Selden, *Titles of Honor*. Exceptional references to James Howell, *Sober Inspections of the Long Parl.*, Daille, *True Case of the Fathers*, Reg. of Writs, MS. in poss. of Lord Holles, MS. in poss. of William Petyt, Faustina A. 3.

f. 105. In margin: Sober Inspections of the Long Parliament dedicated to his Highness the Lord Protector, by Mr. James Howell, after Historiographer Royal to his now Majesty.

f. 106. In margin: Against the position that the Commons House of Parliament had its first beginning Anno 49 H. 3.

f. 106v. Quadam Adversaria.

f. 108. 'But now to my Answer'. In margin: This first mention and use of Parliamentum in any writ or record I have perused is the writ of summons to the Cinque Ports, Close Roll, 49 Henry III.

f. 114v. In margin: 'These Rolls are lost or destroyed' referring to a reference in the text Rotulis Cancellaria about burgesses of St. Albans coming to Parliament. 'Semper irrotulata fecerunt'.

ff. 132, 133. Cap. (blank). Headings only 'Animadversions on the paraphrase Titulo Parliamentum in Sir Henry Spelman's Glossary and upon the clause in the Great Charter, Et habendum Commune Consilium Regni de Auxiliis assidentis . . .'.

ff. 136–63. Cap. (blank), with like references to Matt. Paris, Matt. of Westminster, Malmesbury, Florence of Worcester, Eadmer, Brompton, Ymagines Hist., Rerum Brit., Mirror of Justice, Patent, Close, Fine Rolls, Parliament Rolls, Spelman, *Gloss.*, *Conc.*, T. Smith, *De Republ. Angl.*, Lambard, *Archion.*, Camden, *Brit.*, Bale, *Script. Brit.*, Selden, *Titles of Honor*, *Ad Eadmer*, Prynne, *Truth Triumphant*, Somner, *Gloss.*, Milles, *De Nobilitate*, *Mon.*, Littleton, *Abridge.*, Pulton, *Stat.*, Fitzherbert, *Abridge.*, Coke, *2nd Inst.*, *4th. Inst.* Exceptional references are to Scutage Roll, 5 Edward I, L.T.R. Memoranda Roll, 17 Edward I, Curia Regis Roll, Hil. term, 11 Henry III, Cartae Antiquae, MS. in poss. of William Petyt.

ff. 164–82. Cap. (blank), with like references to Matt. Paris, Reg. of Malmesbury, Patent, Close, Gascon Rolls, Parliament Rolls, Somner, *Gloss.*, Selden, *Titles of Honor*, Prynne, *Parl. Writs*, Fitzherbert, *Abridg.*, Moore, *Reports*. Exceptional references are to Year Book, 27 Edward III, Faustina B. 9 (Chron. de Mailros), Vowell, *Order of Parl.*, Skene, *De verb. signific.*

ff. 184–222. (Cap. blank). Begins: The Several Constituent Parts of Parliament in the Reigns of E. 1, E. 2 and E. 3. Like references to Walsingham, Charter, Patent, Close Rolls, Parliament Rolls, Selden, *Titles of Honor*, *Plac. Parl.*, Totell, *Stat.*, Rastell, *Stat.*, Coke, *3rd Inst.*, *4th. Inst.*, *Reports*, Jones, *Reports*, Broke, *Abridg.* Exceptional references are to Coram Rege Roll, Hil. term, 2 Edward III, Red Book of the Exchequer, MS. Statutes in poss. of William Petyt, *Jurisdiction of House of Lords asserted.*

ff. 225–74. (Cap. blank). The various forms of penning Statutes with some observations of the omission of the word Commons in the Printed Statute Books yet explained and confirmed by recitals in Records. Like references to Bede, On Luke, Register of Selby, Patent, Close, Welsh, Gascon Rolls, Parliament Rolls, Statute Rolls, Coke, *2nd Inst.*, Pulton, *Stat.*, Rastell, *Stat.*, Prynne, *Records*, *Plac. Parl.*, Crompton, *Juris.*, James I, *Works*, Broke, *Abridg.*, Selden, *Privileges of Boroughs*, *Titles of Honor*, Camden, *Brit.*, Howell, *Sober Inspections*. Exceptional references are Memoranda de Parliamento, 9 Edward II, Rot. de Superioritate, Bundles of Writs, 12 Edward II, 15 Edward II, Brevia Regis, 9 Edward II, Journal of House of Lords, 28 Henry VIII, Common Plea Roll, Hil. term, 8 Henry VIII, MS. Stat. in poss. of William Petyt, *Cabala of Letters.*

f. 270v. In margin: 'The Articles or Act tempore H, 5 are not in the Parliament Roll unless it be included in that of 9 Henry V before mentioned'.

f. 296. A note or extract only from Parliament Roll, 1 Henry IV, on cos. Salop and adjoining. Inset at end the printed text: The Pillars of Parliament, by William Petyt, 1681.

A part of the material in this volume has been used in the Petyt tract, *The Pillars of Parliament*.

This draft work has not been as much corrected as the draft volume H above. Apart from references there are notes in the margin but in this case they are in the same hand as the references.

VOLUME K

The manuscript of the posthumously published work by William Petyt, *Jus Parliamentarium*. On flyleaf: The Ancient Jurisdiction of the High Court of Parliament over Inferior Courts. $12\frac{3}{4}'' \times 8\frac{1}{8}''$. 263 ff.

f. 1. Jus Parliamentarium or the Ancient Jurisdiction of the most High Court of Parliament over the Inferior Courts in Westminster Hall Revised and Asserted in two Parts by William Petyt of the Inner Temple esq. This book was published in folio in 1739 as *Jus Parliamentarium* or the Ancient Power and Jurisdiction, Rights and Liberties of the Most High Court of Parliament revised and asserted By William Petyt Esqr., late of the Inner Temple and Keeper of the Records in the Tower of London, with a dedication to Charles, Duke of Somerset, and a lengthy preface by the anonymous editor. In this Preface the editor states that 'There is a fair copy of part of it in the Library of the Inner Temple, as of an entire work but it wants one hundred pages of our text and all our Second Part, which therefore (we may reasonably conjecture) were completed after that copy was taken'. This is only partly correct, as will appear below. The editorial work was carelessly done, as can easily be seen by comparing the chapter headings in the Summary at the beginning of the printed text with the chapter headings in the printed text. Chapter 7 is duplicated as a number and pp. 182–97 of the pagination are repeated so that there are really 13 not 12 chapters in the printed text. The manuscript has the first 11 of the 13 chapters of the printed text only, although the chapter headings of 12 and 13 appear in the Table of Contents. The details of the variations are as follows:

ff. 2–26. The Preface. In the printed text this is called the Introduction and is preceded by the Table of Contents.

ff. 27–31v. Table of Contents in 13 Chapters.

ff. 31–159. Chap. I to Chap. VII agrees with pp. 1–81 of the printed text, but sections III, IV, and V of the printed text pp. 82–181 are omitted in manuscript, but these appear in the Table of Contents as follows:

ff. 29v–30. III. Whether no Judges in former Ages took the law to be that the King had such an Inherent Power vested in him as that by a non obstante put in to his grants he might suspend and dispense with General Acts of Parliament made pro bono publico.

IV. More Particularly whether the King by his Prerogative could dispense with the Statute of xiiid. of Henry VI which enacted

That no man should continue Sheriff or Under sheriff longer than for a year
And that All Patents which should after be made of these Officers should be void

Any clause or word of Non Obstante in any wise put or to be put into such Patent notwithstanding.

V. The Case in the Year Book Anno 11 to Henrici VIImi touching the Matter Considered and Proved by Several Arguments and Reasons That as represented and understood in Later Times It could never be Good Law.

ff. 31–31v. Chap. XII. A Record of some memorable Proceedings in the Honourable House of Commons in the Parliament held Anno MDCX i.e. vii year of King James the 1st with some necessary reflections thereupon. Chap. XIII. The Impeachment exhibited by the Commons in the Parliament xviii and xix Jacobi Imi against the Lord Chancellor Bacon for Great Bribery and Corruption committed by him.

And the judgement which the Lords gave upon him for the same.

There are a few verbal differences in the Table of Contents of the manuscript and the printed text and there are similar verbal differences in the letter press. The marginal notes and references in the manuscript are generally found in the printed text, either in the margin or as footnotes. There is, however, an occasional omission in the printed text, e.g.:

f. 201. In margin: Two reasons given for relating these Proceedings in Parliament at length: But I have two reasons to offer in my excuse. The One is That I never met with these Particular Impeachments, Answers, Replies and Judgement in print and therefore thought it fit they should be set down.

f. 209. In margin (apparently in Petyt's hand): The King's Dispensing Power of his sole uncontrollable Prerogative unknown in H. 8's time. Otherwise though there are a few minor marginal omissions and some verbal differences in the marginalia they are not of any special moment. Also the whole of Part II, pp. 245–400 of the printed text is omitted in this manuscript. It is clear, therefore, that from whatever MS. the printed text was derived it was not from here, though the omission can be supplied substantially from Petyt MSS., which were those from which he drew his material, though the final draft of his work, as amended by the editor, was with him or the printer.

Part II of the printed text has the following title: A short History or Series of the Invasions upon the Privileges of Parliament as to Freedom of Speech for the Redress of Grievances, first begun in the reign of Richard II, Secondly revived by Queen Elizabeth, Thirdly continued and improved in the reign of King James I, and Fourthly completed in that of Charles I, by the bold Resolutions of the Judges of the King's Bench; which was one main and principal Cause of those direful Calamities, which afterwards fell upon King and Kingdom. The completion by Charles I is not reached in the printed text. The Table of Contents contains only the instances from the reigns of Richard II, that of Thomas Haxey, Proceedings in Parliament 13, 23, and 35 Elizabeth I and in 18 & 19 James I. The material for these instances William Petyt had available as follows: for Richard II, 535/31, 32; for Elizabeth I, 537/6, 7; for James I, 537/10, 15, 538/1, 2.

VOLUME L

A draft by William Petyt in his historical controversies with Dr. Robert Brady on the rights of the Commons. On flyleaf: Differences between Mr. Petyt and Dr. Brady. $12\frac{3}{4}'' \times 8\frac{1}{8}''$.

134 ff.

Title-Page: The Ancient Right of the Commons of England Reasserted in reply to a book written by Robert Brady, Dr. of Physic, against a Discourse proving by records and the best historians that the Commons of England were ever an essential part of Parliament.

The First Part. By William Petyt, of the Inner Temple, Esquire.

f. 1. 'The State of the main question between me and Dr. Brady'.

In margin: My Discourse. The State of the main question between Mr. Petyt and Dr. Brady whether the Commons in Parliament compounded of knights, citizens and burgesses had or had not their birth and beginning by rebellion, 49 Henry 3.

f. 1. Chap. 1. 'An Answer to the charge against me for adding to and taking from records or leaving unrecited such words and matter as I thought would either advance or destroy my assertion'.

f. 2. Dr. Brady, Article I. The first argument considered with reference to the petition of St. Albans, Parl. Roll, 8 Edward II, with translation. 'The petition declared that the names of such burgesses coming to parliament were always enrolled on the Rolls of Chancery'. In margin: 'These Rolls are lost or destroyed. The Statute of Articuli Cleri made the next year after this record tells us that there were diverse parliamenta temporibus progenitorum suorum Regum Anglie (with reference to Coke, *2nd. Inst.*) The Rolls of Summons to Parliament are extant for this very Parliament (reference to Close Roll, 8 Edward II). Reference to Selden, *Tit. of Hon.* It appears from the Patent Rolls of 26 Edward III that there were Parliaments and Summons to Parliament temporibus progenitorum et ante 29 Henry III.

f. 8. Recordum, from Bundle of Writs, 5 Edward II. Writ to Sheriff of Hertf. on bailiffs of St. Albans, with reference to Selden, *Jani Angl.*

f. 11v. Margin: All formal writs of summons, both to the Lords and Commons, lost or perished as well before 49 Henry III as after till 23 Edward I, that of 49 Henry III only excepted.

f. 13. The First Precedent, from L.T.R. Mem. Roll, Comm. Trin. 8 Edward II, petition of tenants of Beverley, with reference to Cart. Antiq., Roll R. (*Cart. Antiq., Rolls 11–20*, p. 131) and K.R. Bundle of Writs, 23 Edward I.

f. 14. The Second Precedent, from L.T.R. Mem. Roll, Comm., Mich. 34 Edward I, from men of town of Coventry, with reference to Coram Rege Roll, Trin. term, 1 Edward III (city of London), K.R. Bundle of Writs, 23 Edward I, Camden, *Brit.*

f. 16. The third Precedent, Charter of Edward I to Ely, from *Mon.*, with reference to Malmesbury and Dugdale.

f. 18. A Fourth Precedent, Parl. Petition, 18 Edward I, from *Plac. Parl.*, with references to Charter Roll, 3 Edward IV, Dugdale, *Baronage*, Escheats 9 Henry V, Prynne, *4th Part. Parl. Writs.*

f. 20v. 'Mr. Prynne, from such fragment Bundles as he had met with in the Tower shows that this borough (Arundel) sent to Parliament 33 Edward I, 1, 2, 3, 4, 6, 7, 12, 15 & 17 Edward II. But we are not to believe that the borough did not send burgesses to all the intervening Parliaments from 30 Edward I till 19 Edward II, except those mentioned above'.

f. 21. 'Because Mr. Prynne found no return for that town (Arundel) earlier than 30 Edward I therefore that must be the first, for in my searches in the Exchequer I discovered a broken bundle of returns of knights of the shire and burgesses to Parliament, 23 Edward I, of which neither he nor any of his clerks knew anything, witness his books. And it is very probable that if further and free search were made there and in some other offices, more, and more ancient, returns might be found, as well as that of 23 Edward I'.

In margin: I shall now proceed to furnish you with a chronological and alphabetical catalogue of the respective cities, boroughs and ports of England which have formerly elected and sent any citizens, burgesses or barons to Parliament or been summoned by Sheriffs to choose and send them from 26 Edward I, when the first bundle of original writs for election yet extant begin and bear date till 12 Edward IV, the last bundle remaining in the Tower etc., with reference to *Brev. Parl. Rediv.*

f. 22v. Concerning the town of Leicester, from the Great Register in the office of the Duchy of Lancaster and K. R. Bundle of Writs, 23 Edward I.

f. 23. 'Mr. Prynne who was Master of the Record Office in the Tower in his Preface to the Ingenuous Reader, especially those of the Long Robe and generous English extraction, before his First Part of a *Brief Register of Parliamentary Writs* tells us of the irreparable loss of all Parliamentary Rolls during the reigns of our ancient Kings from William 1st till 5 Edward 2, the first Roll of that kind extant'.

f. 23v. 'And from his indefatigable industry and pains taken in searching in his Fourth Part of his Kalendar of Parliamentary Writs giving us this observable account, that out of the rubbish and dust wherein the decayed broken and defaced Bundles of Writs and Returns of the names of knights, citizens and burgesses had for many years been interred in the White Tower Chapel, like dead men out of mind, whom we remember no more, he had rescued from eternal oblivion, several bundles, amongst which he shows that the borough of Leicester sent 2 burgesses to Parliament, 28 & 35 Edward I, 1, 2, 4, 5, 6, 7, 8, 12, 15, 16, 19 Edward II etc.'.

f. 24. 'By which it is evident that he never saw the Record of the Returns of Knights, Citizens and Burgesses to the Parliament, 23 Edward I, which I discovered in the Exchequer, his Kalendar beginning but at 26 Edward I, as I have shown before from his *Brevia Parliamentaria Rediviva*'.

ff. 33–80v. Chap. II. In margin: That the Commons were represented in Parliament by knights, citizens and burgesses before 1 Richard I, brother of King John, father of Henry III. In this chapter Petyt cites Authority I to Authority XVIII. References to Coram Rege Roll, Mich. term, 19 Edward I, Patent Roll, 17 John, Close Roll, 28 Henry III, Like, 29 Edward I, *Plac. Parl.*, Spelman, *Conc.*, Coke, *1st Inst.*, Register of Writs, Fitzherbert, *Nat. Brev.*, Coram Rege Roll, Trin. 17 Edward II, Close Roll, 17 Edward II, Dugdale, *Chron. Ser.*, Pulton, *Stat.*, Rastell, *Stat.*, Parl. Roll, 51 Edward III, Plowden, *Comm.*, Coke, *4th Inst.*, Parl. Roll, 6 Richard II, Fitzherbert, *Grand Abr.*, Close Roll, 11 Richard II, Parl. Roll, 11 Richard II, Plac. coram Consilio Regis, 1 Edward I, Close Roll, 21 Henry III, Parl. Roll, 9 Henry IV, Year Book, Trin. 1 Edward II, Parl. Roll, 11 Henry IV, Like, 2 Henry V, Rolle, *Abridg.*, *Dial. de Fund. Leg. Angl.*, Crompton, *Jurisdiction*, Camden, *Brit.*, Spelman, *Conc.*, Lambard, *Arch.*, Dugdale, *Juris Orig.*, Sir Robert Leicester, *Hist. Antiq.*, *Cheshire*, Coke, *8th Reports*, Davys, *Reports*.

f. 82. Chap. III, Dr. Brady, Article II. The second argument considered. In margin: Touching the records produced by Dr. Brady, 15 John, omitting one most necessary.

f. 84. Recorda I. Close Roll, 15 John, to William, Earl Marshal, 8 March 1214.

f. 85. Recorda II. Patent Roll, 15 John, to men of Canterbury, 8 March 1214.

f. 86. Recorda III. Like, to all knights etc. 6 March 1214.

f. 87. Reference 'To the transcribing of these writs, about ten or eleven years past, by Mr. Henderson, then my clerk, but since Attorney of the Common Pleas, the very original copy whereof being lately showed him, he gave his testimonial under his hand, which the Reader will find at the end of the Argument. That at the time of the transcribing and till 27 July last he did believe his copy had agreed with the record'.

f. 87v. References to Selden, *Tit. of Hon.*, Domitian A. 10, a Chronicle in possession of William Petyt, Patent Roll, 38 Henry III, Selden, *Jani Angl.*, Parl. Roll, 8 Edward II, Like, 2 Henry V, L.T.R. Mem. Roll, Comm., Mich. 18 Edward I, Like, Trin., Patent Roll, 19 Edward I, Charter Roll, 5 John.

f. 98. Recordum. References to Charter Roll, Like, 17 John, Coke, *2nd Inst.*, Rastell, *Stat.*, Selden, *Tit. of Hon.*, Close Roll, 5 John, L.T.R. Mem. Roll, Comm., Mich. 18 Edward I, Patent Roll, 19 Edward I.

f. 104v. 'I, William Henderson, one of the Attorneys of H.M.'s Court of Common Pleas at Westminster, do hereby attest that ten or eleven years ago, being ordered by Mr. William Petyt, to whom I was clerk, to transcribe from the Rolls in the Office of Records in the Tower of London, several copies, among others the above mentioned copy anno 15to Johannis was one, and having now carefully compared it with the very original paper I had at that time writ, which Mr. Petyt hath showed me, do hereby solemnly declare that at the time of transcribing and till this present day I did believe my copy had agreed with the Record, W. Henderson, 27 July 1684'.

f. 105. 'I, William Towne, of Symonds Inn, London, gent., do hereby attest that I have this day seen and compared the original copy of the above mentioned writ, anno 15th Johannis, and well know it to be the handwriting of Mr. William Henderson and verily believe it was transcribed by him from the Rolls in the Office of Records in the Tower, about 10 or 11 years since, I, being at that time also employed with Mr. Henderson, by Mr. Petyt, to copy out several records in the reigns of King John and Henry the Third, the original papers of some of which Mr. Petyt hath now showed me. W. Towne, 19 July 1684'.

f. 108. Chap. IV. Dr. Brady's Article III. References to Parl. Roll, 40 Edward III, Matt. Paris, Patent Roll, 15 John, Selden, *Tit. of Hon.*, Adam Murimuth, Cleopatra A. 16, Close Roll, 23 Edward I, *Plac. Parl.*, Leslie, *De orig . . . Gest. Scot.*, Close Roll, 15 John, Charter Roll, 15 John, Close Roll, 3 Edward I, Like, 17 Edward I, Liberate Roll, 17 Edward I. Recordum. Parl. Roll, 40 Edward III.

f. 128. Chap. V. Dr. Brady, Articles VI. the Fourth Argument. References to Matt. Paris, Caves, *Desc. of Anc. Church Govt.*, Camden, *Brit.*, *Plac. Parl.*, *Rer. Angl. Script. Vet.*, Patent Roll, 15 John, Walter of Coventry, ancient MS. Chron. Laud MSS. in Bodl., Matt, of West., Patent Roll, 17 John, Close Roll, 17 John, *Cat. Glor. Mundi*, Close Roll, 25 Henry III, Close Roll, 42 Henry III.

VOLUME M

A draft unpublished work by William Petyt in his historical controversies with Dr. Robert Brady. On flyleaf: The Rights of the Commons of England reasserted against Dr. Brady.

2,163 ff.

f. 1. Title-Page: A Review of the Ancient Right of the Commons of England reasserted by way of a reply to Dr. Brady's full and clear answer, by Willam Petyt, of the Inner Temple.

f. ix. Considerations (apparently written by a friend to whom the draft had been sent for advice).

'1. Whether the British government be not too long and too loose. The design being to show 1st. the freedom of the nation in general, 2ndly. That the citizens or Freemen were part of their Common Council or Parliament.
2. Whether the Chapters and Heads under the Saxon Government be orderly disposed.
3. If there be not too many reflections not necessary upon Dr. Brady.
4. To observe whether the words, phrases and inferences in the whole discourse be properly pertinent.'

f. 2. The Preface. The 3 grand designs Dr. Brady had in writing his Answer, followed by the Heads of the Chapters (as under).

f. 1. Begins: About (blank) months ago after a year's expectation and more, the Book of Dr. Brady (the King's Professor of Physic and head of Gonville and Caius College in Cambridge) was published to the world, though without his name prefixed to it. It is pretended to be a full and clear answer to one written by me. The title of mine (though the Dr. hath left it out of his book) is The Ancient Right of the Commons of England asserted or a Discourse proving by Records and the best Historians that the Commons of England were ever an essential part of Parliament.

f. 6. Chap. I. That under the British Government the free men, or as we call them the Commons were an essential part of the Kyfr y then, Common Council or Parliament. References to Gildas, Cassius, Life of Severus, Tacitas, Camden, *Brit.*, Discourse written by an ingenious and learned Gentlemen, called *Patriarcha non monarchia* in Answer to Sir Robert Filmer, Matt. of Westminster, Ptolmey, Spelman, *Conc.*, an old parchment in possession of James Warenn, *Mon.*, Burton, *Commentary on Antonius' Itinerary*, Selden, *Notes on Fortescue*, Selden, *Poly. Cant.*, Cicero, Parsons, *Conversions*, Bede, *Eccles. Hist.*

f. 20. Chap. II. More authorities to prove that the freemen or commons were part of the Common Council of England before Dr. Brady's marvellous year of 49 Henry III. References to S. Taylor, *Hist. of Gavel.*, Enderby, *Cambria Triumphans*, *Divi Brit.* dedicated to H. M., Huntingdon, Bede, *Eccles. Hist.*, Ingulph, Camden, *Brit.*, Caesar, *Gallic War*, Laws of William I, Somner, *Gloss.*, Symeon of Durham, Malmesbury, Florence of Worcester, The Author of the *Grand Question*, *Regiam Maiestatem*, Parliament Roll, 2 Henry V, and several foreign works.

f. 30. Chap. III. The Rights of the Commons of England in Saxon Times. The right of the government of the old Germans from whence our Saxon ancestors descended by way of Introduction, References to Camden, *Brit.*, Bede, *Eccles. Hist.*, Tacitas, Lambard, *Archion*.

f. 38. Chap. IIII. Nineteen Refutations of Dr. Brady's Position, vizt. That there were no Commons to be found in the Saxon Great Council nor anything that tends towards the proof of the Commons of those times to have had any share of making laws in these Councils. Grounded upon Records, the Testimony of ancient Historians and the authority and judgement of learned men. References to Lambard, *De Prisc.*, Spelman, *Conc.*, Sir Tho. Ridley, *A view of the Civil and Eccles. Law*, *Antiq. Brit.*, Dr. Tillesley, *Animadversions upon Mr. Selden's History of the Tithes*, Ingulph, Matt. of Westminster, Caesar, Bede, *Eccles. Hist.*, Ailred of Rievaulx, *Mon.*, Brompton, Malmesbury, Somner, *Gloss.*, Selden, *Hist. of Tithes*, *Titles of Honor*, W. Thorne, Pulton, *Stat.*, Symeon of Durham, Camden, *Brit.*, Florence of Worcester, Hoveden, *Life of Alfred the Great*, Matt. Paris, Close Roll, 32 Henry III, K.R.

Mem. Roll, 17 Edward III, Patent Roll, 42 Henry III, Patent Roll, 53 Henry III, *The Law of Tithes*, L.T.R. Mem. Roll, 7 Edward II, Spelman, *Gloss.*, Somner, *Gloss.*, Atwood, *Jus Angl.*, Close Roll, 3 Edward II, Prynne, *Truth Triumphant over Falsehood, Antiquity over Novelty*, Lambard, *Archion.*, Dugdale, *Orig. Jurid.*, and foreign printed sources.

f. 97v. Chap. V. Dr. Brady's Quere. Where are the Commons to be found in the Prefaces of the Saxon Laws or out of history or any that represented them. 1. The Word Commons. 2. The Prefaces of the Saxon Laws. 3. History. References to Rastell, *Stat.*, Pulton, *Stat.*, Camden, *Brit.*, Malmesbury.

f. 101. Chap. VI. 4. The General Words and Phrases whereby the parts of the Saxon Witenagemotes or Parliaments were expressed considered under five heads. A Glossary. 1. Aldermanni, Aldermen. 2. Thani, Thanes. 3. Gereves, Greves and Sheriffs. 4. Nobiles, Noblemen. 5. Sapientes, Wites or Witen, Wisemen. References to Spelman, *Gloss.*, Lambard, *De Prisc.*, Selden, *Titles of Honor*, Lambard, *Peramb. of Kent*, Somner, *Glos.*, *Sax. Dict.*, Spelman, *Conc.*, Selden, *Hist of Tithes*, Malmesbury, Brompton, Florence of Worcester, Milles, *De Nobilitate*, Patent Roll, 37 Henry III, Coke, *2nd Inst.*, Rastell, *Stat.*, Lambard, *Archion*, Giraldus Cambrensis, Rolls of Essoins 10 Richard I, *Jani Angl.*, Crompton, *Jurisdiction.*

f. 125. Chap. VII. A Supplemental Proof from the evidence of Grotius and Witchindus, great and learned authors. That the ancient Governments of the Germans from whence the English Saxons were descended was the same in substance with that here and that the People was an essential part of their Great Councils. With references to Grotius, *Hist. Goth.*, *Vita Witchindus*, *Primi et antiq. Hist. Sax.*, *Rerum Brit.*, Florence of Worcester, Matthew of Westminster, *Ingulph*, Huntingdon, Verstigens, *Restitution of decayed intelligence*, Eadmer.

f. 136. Chap. VIII. Dr. Brady's Title of Sapientes, Wite or Witen and his exposition and application thereof in the Glossary observed and corrected. With references to Bale, Somner, *Sax. Dict.*, Selden, *Titles of Honor*, *Hist. of Tithes*, Camden, *Brit.*, Lambard, *Kent.*

f. 141. Chap. IX. The different phrases used in the Saxon Laws whereby they represented all the part of their Witena Gemot or Parliament by general words. And that Wites and Populus were differently used to signify the members not noble that made and integrated their Great Council. References to Bede, *Eccles. Hist.*, Spelman, *Conc.*, Lambard, *De Prisc.*, Charter Roll, 7 & 8 Richard II, Malmesbury, Florence of Worcester.

f. 145. Chap. X. The pretended reasons and authorities of Mr. Sheringham (late Fellow of Gonville and Caius College in Cambridge) against the Right of the Commons to be an essential part of the Saxon Great Council examined and confuted. References to Matt. Paris, Camden, *Brit.*, Bede, *Eccles. Hist.*, Lambard, *Archion.*, Spelman, *Conc.*, Matthew of Westminster, Brompton, Coke, *1st Inst.*

f. 161xv. Chap. XI. The conclusion with a 20th Refutation against Dr. Brady by proving my assertion That the Commons was an essential and constituent part of the Parliament in the Saxon times. References to Rerum Brit. Script., Parliament Roll, 40 Edward III.

This volume is a corrected draft with notes and references in the margin.

VOLUME N

A draft by William Petyt correcting what he considered to be errors of recent English historians or authors on Parliament. On flyleaf: Several erroneous and novel positions and assertions against the King and honour of Parliament by Sir Robert Filmer and others. The authors as detailed below are listed on a flyleaf. On another flyleaf: Erroneous Positions against the King and Honour of Parliament. 353 ff.

f. 1. Title-Page: Several Erroneous Novel Positions and Assertions against the King and Honour of Parliament, the Rights of the Peers and Commons of England, and Destructive of the ancient fundamental Laws, Privileges and Customs of the Realm. Collected out of the writings of some modern authors.

(1). The Freeholders Grand Inquest touching our Sovereign Lord the King and his Parliament. By the learned Sir Robert Filmer, kt., first printed Anno 1647, Reprinted 1679.

f. 9. (2). Patriarcha, or the natural power of Kings. By the learned Sir Robert Filmer, bart., printed 1680.

f. 12v. (3). The Royalist's Defence, the author whereof (as I have been informed) was Sir Cha. Dallison, printed 1648.

f. 13. (4). Sober Reflections of the late Long Parliament, by James Howell, by way of dialogue, printed 1655.

f. 19. (5). Mr. Prynne's Second Part of his Brief Register of Parliamentary Writs, published 1660.

f. 19v. (6). Mr. Sheringham in his book The King's Supremacy Asserted, Anno 1660.

f. 20. (7). The Civil Wars of Great Britain, written by an Impartial Pen, John Davies, printed 1661.

f. 23v. (8). The Author of a certain discourse, his Epistle to the Reader, published of late Years.

f. 24. (9). A Discourse of the rise and power of Parliament, printed 1677.

f. 27. (10). Dugdale's Origines Juridiciales, Anno 1666.

(11). The publisher of the 2nd Part of Sir Henry Spelman's Glossary. Title Parliament, printed Anno 1664 (from flyleaf).

f. 29. 'Sir Henry Spelman, having in his lifetime, Anno 1626, published his learned and elaborate Glossary unto the letter M, since H.M.'s happy Restoration there hath been printed a continuation thereof to the end of the alphabet, and in the letter P the title or word Parliament, with a discourse thereupon hath been added and published which I have translated into English thus:'.

ff. 1–41v. Consists mainly of extracts from the respective works and is heavily annotated and referenced in the margins.

f. 42. 'From all which I shall deduce and draw these following positions as the sense of those authors and after that impartially consider their weight and soundness by the certainest rules of the best historians and records'.

ff. 42–323v. William Petyt examines the arguments in nine positions, Positions 1 to 3 and 8 to 9 are not dealt with in detail in this volume. For Positions 4 to 7 he provides his answers to each with very frequent references to the Public Records, especially including Patent Rolls, 6 John to 4 Edward IV, Close Rolls, 28 Henry III to 7 Richard II, Parliament Rolls, 19 Edward II to 31 Henry VI, a single reference each to Charter, Welsh and Norman Rolls. There are references to Coram Rege Rolls, Common Bench Rolls, Rolls of Inquisitions, the Statute Rolls, Acts in the custody of the Clerk of Parliament, the Journals of the House of

Commons, and to Bundles of K.R. Writs, Writs in the Tower, and Petitions to Parliament. The references to manuscripts are few, but include some to those in his own possession and one each in the possession of William Pierpoint, Samuel Baldwin, Serjeant at Law, John Peachey of the Inner Temple, and Evan Seys, Serjeant at Law, and the Register of the Prior and Chapter of Bath, described as being in the possession of the Library of Lincoln's Inn. Of the references to printed works almost all have been noted in his various other collections above.

The following marginalia are of some interest:

f. 65. The Commonwealth of England compiled by the Honourable Sir Thomas Smith, kt., Doctor of both Laws and Principal Secretary unto the two most worthy Princes King Edward and Queen Elizabeth.

f. 108. A considerable clause in the end of the Commons writ for electing members which Sir Robert Filmer takes no notice of.

f. 213v. Ends somewhat abruptly with a section on forms of addressing petitions to the Commons and there is no recapitulation of the chapter.

f. 218. 'And now I will, according to my promise and best of my observation speak of the ancient form and method of proceeding in Parliament in ordaining and making laws under the following heads' (7 heads).

ff. 218–308. Though 7 heads are mentioned only the 2nd, 3rd, 4th, and 7th heads are dealt with at length. The references are here comparatively few and mainly to Parliament Rolls and printed Statutes. An exceptional reference is to Manwood, *Forest Laws*.

f. 266. Begins: But I look back and conclude the general point upon the Statute of Provisors. In margin: 17 E. 3. The Commons told that they could nor would any longer suffer or endure the intolerable oppressions of the Provisors.

ff. 319–342v. A transcript without title or reference of a Latin chronicle beginning: Hinc paucis diebus interpositis Matheildis filia Malcolmi nobilissimi Regis Scotorum. Ends: talis in prefinito termino induciarum definienda in medium revocetur.

ff. 344–350v. 1162. Hoc anno sopita est discordia et amicabili fine terminata inter ecclesiam Lincoln. et cenobium beate Albani. Ends: Henrico filio Geroldi Camerario plurimisque aliis.

ff. 351–352v. Charter of Henry III to citizens of London, 22 December 1226, from Liber C in Archives of City of London. (*Cal. Lett. Book C*, pp. 41–2.)

VOLUME O

A composite volume containing transcripts of the sixteenth century in five main sections as detailed below. On flyleaf: What the Crown of England is and how to be disposed or ordered. $12\frac{7}{8}'' \times 8\frac{3}{4}''$. 158 ff.

1. ff. 1–26v. A tract of the time of Elizabeth I, in a contemporary hand, on 'What the Crown of England is and how to be disposed of or ordered', beginning 'These are the three principal divisions or grounds of your arguments that I intend to deal with'. It has marginal captions and also a few references in the margins, of which the following give an indication of the argument: Whether the crown is ordered by the rules of the common law; Many differences between the title of the crown and common inheritances; The title of the crown subject to

the common laws; Whether Scotland be out of the allegiance of England; Whether the crown go by succession or descent.

2. ff. 28–30v. Transcripts of the articles against Mary, Queen of Scots and her answers. In a contemporary hand.

June 1572. Articles with which she was to be charged by Lord de la Warr, Sir Ralph Sadler, kt., Mr. Wilson and Thomas Bromley, Solicitor General.

17 June 1572. Her protestation being her answers to the above articles. Given at Sheffield Castle.

3. ff. 40–46v. A tract touching the Kingdom of France, the Netherlands, the States of Italy, Modena, Geneva, Switzerland, Burgundy, Lombardy, describing these countries. In a hand of the late sixteenth or early seventeenth century.

4. ff. 110–16. A tract on 'The Causes and Affairs between the Emperor and his allies against the French King and his and their claims to several provinces and their pedigrees and by whom they claim'. In a hand of the second half of the sixteenth century.

5. ff. 120–158v. Transcripts of letters from Cardinal Wolsey and other communications to Richard Pace, Chief Secretary to Henry VIII, 1524–8, described as 'Letters written by Cardinal Wolsey touching the advancement of the Duke of Bourbon'.

f. 120. i. To Mr. Gregory, at the Mowthe, 31 August 1524. (*L. & P., Henry VIII*, IV, i, pp. 269–70.)

f. 127. ii. To Mr. Secretary. At my manor of Hampton Court, 7 August (1524). (Ibid., pp. 247–8.)

f. 130. iii. To Mr. Secretary. At my place besides Westminster, 18 May (1524).

f. 134v. iv. To Mr. Secretary. At the King's manor of Bradwell, 5 March 1524/5. (Ibid., pp. 506–7.)

f. 136. v. To Mr. Secretary and Sir John Russell. At my place besides Westminster, 15 January (1524). (Ibid., p. 264.)

f. 139v. vi. To Mr. Secretary. At my place besides Westminster, 28 June 1524. (Ibid., p. 191.)

f. 143v. 'Instructions given by the King's Highness to his trusty and well beloved Councillor and Chief Secretary, Mr. Richard Pace, containing such charge and matters as he shall disclose to the Duke and Senate of Venice or to their principal authority in the government of their being public of that dominion' (1523). (Strype, *Memorials*, I, ii, pp. 36–45; *L. & P., Henry VIII*, III, ii, pp. 1056–8.)

f. 148. vi. 'Instructions given by the King's Highness to his trusty and well beloved Chief Secretary, Mr. Richard Pace, whom his Grace doth send over his special Ambassador to the Swiss for certain matters to be treated with them as hereafter followeth', (19 March) 1523. (*L. & P., Henry VIII*, III, ii, pp. 1223–5.)

f. 152v. vii. To Mr. Secretary (no place or date).

f. 155v. In margin: The State of the Duke of Cleves, from Bradford. A note of the full title of the Duke.

f. 157v. Petition of the Merchant Adventurers that 'the Company of Merchant Adventurers have been a corporation privileged by the Kings of this realm and by the potentates of Flanders these 400 years and more . . . the great benefit of the realm and augmentation of His Majesty's customs'.

VOLUME P

Draft of a treatise, probably by William Petyt, on the manner of succession to the Crown of England. On flyleaf: The Course of Settling the Succession of the Crown of England. $12\frac{3}{4}'' \times 8''$. 121 ff.

ff. 1–105. The Treatise, beginning: To begin, my Lord, with my first point, That it hath been a universal course of settling the succession by the General Council or Parliament of the Kingdom. The Norman Succession, continuing with marginal captions and references in the margin. References to Brevis Relatio de Willelmo Rege, at end of S. Taylor, *Tract on Gavel.*, William of Poitou, Gesta of William, Duke of Normandy, *A true and exact history of the Succession of the Crown of England*, William of Jumieres, Malmesbury, Huntingdon, Matt. of West., Florence of Worcester, Hoveden, Symeon of Durham, Brompton, Higden, Fabian, Holinshed, Fox, *Acts*. Camden, *Brit.*, Ordericus Vitalis, Eadmer, Flores Hist., Spelman, *Gloss.*, Polydore Vergil, Close Roll, 3 Edward II, Matt. Paris, *Divi Brit.*, Knighton, Richard of Hexham, Gervase of Canterbury, Daniel, *Hist. of Engl.*, Gesta Stephani, *Insolence of the Popish Clergy*, Dr. Tillotson, Sermon before the King, 2 April 1680, entitled *The Protestant Religion Vindicated*, Chron. Norm, Ralph de Diceto, Speed, *Chron.*, Sir Richard Baker, *Life and Reign of Richard I*, from Old Register in Archives of Archbishop of Canterbury, MS. Chron. Abbrev. of time of King Edward, Newburgh, Walsingham, *Plac. Parl.*, Close Roll, 23 Edward I, Mr. Hunt, *Argument for the Bishops' Rights*, Patent Roll, 17 John, Dugdale, *Baronage*, *Letter from a Gentleman of Quality in the Country to his Friend*, Dr. Brady's *Answer to Mr. Petyt's Book of the Ancient Rights etc.*

f. 107. (no heading). Begins: Convenerunt interius die statuto ex mandato Regis.

f. 108. On the coronation of Richard I, from Matt. Paris.

f. 110v. Order of coronation of Richard I, from Hoveden.

f. 115. The manner of choosing the King, from Matt. Paris.

f. 116. The Barons of England choose Louis as King, from same.

f. 118. Letter from Louis to Abbot Alexander, from W. Thorne.

f. 120v. The Earl Marshal's speech to the Barons to choose Henry, son of King John, as King, from Knighton.

The draft has a few corrections and additions in the text and notes and references in the margin.

VOLUME Q

A volume of miscellaneous drafts and transcripts on the Norman Conquest of England, Laws of Countries and Speeches of James I etc. On flyleaf: Touching the Pretended Conquest, Laws of Countries, King James the 1st Speeches in Parliament etc. $12\frac{3}{4}'' \times 8''$. 261 ff.

f. 1. Brevis Refutatio: Quarumdam Positionum Anti Anglicarum de Absoluto Conquestu Anglie per Gulielmum 1m. et Normannos suos. Una cum Appendice.

ff. 1v–6. Testimonium Illustrissimi Domini Edwardi Clarendonis Comitis summi Anglie Cancellarii contra Hobbesium. In margin: A Brief View or Survey of the Dangerous and Pernicious Errors to Church and State in Mr. Hobbes Book entitled Leviathan, By Edward, Earl of Clarendon.

f. 7. Brevis Refutatio (as above), with references to Matt. Paris, Spelman, *Conc.*, Bracton,

Bale, Fortescue, *De Laud.*, Coke, *Reports*, Preface to Selden, *Tit. of Hon.*, Twysden, Preface to Laws of William I etc. in Lambard, *De Prisc.*, *Memorials of English Affairs*, *Hist. Brit. Saxon.*, Ordericus Vitalis.

f. 15. Testimonium H. de Bracton, De Leg. et Consuet. Angl.

f. 17. Testimonium John Fortescue, kt., Chief Justice and after Chancellor of England of Henry VI, *De Laud.*

f. 20. Testimonium Edw. Coke, Preface to *8th Reports*, with references to Life of St. Alban, from Book of Monastery of Lichfield, Ingulph, Lib. de Antiq. Leg., Matt. Paris, Hoveden, Florence of Worcester, Malmesbury, Roger Bacon, De impedimentis sapientibus, Stephen of Canterbury, Matt. of West.

f. 26. Testimonium John Selden, *Hist. of Tithes*, with references to Quintilian, Institutions, Calvin's Case, Hoveden, Abingdon MS. in Cotton Library, Coke, *8th Reports*, Hist. Cad., Westminster Charter inspected 1 Edward IV, William of Poitou, Malmesbury, Matt. Paris, Chard in Cas. in Itin. t. Edward III, Bocquet, *De domaine de Fran.*, Reyner, *De Antiq. Mon. S. Bened.*

f. 32. Charter of William I, in Dugdale, *Hist. Eccl. Cath. S. Pauli.*

f. 33. Testimonium Roger Twysden, Preface to Laws of William I etc. in Lambard, *De Prisc.*, with references to Matt. Paris, Ordericus Vitalis, Hoveden, Dialog. de Trechar., Huntingdon, Malmesbury.

f. 37. Hinemar, *Archiep. Remen.*

f. 43. Livy, Hist., printed in Frankfurt, 1588.

f. 51. Dissertatio Brevis de Monarchia scilicet et absoluta utrum mixte monarchie Regimen non sit cum Principi tum Populo tutius et melius monarchis Absoluta sive Despotica.

ff. 52–63. Extracts from various foreign authors including Bodin, *De Republic.*

ff. 68–97. Collections including extracts from Glanvill, *Tract. de Leg. Angl.*, Red Book of the Church of Bath in poss. of Thomas Guidott, M.D., *Hist. Goth. Vand.*, *Sphera Civit.*, Spelman, *Gloss.*, Close Roll, 45 Henry III, Staunford, *Plees del Coron*, Mirror of Justice, Pleas, Hil. t22 Edward III, Hil. 24 Edward III, Trin. 43 Edward III.

ff. 110–38. Collections including extracts from Fortescue, *De Laud.*, T. Smith, *De Republ.*, *An Exact Abridg. of Records in the Tower of London*, 'said to be collected by Sir Robert Cotton, kt. and bart.' with notes from Dyer, *Reports*, Plowden, *Comm.*

f. 139. Censura John Spelman Henrice F. de Imperio Anglo Saxonico with reference to *Life of Alfred the Great.*

f. 145. Evidentia Memorabilia, Patent Roll, 11 Edward III.

ff. 148–52. De Comitiis veterum Suebo Goth.

ff. 153–8. Collectanea ex nonnullis Jac. I orationibus habitis in Comitiis Parliamentariis Anglie et postea reddita fuerunt Latine et in lucem editi a Rich. Montagu D.D., Bishop of Chichester, with parts of first and second speeches and fourth speech, 21 March 1610 (King James, *Works*).

f. 160. Ex Libro Statutorum, 25 H. 8, cap. 21, Latine redditum.

ff. 162–183v. Collections from Lambard, *Arch.*

Quedam Positiones Antianglicane R. Brady M.D., de Conquestu Anglie. *A Full and Clear Answer to a book by William Petyt esq.* Printed in the year 1680, London, for Samuel Lowndes over against Exeter Exchange in the Strand, 1681, Positiones and translation into Latin.

ff. 184–186v. The Preamble to an Act of Parliament made 25 Henry VIII, cap. 21, from Rastell, *Stat.*

Concerning Courts and Councils in the Saxon and Norman times and after.

ff. 189–190. De Aldermanno et multiplici eius Magistratu apud Anglo-Saxones, with reference to Spelman, *Gloss.*

f. 200. 'To search what authorities may be found either in Glossaries or Dictionaries to prove that the chief and principal men or magistrates of cities were indifferently called by and included under (list of names)'.

f. 202. Nobilitas est Duplex, Superior et Inferior, with references to Chasney, *Catalogus Gloria Mundi.*

ff. 204–9. Diatriba de Baronibus cui adjungitur duo consilia universalis Baronii Regni sive Parliamenti Generalissimi que tenta fuit apud Westmonasterium, 29 & 30 Henry III, with references to Camden, *Brit.*, Selden, *Tit. of Hon.*, Spelman, *Gloss.*, Close Roll, 4 Henry III, Matt. Paris, inset in Cleopatra E. 1, Close Roll, 29 Henry III.

ff. 211–213v. 'A Collection made by Mr. Camden concerning the different sense and meaning of the word Baro in several ages'.

f. 212. 'The following Collection was communicated to by me the learned Dr. Thomas Smith who collected and published the Catalogue of the Cottonian Library'.

ff. 214–223v. 'What the Laws of England are and by whom made', with references to Bracton, Matt. of West, Parl. Roll, 15 Edward III, Patent Roll, 11 Edward III, Parl. Roll, 22 Edward III, Year Book, East. term, 39 Edward III, *Plac. Parl.*, Parl. Roll, 51 Edward III, Coke, *3rd Inst.*, Stat. Roll, 5 Richard II, cap. 5, Parl. Roll, 6 Richard II, Like, 9 Richard II, Like, 2 Henry V, Plea, Mich. term, 9 Henry VII, Rastell, *Stat.*

ff. 225–31. De Significatione verbi Parliamentum, with references to Spelman, *Gloss.*, du Fresne, *Gloss.*, Hotoman, *Francogallia*, Gloss at end of *Dec. Script.*, Camden, *Brit.*, T. Smith, *De Republ. Angl.*, Plowden, *Comm.*

ff. 232–234. De verbo Parliamentum usitato in Anglia quam in Scotia, with reference to Close Roll, 42 Henry III.

ff. 236–240v. De Antiquitate et usu verbi Parliamentum hic in Anglia et de Concilio illius tam membris integrantibus quam potestate et Jurisdictione, with references to Hotoman, *Franco Gall.*, Gloss at end of *Dec. Script.*, Camden, *Brit.*, *Dial. de fund. Leg. Angl.*, T. Smith, *De Republ. Angl.*, *An Exact Abridg. of Rec.*, Dyer, *Reports*, Plowden, *Comm.*

ff. 241–4. 'Of a General Council or Full Parliament held 10 Henry II in which the Assize or Statute of Clarendon were made and sworn to', from Collection of Robert Glover, Somerset, in poss. of Peter le Neve, Rouge Croix.

f. 244. 'Note, Touching diverse phrases or words by which learned men and historians express General and Common Councils or Parliaments' with references to Gerv. of Canterbury, Hoveden, Matt. Paris, Ralph de Diceto, Quadrilogus, fitz Stephen, Matt. of West., *Antiq. Brit.*, Godwin, *De Presul.*, Spelman, *Gloss.*, Twysden, *An Historical Vindication of the Church of England*, Selden, *Tit. of Hon.*, John Clerk, *Ars Critica.*

ff. 246–247v. Officium Regis Anglie. Quoad Politicum Regimen Subditorum secundum Bonas et Antiquas Leges et Justas Consuetudines Anglie uti Demonstratum est, Ab authenticis Historiographis Legum Libris et Recordis Regni, with references to Patent Roll, 27 Edward I, Like, 31 Edward I, Like, 1 Edward II, Close Roll, 50 Henry III, Gascon Roll, 21 Richard II, Lambard, *De Prisc.*

ff. 248–56. 'The opinion and judgement of Mr. Selden and Mr. Prynne concerning the deplorable loss of our ancient Parliamentary Records' with references to Selden, *Tit. of Hon.*, Cotton, *Exact Abridg.*, with Prynne's Preface, Prynne, Epistle Dedicatory to the King before his *Brevia Parliamentaria Rediviva*, Part 2, First Part of *Parliamentary Writs*, with note on Richard II changing Parl. Roll, from Parl. Roll, 1 Henry IV.

f. 257. De Communi Concilio Regni tento 6 John in que assisa sive Statutum de Moneta ordinata fuit, from Patent Roll, 6 John.

ff. 258v.–261. Notes from Mirror of Justice, Coke, *2nd Inst.*, Hoveden, Matt. Paris, Close Roll, 23 Edward I, MS. Stat. in poss. of William Petyt, Pynson, *Antiq. Stat.*, Various Statutes and Constitutions of England, Henry III to Edward II, Vespasian B. 7, Totell, *Magna Carta* etc., Close Roll, 27 Edward I, Parl. Roll, 5 Edward III, Fine Roll, 9 Edward III, Parl. Roll, 2 Henry V, Davys, *Reports*, Trin. 2 James I.

VOLUME R

Draft of a work by William Petyt in his historical controversies with Dr. Robert Brady on English Saxon Parliaments. On flyleaf: The Antiquity, Parts and Power of the English Saxon Parliaments, Vol. 1: Mr. Petyt's assertion of the Power of Parliament against Dr. Brady. 254 ff.

f. 1. The Antiquity, Parts and Power of the English Saxon Great Councils or Parliaments in reply to A Pretended Full and Clear Answer to the Ancient Rights of the Commons of England asserted, written by Robert Brady, Doctor in Physic, with several remarks upon his Introduction to the Old English History and his Compleat History of England. By William Petyt of the Inner Temple, esq.

ff. 11–16. The Contents. The State of the Question between Dr. Brady and me touching the English Saxon Witenagemots, Great Councils or Parliaments and who were parts thereof.

The Introduction reduced to four Heads.

The First to show how the English Saxons were descended from the Germans.

The Second That the Populus as opposed to the other orders were part of the German Great Councils both before and after they received the Christian faith.

The third is That the Civitates or Urbes Germanicae sent their Delegates or Representatives to those Councils.

And the Fourth and last Head is That the Saxons brought with them hither their country laws and customs, which prove

1. In general the Antiquity, Parts and Power of our English Saxon Great Councils or Parliaments.
2. And in particular That the Delegates or Representatives of their Cities or Great Towns were part of such Parliaments.

To evidence the Truth whereof I have given the Reader Comparisons of Great Councils or Witanagemots held in England during our Saxon Government.

f. 18. The State of the Question.

ff. 20–64v. The Introduction. The First Head, with characteristic references mainly to foreign printed sources including Florence of Worcester, Ingulph, Camden, *Brit.*, Bede, *Eccl. Hist.*, Brady, *Compl. Hist. of Engl.*, Selden, *Hist. of Tithes*, *Titles of Honor*, du Fresne, *Gloss.*, Somner, *Dict.*, Spelman, *Gloss.*, Usher, *De Brit. Eccl. Primod.*, Lambard, *Archion.*, Burnet, *Hist. of Rights of Princes in disposing of Eccl. Benefices.*

ff. 65–74. The First Comparison. Of a Common Council held at Canterbury A.D. DCV, under King Ethelbert, the First Christian King, of the English Saxons, In which the Monastery of St. Peter and St. Paul founded by Augustine the Monk in Canterbury and the Donation and Liberties granted to the Monastery by King Ethelbert were all confirmed, with like to Cartae Antiquae, Spelman, *Conc.*, Bede, *Eccl. Hist.*, Lambard, *De Prisc.*, Heylin, *Stumbling Block*, Tillesley, *Animad. on Selden's Hist. of Tithes*, Comber, *Hist. Vindication of Divine Right of Tithes*, and foreign printed works.

ff. 75–88v. The Second Comparison, In a General Council of all Britain held at Hatfield A.D. DCLXXX when were present 1. Egfrid, King of Northumberland, 2. Ethelred, King of Mercia, 3. Aldwulf, King of East Saxons, 4. Hlothere, King of Kent, In which 1. The Canons of V General Councils were received, 2. And several Constitutions which had been made at Rome and sent thence into England were allowed and confirmed to be used here, with like to Matt. of Westminster, Fleta, Close Rolls, Spelman, *Conc.*, Bede, *Eccl. Hist.*, Camden, *Brit.*, Somner, *Dict.*, Preface to *Monition to all Churches.*

ff. 89–100v. The Third Comparison. Of a Witenagemot or Parliament called by Ini, King of West Saxons, in his time the most puissant of all the English Saxon Kings, with like to Spelman, *Gloss.*, *Conc.*, Lambard, *Archion.*, *Perambul. of Kent*, *Eirenarcha*, *Mon.*

ff. 101–119v. The Fourth Comparison. Of a General Synod or Council of All England held at Alnes near Evesham in Worcestershire A.D. DCCIX wherein The Grants which Coenred, King of Mercia, and Offa, King of East Saxons, had made at Rome of several lands in England to Ecgwine, Bishop of Worcester, were ratified and confirmed, with like to Register of Selby, Capgrave, *Mon.*, Cressy, *Hist. of Church of Brit.*, Tillesley, *Animad.*, Bale, *Script. Brit.*, Harpsfield, *Hist. Eccl. Angl.*, Somner, *Dict.*, Stillingfleet, *Orig. Brit.*, Malmesbury.

ff. 120–37. The Fifth Comparison. Of a Synod or General Council of All England held at Chelsea A.D. DCCLXXXVII, in the reign of Elfwald, King of Northumberland, 1. which besides the confirmation of several laws which related to the State, 2. And of several canons which Gregory, Bishop of Ostia, and Theophilus, Bishop of Tody, had, as Legates from Pope Hadrian the 1st brought hither from Rome for reforming and establishing Church laws., 3. A law was made whereby all men were commanded to pay tithes of whatever they possessed because it was God's special part and for that reason they ought to live on the nine parts and give alms out of them, with like to *Vocab. Scot.*, Selden, *Hist. of Tithes*, *Ad Fletam*, Tillesley, *Animad.*, Huntingdon, *Illustr. on Polybolion.*

ff. 138–54. The Sixth Comparison. Of a Synodical Council or Parliament held at Clovesho about the year DCCCXXVI under Beornwulf, King of the Mercians, wherein were debated 1. Such matters as concerned the good advancement of Churches, 2. The Rule and Observance of a monastical life, 3. And the stability and amendment of the Realm, with like to Spelman, *Gloss.*, Lambard, *Perambul. of Kent*, Camden, *Brit.*, Somner, *Dict.*, Selden, *Titles of Honor*, and foreign printed works.

ff. 155–62. The Seventh Comparison. Of another Synod or Parliament held at Clovesho Anno Christi DCCCXXIV, under the same King, In which among other things were done, A suit between Heahbeorht, Bishop of Worcester, and the Nuns of Berlea concerning the inheritance of Æethelric, son of Æthelmund was heard and adjudged, with like to *Mon.*, Selden, *Jani. Angl.*, du Fresne, *Gloss.*, Bede, *Eccl. Hist.*

ff. 163–188v. The Eighth Comparison. Of the harmony which is to be found between the English Saxons and the Old Germans touching their Great Council, 2. As also the agreement between the Germans and their neighbour Northern Nations in their Public Assemblies, with like to Spelman, *Gloss.*, and foreign printed works.

ff. 189–192v. The Ninth Comparison. Of a Parliament held at Winchester about the year DCCCXXIII in which 1. Egbert, King of the West Saxons, was by common consent crowned King of All Britain, 2. Which from thenceforth by a General Decree was to be called England, with like to Matthew of Westminster, Ailred of Rievaulx, Reg. York, Ingulph, Malmesbury, Domitian A. 13, Lambard, *Archion.*, *Mon.*

ff. 193–228v. The Tenth Comparison. Of a Great Council held at Dinningdon A.D. DCCCL under Beorhtwulf, King of the Mercians, to consult how to resist the Danes, of another Great Council or Parliament held A.D. DCCCL at Kingsbury under the same King wherein 1. They consulted touching the affairs of that Kingdom, 2. And confirmed a charter of privilege then granted by King Beorhtwulf to the monastery of Croyland, with like to Huntingdon, Brompton, Florence of Worcester, Spelman, *Conc.*, *Gloss.*, Camden, *Brit.*, du Fresne, *Gloss.*, Bede, *Eccl. Hist.*, Bale, *Script. Brit.*, *Antiq. Brit.*, Selden, *Titles of Honor*, Heylin, *Hist. & Misc. Tracts*, Usher, *De Brit. Eccl. Primord.*, Prynne, *Truth Triumphant.*

ff. 229–241v. The Eleventh Comparison. Of a Council of All England held at Winchester Anno Christi DCCCLV under Ethelwulf, King of the West Saxons, at which Council A General Law was established 1. For the payment of tithes, 2. And that freed from all services, charges and taxes made in the State, with like to W. Thorne, Selden, *Titles of Honor*, *Hist. of Tithes*, *Life of Alfred the Great*, Tillesley, *Animad.*

ff. 242–254v. The Twelfth Comparison. Of a Great Council held A.D. DCCCCV under King Edward the Elder wherein 1. Of two Bishoprics which formerly were in the Province of the Gewisi or West Saxons, three were erected out of them, 2. To fill all which five Bishops were constituted and elected, with like to Malmesbury, Liber Landavensis, *Antiq. Brit.*, Spelman, *Gloss.*, *Conc.*, Somner, *Dict.*, *Mon.*, Camden, *Brit.*, Grafton, *Chron.*, Harpsfield, *Hist. Eccl. Angl.*, J. Cass, *Sphera Civit.*, Usher, *Discourse on Religion professed by Irish and Welsh.*

Vide Vol. 2 pro resid.

There are references and notes in the margin in both volumes R & S and both volumes are written in the same hand.

VOLUME S

The second volume of the draft of a work by William Petyt in his historical controversies with Dr. Robert Brady on English Saxon Parliaments. On flyleaf: Antiquity, Parts and Power of English Saxon Parliaments, Vol. 2. $12\frac{3}{4}'' \times 8\frac{1}{8}''$. 312 ff.

f. 1. Title-Page as in volume R above, vol. II.

ff. 1x–24. The Thirteenth Comparison. Of a famous Council held by Athelstan, King of

England, or All Britain, wherein certain Ecclesiastical Laws were established, with characteristic references to Malmesbury, Matt. of Westminster, Ingulf, Brompton, *Mon. Angl.*, Spelman, *Conc.*, Selden, *Analect. Anglo-Brit.*, *Titles of Honor*, *Jani Angl.*, *De Synedriis*, Lambard, *De Prisc.*, *Archion.*, Bede, *Eccles. Hist.*, Heylin, *Hist. & Misc. Tracts*, and foreign printed sources.

ff. 26–34. The Fourteenth Comparison. Of a Public Council held A.D. DCCCXCVI, about the XIIth year of King Ethelred wherein 1. The charter of Walfrena, a devout woman, who founded the monastery of Wolverhampton in Staffordshire, was by a particular law settled, 2. And by that law several liberties and privileges which had been granted by the Pope to that religious house were likewise ratified and confirmed, with references to his own autograph in possession of R. Windsor, 1640, *Mon. Ang.*, du Fresne, *Gloss.*, Selden, *Jani Angl.*

ff. 36–61. The Fifteenth Comparison. Of a General Council of the whole Kingdom held at Fenham, A.D. MIX, about the XXXth year of King Ethelred, at which several laws, both Ecclesiastical and Civil, were ordained and confirmed, with characteristic references to Malmesbury, Spelman, *Conc.*, Usher, *De Eccles. Angl. Primord.*, Camden, *Brit.*, du Fresne, *Gloss.*

ff. 62–92v. The Sixteenth Comparison. Of a General Council held under King Canute at Winchester, A.D. MXXI, at what time a law was made that the monastery of Briadilesworth, afterwards St. Edmundsbury, should for ever remain and be 1. A House of Monks, 2. Exempt from Episcopal Jurisdiction. 3 and from the County and King's Ministers, 4. and should have cognizance of all causes within those vills which belonged to them, with references to Malmesbury, Florence of Worcester, Brompton, Matt. of Westminster, Matt. Paris, Symeon of Durham, Patent and Close Rolls, Parliament Rolls, L.T.R. Memoranda Rolls, Chron. of St. Benet of Hulme in Galba E 2., Hist., of Church of Ely in Nero A. 15, Reg. of St. Benet of Hulme (in Galba E. 2), Camden, *Brit.*, Spelman, *Conc.*, *Mon. Angl.*, Coke, Pref. to *9th Rep.*, Selden, *Titles of Honor*, *Hist. of Tithes.*, Heylin, *Hist. & Misc. Tracts*, *Plac. Parl.*, Cotton, *Posthuma.*

f. 92. In margin: This Parliament Roll (1 Edward III) is lost, but in a Collection of Petitions in Parliament made by Mr. Selden and transcribed by Mr. Elsyng, Clerk to the House of Lords, I met with the petition entitled: pro Elizabeth de Burgo.

ff. 94–120. The Seventeenth Comparison. Of another Witanagemot or Common Council of the Kingdom held likewise under that King at Winchester Anno MXXXII in which Council, 1. Several Laws as well Ecclesiastical as Civil were enacted, 2. Diverse Laws which had been made under former Kings were revived and confirmed, 3. And severe Penalties ordained against the infringers thereof, with like to Brompton, Malmesbury, Charter Rolls, Lambard, *De Prisc.*, Spelman, *Conc.*, Camden, *Brit. Mon. Angl.*, Broke, *Abridg.*, Staunford, *Pleas of Crown*, Coke, *Rep.*

ff. 123–47. The Eighteenth Comparison. Or some other considerations upon Dr. Brady's Assertion vizt. That it plainly appears the Saxons did in their subjection of and submission to their Princes acknowledge the nomination and appointment of preceding Kings as a Rule of Succession to the Crown, with like to Malmesbury, Huntingdon, Florence of Worcester, Brompton, Parliament Roll, Selden, *Titles of Honor*, Spelman, *Conc.*, Speed, *Chron.*, Bale, *Script. Brit.*, *Life of Alfred the Great*, *Sermon preached at the Magnificent Coronation of Charles II*, by George, Bishop of Worcester, *Mon.*, Fortescue, *De Laud.*, Pulton, *Stat.*, Johnson, *Excellency of Monarchical Govt.*, and foreign printed works.

ff. 148–58. The Nineteenth Comparison. Of a Common Council of the Kingdom held in the Reign of Edward the Confessor wherein the great law concerning the Payment of Tithes to the Church enacted and ordained A rege Baronibus et Populo was renewed and confirmed, with like to Register of St. Augustine's, Canterbury, in Claudius D. 10, Lambard, *De Gavel.*, *The Law of Tithes affirmed against all opposition.*

ff. 160–274v. The Twentieth Comparison. Diverse Assertions of several of our modern writers touching the Constituent Parts of the Saxon Parliament summarily considered, with like to Polydore Virgil, Huntingdon, Florence of Worcester, Malmesbury, Parliament Rolls, Westminster Cart., in Faustina A. 3, *The Royalist's Defence*, Howell, *Sober Inspections*, Bede, *Eccl. Hist.*, Selden, *Titles of Honor*, *Jani Angl.*, *De Synod.*, *Ad Fletam*, Lambard, *Archion.*, *Perambul. of Kent*, *Eirenarcha*, *De Prisc.*, John Spelman, *Life of King Alfred*, Johnson, *Excell. of Monarch. Govt.*, Spelman, *Conc.*, *Gloss.*, *Tithes too hot to be Touched*, Howell, *Fourth Part of Instit. of Gen. Hist. of World*, Verstigan, *Restitution of decayed Intelligence on Antiquity*, Somner, *Dict.*, *Antiq. of Canterbury*, Pulton, *Stat.*, *Liber Stat. Gall.*, Crompton, *Jurisdiction*, Hooker, *Eccl. Polity*, Camden, *Annal. of Q. Eliz.*, D'Ewes, *Journ. of Parl. of Q. Eliz.*, Usher, *De Eccl. Brit. Primord.*

ff. 275–294v. The Twenty First Comparison. A Recapitulation of several of the Saxon Parliaments which have been mentioned in the foregoing Comparisons reduced into series of time. Scriptura: The Will of King Alfred, from *Life of Alfred the Great*, with notes from same, with like to Crompton, Spelman, *Concil.*, *Gloss.*, Lambard, *Perambul. of Kent*, *Antiq. Brit.*, *Mon. Angl.*

ff. 295–297. Scriptura: Gift of Caedwalla to Church of Chichester, from Reg. of Cathedral Church of Chichester in possession of Dean and Chapter.

ff. 299–301. Scriptura: The copy of an Ancient MS. showing the form of trial among the English Saxons, from Somner, *Antiq. of Canterbury*.

ff. 303–308v. Scriptura: The Charter of Bishop Brithelm, from *Mon. Angl.*

ff. 309–312v. Scriptura: Letter of Canute, from Spelman, *Conc.*

VOLUME T

A collection of transcripts and extracts, mainly from the Public Records with some from printed and manuscript sources. On flyleaf: 'Touching the time of prescription, Grants, Pardons, de Expensis Militum, Privileges of Towns, Summons to Parliament, Alliances, Cases etc.' $12\frac{3}{4}'' \times 8\frac{1}{8}''$. 261 ff.

f. 1. Definition of time of prescription, from Rolle's *Abridg.*

f. 3. Extract from Coram Rege Roll, York, Trin. term, 1 Edward III, on grants to the Archbishop of York and his successors of liberties in the River Hull etc.; to Richard de La Pole, Butler, 4 June 1327, and a writ of privy seal to Geoffrey le Scrope, 24 June 1327 (French). Certificate it agrees with the record, 17 June 1689.

f. 11. Letters Patent on dower of Queen Isabella, King's mother, 23 March 1327.

ff. 13, 17. Letters patent of pardon to citizens of London, 28 February 1327.

f. 15. Like for Andrew de Setchford, 28 February 1327.

f. 19. Writs de expensis, knights, 9 March 1327.

f. 19v. The like, citizens, 23 September 1327.

f. 20. The like, knights, 23 September 1327.

f. 20v. The like, citizens, 23 September 1327.

f. 22. Mandate for Bishop of Hereford concerning Mortimer, 16 February 1327

f. 24. Like for men of Hedon, 3 February 1327.

f. 25. Letters patent to Justice of Ireland on restitution of temporalities, 15 August 1327.

f. 26. Inquisition on privileges of city of Lincoln, 1 Edward III, from Bundle of Escheats, 1 Edward III.

f. 30. Letters Patent for Edward, King of Scotland, 1 March 1334 (French), from Scottish Roll.

f. 32. The case of the burgesses of the town of Barnstaple that they have sent burgesses to Parliament time out of mind, 18 May 1343.

f. 36. Extract from case on ancient demesne, 22 Edward III, from *Liber Assisarum*, with extract from Broke's *Abridg*.

f. 38. Extract from Statute of Provisors, 25 Edward III.

f. 40. Extract from Year Book, East. term, 39 Edward III.

f. 41. Letters patent for Archbishop of Canterbury (extract only).

f. 43. Extracts from Bede, *Eccles. Hist.*, and Huntingdon, names of cities.

f. 46. Concerning men of ancient demesne, from MS. Reg. in poss. of William Petyt, with notes from Close, Patent, Charter, and Parliament Rolls, Edwards I–III, etc.

f. 51. On the time of general prescription according to the law and custom of England, from Parliament Roll, 43 Edward III, Select Bundle of Writs and Records, t. Edward III, Year Book, Trin. term, 11 Edward III and Rolle's *Abridg*.

f. 59. Extract from Fitzherbert's *Natura Brevium*, on tenants of ancient demesne.

f. 64. Extract from Preface to Coke, *9th Reports*, on antiquity of and sending representatives to Parliament.

f. 66. Extract from Parliament Roll, 51 Edward III, the Commons petitions that by general prescription they ought to be present in Parliament represented by knights, citizens, and burgesses (French), with translation.

f. 69. Petitions of city of London and of William de Widdeslade, citizen of London (French), from New Misc. Bundle, t. Henry III.

ff. 73–96v. Process at the coronation of Richard II and the claims of all persons who held lands or offices to do service at his coronation. (No reference.)

f. 98. Extract from Statute Roll, 5 Richard II.

f. 99. Extract from protestation of prelates, 11 Richard II.

Ordinance made in Parliament on representation there, from Rastell, *Stat*.

ff. 109–119. Proceedings in Parliament, 7 Richard II. Pronouncement on cause of summons by Chancellor.

f. 120. Extract from Fitzherbert's *Grand Abridg*. on avowry.

f. 122. Extract from Statute Roll, 13 Richard II, with writ to Sheriff of Kent, 16 May (1390).

ff. 124–7. 'A mighty authority to prove that Lords and Commons had writs of summons long before 5 Richard II by general prescription'. Rastell, *Stat.* with translation.

ff. 128–48. Roll of Services on the coronation day, 1 Henry IV. (No reference.)

f. 149. Extract from Proceedings in Parliament, 1 Henry IV.

f. 150. Petition on the adjournment of Parliament, 12 Edward IV (English), from Bundle of Petitions in Parliament, 12 Edward IV.

f. 151. Letters patent on ancient demesne, 26 May 1476.

f. 153. Petition on general prescription (English), 17 Edward IV.

f. 155. Protestation by community of realm, 2 Henry V.

f. 156. Mandate for tenants of ancient demesne, 29 November 1435.

f. 158. Proceedings in Parliament, 4 Henry VII.

f. 160. Act concerning peace between Kings of England and France.

f. 163. Extract from Plowden's *Comm.*

f. 165. Extract from Ralph de Diceto.

ff. 171–8. Extracts from the following works on the loss of Parliamentary records: Selden, *Titles of Honor*, Cotton, *Exact Abridg. of Records in the Tower*, with Prynne's Preface, Prynne, Epistle Dedicatory of his *Brevia Parliamentaria Rediva*, Prynne, *First Part of Parliamentary Writs.*

f. 180. Extract from Camden, *Brit.*

f. 182. Extract from Bracton, De Legibus.

f. 184. Extract from Vespasian B. 7, on who is Steward of England and what is his office.

ff. 188–96. 'The remarkable case of Thomas Merke, Bishop of Carlisle, found guilty of high treason against Henry IV, together with the King's pardon'.

Extract from Coram Rege Roll, Hil. term, 2 Henry IV.

ff. 197–206. 'Of the laudable Statute of Magna Carta in the reign of Edward IV and preceding Kings', from MS. Book of Stat. in poss. of William Petyt, with note from Patent Roll, 18 Edward IV.

ff. 208–18. Alliances made between Henry V and Sigismund, King of Romans, 4 Henry V.

ff. 219–22. Peace concluded between England and France, Henry V.

ff. 223–7. On treaty, 14 January 1422, from French Roll.

ff. 228–36. 'The famous case of Thomas Thorp, Speaker of House of Commons in the time of Henry VI, in time of prorogation, taken in execution, at suit of Richard, Duke of York'.

ff. 247–251v. 'The memorable case of George Ferrers, servant of Henry VIII 34 & 35 Henry VIII', from Crompton, *Jurisdict.*, with note from Plowden, *Comm.*

ff. 252–8. 'The notable case of Trewynnard concerning privilege of High Court of Parliament', from Dyer, *Reports*, 36 & 37 Henry VIII.

ff. 259–261v. The Proclamation of the Earl of Tyrone when he stirred rebellion in Ireland, Dungaron, 15 November 1599. (no references.)

VOLUME U

Transcripts of extracts etc. from manuscripts and printed sources, with some from the Public Records, relating to Scotland, a draft probably by William Petyt. On flyleaf: The Short View of the Government of Scotland compared with that of England by way of parallel. On next flyleaf: A Short View of the Ancient and Modern Government of Scotland. Old red leather label inset: Speculum Scotiae. 526 ff.

Title-Page: Speculum Scotiae or A Short View of the Ancient and Modern Government of Scotland together with a Brief Account of that of England by way of parallel. The First Part.

f. 1. To the Reader. Begins: We are told by the Reverend and Pious Author of the Whole Duty of Man.

ff. 1–22. References to Rastell, *Stat.*; Coke, *2nd Inst.*, *4th Inst.*; Bacon, *Resuscitatio*; Petition of Right; Pulton, *Stat.*; Charles I's Declaration from *Exact Collection of Declarations*; Brompton; James I, *Works*; Fortescue, *De Laud.*; Bracton; Hooker, *Eccles. Polity*; *Patriarcha non Monarchia*; *The True Principles of Government and Property asserted by a Lover of Truth and his Country*; Camden, *Ann. of Q. Eliz.*

ff. 24–30. The Contents of the Chapters of the First Part:

Chap. I. There was an affinity between the constituent parts of the Scottish and English Parliaments . . .

Chap. II. A Brief Account of the Original of the Saxons and their Government.

Chap. III. A Continuation of the View of the Government of Scotland during the reigns of Alexander the 1st etc.

Chap. IV. An Account of the Government of England from William the 1st to Edward the 1st.

Chap. V. A Further Continuation of the View of the Government of Scotland.

Chap. VI. The Scots being very uneasy under the superiority of England procured themselves to be absolved by the Pope from their Fealty.

Chap. VII. The insurrection of the Scots under William Wallis who at first beat the English afterwards was taken himself and at last drawn, hanged and quartered.

Chap. VIII. Two Regents or Governors appointed by Parliament to take care of King David and the Kingdom.

Chap. IX. Upon the death of King David Bruce without issue of his body Robert Stuart, by the name of King Robert the ii nd., succeeded to that Kingdom.

Chap. X. Upon the miserable death of King Robert the Parliament of Scotland convene wherein they commit the Kingdom to Robert, the Brother (sic) of the deceased King.

ff. 31–37. The Contents of the Chapters of the Second Part:

Chap. I. Sir George Mackenzie, the King's Advocate in Scotland, says that there were assemblies of the Chief of the Clans called to give the King advice upon all occasions before Kenneth the iiird's time, but gives little or no Proof of it.

Chap. II. Dr. Brady, Master of Gonvile and Caius College in Cambridge, who since the writing of his Books is made Physician Extraordinary to the King and Keeper of the Records in the Tower, with the annual salary of three hundred pounds from the crown asserts . . .

Chap. III. That the Scottish Parliaments were in former ages numerous.

f. 37. At end in a different hand: The Appendix containing several authorities at large referred to in the preceding Discourse.

ff. 38–41. A Catalogue of what authors, records and other authorities are cited in this book, arranged alphabetically, of which the only noted as manuscripts are Cart. of Westminster, Walter of Coventry, Fordun, Parliament, Close, Patent and Charter Rolls, the Rotulus de Superioritate Regis Angliae in Regno Scotiae, Records of the Exchequer and the Scotichronicon.

f. 1. Chapter 1, begins with a new foliation and continues to f. 218v.

ff. 1–218v. The chapters above Part I, 1–8 only are given with references to authorities English, Scottish, and foreign, of which the following are of special interest: Brady, *Old English Hist.*; Leslie, Bishop of Ross, *De Origine Moribus et Rebus Gestis Scotorum*; Buchan, *Rerum Scotor. Hist.*; Sir G. Mackenzie, *Jus Regimen;* Brady, *Compl. Hist. of Eng.*; Burton, *Commentary on Antonius' Itin. of Brit.*; Ussher, *Discourse on the Religion anciently professed by the Irish and British*; *Regiam Maiestatem*; Brady, *Answer*; *Scotia Juriculum or the Perfect State of Scotland*; Sir G. Mackenzie, *Defence of the Royal Line of Scotland.*

ff. 221–343. The three chapters above Part II, with references to authorities as above and also to Scottish Statute Book; *Scotor. Regum Catalog.*; Docket of Warrants at the Signet Office, 1686 (a note that the King had given Dr. Brady an annual salary of £300 for his care and pains about records); Holinshed, *Hist. of Scotl.*; *The Laws and Acts of Parliament of Scotland.*

ff. 346–526. The Appendix containing several authorities at large referred to in the preceding Discourse, containing Scriptura I–XXIV.

f. 347. I. Foundation Charter of Abbey of Dunfermline, from Original Charter. (*Mon.*)

f. 348. II. The election of Eadmer as Archbishop of St. Andrews. (Eadmer.)

f. 352. III. Statute or Assize of William, King of Scotland. (*Regiam Maiestatem.*)

f. 353v. IV. Charter or Letters Patent of William, King of Scotland, for Morgund, son of Gilchrist, who claimed the Earldom of Mar. (Selden, *Titles of Honor.*)

f. 355v. V. Statute of King Alexander II. (*Regiam Maiestatem.*)

f. 357v. VI. Bull of Nicholas IV of dispensation. 16 November 1289.

f. 359. VII. Letter of Edward I to Eric, King of Norway, 17 April 1290.

f. 360. VIII. Articles made by Edward I with the Parliament of Scotland on the marriage of the Maid of Norway, 20 July 1290.

ff. 368–438v. IX. Rotulus de Superioritate, 19–23 Edward I, mm. 1–18.

ff. 439–63. X. Persons claiming the Kingdom of Scotland put in the following claims before the King of England at Berwick on Tweed and the Proceedings thereon. Ibid., mm. 19–24.

ff. 464–75. XI. The Judgement of Edward I on the above claims. Ibid., mm. 24–7.

ff. 478–92. XII. Treaty between John Balliol and the King of France, 1295.

f. 492. XIII. Mandate to publish the laws of Robert I, King of Scotland. (*Regiam Maiestatem.*)

ff. 494–501v. XIV. Letter to the Pope by the community of Scotland, 6 April 1320, from the Original. (Burnet, *Hist. of Reform.*)

ff. 502–509v. XV. Letter to Boniface VIII by the ecclesiastics of the whole of France, 10 April. (Registre du Trésor des Chartes.)

f. 510. XVI. Approval of Peace between England and France, Parliament Roll, 5 Henry V.

f. 513. XVIII. Third Charter of William I to St. Peter's, Westminster. From Cart. of Westminster, Faustina A. 3.

f. 519v. XIX. Grant of dower to Queen Isabella, 5 May 1204.

f. 520v. XX. Writ to Sheriff of Kent on coronation of Edward II, 18 January 1308.

f. 522. XXI. Writ of summons to Parliament, 30 September 1295.

f. 523. The like, 2 November 1295.

f. 524. XXIII. Extract from Scotichronicon, 1390. (Leslie, *De Origine.*)

f. 525. XXIV. An Act for the subsidy of the Temporalty, 34 & 35 Henry VIII, cap. 27, from Rastell, *Stat.* (English).

This volume appears to be undoubtedly a draft of a work by William Petyt which was never completed or published. It has all the characteristics of method and references of such a work.

VOLUME W

A volume of transcripts and extracts from manuscript and printed sources, with some few from the Public Records relating to Scotland, full bound in dark blue morocco, with Inner Temple coat of arms on both covers. On original flyleaf: De Regno Scotiae. On flyleaf: Historica Collectanea de regno Scotiae ex cartis etc. in archivis Turris Londoniensis. 301 ff.

Title-Page: Historia Collectanea de Regno Scotiae ex Chartis antiquissimis, Codicibus, Manuscriptis, Chronicis, Typis Publicis extractis, Rotulis, Schedulisque pervetustis in Archivis Turris Londoniensis Aliisque Monumentis membranaceis alibi conservatis cum Appendice in qua varia instrumenta authentica conjiciuntur Auctoritas quorum in his Collectaneis passim laudatur. Quibus Alia superadiciuntur notis ac animadversionibus illustrata.

ff. 1–17. Transcript from a printed book (no reference given) beginning: How reason doth lead men unto the making of human laws, whereby political societies are governed. Ends: admiring her as the mother of their peace and joy.

ff. 21–301v. The collection relating to Scotland with references to John Lesley, *De origine moribus et rebus gestis Scotorum*; Buchan, *Rerum Scotiarum Hist.*; Fordun, *Chronicon*; Life of Alfred the Great; Matt. of Westminster; Hoveden; J. Bodin, *De Republica*; *Regiam Maiestatem*; Spelman, *Gloss.*; Symeon of Durham; *Mon.*; Junii, *Observations*; Camden, *Brit.*; Eadmer; St. Leo the Great; Usher, *Brit. Eccles. Primord.*; Bale; Florence of Worcester; Selden, *Titles of Honor*; Matt. Paris; Knighton; Patent Rolls, 17, 18 Edward I; Rotulus de Superioritate; Ingulph; Charter Roll, 36 Edward III; L.T.R. Mem. Roll. 7 Edward II; Close Roll, 29 Edward I; Walsingham; Buchanan, *Account of Trans. of Parl.*; *Plac. Parl.*; Close Roll, 33 Edward I; Transcript of Treaty between John Balliol and King of France; Close Roll, 34 Edward I; Edward I; Grafton, *Chron.*; Letter of Pope, 1320; Holinshed, *Hist. of Scotl.*; Scotch Roll, 8 Edward III; Scotch Roll, 30 Edward III; Patent Roll, 29 Edward III; Patent Roll, 26 Edward III; Boethius; Polydore Vergil; Patent Roll, 2 Henry V; Holinshed, *Chron.*; Lib. Stat. Scot.; Stat. Regn. Scot.; Drummond, *Hist. Scot.*; *Scotor. Hist.*; Cardan, *Lib. de Utilit.*; Parliament Roll, 12 Henry VII; Parliament Roll, 3 Henry VIII; Rastell, *Stat.*; Act Parl. de iure successionis ad Imp. Scot., 1681; Camden, *Ann. Rer. Anglie. et Hibern.*

VOLUME X

A collection of transcripts etc. from the Public Records, with a few extracts from printed sources, relating to Ireland, John to Henry VI, with a preliminary folio of index. On flyleaf: Touching King John, Henry III, Ireland, Releases, Pardons, Parliaments. 190 ff.

f. 1. Letters to clergy of Ireland etc. on actions of King of France, 10 February 1204.

f. 3. Letters Patent, on writs to be issued by the Justiciar of Ireland, 2 November 1204.

f. 5. Like to Justice of Ireland on taking lands into King's hands, 23 May 1207.

f. 7. Like to same to expel thieves, 23 May 1208.

f. 8. Like to same to do judgement on Earl of Dublin and others for non appearance coram Rege in England, 13 November 1207.

f. 9. Letter to same on Henry III's coronation, 5 January 1217, from Close Roll.

f. 14. Letters Patent to be indendant to Eustace de Es, 6 April 1217.

f. 14v. Like committing senescalcy and customs of Poitou and Gascony to Archbishop of Bordeaux, 28 March 1217.

f. 16. Like granting liberties of Kingdom of England to Ireland, 6 February 1217.

f. 17. Mandate to Justice of Ireland on collection of tallage and aid, 10 November 1217.

f. 18. Letters Patent requesting aid in money, 10 November 1217.

f. 18v. Like to Sheriffs (in England) not to allow vexation of those who were in King John's service, 6 March 1218.

f. 19. Mandate to Justice of Ireland to come to England to do homage, 12 February 1218.

f. 20. Like on payment of fines in Exchequer at Dublin, 18 July 1221.

f. 21. Letters Patent to Archbishop of Dublin and Justice of Ireland on limitation on writs of mort d'ancestor, 18 July 1222.

f. 23. Mandate to Archbishop of Dublin for Reginald de Barbwell, 5 February 1223.

f. 24. Letters Patent for Abbots etc. of Province of Ireland on aid, 21 December 1226.

f. 25. Like to Archbishop of Dublin and his suffragans that aid shall not prejudice, 21 December 1226.

f. 27. Like on husband's custody for life of late wife's inheritance, 10 December 1226.

f. 28. Mandate to Richard de Burgh, Justice of Ireland, on observance of laws and customs of England, 8 May 1228.

f. 30. Like to same on payment of 300 marks, 26 April 1228.

f. 31. Letters Patent on aid from clergy of Ireland, 10 May 1228.

f. 32. Like granting to Hubert de Burgh Justiciarship of Ireland for life, 16 June 1232.

f. 33. Like on provision of new writs de cursu, 20 March 1237.

f. 35. Mandate to Justice of Ireland on aid of 2 marks ad scutum, 5 October, 1237.

f. 38. Letters Patent to Maurice Fitz Gerald, Justice of Ireland, to be intendant to Walter, Archbishop of York, to whom King in absence has committed government of England, 5 May 1242.

f. 39. Like on observance of laws and customs of England in Ireland, 9 September 1246.

f. 40. Petition of John de Kenley, Archdeacon of Mayo (Latin), from New Misc., t. Henry III etc.

f. 41. Petition of Archbishop of Cashel (Latin), from same.

f. 42. Petition of Walter de Hauberger (French), from same.

f. 45. Letters Patent for Maurice fitz Gerald to be quit of receipts etc. while Justice of Ireland, 8 August 1248.

f. 47. Mandate to Barons of Ireland on liberties asked for, 28 July 1248.

f. 48. Like to Justice of Ireland on remission of anger to Henry fitz Gerald, 2 July 1248.

f. 49. Letters Patent on assessment of tallage, Ireland, 20 June 1249.

f. 50. Mandates on restoration of lands to Prior and Chapter of Holy Trinity, Dublin, 29 May 1250.

f. 51. Like on dower of Margaret, Countess of Lincoln, widow of William Marshal, late Earl of Pembroke, 15 June 1250.

f. 53. Charter for Oliver de Asprevill, 16 May 1252, from Charter Roll.

f. 55. Like to Justice of Ireland on error in judgement on suit between John Malet and Hugh, son of Lucian, 28 March 1253.

f. 56. Like on record on suit Adam le Petit and William Baret, 9 August 1253.

f. 57. Letters Patent to John, son of Geoffrey, Justice of Ireland, on aid, 2 February 1254.

f. 57v. Like sending Nicholas de St. Neots, brother of Hospital of St. John of Jerusalem in Ireland, on same. 17 February 1254.

f. 59. Like on impoverishment of Ireland by discords and wars there, 12 August 1275.

f. 61. Mandate to Roger de Clifford, Justice of Ireland, to receive mainprise of Hubert de Burgh, 10 June 1281.

f. 63. Letters Patent to Justice of Ireland that the custumanni of Waterford shall have the laws of the English in Ireland, 5 October 1283.

f. 64. Like for crusaders, Ireland, 17 January 1251.

f. 65. Mandate to Justices of Bench, Ireland, on record and process of suit between Walter de Hougberg and Christiana, his wife, and Stephen Talun and Juliana, his wife, from New Misc. Bundle, t. Henry III etc.

f. 67. Like to T(homas), Bishop of Meath, on complaint of William de Baltesdoile on church of Kilskir, 18 February 1290.

f. 68. Letters Patent on aid with horses and men for Scottish war, 28 March 1301.

f. 69. Like to Justice and Treasurer of Ireland on same, 3 April 1301.

f. 70. Mandate to John Wogan, Justice of Ireland, on letters patent to men of Ireland in King's company in Scotland, 15 February 1302.

f. 71. Petition of Thomas, Bishop of Down in Ireland (French), with answer (Latin) and mandate to John Wogan, Justice of Ireland, 16 September 1312, from Close Roll.

f. 72. Mandate that several Irish leaders should come to England, 22 March 1314, from Scottish Roll.

f. 79. Like to Ralph le Botiller, Justice of Ireland, on security of clergy in Ireland, 1 September 1315.

f. 81. Like to Roger Mortimer of Wigmore, keeper of land of Ireland, to certify King and Council on capture of Earl of Ulster etc., 23, 27, 22 April 1317.

f. 87. Letters Patent for University of Cambridge and the removal of women out of the town of Cambridge, 23 October 1327.

f. 88. Letters of credence for John Dufford, Escheator of Ireland, c. 10 Edward II. from New Misc. Bundle, t. Henry III etc.

f. 90. Mandate to Roger Mortimer, keeper of land of Ireland for Mayor and citizens of Dublin, 10 December 1310.

f. 92. Like to Alexander, Archbishop of Dublin, on annual tenth in Ireland, 9 June 1320.

f. 93. Like to Thomas, son of John, Earl of Kildare, etc. as Justices, to enquire who aided invasion of Edward de Brus, 3 February 1320.

f. 95. Like to Justice of Ireland to implement ordinance of Abbots of Dore and Margam, 7 October 1321.

f. 96. Like to Prior and Chapter of St. Patricks, Dublin, to collect clerical tenth, 3 July 1323.

f. 98. Like to Treasurer and Barons of Exchequer, Dublin, to deliver rolls etc. of Chancery of Ireland to Chancellor, 25 July 1323.

f. 99. Like to Treasurer and Barons of Exchequer for men of Hamburgh, 9 March 1324.

f. 100. Letters Patent to Brother Thomas Scurlag, Abbot of St. Thomas the Martyr, Dublin, etc. on election of 2 lay persons to appear before Council in England, 1 December 1375, from Roll of doings of Ministers of Edward II in Ireland, various years, with return thereon.

f. 102. Writ of William de Windsor, Governor and Keeper of land of Ireland, to Sheriff of Dublin, on indenture between King and Nicholas de Dagworth, kt., on message to Ireland concerning expense incurred on Ireland, part of expense should be met from that country. Parliament summoned at Kilkenny to deal with matter, 29 November 1375, with return by Reginald Talbot, Sheriff of Dublin, from same.

f. 108. Writs on above matter to Archbishop of Armagh etc., 12 November 1375, from same.

f. 116. Mandate to Justice of Ireland to deliver to Roger Mortimer, the records of the Chancery and Exchequer of his liberty of Trim, 1 Edward III, from New Misc. Bundle, t. Henry III etc.

f. 118. Letters Patent appointing Thomas, son of John, Earl of Kildare, Justice of Ireland, during pleasure, with mandate to be intendant, 12 March 1327.

f. 120. Mandate to Roger Atlagh, Chancellor of Ireland, on process against Maurice, son of Thomas, Earl of Desmond, with mandate thereon, 28 September 1330.

f. 122. Like to Justice of Ireland for Prior of Holy Trinity, Dublin, on custody of manor of Kyneshale held of him by John Comyn, with mandate thereon to Justices of Bench, Dublin, 18 February 1331.

f. 126. Letters Patent for John, son of George de Rupe, reducing amercement for not coming to Parliament from 200 to 10 marks, 20 June 1334, from Rot. Hibern, 1–12 Edward III.

f. 127. Mandate by John Darcy, Justice of Ireland, to Treasurer and Barons of Exchequer of Dublin, for Maurice, son of Nicholas, 17 January 1336, from same.

f. 128. Mandate to Nigel Duhanlam, Duke of Ichre etc. List. 14 March 1334.

f. 131. Like to Chancellor, Justice and Treasurer of Ireland for men of Ireland, with letters thereon to all Archbishops etc. 2 June 1336.

f. 135. Like to men of Ireland (French), 14 April 1342.

f. 139. The petition upon which the above was based, with answer.

f. 140. Heading: A collection of Records concerning Ireland, with a note of pardon of certain trespasses to Archbishop of Dublin, 18 Edward III. Ordinance made on the state of the land of Ireland, 31 Edward III, from Stat. Roll, with note of ratification and confirmation, 17 Richard II, from Patent Roll.

f. 142. Plea concerning the Master of the Temple in Ireland, Coram Rege Roll' East. term 8 Edward I, Trin. 13 Edward I, Mich. 17–18 Edward I, Trin. 18 Edward I, East. 21 Edward I, Mich. 21–22 Edward I, East. 30 Edward I, Mich. 31 Edward I, Mich. 16–17 Edward I, Hil. 35 Edward I, Hil. 5 Edward III, Mich. 5 Edward III.

f. 146. Letters Patent of pardon for trespasses for Archbishop of Dublin, 14 June 1344.

f. 150. Mandate to Justice of Ireland and Treasurer and Barons of Exchequer of Dublin for mayor and community of city of Cork, 24 May 1354.

f. 151. Like to Justice and Chancellor of Ireland on correction in Parliament in Ireland, 30 August 1355.

f. 153. Like to John de Pembroke, Escheator of Ireland, on certification of liberties and privileges of cities and boroughs in Ireland, 23 August 1360.

f. 155. Letters Patent to men of Ireland of pardon of debts and accounts, with mandates thereon, 20 February 1367.

f. 158. Mandate to Robert de Ashton, Justice of Ireland, on revocation of customs and charges, with mandate thereon, 28 May 1372.

f. 162. Like to mayor and bailiffs of city of Dublin etc. on levying subsidy in Ireland, 6 May 1374.

f. 164. Writ etc. as above f. 102.

f. 170. Mandate to James le Boteller, Earl of Ormond etc. on process against William de Windsor, late Justice of Ireland, 4 December 1376.

f. 172. Letters Patent to Roger Mortimer, Earl of March, Lieutenant in Ireland, to summon a Parliament in Ireland, 29 March 1382.

f. 174. Mandate to James le Boteller, Justice of Ireland, etc. to choose and send Parliament men out of Ireland to the Parliament of England, 25 July 1376.

f. 175. 'These be the Answers against the Articles the which John Corn-Walsh hath set on Mighell Gryffyn unto the King'. In margin: Touching an appeal in Ireland which ought to be tried there.

f. 177. Mandate to Lieutenant of Ireland for Thomas, Archbishop of Dublin, 2 July 1403.

f. 180. Letters Patent appointing James le Boteller, Earl of Ormond, Lieutenant of Ireland, from Roll of Ordinances for King's Council, 1, 2 & 3 Henry VI.

f. 183. Mandate to Sheriffs of London to make proclamation that all Irish men within London and the suburbs thereof do forthwith transport themselves to Ireland for the defence thereof, 3 September 1430.

f. 185. Memorandum touching writs of error from the King's Bench in Ireland to the King's Bench in England, on searching the King's Bench Rolls of Richard II, Henry IV, V, and VI and Henry VII and VIII, Edward VI and Mary none found. Trinity term, 6 Henry VI, whole proceedings in case of Prior of Llanthony entered upon 3 or 4 rolls, Records in Tower, Henry VI Edward IV and Richard III for appeals which are for the most part entered on the backs of the Bills: but no appeal.

f. 187. Extract from Selden, *De Syn.*

f. 188. Extracts from Anderson, *Reports*, that treason committed in Ireland might be tried in England.

f. 190. Notes about writs of error brought to reverse judgements in Ireland returnable in King's Bench in England, from Yelverton, *Reports*, Rolle, *Abridg.*, Croke, *Reports*, Keble, *Reports*, etc. (13 Charles I to 8 William III).

VOLUME Y

A collection of selected records, 1–15 Edward II, almost all from the Public Records, relating to such subjects as Summons to Parliament, Safe Conducts, Taxation etc. On flyleaf: 'Collectanea Selecta Annorum, 1, 2, 3, 4 & 5 Edwardi II'. On another flyleaf: 'Selecta Annorum E. 2. Summons to Parliament'. 338 ff.

f. 1. A brief note on the reign of Edward II from Walsingham and Knighton. Writs of summons to Parliament, 9, 10 March 1308, Lists.

f. 5. Letters patent on repairing walls and ditches, 9 March 1308.

f. 6. Letters patent appointing keepers of peace in counties, 17 March 1308, List.

f. 10. Writs of summons to Parliament, 19 January 1308, Lists.

f. 13. Mandate prohibiting tournaments, 4 October 1308.

f. 15. Writs of summons to Parliament, 4 March 1309.

f. 16. The like, 16 August 1308. Lists.

f. 18. The like, 10 August 1309. Lists.

f. 19. Writs of summons to treat with King, 11 June 1309. Lists.

f. 21. The like, 8 January 1309. Lists.

f. 24. Mandate to Robert de Kendale on crossing without licence, 4 October 1308.

f. 25. Writs to supersede collection of custom on wine, 20 August 1309. List.

f. 26. The like, of new custom, 20 August 1309. List.

f. 28. Letters on provision of victuals, 28 August 1309, (French). List, from Scottish Roll.

f. 30. Mandate to Sheriff of York on sending victuals to Berwick on Tweed, from same.

f. 30v. The like, to taxors and collectors of 25th for community of Yorks, from same.

f. 32. Letters of safe conduct for Pope's messengers, 29 September 1309.

f. 33. Letter from John, Bishop of Llandaff to King, 22 July 1309, from Brevia Regis, t. Edward II.

f. 34. Mandates on Templars, 14 September 1309.

f. 36. Mandate on Templars in Ireland, 29 September 1309.

f. 38. Letters patent to Henry de Cobham etc., 18 December 1309.

f. 40. The like, for William, Archbishop of York, 21 October 1309.

f. 41. Writ to Barons of Exchequer, 18 June (1309), from Brevia Regis, t. Edward II.

f. 43. Writs of summons to Parliament, 26 October 1309, Lists.

f. 46. The like, 12 December 1309. Lists.

f. 48. Writs on collection of new custom, 14 December 1309.

f. 50. Letters patent for Peter Auger, beard and pilgrimage, 17 February 1311.
f. 53. Writ on temporalities of Archbishop of Dublin, 6 January 1311.
f. 54. Mandates on Constable of Tower etc. on Templars, 12 December 1310.
f. 57. Writs on choosing foot for war with Scotland, 20 May 1311, from Scottish Roll.
f. 59. Letters patent on ships for war with Scotland, 23 May 1311, List.
f. 63. Letters to Sheriffs on war with Scotland, 5 July 1311, from Scottish Roll.
f. 64. Writs of summons, service of ships, 2 August 1310, from same.
f. 66. Letters to Philip, King of France, 10 October 1310.
f. 67. The like, 16 October 1310.
f. 68. Mandates to Sheriffs on taking corn, 1 November 1310 (French), from Scottish Roll.
f. 69. Mandate to Sheriffs, 10 February 1311.
f. 70. Letters patent to the Bishops in Council, London, 18 April 1311.
f. 74. Mandate to William, Archbishop of York, 26 July 1311.
f. 75. Mandate to Sheriffs, 11 October 1311. Lists.
f. 79. Mandate to Robert, Archbishop of Canterbury, 24 October 1311.
f. 80. Mandate to Chancellor, University of Oxford, 9 December 1311.
f. 81. Mandate on privileges on University of Cambridge, 29 March 1312.
f. 83. Writ on complaints of Lynn, 16 December 1311, with return, from Brevia Regis, 5 Edward II.
f. 85. Mandate to city of York etc., 18 December 1311.
f. 88. Note on dissolution of Templars, from Walsingham and Stubb's Hist. of Thomas, Archbishop of York.
f. 91. Mandate on Templars, examination of (French).
ff. 92–115v. Note on the treaty in the Provincial Council on the Templars, from Annal. Achp. in Otho B. 3.
f. 117. Letters patent for John de Conyngeston etc. on Templars, 22 July 1311.
f. 118. Mandates on issues of Templar's lands, 19 December 1311. List.
f. 120. Writ to Roger Mortimer to be present at Parliament, 17 January 1316.
f. 121. Mandate to Henry Spigurnel not to take assizes during Parliament, 4 January 1316.
f. 122. Mandate not to take inquisitions on prises etc. 10 April 1316.
f. 124. Letters patent on King's business, Ireland, 1 September 1315.
f. 125. Letters patent to John Inge etc. to enquire on evil doers, 11 August 1315.
f. 127. Letters of credence for King, 17 July 1315. Lists.
f. 133. Mandate for Mayor and city of London, 1 September 1315.
f. 134. Mandate on Staple in France, 16 December 1315.
f. 135. Mandate for Amaneno de Lebreto, 14 March 1316.
f. 136. Letters Patent to Bishops, Chapters etc. on money, 21 March 1316.
f. 138. Mandates on gifts on Ordinances, 1, 26 April 1316.
f. 141. Writs on bringing money to Exchequer, 12 April 1316. List.
f. 143. Writs on fines on taxors, 7 May 1316.

f. 145. Proclamation on sale of victuals, 20 February 1316.

f. 146. Letters patent on aid of foot granted, 5 August 1316.

f. 148. Mandate for John de Boyland, 26 December 1313.

f. 149. 25 December 1321. Letters patent on Hugh le Despenser, the elder and the younger, 25 December 1321.

f. 154. Writs of summons to Parliament, 8 July 1312.

f. 157. Letters patent on safe keeping of town of Lynn, 15 July 1312.

f. 159. Letters patent prohibiting unlawful assemblies, 20 July 1312.

f. 160. Mandates on distraint of knighthood, 31 July 1312.

ff. 161–73. Extract on the life and beheadal of Peter Gaveston, from Walsingham.

f. 174. Letters patent on arrest of Henry de Percy, 31 July 1312.

f. 175. Mandate on Templars' goods, 1 August 1312.

f. 176. Mandates ordering knights to remain in own county, 26 August 1312.

f. 177. Letter to Mayor and city of London, 18 September 1278, from Liber A in archives of city of London.

f. 178. Letters patent for Isabella, Queen of England, 20 October 1312 (French).

f. 179. Letters patent on taking fines, 28 October 1312.

f. 180. Writs on respite of knighthood, 24, 28 October 1312.

f. 183. Mandates to Walter, Bishop of Exeter etc. to send in processes, 6 November 1312.

f. 185. Memorandum on birth of Prince Edward.

f. 186. Letters patent for Peter de Watle of Winchester, 2 December 1312.

f. 187. Letters patent for John Abel etc. on tallage, 16 December 1312.

f. 188. Proclamation on peace and prises, 22 December 1312.

f. 189. Proclamation on confirmation of Charters, 1 January 1313.

f. 190. Extract, 1313, from Walsingham.

f. 192. Writs of summons to Parliament, 8 January 1313. Lists.

f. 197. Writs prohibiting jousts etc., 1 April 1313.

f. 199. Writs committing Templars' lands, 16 April 1313.

f. 200. Mandates on Templars' wages, 18 April 1313.

f. 201. Letters of safe conduct for Thomas, Earl of Lancaster etc., 3 May 1313.

f. 202. Writs committing Templars' lands, 5 May 1313.

f. 203. Writs of summons for the Eyre of Kent, 11 May 1313.

f. 205. Mandate to Archbishop of Canterbury on Gascony etc., 21 May 1313.

f. 206. Letters of safe conduct for the Bishop of Samaria, 22 May 1313.

f. 208. Writs of summons to Parliament, 23 May 1313.

f. 209. Letters patent giving power to open Parliament, 1 July 1313.

f. 212. Mandate for David de Cotesbrook, citizen of London, 17 July 1313.

f. 214. Mandates to William, Archbishop of York etc., 26 July 1313.

f. 216. Mandates on changing money, 26 July 1313. Lists.

f. 218. Writs of summons to Parliament, 26 July 1313.

f. 219. Writs on request for loan, 13 August 1313. List.

f. 221x. Mandate not to go towards Bristol, 18 August 1313.

f. 222. Letters patent for Abbot of St. Albans, 2 May 1314.

f. 224. Writs prohibiting tournaments, 16 September 1313. List.

f. 226. Letters patent that none to be imprisoned for death of Peter Gaveston, 6 November 1313 (French).

f. 229. Letters patent expelling the Jews from Aquitaine, 15 November 1313. (*Gascon Rolls*, p. 315.)

f. 231. Letters patent on Premonstratensian Houses in England, 18 November 1313.

f. 233. Mandate to Prior and Convent of Ely on Bishop of Glasgow, 20 November 1313.

f. 234. Writs of summons to Parliament, 26 November 1313.

f. 236. Letters patent on transfer of Templars' lands to Hospitallers, 28 November 1313.

f. 238. Mandates on same, 28 November 1313.

f. 240. Letters appointing John de Gisors etc. to assess the tallage, with form of tallage (French), 1 December 1313, from Laudes Brit. in archives of city of London.

ff. 244–259v. Instrument on restitution of goods of Templars, 1313, 25 November 1313, 9 December 1313.

f. 260. Writs of summons to Scottish war, 23 December 1313. List.

f. 262. Letters patent on retaining to King's Council, 27 January 1314.

f. 263. Letters Patent on discord between the Seneschal of Gascony and Bayonne, 12 March 1314. (*Gascon Rolls*, p. 335.)

f. 265. Mandate for late Templars, 8 February 1314.

f. 266. Letters patent to William de Grey on diversion of highway, 8 March 1314.

f. 267. Letters patent to Henry le Scrope etc., 20 March 1314 (French).

f. 269. Writs for King taking fines, 13 April 1314.

f. 271. Mandate on taking assizes in the Eyre, 28 April 1314.

f. 272. Letters of credence for King, 10 May 1314, List.

f. 273. Letters patent for delivery of money to Ireland, 28 May 1314.

f. 274. Mandate for Archbishop of Canterbury, 13 June 1314.

f. 275. Letters of pardon and remission made by Philip, King of France, 2 July 1313. (*Gascon Rolls*, pp. 295–6.)

f. 279. Letters of renunciation of an appeal by the King of England, 2 July 1313. (Ibid., p. 296.)

f. 280. Letters patent acknowledging money for King, 17 July 1314. List.

f. 283. Mandates on trespasses by taxors and collectors of aids, 20 July 1314.

f. 285. Writs of summons to Parliament, 29 July 1314.

f. 286. Mandates for Bishop of Salisbury etc. on money, 1 September 1314.

f. 290. Letters patent on repair of walls and ditches, co. Essex, 20 September 1314.

f. 292. Letters patent concerning Gerard Salveyn, 8 October 1314.

f. 294. Writs of summons to Parliament, 24 October 1314.

f. 295. Letters patent on preservation of King's rights on prebends, 3 November 1314.

f. 297. Writs concerning death of King of France, 15 December 1314.

f. 298. Writs concerning John de Eure, 4 January 1315. List.

f. 300. Letters to William, Archbishop of York, 9 January 1315, from Scottish Roll.

f. 302. Mandates on making a regard, 10 June 1315.

f. 305. Letters patent for Chancellor of Church of Exeter, 30 January 1315.

ff. 307–14. Letters patent on agreement between the Scholars of Oxford and the town, 11 March 1315.

f. 315. Ordinance on sale of cattle, 14 March 1315.

f. 317. Writs appointing collectors of clerical tenth, 15 March 1315.

f. 318. Writs on loaning of money, 15 March 1315.

f. 320. Writs taking the Isle of Man into the King's hands, 2 April 1315. (*C.F.R., 1307–1319*, p. 238.)

f. 321. Mandates on collection of tenth, King's chapels, 15 April 1315.

f. 323. Letters patent concerning Robert, son of Robert Bottel of Merston, 18 April 1315.

f. 324. Mandate to Sheriff of Salop for King of Scotland, 20 April 1315.

f. 326. Writs on resumption of castle of High Peak, 20 April 1315.

f. 328. Letters patent for Aymer de Valence, Earl of Pembroke, 3 May 1315.

f. 329. Writs on goods and chattels of Anthony, late Bishop of Durham, 20 May 1315.

f. 332. Letters patent for Thomas, Earl of Lancaster, 23 May 1315.

f. 334. Letters patent on enquiry on forestallers after Ordinance, 28 May 1315.

f. 336. Writ to Barons of Exchequer concerning men of Beverley, 11 June 1315, from L.T.R. Mem. Roll, Brev. dir. Bar., Trin. term, 8 Edward II.

f. 338. Letters to Henry de Lancaster etc., 30 June 1315, from Scottish Roll.

VOLUME Z

A collection of transcripts, mainly from the Public Records, largely from Parliament Rolls. On flyleaf: 'Touching Pardons, Privileges, Alliances and Causes'. Richard II to Henry VII. 273 ff.

ff. 1–13v. Letters patent of pardon for William of Wykeham, Bishop of Winchester, 31 July 1377.

f. 14. Ordinances, 5 Richard II, cap. 4, from Statute Roll, 5 Richard II with translation from Rastell, *Stat.*

f. 16. Letters to Sheriff of Cornwall enclosing the above Ordinances, 26 May 1382.

f. 18. Writs of summons to Parliament to Sheriffs, 1 January 1388.

f. 19. Extract from Parliament Roll, Henry IV.

f. 20. Claim and protestation made in Parliament by the Archbishop of Canterbury on behalf of himself and his fellow Bishops, from Parliament Roll, 11 Richard II.

f. 25. Claim and protestation made in Parliament by the Bishops on their sitting in and their privileges of Parliament, from the same.

f. 29. 'An unusual clause in the writs of summons to Parliament contrary to ancient forms' and a new writ sent to Sheriffs, 17 December 1387.

f. 32. The amended writ issued, 1 January 1388.

f. 34. Statement that the election of knights of the shire ought to be free and that they were entitled to lay open their counties' grievances and to prosecute for remedies, with translation, from Parliament Roll, 1 Henry IV.

f. 36. 'The remarkable case of Thomas Merke, Bishop of Carlisle, found guilty of high treason against Henry IV', from Coram Rege Roll, Hil. term, 2 Henry IV, and the King's pardon, 28 November 1400.

f. 45. Dispute between the Earl of Rutland and Fitzwalter, from Parliament Roll, 2 Henry IV.

f. 47. The writ de expensis militum, from the *Reg. of Writs*, and letters patent for the men of Witley co. Surr., 14 April 1402.

f. 49. 'The Crown of England entailed', 7 Henry IV, giving the text of letters, 7 June 1406, from a New Misc. Bundle, t. Richard II, Henrys IV, V & VI and Edward IV.

f. 54. 'Succession to the Crown of England entailed', a petition (French), 22 December 1406.

f. 65. Grant of a subsidy made to the King in Parliament for guarding the sea, from Parliament Roll, 13 Henry IV.

f. 69. 'The claim of the Commons that it has ever been their liberty and freedom that no statute or law can be made without their assent', from Parliament Roll, 2 Henry V (English).

ff. 71, 76. The claim by the Commons of general prescription, from Parliament Roll, 2 Henry V, with notes from Selden, *Mare Clausum*, and on the making of balingers, from Close Roll, 1 Richard II, 30 November 1377.

f. 80. 'The observable proceedings in Parliament, 2 Henry V, concerning Thomas Paunfeld, one of the King's free tenants in the town and manor of Chesterton, co. Cambridge', the text of petition (French), with translation, from Bundle of Petitions, 2 Henry V.

f. 89. 'Act was made, schism at Rome, elections in Catholic Churches in England should be confirmed by Metropolitan, and that by authority of King's writ grounded upon the Act of Parliament', from Parliament Roll, 3 Henry V.

f. 92. Alliance between Sigismund, King of the Romans, and Henry V, was ratified by Parliament, 19 October 1416.

f. 103. Confirmation of this alliance, 15 August 1416, from Parliament Roll, 4 Henry V.

f. 116. By petition by the Commons Act that the realm of England should never be subject to that of France, from Parliament Roll, 8 Henry V.

f. 120. The three estates of the Duchy of Normandy and other parts adjacent summoned to appear at Rohan etc., 24 January 1421, from Norman Roll, 8 Henry V.

f. 127. Conclusion of peace between Charles, King of France, and Henry V agreed to be approved by the three estates of the realm, from Parliament Roll, 9 Henry V.

f. 130. The controversy between the Lords and Commons in Parliament concerning granting of subsidies and aids to the crown agreed and settled by King, from same.

f. 138. The great commotion in England and Ireland between the Earl of Ormond and the Lord Talbot and Furnival and their adherents at last settled by a Parliament of England, from Parliament Roll, 2 Henry VI.

ff. 145–171v. 'The great case between John, Earl Marshal, and Richard, Earl of Warwick, touching their places in Parliament. The arguments are entered in the Parliament Roll for that year (8 Henry VI), the first precedent of that kind I ever yet saw in my researches and enquiries'.

f. 173. Letters from Pope Martin (V) to Henry VI for abolishing 'the detestable Statute of Premunire of 16 Richard II'. Letter sent to Parliament, 13 October 1427, from a MS. in poss. of William Petyt.

f. 177. Pope Martin (V)'s Bull sent to the Archbishop of Canterbury, 6 Henry VI, commanding him at the next Parliament to endeavour to get it repealed, letters 5 December 1426, 13 October 1427, and the Archbishop's speech, from same.

f. 189. 'The office and duty of a House of Commons in the reigns of Edward II and Henry VI to enquire into the grievances of the people and to seek for remedy and redress in Parliament, from Parliament Roll, 11 Henry VI and the promise made to the King in Parliament, 17 March 1315, to John, Bishop of Chichester.

f. 196. The proceedings concerning Richard, Bishop of Lincoln, in Parliament. Petition (French), from Bundle of Petitions to Parliament, 6, 7 & 8 Henry IV.

f. 201. An Act made concerning the executors of the Will of Henry V, from Statute Roll, 1 Henry VI, 18 December 1422.

f. 205. Concerning the settlement of the dowers of Joan, Queen of England, 20 February 1423, and Katherine, Queen of England, 9 November 1422.

f. 209. Act that clergy coming to Convocation, by the King's writ, and servants should have liberties as the great men and Commons coming to Parliament, from Statute Roll, 8 Henry VI, with translation from Rastell's *Stat.*

f. 213. 'Doubt whether, in point of law, Duchesses etc. being indicted of treason, or felony, should be tried by a common jury or peers', 20 Henry VI. Parliament should be judged by peers, from Statute Roll, 20 Henry VI, from MS. Book of Stat. in poss. of William Petyt, with translation from Pulton, *Stat.*

f. 218. Parliament incorporated the Brethren of the House or Hospital of St. Thomas de Acre, Martyr, London, from Parliament Roll, 23 Henry VI.

f. 223. Act of Parliament made concerning Edmund, Marquis of Dorset, from Patent Roll, 24 Henry VI, 12 April 1446.

f. 227. 'An extraordinary Act of Parliament for suppressing riots etc. If Duke etc. refuse to appear to lose for life the name of lord and place in Parliament', 31 Henry VI, from Statute Roll, 25–36 Henry VI.

f. 233. Famous case of Thomas Thorp, being Speaker of House of Commons, in time of Henry VI, was in time of prorogation, taken in execution at suit of Richard, Duke of York, from Parliament Roll, 31 & 32 Henry VI, Patent Roll, 33 Henry VI, 24 March 1455, Close Roll, 34 Henry VI, 2 February 1456, Petition (English).

f. 244. Petition by Commons, on behalf of Roger Thorp esq., son and heir of Thomas Thorp, taken prisoner, beheaded at Harringay Park, co. Midd., from Parliament Roll, 1 Henry VII.

f. 252. Statute, 1 Richard III, caps. 3 & 4, 1 Richard III, with translation.

f. 261. The title by which Richard III claimed the throne, from Parliament Roll, 1 Richard III.

f. 268. 'Touching the title of Henry VII', 4 Henry VII, from Finch, *Nomotexemia*, Dyer, *Reports*, Plowden, *Comm.*

f. 270. Peace or truce between Henry VII and Charles, King of France, confirmed by Parliament, from Parliament Roll, 11 Henry VII.

PETYT MS. 515

The nine volumes grouped under this pressmark have little organic or subject relationship. Volumes 1–5 are transcripts or extracts from Assize Rolls, or Coram Rege Rolls, 3 Edward I to 37 Edward III. Volume 6 consists of an index to pleas, mainly Coram Rege, from the reign of John to that of Henry V. All these volumes were written in the late seventeenth century, probably to William Petyt's order. Volumes 7 and 8, which are bound together, consist of accounts, and volume 9 is a tract on the Court of Exchequer. The volumes vary very much in size. Volumes 1 and 6 have the Petyt coat of arms on both covers; the remainder have the Inner Temple coat of arms on both covers. All are full bound in dark green morocco. Volumes 1 to 6 are in part transcripts of Agarde's Indexes as follows: volume 1, Agarde Index 17; volume 2, Agarde Index 30; volume 3, Agarde Index 34; volume 4, Agarde Index 36; volume 5, Agarde Index 35; volume 6, Agarde Index 43. Parts of volumes 2 and 3 are printed in *Abbrevatio Placitorum*, Richard I to Edward II (R.C.).

VOLUME 1

This volume consists of transcripts and extracts from various Assize Rolls for the counties of Worcester, Salop, and Northumberland of the reign of Edward I, made up in three distinct sections, one for each of the three counties, and bound together later. $14\frac{1}{2}'' \times 9\frac{1}{8}''$. 295 ff.

f. 1. Worcester. Pleas of Juries and Assizes before Nicholas de Stapleton and his fellow Justices in Eyre, 3 Edward I. This is a straight transcript of the roll, with membrane references in the margins, mm. 1 to 28d, including the marginal notes in the original roll. Ends f. 78v.

f. 79. Pleas of Juries and Assizes at Worcester (as above), Morrow of Ascension, 3 Edward I (23 May 1275). Saham. Pleas of the Crown. Ends f. 83v. These are brief extracts only from mm. 33 to 51.

ff. 85–108. Alphabetical index of the roll.

f. 109. Salop. Pleas of Juries and Assizes before John de Berwick and his fellow Justices in Eyre, Octave of Michaelmas 20 Edward I (6 October 1292).

f. 169v. Rot. xlvii. Pleas of the Crown, co. Salop, before John de Berwick, Thomas de Normanvill, John de Lethgreynes, William de Bereford and Hugh de Cave, Justices in Eyre, at Shrewsbury (as above). Rex. Transcripts and extracts from mm. 1 to 82, with membrane references in the margins, including the marginal notes in the original roll.

f. 215. Rot. xxxviii. Foreign Pleas at Shrewsbury. Ends f. 216.

ff. 217–217v. Index rerum to the transcripts and extracts.

f. 221. Borough of Ludlow. Rex. Ends f. 226. The last entries are Rot. lxxxxi. Delivery of the Gaol of the Borough of Shrewsbury and Rot. lxxxxv. Roll of Complaints etc. Rex. Finis. Extracts to m. 95.

f. 227. Pleas of the Crown before Hugh de Cressingham, William de Ormesby, John Wogan, Master John Lovel and William de Mortimer, Justices in Eyre, at Newcastle upon Tyne, co. Northumberland, Morrow of St. Hilary 21 Edward I (14 January 1293). Transcript of cases and extracts from mm. 1 to 13. Ends f. 270.

ff. 272–95. 'Names of persons between whom the pleadings were'. Alphabetical index of persons and places.

VOLUME 2

This volume contains transcripts and extracts from the Coram Rege Rolls, 1–35 Edward I, with a few transcripts and extracts from the Common Bench Rolls etc. for part of that period. The volume is prefaced by an alphabetical index of persons and places of 3 ff. The transcriber appears to have been through all the Coram Rege Rolls of the reign twice. He gives references to term, regnal year, and membrane. $11\frac{3}{4}'' \times 7\frac{5}{8}''$. 338 ff.

ff. 1–166. Transcripts and extracts from Coram Rege Rolls, Michaelmas term, 1 Edward I, to Trinity term, 35 Edward I.

f. 167. Extract from Assize Roll, 7 Edward I, taken before William de Saham, in co. York.

f. 168. Extract from Common Bench Roll, Trinity term, 4 Edward I, before Roger de Seyton.

ff. 170–6. Extracts from Coram Rege Rolls, Michaelmas term, 1 Edward I, to Hilary term, 2/3 Edward I.

f. 177. Extracts from Common Bench Roll, Michaelmas term, 2/3 Edward I.

ff. 180–256. Extracts from Coram Rege Rolls, Michaelmas term, 3/4 Edward I, to Easter term, 20 Edward I.

f. 258. Pleas of King at Berwick on Tweed, Trinity term, 20 Edward I, before Gilbert de Thornton, Roger Brabazon and Robert Malet, Justices assigned.

ff. 260–338. Extracts from Coram Rege Rolls, Michaelmas term, 20 Edward I, to Trinity term, 35 Edward I.

(It is noted on f. 284 that the roll for Hilary term, 24 Edward I, was not found and that the Coram Rege Rolls for Hilary term, 28 Edward I (f. 304), and Trinity term, 28 Edward I, were missing.)

VOLUME 3

A similar volume of transcripts and extracts from Coram Rege Rolls, Michaelmas term, 1 Edward II, to Easter term, 19 Edward II. $12\frac{1}{4}'' \times 7\frac{5}{8}''$. 131 ff.

There are references to term, regnal year, and membrane. Every terminal roll 1 to 19 Edward II has contributed extracts, except Trinity term, 4 Edward II.

VOLUME 4

A similar volume of transcripts and extracts from Coram Rege Rolls, Hilary term, 23 Edward III, to Michaelmas term, 37 Edward III. $11\frac{1}{4}'' \times 7\frac{5}{8}''$. 156 ff.

There are references to term, regnal year, and membrane. Every term 23 Edward III to 37 Edward III has contributed extracts. There is no roll for Trinity term, 35 Edward III, because of the Black Death.

VOLUME 5

A similar volume of transcripts and extracts from Coram Rege Rolls, Hilary term, 1 Edward III, to Michaelmas term, 22 Edward III. $12\frac{3}{8}'' \times 7\frac{7}{8}''$. 170 ff.

There are references to term, regnal year, and membrane. Every term 1 Edward III to 22 Edward III has contributed extracts. On f. 8 there are Pleas at Westminster, before the Chancellor, Sunday in Mid Lent, 1 Edward III.

VOLUME 6

This volume contains indexes to Pleas, mainly Coram Rege, for the reigns of John, Edward I, Edward II, Edward III, Richard II, Henry IV, and Henry V, with a few miscellaneous items. There is a table of contents on the flyleaf. $12\frac{1}{8}'' \times 8''$. 154 ff.

ff. 1–11. Alphabetical index, subjects, Pleas in the time of King John.

ff. 12–52. Like, with judgements given, with county and number in margin, with regnal year, term, and membrane, for Pleas Coram Rege in the time of Edward I, with brief subject references.

f. 53. Like, for Pleas of King's Army.

ff. 66–72. Like, for Common Bench, Hilary term, 15 Edward I.

ff. 73–85v. Alphabetical index and summaries of cases, Pleas Coram Rege, in the time of Edward II.

ff. 86–92v. Like, Pleas Coram Rege, in the time of Edward III.

ff. 93–100v. A glossary of obsolete and other words used in this volume, alphabetically arranged, under the title Verba Obsoleta et alia in hoc libro exposita.

ff. 101–138v. Judgements given Hilary term, 23 Edward III, Coram Rege, with alphabetical index.

f. 139. Like, Hilary term, 44 Edward III.

ff. 141–7. Like, Coram Rege, in time of Richard II.

ff. 147v–151v. Like, Coram Rege, in time of Henry IV.

ff. 152–154v. Like, Coram Rege, in time of Henry V.

Some of these indexes and tables of contents are to some of the above volumes 1 to 5; others to volumes not now in the Petyt Collection.

Volumes 7 and 8

This book consists of two separate volumes which have been re-bound together, the first consisting of 68 ff., the second of 38 ff. The first volume consists of the original entry book of the Lord Chamberlain, covering the period 1 October 1621 to 30 September 1622; the second of Annuities and Payments in the Exchequer, 1599. $11\frac{3}{4}'' \times 7\frac{7}{8}''$.

VOLUME 7

Lord Chamberlain's Entry Book, 1 October 1621 to 30 September 1622, has the following on the original flyleaf: 'A Book containing several particulars with relation to the King's servants, petitions, warrants, bills etc. and may be supposed to be a copy of some part of the Lord Chamberlain of the Household's Book in and about the year 1622'.

f. 2. Petitions: Begins: 'An Answer to the petition of William Wilbloud against one of the 40ty messengers, viz. his Lordship ordered that the petitioner should be relieved out of the pay of the said Barefoote and that the Clerk of the Cheque should make stay thereof for that purpose and receive and pay to the petitioner till the due debt were fully satisfied'. Petitions and adjudications upon them continue to f. 17v.

f. 20. Warrants: Begins: A warrant for allowance of £90 to Vanzomer, for the King's picture all at length, to be sent to Humfrey Handford and the like of Prince Henry to be given to the King of Bohemia. Other warrants include one to Inigo Jones, Surveyor of H.M.'s Works, for the reparation of the Lord Steward's Lodging at Whitehall; to the same for erecting scaffolds in the Banqueting Hall against Christmas; for £11–11–6 to Andrea Bassano for mending and tuning the organs at Hampton Court and Greenwich for three years; to the Master of the Jewel House for a chain of gold of £100 value and a medal of £5 to be given to the King of Denmark's Ambassador that came over when he stopped the English from going to Polonia; of £4 to Caesar Galliardello and his fellow musicians for string for their violins for one whole year ended at Christmas 1621; to the Signet Office for a privy seal for £400 to be delivered to Mr. Michael Ollisworth for the charge of the Prince's masque at Christmas 1621; for a New Year's gift of 20 ozs. of plate for Mr. Laurence Hillyard, H.M.'s Limmer; a warrant to be signed by other of the Lords of the Council, as by his Lordship, for the allowance of £16 for Mr. Laurence Hilliard for making and delivering four of H.M.'s pictures in small for H.M.'s service, the one given to Sir Arthur Ashton in a tablet, the second to Sir Robert Mansfield, the third for Lord Cranfield, and the fourth to Lady Margaret Buckingham; 40 marks annuity and £18–2–6 for apparel or livery to Thomas Lupo, composer for H.M.'s violins, for variety of music for H.M.'s service; for allowance of 20 marks for two plays to the Prince's servants, the one, 27 December 1621, called the Man in the Moon drinks Claret, the other 29th of the same month, called the Witch of Edmonton, and a reward for both 20 nobles; for allowance of 20 nobles for one play acted by Ellisworth and his fellows, late servants to Queen Anne, and now the Company of the Revels, the play called Gramarcy, on 30 December 1621, and £3–6–8 by way of reward; for allowance of £60 to John Hemmings and his fellows, the King's Majesty's players for 6 plays, viz. The Women's Plot, played before H.M. 5 November last, the Woman is too hard for him, 26th of same month, The Island Princess, on St. Stephen's Day, The Pilgrim, on New Year's Day, The Wildgoose Chase, the 24th of January, The Coxcomb, the 5th of this instant March; for a gold chain and a medal of £200 or thereabouts to be given to Captain Kenett, for bringing news of the Queen of Bohemia's safe deliverance of a child; warrant to the Signet Office for a privy seal for H.M.'s signature for the licencing of Robert Lee, Richard Perkins, Ellisworth, Thomas Basse, John Blany, John Cumber and Will. Robins, late comedians to Queen Anne, deceased, to bring up children in the quality and exercise of playing comedies, histories, interludes, morals, pastorals, stage plays and such like other, as well for the solace and pleasure of H.M., as for the honest recreation of such as shall desire to see them, to be called by the name of the Children of the Revels, and to be drawn in such manner and form as hath been used in other licences of that kind. Ends f. 53v.

f. 56. Letters: A letter to Doctor Langton, of Magdalen College, Oxford, for a place for the son of one Vernon, at the request of the Lady Bedford, 1 October 1621; to the Governor and Council of Virginia, on behalf of Willm. Whitehead, whose parents died there, that order may be taken for the preservation of such estate to his use as was left at the death of his said parents; to the Council of Virginia, on behalf of Captain Leeke, to be one of H.M.'s Council in Virginia and to have a colonelship there; to Alderman Hollyday, on behalf of John Forest, to be made Steward of one of their East Indy ships; on the behalf of Captain Leeke, to his brother, Sir Francis Leeke, to do something for him against his going to Virginia; to Mr. Clarencieux Camden, on the behalf of Mr. Meare, to be Reader of his new historical lecture at Oxford; from his Lordship to Mr. Doctor Pinck, Warden of New College, Oxford, on the behalf of Thomas Browne, a child of Winchester, to be elected into New College, Oxford, this next election. Ends f. 60v.

f. 62. Miscellaneous Entries, Acquittances, Certificates: A key of the garden at Whitehall which had been made for the Lord of Buckingham was delivered to Mr. Forte; a licence under his Lordship's hand and seal to Martin Slatier, servant to the late Queen Anne, and the rest of his associates to use and exercise the acting of tragedies, comedies, histories etc. in London or any other town, demeaning themselves orderly and continuing not above 14 days in a year in any city or other place where they shall travel, and not to exceed the number of eighteen persons; certificate for Mr. Laurence Hilliard that he is the King's Limmer and therefore to be exempted from all payments and taxations any where but in Court, according to the privileges of other H.M.'s servants in ordinary. Ends f. 67.

VOLUME 8

On the original parchment cover, bound in: 'Receipt of the Exchequer. Annuities, Fees and other payments paid there, 1599, 41 Elizabeth'.

f. 1. Annuities or Pensions granted for various considerations. The entries are arranged alphabetically under surnames of grantees. Ends f. 12v.

f. 13. Fees and Wages for various offices and services. Arranged alphabetically as above. Ends f. 24.

f. 24v. Officers of the Queen's Works.

f. 25. Queen's Heralds or Pursuivants.

f. 25v. Queen's Musicians.

f. 26v. Queen's Sergeants.

f. 27. Annual payments to various late footmen and grooms of Queen's Chamber.

f. 28. Officers of the Admiralty.

f. 30. Officers at Arms.

f. 31. Master, Surveyor and other officers of the Ordnance.

f. 32. Drummers at the Tower of London.

f. 35. Officers of the Queen's Court of Exchequer.

f. 37. Queen's Justices of Assize etc.

f. 38. To Ecclesiastical Bodies etc., Schools, Universities etc.

VOLUME 9

A transcript of Sir Thomas Fanshaw's Practice of the Court of Exchequer, made in the first half of the seventeenth century. $10\frac{7}{8}'' \times 7''$. 89 ff.

f. 1. Title Page: A Short Compendium or Brief Declaration of what every Officer of H. Majesty's Court of Exchequer ought to do by virtue of his office in England, as also The Articles of the uniting of the late Court of Augmentations and Revenues of the Crown and the late Court of First Fruits and Tenths to the Court of Exchequer at Westminster, written at the request of the Rt. Hon. the Lord Buckhurst, Lord Treasurer of England in the Reign of Our Sovereign Lady Elizabeth.

f. 2. A Table of Contents.

f. 5. The Lord Treasurer: Questions concerning the Lord Treasurer's Office with several Answers made by Mr. Fanshaw, or rather a declaration of his opinion touching the same made at the request of my Lord Buckhurst (26 questions). This is followed by sections on the following: f. 15v. The Chancellor; f. 17. Under Treasurer; f. 18. The Lord Chief Baron; f. 22. The Second Baron; f. 24. The Third Baron; f. 24v. The Fourth Baron; f. 26v. The Two Chamberlains; f. 27v. The King's Attorney; f. 29. The King's Remembrancer; f. 37. The Lord Treasurer's Remembrancer; f. 47. Sheriffs' Accounts; f. 48. Escheators' Accounts; f. 48v. Roll of Accounts, Customers' Accounts; Rolls of Subsidies and Fifteenths; f. 49v. Rolls of the Wardrobe and Cofferers, Rotulus Examinatus; f. 50. Clerk of the Pipe; f. 51. Fee Farm rents and services; f. 51v. Oblate or Old Debts; f. 54. Clerk of the Estreats; f. 54v. The Auditors of the Prests; f. 55. Remembrancer of the First Fruits and Tenths; f. 55v. The Controller of the Pipe; f. 56. The Clerk of the Pleas; f. 57. The Foreign Opposer, The King's Attorney General; f. 61. The King's Solicitor General; f. 61v. The Auditors of the Exchequer; f. 63. The Receivers; f. 63v. The Surveyors; f. 64. The Attorneys and Clerks of the King's Remembrancer's Office, The Attorneys of the Clerk of the Pipe; f. 64v. The Attorneys and Clerks of the Clerk of the Pleas Office; f. 65. The Joiners of the Tallys; f. 65v. The Two Parcel Makers; f. 67. The Clerk of the Nihills; f. 67v. The Sealer of the Court; f. 68. The Chief Usher; f. 68v. The Marshal of the Court; f. 69v. The Four Ordinary Ushers, The Praisor of the Court; f. 70. The Four Tellers of the Receipt; f. 72v. The Clerk of the Pells; f. 73. The Cutter of the Tallys; f. 73v. The Controller of the Pells; f. 74. The Auditor of the Receipt; f. 76. The Two Under Chamberlains; f. 77. The Four Ordinary Messengers of the Receipt.

f. 78. The Articles of the late Court of Augmentations and Revenues of the Crown annexed to the Court of Exchequer at Westminster. (27 articles.)

f. 85. The Articles of the Uniting of the late Court of First Fruits, and Tenths to the Court of Exchequer at Westminster. (20 articles.) See Sir Thomas Fanshaw's *Practice of the Exchequer*, printed in 1658.

PETYT MS. 516. Volumes 4–9

This group of manuscripts now consists of six volumes of Law Reports, covering the following years: 13–18, 37–43 Elizabeth I, 2–3, 15–22 James I, 1 Charles I. They are of varying sizes but are uniformly bound in greenish-brown morocco, with Inner Temple coat of arms on both covers. The volumes are numbered 4 to 9, so volumes 1 to 3 are presumably lost. On flyleaves each volume has: Presented by W. Barnesley, and the signature: W. Barnesley.

VOLUME 4

Reports of cases in the Courts of King's Bench and Common Pleas, Hil. 39 Elizabeth I to Mich. 43 Elizabeth I (1597–1601), arranged in terminal order. On ff. 92–3 is an alphabetical index of parties. $7\frac{1}{2}'' \times 5\frac{5}{8}''$. 94 ff.

(Cf. *English Reports*, vols. 73–5, 97, 123.)

VOLUME 5

Reports of cases in the Courts of King's Bench and Common Pleas, Mich. 37 Elizabeth I to Mich. 43 Elizabeth I, with a number of notes etc. added at the end of the volume, as set forth below. $7\frac{5}{8}'' \times 5\frac{3}{8}''$. 375 ff.

ff. 347–62v. Darcy's Case of Monopolies, 44 Elizabeth I.

ff. 363v–368v. Instructions given by H.M.'s Commissioners for the levying of an aid to make the most noble Prince Henry, H.M.'s eldest son, knight, in April 1609.

In margin: In April 7 James I (1609) this commission was executed. Robert Houghton, Serjeant at Law, and Thomas Richardson esq. being the only lawyers in Norf. that were in commission, and they sat at Norwich, Fakenham, Thetford and Yarmouth.

Begins: First that your meeting and sitting be at the most public place in the county and the same to be in more or fewer places according as the county is great or small.

Ends: From Lincoln's Inn, this 25 April 1609. Your loving and assured friend, Henry Hobarte.

ff. 346, 369–70, 375. Brief notes and jottings.

ff. 371–4. Alphabetical index of cases.

(Cf. *English Reports*, as above.)

VOLUME 6

Reports of cases in the Courts of King's Bench and Common Pleas, Trin. 13 Elizabeth I to Mich. 18 Elizabeth I (1571–6), and in the Court of Common Pleas, East. 22 James I to Hil. 22 James I and East. to Trin. 1 Charles I (1625). $12'' \times 7\frac{3}{4}''$. 155 ff.

(Cf. *English Reports*, vols. 73–5, 79–82, 123–4.)

VOLUME 7

Reports of cases in the Courts of King's Bench, Common Pleas, Exchequer, Star Chamber, Court of Wards, Duchy of Lancaster, and Exchequer Chamber, East. 17 James I to Hil. 22 James I (1620–5). $12'' \times 8''$. 14 ff. 449 ff.

f. 2. Recipes for the stone and gravel.

f. 5. Signature: W. Barnesley, and a note: 'A book of Mr. (John) Ward's hand, the first leaves of my hand'.

f. 7. At top: Tho. Richardson, the 28 of April 1635.

Brief notes of cases from 30 Elizabeth I to 16 James I.

ff. 448–9. Alphabetical index of part of volume only.

(Cf. *English Reports*, vols. 82, 124, 145.)

VOLUME 8

Reports of cases in the Courts of King's Bench and Common Pleas, Hil. 2 James I to Mich. 3 James I (1605). $14\frac{1}{8}'' \times 8\frac{7}{8}''$. 282 ff.

f. 1. At top: Tho. Richardson, the 28 of April 1635.

ff. 281–2. Alphabetical index of cases.

(Cf. *English Reports*, vols. 80, 123.)

VOLUME 9

Reports of cases in the Court of Common Pleas, Trin. 15 James I to Hil. 17 James I (1618–20), with report of one case in Star Chamber, Hil. 15 James I (1618). $11\frac{5}{8}'' \times 7\frac{1}{4}''$. 214 ff.

ff. 213–214v. Alphabetical index of cases.

(Cf. *English Reports*, vol. 124.)

PETYT MS. 517

Instructions for the Master of Wards and Liveries, full bound in light brown morocco, with Inner Temple coat of arms on both covers. On flyleaf: Presented by W. Barnesley. Price 4s. Signature: W. Barnesley. $12'' \times 7\frac{5}{8}''$. 54 ff.

f. 1. Instructions for the Master of our Wards and Liveries, for the better authorising and directing of him in the execution of his office and performance of our service (1618).

Begins: First our pleasure is and we do declare that the Master of our Wards shall and may survey and dispose of all and every of our Wards, idiots and lunatics, and respectively of their lands.

The main sections are as follows: 1. Tenures; 2. Tenures in capite by knights service; 3. Socage in capite; 4. Common knights service of the King; 5. Common socage of the King; 6. Wards; 7. Wardship and primer seisin by the Statutes, 32 Henry VIII, cap. 1, and 34 Henry VIII, cap. 5; 8. Collusion to avoid wardship; 9. Marriage; 10. Relief; 11. Of livery; 12. Commissions; 13. Ouster le main; 14. Office.

f. 53. Ends: shall be restored to the profit of his lands from the time of his very full age, notwithstanding such an untrue office.

The volume has marginal notes, captions, and references. There are additions to the text at the top, bottom, and margins of several folios.

(Cf. also Petyt MS. 538/32 below.)

(Printed 1618; cf. also Sir James Ley, *Learned Treatise concerning Wards and Liveries*, 1641, 1642, and reissued in his *Reports, 1608–1620*, in 1659.)

PETYT MS. 518

A volume containing notes and arguments on the disputes between the Ecclesiastical and Temporal Jurisdictions, with special reference to Prohibitions, in the controversies of the reign of James I etc. On flyleaf: 'Presented by W. Bardesley. William Watts', with signature: W. Barnesley. $12\frac{1}{4}'' \times 7\frac{3}{4}''$. 100 ff.

ff. 1–7. Notes on cases in the Common Pleas, Mich. term, 6 James I to Trin. term, 7 James I.

f. 9. 'The second question propounded on behalf of the Lord Archbishop of Canterbury touching the exposition of Statutes concerning ecclesiastical causes, whether the same belong to the Judges of the realm, or to the interpretations of the Civilians and Canonists. A question never made in any of the books nor moved by any in any time heretofore'. In margin: 'That Acts of Parliament touching ecclesiastical causes are to be interpreted by the Judges of the common law'.

f. 15. 'The 3rd question that hath been made on behalf of the Lord Archbishop of Canterbury is whether if tithes in kind be not divided and set forth an action may be brought in any of the King's Courts at Westminster by the party aggrieved for treble damages grounded upon the Statute of 2 E. 6, cap. 13'.

f. 20. 'The 4th position or question on behalf of the Lord Archbishop of Canterbury concerning prohibitions given out of the Court of Common Pleas, which was debated before H.M. was not prohibition out of the Common Pleas, but upon suit depending there by original'.

f. 37v. 'An answer to the chief proofs selected touching Modus decimandi where the question is whether in the suit in the spiritual court for them in specie and prescription or custom de modo decimandi pleaded, a prohibition may be brought in the temporal court, or whether the spiritual court may not try that issue and so sentence the entire cause'.

f. 44. 'Authorities in law as proving the point in question and the reasons first set down'.

f. 64. Jurisdiction of the Stannaries, beginning with the inspeximus of a deed, 26 November 6 James I (1608), on the stannaries in co. Devon, in the rolls of the Court of Chancery.

f. 68. Question 1. Whether the High Commissioners may legally proceed to censure men for a breach of a decree of Star Chamber, made 28 Elizabeth I, for the better ordering of Printers and Stationers.

f. 68v. Whether the High Commission may fine and imprison by virtue of 10 Elizabeth I, cap. 1, unless it be in case of heresy or incontinency of ministers.

f. 72. A declaration of the true grounds of prohibition to the High Commission and the authority and reasons approving the same with answers to the objections made to the contrary.

f. 85v. A short report of the case Symons *v.* Wood.

f. 86. The grounds of the prohibitions to the High Commission and the answers to them.

f. 94. Prohibitions at actions upon the Statute for suing in the Admiralty Court for contracts made upon the land and upon the main sea.

f. 95. Prohibitions granted or stay in proceedings in causes pleadable before the Commissioners in Causes Ecclesiastical upon the Statute of 1 Elizabeth I, cap. 1.

f. 95v. Prohibitions granted upon the Statute of 23 Henry VIII, cap. 9, that no person shall be cited out of the diocese but in certain cases. Certain observations concerning prohibitions for the ease of H.M.'s subjects in Wales and the Marches of the same touching suits in that Court held before the Lord President and Council there.

f. 97v. Propositions presented to the consideration of the reverend Judges by direction of H.M. sitting in Council, 13 February 1632/3.

f. 100. List of cases.

PETYT MS. 519

Arms of the Nobility and Gentry, William I to James I. On old red label inset: 'Coats of Arms of the Nobility'. 'Presented by John Hales, A.D. 1716'. On flyleaf: 'This valuable manuscript of Arms curiously emblazoned was presented to this Honourable Society by John Hales, esq., a Bencher of the same Society. It contains the Arms of the Ancient Britons, Romans, Saxons and Danes, together with the Arms of our several Kings and Nobles, in each successive reign, beginning with William, Duke of Normandy and ending with King James the First'. On another flyleaf (f. 1) the same corrected and signed: Wm. Jeffs. 16″ × 11″. 102 ff.

The coats of arms start on f. 2v, which has the arms of the Britons, the Romans, the Saxons, and the Danes at the corners and the arms of William, Duke of Normandy, in the middle, numbered 1 to 5. Thereafter the arms are three on a page, numbered 6 to 548 (f. 102v). The name of the noble appears under the arms, with notes on the first holder and his successors, arranged chronologically under Kings, William I to James I. The last creations recorded are those of 4 May 1605 (ff. 101v, 102). The colours used in the coats of arms are red, blue, black, and yellow. The execution of the work is not of a high standard. The original hand of the letterpress ends f. 95v (no. 511). The additions of James I's reign are in a different hand. The volume seems to have been compiled towards the end of Elizabeth I's reign, with the creations of James I added.

PETYT MS. 520

Catalogue of Books given to the Inner Temple Library by Silvester Petyt in 1715. 12¼″ × 8″. 4 ff. 42 ff.

f. 1. 'Books given by Silvester Petyt, of Barnard's Inn, gent., towards the augmentation of the Inner Temple Library, to the building, furnishing and perfecting whereof, his brother, William Petyt, esq., heretofore one of the Masters of the Bench and Treasurer of the same Inner Temple, was a principal contributor and benefactor'.

There is a summary description of the eighteen volumes given, followed by a detailed description of each of them, with a list of the plates in each.

PETYT MS. 523

This pressmark consists of two volumes of the original Catalogue of the Books and Manuscripts of William Petyt. The two volumes are uniformly full bound in faded red morocco, with the Petyt coat of arms on both covers. 12⅞″ × 8″. Each volume has as a frontispiece an engraving of the head and shoulders of William Petyt, with the caption: William Petyt esq., Fellow of the Inner Temple and Keeper of the Records and Archives in the Tower of London. Each volume has the following Title-Page: 'The Books of Law, History, Antiquity, Manuscripts and Parliamentary Proceedings of William Petyt esq., heretofore Treasurer of the Honourable Society of the Inner Temple, London, and late Keeper of Her Majesty's Records in the Tower of London, with an index to the contents of the respective volumes'. Each volume opens with a transcript of the 'Act of Parliament of the Honourable Society of the Inner Temple touching the said Books, Manuscripts etc.' and proceeds to list the same in detail, the main particulars of which appear below. The descriptions of the manuscript volumes generally give a fairly detailed account of the contents of the various volumes; the descriptions of the printed books give full titles, name of author, and date of publication. In both manuscripts and printed books, when the volume is composite, the various items or sections are described. The pressmarks and other details have been entered later in a later hand. There are occasional marginal notes and comments, sometimes under the initials 'J.B.', that is Joshua Blew, Chief Butler and Librarian of the Inner Temple, who appears to have been responsible for the arrangement of the manuscripts and books in the library. The Act referred to above contains the following statement: 'the said William Petyt, in his life time, when Keeper of the Records in the said Tower of London, did invite many students in the law to go to the Tower to search and see the records there and take out of them what notes or extracts they pleased gratis'.

VOLUME I

The first volume contains the following classes or groups of Manuscripts and Printed Books: 364 ff.

ff. 4–5. Parliament Rolls, 534/ 33 volumes.

'The particulars contained in these Rolls may be seen in Mr. Prynne's *Abridgment of the Records in the Tower of London*, printed in 1657, and is amongst the History books, n. 67'.

ff. 8–9. Journals of Parliament, 537/ 46 volumes.

ff. 14–124. Records extracted, 533/ 38 volumes.

ff. 128–75. Transcript from the Rolls, 536/ 14 volumes.

ff. 178–296. Proceedings in Parliament and Miscellanies, 538/ 56 volumes.

f. 254. Volume 36. 'The particular contents of this volume you may see in the first page of this Book more at large'.

f. 282. Volume 49. 'You may see the contents of this volume in the first leaf by me J.B.'.

ff. 297–317. Charters, Privileges, Coronations etc. 535/ 7 volumes.

ff. 319–37. Placita de Juratis et Assisis etc., 515/ 9 volumes.

ff. 340–43v. History Books in print, 91 volumes.

ff. 346–9. Law Books in print, 88 volumes.

ff. 352–63. An Abstract of some Journals in Parliament in the reigns of King James and King Charles, 537/ (see above). A more detailed list of certain volumes.

Law Common Place Books, 6 volumes (this appears at end of index of Contents only).

VOLUME 2

The second volume contains the following classes or groups of Manuscripts and Printed Books: 198 ff.

ff. 5–153v. Manuscripts in folio touching the Government of England, 512/ 26 volumes.

f. 106v. Volume R. 'In which comparisons Mr. Petyt hath truly stated Doctor Brady's assertions and refuted and answered the same by good authorities, as by reading them will sufficiently appear. And that our ancestors were not beasts of burden, but a generous and free people, willing and able to supply their King and government when they met in Great Councils and Parliaments circa ardua negotia Regni'.

ff. 155–6. Manuscripts in vellum in folio, 511/1–10.

f. 155. In margin against 511 (Robert of Gloucester): 'March 26th. 1716. The learned Jno. Anstis esq. informed me that this Book is a translation from the French by Robert de Mannyng of Peter de Langtoft's book'.

ff. 157–73. Manuscripts in vellum and paper in folio, quarto, and octavo, 511/11–23.

ff. 179–85v. Parliament, Law and History, in quarto, printed, 71 volumes.

ff. 187–92. History and Proceedings in Parliament, printed, 88 volumes.

ff. 195–7. Law, in octavo, printed, 47 volumes.

PETYT MS. 524

Scala Perfectionis written in English before 1296 by Walter Hilton, full bound in dark blue morocco, with Inner Temple coat of arms on both covers. On flyleaf: There is no reference, nor does this manuscript appear in the Petyt Catalogue so it is probably not a Petyt manuscript. On a first leaf of binding are some verses in English in a hand of the fifteenth century, being part of Lydgate's prologue to his Seige of Troy. $11\frac{1}{2}'' \times 8\frac{1}{8}''$. 149 ff.

f. 1. Sal. Consolium Junerum Singulare Comodum Latens Odium Destruit Regnum. This Booke is Cleped Scala Perfectionis said to be founden in Maister Lowis de Fontibus Book at Cantebrige and turned into English bi Maister Waultier Hilton de Turbaton. Jos. Blew, 1730. Since printed by Wynkyn de Worde in Wm. Caxton's House. See Thoresby's Cat. of Ancient Printed Books . . . anno Dni 1484. J. B. 1730.

ff. 2 and 3 are blank and one leaf or more of the text missing.

f. 4. Begins: We take not upon us bi oure owne traveille ne bi oure owne witte. Where bigynnen viii chapitres necessarie for men that yeven hem to perfeccion whiche weren founden in Maister Lowis de Fontibus book at Cantebrigge and turned into English bi Maister Waultier Hilton de Turbaton of tokens and wishynges of love.

f. 11v. Here begynneth the boke that is cleped Scala Perfeccionis and it hath two parties whereof heere sueth the table of the first partie. (91 chapter headings.)

f. 14. Begins: Hereinne is tolde the cause whi thise writynges is made and hou she shal have her in the redynge that it was made unto.

f. 71v. Heere endeth the first partie and after sueth the table of the second partie. (46 chapter headings.)

f. 73. Thus endeth the table and after sueth the second partie of the boke.

f. 147v. Ends: may seen moore in an houre of such goostli matier than myght be writen in a greet boke. deo gracias.

f. 148. The signature of Stephen Gardiner, Bishop of Winchester (1531–51, 1553–5): Stephani Winton. et amicorum.

f. 149v. 2 verses in Latin (repeated) and 10 verses in English followed by four lines of numerals and Greek letters as if a cypher.

(The *Scala Perfectionis* was edited by Robert E. Grey, London, 1869, and by J. R. Dalgarius, London, 1870.)

The manuscript is well written in a good hand, well-formed, in good black ink, on good parchment. There are references in the margins, almost all to Books of the Bible. There are also a few nota in the margins but all marginalia seem to be contemporary not later additions. The manuscript may be dated the first half of the fifteenth century. There is good illumination in gold, blue, green, red, and purple in the capital letters and there are paragraph marks in the text and margins in red and blue or blue and gold. There are large capitals, the length of the ff., on ff. 11v, 53v, 70v, and illumination and decoration all round the ff. at the beginning of the text of the First and Second Parts, on ff. 14, 73.

PETYT MS. 525

A Collection of Appeals to the House of Lords, 1701–28, a Table of Points, and an Index of Cases. Full bound in light brown morocco with the Inner Temple coat of arms on both covers. $12\frac{3}{8}'' \times 7\frac{7}{8}''$. 148 pp.

Title-Page: 'A Table of the Most Remarkable Points in the Printed Cases upon Appeals to the House of Lords since the year 1701, upon which the Decrees and Judgements were Affirmed, Varied or Reversed, Together with another Alphabetical Index of the Names of the Cases referring to the Day and Year and likewise to the Title under which they are placed in the 1st Table, with notice taken whether Affirmed, Varied or Reversed'. At foot of Title-Page: 'This Common Place includes the year 1728'. The Titles are arranged alphabetically, Abatement to Witness. The earliest case is 6 March 1700/1, the latest 23 November 1728.

PETYT MS. 526

A volume containing transcripts of (1) Sir Francis Vere's account of the expedition to Cadiz, 1597, the Island Voyage, and the battles of Turnhout and Newport; (2) Francis Bacon's dedication of his Maxims of Law to Queen Elizabeth I; (3) Sir Walter Rayleigh's Apology. Full bound in light red morocco, with the Inner Temple coat of arms on both covers. $12\frac{1}{8}'' \times 7\frac{7}{8}''$. 50 ff.

1. f. 1. The Cadiz Journey. Begins: 'In the year of our Lord etc. I was sent for into England; at that time the journey to the coast of Spain was resolved on, what by the taking of Cadiz was after commonly called the Cadiz Journey'.

f. 8. Ends: 'The troops dissolved. I went to the Court and there attended the most part of that winter'. (Sir Francis Vere, *Commentaries* (1657).)

f. 9. The Island Voyage. Begins: 'In the year of our Lord etc. being the next year after the Journey of Cadiz, another journey was made by the Earl of Essex to the coast of Spain and the Island'.

f. 17. Ends: 'I stayed the winter in England, in which time my Lord Sheffield making resignation of his government of the Brill into H.M.'s hands, I was advised and encouraged by my good friends to make means to H.M. for that charge'. (Ibid.)

f. 18v. The Slaughter at Turnhout. Begins: 'That winter the enemy being at Turnhoult, an open village, with 1,000 foot and 600 horse, one day amongst other speeches I said to Monsieur Barnevelt'. (Sir Francis Vere, *Commentaries* (1657).)

f. 23. The Battle of Newport. Begins: 'In the year of our Lord etc. the enemies being weakened in mutinies and his affairs in disorder, the States resolved to make an offensive war in Flanders'.

f. 32. Ends: 'Wherein I will charge none and excuse none but the messengers of their slackness'. (Ibid.)

2. f. 33. To her sacred Majesty. Begins: 'I do here most humbly present unto your Majesty a sheaf and cluster of fruit of that good and favourable season which by the influence of your happy government we enjoy'.

f. 34. Ends: 'I most humbly crave pardon and commend your Majesty to the divine preservation. January 8th 1596/7.

Your Majesty's most humble and obeying subject and servant Fr. Bacon'.

f. 35. The Preface. (Bacon's *Works*, Vol. VII.)

3. f. 43. Sir Walter Rayleigh's Apology. (Heading.)

Begins: 'If the ill success of this enterprise of mine had been without example I should have needed a long discourse'.

f. 50. Ends: 'By doing the one I had robbed the King of Spain and been a thief, and by the other a disturber or breaker of the peace'. (Rayleigh's *Works*, Vol. VIII.)

The three transcripts are by three different hands, all written early in the seventeenth century.

PETYT MS. 527

A transcript of Sir Francis Vere's Commentaries, with a transcript of Letters of John van Olden Barneveldt, 1619. Full bound in light red morocco, with the Inner Temple coat of arms on both covers. $12\frac{1}{2}'' \times 7\frac{3}{4}''$. 39 ff.

f. 1. Begins 'The Count Charles Blaunefylde passed with part of this army into the Romnells ward, the rest being in Brabant'.

f. 37v. Ends: 'the difficulty they found in passing there grosse over the Creikes with some loss to us yet much more to them they retired to the redoubt they had gotten'. (Ptd. in 1657.) (Ff. 6–32 was in volume 526 above, ff. 1–32.)

f. 39. A transcript of Barneveldt's first letter to 'very loving children, sons in law and childrens' children'. 'From my chamber of sickness, 12 May 1619. John van Oulden Barnefelt'.

f. 39v. A transcript of his second letter to 'very loving wife and children'. 'From my chamber of sadness, the 13th of May 1619. John van Oulden Barnefelt'.

(These two letters are written in a hand different from the previous transcript.)

PETYT MS. 528

Translations out of Dutch of the Treaty of Munster, 30 January 1648, and out of French of the Treaty of Commerce, 17 December 1650. Full bound in light red morocco, with the Inner Temple coat of arms on both covers. $8\frac{7}{8}'' \times 6\frac{3}{4}''$. 29 ff.

1. Title-Page: 'Articles and Conditions of the Everlasting Peace concluded between the most potent King of Spain etc. on the one side and the High and Mighty Lords, the States General of the United Provinces, on the other side, and sealed the 30th of January 1648 at Munster. Translated out of the Dutch'.

f. 1. The Lords States General of the United Provinces. In the name of God and to his Glory, be it known to all men that after long sequel of bloody wars, which for so many years have oppressed the people, subjects, realms and countries under the obedience of the King of Spain and the States General of the United Provinces. 79 articles or sections.

f. 17v. lxxix. The said Treaty is to be published everywhere upon the delivery of the said ratification and then all acts of hostility are to cease.

f. 18. A copy of the Full Power the King's Majesty of Spain delivered to the High and Mighty the Lords States General of the United Provinces, now assembled at Munster, wherein H.M. doth declare these United Provinces to be free, without having any pretensions thereupon in no manner whatsoever . . .

f. 19. In witness whereof I have commanded these presents to be dispatched signed with my hand and contrasigned with the superscription of my Secretary of State. Dated at Saragossa, the 7th July 1646.
I the King. P. Coloma.

f. 20. Here followeth the Procuration of the Plenipotentiaries of the Lords States General. Done at Munster in Westphalia, the 30th January 1648. (9 names.)

2. f. 23. Title-Page: 'A Treaty concerning the Navigation and Commerce at Sea, between the Lords, the King of Spain and the States General of the United Provinces. Concluded the 17th December 1650. Translated out of French'.

f. 24. Begins: 'Whereas after the conclusion of the Treaty of Munster'. 18 articles or sections. Ends: 'xviii. Finally that this present Treaty is to be approved and confirmed by the said King of Spain and the States General of the United Provinces of the Low Countries within 4 months after the date hereof'.

f. 27. The Form of the Sea Letter: By the Burgomaster and Governors of the city of (blank). Certificate of Master of Ship.

f. 27v. Here followeth the copy of the power of the Lord Anthony Brun, Ordinary Ambassador of the King of Spain, translated out of the French. From Madrid, 18 August 1650.

f. 28v. Here followeth the powers of the Lords Deputies of the States General. Given at the Hague in our Assembly, 7 December 1650, under our Great Seal and signed by our Secretary.

PETYT MS. 529

Transcript of Richard Hakluyt's translation of Grotius's *Mare Liberum*. On flyleaf: 'Mare Librum. The Free Sea'. On another flyleaf: 'Translated into English by Mr. Richard

Hakluyt etc.'. Full bound in red morocco, with Inner Temple coat of arms on both covers. $8\frac{5}{8}'' \times 6\frac{3}{4}''$. 24 ff.

f. 3. The Free Sea or A disputation concerning the right which the Hollanders ought to have of the Indian merchandize for trading.

The Chapters of the Disputation. (13 chapters.)

f. 24. Ends: 'Who for the only respect of their own gain oppose themselves against the common benefit of mankind. Finish. Soli Deo laus et gloria'.

'Seeing about this time very many of the King of Spain's letters came to our hands wherein his and the Portugal's purpose is manifestly discovered, I thought it useful of those (whereof there were many of the same argument) to translate two of them into the Latin tongue'.

First written at Lisbon, 28 November 1606.

Second written at Madrid, 27 January 1607.

PETYT MS. 529A

Transcript of 'The Life and Death of Henry, our late famous Prince, together with his Funerals', by Sir Charles Cornwallis. The Title-Page: 'The Life and Death of Henry, our late famous Prince, together with his Funerals, who was born at Stirling Castle, on Tuesday, the 19th of February 1594/5, and deceased at St. James, on Friday, the sixth of November 1612'. Full bound in red morocco, with the Inner Temple coat of arms on both covers. $7\frac{3}{8}'' \times 5\frac{7}{8}''$. 48 ff.

f. 1. Begins: 'To live and to live well are two things so distinct in themselves as Contemplation and Action'.

f. 48v. Ends: 'with the love, prayers and tears of all he was attended into Heaven'.

(Ptd. in 1641, and in Somers' *Tracts*, II, p. 226, where it has a different Preface.)

PETYT MS. 530

A group of six volumes of different sizes (given below), which are lettered A to F. Volume A is full bound in red morocco, volumes B and C in full chocolate-coloured calf, and volumes D, E, and F in full light brown calf. All the volumes have the Inner Temple coat of arms on both covers. Volume A is a draft or revised copy of John Leslie's History of Scotland, volumes B to E are sermons, and volume F a student's notebook on logic.

VOLUME A

An author's copy or draft of John Leslie, Bishop of Ross's History of Scotland, with corrections and notes. $7\frac{7}{8}'' \times 5\frac{7}{8}''$. 194 ff.

f. 1. Original flyleaf: The brief history of Scotland from the death of King James the First to the year of God 1m. four hundred thirty six years to the 1561 and so of Kings James the Second, James the Third, James the Fourth, James the Fifth and Mary now Queen of Scotland. (Ptd. by the Bannatyne Club in 1830.)

Followed by the following note: This copy is not perfect and therefore to be reformed in divers places conform to the principal, which is in the Queen Majesty's hands.

f. 3. Dedication: To the right high, right virtuous and excellent Princess Mary, by the grace of God, Queen of Scots and Dowager of France, Your most humble servant and servitour, John Leslie, Bishop of Ross, prays prosperous health, increase of honour and perpetual felicity.

Begins: The noble, wise and prudent senator Roman, scilicet Cato (most excellent and gracious Sovereign Lady).

f. 6. Ends: The (blank) day of April 1569. Your mistress's most humble and obedient subject and servitour.

f. 8. James the Second. (In margin: the year of Christ 1436.)

f. 19. James the Third. (In margin: the year of Christ 1460.)

f. 33. James the Fourth. (In margin: 1488.)

f. 59. James the Fifth. (In margin: Anno Christi 1513.)

f. 102. Two paragraphs cancelled by striking through.

Follows the History of Queen Mary, 1542.

f. 103. Queen Mary. (In margin: 1542.)

f. 194. Ends: and all happened and thus I finish and make end the xxv day of March 1 m. v lxx.

The volume has marginal notes of three kinds: (1) paragraph headings; (2) the year of Grace; (3) additions and corrections. (1) run from f. 3 to f. 109 (1544), after which there are none to f. 171 (1558), after which they continue to f. 187 (1561). (2) run throughout from f. 8 (1436) to f. 187 (1561). (3) There is a long insertion to the preface under sign +.

There are also a number of corrections in the text, including some words, some phrases, and sometimes several lines cancelled, e.g.: f. 8, 4 lines; f. 11. 'In the meantime' altered to 'the next winter following'; f. 30v, 5 lines cancelled; f. 34, marginal caption; f. 41 consists of two whole paragraphs for insertion into f. 40v, the first of 12 lines at the end of 1503, the second of 10 lines for insertion after the above for the year 1505, which is not represented otherwise in the original text; f. 62v. 'My Lord' governor corrected to 'The' (1515); f. 86. The last paragraph here (1530), appears to be an addition beginning 'There was a Parliament holden in Edinburgh in the month (cancelled) of 9br'.; f. 86v, The following addition at the bottom of the folio, 'in the year of Christ 1436. This is in so eloquent style, so diligently and truly collected yet now of all the matters is at that time cast away'; f. 90v, under 1537, The King is etc.; f. 91, 1538, addition in margin, Melrose he too during all the days of his life etc.; f. 96, addition at bottom of folio, partly cut away; in text, At the same time (cancelled) there came one doctor, altered to, during the time the Queen Dowager and ladies of the nobility of Scotland were of course there came one doctor (1551); f. 172, nearly 4 lines in text cancelled, with six hundred soldiers and the Queen with her whole retinue etc.; f. 190, only her friends 'received' in good part altered to 'excepted'.

The paper on which the volume is written is very thin, almost Indian paper, entirely different from the paper used at that time in England. Many headings are almost cut away. The hands used are very neat. The title and the note given in f. 1 above are written in a definitely Scottish hand, probably by John Leslie. The second hand of the text begins with the section beginning with Queen Mary (f. 103), as if this section is a later addition by the author.

VOLUME B

A volume containing three sermons by Alexander Strange, 8″×6″. 61 ff.

f. 1. Title-Page: Three Sermons made upon several occasions: The first at St. Mary's in Cambridge; The second at the Assizes at Hertford; The third at Woodhall Hatfield. By Alexander Strange, Bach. in Divinity.

f. 1v. Dedication to Sir Ralph Sadleir, kt.

f. 2v. Preface in Latin ends: Vale. Kalend. Januar. Anno 1610. Alex. Strange.

ff. 3–19. A sermon preached at Cambridge. Coloss. 3. 16, in Greek and translated.

ff. 19v–46. A Sermon preached at Hertford, the 4th day of March 1607/8, before Sir John Leventhorpe, kt., being High Sheriff, Sir Thomas Walmysley, kt., and Sir John Croke, kt., being Judges of the Assize, and other knights and gentlemen of the shire.

ff. 46v–61. A sermon preached at Woodhall Hatfield, before Sir Ralph Coningsby, kt., and other knights and gentlemen of quality, at the anniversary commemoration of that worthy knight, Sir Henry Butler. 1 John 3. 18.

Throughout the volume there are marginal references to the Books of the Old and New Testaments, with a few to the Fathers and Classics (Latin and Greek).

VOLUME C

A sermon for Christmas, presented to Mrs. Anne Sadleir. $5\frac{7}{8}''\times3\frac{7}{8}''$. 40 ff.

Title-Page: A Sermon for Christmas. To the virtuous and therefore worthy Mrs. Anne Sadleir, of Standon, all increase of spiritual graces and temporal blessings is wished, By her true and loving friend, Alexander Strange.

ff. 1–40. A sermon. Galat. 4. 4. n.d. (first quarter of seventeenth century).

The volume has running headings and marginal references to the Books of the Old and New Testaments.

VOLUME D

A volume containing two sermons by Thomas Newcomen. $7\frac{1}{2}''\times5\frac{3}{8}''$. 4 ff. 48 pp.

(f. 1). 'To the greater example of lovingful and Christian piety. Mrs. Sadleir, when I last had the honour to wait on you at Standon my text was a prayer'.

(f. 1v). Ends: Your humbly devoted servant: Tho. Newcomen, Clothall, July 9th 1660.

(ff. 2–3v). A prayer.

pp. 1–48. A sermon. Psalm 144. 5.

The volume has a few notes and many marginal references to the Books of the Old and New Testaments.

VOLUME E

A volume containing a translation of Philip de Mornay's Meditation on the Lord's Supper. 8″×6″. 40 ff.

f. 1. Title-Page: A Meditation upon the first to the Corinthians, chapter 11, verse 24. By Philip de Mornay, Seigneur du Plessis Marly, translated into English by R( ) C( ), Paris. 1609, September 22.

ff. 2–39v. The translation of the Meditation.

f. 40. A short prayer of 6 lines written in a different hand.

Besides the text at the beginning, where there are marginal references to the Books of the Old and New Testaments, the words in the text are written in red ink, as well as odd words and phrases throughout. The red ink has faded badly.

VOLUME F

A volume containing a student's notes or extracts on logic. $6\frac{3}{8}'' \times 4\frac{1}{2}''$. 287 pp.

The volume is described as Artis Logicae. Libri Duo etc. Before the pagination begins there is a rough table of contents, followed by titles or headings and notes on de logicis natura ac divisione, de fallaciis in genere, an logica sit necessaria, de substantia, de qualitate, de numero praedicabilium. The whole volume appears to be a student's notebook. Throughout there are many blank pages and from p. 119 onwards most pages have letters, words, or phrases in faded red ink. n.d. (Early seventeenth century.)

PETYT MS. 531

A group of seven volumes, of varying sizes (which are given below), of which six are uniformly bound in chocolate-coloured calf, with the Inner Temple coat of arms on both covers. The exception, volume F, is full bound in its original brown calf, with the Tudor rose, Garter motto, and crown on both covers. The volumes are lettered A to F. Volume A contains a collection on Coronations and one concerning the peerage, and the remaining six volumes contain sermons, four of them of the first half of the seventeenth century or a little later.

VOLUME A

A volume containing two items, the first on the form of coronation oaths and the second on the creation, succession etc. of Dukes, Marquises, and Earls in England. $7\frac{1}{8}'' \times 5\frac{5}{8}''$. 60 ff.

1. ff. 1–3v. 'The manner and form of the coronation of Kings and Queens of England', described as a transcript from the old chronicle called the Brut. It has the signature: Fraunces Morre, 1590, at the top of f. 1. In a hand of the second half of the sixteenth century.

2. ff. 4–60. 'A Collection of the creation, succession and decease of the Dukes, Marquises and Earls of England since the Conquest, gathered by C(   ) P(   )'.

It begins with Albemarle and proceeds more or less in alphabetical order to Shrewsbury. It was compiled 1588–9, as Roger was Earl of Rutland (f. 55), who did not succeed until 1588, and George was Earl of Shrewsbury (f. 59), who died in 1590, and his son Francis, who predeceased him, was still alive.

VOLUME B

A volume of four sermons, written in an unusual somewhat spiky hand, with a relation of the life of Francis Spira added, probably written in the early part of the second half of the sixteenth century. $7\frac{3}{8}'' \times 5\frac{7}{8}''$. 87 pp., 22 pp.

p. 1. A sermon beginning: Likewise I say unto you there is joy in the presence of the Angels of God over one sinner that repenteth. Luke 14. 10.

p. 17. A sermon beginning: Why art thou cast down Oh my soul and why art thou disquieted within me. Psalm 42. 6.

p. 35. A sermon beginning: In whose heart are thy ways. Isaiah 84. 5.

p. 59. A sermon beginning: They that love the Lord hate evil. Psalm 97. 10.

This is followed by an unpaginated sheet which has 'Fr. Spira' on the recto and on the verso: Proverbs 14. 14. The backslider in heart shall be filled with his own ways. Then begins a new pagination.

p. 1. 'A Relation of the desperate estate of Francis Spira in the year 1548'. Begins: In the year 1548, when the glorious sun of the Gospel was but newly risen in Europe, in the days of the reign of Edward the VIth. of that name, King of England, in the territory and under the jurisdiction of the city of Venice, being the very border of Italy, in the town of Citadella, lived one Francis Spira, an advocate of great rank and esteem.

p. 22. Ends: Yet an occasion to make us remember that secret things belong to the Lord our God, but charity to man to teach him to hope all things.

VOLUME C

A sermon by Andrew Marvell, the elder, 1626. $5\frac{1}{2}'' \times 3\frac{3}{8}''$. 4 ff. 56 pp.

f. 1. Title-Page: Israel and England paralleled, or some of their sins balanced. 1 Corinthians 10. 7. Be yet not idolators as were some of them.

f. 2. 'To the truly noble, religious and right virtuous gentlewoman Mrs. Anne Sadleir, health and happiness'.

f. 4. 'From my poor study, April 28, 1626. Ever devoted to your service: And. Marvell.'

pp. 1–56. Judges 5. 8. They chose new Gods. A sermon with references in the margin to Books of the Old and New Testaments and one to the classics.

VOLUME D

A sermon. $6'' \times 4\frac{1}{2}''$. 14 ff.

ff. 1–14v. A sermon on Psalm 94, v. 19. In the multitude of the sorrows that I had in my heart thy comforts have refreshed my soul. With references in the margins to Books of the Old and New Testaments and to the classics. Written in the first half of the seventeenth century.

VOLUME E

A sermon by Robert Tounson, at the funeral of Sir Thomas Sadleir, prefaced by a short biography. $7\frac{1}{2}'' \times 5\frac{1}{2}''$. 23 ff.

On the original flyleaf is the signature: Anne Sadleir.

f. 1. 'The copy of a sermon preached at the funeral of Sir Thomas Sadleir, kt., at Sandon, in Hertfordshire, upon Shrove Tuesday, being the 17th of February 1606/7. By Robert Tounson'. (Probably written by Anne Sadleir.)

f. 2. The Preface: It hath so pleased Almighty God.

ff. 4–10. 'The Narration of the Life and Death of Sir Thomas Sadleir.'

ff. 11–23. A sermon on Genesis 25. 8. Then Abraham yielded the spirit and died, in good age, an old man, and of great years, and was gathered to his people.

It has notes or headings only in the margins.

VOLUME F

A volume containing four sermons, 1654, 1655, the first and second being in one hand and the third and fourth in another. $5\frac{3}{4}'' \times 3\frac{7}{8}''$. 79 ff.

ff. 1–15. A sermon on Proverbs 31. 30. Favour is deceitful and beauty is vanity, but the woman that feareth the Lord she shall be praised.

ff. 17–39v. A sermon on 2 Esdr. 7. 48. Oh Adam what hast thou done in that thou hast sinned.

ff. 42–59. A sermon preached at Corby on the Feast Day, 1654. Luke 15. 23. Bring the fat calf and kill him and let us eat and be merry.

ff. 62–79v. 'The first sermon that an aged minister preached after the death of his dear son and only child, June 3, 1655. Isaiah 26. 19. Thy dead men shall live, with my body shall they arise. Awake and sing ye that sleep in the dust, for thy dew is as the dew of herbs, and the earth shall cast forth her dead.

VOLUME G

A sermon preached at the funeral of Anthony Cookson, 1624. $4\frac{1}{4}'' \times 3\frac{1}{8}''$. 87 pp.

Title-Page: A Sermon at St. Sepulchres, the 29 of January 1623/4, at the funeral of that worthy citizen vintner Mr. Anthony Cookson, by that famous divine Mr. Nathaniel Shute, resident at (blank) in Lombard Street, London.

p. 1. Preface.

pp. 5–87. A sermon on Psalm 39. 5. Behold thou hast made my days as a hand breadth.

PETYT MS. 532

A volume of tracts and letters in French, with Inner Temple coat of arms on both covers. On flyleaf: Des Remarques de la France. This volume is not in the Petyt Catalogue. $8\frac{5}{8}'' \times 6\frac{7}{8}''$. 100 ff.

f. 1. Remarques sur l'estat de France. Begins: Cest une vraye et absolue Monarchie.

f. 45. Ends: la quelle monterson et nombre d'autres y ont de lettre.

f. 49. Lettre de Monsieur le Cardinal d(u) P(erron) au Roy sur l'estat de Venise. Begins: Sire l'escaus por le dernier ordinaire.

f. 59. Monsieur du Perron a Monsieur le Chancelier de Sillery sur sa promotion.

f. 61v. Monsieur du Perron a Monsieur de Rosny.

f. 62. Response de Monsieur de Rosny.

f. 65. Monsieur du Plessis estant a Angers par le commandement du roy pour traiter dune treue avec les deputez de Monsieur de Mereur fut offence de quelques coups de baton par derriere par un gentilhome son enemy.
Le Roy luy escrit. 8 Novembre 1597.

f. 65v. Je seay le sixieme du prochein sans faillie a Bloys lieu resolu dapprendre le passepiet de Bretaigne.
Madame la Marquise de Vernueil au roy.

f. 67. Lettre de Monsieur Ar. a Monsieur de Bethune Cousin de Monsieur de Sailly estant en Hollande sur le suiet de son changement de Religion.

f. 71v. Lettre de Monsieur Ar. a Monsieur de Beaumont sur le suiet de quelques vers de sa fawn plaignans sa disgrace.

f. 73. Epitaphe sur le tombeau du Sieur Marton Conseiller du roy en son conseil destat et advocat general en son parlement de Paris.
Par Monsieur le Cardinal du Perron.

f. 74. Replicque par Monsieur Ar.
Lettre remerciemens de Monsieur Ar. a Monsieur du Perron.

f. 75v. Lettre de Monsieur de Sailly au gouverneur d'Orange.

f. 79. Touchant M. de Bouillon.

f. 85v. Harangue des Ambassadeurs d'Alemayne au roy environ le mois de Juing 1605.

f. 87v. Sommaire de la response du Roy.

f. 89. Comparison des trois roys.

f. 91. Harrangue a la Noblesse de Provence par Monsieur M. Gentilhomme du Paris.

Ends f. 100v.

This manuscript is written in a foreign hand on foreign paper and is of the first half of the seventeenth century.

PETYT MS. 533

This group consists of 38 volumes, all full bound in grained calf, with the Petyt coat of arms on both covers. The size of the volumes is fairly uniformly $12\frac{5}{8}'' \times 8''$, with slight variations due only to rebinding. The whole group consists of transcripts or extracts, some with translations, of Public Records, especially from the Chancery Rolls and the King's Remembrancer and Lord Treasurer's Remembrancer Memoranda Rolls of the Exchequer (then and since a little-used source), and from manuscript and printed chronicles and other manuscript and printed sources. The manuscript sources included transcripts and extracts from twenty-two manuscripts in the Cotton Collection, many of the Archives of the city of London, and many manuscripts then in other public and private possession. The Public Records also include transcripts and extracts from Assize Rolls, King's Bench Rolls and Common Plea Rolls, bundles of writs and returns, and other Chancery and Exchequer rolls. The whole collection was made by or for William Petyt and some volumes contain notes by him. The whole range is from the reign of William II to that of Edward IV. The whole group is generally described as 'Recorda'. Volume 1 relates to the reign of John, continuing with the reigns of Henry III, volumes 2–10, Edward I, volumes 11–15, Edward II, volumes 16–21, Edward III, volumes 22–8, Richard II, volumes 29–31, Richard II and Henry IV, volume 32, Henry V, volume 33, Henry VI, volumes 34–5, William II to Edward IV, volumes 37–8. The following volumes are specifically entitled 'Recorda', volumes 1–7, 10–14, 16–18, 22–6, 30–5. Of the remaining volumes, volume 8 describes itself as 'Parliamenta', volumes 9, 20, 28, 29 as 'several writs, records, commissions etc. and transactions in Parliament', volumes 15, 19, 27 as 'The Rights of the Commons in Parliament by Prescription', volume 21 is a volume of lists and excerpts from the Chancery Rolls, John to Edward II, volume 36, brief extracts mainly from Chancery Rolls, volume 37, transcripts from chronicles and other printed and manuscript sources, William II to Richard I, volume 38, the like, mainly from the Public Records, Edward III to Edward IV. The volumes, other than those marked 'Recorda', seem to have been prepared specifically for William Petyt's printed and manuscript works on Parliament.

VOLUME I

A volume of transcripts from the Public Records, mainly from the Charter, Patent, Close, Oblate, and Fine Rolls, with a few extracts from printed and manuscript sources, 1–17 John. On flyleaf: 'Records from the 1st of King John to the 17th year'. On another flyleaf: 'Recorda tempore Regis Johannis'. 407 ff.

f. 1. A short introductory note to the reign of King John.

f. 5. An account of the election and coronation of King John, at London, 1199, from Matthew Paris, and an account of the whole reign from the same, Hoveden, Brompton and Hemingford and an ancient Register in the Archives of the Archbishop of Canterbury

f. 9. Grant to Geoffrey de Ver of the Sergeanty of Caen, 14 July 1199.

f. 10. Confirmation to citizens of Lincoln, 21 July 1199.

f. 12. Grant to Agatha, nurse of Queen Eleanor, 18 July 1199.

f. 13. Confirmation to men of Fontevrault, 31 August 1199.

f. 17. Confirmation to knights and free tenants in King's forests in Honor of Lancaster, 9 October 1199.

f. 18. Grant to Richard de Belhus of land in Sledmere, 3 September 1199.

f. 19. Confirmation of exchange of lands between the Archbishop of Canterbury and the monks of Rochester, 26 September 1199.

f. 21. Grant to burgesses of Dundee of quittance of toll in England except in London, 26 October 1199.

f. 22. Grant to John de Gray of 3 knights fees. 15 October 1199.

f. 23. Grant to Geoffrey, son of Robert, of 5 knights fees, 14 October 1199.

f. 24. Grant to Elias, son of Robert, of Master Sergeanty of wapentake of Salford, 10 October 1199.

f. 25. Confirmation to Gerold de Claiton of Sergeanty of Leylandshire 10 October 1199.

f. 26. Grant to Queen Isabella of city of Saintes etc. in dower, 30 August 1200.

f. 26v. Grant to William Marshal, Earl of Pembroke, of the pastoral staff of the Abbey of Nutley, 16 August 1200.

f. 27. Grant to Gamel, son of Gamel, and descendants, to be free men and have liberties of free borough of Preston, 10 October 1199.

f. 28. Confirmation to burgesses of Preston of liberties with additional grant, 10 October 1199.

f. 29. Confirmation to Elias, son of Robert, of land, Pembury, 10 October 1199.

f. 30. Agreement between King and Baldwin, Count of Flanders, not to make peace with King of France. n.d. (1199).

f. 31v. Letter to Innocent III appointing Master P(eter) Barell his proctor in a cause. 14 June 1200.

f. 32. Offer of 15 marks by Stephen de Cruwes to have lands of which he was disseised with mandate to Justice of Ireland, 1 John. From Oblate Roll (to f. 33v).

Offer of £200 by Abbot of St. Edmunds for confirmation of charter of Richard I, 1 John.

f. 32v. Offer of 1,200 marks by Bishop of Durham for confirmation of Sadberg etc. 1 John.

f. 33. Offer of 15 marks by Ernald Ruffus for market at Wittenham, 1 John.

Offer of 60 marks by Sibyl de Blugeney and Hawis de Dinant for having right in curia regis in vill of Stanton, 1 John.

f. 33v. Offer of 200 marks by knights, thanes and free tenants of Honor of Lancaster for confirmation of charter on right in forests etc. 1 John.

Offer of 30 marks from Abbot of Malmesbury for scutage of his knights, 1 John.

f. 34. Extract from Hoveden on Poitou, 1199.

f. 36. Charter on moderating the fees of the great seal, 7 June 1199, from an ancient Register in Archives of Archbishop of Canterbury.

f. 39. Confirmation to William, son of Roger de Flamvill, of land in Wittenham, 30 March 1200.

f. 39v. Grant to William Marshal, Earl of Pembroke, of Marshalsea, 20 April 1200.

f. 40. Grant to William, son of Wakelin, of manor of Stainsby, 4 April 1200.

f. 41. Grant to Mayor etc. of London that all merchants shall safely come and go with their wares in England, 5 April 1200.

f. 41v. Grant that merchants of Flanders, etc. shall come and go with their wares in England. n.d. (1200).

f. 42. Offer of 3 marks by Roger de Rames for partition of Barony, 1 John. From Oblate Roll.

Grant to Hubert, Archbishop of Canterbury, that his Will shall stand, n.d. (1199).

f. 43. Confirmation to William de Fengeriis of land called le Buse, 30 January 1200.

f. 44. Confirmation to Thomas Basset, King's knight, of manor of Collaton, 19 January 1200.

f. 45. Confirmation to Meurig, son of Roger of Powis of Whittington and Overton, 11 April 1200.

f. 45v. Offer of 50 marks by Meurig of Powis for above confirmation, 1 John. From Oblate Roll.

f. 46. Grant to Master Alan, King's clerk, of land in Clay etc. 7 April 1200. (*Rot. Chart.*, p. 48.)

f. 47. Grant to William Marshal, Earl of Pembroke, and Isabella, his wife, daughter of Earl Richard, and to Richard de Clare, Earl of Hertford, lands of Earl Giffard in England and Normandy, 20 April 1200.

f. 48. Grant to William Marshal, Earl of Pembroke, of Bosham etc. 19 April 1200.

f. 49. Grant to Ralph, son of May, of his land in Northumberland which he holds by sergeanty to be held as 1 knight's fee, 1 April 1200.

f. 49v. Grant to William Bardolf and Elizabeth, his wife, of the land her father held in thegnage in Hepdale etc. 25 April 1200.

f. 50. Grant on agreement made between William de Vernon, Earl of Devon, and Hubert de Burgh, King's Chamberlain, on latter's marriage to Joan, daughter of former, 28 April 1200.

f. 51. Letters Patent on statement by Barons of Hastings that the men of Winchelsey and Rye ought to aid King with 5 ships, 2 May 1200.

f. 52. Grant to Ralph de Faya of land of Bromley, 4 December 1200.

Grant to Robert de Turnham of additional day for his fair at Doncaster, 9 May 1200.

f. 53. Grant to Gwenwynwyn of manor of Ashford, co. Derby, 11 April 1200.

f. 54. Grant to Peter de Brimenton of manor of Whittington, 10 April 1200.

f. 55. Grant to William de Stutvill of Knaresborough etc. 22 April 1200.

f. 56. Confirmation to Alan, son of Henry, Count of Britanny, of Waltham etc., 27 April 1200.

f. 56v. Grant to Simon de Pateshull of 2 messuages in Northampton, 26 April 1200.

f. 57. Extract from Hoveden about payment of 300 marks to King John for giving judgement of Barony of William de Mowbray.

f. 59. Letter to A(mery), Viscount of Thouars, asking him to visit Eleanor, the King's mother, who is ill at Fontevrault. n.d. (March 1201).

f. 60. Letter to King from Eleanor, his mother, about Guy de Diva, from Fontevrault. n.d. (March 1201).

f. 61. Offer of £100 by burgesses of York for not going to meet the King on his arrival at York etc. 2 John, from Oblate Roll.

f. 62. Perambulation made between the church of Rouen and Walter, Archbishop of Rouen, the King giving all mills he has in Rouen, from Norman Roll.

f. 64. Confirmation to William Brewer that Bridgwater shall be a free borough etc. 26 June 1200.

f. 65. Notification of grant of officiality of Bishopric of Lincoln to Hugh de Wells, King's clerk, 29 November 1200.

f. 65v. Pardon to Roger de Swerford for flight and banishment pronounced against him, 10 December 1200.

Letter from B(aldwin) de Bethune, Count of Albemarle, on request of his burgesses of Hedon to replevy them for 70 marks promised to King. n.d. (December 1200).

f. 66. Grant to citizens of Exeter of their customs, 5 June 1200.

f. 66v. Confirmation and grant to burgesses of Ipswich, 25 May 1200.

f. 68. Grant to Nicholas Salsarius of land in Anstey etc. 28 January 1201.

f. 69. Grant to men of Pickering of town of Pickering, 5 February 1201.

f. 69v. Grant to men of Scalsby of town of Scalsby, 5 February 1201.

Grant to men of Pocklington of town of Pocklington, 5 February 1201.

f. 71. Grant to Abbot of Whitby that the King will not confirm the charter that the burgesses of Whitby have, 13 January 1201.

f. 72. Grant to burgesses of Cambridge of a gild merchant etc. 8 January 1201.

f. 74. Confirmation to burgesses of Dover of quittance of toll, 1 January 1201.

f. 74v. Confirmation to Portsmouth that borough shall be retained in King's hand, 23 October 1200.

f. 76. Grant to William de Stutvill of Bardsey etc. 2 March 1201.

f. 77. Grant to William Brewer of lands of Merton etc. 23 February 1201.

f. 78. Grant to burgesses of Corbridge of town of Corbridge, 20 February 1201.

Grant to men of Newburn of town of Newburn, 10 February 1201.

f. 79. Confirmation of grant to men of Newcastle upon Tyne, 9 February 1201.

Grant to men of Hartlepool of liberties of burgesses of Newcastle upon Tyne, 8 February 1201.

f. 80. Grant to Richard de Rushale of lands his father held, 10 March 1201.

f. 81. Grant to William de Stutvill of forest of Millburn, co. Westmorland, 4 March 1201.

f. 82. Confirmation to burgesses of Grimsby of liberties, 11 March 1201.

f. 84. Grant to William de Ferrers, Earl of Derby, of service for land of Drakelow, 17 March 1201.

f. 85. Grant to all Jews of England on residence and suits, 10 April 1201.

f. 87. Letters Patent to burgesses of Helston on town of Helston, 18 April 1201.

Grant to same of free borough, gild merchant, etc., 15 April 1201.

f. 88v. Grant to burgesses of Andover of town at old farm, 18 April 1201.

f. 89. Final Concord in the Exchequer at Caen, John de Manbis, tenant, and Robert, monk, his brother, claimant of portion of hereditary lands, from Norman Roll.

f. 91. Grant to Payn de Mehoudon of fee of Aissel etc., 2 John, from same.

f. 91v. Grant by Robert de Ponte in Exchequer at Caen of sale of half his vavassor at Beuiler, 2 John, from same.

f. 92. Writs to Sheriffs of Kent etc. on scutage of 2 marks. (Wrongly given as Pat. 2. John, for which there is no roll.)

f. 92v. Appointment of Hamo de Valon' as Sheriff of cos. Cambridge and Huntingdon, 13 December 1201.

f. 93. Confirmation to William de Braose of Honor of Limerick, 12 January 1201.

f. 95. Mandate to all Sheriffs to allow Archbishops etc. to sell their corn by weight until Feast of St. Catherine.

f. 96. Letters Patent to give no counsel to G(erald), Archdeacon of Brecon, who claims to be elect of St. David's, 10 April 1202.

f. 96v. Letters Patent to clergy and people of England as above, 17 December 1201; like to Chapter of St. David's.

f. 98. Letters Patent to Chief Justice of England and Justices de Banco. King's wish that Hubert, Archbishop of Canterbury, should recover in court what was unjustly alienated from his Archbishopric, 15 February 1202.

Letters Patent on same matter, 6 March 1202.

f. 100. Letters Patent to all Abbots of Cistercian order for aid against King of France on breach of treaty, 11 December 1202.

f. 101. Letters Patent pardoning William, son of Owen, for flight and outlawry, 18 December 1202.

f. 101v. Like, pardoning Nicholas Poneire for like, 26 April 1203.

f. 102. Letters Patent on regulation or assize made by King with common counsel of his barons on white bread made in city of Winchester, 15 April 1204.

f. 104. Grant of dower to Isabella, Queen of England, 5 May 1204.

f. 106. Notes concerning Parliament, 1 Edward II, 12 Edward III.

f. 107. Letters Patent to men of Bishopric of St. David's against G(erald), Archdeacon of Brecon, 11 September 1203.

f. 107v. Letters Patent to suffragans of see of Armagh against elect of Armagh against King's assent, 27 May 1203. Like to men of Bishopric.

f. 109. Request to all clergy in Ireland for aid against the King of France, 10 February 1204, from Charter Roll.

f. 110. Extracts from Pleas of Assize and of the Crown, at Lichfield, 5 John, Essoins, St. Matthew the Apostle (21 September 1203) before Simon de Pateshull, Hundreds of Pirehill and Offlow.

f. 110v. Extracts from Pleas of Assize of Novel Disseisin, taken at Lincoln, 3rd day after Assumption (18 August) t. John.

f. 111. Extract from Plea Roll, Trin. term, 15 John, Pleas Morrow of Trinity, Midd.

f. 112. Extracts from Assizes and Pleas of the Crown, Essoins (as above f. 110), Hundred of Totmonslow, Assizes and Pleas of the Crown 4 John, cos. Northants, Warw., Lincs. and Rutl., Verdict of Northants. Hundred of Willybrook, Pleas of Crown at Northampton, Octave of Nativity of St. Mary (15 September 1202), Hundred of Cleley. Letters of Geoffrey fitz Peter produced, of pardon of Hugh, son of the priest, for flight and outlawry.

f. 114. Letters Patent to Sheriff of Rutland on finding of a tenth knight by nine knights. Summons to London 3 weeks from Easter. Like to all Sheriffs, 3 April 1205.

f. 118. Writ to Walter de Lacy to take into King's hand the city of Limerick and the cantred, 12 November 1204.

f. 119. Letters Patent to Sheriff of Lincoln on carrying and having clipt money. Like to all Sheriffs, 9 November 1204.

f. 121. Letters Patent to men of Yarmouth on provision of galleys for King's service, 18 April 1205.

f. 123. Payment of 60 marks by men of rape of Hastings to be quit of common summons of the forest, 7 John, from Oblate Roll.

f. 124. Letters Patent to H(enry), Archdeacon, T(homas), Official, and clergy of Archbishopric of Canterbury requesting aid, 30 April 1207.

f. 124v. Letters Patent to Justiciar of Ireland concerning offer of 300 marks of silver and 3 marks of gold to have lands and liberties of Archbishopric of Armagh, 30 August 1207.

f. 125. Letters Patent on aid granted on rents and chattels, 17 February 1207.

f. 127. Letters Patent to all clergy in convention at St. Albans on Peter's Pence, 26 May 1207.

f. 128. Note on similar prohibition, 11 Edward II, from Patent and Close Rolls.

f. 129. Letters Patent for all those who take burgages at Liverpool, 27 August 1207.

f. 130. Mandate on expulsion of thieves from Ireland, to be dealt with according to the law of England, 23 March 1208.

f. 131. Mandate of proclamation concerning religious and clerks, 11 April 1208.

Letters Patent committing the custody of Christ Church, Canterbury, and the manors of the Priory and Archbishopric, 23 January 1208.

f. 131v. Letters Patent to men of Kent on request that Master Stephen Langton should be received as Archbishop of Canterbury, 14 March 1208.

f. 132. Letters Patent to all of Bishopric of Lincoln on committal of all lands of Bishopric, 18 March 1208. Like to all of Bishopric of Ely.

f. 133. Mandates of delivery of manors of Bishopric of Coventry etc. 21 March 1208.

f. 133v. Payment of 500 marks by men of Cornwall to have Sheriff and 200 marks for remission of King's anger, 9 John, from Oblate Roll.

f. 135. Mandates to return Bishopric to Bishop of Winchester, 5 April 1208.

f. 135v. Mandate to cause Earl Roger to have all rents etc. of clergy of his fee, (April) 1208.

Mandate to return his regality to Bishop of Norwich, (5 April) 1208.

f. 136. Mandates to Sheriff of Midd. and all sheriffs to take all churches etc. of clergy who are beyond seas, 5 June 1208.

f. 137. Extract from Cleopatra E. I on King John's affliction of religious, especially those of the Cistercian order and letter of Innocent III concerning Fulk de Cantilupe and Reginald de Cornhill, 6 Kal. September 10 Pont. (27 August 1208).

f. 139. Extract from Matt. of Westminster on King John's treatment of church.

f. 140. Similar extract from Roger of Wendover, 1210.

f. 141. Letters Patent to Bishops of London, Ely and Worcester that King is prepared to obey Pope, 21 January 1208.

f. 141v. Mandates to Sheriffs concerning religious and clergy, 11 April 1208.

f. 142. Mandates as above, f. 135.

f. 143. Mandate to Brian de Insula concerning hunting in his bailiwick, 11 June 1207.

f. 143v. Payment of 60 marks by Barons etc. of rape of Hastings to be quit of summons of pleas of forest, 9 John, from Oblate Roll.

f. 144. Charter of disafforestation of Forest of Essex, 25 March 1204.

f. 145. Note on the Great Council, London, 14 John, on release of interdict in England.

f. 146. Mandate to cross the sea when the King shall command them (15 June 1212).

Mandate to bailiffs and men of Canterbury for 40 horses and men to cross the sea. Like to others (long list).

f. 149. Letters Patent on release of interdict in England, 6 March 1214. With translation into English.

f. 151. An account of King John's journey into France and his successes there. Letters Patent to men of Canterbury on release of interdict, 8 March 1214. Like to others (list). With translation into English.

f. 153. Note from Selden's *Titles of Honor*, 16 John.

f. 154. Mandates to William, Earl Marshal, and to other Earls and Barons on release of interdict, 8 March 1214. With translation into English.

f. 156. Note from Matthew Paris on calling of a Great Council by the Papal legate by the King's authority.

f. 157. Writ sent to Barons of Exchequer on the taxation of aids, tallages or contributions in counties, cities etc. 18 October 34 Edward I (1306), from L.T.R. Mem. Roll, 34 Edward I, Brev. Mich. term, with translation into English.

f. 160. Writ of summons for 4 knights from counties to come to King at Oxford, 11 November 1213.

f. 161. Extract from Cleopatra E. 1. The Bull of Innocent III incorporating the charter of King John by which he offered the Pope the kingdoms of England and Ireland, 15 May 1212. Lateran, 2 Non. November 16 Pont. (4 November 1213).

f. 166. Letters Patent to all of cos. Lincoln and Yorks, on mission of Robert de Ros and others, 25 February 1213.

f. 168. Letters Patent concerning the customs in co. Essex and proclamations thereon, 2 January 1213.

f. 169. Charter of King John for Innocent III, St. Paul's, 3 October 1213.

f. 172. Note on grant to Innocent III of kingdom of England, with reference to 1245, 29 Henry III.

f. 174. Letters Patent to Stephen, Archbishop of Canterbury, on outlawry of the clergy, 15 May 1214.

f. 175. Letters Patent to same and other Bishops beyond seas, 24 May 1214.

f. 177. Letters Patent revoking the interdict or outlawry against ecclesiastical persons, 13 June 1214.

f. 178. Mandates to William, son of Roselin, and others on inquisitions, 6 October 1214.

f. 181. Writs to Sheriffs to summon knights to Oxford, 7 November 1214.

f. 181v. Letters Patent to be intendant to Peter, Bishop of Winchester, 6 March 1214.

f. 182. Note on the Great Council or Parliament called at London, 16 John, on the business of the interdict and its release in England.

f. 183. Letters Patent as above, f. 151, with translation.

f. 185. Note as above, f. 153.

f. 186. Letters Patent as above, f. 181v.

f. 187. Mandates as above, f. 154.

f. 190. Note from Matt. Paris as above, f. 156.

f. 191. Writ as above, f. 157.

f. 194. Note from Matt. Paris as above, f. 156.

f. 196. Charter granting that lending the King money shall not be drawn into an evil custom.

f. 198. Transcript of the letters patent by which King John resigned the crown of England to the Pope.

f. 201. Charter as above, f. 169, followed by note from Matt. Paris 1245 on the complaint of the proctors of England at the Council of Lyons.

f. 203. A record referring to the time of King John, from Parliament Roll, 40 Edward III.

f. 205v. Note from Selden, *Ad Fletam*.

f. 207. Mandate as above, f. 154.

f. 208. Letters Patent as above, f. 151.

f. 209. Letters Patent as above, f. 149.

f. 211. Letter written to King John by William Mauclerc, King's clerk, 16 John, from Bundle 16 & 17 John in Tower, from Prynne, *Records*, III, f. 29.

f. 215. Letter of Innocent III sent to the Archbishop of Canterbury and his suffragans. Lateran, 14 Kal. April 18 Pont. (20 March 1213).

f. 217. Charter granting the Archbishop of Canterbury the patronage of the episcopal church of Rochester, 22 November 1214.

f. 219. Letter of Innocent III reprobating the dispute newly arisen between the King and clergy. Lateran, 14 Kal. April 18 Pont. (20 March 1214).

f. 221. Extract from Selden's *Titles of Honor*, the Parliament of London releases the King from fealty and homage to Pope, 16 John.

f. 222. Notification to Peter, Bishop of Winchester, that the King has committed the castle of Donnington to John, Constable of Chester, 26 July 1214.

f. 222v. Summons to Prior and Convent of Glastonbury to Council at Reading, 30 October 1214.

f. 223. Mandate to men of Cornwall to elect a Sheriff. n.d. (1214).

f. 224. Extract from Matt. Paris on a meeting in which the Archbishop of Canterbury produced the Great Charter of Henry I.

f. 225. Letters as above, f. 215.

f. 226v. Letter as above, f. 219.

f. 229. Letters of Innocent III to John, Bishop of Norwich and others. Lateran.

f. 231. Letter as above, f. 219.

f. 233. Undertaking by King John to pay 40,000 marks to Archbishop of Canterbury and others, 17 June 1214.

f. 234. Undertaking by William, Earl of Ferrers, on above undertaking, 17 June 1214.

f. 237. Mandate as above, f. 223.

f. 238. Extract from William of Britanny on peace between King John and Barons.

f. 239. Extract from Walter of Coventry, Life of King John, 1217.

f. 240. Extract from Matt. Paris, 1216, the Barons chose Louis, son of King of France, and on the charter of the King to settle dispute between King and Barons, 15 June 1215.

f. 246. Letters Patent to Stephen, Archbishop of Canterbury, on castle of Rochester, 9 August 1215.

f. 246v. Letters Patent to Sheriffs etc. on peace between King and Barons, 19 June 1215. Letters Patent of safe conduct to Richard, Earl of Clare, and others, 9 November 1215.

f. 247v. Mandate to bailiffs of Southampton to remit toll to Wydd, merchant of Rouen, 28 June 1215.

f. 248. Extract from Roger of Wendover, 1216.

f. 252. Extract from Chronicle of Hagneby, co. Lincs., from Vespasian B. 11, on discord between King and Barons.

f. 254. Extract from Chronicle of W. Thorpe, 1216. Letter of Louis, eldest son of King of France, to Abbot and Convent of St. Augustine's, Canterbury.

f. 258. Fine with King in 40 marks by John de Nevill to have King's grace, 17 John.

f. 258v. Like in 30 marks by Walter de Percy.

f. 259. Like in 1,200 marks by Gilbert, son of Reinfrid, from Oblate Roll to f. 260.

f. 260. Like in 100 marks and his war horse by Simon, son of Walter.

Like in 20 marks by Walter de Carthorp, 24 February 1216.

f. 261. Letter from King John to Innocent III seeking aid against the Barons, 4 September 1215.

f. 261v. Like to Innocent III sending messengers to Rome, 13 September 1215.

f. 263. Letters Patent to Stephen Harengod on peace between King and Barons, 18 June 1215.

f. 264. Undertaking by Gilbert, son of Reinfrid, to King and giving of hostages, 17 John.

f. 266. Extract from Matt. Paris, 18 John, the tyranny of King John after Magna Carta.

f. 268. Letters of Innocent III to the Barons of England. Anagni, 8 Kal. September 18 Pont. (25 August 1215).

f. 270. Extracts from Matt. Paris and Walter of Coventry on choice by Barons of England of Louis of France as King.

f. 270v. Mandate to Sheriff of Norfolk and Suffolk on proclamation of coming to King's peace, 14 April 1216.

f. 271. Fine with King in 50 marks by William, son of Hamo, 17 John, from Oblate Roll.

Like, 40 marks by John de Nevill, from same.

f. 272. Letters Patent to Sheriff of Warwick etc. General proclamation on better observance of Charters, 27 June 1215.

f. 273. Agreement between King John and Robert, son of Walter, Marshal of Army of God and the Holy Church of England etc.

f. 275. Bull of Innocent III. Anagni, 8 Kal. September 18 Pont. (25 August 1215).

f. 281. Chapters or Articles sought by Barons and granted by King John, from the original of Gilbert, Bishop of Salisbury, taken 21 May 1689.

f. 290. Extract from Roger of Wendover, 17 John.

f. 291. Mandate to Barons of Rye etc. on ships, 14 April 1216.

f. 293. Extract from Matt. Paris about John making forged seals of Bishops of Ely.

f. 294. Material on the grant and confirmation of Magna Carta from Close Roll, 28 Henry III, Matt. of Westminster, Roger of Wendover, Otho B. 5. Close Roll, 17 John, Magna Carta in Augustus A. 2, and Walter of Coventry, Life of King John in Vitellius E. 13.

f. 298. Extracts from Walter of Coventry, Life of King John, and William of Britanny on the rejecting of King John and the election of Louis, son of King Philip of France.

f. 301. Extract from William Thorne on the same, Letter of Louis, 17 John.

f. 309. Extracts from Matt. Paris, Roger of Wendover, Matt. of Westminster, Close Roll, 28 Henry III, on grant of Magna Carta.

f. 319. Pleas coram Rege, Mich. term, 19–20 Edward I, Assizes at Hereford, plea of novel disseisin, Mabel, widow of Roger Mortimer, and Ralph de Tany and others on free tenement in Bridchurch etc.

f. 328. Magna Carta as in Matt. Paris' Historia.

f. 341. Charter of the Forest as in Matt. Paris, divided into articles or chapters as in Brady, *Compleat Hist. of Engl.*, p. 141.

f. 345. 'King John's desperate message sent to the King of Morocco (1) to offer him his kingdom (2) to hold it under tribute as his vassal (3) and to relinquish the Christian religion and embrace the Mohametan' from Daniel, *Hist. of Engl.*, p. 119, derived from Matt. Paris.

f. 350. Matt. Paris, the charter granted by King John to all men of the kingdom, 25 June 1215.

f. 356. Letters Patent to men of Seaford, 3 September 1216.

f. 357v. Letters Patent to sworn men of cos. Suss. etc. 2 September 1216.

Letters Patent to Barons of Hastings etc. 2 September 1216.

f. 360. Extracts from Matt. Paris and Roger of Wendover and Close Roll, 17 John.

f. 366. Notes on the tyranny of John (28 articles).

f. 381. Notes on the depositions of Edward II, Richard II and Edward V.

f. 385. Letter from King John to Pope on crusade, 29 May 1215.

f. 390v. Letter from King John to Pope seeking counsel and aid, 13 September 1215.

f. 391. Letter from King John to Pope on disobedience of English prelates, n.d. (1215.)

f. 393. Letters Patent to Stephen, Archbishop of Canterbury, 9 August 1215.

f. 394. Extract from Matt. Paris, letter from Richard, Earl of Cornwall, Simon de Montfort, Earl of Leicester, and others to Pope.

f. 396. Letters Patent as above, ff. 356, 357v.

f. 399. Extract as above, f. 254.

f. 400v. Letters Patent as above, ff. 357, 357v.

f. 402v. Extract from Roger of Wendover on the oath of Louis to the English.

f. 403. Extract from same on progress of Louis.

f. 404. Extract from same and Matt. of Westminster on the death of King John and succession of Henry III.

VOLUME 2

A volume of transcripts from the Public Records and other sources, 1–8 Henry III. On flyleaf: Recorda H. 3 ab anno lo usque 9m. Vol. I; on other side: Tempore H. 3. Vol. V. 275 ff.

f. 1. Mandate to Sheriffs to cause to come to Exeter with horses and arms to go with William Marshal etc., 4 July 1217.

f. 1v. Like to Sheriff of Berks. to come to Oxford to serve, 22 July 1217.

f. 2. Like to Sheriff of Devon to come to Exeter with 4 etc. 1 November 1216.

Like to same to cause to come to Oxford, 4 July 1217.

f. 2v. Like to proclaim coronation in church of St. Peter's, Gloucester, 28 October 1216.

Day given to Philip de Ulcotes and Roger Bertram to come to London coram consilio domini Regis, from Close Roll, 1 Henry III.

f. 3. Notification of grant to Baldwin de Due of first marriage to come to King's hands, 16 January 1217, from Patent Roll.

Letters Patent to Philip Martel of grant to William, Lord of Ferrers, of manor of Melbourn, 16 January 1217.

Letters Patent that Ireland to have liberties granted by King John to England, 6 February 1217.

f. 4. Like that Reginald de Braose has come to King's faith and service and mandates to deliver castles of Barnstaple and Totnes, 27 June 1217.

f. 5. Like to Barons of London, to have liberties granted by King's predecessors, 4 October 1217.

Note that Barons of Rye and other ports omitted only because space is not enough, 14 April 1216, from Close Roll, 17 John.

f. 6. Letters Patent to Hugh de Lacy to come to faith and service, 18 November 1216.

f. 6v. Mandate to John Marshal, Justice of Ireland, 1 Henry III.

f. 8. Letters Patent to Archbishops etc. of Ireland, 6 February 1217.

f. 8v. Mandate to Sheriff of Worcs. to cause Magna Carta to be read, 23 June 1217.

f. 9. Letters Patent to Robert de Gaugy on surrender of Castle of Newark to Hugh de Wells, Bishop of Lincoln, 23 June 1217.

f. 10. Mandate to cause Magna Carta to be observed, 23 June 1217.

f. 11. First coronation of Henry III, from Knighton.

f. 13. As f. 3 above.

f. 17. Letters Patent to Falkes de Breaute to deliver Osbert, son of Nigel, 2 October 1217.

f. 17v. Like for Henry, son of (blank) to hold co. Cornwall, 23 January, 7 February 1217.

f. 18. Like to H(ugh), Bishop of Lincoln, Prior and Convent of Newenham, 4 February 1217.

f. 19. As f. 2 above.

f. 21. Oath of Henry III when he was crowned, from Matt. Paris.

f. 23. As f. 4 above.

f. 25. Letters Patent to all in co. Kent to be intendant to Philip de Aubigny, 20 January 1217.

f. 26. As f. 4 above.

f. 27. Mandate to J(ocelin), Bishop of Bath and Wells, and Prior and monks of Glastonbury on coronation, 9 September 1217.

f. 28. Letters Patent to Philip de Mauley etc. on mainprise of John, Giles, Philip and Walter, sons of William de Braose, 24 January 1218.

f. 29. On the Common Council of the Realm, London, 1218. Magna Carta confirmed, from MS. Stat. in poss. of William Petyt, with reference to first letters of new seal of King, from Patent Roll, and to mandates on adulterine castles and writs to Sheriffs on Magna Carta, from Close Roll.

f. 31. Letters Patent for those who were with the King in war, 6 March 1218.

f. 32. Mandates to Sheriffs to distrain for scutage, 22 January 1218.

f. 33. Like to Llewelyn, Prince of Wales, etc. to do homage, 12 February 1218.

f. 35. Like to direct letters on Magna Carta and Charter of Forests to Sheriffs, 2 Henry II. As f. 28 above.

f. 35v. Like to Sheriff of Hertf. to summon John de Bassingbourne to be before Council in London, 2 Henry III, from Fine Roll.

f. 36. On Common Council, 1218. Scutage. Mandates to Sheriffs to aid to distrain, 30 October 1218.

f. 46. Letters Patent to Falkes de Breaute on custody of castle of Wisbech etc. 6 November 1218.

Like on render of scutage of fees of Wallingford to Richard, son of Reginald, 10 November 1218.

f. 46v. Like to officials of rape of Hastings to pay expenses in time of war, 6 March 1218.

f. 47. Like on Seneschalcy of Poitou and Gascony etc. 8 May 1218.

f. 49. Mandate on barony of Robert de Mesvill for Archbishop of Canterbury, 13 May 1218

f. 50. Like to Sheriff of Lincs. to elect coroners, 31 (*sic*) June 1218.

f. 51. Like to Robert de Albemarle on co. Devon for Robert de Courtney, 8 May 1218.

f. 52. Letters Patent on Exchequer of Jews, 18 May 1218.

f. 52v. Like to Sheriffs on Jews to remain as in time of King John, 5 November 1217.

f. 54. Notification to Falkes de Breaute of commission to Priors of Ely and Barnwell of custody of all manors of bishopric of Ely, 5 November 1217, from Charter Roll.

Like of commission to R(ichard), Bishop of Salisbury, of castle of Ely etc. 6 November 1217.

f. 55. Letters Patent to Sheriffs. Jews to have communia accustomed between Christians, 19 June 1218.

f. 56. As f. 35 above.

f. 56v. As f. 35v above.

f. 58. As f. 29 above.

f. 62. General Proclamation sent to all Sheriffs on disafforestation according to Charter of Forests, 24 July 1218, from Patent Roll.

f. 64. General Commission to summons to Eyre, 2 Henry III, from Close Roll, with references to Close Rolls, 5, 10, 45, 46 Henry III and Patent Roll.

f. 68. The first public grant of Magna Carta and Charter of Forests by Henry III in a Common Council, London, 2 Henry III, from MS. Stat. in poss. of William Petyt, with references to Close Roll, 2 Henry III, Matt. Paris, Ann. of Waverley, Phrasis Hist.

f. 72. Magna Carta, 2 Henry III, from MS. Stat. in poss. of William Petyt with note Hil. 5 Henry IV from Fitzherbert, *Grand Abridg*.

f. 82. Charter of Forests, 2 Henry III (as above).

f. 86. Common Council, London, 2 Henry III, with references to Ann. of Waverley, Stat. (as above), Patent Roll, 3 Henry III, Close Roll, 2 Henry III. Lauds Britanniae in Archives of city of London, Red Book of Church of Bath in poss. of Thomas Guidot M.D.

f. 90. The first solemn grant and confirmation of Magna Carta and Charter of Forests, 6 November 1217, text from MS. Stat. (as above), with examples from (1) MS. in poss. of Samuel Baldwin (2) in custody of John Cook, esq., one of Prothonotaries of Court of Common Bench (3) William Petyt.

f. 107. Mandate to Sheriff of Yorks, 22 February 1218.

f. 107v. Hugh Despenser owes 25s. relief for fourth part of knight's fee, 2 Henry III, from Fine Roll.

f. 109. Agreement between Henry III and Prince Louis, from Matt. Paris.

Fine by Robert de Insula, £100 for half barony of Deyncourt.

f. 113. Charter of Forests, confirmation, 2 Henry III, in same form as 9 Henry III, witnesses and date excepted, exemplified and confirmed, 12 October 1297, from contemporary MS. Stat. in poss. of Samuel Baldwin.

f. 120. Submission of Llewelyn, Prince of Wales, 16 March 1218, from Close Roll.

f. 122. Letters Patent to Prior and Convent of Newenham of church of Tindon.

f. 123. As f. 86 above.

f. 127. Common Council, 2 Henry III, with references to MS. Stat. (as above), Patent Roll, 3 Henry III, Close Roll, 2 Henry III, Bracton, Walter of Coventry, Hale, Matt. Paris, Spelman, *Gloss.*, Stat. 25 Edward I, Patent Roll, 11 Edward III, Stat. 15 Edward III, Parl. Roll, 2 Henry V, Rastell, *Stat.*, Broke, *Grand Abridg.*, Coke, *8th Reports*, Camsus, *Principis*, Letters Patent of disafforestation, 24 July 1218.

f. 132. Mandate on 2 knights of neighbourhood of Dartmoor, 28 June 1219.

Mandate to Sheriff of Devon to cause Falkes de Breaute to have third penny of co., 19 July 1219.

f. 132v. Like to Hugh, Bishop of Lincoln, and fellow Justices in Eyre, cos. Lincs. etc. on amercements of earls etc. 2 February 1219.

f. 133. Second coronation of Henry III, 3 Henry III, from Matt. Paris.

f. 135. Letters Patent on sealing perpetuities during King's minority, 3 Henry III.

f. 135v. Like to Hugh de Wells, Bishop of Lincoln, etc. (as above) on suit before them, 24 June 1219.

f. 137. Like of pardon for Isaac, son of William Widher, 20 August 1219.

f. 137v. Like of pardon for Roger Wastehoess, 12 May 1227.

Like of pardon of outlawry for John de Newenham, 2 July 1227.

f. 139. Like to enquire on trespass, 11 Henry III.

Memorandum concerning Simon de Montfort, Earl of Leicester, 14 December 1257, from Patent Roll.

f. 141. As f. 132 above.

f. 142. As f. 132v. above.

f. 144. Letters Patent to Philip de Ulcote and fellow Justices in Eyre, cos. Cumberland etc. 26 June 1219.

f. 146. Common Council, 3 Henry III. First letters of King's new seal, from Patent Roll.

f. 147. Extract from Walter of Coventry, with notes (struck through).

f. 148. As f. 146 above.

f. 149. Letters Patent on verderers, on perambulation of forests, cos. Notts. and Derby, 1 May 1219.

f. 150. Fine, Robert de Veteri Ponte, Tyndale, belonging to King's castle of Carlisle, 29 January 1219, from Fine Roll.

Like, Richard Pletun, Constable of Richmond.

f. 151. Mandate to Justices in Eyre, co. Kent, on amercements, 9 December 1218.

f. 152. Letters Patent to Pandulf, Bishop of Norwich, Papal Legate, on appointment of proctors, 21 July 1219.

f. 154. Letters to Philip, King of France, 25 July 1219, from Close Roll.

f. 155. Mandate on lands of Daniel de Sules for Philip de Ulcote, 14 December 1218.

f. 156. Like to Hugh, Bishop of Lincoln etc. to distrain citizens of Lincoln, 9 November 1218.

f. 157. Letters Patent to William de Leiha, clerk, 20 January 1219.

f. 159. Like to Philip de Ulcote and fellow Justices etc. 26 January 1219.

f. 161. As f. 146 above.

f. 163. Like for Queen Berengar, 20 July 1220.

f. 167. Like to Hubert de Burgh, Justiciar of England, etc. 4 Henry III.

f. 168. Like concerning King of Scots, 15 June 1220.

f. 170. Mandate to G( ), Viscount Le Mans, 7 September 1220.

f. 171. Like to John Marshal etc. on forests, 8 November 1219.

f. 173. Like to Prince of North Wales, 5 October 1220.

f. 176. Like to Sheriff of Suss. on carucage, 7 September 1220.

f. 178. Like to Hugh de Vivon on seisin, 12 September 1220.

f. 179. Like to E(ustace), Treasurer, and Chamberlains on 3 writs of liberate, 25 April 1220.

f. 181. Writ to Sheriff of Lincs. Judgement by Council that Robert Marion ought not to answer on debts of £20 and £160, 3 February 1220, from L.T.R. Mem. Roll, Comm., Rec., Hil, 4 Henry III.

f. 182. Mandates to Sheriffs, 9 August 1220.

f. 183. Writ that Fulk fitz Warin had made security, 30 June 1220, from L.T.R. Mem. Roll, Comm., 4 Henry III.

f. 184. As f. 182 above.

f. 186. Mandate to Escheator North of Trent etc. on lands taken into King's hands, 17 April 1220, from Fine Roll.

f. 188. Like to Sheriff of Cornwall on quittance of fine, 15 May 1221.

Like to Robert Bacon, 5 Henry III.

Like to Ranulf, Earl of Chester and Lincoln, 1 May 1221.

f. 189. Writs on manor of Newburn, on men of Mayfield, Jordan Oliver, fee of honor of Stafford, Milisent de Stafford, from K.R. Mem. Roll, 5 Henry III.

f. 190. Mandate to Sheriff of Westmorland, 3 February 1221.

f. 192. Like on scutage of Byham, 5 Henry III.

f. 196. Like on quittance of carucage, 23 November 1220.

f. 197. Letters Patent to Sheriff of Northumberland on pulling down of castle, 1 May 1221.

f. 197v. Letters Patent on peace granted to John de Torrington, 2 May 1221.

f. 198. Like on Mint of England committed, 8 December 1221.

f. 200. Mandates to Sheriffs on royal demesne, 24 June 1221, from Fine Roll.

f. 202. Like to Sheriff of Somerset for Richard Revel, 16 August 1222, from same.

Like to Sheriff of Yorks., for Robert de Guiedell, from same.

Fine £100, Peter de Brus, son and heir of Peter de Brus, from same.

f. 204. Siege of castle of Bisham and disturbance of realm, from Matt. Paris.

f. 212. Letters Patent, Falkes de Breaute on his excommunication for detention of Henry de Braibroc, King's Justice, in castle of Bedford, 1223.

f. 214. Mandates to Sheriffs on aid, Holy Land, 26 June 1222.

f. 214v. Like to Sheriff of Essex, 17 August 1222.

f. 215. Like to Sheriffs on money, 20 February 1222.

f. 216. Like for Eustace de Fauconberg, Bishop of London, 13 April 1222.

f. 217. Writ on scutage, land of Upton; Richard de Aslaceby, Mayor of London, presentation of Sheriffs, from K.R. Mem. Roll, Comm., Hil., 6 Henry III.

f. 217v. Mandate for Hugh de Beauchamp, 30 April 1222, from Fine Roll.

Letters Patent to Henry de Loundres, Archbishop of Dublin, Justiciary of Ireland, 18 July 1222.

f. 218. Like to Llewelyn, Prince of Wales, 20 April 1222.

f. 218v. Like for Eustace de Fauconberg, Bishop of London, 14 August 1222.

f. 219. Mandate to Sheriff of Suss. to enquire what customs and liberties King John had in that co. day war began, 30 January 1223.

f. 220. Like not to distrain men of Bishop of Ely, 3 November 1223.

Letters Patent, men of Ipre, 7 Henry III.

Mandates to Sheriffs to enquire on King's liberties, 9 April 1223.

f. 222. Like to Sheriffs, aid, Holy Land, 24 November 1222.

f. 223. Like to Henry de Loundres, Archbishop of Dublin, Justiciary of Ireland, 4 June 1223.

f. 223v. Like to Mayor and Sheriffs of London on markets, 24 May 1223.

f. 224. Form of letters to summon army at Gloucester, 12 September 1223, from Close Roll

f. 226. Mandates to Bailiffs of towns, aid, Holy Land, 7 Henry III.

f. 227. Like to Michael, son of Michael, same.

f. 227v. Like to Ralph de Monasterio, same.

f. 228. Like for quittance for Brian de Insula, 16 November 1222.

f. 229. As f. 220 above.

f. 231. Writs on King's demesnes, 27 April 1223, from Patent Roll.

f. 232. Letters Patent for Ruffin, nephew of Lord Walter, 12 November 1222.

f. 232v. Like on Chamberlainship of London, 29 January 1223.

f. 233. Like on appointment to take thieves and malefactors, 16 February 1223.

f. 235. Like, safe conduct for Llewelyn, Prince of Wales, 22 June 1223.

f. 236. Mandate to Keeper of honor of Wallingford for Isabella, widow of Robert Mauduit, 29 January 1223.

f. 238. Like to Sheriff of Berks. on pleas of forest, 8 Henry III, from Fine Roll.

f. 238v. Like to same on assize of novel disseisin, same.

f. 240. Like on carucage to Archbishops and Bishops, 7 October 1224, same.

f. 241. Like on aid granted to King by Bishops, 18 August 1224, same.

f. 242. As f. 238v above.

Like to Barons of Exchequer for Roger Clifford, same.

f. 243. Carucage in honor of Wallingford. Roll of carucage assessed and collected in bailiwick of Windsor, by assessors elected according to form of King's mandate. Manner or form of assessing carucage or aid granted by Common Council of realm, in Windsor, Bray, Cookham, Rainham, Finchampstead, Swalfield, Berkham, Harleigh, Dydewig, Ellington, Dynwar, Chedbury, Setbrook, Honford. From a roll of uncertain date. t. Henry III, perhaps 8 Henry III. (Cf. *Book of Fees*, I, pp. 302–6.)

f. 248. As f. 243 above.

f. 254. Liberties exacted from King by Stephen Langton, Archbishop of Canterbury, 1223, from Matt. Paris. Also on certain Barons who wished to excite a schism.

f. 256. Mandate to Constable of Marlborough on suits at hundred of Salkell, 8 Henry III.

f. 258. Letter to Pope, 19 December 1224, from Close Roll.

f. 270. Extract from Matt. Paris on exile of Otto Falast, traitor, 1225.

f. 273. Mandate on remission of King's anger to Robert Beaumais, 3 August 1224.

f. 274. Like on new writs de cursu on prohibition to William de Carmarthen, 25 September 1224.

f. 275. As f. 270 above.

VOLUME 3

A volume of transcripts etc. from the Public Records and other sources. On flyleaf: Recorda H. III ab anno 9 usque ad 18 (repeated). 258 ff.

f. 1. Mandate to Sheriffs on half 15th, 14 May 1225.

f. 2. Mandate to Sheriffs on liberties in Magna Carta, 8 May 1225.

f. 3. Mandates to Sheriffs on observation of liberties not mentioned in Magna Carta, 8 August 1225.

f. 5. Thurstan Despenser rendered gilt spurs for land of Kingsworm. (K.R. Mem. Roll, Communia, Mich. term, 9 Henry III.)

Mandate on election of Sheriff, co. Cornwall, 30 March 1225.

Form of 15th on moveables granted in England, 14 May 1225.

f. 6. Letters Patent for Bishop of Carlisle and Brothers and Master of Knights Templar, 3 January 1225.

f. 6v. Mandate to Sheriff of Southampton for John de Insula, 15 August 1225.

f. 7. Mandate on Magna Carta for co. Yorks., 7 July 1225.

f. 8. Provision by Justiciar and Council on William de Earlward, Sheriff of Essex and Hertford. From Roll entitled Essex. K.R., 9 Henry III.

f. 11. On grant of 15th of moveables. Extract from Matt. Paris.

f. 13. Mandates to Sheriffs about extreats, 16 November 1224.

f. 14. Mandate on collection of 15th of Abbot of St. Edmunds, 4 March 1225.

f. 15. As f. 5 above.

f. 15v. Mandates to Sheriffs on assessment of 15th, 14 May 1225.

f. 17. Mandates to William de Basset and others, 14 May 1224.

f. 18. As f. 15v above.

f. 19. Mandate on liberties of Bishop of Ely, 17 February 1225.

f. 20. Mandates to Sheriffs.

f. 21. Form of 15th of moveables in England, 20 May 1225

f. 22. Mandates to others, 14 April 1225.

f. 24. On Magna Carta and Charter of Forests. Extracts from Walter of Coventry and Matt. Paris.

f. 30. As f. 14 above.

f. 32. Of a Common Council of the whole realm, held at London, 9 Henry III, wherein Magna Carta and the Charter of the Forests were read a second time and granted and confirmed, for which a second subsidy of a 15th was given to the King. References to Harpsfield, *Hist. Angl. Eccles.*, Matt. Paris, Spelman, *Gloss.*, certiorari of trespass between the Bishop of Winchester and John Giffard, 3 Richard II, on disafforestation, (in a bundle in the Tower), Statute Roll, 25 Edward I, Confirmatio Cartarum.

f. 42. Mandate to Simon de Braket, Sheriff of Cornwall, 30 May 1225.

f. 43. Mandates to William Russell and others, 14 May 1225.

f. 45. On Common Council, Westminster, 9 Henry III.

f. 47. Mandate to Hugh de Nevill on bailiwick of Plympton, 12 May 1225.

Mandate of respite for Hugh de Chastillon.

Mandate to William de Burnley, keeper of Richard, son of William.

Writ to Walter de Clifford, 7 August 1225, from Fine Roll.

f. 48. As f. 8 above.

f. 49. Form of assessing and collecting 15th. Letters Patent to William Basset etc. 15 February 1225.

f. 53v. Letters Patent to Justices, co. Kent, on 15th.

f. 56. As f. 45 above.

f. 59. Extracts from Walter of Coventry and Matt. Paris, 9 Henry III.

f. 62. Magna Carta of Henry III which agrees with the original charter under King's great seal in possession of Sir Nathaniel Powell, bart., one of the assessors of the Inner Temple, London, 6 February 1689/90, but not arranged in chapters as in this transcript. 11 February 1225.

f. 74. Extracts from Harpsfield, *Hist. Angl. Eccles.*, and Spelman, *Gloss.*

f. 75. On altercation between Hubert de Burgh, Earl of Kent, and Master Laurence of St. Albans. Extracts from Matt. Paris's Additamenta.

f. 76. As f. 49 above.

f. 80. Mandates on Magna Carta, 7 July 1225.

f. 81. Extract from Bracton, De Legibus, De Exceptionibus, and note on Spelman, *Gloss.*

f. 82. Confirmation by Edward I of Henry III's confirmation of Magna Carta and Charter of Forests, with references to Patent Roll, 25 Edward I, Statute 34 Edward III, Statute 5 Richard II, Christopher de St. German, *Dialogus*, answer of Edward I to the Archbishop of Canterbury on Pope's letter (Matthew of Westminster) and Statute 1 Henry IV.

f. 86. Confirmations of Magna Carta and Charter of Forests, 38 Edward III, 5 Richard II, 12 Richard II, 11 Henry IV, 4 Henry V, 12 Edward IV, from a Book of Statutes in French in possession of William Petyt, cf. Rastell, *Stat.*, and notes from Year Book, East. term, 39 Edward III, Petitions in Parliament, 2 Edward III (*Plac. Parl.*, pp. 636–7) and Dyer, *Reports*, *Privilege of Parliament*.

f. 89. Extracts on Magna Carta from Broke, *Le Second Part du Grand Abridg.*, and Coke, *8th Reports*, and note from *Reports* of Sir William Jones.

f. 92. Of the sacroscant authority of Magna Carta, with references to Matt. Paris, Book of Exodus, Statute, 25 Edward I, Parliament Roll, 15 Edward III, Pupilla Oculi, Close Roll, 10 Edward II, and Tacitus, *Agricola*.

f. 94. Mandates to Sheriffs on proclamation of a single measure, 20 February 1316.

f. 95. Mandate to Hugh de Nevill and others on perambulation of forests, 8 May 1225.

f. 96. Mandates to Sheriffs to make proclamation, 21 January 1227.

f. 96v. Letters Patent to all barons etc. 10 December 1226.

f. 97. Mandate to Barons of Exchequer on pleas with like mandate to Sheriff of Oxford on Henry, son of Simon.

f. 99. Letters Patent to Stephen Langton, Archbishop of Canterbury, and Walter de Gray, Archbishop of York, 2 November 1226.

f. 99v. Letters Patent on confirmation by William Brewer to Hubert de Burgh of land of Treglaston.

f. 100. Letters Patent to Stephen Segrave and other Justices in Eyre, cos. Warw. etc. 29 October 1226.

f. 102. Of the Common Council of the whole realm and the nature thereof, with references to Matt. Paris's Additamenta, Charter Roll, 11 Henry III, Statute, 25 Edward I, Bracton, De Legibus, and Spelman, *Gloss*.

f. 106. Mandate to Prior and Convent of Christ Church, Canterbury, 26 June (1242).

f. 108. Extract from Chronicle of Dunstable (Tiberius A. 10).

f. 113. Charter of Henry III to Barons of London, 11 Henry III, that the aid they had granted him should not prejudice them or their heirs as a precedent, from Laudes Britan. in archives of city of London, 22 December 1226, with reference to Matt. Paris.

f. 117. Letters Patent on tallage of King's Lynn to use of Bishop of Norwich, 28 March 1227.

f. 118. Charter to Hubert de Burgh not to render account, 22 July 1227.

f. 119. Mandates to Barons of Exchequer on pardons for Hubert de Burgh and others, 10 May 1228.

f. 121. Plea, Hil. term, 11 Henry III, between King and Archbishop of Canterbury on certain liberties.

f. 123. Mandate to men of cos. Notts. and Derby, 30 January 1227.

f. 123v. Mandate to Sheriff of Cornwall on quo warranto, 7 April 1227.

f. 124. Mandate to Sheriff of Devon, 18 March 1227.

f. 124v. Mandate to Simon de Ropell and others on tallage, city of Lincoln.

f. 125. Mandate to Geoffrey de Mariscis, Justiciar of Ireland.

Mandate to Stephen de Segrave and others, 8 November 1226.

f. 127. Mandates to Sheriffs, 2 knights to choose 4 to be at Westminster, 13 August 1227

f. 129. Mandate to Hugh de Nevill on perambulation cos. Leics. etc. 9 February 1227.

f. 129v. Mandates to Sheriffs to make proclamation, 9 February 1227.

f. 132. Mandates to Sheriffs on confirmation of charters, 21 January 1227.

f. 132v. Letters Patent to barons etc. 10 December 1226.

f. 133. Letters Patent to Stephen Langton, Archbishop of Canterbury, on assizes etc 2 November 1226.

f. 133v. As f. 99v. above.

f. 134. Mandate to John de Channy and wife.

Mandate to Sheriff of Southampton to extend manor of Freshwater, 20 July 1227.

Mandate to Barons of Exchequer on William de Cornbury.

f. 134v. Mandate to Prior of Holy Trinity, London, on John, son and heir of Geoffrey fitz Peter.

As ff. 123v., 124v. above.

f. 135. Mandate to Constable of castle of Knaresborough, Robert de Veteri Ponte, 9 February 1227.

f. 135v. As f. 125 above.

f. 136. As f. 125 above.

f. 138. Fine, 100 marks, Abbess of Dunkeswell, for confirmation of manor of Hembir', from Fine Roll.

Mandate to Sheriff of Cornwall to assess aid, 16 February 1227.

f. 139v. As f. 123v. above.

Mandate to Sheriff of Devon on land of barony of William de Torrington, 3 August 1227.

f. 140. Mandate on pardon, appeal of Edith, wife of William Leominster, 8 September 1227.

f. 140v. Letters Patent, pardon for flight to Jordan de Tid, 22 August 1227.

f. 141. As f. 127 above.

f. 143. Extract from Matt. Paris on extortion of King of much money, 1227.

f. 144. Charter to burgesses of Stafford, 11 April 1228.

f. 146. Charter on Justiciary of England and castles of Dover, Rochester and Montgomery, 27 April 1228.

f. 149. Summary of charter on f. 146.

f. 150. Mandate to Martin de Patshull and Stephen de Segrave on Cinque Ports, 24 June 1228.

f. 152. Mandate to Richard de Burgh, Justiciar of Ireland, on observance of laws and customs, 8 March 1228.

f. 154. Extract from Matt. Paris on tenths collected in England for Gregory IX, 1229.

f. 157. As f. 143 above.

f. 160. Extract from Matt. Paris on grievous exaction of tenth, 13 Henry III. Repeated f. 162.

f. 163. Mandate to Ranulf, Earl of Chester, and Lincoln, on rumours.

f. 163v. Mandate to Barons of Sandwich etc.

f. 165. Mandates to Sheriffs on quo warranto, 11 January 1229.

f. 166. Mandate to Falkes de Breaute on detention of Henry de Braybrook, 12 June 1224.

f. 167. Writ on tallage of King's demesnes, co. Lancs., 27 January 1229, from Fine Roll to f. 170.

Writ to Sheriff of Lancaster, 20 March 1229.

f. 167v. Writ to same, forest of honor of Lancaster, 15 March 1229.

f. 168. Mandate for certain Welsh of co. Lancs., 15 March 1229.

f. 169. Fines of men of Norwich and Marlborough and burgesses of Derby.

f. 170. Writ to Sheriff of co. Lincs. to tallage.

Mandate to Bailiffs of Bristol to pay fee farm of town, from Oblate Roll.

Letters Patent to cause ships to come to St. Gildas, 16 September 1230.

f. 173. Mandates to Abbots of Cistercian Order, Ireland.

f. 175. Mandate that men dwelling outside the forest shall not come to pleas of forest by common summons, 5 December 1230.

f. 178. Extract from Matt. Paris on the great preparations for the King to cross overseas, 14 Henry III.

f. 180. Extract from Matt. Paris on the tenths collected from England for Gregory IX, 14 Henry III.

f. 182. Confirmation by Richard le Grant, Archbishop of Canterbury, Richard Poore, Bishop of Salisbury, and Chapter of tenths, pensions and portions to Abbot and Convent of Malmesbury, July 1230, from Register of Charters of monastery of Malmesbury, in possession of Evan Seys, Sergeant at Law.

f. 184. Like confirmation by John Peckham, Archbishop of Canterbury, 30 June 1285, from same source.

f. 185. Letters Patent on custody of land of England, 28 April 1230, and mandate to Walter Mauclerc, Bishop of Carlisle.

f. 187. Extract from Matt. Paris on exaction of scutage for expedition overseas, 15 Henry III, 1230.

f. 188. Concerning those who remain outside the forest (in K.R. co. York).

f. 189. Letters Patent on the immunity of the prelates of England, 14 April 1231.

f. 189v. Mandate on wounding of Mayor of Exeter, 2 April 1231.

f. 191. Extract from Matt. Paris on aid sought by King from the whole of England, 16 Henry III, 1232.

f. 192. Extract from Matt. Paris on demands from Hubert de Burgh and others, 16 Henry III, 1232.

f. 194. Extract from Matt. Paris on grievances objected against Hubert de Burgh, 16 Henry III. Repeated f. 195.

f. 196. Extract from Matt. Paris on removal by King of certain ministers, 16 Henry III, 1232.

f. 197. Mandates to Peter de Thaneo and others.

f. 199. Letters Patent on vill of Colishall, 16 June 1232.

f. 201. Letters Patent prohibiting a tournament, 8 May 1232.

f. 202. Letters Patent prohibiting certain Mints, 28 September 1232.

f. 203. Mandates to William de Vescy and others on a tournament, 10 February 1232.

f. 204. Mandates to Sheriffs on aid, 28 September 1232.

f. 207. As f. 204 above.

f. 209. Extract from Matt. Paris on removal by King of his natural ministers, 17 Henry III, 1233.

f. 211. Letters Patent prohibiting a tournament, 9 July 1233.

f. 212. Letters Patent on case against Hubert de Burgh.

f. 215v. Letters Patent, 12 October 1233.

f. 218. Extracts from Matt. Paris, 17 Henry III, 1233.

f. 254. Mandate to Abbot of Coggeshall, 8 June 1233.

f. 255. Extract from Chronicle of monastery of Hagneby, co. Lincs., from Vespasian B. 11., 17 Henry III.

f. 257. Mandate to Sheriff of Cornwall, watch, 1 June 1233.

VOLUME 4

A volume of transcripts etc. from the Public Records and other sources, 18–29 Henry III. On flyleaf: Recorda ab anno 18 Henr. ad annum 30 (repeated). 278 ff.

f. 1. In Curia Regis apud Glouc'. Mandates to Sheriffs on revocation of outlawry promulgated on Hubert de Burgh, Geoffrey Basset and others, 8 June 1234.

f. 2. Extract from Matt. Paris. The Marshal rebukes the King, 1233.

f. 3. Final Concord, 18 Henry III, Mayor and burgesses of Lynn, complts. and Thomas Blundeville, Bishop of Norwich, from Fines, co. Norf. in Exchequer of Receipt, t. Henry III.

f. 5. Mandate to Justices in Eyre, co. Lincs., 12 October 1234.

f. 6. Like to Constable of castle of Wallingford, 17 September 1234.

f. 6v. Like on hundreds in cos. Cornwall and Devon, 11 October 1234.

f. 8. Like to Sheriff of Suss. on castles of Brevil, La Cnapp and Pevensey, 30 June 1234.

f. 9. Like to Walter de Clifford on castles in hands of Peter de Rivaux, 1 July 1234.

f. 11. Like on scutage of Honor of Richmond, tallage, 6 September 1234.

f. 13. Like to Sheriff of Lincs. on interpretation of certain clauses of Magna Carta, 11 October 1234.

f. 15. Like to Sheriffs on hundreds of St. Edmund's, 12 February 1234.

f. 16. Like to Sheriffs on liberties, 29 August 1234.

f. 17. Letters Patent to all barons of Ireland and mandate to Justiciar of Ireland, 29 August 1234.

f. 17v. Like for Eva de Braose, 15 May 1234.

Like to Henry de Tracy, keeper of coast of Devon, 13 November 1233.

Like to Sheriffs, knight's fees co. Hereford, 3 November 1233.

f. 18v. Like to Hubert de Burgh, 17 Henry III.

f. 21v. Mandate to Abbot of Missenden etc., 11 July 1234.

f. 22. Like to Sheriff of Somerset and Devon on liberties, 29 September 1234.

f. 23. Letters Patent to Constable of castle of Bramber to take sea coast castles into King's hands, 30 June 1234.

f. 24. Like to Archbishops etc., 4 May 1236.

f. 25. Like on provision of new writs, Ireland, 20 March 1237.

f. 26. Like to Archbishops etc. in Ireland and Gascony, 11 June 1245.

f. 27. Like to Abbots of Stratford and Boxley on Priory of Winchester, 18 June 1255.

f. 29. Like to all clergy and laity, 18 October 1258 (French).

f. 29v. Like to all in co. Rutl., 20 October 1258 (French).

f. 31v. Like on commission of cos., 23 October 1258.

Like, 3 November 1258.

Like, 14 November 1258.

f. 34. Like on inquisitions in each co., 4 August 1258.

f. 38v. Like on affairs of Scotland, 4 August 1258.

Letters Patent (French), 42 Henry III.

f. 41. Mandate to Mayor and Sheriffs of London, 8 March 1234.

f. 42. Charter for monks of St. Andrews, Tywardreath, co. Cornwall, inspeximus, 6 May 1235.

f. 44. Writ to Barons of Exchequer for Walter de Gray, Archbishop of York, 5 September 1235.

f. 45. Mandate to Sheriff of Lincs. on liberties, 14 August 1235.

f. 46. Like on marriage of Queen, Eleanor of Provence, 15 October 1235.

f. 50. As f. 13 above.

f. 51. Like to Queen of Scots, 23 February 1235.

f. 52. Letters to Gregory IX and to Cardinals, 25 February 1235, from Close Roll.

f. 53v. Mandate to keeper of Honor of Richmond on tithes, 6 September 1235.

f. 54. Like to Sheriffs on common aids, 10 July 1235.

f. 56. Like to Sheriff of Somerset on aid, 17 July 1235.

f. 57. As f. 54 above.

f. 57v. Like to Sheriff of Oxf. on aid, 16 July 1235.

Like to Sheriff of Cornwall and Devon on aid, 17 July 1235.

f. 59. Notification on marriage of King, 19 Henry III, from Close Roll.

Mandates to Sheriffs on making of knights, 7 November 1234.

Like to Sheriffs on doing justice to malefactors, 28 August 1235.

f. 60. As ff. 57, 57v above.

Mandate to Justices in Eyre co. Lincs., 12 October 1235.

As f. 57v above.

f. 64. Like to Robert de Langton, Archdeacon of Canterbury etc. 27 January 1235.

f. 66. Like to Robert Grosseteste, Bishop of Lincoln, on maintenance of royal liberties, with mandate to Justices of Bench, 17 January 1236.

f. 68. Extract from Matt. Paris, 21 Henry III.

f. 72. Letters Patent for Archbishops etc. 4 May 1236.

f. 73. Like on aid, 4 May 1236.

f. 74v. Like, same, 2 May 1236.

f. 75. Stat. of Merton, 20 Henry III.

f. 81. Writs to Sheriff of Worcs. for Peter de Norwich; to same on manors of Tenbury and Savenak; to Sheriff of Warw. and Leics. for William de Stutville; to Sheriff of Yorks; to Sheriff of Midd. to put John de Ray in pledge; for Nicholas de Beauchamp and William de Raleigh, 12 May 1236; on scutage of Poitou, 16 October 1236; on William Methenby and Hugh Wake; on Geoffrey Balister; on land of Bartholomew de Cheney, 22 October 1236; on Stephen de Segrave, 25 October 1236; on Gerard, son and heir of Gilbert de Sutton; Hugh Tanmache, 23 October 1236; on Henry de Pinkeney, 9 November 1235; on Bishop of Lincoln for Richard de Wiverton; to same for John Perteman, son and heir of Russell de St. Mayence, 18 December 1235, from K.R. Mem. Roll, 20 Henry III.

f. 89. Mandate on lands which indict malefactors etc., 21 July 1236.

f. 90. Like to Sheriffs to take oaths, 24 February 1240.

f. 91. Like on provisions on Justices in Eyre, 1 April 1236.

f. 92. Like to Sheriffs, 29 January 1236.

f. 94. Charter to citizens of Exeter, 24 March 1236.

f. 95. Mandate to Sheriff of Devon on custody of demesne woods and parks, 12 July 1237.

f. 96. Charter of confirmation of liberties, 28 January 1237.

f. 98. Extract from Matt. Paris, 21 Henry III.

f. 101. Letters Patent to John, Earl of Lincoln and Constable of Chester, 26 October 1237.

f. 102. Letters, Henry, King of England, and Alexander, King of Scotland, 21 Henry III, from Patent Roll.

f. 108. Letters Patent on tournament, 26 June 1237.

f. 109. Grant of aid, Council at London, 21 Henry III, from Misc. Bundle.

f. 111. As f. 94 above.

f. 113. Mandate on marriage of King's sister, Isabella, 21 Henry III.

f. 114. Note on treaty concerning forests etc., 21 Henry, from Close Roll.

f. 116. Note on Henry de Balliol and others coming to King that he should render to King of Scotland co. Huntingdon, 21 June 1237, from same.

f. 118. Mandate on assessment and collection of 30th in Cornwall, 10 July 1237.

f. 120. Like to Sheriff of Cornwall, 26 March 1237.

As f. 114 above.

f. 120v. Like on restoration of foresters disseised and restored to seisin, 21 Henry III.

f. 122. Like on Chester to Stephen de Segrave, 22 June 1237.

f. 124. Like on reading Magna Carta in full county, 4 March 1237.

Mandates on reading Magna Carta granted by King while under age, 26 March 1237.

f. 127. Letters Patent on assessment of aid in Bishopric of Winchester, 6 July 1238.

f. 128. Extract from Matt. Paris Additamenta on the altercation between Hubert de Burgh, Earl of Kent, and Master Laurence de St. Albans, with answers of Master Laurence.

f. 142. Mandate to Richard de Montfichet on reading of Magna Carta, 22 Henry III.

f. 143. Bull of Gregory IX, 20 February 1238, from Bull in Tower.

f. 144. Form of letters of prohibition to earls and barons on beasts taken in King's forests, 27 June 1238, from Close Roll.

f. 146. As f. 142 above.

Mandate to Barons of Dover etc. 28 September 1238.

f. 148. Form of letters to extend King's demesnes for use of King of Scotland, 29 May 1238, from Patent Roll.

f. 150. Writ for Henry de Merston, 25 June 1239, from Fine Roll.

f. 151. Renders of hawks etc. under various co. captions; Nicholas de Milis, Paulin de Pamer, 220 marks, profits cos. Bedf. and Bucks., from K.R. Mem. Roll, Comm., Mich., 24 & 25 Henry III.

f. 153. Mandates to Sheriffs, making of knights, 25 July 1240.

f. 155. Letters Patent (French), 24 Henry III.

Mandate to Abbot of St. Augustine's, Bristol, 30 September 1240.

Like to Sheriff of Yorks. on oath, 24 February 1240.

f. 156. Appointment of Master Walter de Dya to custody of Edward, the King's son, 23 March 1240, from Close Roll.

f. 156v. Mandate to Maurice fitz Gerald, Justiciar of Ireland, for Archbishop of Dublin, 8 February 1241.

f. 157. As f. 151 above.

f. 159. As f. 153 above.

f. 160. Like to Sheriff of Bucks. on pleas of forest, 10 October 1240.

f. 161. Like to Sheriffs on making of knights, 25 July 1240. List.

Like to Sheriff of Northants. on those who have 20 librates, 26 Henry III.

f. 161v. Like to Sheriffs on Prince Edward, 27 March 1240.

f. 162. Like to men of town of Oxford, 24 Henry III.

Mandate to Sheriffs, 24 February 1240.

f. 163. Letters Patent on wards and escheats, 11 February 1242.

Mandates on making knights, 22 July 1242.

f. 164. Like to Abbot and Convent of Roche, 21 February 1240.

f. 165. Like on assizes in cos. Norf. and Suff., 8 June 1242.

f. 165v. Like for David, Jew of Oxford, 27 August 1242.

f. 166. Like to men of Yarmouth on keeping peace at seas, 10 September 1242.

f. 166v. Like to Sheriffs of Norf. and Suff. on arrest of ships, 19 September 1242.

f. 167. Like to Sheriff of Suff. for Flemish merchants, 20 October 1242.

f. 167v. Like to Archbishop of York and others of Council for Richard Seward, 26 Henry III.

f. 169. Extract from Matt. Paris on death of Eleanor, sister of Arthur of Britanny.

Letters Patent to Prior and Convent of St. James, Bristol, on removal of body of Eleanor of Britanny, 20 October 1241.

f. 170. Like on assessing tallage, 6 April 1241.

f. 171. Like to Archdeacon of Gloucester on prohibition of contribution for Pope's use, 11 June 1241.

f. 172. Writs on tallaging boroughs and King's demesnes, 17 February 1241, from Fine Roll.

f. 173. Mandates to Archdeacons of Northampton etc., 26 July 1241.

f. 175. Extract from Matt. Paris, 26 Henry III.

f. 182. Charter of Plympton of enfeoffment of Baldwin, Earl of Devon, 25 March 1242, from Cart. Antiq., Roll JJ.

f. 183. Letters Patent on King's wards, 5 May 1242.

f. 184. Like to David, son of Llewelyn, 5 May 1242.

f. 185. Like on subsidy made to King, 8 April 1242.

f. 186. Charter to Warin fitz Gerald and Agnes, his wife, of manor of Mursle, 21 December 1242.

f. 187. Letters Patent committing Kingdom of England to Walter de Grey, Archbishop of York, 26 Henry III.

f. 189. Letters to the Emperor, 15 June 1242, from Gas. Pat. & Cart.

f. 191. Mandate to Archbishop of York etc. on contributions to King's subsidy, 14 October 1242.

f. 192. Writ on suit at county court of Surr., 13 February 1242; like to Barons for Walter de Mere, for William de Hatfield, for Roger de Wylie, 14 May 1242; for Henry de Wangham, on manor of Mutford, 7 July 1242; for Robert de Tok, 9 July 1242; for Monmouth and 4 coroners co. Heref., 19 July 1242; on land of Robert de Basingham on Harperham, 21 July 1242; from K.R. Mem. Roll, 26 Henry III.

f. 195. Mandate to Maurice fitz Gerald, Justiciar of Ireland, on tallages, 23 March 1242.

f. 196. Extract from Matt. Paris on Parliament, 1242 etc. with reference to Spelman, *Gloss.*

f. 202. Mandate to Sheriff of Cornwall on knighthood; to Sheriff of Devon on 8 February 1242; to Sheriffs on wards, 24 March 1242; to Sheriff of Devon for Thomas Peverel, 15 July 1242; to all Bishops etc. 14 December 1241.

f. 203v. Writs for William de Ferrers, 21 January 1242; for William de Chaumpeneys, 1 February 1242, from K.R. Mem. Roll, Comm., Hil., 26 Henry III.

f. 204. Mandates to Sheriffs on distraint of knighthood, 26 Henry III.

f. 205. Letters Patent for Abbots etc. 13 February 1242.

f. 206. Mandate to Sheriffs, 21 February 1242.

f. 207. Like to John de Segrave etc., Justices of Forests etc. 20 June 1242.

f. 208. Like to Archbishops etc. to be at London to treat, 14 December 1241.

f. 209. Letters Patent to Ralph Neville, Bishop of Chichester, etc. 26 June 1243.

f. 211. Writ to Archbishop of York to write to Sheriffs on distraint of knighthood, 1 September 1243, from Fine Roll.

f. 212. Mandates to Prior and Convent of Christ Church, Canterbury, etc. 26 June 1243.

f. 214. Like to Sheriffs of Lincs. to proclaim St. Botolph's Fair, 15 June 1243.

f. 215. Like to Sheriffs on arms, 27 Henry III.

f. 216. As f. 212 above.

f. 218. Like to John, Duke of Britanny and Earl of Richmond, 10 November 1242.

f. 219. Like to Sheriffs, 18 September 1243.

f. 220. The great dispute between the Prior and Convent of Christ Church, Canterbury, and Walter de Grey, Archbishop of York, Walter Mauclerc, Bishop of Carlisle, and William de Cantilupe on the archiepiscopal dignity. Mandate to Prior and Convent of Christ Church, Canterbury, 26 June 1243.

f. 222. Like to Archbishop of York etc., 26 March 1243.

f. 224. Writ, Cornwall, 1 September 1243, from Fine Roll etc.

Mandate not to sell wines contrary to Statute, 15 June 1243.

f. 224v. Like to barons of Aquitaine etc., army, 24 May 1243.

Like to Sheriffs, army cancelled. 2 June 1243.

f. 225. Like to Sheriffs on truce with King of France, 28 April 1243.

f. 225v. Like to Sheriffs on King's return, 18 September 1243.

f. 228. Letters Patent to Chancellor of Amiens, Judge Delegate of Pope, 25 May 1244.

f. 229. Like on subsidy for Holy Land, 28 Henry III.

f. 230. Writ for Abbot of St. Edmunds, 26 June 1244; for Abbot of Abingdon, 3 July 1244; for Robert Grosseteste, Bishop of Lincoln, 14 July 1244; from Fine Roll.

f. 232. Mandate to Sheriffs on wards, 28 January 1244.

f. 233. Like to Sheriffs on plea de namio vetito, 15 April 1244., with note on Close Roll, 42 Henry III, for Bishop of Rochester.

f. 234. As f. 220 above.

f. 236. As f. 233 above.

f. 237. Like to earls, barons etc. 7 May 1244.

f. 238. Like to Barons of Dover etc. 7 May 1244.

f. 241. Extract from Liber Albus in Archives of city of London, Plea of city of London arramed at Tower of London, Quindene of East. 28 Henry III.

f. 243. Mandate to Sheriffs on enquiries on Articles of Forest, 25 April 1244.

f. 245. Letters Patent for Walter de Grey, Archbishop of York, on his Will, 22 May 1245.

f. 245v. Like, 5 July 1245.

f. 246. Extracts from Matt. Paris on messengers of Universality of England to Council of Lyons.

f. 249. The Council of the whole baronage of England at Westminster, 29 Henry III, with references to Matt. Paris, Ann. of Burton, insertion in Cleopatra E. 1, Close Roll, 29 Henry III.

f. 252. Extract from Matt. Paris on observance of Magna Carta, 29 Henry III.

f. 253. As ff. 249–251v above, with further note from Plac. Parl. on petitions against William de Testa and the letter to Pope.

f. 255. Extract from Matt. Paris including the transcript of the letter on the extortions of the Roman curia.

f. 259. Extract from the Ann. of Burton on the grievances of the Kingdom of England by the Pope.

f. 261. The King's letter to the Pope for the liberation of England from Papal oppressions, with notes from Plac. Parl., Fox, *Acts*, Roman Roll, 17 Edward I.

f. 264. Extract from Matt. Paris, letter from Abbots and Priors to Pope and their meeting of Provinces of Canterbury and York, the letter to Pope of the Universality of England, letter of the Bishops of Province of Canterbury and many complaints of the King, nobles and People in Parliament on papal oppression and grievances.

f. 270. Writ to William Passelawe, keeper of lands late of William de Insula, Earl of Devon, on the collection of aid to King's use, 14 July 1245, from Fine Roll.

f. 271. Charter for the Converts, London, 30 April 1245.

f. 272. Mandates to Sheriffs etc. 7 June 1245.

f. 273. Like to John Lestrange, Justice of Chester, concerning letters sent to him to direct to David, son of Llewelyn, late Prince of Wales, 6 January 1245. Like to John de Monmouth concerning the Welsh of South Wales who did homage to the King.

f. 275. Like to Abbot of St. Edmunds on papacy, 29 Henry III.

f. 276. Like to Sheriffs on distraint of knighthood, 8 June 1245.

f. 277. Like to Maurice fitz Gerald, Justiciar of Ireland, 1 June 1245.

f. 278. As f. 275 above.

VOLUME 5

A volume of transcripts etc. from the Public Records and other sources 30–40 Henry III. On flyleaf: Recorda H. 3 ab anno 30 usque as 40 (repeated). 298 ff.

f. 1. Charter for Peter of Savoy of the whole honor of Laigle in England, advowsons etc. 20 July 1246.

f. 5. Tallage of the King's demesnes. Various men of various vills make fines for tallage.

f. 10. Extract from Matt. Paris on letter sent to the Pope. (As vol. 4, f. 266 above.)

f. 14. Extract from insertion in Cleopatra E. 1. Letter sent to Cardinals of Roman Church at Lyons.

f. 19. Another General Council of the baronage of England or General Parliament, at Westminster, 30 Henry III, from Fox, *Acts*.

f. 20. Letter to Clement VI (in English) from same source, 18 May 1343.

f. 24. Letter to the same from the Archbishop of Canterbury on the prejudice of provision, 30 August 1343.

f. 26. Letter to Pope, 10 September 1343.

f. 34. As f. 19 above, with references to Matt. Paris, Cleopatra E. 1, Liber F. in Archives of city of London, Fox, *Acts*, Roman Roll, 17 Edward III, with appendix from insertion in Cleopatra E. 1.

f. 41. Extract from Matt. Paris on the complaint of all England on papal oppressions with references to Matt. Paris, *Plac. Parl.* (p. 355), Liber F in Archives of city of London, and Fox, *Acts*.

f. 43. Extract from Matt. Paris, letter of universality of England to Pope.

f. 45. Relation of the General Parliament called 30 Henry III, with references to Matt. Paris, *Plac. Parl.* (p. 373), Fox, *Acts*, Roman Roll, 17 Edward III.

f. 56. As ff. 34–8 above.

f. 61. Like.

f. 69. Mandates to Justice of Chester and John de Monmouth, 6 January 1246.

f. 71. Mandates to Sheriffs on sergeanty, 10 November 1245.

f. 73. Letters Patent for Richard, Earl of Cornwall, on coinage, 27 July 1246.

f. 74. Charter on Cinque Ports, 15 May 1247.

f. 78. Mandate to Sheriff of Gloucester on pleas of forest.

f. 80. Mandate to Roger de Thirkill and fellow Justices, 25 May 1247.

f. 81. Mandate to certain Sheriffs on matrimonial causes. Writs to Barons of Exchequer for Mabel Revel, on marriage of sister, for Adam, son of Hervy (K.R. Mem. Roll, Comm. Mich. term, 31 Henry III); on marriage of King's daughter, 5 February 1247, for Geoffrey de Mandeville, custody of King's die, in place of Walter de Fleming (ibid., Hil. term); on oath of Agnes, widow of William de Lancaster (ibid., East. term).

f. 83. Letters Patent on Priory of Lewes, 7 September 1248.

f. 84. Writ of prohibition to William Suffield, Bishop of Norwich, not to compel rectors of churches to confer on grant of subsidy to Pope, 9 March 1248.

f. 85. Mandates to certain Sheriffs on escheats, 28 January 1248.

f. 86. Mandates to mayors etc. on coinage, 26 February 1248.

f. 88. Outlawry against William de Hastincot reversed by judgement of King's court because not made according to law and custom of realm, 16 February 1248.

f. 89. Mandates to Sheriffs on election of verderers, 9 May 1248.

f. 90. Mandate to Sheriff of Cumberland that no free man shall be disseised without judgement, 23 December 1247.

f. 91. Extract from Matt. Paris, 33 Henry III.

f. 97. Charter for converted Jews, 8 March 1248.

f. 99. Letters Patent to Abbots etc. seeking a subsidy, 10 December 1248.

f. 100. Letters Patent on King's escheats, 12 November 1248.

f. 102. Mandate to Sheriff of Lincoln for Robert Grosseteste, Bishop of Lincoln, 2 May 1249. Mandate to same on matrimonial causes.

f. 104. Tallage assessed on cities, boroughs and King's demesnes.

f. 107. Mandate on complaints of barons and community of Chester, 30 July 1249.

f. 109. Letters Patent on extending King's manors, 12 July 1250.

f. 109v. Extract from Chron. of Thomas Wykes, 34 Henry III.

f. 110. Inquisition made in co. Heref. on knight's fees, arranged in hundreds. (K.R. Mem. Roll, see below.)

f. 118. Plea in Exchequer, t. Henry III, John de Lexington; for Ralph Briton; to Bishop of Winchester or his Official; to answer Henry Enveyse; to Archbishop of Canterbury or his Official; to Bishop of London; to Bishop of Norwich; William Marmiun; Richard de Merton; Brother Roger, attorney of the Templars; Madoc de Sutton; William le Rus; William de Kyme; William de Cardiff; Charter of Peter de Watville (K.R. Mem. Roll, Comm. Trin. term, 34 Henry III).

f. 122x. The like Walter Camerarius; Sir Robert de Walton and others; John de Nevill; William de Ferrers, Earl of Derby; Herbert de Nevill (ibid., East. term).

f. 124. The like Alan de Maidwell; Thomas, son of Alexander; John de Hampton; Roger Bigod, Earl of Norfolk, Earl Marshal; Robert de Gregat; Robert Tresgoz; on scutage of Deganwy; John de Dunton; John de Lanfar; on aid for marriage of King's sister; on manor of Middleton; on son and heir of John de Esse (ibid., Mich. term).

f. 128. Inquisition for King on grant of Henry II to predecessors of John Gravenell; Thomas de Putteridge; on scutage of Deganwy (ibid., Hil. term).

f. 130. Writ that Sheriff shall cause to come all foresters and regarders before the arrival of Justices of the Forest, 23 March 1250.

f. 131. Mandate for Richard de Ortiay and his men, 10 August 1250.

f. 133. Fine for Hugh de Aubigny, 6 July 1252.

Fine for John de Boulton, 26 July 1252.

f. 132. Mandate for men of co. Lancs., 24 June 1250.

f. 135. Fine for burgesses of Newcastle upon Tyne, 23 September 1252.

f. 136. Fine for burgesses of Bristol, 17 August 1252.

f. 137. Extract from Matt. Paris on scandals said of Henry de Bath, 36 Henry III.

f. 139. Writ to Sheriff of Kent on cap. 29, Magna Carta, from MS. of Sir Ciriac Petyt, in possession of Thomas Petyt, of Colkins, near Faversham, co. Kent, esq.

f. 141. Grant by King to all Archbishops etc. and all of realm of liberties, 21 February 1252.

f. 151. Writ to Master Simon de Wanton and Richard de Braycote, to take assize which Roger Weseham, Bishop of Chester arramed, 16 May 1252 (Misc. Bundle, t. Henry III, in Tower of London).

f. 152. Charter of Andrew Turbut, 28 February 1252.

f. 153. Fine for citizens of Canterbury after paying 2½ marks of gold, 28 September 1252.

f. 154. Charter of inspeximus for Prior and Canons of Bodmin, 15 March 1252.

f. 155. Mandate to Robert de Thirkelby and fellow Justices on pleas on sergeanties, 24 June 1251.

f. 156. Charter for Philip, son of Alexander of Montgomery, 1 May 1251.

f. 158. Fine for Henry de Bath.

f. 159. Letters Patent on peace for Henry de Bath, 8 July 1252.

f. 160. Letters Patent for men of Gascony and Isle of Oleron, 6 June 1252.

f. 161v. Mandate for men of Hythe, 5 March 1252.

f. 162. Letters Patent for Philip Lovel, 5 February 1252.

f. 163. As f. 160 above.

f. 164. Letters Patent for Roger de Leyburn, 20 October 1252.

f. 165. Letters Patent for vicar of Geddington, 22 January 1252.

f. 166. Letters Patent for Alan, son of Thomas, 30 January 1252.

f. 167. Letters Patent on form of peace between King and men of Bordeaux, 18 January 1251.

f. 168. Letters Patent touching the dispute between Simon de Montfort, Earl of Leicester, and certain magnates, barons, citizens and burgesses of King's land of Gascony.

f. 169. Letters Patent of pardon for William Goldwell condemned for death of Roger Bishop, 22 June 1251, and mandate thereon.

f. 170. Mandate to Geoffrey de Langley, Justice of Forest, 12 May 1251.

f. 171. Mandate to burgesses of Rhuddlan, 19 October 1252.

f. 172. Mandate on the privileges of the Hospitallers and Templars on tallage, 22 October 1252, and mandate thereon to Barons of the Exchequer, 23 October 1252.

f. 173. Mandates on tallaging a tallage, 20 June 1252.

f. 174. Mandates on tallaging the King's demesnes, 24 April, 28 April, 2 May 1252.

f. 179. Mandate to Robert Grosseteste, Bishop of Lincoln, on oath of office, 14 June 1252.

f. 180. Mandate to Boniface of Savoy, Archbishop of Canterbury, 16 May 1252.

f. 180v. Mandates to Archbishops etc. on preaching the Cross, 26 May 1252.

f. 181. Mandates to Archbishop of Canterbury etc. on subsidy for Holy Land.

f. 182v. Mandate to Patriarch of Jerusalem, 6 June 1252.

f. 184. Letter to Pope, 27 December 1252.

f. 185. Mandate on Jews, 23 November 1251.

f. 186. Sentence on those who infringed Magna Carta, 13 May 1252. City gave 500 marks, from Lib de Ant. Leg. in Archives of city of London.

f. 188. Letters Patent on marriage of King's eldest daughter, 27 December 1251.

f. 189. Extract from Matt. Paris, 37 Henry III.

f. 194. Letters Patent on sentence of excommunication, 13 May 1253.

f. 196v. Mandate to Barons of Exchequer to distrain Archbishops and others, 2 November 1254.

f. 196. Letters Patent to Queen and Richard, Earl of Cornwall, on observance of Magna Carta, 24 March 1254.

Mandates to Sheriffs on the same, 23 June 1253.

f. 198. Mandate for Archbishop of Canterbury on return of writs etc. with mandate to Richard, Earl of Cornwall, 24 August 1253.

f. 200. Mandates on articles of watch, 24 July 1253.

f. 203. Mandate for Gilbert Saloman, 12 December 1252.

f. 204. Mandate to Sheriff of Devon for William Arthur, 22 February 1253.

f. 205. Mandate for Thomas le Waleys, Bishop of St. David's, 27 January 1253.

f. 206. Mandate to Barons of the Exchequer for knighting of King's eldest son, 14 May 1253.

f. 207. Mandate on John, son of Martin of Aldburgh, on forgery of King's seal, 12 October 1253.

f. 208. Mandate to Sheriff of Cambridge for Roger de Scaccario, 21 July 1253.

f. 209. Mandates on provision made by King for Jews of England, 31 January 1253.

f. 211. Mandates on record of suit sent to Westminster to Master Simon de Walton and fellows, 3 February 1253.

f. 212. Mandate for Matilda de Chabbenham on death, childbirth, 16 August 1253.

f. 213. Mandates on prest aid to Thomas de Staunford, Escheator etc. 29 May 1253.

f. 214. Mandates to all Sheriffs on same, 21 July 1253.

f. 215. Mandates on distraint of knighthood, 17 November 1252.

f. 216. Mandate on men of Reading, 19 June 1253.

f. 217. Extract from Matt. of Westminster on general sentence of excommunication in Parliament, 37 Henry III.

f. 217v. Letters Patent to Roger, Earl of Norfolk etc.

f. 219. On the great Parliament, 37 Henry III, Confirmation of Magna Carta and Charter of the Forests, 9 Henry III, from Statute, 25 Edward I (French).

f. 223. Statute de tallagio non concedendo, 25 Edward I, from Coke, *2nd Inst.*

f. 224. Extract from Parliament Roll, 6 Edward III (French).

f. 225. Statute 12 Edward IV, cap. 7 (Kedels), from Rastell, *Stat.*

f. 226. Plea, Henry de Tracy, on barony of Torrington. (K.R. Mem. Roll, Comm. Mich. term, 37 & 38 Henry III.)

f. 226v. Letters Patent on church of Regula, 22 March 1254.

f. 228. For men of Bridport. (K.R. Mem. Roll, Comm. Mich. term, 37 & 38 Henry III.)

f. 229. Mandates to Sheriffs, aid against King of Castile, 11 February 1254.

f. 231. Mandate on amendment of Scottish coinage, 1 November 1253.

Mandate on removal of Peter de Goldington from office of coroner, co. Essex, because young and insufficient, 12 February 1254.

f. 231v. Plea, 38 Henry III, community of city of Bath.

f. 233. As f. 229 above.

f. 235. Letters Patent on Irish matters and aid against King of Castile, 2 February, 17 February 1254.

f. 238. As f. 235 above.

f. 240. Letters Patent to Archbishops etc. of Ireland on King's business. 10 December 1253.

f. 242. Extracts from Matt. Paris on money for business of Apulia, 1255, and Parliament of London, 1255.

f. 247. Pleas in Exchequer: Prior of Newenham came before Barons; for Richard Blund, Bishop of Exeter; on impleading Barons of Exchequer elsewhere; William, son of Paul etc.; for citizens of London on receiving their mayor (K.R. Mem. Roll, Comm. Mich. term, 39 Henry III); for Walter de Cantilupe, Bishop of Worcester; to distrain Nicholas, son of Guy; for Barons of Exchequer; Hamo and John Petit, bailiffs of Hundred of Tandridge; for King against citizens of London (ibid., Hil. term); Robert de Fulham, Constable of Exchequer; mayor and citizens of London and merchants of Lucca; production of charter of Henry II to London; for Abbot of Westminster; Richard de Clare, Earl of Gloucester (ibid., East. term).

f. 255. Memorandum on monstrous fish, King sitting in Exchequer, William de Pakeham, steward of Bishop of Norwich. (K.R. Mem. Roll, Comm. Hil. term, 39 Henry III.)

f. 257. Extract from Ann. of Burton, Parliament at Westminster, 1255, 39 Henry III; letter on execution of papal mandate by Master Rostrand.

f. 287. Mandates to Henry de Bath etc. on tallage of city of London, 26 January 1255.

f. 289. Mandates on assessment of same, 14 February 1255.

f. 293. Mandates to Sheriffs on knighting of King's eldest son, 3 May 1255.

f. 294. Letters Patent sent to King by Alexander, King of Scotland, 20 September 1255.

f. 297. Letters Patent on same matter, 21 September 1255, with note from Close Roll, 40 Henry III.

VOLUME 6

A volume of transcripts etc. from the Public Records and other sources, 40–6 Henry III. On flyleaf: Recorda H. 3 ab anno 40 usque ad 47. 265 ff.

f. 1. Extract from Ann. of Burton, reciting papal mandate, 1256.

f. 2. Mandate for Abbot of Glastonbury, 20 February 1256, with like to be intendant.

f. 4. Like to Sheriffs on subsidy to Pope, 20 May 1256.

f. 6. Like to Boniface of Savoy, Archbishop of Canterbury, etc. 22 November 1256.

f. 7v. Like, 3 January 1257.

f. 8. Letters Patent to Stephen Lungespere, Seneschal of Gascony (4), 15 June 1257.

f. 10. Like to collectors of money of Cross, 24 June 1257.

f. 11x. Like to persons appointed to fruits of bishopric of Winchester, with mandate thereon, 3 April 1258.

f. 13. Venire facias to Dean and Chapter of St. Mary of Penfold; William de Warner etc.; John de Threshall etc.; Henry Lovel; Robert de Chille; memorandum for citizens of London; William de Lessebarwe; Henry de Codham; memorandum on Simon de Montfort, Earl of Leicester, 13 December 1257; Everard de Holbech; on levying of scutage; memorandum on manor of Gynebury which Gerard de Talbot held; for William de Eboriciis; Hugh de Scour for Thomas de Pouvilly; writ to Barons for William de Hareng; commission of cos. Essex and Hertf.; to Constable of Dover for Abbot of Pershore; writ to Barons for Abbey of Hyde near Winchester; Archdeacon and Official of York for King; memorandum for Philip de Aubiny; Baldwin de Insula; John le Fraunceys, Baron of Exchequer, from K.R. Mem. Roll, 42 Henry III.

f. 23. Pledge of money paid by the King of France to have peace pledges of King on his agreement between Henry III and Simon de Montfort, Earl of Leicester, and Eleanor, his wife, 26 July 1259, from New Misc. Bundle t. Henry III.

f. 25. Extract from Ann. of Tewkesbury, in Cleopatra A. 7, 1258.

f. 26. On Parliament, London, 42 Henry III, with reference to Matt. Paris.

f. 33. Letters Patent for King and Baronage of England, 2 May 1258.

f. 33v. Like (French), note on Provisions of Oxford, 2 August 1258.

f. 36. As f. 25 above.

f. 39. Extract from Ann. de Gestis Angl., from Cleopatra D. 9. on Council of Oxford, 42 Henry III.

f. 41. Letters Patent, 18 October 1258, Anglo Saxon charter of Henry I to men of Huntingdon, with translation and note from Somner, *Saxon Dict*.

f. 43v. Parliament, 42 Henry III, with references to Matt. Paris, Patent Roll, 42, 43 Henry III, Ann. of Tewkesbury, Ann. de Gestis Angl., Papal Bull in Cleopatra E. 1, Close Roll, 46 Henry III, Ann. of Burton.

f. 48. Extract from Matt. Paris on continuation of Parliament, 1258.

f. 53. Roll of Parliament abridged by Mr. Selden out of the original roll which he borrowed from Mr. Edward Coke. Letters of Kings' Councillors and 12 elected on behalf of the community, May 1258; letters of King directed to 4 knights; writ to Sheriffs to proclaim certain liberties.

f. 57. Mandate to Mayor and Sheriffs of London, 7 July 1258.

f. 58. Letters Patent to Aymer de Valence, Elect of Worcester, etc. 28 June 1258.

f. 61. Like on rectification and reform of state of realm, 2 May 1258.

f. 63. As f. 61 above.

f. 64. Like, Edward, eldest son of King, to Archbishop etc. 12 July 1258.

f. 66. Like of prohibition to Boniface of Savoy, Archbishop of Canterbury, 7 January 1258.

f. 67. On all trespasses, excesses etc., Parliament of Oxford, 42 Henry III.

Letters Patent on inquisition in each co., 4 August 1258.

f. 71. Form of oath of keepers of castles in England (French). Letters Patent, 22 June 1258.

f. 75. Like (French), 42 Henry III.

f. 76. Mandate to Robert de Nevill, same.

Like to William de Latimer, Sheriff of Yorks., 12 May 1258.

f. 78. Letters Patent for Henry Wingham, Elect of London, 18 June, 4 August 1259.

f. 79. Mandate to Peter d'Aigueblanche, Bishop of Hereford, 26 November 1258.

f. 82. Like on Welsh expedition, 18 March 1258.

f. 84v. Like to King of Scotland, 27 August 1258.

f. 86. Like concerning King of Scotland, 18 January 1258.

f. 88. Like to Constable of castle of Winchester, 24 October 1259.

Like to Constable of Dover.

Memorandum on business of Rome, 1 August 1258, from Close Roll.

f. 90. Mandate to Mayor and Sheriffs of London, 42 Henry III, with reference to Close Roll, 44 Henry III.

f. 92. Like to Sheriffs de expensis for 4 knights, 4 November 1257.

f. 94. As f. 88 above.

f. 95. Letter to Pope, 1 August 1258, from Close Roll.

f. 100. Mandate on Sheriff's turn, 9 January 1258.

f. 101. Like to Sheriffs on reasonable expenses to 4 knights, 4 November 1258.

f. 103. Like to Sheriffs on prorogation of assizes etc. 4 June 1258.

f. 103v. Like to Mayor etc. of Lincoln etc. 14 March 1259.

f. 104. As f. 95 above.

f. 106. Writ for Llewelyn, son of Maredudd, 1 November 1258; for Andrew de Luk, 3 November 1258; for James Danemtato and fellows, 3 November 1258; for Robert de Foleham, 7 November 1258; for Punzard Duymes, 20 February 1259, from Liberate Roll, 43 Henry III.

f. 108. Plea on Robert Burnell, co. Salop, from K.R. Mem. Roll., Comm., Mich. 43–4 Henry III; writ to Barons for various Sheriffs; judgement against Simon Walton, Bishop of Norwich, on amercement, same East.

f. 112. Great and Long Parliament in the Great Hall, Westminster, 43 Henry III, from Liber D and Lib. de Antiq. Leg. in Archives of city of London.

f. 114. Letters Patent for Master John Mansel on prebend of Fenton, 11 May 1259.

f. 115. Like on forestry beyond Trent to Thomas Gresley, 11 September 1259, with mandate.

f. 115v. Like for Henry Wingham, Elect of London, 4 August 1259.

f. 116. Like on commission of forest of Clarendon, 14 June 1259.

f. 117. Like to all cos. (French), 28 March 1259.

f. 120. Like for Henry Wingham, Elect of London, 12 July 1259.

f. 120v. As f. 115v above.

f. 121. As f. 79 above.

f. 123. Like of commission of castle, 29 March 1259.

f. 124. As f. 41 above.

f. 125. Like on commission of escheatry, South of Trent, 2 June 1259.

f. 128. Mandate on bishopric of Carlisle, 6 November 1259.

f. 131. Like for Prior of Llanthony, 4 November 1258.

f. 132. Letter to King of Almain, King's brother, 4 November 1258, from Close Roll.

f. 133. Names of those sworn of King's Council, 43 Henry III, from same.

f. 134. Mandate for Robert de Ros, 6 November 1259.

f. 135. Like to Walter Kirkham, Bishop of Durham, 11 September 1259.

f. 136. Letters to Pope and to Cardinals, 23 September 1259, from Close Roll.

f. 139. Stat. de anno et die bisexili, 44 Henry III, from MS. Stat. in poss. of J. Peachey, of Inner Temple, Esq.

Mandate for Peter d'Aigueblanche, Bishop of Hereford, 5 June 1260.

f. 139v. Memorandum of Barons etc. of Chester, 44 Henry III, from Patent Roll.

f. 140. Mandate to Philip Basset, 7 June 1260.

f. 141. Fine for custody of lands and heirs of Hugh de Morwich, with mandate, 4 November 1260, from Fine Roll.

f. 143. Writs to Barons for Abbot of Osney; community of Guidon; memorandum on manor of Pocklington; writs to Barons for John de Balliol and wife; 9 November 1260; summons for King; inquisition for Alice Clement; attorney for John de Wendon; for Henry de Whitingdon, from K.R. Mem. Roll, 44–5 Henry III.

f. 150. Letters Patent for King of Almain, 15 June 1260.

f. 150v. Like for merchants of Germany, 15 June 1260.

f. 151. Like for Henry, son of King of Almain, 20 October 1260.

f. 151v. Like for Edward, the King's son, 18 October 1260.

f. 152. Like to Bailiffs of Ipswich prohibiting export of grain, 20 May 1260.

f. 152v. Like on France, 4 July 1260.

f. 153. Like to Abbot of Newminster for Bishop of Durham, 1 August 1260.

f. 154. Like on commission of King's castle and mill of Oxford and meadow of Woodstock, 6 November 1259.

f. 156. Like for Earl of Leicester (French), 44 Henry III.

f. 157. Mandate to Hugh le Despenser, 4 December 1259.

f. 158. Like to collectors of 10th, diocese of Norwich, 4 June 1260.

f. 160. Like to Hugh le Bigod, Justiciar of England, 44 Henry III.

f. 162. Like to same, 16 January 1260.

f. 165. Mandate on army of Wales, 1 August 1260. List.

f. 169. Letters to Pope and to Cardinals, 16 January 1260, from Close Rolls.

f. 171. Like to Pope, 18 January 1260, same.

f. 173. Mandate on mill of Bishop of Ely, 44 Henry III.

f. 174. Like to Peter d'Aigueblanche, Bishop of Hereford, to deliver excommunicate from prison, 15 September 1260; like to Sheriff of Norf., 15 September 1260.

f. 177. New writ provided on account. Mandate to Mayor and Sheriffs of London, 7 May 1260, with notes from Spelman, *Gloss.*, Reg. of Writs.

f. 182. Mandate to Sheriff of Somerset for Roger, Abbot of Glastonbury, 21 July 1260.

f. 184. Like on provision made by King and Council, 44 Henry III.

f. 190. Like to Sheriffs on appointment of Justices, 28 November 1259.

f. 192. Letters Patent to Justices in Eyre, co. Cambridge, 11 February 1261.

f. 194. Letters Patent on service, 18 October 1261. List.

f. 198. Like on knights to come to King, 17 February 1261.

f. 200. Mandates on same, 18 February 1261.

f. 201. Letters Patent on safe conduct on Barons coming to Kingston, 20 October 1261.

f. 202. Like appointing proctors in Roman curia, 27 May 1261.

f. 204. Like for each co., 5 August 1261.

f. 209. Charter for Ingelram de Fenes, inspeximus, 7 January 1261, with mandate.

f. 210. For Alan de Ospergrave; writ to Barons for Abbot of Osney; render by William de Englishvill; Letters Patent appointing proctors in Roman curia; to Abbot of Chertsey for King; writ to Barons for Richard de Grey; to Mayor and Bailiffs of Canterbury; for Richard, Earl of Gloucester; memorandum for citizens of London; debt on aid for King's sister; memorandum on seal of Geoffrey de Rus; to William Huse for King; to Bailiffs of Abbot of Fecamp; for John de Bath; to Henry de Whitington, from K.R. Mem. Roll, 45 Henry III.

f. 219. As f. 200 above.

Mandate to William Maudit of Warminster, 45 Henry III.

f. 220. Writs for Hugh le Despenser, 9 November 1260; for Alenard de Semingham; on delivery of money to make a wall, 28 November 1260; for Chancellor (Nicholas of Ely, Archdeacon of Ely), 28 November 1260; for Emery of Somevill, 4 December 1260; for Simon de Romano, 8 December 1260, from Liberate Roll.

f. 224. Writs to Mayor and Bailiffs of Bristol; Sheriff of Cambridge and Hunts.; Mayor etc. of London; Gilbert de Clare, Earl of Gloucester; Llewelyn ap Gruffydd, Prince of Wales; Boniface of Savoy, Archbishop of Canterbury; John de Balliol, from Extract Roll, 45–9 Henry III.

f. 224v. Writ to Boniface of Savoy, Archbishop of Canterbury, 30 August 1261, from Bundle of Certificates, 49 Henry III.

f. 238. Writ to Justiciar etc. of Ireland, from Extract Roll, 45–9 Henry III.

f. 238v. Mandate to Sheriff of Southampton, 3 April 1264.

f. 239. Like to Robert de Nevill, Sheriff of Yorks., 26 May 1264.

f. 240. Writ to Sheriff of Cambridge and Hunts., from Extract Roll, 45–9 Henry III.

f. 242. Mandate to Llewelyn ap Gruffydd, Prince of Wales, 8 July 1261.

f. 244. Like to Sheriffs, 11 September 1261.

f. 245. Bull of Alexander IV, 13 April 1261, from original in Cleopatra E. 1.

f. 246. Mandates to Sheriffs, 2 May 1262.

f. 248. Letters to Pope, 11 December 1261, from Close Roll.

f. 250. Mandates for citizens of London etc. 2 May 1262.

f. 251. As f. 242 above.

f. 252. Like for Prior of Wenlock for King, 23 February 1262.

f. 254. Fine of city of Lincoln, 2 March 1262, from Fine Roll.

f. 254v. Fine for city of York, 9 May 1262, same.

f. 256. Letters to Pope, 1 January 1262, from Close Roll.

f. 256v. Letters to Cardinal Ottobon and other Cardinals, 1 January 1262, from Close Roll.

f. 258. Letters to Alphonso, King of Romans, 16 August 1262, from Close Roll.

f. 261. Mandates to Earl Marshal and others, 16 December 1261.

f. 262. Letters Patent on disputes between King and Barons, 7 December 1262 (French).

f. 265. Like for community, co. Bucks., 29 January 1262.

VOLUME 7

A volume of transcripts etc. from the Public Records and other sources, 47–56 Henry III. On flyleaf: Recorda ab anno 47 Henr. 3 ad finem regni sui. 331 ff.

f. 1. Writs to Earl of Winchester etc. to come to King at Windsor, with horses and arms, to treat on certain matters touching the realm, 17 October 1263, from Patent Roll.

f. 2. Mandates to Bailiffs etc. of Yarmouth etc., 11 August 1263.

f. 3. Letter of Llewelyn ap Gruffydd, Prince of Wales, to King, from Close Roll.

f. 4. Mandate to Sheriff of Staffs. on Isabella de Fengers, 24 March 1263.

f. 5. Like on summons of army of Wales against Llewelyn ap Gruffydd, 25 May 1263.

f. 9. Bull of Urban IV, 21 March 1263, from original in Cleopatra E. 1.

f. 11. Confirmation of King of France of promise made by reason of Ordinances made at Oxford, 47 Henry III. Notarial Instrument including above Bull, from same.

f. 17. Letters Patent to Sheriffs on Oaths, 10 March, 22 March 1263.

f. 19. Proclamation of peace between King and Barons, from Patent Roll.

f. 20. Disputes arising in various cos. by occasion of non-observance of Provisions of Oxford, the King wishing them to be observed and kept.

Letters Patent appointing keepers of the peace in each co., 20 July 1263.

f. 21. The same year the King gave power to certain commissioners to treat and make peace between him and his Barons on the constitutions and statutes of Oxford, 4 July 1263, from Patent Roll.

f. 22. Letters Patent on preservation of liberties of church, 6 August 1263.

f. 23. As f. 4 above.

f. 24. Like to Sheriff of Somerset on dispute between Roger, Abbot of Glastonbury, and William Button, Bishop of Bath and Wells, 47 Henry III.

f. 26. Letters Patent about King of France, same.

f. 30. Stat. of Marlborough beginning at cap. 9, from Patent Roll.

f. 32. Letters Patent of pardon to Mayor and citizens of London, 17 September 1263.

f. 33. Like giving powers to confirm, 16 July 1263.

f. 35. Like to Chancellor of University of Oxford, 48 Henry III.

f. 37. Renders of Robert le Mercer of Northampton, Laurence St. Michel, Henry de Wayte, John le Moyne, from K.R. Mem. Roll, Comm., Mich., 47–8 Henry III.

f. 38. Confederation made at London, 48 Henry III, between Simon de Montfort, Earl of Leicester, and the Mayor etc. of London, from Lib. de Antiq. Leg. in Archives of city of London.

f. 40. Inquisition made at Parliament at Tristel, 18 June 1264, from Reg. of Archbishop of Dublin. (Fragment only.)

f. 41v. Extract from Chron. of Melrose, on battle of Lewes, 48 Henry III and from Chron. Wykes, on treaty between King and Barons.

f. 50. Letter to Louis, King of France, 10 July 1264, from Close Roll.

f. 52. Mandate to Sheriff of Southampton to summon to King at Oxford, 3 April 1264.

f. 54. Like to citizens of London, 8 December 1263.

f. 57. On the Parliament of London, 48 Henry III. Form of peace between King and Barons, June 1264, with Letters Patent of revocation, 3 July 1264.

f. 65. On the Parliament at London, 48 Henry III, translation of form of peace (as above), with references to Dr. Brady, *Intro. to Old Eng. Hist.*, Patent Roll, 48 Henry III, Parl. Roll, 40 Edward III, Close Roll, 28 Edward I, Patent Roll, 48 Henry III, Coke, *1st Inst.*, Patent Rolls, 9 Edward II, 48 Henry III.

f. 78. Letters Patent to all Sheriffs, 20 December 1263.

f. 81. Like on coming to King at Oxford with horses and arms, 4 July 1264.

f. 83. Like on preservation of peace, 4 July 1264.

f. 84. Like on trespasses done against the church in England (French), 48 Henry III.

f. 86. Like of commission of cos., 27 June 1264.

f. 88. Like for community of prelates of kingdom of England, 18 October 1264.

f. 90. On disturbances in the kingdom and Battle of Lewes, to Archbishops etc. of Ireland.

f. 92. Letters Patent to Stephen Berksted, Bishop of Chichester, etc. 23 June 1264.

f. 93. Like to John de St. Valery on Provisions of Oxford, 48 Henry III.

f. 94. Like to Simon de Montfort, Earl of Leicester, etc., 11 September 1264, with note from Matt. of West.

f. 98. Like giving power to treat on reform of Kingdom, 13 September 1264.

f. 100. Like of safe conduct for Barons to Oxford, 18 March 1264.

f. 100v. Like for the King's proctors, 20 March 1264.

f. 101. As f. 98 above.

f. 102. Like to Roger de Clifford, 3 July 1264.

f. 103. Charter to citizens of London that the aid freely granted to King should not prejudice them in future, 22 December 1226, from Laud. Brit. in Archives of city of London.

f. 105. Extract from Chron. of Melrose on escape of Prince Edward from custody of Simon de Montfort, 49 Henry III.

f. 111. Letters Patent of pardon to Earl of Gloucester, John Giffard etc. 9 October 1265.

f. 112. Letters to Louis, King of France, on business of England, 14 April 1265, from Patent Roll.

f. 113. Letters Patent for King of Almain, 12 September 1265.

f. 114. Like that the Irish should use the laws of England, 22 May 1318.

f. 115. Like to Godfrey Ludham, Archbishop of York, etc. 8 December 1264.

f. 116. Mandates to same, 3 September 1264.

Like to Simon Walton, Bishop of Norwich, 1 September 1264.

f. 117. Letters Patent to Bishop of Hereford, 1 June 1265.

f. 119. Like for King touching Battle of Lewes, 10 March 1265.

f. 120. Like prohibiting tournaments, 16 February 1265.

f. 121. Like to Gilbert de Clare, Earl of Gloucester and Hertford, and to Simon de Montfort, Earl of Leicester, 16 February 1265.

f. 122. Like for Roger Mortimer, 27 February 1265.

f. 123. Like to Keepers of Peace in all cos., 7 June 1265.

f. 126. Writ to Justices of Jews, 5 March 1265, from Fine Roll.

f. 128. Mandate to Sheriff of Salop and Staffs., 23 February 1265.

f. 130. Like with writ attached, 49 Henry III.

f. 131. Provision made 19 January 1268, from Close Roll.

f. 132. Writ de expensis, 15 February 1265.

f. 134. Mandate on provision of wine for King's use, 3 May 1265.

f. 135. Writs of summons to Parliament, 13 December 1264, 20 January 1265, 15 February 1265, 23 February 1265.

f. 142. Mandate to Dean and Chapter of York, 15 May 1265.

f. 143. Form of peace between King and Barons, Parliament, London, 49 Henry III, from Close Roll.

f. 147. Mandate for William de Colevill, 12 April 1265.

f. 147v. Letter to Countess of Flanders, 15 April 1265, from Close Roll.

f. 149. Mandate on suspension of pleas de Banco, 1 June 1265.

f. 150. Like to Richard, Bishop of Bangor, on mandate to Llewelyn ap Gruffydd, 15 May 1265.

f. 151. Like for Robert de Grendon, 5 March 1265.

f. 151v. Like restitution Robert Aguilion, 20 February 1265.

f. 152. Like on carriage of herrings for King's use, 7 March 1265.

f. 152v. Like for Eleanor, consort of Prince Edward, 5 March 1265.

f. 155. Form of writ of summons to cities and boroughs, Parliament, London, 14 December 1264.

f. 157. Mandate to Henry of Sandwich, Bishop of London, for delivery of Prince Edward, 12 June 1265.

f. 158. Like to various Bishops to come to King, 2 June 1265.

f. 158v. Extract from Ann. of Waverley on inquisition on rebels after Battle of Evesham, 49 Henry III.

f. 159. Form of summons to Earl of Leicester and 22 temporal lords to Parliament, London, 13 December 1264, with translation.

f. 161. Mandate to Roger Bigod, Earl of Norfolk, and Gilbert de Clare, Earl of Gloucester, 7 June 1265.

f. 163. Letters Patent, Ireland, 18 June 1265.

f. 166. Extract from Chron. of Melrose on Battle of Evesham, 49 Henry III.

f. 172. Stat. of Parliament of Winchester, Inquisitions de rebellis, 49 Henry III.

f. 175. Dr. Brady's Propositions against the Ancient Right of the Commons of England to be an essential part of Parliament before 49 Henry III and then began by rebellion. Dr. Brady's two contrary propositions to Mr. Petyt concerning the Parliament to meet at London, 49 Henry III, with references to Dr. Brady, *Full and Clear Answer to Mr. Petyt*, Pulton, *Stat.*, Stat. of Gloucester.

f. 179. Letters Patent to William de Engleby etc. 10 March 1265.

f. 180. King's peace proclaimed throughout England, from Claudius, D. 6.

f. 182. Form of Peace between King and Barons, from Charter Roll, and King's oath on same.

f. 196. Letters Patent to Henry of Sandwich, Bishop of London, 6 June 1265.

f. 200. Like concerning differences between Simon de Montfort, Earl of Leicester, and Gilbert de Clare, Earl of Gloucester and Hertford, 8 June 1265.

f. 202. Like to co. Lancs., 49 Henry III.

f. 204. Like for Gilbert de Clare, Earl of Gloucester, 12 January 1266.

f. 205. Like for earls, barons and others on their fees, 12 January 1266.

f. 206. Mandate for Sheriff of Yorks., 3 May 1266.

f. 208. Form of proclamation for reading Magna Carta in full county court, 50 Henry III, from Close Roll.

f. 209. Writ to Barons for Thomas Passelaw, from K.R. Mem. Roll, Comm., Mich., 50 Henry III.

f. 211. Charter, Ottobon, 16 January 1267.

f. 217. Mandate on John de Burgh, Earl of Kent, etc. 23 January 1267.

f. 218. Like to Sheriff of Berks. on Abbot of Abingdon, 23 December 1266.

f. 219. Like for John de St. Valery, 25 February 1267.

f. 220. Letters Patent on clergy of Bishopric of Norwich on fine, 2 August 1267.

f. 221. Like on peace between King and Gilbert de Clare, Earl of Gloucester, 16 June 1267.

f. 226. Like of pardon to citizens of London, 1267.

f. 228. As f. 221 above.

f. 229. Like for the disinherited (French), 51 Henry III.

f. 230. Like for Roger le Poitevin etc., 25 June 1267.

f. 231. Like for Robert de Ver, Earl of Oxford, 5 December 1266.

f. 232. Like for citizens of Lincoln, 10 February 1267.

f. 233. As f. 228 above, with notes from Patent Roll, 7 Edward II, Pleas coram Rege, Trin. term, 12 Edward II.

f. 234. As f. 221 above.

f. 236. Mandate for Walter de Huntingfield etc. (French), 13 June 1267.

f. 237. As f. 228 above with note.

f. 239. Letters Patent for John de Eyvill and other disinherited, 1 July 1267.

f. 241. Like for William de Monte Casino, 2 February 1267.

f. 243. On Parliament or General Plea, London, Quindene Mich. 52 Henry III, on cause or business of Cross. Letters to King of France, 20 September 1268, with note from du Fresne, *Gloss.*

f. 245. Mandate to Barons of Exchequer for burgesses of Dunwich, 13 March 1268.

f. 246. Mandate to Sheriff of Lincs., 22 November 1267.

f. 247. Letters Patent on compromise with King of France, 6 April 1268.

f. 248. Like for William de Tracy, 20 June 1268.

f. 249. Like for Prior and Convent of Whitby, 27 March 1268.

f. 251. Like for community of co. Cambridge and Isle of Ely, 21 November 1267.

f. 252. Like of pardon for Roger de Leyburn etc. 10 March 1268.

f. 254. Mandate on tallage assessed beyond Trent, 52 Henry III.

f. 260. Preamble of Stat. of Marlborough, 52 Henry III, from Coke, *4th Inst.*

f. 261. Letters Patent for Sweteman, the Jew of Winchester, 20 July 1269.

f. 262. Like for clergy of Bishoprics of Lincoln and Norwich, 14 July 1269.

f. 263. Like (French), 53 Henry III.

f. 265. Parliament, London, 53 Henry III. Letters Patent, 21 June 1269, with note from Close Roll, 3 Edward I.

f. 266. Pleas of Juries and Assizes, 53 Henry III, co. Cambridge. Letter of Gilbert de Clare, Earl of Gloucester and Hertford, concerning Lady Dionisia de Monte Casino, 7 February 1269.

f. 268. Writs to Barons for Richard de Monet; for Hugh de Balliol; on grange of John de Padham; for King; Philip de Aulton; Poncio de la More; Prior of Braxton; from K.R. Mem. Roll, Comm., Mich., 53–4 Henry III.

f. 271. Mainprise of Robert de Ferrers, Earl of Derby, 53 Henry III, from Close Roll.

f. 271v. Provision for Jews, same.

f. 272. Letters Patent on Jews, 20 July 1269.

f. 273. As f. 271v above.

f. 275. Mandate to Justices in Eyre to put in respite, 24 April 1269.

f. 276. Like on inquisition between Abbots of Bury and Crowland, 30 July 1269.

f. 277. Letters Patent for Steward and Marshal of King's Household, 25 March 1269.

f. 279. Charter, inspeximus for Abbot of Cluny, 26 February 1270.

f. 283. Writs on commissions on various cos. and castles, 3 June 1270, from Fine Roll.

f. 286. Mandate to taxors of 20th, co. Dorset, 14 December 1269.

f. 287. Letter to Llewelyn ap Gruffydd, 16 October 1270, from Close Roll.

f. 290. As f. 286 above.

f. 291. Mandate against the Jews, 14 May 1270.

f. 293. Like to Llewelyn ap Gruffydd, Prince of Wales, 24 August 1270.

f. 295. Letters Patent to Master John de Chishill, Dean of St. Paul's, on state of Exchequer, 12 February 1270.

f. 298. Grant of 20th, Holy Land, Parliament, 54 Henry III. Letters Patent, sign of Cross, Prince Edward, 4 August 1270, with note from Lib. de Antiq. Leg. in Archives of city of London.

f. 301. Extract from Chron. of T. Wykes, on translation of Edward the Confessor, 54 Henry III.

f. 304. Letters Patent for John de Warenne, Earl of Surrey, 4 August 1270.

f. 305. As f. 286 above.

f. 307. Writs for Barons for Philip de Champnent and Robert de Waleyns; Henry de Stanhow; Prioress of Wroxhall; Robert de Timberhough; Abbot of Waltham; from K.R. Mem. Roll, Comm., Hil., East. 54 Henry III.

f. 309. Letters Patent for preservation of peace, 18 March 1271.

f. 311. Like on Jews, 26 October 1271.

f. 312. Writ to collectors of 20th, co. Wilts., 28 January 1270, from Reg. of Malmesbury in poss. of Evan Seys, Serjeant at Law.

f. 313. Mandate to Sheriff of Lincs., 28 July 1271.

f. 314. Like to Pontius de Mora on market of St. Botolph, 18 August 1272.

f. 315. Like to Sheriff of Suss. to assign £100 to Queen Eleanor, Consort, for her expenses, 15 August 1272.

f. 316. Note from Close Roll, 9 Edward II, not to take assizes during Parliament.

f. 317. Memorandum, Keeper of lands of John de Grey, 5 January 1272, from Patent Roll.

f. 318. As f. 312 above.

f. 319. Mandate to Ralph, Preceptor of New Temple, London, 25 March 1272.

f. 320. Like against outlaws in cos. Notts., Leics., and Derby, 11 February 1272.

f. 322. Like to Gilbert de Clare, Earl of Gloucester, on dispute with Llewelyn ap Gruffydd on castle of Caerphilly (French), 56 Henry III.

f. 324. Letters Patent on wards and escheats, 11 February 1272.

f. 325. As f. 320 above.

f. 327. Like against those who attack monks of Priory of Norwich, 6 September 1272.

f. 329. Like for Thomas, Abbot of Selby, 23 February 1272.

f. 330. Like against Jews, 18 April 1272.

f. 331. As f. 317 above.

Mandate to Ralph de Hengham, etc., Justices in Eyre, for Roger Mortimer, 17 September 1272.

VOLUME 8

A volume of transcripts etc. from the Public Records and other sources, 1–56 Henry III etc. On flyleaf: Parliamenta tempore H. 3. Pars 1a et 2da. 310 ff.

f. 1. On election and coronation of Henry, son of King John, with references to Wendover and Knighton.

f. 4. On the coronation of Henry III at Gloucester and the state of Ireland. Mandate to John de Marisco, Justice of Ireland, 1 Henry III, with note from Patent Roll, 1 Henry III.

f. 7. The Second Coronation of Henry III at Westminster, 4 Henry III, from (Domitian) A. 10, Letters Patent to Barons of London, 4 October 1217.

f. 9. Letters Patent of safe conduct to Hugh de Lacy, 18 November 1216.

f. 10. Mandate to Sheriffs on Magna Carta and Charter of Forests, 22 February 1217.

f. 11. Like on proclamation of charters, 7 July 1225.

f. 14. Extracts from Walter of Coventry, Matt. Paris and Stat. 25 Edward I, on charters, 9 Henry III.

f. 17. Extract from Matt. Paris on confirmation of charters. 7 or 8 Henry III.

f. 18. Writ to Barons of London, 22 December 1226, from Laud. Brit. in Archives of city of London.

f. 20. Exemplars of Magna Carta and Charter of Forests, 9 Henry III, agreeing with original charter in possession of Sir Nathaniel Powell, bart., Treasurer of Inner Temple, London, 1672, but not arranged in chapters as in the manuscript, 11 February 1225.

f. 29. Transcript of Charter of Forests, 11 February 1225, from Stat. Roll, 25 Edward I.

f. 37. On the custody of Eleanor, sister of Arthur, Duke of Britanny, in castle of Bristol. Mandate to William Talbot etc. 6 May 1234.

f. 39. Mandate on marriage of Queen, 15 October 1235.

f. 41v. Letters Patent to John, son of Philip etc. 11 October 1235.

f. 42. Writ to Hugh of Northwood, Bishop of Ely, and Ralph Maidstone, Bishop of Hereford, 19 December 1235.

f. 43. Writ of summons to Eyre, co. Surrey, 24 January 1229.

f. 45. Of the reading in full County Court of Magna Carta and Charter of Forests

21 Henry III. Charter of Liberties, 28 January 1237, from Charter Roll. Mandates to Sheriffs, 26 March etc. 1237.

f. 53. Extract from Matt. Paris, 28 Henry III, on summons of magnates to London on liberties.

f. 61. Mandates to Sheriffs, 15 April 1244.

f. 63. Council of Barons, Westminster, 29 Henry III, on papal exactions, with references to Matt. Paris, Ann. of Burton, insertion in Cleopatra E. 1., Close Roll, 29 Henry III, Camden, *Brit.*, Selden, *Tit. of Hon.*

f. 71. Mandate to Abbot of St. Edmund's, 29 Henry III.

f. 72. As f. 53 above.

f. 79. Another Council of the Baronage, 30 Henry III, Articles of Grievances, from insertion in Cleopatra E. 1.

f. 84. Another Council of the Baronage, Westminster, 30 Henry III, with references to Cleopatra E. 1., Matt. Paris, *Plac. Parl.*, Liber F in Archives of city of London, Fox, *Acts*, Roman Roll, 17 Edward III.

f. 87. Mandate on reversal of outlawry of William de Hastingcote, 16 February 1248.

f. 89. Mandates to Sheriffs on keeping Magna Carta, 23 May 1255.

f. 90. Of the Common Council of the Realm, Law and Custom, t. Henry III, certain writs formed, granted and approved, with references to Bracton, Spelman, *Gloss.*

f. 92. Extract from Ann. of Burton, 36 Henry III, Grievances, Pope and King, with note from Close Roll, 3 Edward II.

f. 94. On sentence of excommunication pronounced in Great Hall, Westminster, against transgressors of liberties of church, 37 Henry III, with references to Matt. Paris, Fleta, Matt. of West., Patent Roll, 37 Henry III with, notes from Close Roll, 49 Henry III, Lib. de Antiq. Leg. and Liber D in Archives of city of London.

f. 104. Of the Great Parliament, London, 39 Henry III, with references to Matt. Paris, Coke, *2nd Inst.*, Camden, *Brit.*, Mills, *De Nob. Polit. Civ.*, Chasney, *Cat. Glor. Mundi.* Ann. of Burton.

f. 111. Letters Patent, 18 May 1254.

f. 113. Marriage of Edward, the King's son, with Eleanor, sister of King of Castile. Letters Patent appointing proctors, 23 July 1254. Letters Patent on contract of marriage, 23 July 1254.

f. 117v. Letters Patent on Magna Carta, 24 March 1254.

f. 118. As f. 104 above.

f. 123. Of two Parliaments, Westminster, 40 and 41 Henry III, on matters of Sicily and Apulia, with references to Ann. of Burton and Patent Roll, 42 Henry III.

f. 126. Mandate to Robert de Cambhou etc. 4 November 1257.

f. 128. Like to King of Almain, 4 November 1257.

f. 129. Letters Patent to same, 22 January 1259.

f. 131. Of Parliament, Great Hall, Westminster, 43 Henry III, with references to Liber D and Lib. de Antiq. Leg. in Archives of city of London.

f. 133. On truces made in Parliament, Oxford. Letters Patent to Llewelyn ap Gruffydd, 20 July 1260.

f. 134. Mandates to Sheriffs on 3 knights from each county, 11 September 1261.

f. 136. General Proclamation that King did not intend to subvert rights and customs. Letters Patent, 5 August 1261.

f. 141. On arbitration of King of France, 46 Henry III, from Lib. de Antiq. Leg. and Liber D in Archives of city of London.

f. 145. Another proclamation against undue and unaccustomed tallages. Letters Patent, 20 December 1263.

f. 150. Mandate on foreigners, 20 August 1264.

f. 152. Letters Patent, 18 October 1264.

f. 155. Letter to King of France, 2 August 1264, from Close Roll.

f. 156v. Mandates to Archbishop of Canterbury and others, 4 August 1264.

f. 158. Confederation, London, 48 Henry III, between Simon de Montfort and London (French), from Lib. de Antiq. Leg. in Archives of city of London.

f. 160. Parliament, London, 48 Henry III, form of peace between King and Barons, June 1264. Letters Patent.

f. 166. Letters Patent to Roger de Clifford, 3 June 1259.

f. 168. Writs of summons to Parliament, 14 December 1264. Lists.

f. 179. Mandate to Simon Walton, Bishop of Norwich, 26 December 1264.

f. 181. Writ de expensis, Parliament, London, 15 February 1265.

f. 182. Mandate, 2 knights, 25 February 1265.

f. 192. More on Parliament, 49 Henry III, with reference to Lib. de Antiq. Leg.

f. 197. Parliament, London, Oct. of Hil., 29 Henry III. Charter, Form of Peace, like from Close Roll.

f. 202v. On the sanctity of the authority of Magna Carta, with references to Matt. Paris, Exodus, Stat. 25 Edward I, Selden, *De Syn.*, Close Roll, 10 Edward II, Parl. Roll, 15 Edward III, *Pupilla Oculi*, Tacitas.

f. 207. As f. 197 above.

f. 219. On the new war arisen in the Kingdom after Parliament, 49 Henry III, together with the writs of proclamation for suppression of insurrection, from Patent Roll, 49 Henry III, Extracts, 45–9 Henry III and Ann. of Waverley.

f. 224. Inquisition at Leverfield, de rebellibus, taken after the Battle of Evesham, 49 Henry III.

f. 226. The King at request of Ottobon summoned Parliament at Kenilworth in which the Dictum of Kenilworth was ordained, from Patent Roll, 50 Henry III, with note from Matt. Paris.

f. 229. Writ of proclamation that Magna Carta should be inviolably observed, 50 Henry III. Mandate, 3 May 1266.

f. 232. Parliament, 51 Henry III. Letters Patent for city of London, with references to Close Roll, 51 Henry III and Patent Roll, 51 Henry III.

f. 234. 28 Edward I, the King at Berwick sent to John de Langton, Chancellor, privy seal on summons to Parliament, 29 December 1300, from New Bundle of Miscellanea.

f. 239. Letter to King of France, 20 September 1268, from Close Roll, with note from du Fresne, *Gloss.*

f. 241. Stat. of Marlborough, 52 Henry III, with references to Coke, *2nd Inst.*, Patent Roll, 7 Edward I, like, 11 Edward III, Year Book, East. term, 39 Edward III, Close Roll, 1 Richard II.

f. 247. 53 Henry III, Parliament, London, Letters Patent, 21 June 1269.

f. 248. Extract from Thomas Wykes, subsidy, 20th Holy Land etc. 54 Henry III.

f. 252. Letters Patent, Cross taken by Prince Edward, 4 August 1270, with note from Lib de Antiq. Leg.

f. 253. Letters Patent on protection and safe conduct for Henry de Borham, 2 May 1270.

f. 253v. Mandate on assize of bread, 28 July 1271.

f. 256. Writ of summons to Parliament, 10 October 1272.

f. 257. Mandate of supersedeas to Ralph de Hengham etc., Justices in Eyre, co. Salop, 17 September 1272.

f. 259. Writ from Bundle of Letters and Writs, 10 Edward II, with note from Prynne, *Records*, III, Close Roll, 8 Edward II, like 9 Edward II and Parl. Roll, 2 Henry V.

f. 262. Of death of Henry III and what happened thereafter, from Matt. Paris and Ann. of Waverley.

f. 265. Letters Patent to Maurice, son of Maurice, Justiciar of Ireland, 7 December 1272.

f. 266. Like on fealty, Archbishops etc. of Ireland, 7 December 1272.

f. 268. Mandate to proclaim the King's peace, 23 November 1272.

f. 272. On protection for those who had taken the Cross and were setting out for the Holy Land, with catalogue of their names (178 names), 19 October 1270 etc. 12 January 1271 (44 names).

f. 289. 'Mr. Selden's confutation of Mr. Camden's Old Authors Relations concerning the exclusion of some earls and barons from our ancient Parliaments and also his complaint of the loss of our Parliamentary records'. Selden, *Tit. of Hon.*, Camden, *Apologia* and *Brit.*

f. 294. Of the time of general prescription according to the law and custom of England, with references to Parl. Roll, 43 Edward III, Year Book, Trin. term, 12 Edward II, Rolle, *Abridg.*

f. 296. Of the deplorable loss of Parliamentary Records: (1) summons to Parliament (2) Parliament Rolls (3) Statute Rolls, with references to Selden, *Tit. of Hon.*, Stat. Roll, Edward I, Rastell, *Stat.*, Prynne, Preface to Cotton, *Records*, *Plac. Parl.*

f. 301. On the significance of the word Parliamentum, with references to Spelman, *Gloss.*, du Fresne, *Gloss.*, Hotoman, *Franco Gallia*, Camden, *Brit.*, T. Smith, *De republ. Angl.*, Plowden, *Comm.*

f. 308. On the word Parliamentum used both in England and Scotland, Close Roll, 42 Henry III, with note that it agrees with record, Geo. Holmes, Tho. Jenkinson.

VOLUME 9

A volume of transcripts from the Public Records and other sources, 1–56 Henry III. On flyleaf: Several writs, records, commissions, patents, grants, summonses and transcripts in Parliament and elsewhere in the reign of Henry III. 190 ff.

f. 1. Letters Patent of absolution to be made to some of the barons, 1 Henry III.

Like granting benefit of Magna Carta to Ireland, 7 February 1226.

f. 3. Like granting Baldwin de Insula first marriage to come to King's hands, 16 January 1217.

Like to Philip Mant, 16 January 1217.

f. 3v. Like of safe conduct for Hugh de Lacy, 18 November 1216.

f. 5. Extract concerning grant and confirmation of Magna Carta, 6 November 1217, from MS. in poss. of William Pierpont, the confirmation of 28 Edward I, 8 March 1300, grants of subsidy of 2 and 9 Henry III.

f. 7. Mandates on Justices Itinerant, 2, 5, 10, 45 Henry III.

f. 7v. Mandate on reading and observance of Magna Carta, 22 February 1218.

f. 8v. Mandate to Sheriff of Oxf., 30 October 1217.

f. 9. Letters Patent on limitation of grants to King's minority, 3 Henry III.

f. 9v. Like for Peter de Mauley, 22 April 1219.

f. 13. Mandate to Sheriff of Surr. on carucages, 7 September 1220.

f. 13v. Like to Sheriff of Northants on assize, 19 October 1220.

f. 14. Like to same on carucage, 9 August 1220.

f. 15. Like to G( ), Viscount le Mans, 7 September 1220.

f. 17. Like to Sheriff of Essex and Hertf. for Robert fitz Walter, 24 November 1220.

Like to Sheriff of Cornwall for William Brewer, 15 May 1221.

f. 17v. Like to Sheriff of Northants for Richard Snard, 9 February 1221.

f. 18. Like to Sheriff of Westmorland on castle of Cockermouth, 3 February 1221.

f. 18v. Like to Mayor and Sheriffs of London on aid debt, 11 June 1221.

f. 19. Like to Sheriffs of Yorks. etc. on aid, Holy Land, 26 June 1222.

f. 21. Like to Sheriffs on making half pence and farthings current, 20 February 1222.

f. 21v. Like to Sheriff of Essex on appointment of verderers, April 1222.

f. 22. Like to Sheriffs on demesnes, manor of Somerton etc., 24 January 1222, from Fine Roll.

f. 22v. Letters Patent on pardon of outlawry, Richard de Sherbiry, 7 July 1322.

Mandates on inquisitions on King's liberties, 9 April 1223.

f. 23v. Like on liberties and customs, 30 January 1223.

f. 25. Like on aid, Holy Land, 24 November 1222.

f. 26. Like to Sheriff of Norf. and Suff. not to molest men of Bishop of Ely, 2 November 1222.

f. 27. Like to Bailiffs of Gloucester etc. on aid, Holy Land, 7 Henry III.

f. 29. Fines, tallage of King's demesnes, in cos. 7 Henry III, from Fine Roll.

f. 31. Fines, pleas of forest, 26 October 1224, from same.

f. 31v. Mandate to Constable of Marlborough on suits at hundred of Selkell, 21 March 1224.

f. 33. Like to Bishop of Durham, 23 May 1225.

f. 33v. Like on 15th, 14 May 1225.

f. 35. Letters Patent on form of assessing and collecting 15th, 15 February 1225.
f. 39. Like to Justices on 15th, 16 February, 29 March 1225.
f. 41. Mandates to choose 4 knights, 8 August 1227.
f. 42. Like for men of Wilton, 16 July 1227.
Like to Barons of Cinque Ports, 22 December 1226.
f. 43. Like to Sheriff of Northants, 21 January 1227.
Like on tallage of King's demesnes, 30 January 1227.
f. 45. Like on observing laws and customs in Ireland, 8 March 1228
f. 47. Charter for burgesses of Stafford, 11 April 1228.
Charter on Justiciar of England and castles of Dover etc. 27 April 1228.
f. 49. Mandates to Robert de Insula, Justice of Forests etc. 15 December 1229.
f. 50. Like on recrossing to Ireland, 14 Henry III.
f. 50v. Like to Dean and Chapter of York etc. 2 November 1229.
Like to Sheriff of Kent on malefactors, 15 Henry III.
f. 53. Letters Patent on custody of land of England, 28 April 1230.
f. 55. Mandate to Abbot of Snelshall, 8 June 1231.
f. 56. Extract from Matt. Paris, 16 Henry III, 1232.
f. 57. Letters Patent concerning Ireland, 28 October 1233.
f. 57v. Mandate to Justices in Eyre, co. Lincs., 11 October 1234.
f. 58. Like to Constable of castle of Wallingford, 6 September 1234.
f. 59. Like to Sheriff of Somerset, 17 July 1235.
f. 59v. Like to Sheriff of Lincs., 24 August 1235.
f. 60v. Like to Robert de Langton, Archdeacon of Canterbury, 27 January 1235.
f. 63. Like to Sheriff of Suss. on aid, 10 July 1235, Henry III.
f. 63v. Like notifying marriage of King to Eleanor, 19 Henry III.
f. 64. Mandate to Justices in Eyre, co. Lincs., 12 October 1235.
f. 65. Letters Patent on ecclesiastical aid, 4 May 1236.
f. 65v. Letters Patent to men of Peak, 20 Henry III.
f. 66. Like on ecclesiastical aid, 2 May 1236.
Like on collectors of 15th in North Riding, 25 September 1236.
f. 67. Mandates of general 30th, 2 July 1236.
f. 69. Charter on Magna Carta, 28 January 1236.
f. 71. Mandate to Abbot of Cluny on 30th, 22 Henry III.
f. 73. Letters Patent (French), 24 Henry III.
f. 75. Like on subsidy, 8 April 1242.
f. 77. Like on safe conduct, Scotland, 6 August 1244.
f. 79. Mandates to Sheriffs, 16 February 1244.
f. 79v. Like, 28 January 1244.
f. 81. Memorandum on Parliament, 3 weeks of East., from Patent Roll, 28 Henry III.
f. 83. Mandate to Abbot of St. Edmund's, 29 Henry III.

f. 85. Letters to Pope, 1246, from Close Roll.

f. 86. Mandate of pardon to summons of Exchequer for Robert de Monte Alto, 25 April 1246.

f. 87. Like on one year's fruits, 32 Henry III.

f. 89. Letters Patent on assessment of tallage, co. Chester, 3 August 1249.

Like to Sheriff of Norf. on manor of Hengham, 18 December 1248.

f. 91. Mandate on amercement, co. Wilts., 28 July 1250.

f. 93. Like on 2 homages, 17 August 1250.

Like to Justice of Chester, 34 Henry III.

Like for Robert, son of Reginald, 30 January 1251.

f. 95. Letters Patent, form of peace, Bordeaux, 18 January 1251.

f. 97. Charter for Edmund de Lacy, 28 April 1251.

f. 99. Letters Patent on Gascony, 8 June 1252.

f. 101. Mandate on Archenfeld, 36 Henry III.

f. 103. Letters Patent for Simon de Montfort, same.

f. 105. Like on liberties etc. 37 Henry III.

f. 106. Like on aid for King's crossing, 28 May 1253.

f. 107. Like on Ireland, 5 May 1253.

f. 108. Mandates to John de Catesden etc. 24 July 1253.

f. 108v. Memorandum on crossing to Gascony, from Close Roll, 27 Henry III.

f. 111. Mandate to Sheriff of Yorks., 30 November 1253.

Like on amending money, Scotland, 1 November 1253.

f. 111v. Like on respite for Roger de Burghill, like for Peter de Goldington, 38 Henry III.

Like for Edward Vyson, 30 August 1254.

f. 113. Letters Patent on oath, marriage of Prince Edward to Eleanor of Castile, 38 Henry III.

f. 113v. Like on King's business in Ireland, 10 December 1253.

f. 115. Mandates to Sheriffs, 11 February 1254.

f. 119. Like for Prince Edward, tallage of Stamford and Gorham, 39 Henry III.

Like on tallage, 14 February 1255.

f. 121. Letters Patent for King's eldest son, 40 Henry III.

f. 122. Mandate not to distrain John de Elek, 47 Henry III.

f. 123. Like to Mayor and Sheriffs of London, 42 Henry III.

f. 124. Like on inquisition on grievances, 4 August 1258.

f. 126. Letters Patent for King and Baronage of England, 7 May 1258.

f. 126v. Like concerning Robert Walerand, 42 Henry III.

f. 127v. Like to John Mansel, Treasurer of York etc. 42 Henry III.

f. 129. The form of oath of keepers of castles (French), from Patent Roll, 42 Henry III.

f. 132. Roll of Parliament, 42 Henry III, at Oxford, abridged by Mr. Selden out of the original roll which he borrowed from Sir Edward Coke (French).

f. 136. Letters Patent to Sheriffs, 5 August 1261.

f. 140. Like for the magnates of England, 15 September 1263.

Like for Nicholas, Archdeacon of Ely, 8 October 1263.

f. 140v. Like for Mayor and Sheriffs of London, 17 September 1263.

f. 142. Like for Adam de Novo Mercato, 4 June 1264.

f. 143. Mandate to Sheriff of Essex and Keepers of Peace, 7 August 1264.

Mandate, 19 October 1264.

f. 144. Letters Patent, 27 January 1264.

f. 146. Memorandum (French) from Patent Roll, 48 Henry III.

f. 148. Mandate to Sheriff of Southampton, 3 April 1264.

f. 150. Letters Patent to Simon de Montfort etc. 13 September 1263.

f. 152. Like to Roger le Bigod on preservation of peace, 8 July 1264.

f. 152v. Like to Roger Clifford etc. 3 July 1264.

f. 153. Like cos. Warw. and Leics., 20 August 1264.

f. 154. Like, 28 Henry III.

f. 155. Memorandum, Patent Roll, 48 Henry III.

f. 156. Form of peace, in Parliament, London, June 1264, from Patent Roll.

f. 157v. Letters Patent to Sheriff of Cambridge and Hunts., 48 Henry III.

f. 159. Like, Ireland, same.

f. 160. Mandate to Sheriff of Yorks., 15 February 1265.

f. 162. Letters Patent to Bishop of London, 8 June 1265.

f. 164. Mandate to Sheriff of Essex, 15 October 1265.

Like to Sheriff of Salop and Staffs., 23 February 1265.

f. 166. Letters Patent to co. Lancs., 8 June 1265.

f. 166v. Like on appointing knights, cos. Warw. and Leics., 21 September 1265.

f. 168. Mandates to Sheriffs of Yorks., etc. 20 December 1265.

f. 170. Letters Patent for Henry, son of King of Almain etc. 50 Henry III.

f. 172. Like (French), 31 August 1266.

f. 174. Like, aid, cos. Cambridge and Hunts., 21 November 1267.

f. 176. Like for John, son of Alan of Arundel, 2 April 1269.

f. 179. Grant of Robert de Ferrers, Earl of Derby, from Close Roll, 53 Henry III.

f. 181. Letters Patent for city of London, 27 February 1270.

f. 183. Like for Prince Edward, 4 August 1270.

f. 185. Like to Abbot of Agen, 55 Henry III.

Like for Bailiff of Yarmouth, 24 March 1271.

f. 187. Like on measure of bushels, etc. 56 Henry III.

f. 189. Mandate to Sheriff of Southampton, 3 April ( )

f. 190. Like to Mayor etc. of Norwich, 26 February ( ).

VOLUME 10

A volume of transcripts etc. from the Public Records and other sources, t. Henry III. On flyleaf: The rights of the Commons in Parliament by Prescription. On another flyleaf:

Antiquata usu qui volvunt
Hi quod in his labor est et sine fruge sciunt. 145 ff.

f. 1. Grant and confirmation of Magna Carta and Charter of Forests, 9 Henry III, at Westminster, with references to Vitellius E. 13, Walter of Coventry, Confirmatio Cartarum, Matt. Paris, Stat., 25 Edward I., certiorari of trespass, Bishop of Winchester and John Giffard, 3 Richard II, on disafforestation, Harpsfield, *Hist. Anglicana*, Spelman, *Gloss.*

f. 7. On the Common Council, writ, with references to Bracton, Spelman, *Gloss.*

f. 9. On the authority of the Council of the whole Realm, mandate, 26 June 1243.

f. 10x. Sentence of excommunication promulgated in the Great Parliament, London, on transgressors of Magna Carta, 37 Henry III. Notes from Fleta, Matt. Paris, Selden, *Syn.*, Close Roll, 49 Henry III, Stat., 25 Edward I, Statute de Tallagio non concedendo, 34 Edward I, as printed in Coke, *2nd Inst.*, Parl. Roll, 6 Edward III, Rastell, *Stat.*

f. 16. Parliament at London, 38 Henry III, on the business of the Cross or Holy Land, Letters Patent, 17 May 1254.

f. 18. 38 Henry III. Edward, the King's eldest son and heir, contracted marriage with Eleanor, sister of the King of Castile, 23 July 1254.

f. 23. Extracts from Ann. of Burton on Parliament, Westminster, after Mich. 1255, 39 Henry III.

f. 25. 42 Henry III. Parliament, Oxford, Letters Patent (French), with translation, with note on making of inquisitions.

f. 29. Parliament, London, Quinden of St. John the Baptist, 44 Henry III, to treat of arduous and urgent business of the realm. Letters Patent, 30 July 1260.

f. 32. 44 Henry III, the great and long Parliament in the Great Hall, Westminster, from Liber D in Archives of city of London, with reference to Lib. de Antiq. Leg.

f. 34. Confederation between Simon de Montfort and the Mayor etc. of London, 48 Henry III (French), from Lib. de Antiq. Leg.

f. 36. Writ of summons to Parliament, 49 Henry III, with catalogue of names of those who were specially summoned, 14 December 1264, 20 January 1265, with notes from Patent Roll, 26 Edward III, Close Rolls, 28 Edward I, 29 Edward I, Coke, *2nd Inst.*

f. 62. On the various Councils of the time of Henry III (1) on Parliament (2) on Curia Regis (3) of King and Council (4) of whole Council, Mandate on Peter of Savoy etc., 19 March 1265.

f. 63. Of the famous Parliament, London, 49 Henry III, Charter Roll, 49 Henry III, with note from Selden, *Syn.*, and extracts from Lib. de Antiq. Leg., Claudius D. 2, charter in which the King granted that 3 men should choose his ministers etc., 14 March 1265, the charter which the King made to his Barons after the disturbance of his realm, 14 November 1265, letter of Prince Edward, London, 10 March 1265, and note from Ann. Acephali, Otho, B. 3.

f. 92. On the escape of Prince Edward from his keepers in Wales, 8 June 1265. Letters Patent etc.

f. 100. The Barons having been overcome at Evesham, Henry III called Parliament at Winchester, 49 Henry III, which decreed that it should be enquired into concerning the King's adversaries, Inquisitions de Rebellibus, 49 Henry III.

f. 102. 50 Henry III. At the request of Ottobon the King summoned Parliament at Kenilworth, at which the Dictum of Kenilworth was ordained, 31 August 1266, from Patent Roll, with note from Matt. Paris.

f. 105. Letters of excuse. Mandate to Sheriff of York to proclaim, 3 May 1266.

f. 107. 51 Henry III. Pardon in Parliament to Gilbert de Clare, Earl of Gloucester, and others, 5 June 1267 (French), from Patent Roll, with references to Close Roll, 51 Henry III, Patent Roll, 7 Edward II, 12 Edward II, 15 Edward II, Stat. 15 Edward II, Close Roll, 1 Edward III.

f. 114. General Pardon granted to the city of London, 51 Henry III, 16 June 1267, from Patent Roll, with notes from Close Roll, 51 Henry III, Patent Roll, 7 Edward II, Plac. coram Rege, Trin. term, 12 Edward II.

f. 117. Stat. of Marlborough agreed and ordained, 52 Henry III, with note Coke, *2nd Inst.*, and translation Rastell, *Stat.*

f. 122. 52 Henry III. Parliament, London, Quindene Mich., or general plea about the cause of the business of the Cross. Letter to King of France, 20 September 1268, from Close Roll, with note from du Fresne, *Gloss.*

f. 126. Concerning protections for those who took the Cross, 54 Henry III, with catalogue of names, 20 October 1270 etc., from Patent Roll.

f. 139. On the protection and safe conduct granted Henry de Boreham and others going to Parliament, 54 Henry III, 2 May 1270, from Patent Roll.
Mandate on assize of bread, 28 July 1271.

f. 141. 56 Henry III. Writ of supersedeas to the Justices in Eyre, co. Salop. Similar writs of supersedeas were granted during Parliament in the times of Edward I and Edward II as follows: 17 September 1262, from Bundle of Writs 10 Edward I (Prynne, *Records*, III), 9 Edward II, Parl. Roll, 5 Henry V, with translation.

VOLUME II

A volume of transcripts from the Public Records and other sources, 1–29 Edward I. On flyleaf: Recorda Anno 1 usque 30 Edward I. On another flyleaf: Several writs, records, commissions, summonses, and transactions in Parliament and other courts from the first unto the 30th year of King Edward the First. 454 ff.

f. 1. Extract from Ann. Hibern. at end of Camden, *Brit.*, 1272.

f. 3. Mandate for proclamation of King's peace, 23 November 1272.

f. 3v. Letters Patent on preservation of King's peace in Ireland, 7 December 1272.

f. 4. Like on Archbishops of Ireland etc., making fealty, 7 December 1272.

f. 5. Prohibition of Prior of St. Mary de Pratis, Leicester, from Common Plea Roll, Mich. term, 2 Edward I. Writ on alienation of barony of Ralph de Valle Torta, 2 Edward I, Brevia emissa pro Rege, East. term.

f. 7. Mandate to Geoffrey de Genville, Justice of Ireland, on retaining liberties in King's hands, 11 October 1274, with memorandum on King's coronation.

f. 9. Writ to Barons of Exchequer for Archbishop of Canterbury, 28 November 1273; like for William Tryvet, from K.R. Mem. Roll, Brev. dir. Bar., Mich., 2 Edward I.

f. 11. Extract from Hundred Roll, Brockleston, co. Notts., 3 Edward I.

f. 13. Plea, Common Plea Roll, Hil. term, 3 Edward I, ne injuste vexes, carucate. Like, East. term.

f. 14. Letters Patent to co. Chester, 3 November 1275.

f. 15. Letter to Pope, 19 January 1275, from Close Roll.

f. 17. Form of taxation and levying 25th (French); Devon, on relief of William Martin, from K.R. Mem. Roll, Comm., Mich., 3 Edward I.

f. 21. Mandate on Llewelyn ap Gruffydd, 4 Edward I.

f. 25. Letters Patent on 15th, co. Chester, 3 November 1275.

f. 27. Like for Abbot of Beaulieu, 24 July 1275.

f. 29. Charter for Robert de Veteri Ponte, 28 October 1203, from K.R. Mem. Roll, Comm., Trin., 4 Edward I.

f. 31. Barons of Exchequer for Robert Marmion, from same, East., 4 Edward I; for Master Henry de Bray, 18 June 1276, from same, Trin.

f. 33. Extract from Common Plea Roll, 4 Edward I, bastard.

f. 33v. Mandate to Sheriff of Norf. for citizens of Norwich; mainprise for Henry de Kirkby in Normanton; to Barons of Exchequer for John de Vernon; for Oliver, son and heir of Nigel de Langford; relief, from K.R. Mem. Roll, Comm., Mich., 4–5 Edward I.

f. 35. On mainprise of Henry de Kirkby in Normanton; co. Lincs., William son of Henry, made fine with Richard I for 100 marks; co. Norf., Barony, Robert Novel; co. Glouc., Godfrey Giffard, Bishop of Worcester; co. Oxf. recognizance of Walter de Huntercombe; like of John le Blund, from K.R. Mem. Roll, Comm., Mich., 4–5 Edward I.

f. 37. Writ for Elias de Rabyn, 28 May 1277; Charter of John de Heham, n.d. from same, East.

f. 39. Mandate on those who owe service in army of Wales, 12 December 1277.

Like on proctors of Mayor etc. of Bayonne, 8 October 1276.

f. 41. Extract from Common Plea Roll, Hil. term, 5 Edward I, on posse Comitatus, amercement, sheriff, sheriff's return; like East. term, on prohibition, contempt, law.

f. 42. Recognizance of Roger le Bigod, Earl of Norfolk and Marshal of England, from K.R. Mem. Roll, Recog., Hil., 5 Edward I; Precepta, cos. Cumberl., Norf., Suff. etc., from same. Prec.

f. 42v. Extract from Scutage Roll, Cumberland, 5 Edward I.

f. 43. Mandates to Robert de Retford etc. 12 September 1277.

f. 45. Letters Patent for communities, cos. Salop and Heref., 6 February 1277. Recognizances of John de Burgo, Ralph de Beauchamp, kt., Robert de Ver, Earl of Oxford, from K.R. Mem. Roll, Recog., Hil., 5 Edward I.

f. 45v. Letters Patent for Ireland, 10 June 1277.

Letters Patent for Edmund, son of Edmund, late Earl of Kent, and Margaret his wife (French), 8 February 1331.

f. 53. Mandate on salaries of Justices, King's Bench, Common Pleas and in Eyre, 6 Edward I.

f. 53v. Form of militia, 26 June 1278, from Close Roll.

f. 55. Letters to Alexander, King of Scotland, 6 Edward I, from same.

f. 57. Extract from Common Plea Roll, Mich. term, 6 Edward I, on monstraverunt.

f. 59. Like, Hil. term, 7 Edward I, on sub custodia etc., extorcio, defamation, Court Baron, assent, droit, Grand Assize, villein, merchet.

f. 61. Like, Trin. term, on sub custodia etc., common etc.

f. 63. Like, Mich. term, on limitation, sub custodia etc., bastardy, garde, Ireland, trial.

f. 67. Extract from Pleas of Juries and Assizes, 7 Edward I, on sub custodia etc.

f. 68. Charter, 8 September 1333, from MS. Book of Abbey of Melrose.

f. 69. Bull of Innocent VI on conservation of Cistercian Order in England, 12 May 1353.

f. 70. Extract from Common Plea Roll, East. term, 8 Edward I, on William, son of Henry, monstraverunt, Domesday Book, ancient demesne, justicies.

f. 72. Like, East. term, on canon, quare nuper.

f. 86. Plea at Cirencester between Abbot William and burgesses of town of Malmesbury, 10 Edward I, from Reg. of Malmesbury in poss. of Evan Seys, Serjeant at Law.

f. 87v. Allowance made to Robert Burnell, Bishop of Bath and Wells, from K.R. Mem Roll, Comm., East., 10 Edward I.

f. 88. Extract from Common Plea Roll, East. term., 10 Edward I, on sub custodia etc., judgement, impeachment, common notary, ut attachet, ley, tabellio, premunire.

f. 90. Writ to Barons of Exchequer on proof of age of John de Hastings, from K.R. Mem. Roll, Comm., Trin., 11 Edward I.

f. 92. On removal of Gilbert de Corwen, Sheriff of Cam., and appointment of another in his place, from same, Commiss., East.

f. 93. Letters Patent that nothing should be attempted against the Crown in Convocation, 16 February 1283.

f. 94. Writ to Barons of Exchequer for John de Columbariis and Henry de Urtiaco, from K.R. Mem. Roll, Comm., East., 12 Edward I.

f. 96. Writ to same for Matthew de Knolle, 28 June 1284; for Abbot and Convent of Hayles and Peter Corbet, castle of Bere, 4 November 1284, from K.R. Mem. Roll, Mich.

f. 98. Recognizances of Henry de Stratton and Thomas Squier, Thomas de Clare, brother of Earl of Gloucester, Master John de Pontoise, Bishop of Winchester, Robert de Esthall, Richard de Burgo, Earl of Ulster, from same Recog.

f. 100. Recognizances of Philip de Montgomery, Prior of St. Swithin's, Winchester, Roger Mortimer, Walter de Beauchamp, from same, 13 Edward I.

f. 104. Oaths, cos. Oxf. and Salop, from same, Affid., Trin.

f. 106. Recognizance of Robert de Crecequer, from same, Recog., Trin.

f. 108. Mainprise of Robert de Rokby; on certain conspirators attached at Exchequer, mainprise of Sear de Huntingfeld etc.; on form in which Sheriff of Westmorland to be admitted at Exchequer; writs to Barons for John de Estington, Howel de Hampton etc.; William de Beauchamp, Earl of Warwick, Roger de Meules, John Lestrange; mainprise of Richard de Patton of Bristol etc; render co. Kent; writ to Barons for Alan de Plogenet; day given to

Roger de Eyly; like for Henry de Hadley; mainprises of John de Villa Mora, Richard de Wakefield, from same, Comm., Trin.

f. 116. Mandate for Reginald de Grey, 8 May 1285; like for Ralph de Vernon, 23 May 1285.

f. 116v. Letters Patent of exemplification for William de Ros and Margery his wife, 20 February 1285.

f. 124. Charter of Walter Wygton, n.d.; recognizance of Walter de Wynton; of Amery de St. Amando; writs to Barons for Geoffrey de Nevill, Simon de Thorp, William de Framlington; for King on 15th granted by clergy, like on 20th, from K.R. Mem. Roll, Comm., Hil., 13 Edward I.

f. 128. Writ to Barons for Jordan Godschep, from L.T.R. Mem. Roll, Comm., Hil., 14 Edward I.

f. 130. Writ to Barons for John de la Gerston; on delivery of Fleet Prison; writs to Barons for heirs of Hubert House, Edmund Mortimer; dispute between Robert Burnel, Bishop of Bath and Wells, and Simon de Insula; writing of Nicholas de Gardiniis; writ to Barons for Hugh de Rupibus; writings of John de Bohun, Thomas de Clare, Richard le Boteler, Robert de Muscgros; quit claim of manor of Wrocwardin by John Lestrange; writ to Barons for men of Henry de Perpunt and Annor, his wife, on manor of Sweynton; writing of Adam le Despenser, from K.R. Mem. Roll, Comm., Mich., 14 Edward I.

f. 140. Mainprise of William de Barnby; memorandum for King; writ to Barons for Master Perswall de Lavanne; on homage of Roger le Bigod, Earl of Norfolk; letter of John Bishop of Ely, from same, Hil.

f. 142. Writs to Barons for John de Bosco, Ralph Pipard, chaplains in chapel of Woodstock, Isabella de Grey, Philip Marmion; writing of Robert Burnel, Bishop of Bath and Wells; writ to barons for Abbot of Quarr, from same, East.

f. 146. Letters Patent for Eleanor, Queen of England, on lands and tenements for life, 23 January 1286.

f. 148. Thomas, Earl of Norfolk; writs to Barons for Owen, son of Gruffydd; Isabella Mortimer, from same, Mich.

f. 150. Extracts from Common Plea Roll, Mich., 14 Edward I, on sub custodia, prohibition, Statute of Marlborough.

f. 152. Extracts from same, East. term, on quare non admisit, procedendo, privy seal, distress.

f. 154. Extracts from same, Mich. term, on vouching to warranty, warranty, homage, collusion, voucher, Statute of Voucher.

f. 156. Statute of Nottingham, 17 Edward I, from MS. Stat. in poss. of (John) Peachey, of Inner Temple, esq.

f. 158. Extract from Chron., 1272–1307, in poss. of (blank) esq., 18 Edward I, with notes from Matt. Paris, Selden, *ad Fletam*, Fine Roll, 18 Edward I.

f. 162. Oath of Justices, from L.T.R. Mem. Roll, Comm., Hil., 18 Edward I.

f. 164. Extracts from Common Plea Roll, Mich. term, 18 Edward I, on auditores querelam, term, cornage, release, tenure.

f. 166. Charters of various liberties which various claim shown by them, 18 May 1290; annulment of fine between Matthew Shake and William de Wasthull, from L.T.R. Mem. Roll, Comm., Trin., 18 Edward I.

f. 168. On aid granted to King for marriage of eldest daughter, from same, East.

f. 168v. Mandate for Earl of Hereford and Essex, 13 February 1290.

f. 170. Extract from King's Bench Roll, Mich. term, 18 Edward I, John de Bosco.

f. 172. Mandate to Barons of Exchequer on Jews, 18 Edward I.

f. 172v. Writ on taxing 15th, 22 September 1290, from L.T.R. Mem. Roll, Comm., Mich., 19 Edward I.

f. 174. Bull of Nicholas II on marriage of heir of Scotland, 16 November 1289, from K.R. Mem. Roll, Comm., Mich., 18 Edward I.

f. 176. Form of 15th and oath of taxors, from L.T.R. Mem. Roll, Comm., Mich. 18–19 Edward I.

f. 180. Extract from Common Plea Roll, East. term, 19 Edward I, on sub custodia etc., thraves, expulsion.

f. 182. Like, Hil. term, 19 Edward I, on Richard de Belhouse, Kenilworth, merchet.

f. 184. Writ to Barons for King's seal for merchants in markets, 23 June 1291; recognizance of John de Beauchamp, kt., from K.R. Mem. Roll, Comm., Trin., 19 Edward I.

f. 186. Extract from Common Plea Roll, Trin. term, 19 Edward I, on sub custodia etc., affray, courts, deceipt, attorney, trial, fine.

f. 188. Writs to Barons for burgesses of Great Yarmouth, 23 November 1290, to Treasurer and Barons on usury, K.R. Mem. Roll, Comm., Mich., 19 Edward I.

f. 190. Writ on taxing of 15th, from same.

f. 192. Writ to Barons on debts of Thomas Dyvelston, 20 October 1291; for citizens of Cork in Ireland, 12 July 1291; mainprise of Matthew, son of John; writ for John de Merk, 26 October 1291; for William de Beauchamp, Earl of Warwick, 30 November 1291; for Richard de Harcourt, 1 December 1291; recognizances of Edmund Deyncourt, John de Segrave, William de Ros of Hamlak, from same.

f. 196. Extract from Common Plea Roll, Mich. term, 19 Edward I, on sub custodia etc., aid, deceipt, attorney, statute, castle, riot, trial, visne.

f. 198. Writ to Barons for Prior and Convent of Royston, 8 November 1290; of office of Usher of Exchequer taken into King's hands; recognizances of Theobald de Verdun, Roger de Huntingfield, Robert de Pinkney, John de Engayn, junior, Roger de Beauchamp, Simon de Montagu, Walter de Huntercumb, from same, Hil.

f. 202. Letters Patent on 15th, 20 January 1291.

f. 204. Extract from King's Bench Roll, Mich. term, 19–20 Edward I, on sub custodia etc.

f. 206. Charter for Ipswich, 23 June 1291, from L.T.R. Mem. Roll, Comm., Trin., 19 Edward I.

f. 216. Letters Patent on inquisition on death of Roger de Drayton, 6 May 1292.

f. 218. Petition on manor of Costeray; on fine for having marriage; writ to Barons on plea between Gett. Honeste and Pelegrim de Luca; on judgement on Thomas atte Water, from K.R. Mem. Roll, Comm., Trin., 20 Edward I.

f. 222. Letters Patent as f. 216 above and on taxation co. Chester, 6 August 1292.

f. 224. Extracts from Common Plea Roll, Hil. term, 20 Edward I, on attorney, clergy, Tower, justices, freehold, King's Court etc.

f. 226. Like, East. and Trin. terms, on sub custodia, slander of judges is contempt of court, jurors on same.

f. 231. Letters Patent quitting Brother Guy, Master of Knights Templar in England, of common summons, 16 September 1292.

f. 232. Fine for relief; mainprise of John de Wigton; writs to Barons for King; for William de Chelfield, 28 April 1291; for Geoffrey de Bysseye, 24 April 1291; for Thomas Bidhay, 6 May 1292; for Hugh de Courtney, 19 September 1291; fine for relief; writ to Barons for John de Chandos; recognizances of Roger de Monte Alto, kt.; Hugh de Audele; Thomas de Hibernia; Hugh Wake, from K.R. Mem. Roll, Comm., East., 20 Edward I.

f. 238. Mainprise of Master Nicholas de Lovetot on office of Constable in Exchequer; Letters Patent for Margery, wife of Geoffrey de Nevill, 24 January 1292; for Ella, widow of Richard Knout, executor of his will; on judgement against Matthew de Scaccario, otherwise sent to prison; writs to Barons for Abbot of Leicester, 6 February 1292; for Walter de Huntercumbe, 6 February 1292, from K.R. Mem. Roll, Comm., Hil., 20 Edward I.

f. 242. On oath of Roger de Hengham, King's Serjeant, from L.T.R. Mem. Roll, Comm., Trin., 21 Edward I.

f. 244. Extract from Common Plea Roll, East. term, 21 Edward I, on sub custodia, justice, contempt.

f. 246. Like, Trin. term, on war, Kenilworth, sub custodia etc.

f. 248v. Mandate for John de Britannia, Earl of Richmond, 14 May 1292, and on quittance of common summons. List.

f. 250. Writs for Prior of Ely, 12 November 1292; Abbess of Malling, 15 November 1292, from K.R. Mem. Roll, Brev. dir. Bar., Mich., 21 Edward I.

f. 252. Writs for John de Offord, 15 April 1293; Maurice de Buye, kt.; Abbot of Westminster; for King, 18 May 1293; Bishop of Worcester, from same, East.

f. 259. Writ to Treasurer for William de Chigwell and Walter de Mundham, 3 September 1294, from L.T.R. Mem. Roll, Comm., Trin., 22 Edward I.

f. 260. Memorandum for William de Marchia, Bishop of Bath and Wells, from same, Rec., East.

f. 262. Concerning Roger le Bigod, Earl of Norfolk, from same, Mich.

f. 264. Writ on prerogative of Earl of Chester, 20 January 1295; inquisition at Chester, 4 February 1295, from Escheats, 22 Edward I.

f. 266. Extracts from Common Plea Roll, Trin. term, 22 Edward I, on attorney, slander of court.

f. 268. Like, Mich. term, on statute.

f. 270. Summons to Parliament, to Sheriff of Cumberland, 3 October 1295; to Sheriff of Westmorland, 2 November 1295, from Bundle of Writs, K.R.

f. 272. Writs of summons to Parliament, 24 June 1295. Lists.

f. 276. Like, 30 September, 13 October 1295. Lists.

f. 280. Writs of prorogation of Parliament, 2 November 1295. Lists.

f. 284. Names of Members of Parliament, Lists, from Bundle of Writs, K.R., 23 Edward I

f. 308. Extract from Common Plea Roll, Trin. term, 23 Edward I, on villein.

Mandate to Robert Winchelsey, Archbishop of Canterbury, on holding of Parliament, 30 September 1296.

f. 310. Letters Patent on levying and collection 11th and 7th, 4 December 1296.

f. 310v. Charter of Roger le Bigod, Earl of Norfolk, 16 December 1295.

f. 314. Writs of summons to Parliament, 25 August 1296. Lists.

f. 318. Mandate on mainprise of Gilbert de Umfravill, 22 August 1296.

f. 320. Extracts from Common Plea Roll, Trin. term, 24 Edward I, on appeal, statute of damages in appeal.

f. 322. Like, East. term, on giving of debet.

f. 324. Like, Mich. term, on distress, justicies etc.

f. 326. Writs of summons to Parliament, 26 January 1297. List.

f. 327v. Like, 9 September 1297. List.

f. 330. Extract from Walsingham, Vita Edward I.

f. 332. Letters Patent on taxors assigned and form of taxation (French), 30 July 1297.

f. 334. Like that 8th granted for confirmation of Magna Carta shall not be to prejudice of people, 28 August 1297.

f. 336v. On prohibition that no clerk shall be admitted to plead in Exchequer; on precept to Barons that they shall hold no plea except for the King; writ to Barons for John de Insula, from L.T.R. Mem. Roll, Comm., Hil., 25 Edward I.

f. 340. Mandate on plea coram Rege on advowson of church of Bridgeford, 8 February 1297.

f. 342. Like to Nicholas de Audley, 12 March 1297.

f. 344. Like on defence of Kingdom of Scotland, 21 October 1297. List.

f. 348. Like on coming with horses and arms, 20 August 1297. Lists.

f. 354. Like to Sheriff of Oxf. and Berks., 24 June 1298, and on coming with horses and arms, 26 September 1299 (French). Lists.

f. 358. Writs of summons to Parliament, 6 February 1299. Lists.

f. 362. Like, 10 April 1299. Lists.

f. 364. Letter to King from Treasurer and Barons for men of Kingston upon Hull and Ravenspur, with form of petition (French), from L.T.R. Mem. Roll, Comm., Rec., Hil., 27 Edward I.

f. 368. Grant of Prior of Bath, dated at Bath, 5 April 1299, and by Prior and Chapter of Bath, dated in Chapter House of Bath, from Reg. of Church of Bath in Library of Lincoln's Inn.

f. 376. Petition of Walter de Dernford and Joan, his wife (French), from L.T.R. Mem. Roll, Comm., Rec., East., 27 Edward I.

f. 378. Letters Patent on subsidy from whole community of Wales, 19 July 1300.

f. 380. Writs of summons to Parliament, 29 December 1299. Lists.

f. 386. Like, 26 September 1300. Lists.

f. 396. Petition, Exeter (French), from L.T.R. Mem. Roll, Comm., Rec., East., 28 Edward I.

f. 398. Writ to Barons on liberties of Bishop of Ely in Isle of Ely, from same, Trin.

f. 398v. Letters Patent to communities of grant made to King, 21 September 1300, with notes from Patent Rolls, 28 Edward I, 12 Edward III.

f. 400. Writs to Barons for King and Thomas Corbridge, Archbishop of York on dies, 28 June 1299, from L.T.R. Mem. Roll, Brev. dir. Bar., Trin., 28 Edward I.

f. 402. Mandates to John de Metingham and others, 26 September 1301.

f. 402v. Writs de expensis, knights, 30 March 1300.

f. 404. Writ to Barons for Abbot of Leicester, 14 May 1300, from L.T.R. Mem. Roll, Brev. dir. Bar., Trin., 28 Edward I.

f. 406. Writs to Barons for Prior of St. Neots, 1 April 1300; Prior of Ogbourne, from same, East.

f. 408. On relief of John de Grey, from same, Fines, Mich.

f. 410. Amercement, co. Somerset, from K.R. Mem. Roll, Comm., Rec., Mich., 28 Edward I.

f. 410v. Writs of summons to Parliament, 26 September 1300.

f. 412. On Abbot of Chester, from K.R. Mem. Roll, Comm., Mich., 28–9 Edward I.

f. 416. Writ to Barons on observing liberties in Magna Carta, the same.

f. 418. Mandate, Prohibition for Abbot of Regalis Loci, 23 February 1301.

f. 420. Ordinance made by King and Council on inquisitions returned to Chancery, 29 Edward I, from Close Roll.

f. 422. Commissions to all cos., 24 April 1301, from K.R. Mem. Roll, Commiss., East., 29 Edward I.

f. 424. Barons Letter to Pope, Lincoln, 12 February 1302, from Julius C. 7, with list of 8 barons in the charter who did not seal.

f. 428. Proceedings in Parliament of Lincoln, 29 Edward I, from *Plac. Parl.*, with list of Justices from Roger de Brabazon, Chief Justice, with reference to Liberate Roll.

f. 432. Letters Patent on assessing and levying 15th, 29 Edward I.

f. 432v. Writs of summons to Parliament, 30 January 1301.

f. 434. Fines of William la Zouch, William Russell, from K.R. Mem. Roll, Fines, East., 29 Edward I.

f. 436. Petition of sisters and heirs of Thomas Peverel (French), from K.R. Mem. Roll, Comm., Rec. et Pet., 29 Edward I.

f. 438. Petition of Gilbert de St. Lifard, Bishop of Chichester (French), from same, East.

f. 444. Writ to Treasurer for John de Metingham, 2 March 1301, from same, Brev. dir. Bar., East.

f. 446. Writ to Treasurer and Barons for Prior and Convent of Merton, 27 February 1301; for Abbot and Convent of Osney, 26 February 1301; for John de Havering, 26 February 1301, from same, Comm., Hil.

f. 448. Writs de expensis, knights, 30 January 1301.

f. 449. Writ to Barons for King, 10 February 1301; for Robert de Stodley, for relief; from K.R. Mem. Roll, Comm., 29 Edward I.

f. 450v. For relief of Thomas, son of Roger de Chandos; to Abbot of Cerne on levying 10th and 15th, from same, East., 29 Edward I.

Inset at end of volume is printed pamphlet: The Pillars of Parliament.

VOLUME 12

A volume of transcripts etc. from the Public Records and other sources 25–35 Edward I. On flyleaf: Recorda Tempore E. 1. On another flyleaf: Several writs, records, pardons, grants, patents, summonses and transactions in Parliament and elsewhere during the reign of Edward I. 282 ff.

f. 1. Writs of summons to Parliament. Lists. 2 June 1302.

f. 5. Writs of summons to Parliament. Lists. 24 July 1302.

f. 9v. Writs of prorogation of Parliament. Lists. 13 September 1302.

f. 15. Letters Patent for marriage of King's eldest daughter, 7 November 1302, and to be intendant to collectors.

f. 17. Letters Patent for John de Kirkby, 11 February 1303. (L.T.R., Mem. Roll, Comm., Commissiones etc., Trin. term, 31 Edward I.)

f. 19. On reliefs of Robert de Tatshull and John Biset. (Ibid., Brev. dir. Bar., 30 Edward I.)

f. 23. Writ to Barons of Exchequer for Adam, son of Adam Bernard, 12 August 1302. (Ibid., Trin. term, 31 Edward I.)

f. 23v. Letters Patent for men and community of co. Northumberland (French), 3 January 1302.

f. 25. Writ to Barons of Exchequer for Hugh Wake and Hugh de Audley, 21 October 1302; on proclamation of peace between Kings of England and France (French). (L.T.R., Mem. Roll, Comm., Rec., Trin. term, 31 Edward I.)

f. 27. On Book of Fees. (Ibid.)

f. 28. Writ to Barons of Exchequer for Ralph de Gorges. (Ibid., Brev. dir. Bar., East. term, 31 Edward I.)

f. 30. Petition of William de Saundervill (French). (Ibid., Comm., East. term, 31 Edward I.)

f. 32. Day at Exchequer for John de Brantingham, clerk. (Ibid., Comm., Rec., Hil. term, 31 Edward I.)

f. 34. For Geoffrey de Crakour and Henry, his son. (Ibid.)

f. 36. Writ to Barons of Exchequer for Hugh de Estcote. (Ibid., East. term, 31 Edward I.)

f. 38. Writs of summons to Parliament. Lists. 12 November 1304.

f. 44. Writs to Barons of Exchequer for Robert de Ver, Earl of Oxford, 22 August 1304; Ralph de Monthemer, Earl of Gloucester and Hertford, 25 August 1304; Robert Stutvill, 12 June 1304. (K.R. Mem. Roll, Brev. dir. Bar., Mich. term, 32 Edward I.)

f. 46. To King on process of Thomas de Furnivall (French). (L.T.R., Mem. Roll, Brev. dir. Bar., Mich. term, 32 Edward I.)

f. 48. On delivery to prison of Sheriff of Salop. (Ibid., Comm., Rec., Hil. term, 32 Edward I.)

f. 50. Writ to Barons of Exchequer for Robert Orford, Bishop of Ely, 5 July 1304 (ibid., Brev. dir. Bar., Trin. term, 32 Edward I); writs on debts of late Archbishop of York and debts of Abbot of Hulme, 4 October 1304 (ibid., Mich. term, 32 Edward I).

f. 52. Writ to Barons of Exchequer for Prior of St. Andrews, York, 18 April 1304; letter from Prince of Wales to Treasurer and Barons, 28 April 1304; writ to Barons for John de Compton, 31 May 1304. (Ibid., East. term, 32 Edward I.)

f. 54. Writs of summons to Parliament. Lists. 27 August 1305.

f. 60. Letters Patent on inquisitions on homicides etc.

f. 60v. Letters Patent on collection of 15th, 19 February 1305.

f. 62. Plea in Parliament, 33 Edward I, from Memoranda de Parliamento. (*Plac. Parl.*, pp. 254–5.)

f. 64. Writs to Barons of Exchequer for Robert Orford, Bishop of Ely, 8 April 1305; Prior of St. Catherine's without Lincoln, 26 April 1305; John Spigurnel, 2 April 1305; Robert de Hereyard, 1 April 1305; Prior of Merton, 25 March 1305. (K.R. Mem. Roll, Comm., East. term, 33 Edward I.)

f. 68. Writs to Barons of Exchequer for Abbot of Bardney, 8 October 1305; citizens of York, 3 October 1305; Richard de Luda, 25 October 1305; John Peverel, 7 November 1305. (L.T.R. Mem. Roll, Brev. dir. Bar., Mich. term, 33 Edward I.)

f. 70v. Writ to Barons of Exchequer for Robert de Stutvill, 12 June 1304. (K.R. Mem. Roll, Comm., Mich. term, 32 Edward I.)

f. 72. Extract from Common Bench Roll, Hil. term, 33 Edward I, on custom.

f. 74. Mandate to Robert Winchelsey, Archbishop of Canterbury. (K.R. Mem. Roll, Comm., East. term, 33 Edward I.)

f. 76. Writs to Barons of Exchequer for John Butetort and others, 6 March 1305; Abbot of Robertsbridge, 4 April 1305 (L.T.R. Mem. Roll, Brev. dir. Bar., Hil. term, 33 Edward I); on delivery of King's seal to William de Hamilton (ibid., Recorda); writs to Barons for Robert Orford, Bishop of Ely, 8 February 1305 (ibid., Brev. dir. Bar., East. term); Pleas before Treasurer and Barons of Exchequer and others of King's Council, at Westminster, 9 May 1305; writ to Barons for Lucy, widow of John de Dievelston, 24 June 1305 (ibid., Trin. term); mainprise of Ralph de Sandwich, Constable of Tower of London; writs to Barons for Robert de Ver, Earl of Oxford, 22 August 1304; Ralph de Monthemer, Earl of Gloucester and Hertford, 25 August 1304 (ibid., Brev. dir. Bar., Mich. term); writs to Barons for John Butetort, 6 March 1305; for citizens of York, 21 March 1305; Abbot of Robertsbridge, 4 April 1305 (ibid., Hil. term).

f. 86. Memorandum on Scotland for King (French).

f. 88. Writs of summons to Parliament of Carlisle. Lists. 3 November 1306.

f. 94. Mandates on aid on marriage of King's eldest son, 5 April 1306.

f. 98. On Roger de Beauchamp. (K.R. Mem. Roll, Rec., Trin. term, 34 Edward I.)

f. 100. On aid granted for knighting of King's eldest son. (L.T.R. Mem. Roll, Rec., Trin. term, 34 Edward I.)

f. 104. For men of town of Coventry, 18 October 1306; writing of Erard de Barr; on 30th and 20th; on William de More, Master of Knights Templar. (Ibid., Mich. term.)

f. 106. On homage made by James, Steward of Scotland. (Ibid.)

f. 110. Recognizance of James, Steward of Scotland. (Ibid., Recogn., Mich. term, 34 Edward I.)

f. 111. Writ to Barons of Exchequer for Henry de Bolebek, 10 September 1306. (K.R. Mem. Roll, Brev. dir. Bar., Mich. term, 34 Edward I.)

f. 112. Writ to Barons of Exchequer for Abbot of (blank), 29 October 1305. (L.T.R. Mem. Roll, Brev. dir. Bar., Hil. term, 34 Edward I.)

f. 114. Mandate to Thomas de Berkeley, 11 July 1288.

f. 116. Form of taxing and levying 30th and 20th (French). (L.T.R. Mem. Roll, Comm., Rec., Trin. term, 34 Edward I.)

f. 122. Form of commission made to taxors and collectors of 30th and 20th, 22 July 1306. (Ibid.)

f. 126. For men of Great Yarmouth and Lothinglond. (Ibid.)

f. 132. On John de Insula. (Ibid., East. term.)

f. 134. Petition of John de Insula. (French.) (Ibid.)

f. 140. Petition of John de Insula (French); writ to Barons of Exchequer for William de Ludlow, 18 April 1306. (Ibid., Brev. dir. Bar., East. term.)

f. 142. Writ to Barons of Exchequer for Baldwin Pycot, 16 June 1306. (Ibid., Trin. term.)

f. 143. Writs de expensis, 3 May 1306.

f. 144. Writs to Barons of Exchequer for John de Berwick, 2 July 1306; Roger de Bello Campo, 8 July 1306. (L.T.R. Mem. Roll, Brev. dir. Bar., Trin. term, 34 Edward I.)

f. 146v. Extract from King's Bench Roll, Mich. term, 33–4 Edward I, on contempt.

f. 148. Fine for relief of Thomas Wylughby. (K.R. Mem. Roll, Fines, etc., Trin. term, 34 Edward I.)

f. 150. Writ to William de Bencote, 20 October 1306 (K.R. Mem. Roll, Brev. Retorn., Mich. term, 34 Edward I); writ to Sheriff of York etc. (ibid., Brevia non Retorn., Mich. term).

f. 152. Writ to Archbishop of Canterbury for John de London, 8 February 1306. (Ibid., Hil. term.)

f. 154. Writ on payment of money, co. Salop, 12 May 1306. (Ibid., East. term.)

f. 156. Writs to Barons of Exchequer for Abbot of de Pratis, 7 November 1306 (L.T.R. Mem. Roll, Brev. dir. Bar., Mich. term, 34 Edward I); delivery to Chamberlains of public instrument on affairs of Scotland (ibid., Rec., Trin. term); writ to Sheriff of Northants. etc. 18 January 1306; Ralph Basset, Lord of Drayton (ibid.); relief Master of Knights Templar; fine of William le Wayte of Grantham (ibid., Trin. term).

f. 160. On respite of scutage to Archbishops etc. (K.R. Mem. Roll, Rec., Trin. term, 34 Edward I.)

f. 161. Enrolment of public instrument from Close Roll.

f. 162. Reliefs of John de Insula, Adam de Tirington, Adam de Wavervill; oath of William de Watlington. (K.R. Mem. Roll, Comm., East. term, 34 Edward I.)

f. 164. Relief of Thomas Bardolf (ibid., Fines etc., Hil. term); Elias Scarlet, Bailiff of Sandwich (ibid., East. term).

f. 166. Writs to Barons of Exchequer for vill of Paulfleet, 15 April 1306; Gilbert de Sauteour, privy seal (French). (K.R. Mem. Roll, Brev. dir. Bar., East. term, 34 Edward I.)

f. 168. Extracts from Common Plea Roll, Mich. term, 33 Edward I, on sewers, suit, aid, quod reddat, rotulus de cartis irrotulatis.

f. 174. Writs to Barons of Exchequer for Abbot of Bardney, 8 October 1305; Walter de Gloucester, 14 October 1305; Roger Springhouse, 8 April 1305; Abbot of Evesham, 6 October 1305; John de la Mare, 24 October 1305; John de Ingham, 4 September 1303, privy seal (French); letter of Aymer de Valence to Constable, Marshal and Keeper of Wardrobe, for Gilbert de Acon, 14 May 1305; Richard de Luda, 25 October 1305; John de Erlegh, 24 February 1301; Fulk Lestrange, 24 October 1306; John de la Mare, 13 November 1305;

Roger le Bigod, Earl of Norfolk, 16 November 1305; Abbess of de la Pre, 7 November 1305. (K.R. Mem. Roll, Brev. dir. Bar., Mich. term, 33–34 Edward I.)

f. 182. Writs to Barons of Exchequer for John, son of Roger de Molis, 22 January 1306; Stephen Hovet and Mary, his wife, 3 January 1306; Master of Knights Templar, 3 January 1306; from Prince for William Trussell, Justice of Chester, 28 April 1305; for Abbot of Maldon, n.d.; Abbot of Faversham, 8 February 1306; Ralph de Monthemer, Earl of Gloucester and Hertford, 20 January 1306; William Gerberg, 8 February 1306; Robert de Brus, 19 February 1306; Alexander de Balliol, 19 February 1306; Abbot of Dunkeswell, 6 April 1306; monks of St. Mary of Thame, 10 February 1306; Ralph Baldock, Bishop of London, 12 April 1306; Abbot of St. Albans, 10 April 1306; Margaret, widow of Edmund, Earl of Cornwall, 8 April 1306; Walter Gainborough, Bishop of Worcester, 21 March 1306; Margery Belet, 15 April 1306; William de Ludlow, 18 July 1306; Master of Knights Templar in England, 13 November 1305; tenants of little fee of Morteyn, co. Cornwall, 3 June 1306; Baldwin Picot, 16 June 1306; Abbot of Abingdon, 26 June 1306; Bartholomew, son and heir of Peter of Poitou, 17 June 1306; Abbot and Convent of St. Mary of Kirkstall, 25 June 1306; John Andrew etc., 13 June 1306; William de Luda, 18 July 1306; Abbot of St. James without Northampton, 3 July 1306; Abbot of Selby, 17 June 1306; Walter de Gloucester, Constable of Tower, 16 July 1306. (K.R. Mem. Roll, Brev. dir. Bar., 34 Edward I.)

f. 202. Ordinance made on business of Exchequer in absence of Treasurer; process touching John de Thorpe; for Abbot of Evesham; letter sent by John de Insula and John de Drokensford, Barons of Exchequer, and whole Council (French); for Ralph de Rothings; letter of William de Ormesby to William de Carleton (French); on Robert de Ver, Earl of Oxford; petition of burgesses of Appleby; writing of Thomas de Berkeley on services done in Scotland; Henry Spigurnel, Justice of Gaol Delivery; on men of Yarmouth etc.; on respite of scutages; relief of Thomas Bardolf; fine of Elias Scarlet; relief of John de Insula; Andrew de Tirington; Adam de Wavervill; William de Watlington. (K.R. Mem. Roll, 34 Edward I.)

f. 228. Letters Patent for Abbot of St. Augustine's, Bristol, not coming to Parliament, 2 May 1307.

f. 230. Writ de expensis, Parliament of Carlisle, 20 January 1307.

f. 230v. Letters Patent on 30th and 20th in liberties of Durham etc., 1 December 1306.

f. 232. On payments assigned for wool and other things taken for King's use. (L.T.R. Mem. Roll, Comm., Rec., Trin. term, 35 Edward I.)

f. 234. Pleas in Parliament, 35 Edward I. Names of those summoned to Parliament of Carlisle, Octave of Hilary.

f. 237. Writ of privy seal, List of proctors etc., 19 January 1307.

f. 244. Writ of summons to Parliament. Lists. 22 February 1307.

f. 246. Money assigned to William Trent, King's Butler. (L.T.R. Mem. Roll, Comm., Trin. term, 35 Edward I.)

f. 248. Mandate (French). 26 February 1307.

f. 249. Letters Patent on assessment of 30th and 20th, co. Midd., 1 December 1306.

f. 250. Form of oath of those of King's Council (French).

f. 251. Pleas in Parliament. Hugh de Lowther appointed Justice. (*Plac. Parl.*, p. 317.)

f. 252. On satisfaction of various creditors of King. (L.T.R. Mem. Roll, Comm., Rec., Trin. term, 35 Edward I.)

f. 254. Writ of privy seal to Barons of Exchequer for Prior and Convent of Durham, 11 May 1307 (French). (Ibid., Brev. dir. Bar., Trin. term.)

f. 256. Statute of Carlisle, 35 Edward I. (*Plac. Parl.*, p. 312.)

f. 260. Letters Patent to men of Coket of liberty of bishopric of Durham, 10 February 1303.

f. 262. Ordinance made for protections in the Exchequer; of surrender of co. Kildare in Ireland to King; writ to Barons of Exchequer for David Martin, Bishop of St. David's, 19 April 1307; petition to Exchequer returned to Parliament, 1 July 1297, for Gilbert de Braunolves (French); mainprise of Henry de Pinkeney; relief of Ab Adam; mainprise of William de Stoke; writ on inquisition on fees of Gilbert de Gant, 26 February 1297; commission made to John Randolf and Henry de Guldford, 7 March 1297; form of taxation of 12th (French); appointment of taxors of 12th. List. 29 November 1296; that Sheriffs shall assist taxors; on removal of taxors and appointment of others, 12 December 1296; Form of assessors and taxors of city of London (French); on oath of same (French); writ to Sheriffs of London, 7 December 1296; on form of passage to various ports, 1 March 1297 (French); writs to Sheriffs. List; writ to Sheriff of Yorks., 1 May 1297; instrument produced in Exchequer; writs (French). (K.R. Mem. Roll, Comm. etc. 25 Edward I.)

f. 277. Letters Patent, 31 August 1297 (French); also 20 March 1297 (French).

f. 282. Letters Patent, 12 September 1297.

VOLUME 13

A volume of transcripts etc. from the Public Records and other sources, 1–25 Edward I. On flyleaf: Recorda tempore Edw. I. Vol. II. On next flyleaf: Records from the 1st of Edw. 1st to the 19th year. 340 ff.

The four preliminary pages contain a Table of Contents, ending with the following paragraph: There are contained in this volume other things, vizt., customs upon wool, taxes, commissions, restitutions, seizures, letters to and from the Pope, inquisitions, subsidies, pardons, Wales, confirmations of charters etc., custodies, Oxford University, letters to and from Kings and to and from Bishops, ad quod damnum, inspeximus.

f. 1. Of the death of Henry III and the succession of Edward I, with references to Matt of West. and Ann. of Waverley.

f. 2. Extract from Coram Rege Roll, Trin. term, 12 Edward I.

f. 3. Letters Patent on preservation of peace in Ireland, 7 December 1272.

f. 4. Of the barony of the Bishop of Chichester in King's hands, 25 May 1273, from Fine Roll.

f. 5. Mandate to Geoffrey de Genevill, Justiciar of Ireland, on retaining liberties in King's hands, 11 October 1274.

f. 7. Writs of summons to Parliament, 27 December 1274.

f. 8xv. On the reading and proclamation of statutes in co. Chester etc., 28 May 1275, from Patent Roll.

f. 8x. Extract from Stat. of West. I, 3 Edward I.

f. 9v. Letters Patent for Abbot of Beaulieu, 24 July 1276.

f. 11v. Mandate to Robert Breton on delivery of Stat., 13 Edward I.

f. 12. Like to Sheriffs on proclamation of Stat. of West. I., 1 April 1335.

f. 13v. Various Statutes and Constitutions, Henry III to Edward III, from Vespasian B. 7.

f. 15. Letters Patent on wool, 15 November 1275.

f. 16. Mandate on New Custom, 3 Edward I, from Fine Roll.

f. 17. Note on Stat. of West. I by J. Vaughan, Chief Justice of Common Pleas, *Reports*.

f. 19. As f. 8xv above.

f. 21. Letters Patent of oyer and terminer on dispute between Mayor and citizens of York and Abbot of St. Mary's, York, 28 May 1275.

f. 23. Mandate on Queen's dower in Gascony etc. 22 October 1275.

f. 27. Like to Treasurer and Chamberlains of Exchequer to make indentures for the receipt of records, processes etc., 22 April 1275, from Brevia Regis.

f. 29. Letters Patent on 15th in co. Chester, 3 November 1275.

f. 30. Like on dispute between Henry III and Count of Flanders, 31 October 1275.

f. 31. On form of peace, 28 April 1274, from Gascon Roll.

f. 35. Letters Patent on examination of measures, 7 December 1274.

f. 37. As f. 29 above.

f. 38. As f. 16 above.

f. 39. Fine on restoration of town of Canterbury, 19 May 1275, from Fine Roll.

Writ on lands of John de Mandevill taken into King's hands, 3 May 1275, same.

f. 40. Letters to Pope, 19 June 1275, from Close Roll.

f. 42. Protestation made by King on subsidy of 15th, 1 November 1275, from Patent Roll.

f. 43. Mandate on 15th from honor of Bergavenny, 24 November 1292.

f. 44. Letters Patent on inquisition on William de Northburgh, 3 July 1276.

f. 46. Writ of aid for lands held in alms and in socage, Abbot of Nostel, 1 May 1274, from old MS. Reg. of Writs in poss. of John Lapthorne.

f. 47. Letters Patent for Barons of Cinque Ports, 5 August 1277.

f. 48. Like on water of Severn, 7 February 1277.

Like to communities of cos. Salop and Heref. on subsidy, 5 February 1277.

f. 50. Like on army of South Wales, 8 August 1277.

f. 51. Homage of Alexander, King of Scotland, 6 Edward I, from Close Roll.

f. 53. Homage on writing of Alexander, at Tewkesbury, 17 October 1278, from Bundle of Letters and Writs, 6 Edward I.

f. 55. Preamble of Stat. of Gloucester, 6 Edward I.

f. 56. Note from Reg. of Writs, de vasto.

f. 57. Original writ formed on Stat. of Gloucester, cap. 5.

f. 58. As ff. 55, 56 above.

f. 60. Revocation of Provisions in Council of Reading, 7 Edward I, from Close Roll.

f. 62. On measure of cloth at Boston, from Bundle entitled on Flemish merchants and cloth at Parliament at Westminster, 7 Edward I, in a certain box No. 10 in Tower.

f. 64. Letters Patent on grant of English Law to Ireland, 10 June 1280.

f. 66. Provision made on petition in Parliament (French), 8 Edward I, from Close Roll.

f. 67. Mandate on Hospital of St. John at Basingstoke, 18 May 1281.

f. 68. On sentence of excommunication on breakers of Magna Carta, among the Constitutions of John Peckham, Archbishop of Canterbury, at Lambeth, 1281, from Spelman, *Conc.*

f. 69. Mandate on Hubert de Burgo, Ireland, 10 June 1282.

f. 70. Letter from Justices in Eyre, co. Devon, to Robert Burnell, Bishop of Bath, from Bundle of Letters and Writs, 6 Edward I (Prynne, *Records*, III).

f. 72. Fine, Prior of Coventry, 10 Edward I, from Scutage Roll, mandate on same.

f. 73. Mandate on John de Kirkby, 19 June 1282, from Welsh Roll.

f. 74. Writ to Mayor and citizens of London sending John de Lovetot on money for Welsh war, 10 Edward I, from New Misc. Bundle, t. Henry III etc.

f. 75. Mandate on levying money arising from subsidy, 20 December 1282, same.

f. 76. Writ to John de Kirkby, from Bundle of Letters and Writs, 10 Edward I (Prynne, *Records*, III).

f. 78. Letters Patent for Prior of Carlisle etc. 7 February 1282.

f. 79. On David ap Gruffydd, from Walsingham and Welsh Roll, with translation.

f. 83. Note on extract from Walsingham with translation.

f. 84v. Writs of summons to Parliament, 28 June 1283, from Welsh Roll.

f. 93v. Writs to Sheriffs, 24 November 1283, same.

f. 97. As f. 93v above.

f. 99. Writ to Robert of Holy Island, Bishop of Durham, 6 January 1283, same.

f. 100. Bull of Martin IV on tenth, 8 January 1283, from Close Roll.

f. 104. People of England and Ireland, from Stat. Roll, 13 Edward I.

f. 106. Letter to John XXI on city of Agen, 13 Edward I, from New Misc. Bundle, t. Henry III etc.

f. 108. Petition in Parliament on confirmation of the Charters, 13 Edward I, from Close Roll.

f. 111. On delivery of Stat., 14 September 1285, with notes, same.

f. 113. Letters of prelates and magnates of Provence to Edward I with his letter in reply, 29 June 1286, from Treaty Roll between Kings of England and France.

f. 116. Letters Patent for men of Chester, 22 July 1286, from Welsh Roll.

f. 117. Writ to Barons for Jordan Godsorp, L.T.R. Mem. Roll, Mich., 14 Edward I.

f. 118. Writ to Edmund, Earl of Cornwall, 24 April 1288, from Bundle of Letters and Writs, 16 Edward I (Prynne, *Records*, III).

Like, 24 May 1288 (French).

f. 120. Writ to John de Metingham for records, 14 June 1288, from New Misc. Bundle, t. Henry III etc.

f. 121. Pleas of Crown before John de Metingham and fellows, Justices in Eyre, at Sherburn, co. Dorset, Oct. of Trin., 16 Edward I, hundred of Cranbourne.

f. 122. Letters Patent on Margaret, daughter of Eric, King of Norway, 6 November 1289.

f. 123. On marriage planned between Prince Edward and Margaret, daughter of Eric, King of Norway, and heiress of kingdom of Scotland, 17 & 18 Edward I.

f. 124. Letters of Nicholas IV to Prince Edward, 16 November 1289, from Patent Roll.

f. 126. Letters of Edward I to Eric, King of Norway, 17 April 1290, same.

f. 128. As f. 122 above.

f. 129. Letters Patent to William, Bishop of St. Andrews etc. 28 August 1290.

f. 131. On the doings, Scotland and Norway, on the marriage, 16 July 1290, from Patent Roll.

f. 138. Conference on the above, 28 August 1290.

f. 139. Letters Patent to Robert Wischard, Bishop of Glasgow etc. (French), 18 Edward I.

f. 142. As f. 126 above.

f. 144. Mandate to Sheriffs on grievances against ministers, 13 October 1289.

f. 145. Writ to Oliver Sutton, Bishop of Lincoln, 30 September 1289, from New Misc. Bundle, t. Henry III etc.

f. 147. Letters Patent on survey and repair of ditches, 10 July 1289.

f. 149. As f. 122 above.

f. 150. Writs of summons to Parliament, cos. Hertf., Oxf. and Lincs., with returns on dorse, 14 June 1290, from Bundle of Writs of Summons, 18 Edward I.

f. 155. Translation of writ to Justices of Bench, 30 October 1279, from Rastell, *Stat.*

f. 157. Writ of summons to Parliament, co. Westmorland, 14 June 1290, with return on dorse, from same Bundle, 18 Edward I.

f. 159. As ff. 131–8 above.

f. 167. As f. 129 above.

f. 169. Declaration on grant of subsidy and Letters Patent on taxing, collecting and levying 15th, 22 September 1290, from L.T.R. Mem. Roll, Mich., 18–19 Edward I.

f. 171. Oath of Justices (French); Oath, same, Hil. & Trin., 17 Edward I.

f. 172. Mandate to Treasurer and Barons of Exchequer, 5 November 1290.

f. 173. Letters to Nicholas IV, 18 Edward I, from Close Roll.

f. 177. Letters Patent on 15th in Wales, 20 January 1291.

f. 179. Writ on taxation of 15th, co. Hunts., for Abbot of Ramsey, 11 January 1291, from MS. Book of Abbey of Ramsey, with reference to Close Roll, 19 Edward I.

f. 180. Provision made by King allowing Charter of Liberties in Exchequer, 6 February 1292, from Close Roll.

f. 181v. Mandate to Sheriff of Heref., 6 February 1292.

f. 183. Peace between the King's men and men of Count of Flanders, 27 May 1292, from Close Roll.

f. 184. Fine of John de Bekingham, 22 June 1292, from Fine Roll.

f. 185. Letters Patent on inquisition on death of Roger Drayton etc. 6 May 1292.

f. 187. Like to Gilbert de Thornton on inquisition, 28 June 1292.

f. 188. Like to Nicholas de Segrave on Isle of Man, 15 July 1292.

f. 189. Letters to King of Hungary, 20 June 1292, from Close Roll.

f. 190. Letters Patent for William de Valence, Earl of Pembroke, 22 October 1292.

f. 191. Like to William de Bereford etc. on bailiff of liberty of Richmond, 10 December 1291.

f. 192. Like on 15th, co. Chester, 6 August 1292.

f. 193. Writs to Gilbert de Thornton etc. 24 April 1292; John de Metingham, 26 April 1292; William Inge, 28 April 1292; Philip de Wylughby, 28 October 1292, from Liberate Roll.

f. 194. Offers, John of Pontoise, Bishop of Winchester, £1,500; cos. Dorset and Somerset, £100; monks of Whitby, 30 marks; citizens of London, 300 marks; Abbot of Malmesbury, 30 marks, from Rot. Oblat.

f. 195. Writ on goods of John de Casthorp, 12 February 1293, from Fine Roll.

Writ to Justices in Eyre, co. Cumberland etc. 3 January 1293, same.

f. 196. Pardon of John le Bailiff of Corfham, 3 November 1293, same.

Writ for Edmund, King's brother, parish of St. Clement Danes, 21 June 1293, same.

f. 196v. Writ for Richard Neel etc. 14 June 1293, same.

f. 197. Memorandum at Tughall before Robert Tibetot etc. 21 Edward I, same.

Writ to John de Cobham on citizens of London, 16 August 1293, same.

f. 199. Mandate for Stephen Pauncefot, clerk, 30 July 1293.

f. 199v. As f. 197 above.

f. 200. Like for merchants of St. Valery etc. at Southampton, 27 August 1293.

f. 200v. Like for merchants of Calais in Ireland, 6 September 1293.

f. 201. As f. 195 above.

f. 203. Certain Ordinances on petitions made in Parliament (French), from Close Roll.

f. 204. Writ for Ralph de Gorges on fine, 3 January 1293, from Fine Roll.

f. 205. Mandates to Sheriffs on proclamation of certain articles, 18 November 1292.

f. 206. Like to John de Wake etc. 6 June 1294, from Gascon Roll.

f. 208. Like to John le Romeyn, Archbishop of York etc. 18 June 1292, same.

f. 209. Like on Duchy of Aquitaine etc. 21 November 1293, from Almain Roll.

f. 211. Writs, Lists, 19 August 1294, from Gascon Roll.

f. 213. Like for Simon de Starstede, 11 December 1293.

f. 214. Letters on Gascony, 1 July 1294, from Gascon Roll.

Like on rolls of Newgate Gaol to Exchequer, 24 November 1293.

f. 215. Writ to William March, Bishop of Bath and Wells, Treasurer, 16 July 1294, same

f. 215v. Like to Bartholomew de Doleriis of Everwarton, 14 June 1294, same.

f. 216v. Like to be intendant to John de Britanny, 1 July 1294, same.

f. 217. Like to merchants of Ireland on wool customs, 28 October 1294, from Fine Roll.

f. 217v. Like of goods of King of France in Ireland, 16 October 1294.

f. 218. Like for merchants of Gascony, 5 December 1293, same.

f. 218v. Like for John de Balliol, King of Scotland, 2 December 1293, same.

f. 219. Like on appointments to various cos., King of France, 6 July 1294 (French), from Gascon Roll.

f. 223. Letters Patent on Minories without Aldgate, 8 November 1294.

f. 224. Writs on merchants of France (French), 18 June 1294, from Gascon Roll.

f. 226. Letters Patent for John de Halton, Bishop of Carlisle, ad quod damnum, 30 October 1294.

f. 226v. Like for University of Cambridge, 30 October 1294.

f. 228. Mandates to Sheriffs on choosing knights, 8 October 1294.

f. 229. Like, 9 October 1294.

f. 230. Letters Patent on plaints against William de Vescy in Ireland, 10 December 1293.

f. 232. Mandate to Sheriff of Lincs., on proclamation of Stat., 13 December 1293.

f. 232v. Like for King to Bishops on prayers, 14 February 1294.

f. 233v. Like on Ireland, William de Vescy etc. 21 April 1294.

f. 234. Letters Patent to knights etc., co. Cumberland, 12 November 1294.

f. 236. Writs of summons to Parliament, 30 September 1295.

f. 239. Like to lay barons, 1 October 1295.

f. 241. Like to Sheriffs, 3 October 1295.

f. 243. Like on prorogation of Parliament, 2 November 1295.

f. 254. Like, 24 June 1295.

f. 258. Like, 26 August 1296.

f. 259. Like, 12 November 1304.

f. 260. As f. 258 above.

f. 263. Letters Patent to Sheriffs on 11th and 7th, 4 December 1295.

f. 265. Writ to men of Galway, 6 March 1296, from New Misc. Bundle, t. Henry III etc.

f. 266. Extract from Matt. of West. on subsidy, 1295.

f. 268. Writs of summons to Parliament, 26 August 1296.

f. 270. Writs on Parliament, 25 Edward I, from New Misc. Bundle, t. Henry III etc.
Confirmatio Cartarum, 10 October 1297 (French), with translation from Rastell, *Stat.*

f. 277. Writ of privy seal, 25 Edward I (French), with return on dorse (Latin), from Bundle of Writs of Privy Seal, 25 Edward I (Prynne, *Records*, III).

f. 279. From among Memoranda in Exchequer, 25 Edward I, printed in Year Book, Edward II, Winchelsey, under privy seal.

f. 281. Extract from Walsingham, 25 Edward I.

f. 284. Letters to Gregory X, 29 January 1275, from Close Roll.

f. 287. Mandate to Sheriffs on knighting of King's eldest son, 5 April 1306.

f. 288. Letters Patent to Sheriff of Suff. on 12th and 8th, 16 December 1296.

f. 290. On Magna Carta, with references to Matt. Paris, Exodus, Stat. Roll, 25 Edward I, Parl. Roll, 15 Edward III, Pupilla Oculi, Close Roll, 10 Edward II, Tacitas, Fleta.

f. 295. Magna Carta, 5 November 1297 (French), with notes from Coke, *2nd Inst.*

f. 301. Part of Stat. de Tallagio non concedendo, 25 Edward I, same.

f. 303. As f. 279 above.

f. 305. Confirmation of Magna Carta, 9 Henry III, from Stat. Roll, 25 Edward I.

f. 307. Original Writ formed on cap. 25, Stat. of West. II, de manutenendo, from Reg. of Writs.

f. 308. As f. 266 above.

f. 312. Writ, 12 October 1297, from Stat. Roll, 25 Edward I.

f. 318. As f. 281 above.

f. 320. As f. 277 above.

f. 322. Mandate to Sheriff of Yorks., on coming for confirmation of Magna Carta, 15 September 1297.

f. 324. Letter Patent on 8th granted for confirmation of Magna Carta, 28 August 1297.

f. 325. Text of Magna Carta, 12 October 1297, from Stat. Roll, 25 Edward I.

Notes on same from same, Patent Roll, 11 Edward III, Parl. Roll, 15 Edward III, 15 Edward II, 2 Henry V.

VOLUME 14

A volume of transcripts etc. from the Public Records and other sources, 25–35 Edward I. On flyleaf: Recorda tempore Edw. I. Vol. II. On next flyleaf: Records from the 1st of Edw. 1st to the 19th year. 311 ff.

f. 1. Sentence of excommunication against all those who go against Magna Carta and the Charter of the Forests. Richard de Gravesend, Bishop of London to Dean and Chapter of St. Paul's, 25 July 1298, from Cleopatra E. 1.

f. 9. Writ of privy seal, from Bundle of Writs of Privy Seals, 25 Edward I, with reference to Patent Roll, 25 Edward I.

f. 12. Writ of summons to Parliament at York, 13 April 1298, from Bundle of Writs of Summons to Parl., 26 Edward I.

f. 13. Like writ, 13 April 1298, from Liber B in Archives of city of London, with reference to same Bundle of Writs.

f. 14. Like writ to Sheriff of London, 13 April 1298, with return on dorse from same Bundle of Writs.

f. 16. Letters Patent for enquiry into grievances of the people, 4 April 1298.

f. 18. Writ to Sheriff of Edinburgh etc. 2 September 1296, from Scottish Roll.

f. 19. Letters Patent for the Bishops of the kingdom of Scotland, 5 October 1296.

f. 20. From a certain roll entitled 'On the superiority of the sea of England and the office of Admiralty', 26 Edward I, with writs, 24 May 1319 etc.

f. 25. Letters Patent for the Abbot of Leicester that he is not bound to come to Parliament, 15 February 1296, certified transcript.

f. 26. Stat. 2 Richard II, c. 7, from *Book of Stat.* in French.

f. 27. Mandate for Archbishop of York, 8 October 1325.

f. 29. Form in which M. de Balliol was bailed by the Bishop of Vicence and how he received him (French), from Brevia Regis, 26 & 27 Edward I.

f. 32. Letters Patent for citizens of London, 22 April 1299.

f. 33. Mandate to Justices of Bench for Abbot of St. Mary's, York, that pleas of quo warranto shall be pleaded and determined in the Eyres of the King's Justices, 20 April 1299.

f. 34. Letters Patent on perambulation between barony of Pevensey and barony of Hastings, 18 October 1299.

f. 35. Like for King to cos. Warw., Leics. etc. (French), 25 June 1299.

f. 38. Writ to co. Southampton, 25 June 1299 (French), from Bundle of Writs, 27 Edward I (Prynne, *Records*, III).

f. 40. Letters Patent committing the King's counterseal on Statute Merchants at Nottingham to Robert Ingram of Nottingham, 19 March 1300.

f. 41. Stat. called Articuli super Cartas, 28 Edward I (French), from Stat. Roll, Edward I–III.

f. 49. Note from Coram Rege Roll, East. term, 30 Edward I, Kent, from Coke, *2nd Inst.*

f. 50. Writ to John Sampson on castle of Scarborough, 28 Edward I, from New Misc. Bundle, t. Henry III etc.

f. 52. Mandate on observance of Magna Carta in the Exchequer, 23 October 1300.

f. 53. Like concerning Ireland, 16 January 1300.

f. 54. Letters Patent to John de Harrington etc. on observance of Magna Carta and Statute of Winchester, 10 May 1300.

f. 56. Like for the Bishops, Abbots etc. of North Wales, 21 September 1300, like for Flint, Builth, Montgomery, and Powys Gruffydd.

f. 57. Plea for Bishop of Ely, from K.R. Mem. Roll, Comm., Trin., 28 Edward I.

f. 57v. Plea concerning Master William de Testa adjourned to Parliament (French), same, Mich., 4 Edward II.

f. 63. As f. 54 above.

f. 66v. Letters Patent to be intendant to Justices appointed on Articles and Statutes, 28 Edward I.

f. 67v. Like to Peter Crok etc. to receive oaths, 10 May 1300.

f. 69. Writ de expensis, burgesses, 20 March 1300.

Like to Bailiffs of Beverley, 20 March 1300, from New Misc. Bundle, t. Henry III etc., with note from Coke, *1st Inst.*

f. 65 (bis). Writ de expensis, knights, 20 March 1300.

f. 66 (bis). Like, 26 September 1300.

f. 68 (bis)x. Fines paid to King by various for confirming their charters: Barons of Cheshire, Bristol, Prior of Bolton, 28 Edward I, from Fine Roll.

f. 69 (bis). Writ of summons to Parliament, to Sheriff of Hertf., 26 September 1300, with return, from Bundle of Writs of Summons, 28 Edward I.

f. 71. Like, 29 December 1299.

f. 72. Mandate to Sheriffs on proclaiming and firmly observing the ordinance on money and others made, 28 Edward I.

f. 75. Like to Sheriffs on keeping the Stat. of Winchester, Magna Carta, and Charter of Forests, 2 May 1300.

f. 76. Letters Patent to community, co. Flint, on subsidy, 21 September 1300.

f. 77. Writs de expensis, knights and burgesses, 20 March 1300.

f. 81. Mandate on returning the standard of St. John of Beverley, 27 November 1301. Like on standard of St. Cuthbert.

f. 82. Letters Patent to men, co. Cumberland on forest of Inglewood, 1 November 1301.

f. 85. Like to Sheriff of Yorks. on election of knights to levy 15th, 8 October 1301.

f. 88. Writ of summons to Sheriff of Kent, Parliament, Lincoln, 30 January 1301.

f. 90. Like to Sheriff of Northants etc. 30 January 1301.

f. 92. Letters Patent to Sheriffs to be intendant to taxors of 15th, 24 October 1301.

f. 94. Letters sent by King to several towns to lend him money, 2 August 1301, from Close Roll.

f. 95v. Mandate to John de Drokensford, Keeper of Wardrobe, etc. on executing the above, 2 August 1301; form of credence on above (French).

f. 100. Letters Patent on assessing and levying 15th, 24 October 1301.

f. 103. Extract from Julius C. 7. Letter of Barons to Pope, 29 Edward I. Sealed 12 February 1301.

f. 107. As f. 81 above.

f. 108. Letter to Pope on rights of King in Scotland, 7 May 1301, from Close Roll.

f. 119x. Letters Patent on fines for 15th to King's use, 2 November 1301.

f. 120. Like to hasten taxation and payment of 15th, 6 October 1301 etc.

f. 122. Ordinance made by King and Council on return of inquisitions to Chancery, 29 Edward I, from Close Roll.

f. 124. Petition by Gilbert, Bishop of Chichester (French), from K.R. Mem. Roll, Comm., Rec. et Pet., East., 29 Edward I.

f. 130. Writ to Barons for John de Metingham on disputes with Mary, widow of William de Braose, from L.T.R. Mem. Roll, Brev. dir. Bar., East., 29 Edward I.

f. 131. The underwritten are the three writs which the King of France and the people of Scotland sent to Boniface VIII to begin the process against Edward, formerly King of England, from certain rolls in the Archives of the Arches of London, of the times of Edward I and Edward III, on the superiority of the kingdom of England over the kingdom of Scotland. (Cf. Prynne, *Records*, III.)

f. 135. Mandate on prohibition of tournament, 13 June 1302.

f. 136. Writs of summons to Parliament, 21 October 1302.

f. 137. Mandate to Sheriff of Lincs., 18 December 1301.

f. 138. Writs on prorogation of Parliament, 13 September 1302.

f. 140. Writs of summons to Parliament, 16 July 1302.

f. 142. Letters Patent for Abbot and Convent of Cirencester, 12 November 1302.

f. 144. Like of credence for King's affairs to commissioners, 18 December 1301.

f. 146. Fines made before Walter de Langton, Bishop of Coventry and Lichfield, Treasurer, in the King's Parliament at Westminster, 1 July 1302: Gloucester, Robert Viry, Norfolk, Prior of St. Stephen of Hampton, Cornwall, Thomas de Pridiad, Norfolk, William But etc., Kent, Barons of Faversham, from Fine Roll.

f. 148. Writs of summons to Parliament, 20 July 1302.

f. 150. Letters Patent on aid for marriage of King's eldest daughter, 7 November 1302.

f. 152. Like of exemplification of Bull by which Pope gave King tenth of ecclesiastical revenues in England and Ireland, 1 September 1302.

f. 154. Like to be intendant to collectors of aid for marriage of King's eldest daughter, 7 November 1302.

f. 156. Mandate to Prior of Merton on aid, 40s., 10 February 1303.

f. 157. Like for William de Campo Arnulphi, 4 February 1303.

f. 159. Like for Sheriffs to come to Exchequer, 7 May 1303.

f. 160. Like to Richard de Ferings, Archbishop of Dublin, 28 January 1303.

f. 161. Like for Ralph de Gorges and tenants of Isle of Wight, 13 May 1303.

f. 163. Writs to Barons for Hugh Wake and Hugh Daudley, 21 October 1301, from L.T.R. Comm., Rec., Trin., 31 Edward I, for Hugh de Escote, 30 October 1301, same East.

f. 165. Letters Patent for men of community, co. Northumberland, 4 January 1303.

f. 167. Like for Ralph Colt, 18 October 1313.

f. 168. Like to John de Langley etc. on collection of aid of 40s., 10 February 1303.

f. 170. Mandate to Coroners, cos. Salop and Staffs. on Sheriffs, 16 April 1303.

f. 172. Writ to Barons for Ralph de Gorges etc., from L.T.R. Mem. Roll, Comm., Brev. dir. Bar., East., 31 Edward I.

f. 173. Mandate for Abbot of Peterborough, 2 July 1304.

f. 175. Writs of summons to Parliament, 12 November 1304.

f. 176. Mandate to Sheriff of Kent for Gilbert de Malherbe, 20 March 1304.

f. 178. Letters Patent to taxors, co. Hunts., satisfaction for corn taken, 28 June 1304.

f. 179. Mandate for tenants of Bishop and Dean and Chapter of Hereford on tallage, 10 June 1304.

f. 179v. Like for various men, quittance of tallage.

f. 181. Like on respite of tallage for various Abbots etc. 28 July 1304.

f. 182. Letters Patent for Henry Urtiaco, 28 July 1304.

f. 183. As f. 173 above.

f. 185. Like for Abbot of Peterborough, 20 July 1304.

f. 187. Mandate for Abbot of Stanley, 26 March 1304.

f. 188. Letters Patent on trailbaston, 6 April 1305.

f. 191. Like to William de Bereford etc. 30 July 1305.

f. 192. On enquiry into homicides etc., from Mem. Parl., 35 Edward I.

f. 194. Ordinance made on settlement of land of Scotland (French), from Close Roll.

f. 202. Parliament, Westminster, 26 September 1305, petition of Margaret, King's daughter, from New Misc. Bundle, t. Henry III etc.

f. 203. Letters Patent to collectors of 15th, Cinque Ports, 19 February 1305.

f. 204. Writ de expensis, 20 March 1305.

f. 205. Form of commission made to taxors, 30th and 20th, 12 July 1306, from L.T.R. Mem. Roll, Comm., Rec., Trin., 34 Edward I.

f. 207. Mandates on aid to knight King's eldest son, 5 April 1305.

f. 209. Writs of summons to Parliament, Carlisle, 3 November 1306.

f. 210. Like to Bishops.

f. 211. Writ to Barons on knighting King's eldest son, from L.T.R. Mem. Roll, Comm., Brev. dir. Bar., Trin., 34 Edward I.

f. 215. Letters Patent that grant of 10th shall not prejudice, 30 May 1306.

f. 217. Writ to taxors, co. Somerset on 30th, 22 July 1306, with execution on dorse, from New Misc. Bundle, t. Henry III.

f. 219. As f. 215 above.

f. 221. From Stat. Roll, 34 Edward I, 27 May 1306.

f. 225. Mandate to William Greenfield, Archbishop of York, etc. 5 April 1306.

f. 227. Mandates on coming to treat on aid for knighting Prince Edward, 5 April 1306.

f. 229. Like to Sheriff of Southampton on William de Lamberton, Bishop of St. Andrews, 7 August 1306.

f. 230v. Like to keeper of castle of Porchester, 7 August 1306.

f. 231v. Like on Robert Wischard, Bishop of Glasgow, a prisoner, 34 Edward I.

f. 232. Like to Sheriff of Southampton on Scottish prisoners, same.

f. 233. Writ to Barons for men of Coventry, 18 October 1306, from L.T.R. Mem. Roll, Comm., Mich., 34 Edward I, with note from Close Roll, 34 Edward I, for Prior of Coventry, 18 October 1306.

f. 235. From an old MS. Book entitled Placita Parliamentaria, 33 Edward I, remaining among the records in the Tower of London.

f. 236. Writs de expensis, 30 May 1306.

f. 237. Mandates to Sheriffs to cause two to come from each co. to treat on sea coasts, 15 February 1307, from French Roll.

f. 238. Part of writ of summons to Parliament, from Plac. Parl.

f. 240. Writ, from L.T.R. Mem. Roll, Comm., Mich., 34 Edward I.

f. 242. Writs of summons to Parliament, Carlisle, 3 November 1306. Lists.

f. 248. List of names of those who were summoned to the Parliament of Carlisle, 35 Edward I, from Plac. Parl.

f. 252. Writ to those at Carlisle (French), 19 January 1307, same.

f. 263. Certificates of the Sheriffs of England of the knights, citizens and burgesses elected, from New Misc. Bundle, t. Henry III.

f. 271. Writ de expensis to Bailiffs of St. Albans, 20 January 1307.

f. 271v. Note on return of burgesses of St. Albans (cf. f. 263 above).

f. 272. Letters Patent for observance of Stat. in town of Kingston upon Hull, 29 January 1307.

f. 274. Form of oath of King's Council (French), from Close Roll.

f. 275. Short extracts from Plac. Parl.

f. 276. Letters Patent for men of community of Bishopric of Durham (French), 10 February 1307.

f. 278. Writ to Barons for Prior and Convent of Durham, 15 May 1307 (French), from L.T.R. Mem. Roll, Comm., Trin., 35 Edward I.

f. 279. Mandate to Mayor of Canterbury for Peter of Savoy, 10 December 1306.

f. 280. Like to Mayor of York, 16 March 1307.

f. 281. Extract from Walsingham on death of Edward I and succession of Edward II, 1307.

f. 284. Mandate to Sheriff of Lancs. on election of verderers, 1 March 1307.

f. 286. Letter to King of Norway, 6 March 1307, from Close Roll.

f. 288. As f. 238 above.

f. 289. Memorandum on King John and Richard, his son, from New Misc. Bundle, t. Henry III etc.

f. 291. Petition on the barony of Greystoke, with answer, from same.

f. 293. Letter to Edward I on castle of Kilkenny, from same.

f. 295. As f. 289 above.

f. 296. As f. 286 above.

f. 299. Letters Patent on subsidies of 30th and 20th, 1 December 1306.

f. 301. Like on assessment of same in liberties of Durham etc., 1 December 1306.

f. 303. As f. 281 above.

f. 307. Mandate to William Martin that conspirators are not to be put on recognitions or assizes, 24 April 1307.

f. 309. Writs de expensis, knights, 20 January 1307.

f. 310. Like, burgesses, 20 January 1307.

f. 311. Writ de expensis to Sheriff of Kent for Bartholomew de Badlesmere etc., 10 March 1307.

VOLUME 15

A volume of transcripts etc. from the Public Records and other sources, 1–35 Edward I. On flyleaf: The Rights of the Commons in Parliament by Prescription. Edward I. No. 3.

269 ff.

f. 1x. On the coronation of Edward I and the oath taken by him.

f. 1. Mandate for the provision made for the coronation of the King, 10 February 1274.

f. 3. On the nobility and display at the coronation of Edward I, from the Lib. de Antiq. Leg. in the Archives of the city of London.

f. 4. Memorandum on the King's coronation, with note from the Annals of Ireland at the end of Camden, *Brit.* and *Hist. Anglic. Quinque.*

f. 7. Letter from Edward I to the Pope, 19 January 1275.

f. 9. Note from Smith, *De Republ. Angl.*

f. 10. Writ to Treasurer and Barons of Exchequer on the Jews, 5 (November 1290).

f. 11. Letters Patent to Hugh de Digneneton on inquisition made on the doings of the Jews, 24 May 1277.

f. 13. Letters Patent for Robert Winchelsey, Archbishop of Canterbury, 1 November 1276.

f. 14. Statute of Gloucester, 6 Edward I, with translation.

f. 16. Memorandum at the Parliament of Westminster, 6 Edward I, on Alexander, King of Scotland.

f. 18. Revocation of the Provisions of the Council of Reading, 7 Edward I.

f. 19. Provision made on petitions in Parliament, 8 Edward I (French).

f. 20. Mandate, Ireland, on Hubert de Burgo, 10 June 1281.

f. 22. Mandate to Sheriffs on proclamation on the army of Wales, 2 July 1282, from Welsh Roll.

f. 24. Writ to Robert Burnel, Bishop of Bath and Wells, from Bundle of Writs and Letters, 10 Edward I. (Prynne, *Records*, III, p. 1252.)

f. 24v. Notes from New Misc. Bundle, t. Henry III, etc. 10 Edward I, Close Roll, 18 Edward I, and Patent Roll, 20 Edward I.

f. 26. Extract from Walsingham on the Parliament of Shrewsbury, 11 Edward I.

f. 28. Writ of summons to Gilbert de Clare, Earl of Gloucester and Hertford, etc. to treat concerning David ap Gruffydd. List. 28 June 1283, from Welsh Roll to f. 37v.

f. 32. Like to Sheriffs, 28 June 1283.

f. 34. Like to Mayors etc. 28 June 1283.

f. 37v. Writ to Sheriff of Norf. and Suff., 24 November 1283.

f. 40. Adjournment of King's Council to Parliament. To Barons of Exchequer for Jordan Godschef. (L.T.R. Mem. Roll, Comm., Mich. term, 14 Edward I.)

f. 41. Writ on dispute between the Bishop of Lincoln and the University of Oxford on jurisdiction, 30 September 1289, from Bundle of Writs, 17 Edward I. (Prynne, *Records*, III, p. 1297.)

f. 42. Writ to Sheriffs for those who wish to complain of King's officers, 13 October 1289.

f. 44v. Writ of summons to Sheriff of Cumberland, 14 June 1290. (Council not Parliament, see Prynne, *Records*, III.) From Bundle of Writs of Summons, 18 Edward I.

f. 46. On the marriage contracted between Edward, the King's son, and Margaret, the daughter of Eric, King of Norway.

f. 47. Bull of Nicholas IV, 16 Kal. December 2 Pont. (16 November 1289.)

f. 49. Letter from Edward I to Eric, King of Norway, 15 Kal. May 18 Edward I. (17 April 1290.)

f. 51. Letters Patent to magnates etc. of Scotland, 6 November 1289.

f. 52. Letters Patent to William Fraser, Bishop of St. Andrews etc. 28 August 1290.

f. 54. Treaty between Scotland and Norway on the marriage, 15 Kal. August (18 July) 1290. Ratification 28 August 1290.

f. 62. Letters Patent to Robert, Bishop of Glasgow, and John Comyn. (French.)

f. 65. Plaint of Master Adam de Fulburn on the church of Slane, Ireland, 16 February 1290, from New Misc. Bundle, t. Henry III.

f. 66. Letters Patent to Robert de Hertford etc. on inquisition on death of Roger Drayton, Treasurer of Earl of Cornwall, 6 May 1292.

f. 69. Ordinance of petitions in Parliament, 21 Edward I.

f. 70. Writs to Sheriffs to choose knights for Council, 8 October 1294.

Writs to Sheriffs for additional knights, 9 October 1294.

f. 72. On the Parliament at St. Edmund's, 23 Edward I.

f. 73. From the Roll of the Superiority of the King of England in the kingdom of Scotland and the fealty and homage of the King and Kingdom of Scotland, to the King of England, 19–23 Edward I. (Cf. Prynne, *Records*, III, p. 537.)

f. 82. Returns of writs of summons to Parliament, 23 Edward I, from Bundle of Writs K.R., 23 Edward I.

f. 83.	Sheriff of	Cumberland.	3 October 1295.
f. 84.	,,	Westmorland.	2 November 1295.
f. 85v.	,,	Northumberland.	3 October 1295.
f. 86.	,,	Cumberland.	,,
f. 87.	,,	Westmorland.	2 November 1295.
f. 87v.	,,	Essex and Hertf.	,,
f. 88.	,,	Lancashire.	,,
f. 89v.	,,	Kent.	,,
f. 90.	,,	Rutland.	,,
f. 90v.	,,	Middlesex.	,,
	,,	Surr. & Suss.	,,
f. 92v.	,,	Cambridge & Hunts.	,,
f. 93.	,,	Lincolnshire.	3 October 1295.
f. 94.	,,	Bedford.	2 November 1295.
f. 94v.	,,	Buckingham.	,,
	,,	Southampton.	,,
f. 96v.	,,	Cornwall.	3 October 1295.
f. 97.	,,	Worcestershire.	2 November 1295.
f. 99.	,,	Leicestershire.	,,
	,,	Yorkshire.	3 October 1295.
f. 101v.	,,	Gloucester.	2 November 1295.
f. 102v.	,,	Somerset.	,,
f. 104.	,,	Dorset.	,,
f. 105.	,,	Hereford.	,,
f. 105v.	,,	Devon.	,,
f. 106v.	,,	Oxfords.	,,
f. 107.	,,	Berkshire.	,,
f. 107v.	,,	Wiltshire.	,,
f. 108v.	,,	Salop.	,,
f. 109.	,,	Staffords.	,,
f. 109v.	,,	Nottinghams.	,,
f. 110v.	,,	Derbys.	,,
f. 111.	,,	Northumberland.	7 October 1295.

f. 112. Memorandum (by William Petyt). 'In my searches in the King's Remembrancer's Office in the Exchequer, near 20 years ago, I met with in a great chest several broken bundles of writs and other records in the reigns of different Kings huddled up together, and amongst them I found an imperfect bundle of writs of summons, with their returns, to a Parliament to be held at Westminster, 23 E. I. The very first precedent of that nature hitherto found out by any man that I heard of.

'This discovery being thus made by me, I ordered my clerk to take a copy of those writs and returns, which I have, and after acquainted Mr. Halsted (then Deputy to Sir Algernon May, Keeper of the Records at the Tower, and after to Dr. Brady) with my discovery, which I believe upon very good reasons Mr. Halsted after told the Doctor of.

'From this account two observations may arise.

'The first is that Mr. Prynne had not, in all his searches in the Exchequer, met with the bundle de Anno 23 E. I, for if he had, he would undoubtedly have taken notes thereof in his book called *Brevia Parliamentaria Rediviva*, as he did of several of the like nature afterwards.

'The second is that that bundle was found amongst the records of the Exchequer, and not amongst the records of the Tower, where the generality of the Parliamentary records are kept, from whence it may be presumed that that bundle of 23 E. I was not the first or only bundle of that kind which was lodged in the Exchequer, but that there may be several others of more ancient time which remain there yet undiscovered'.

f. 114. From Writs of Summons to Parliament at Westminster, 23 Edward I.

f. 115. Writs of summons to the Archbishop of Canterbury etc. 30 September 1295. Lists.

f. 119. Writs of summons to Edmund, Earl of Cornwall etc. 1 October 1295.

f. 121. Like to Sheriffs, 3 October 1295.

f. 122. Further of the Returns to Writs of summons to Parliament, 23 Edward I.

f. 123. Writ of summons to Sheriff of Northants, 3 October 1295.

f. 124. Return to writ of summons, co. Devon, from Bundle of Writs K.R., 23 Edward I.

f. 125. The like, co. Cumberland. (Ibid.)

f. 127. Letters Patent appointing collectors co. Cornwall, 14 October 1297.

f. 129. Letters Patent appointing taxors in various cos., 30 July 1297.

f. 130. Writs appointing taxors in various cos., 29 November 1296. (K.R. Mem. Rolls, Comm., Mich. term, 25 Edward I.)

f. 132. Letters Patent that the grant of 8th shall not prejudice, 28 August 1297.

f. 133. Writ to Sheriff of Yorks. concerning confirmation of Magna Carta, 15 September 1297.

f. 135. Statute de tallagio non concedendo, 34 Edward I, as printed in Coke, *2nd Inst.*, and note that it is in error dated 25 Edward I, with other notes on the same.

f. 140v. Sentence of excommunication by Robert Winchelsey, Archbishop of Canterbury, etc. 26 Edward I, 1 Ides July 1298 (15 July); 8 Kal. August 1298 (22 July), from Cleopatra E. 1.

f. 148. Returns to Writs of Summons to Parliament, 26 Edward I. The writs are all dated 13 April 1298 and the returns are from Bundle of Summons to Parliament, 26 Edward I.

f. 149. Cambridge.
f. 150. Essex.
f. 151. Bedford.
f. 151v. Buckingham.
f. 152. Cornwall.
f. 153. Dorset.
f. 154. Derbyshire.
f. 154v. Devon.
f. 156. Yorkshire.
f. 156v. Gloucestershire.
f. 157v. Hertfordshire.
f. 158. Huntingdonshire.
f. 158v. Lancashire.
f. 160v. London (10 April 1298).
Lincolnshire.

f. 161. Middlesex.
Norfolk.
f. 161v. Northants.
f. 162. Rutland.
f. 162v. Nottinghamshire.
f. 163. Northumberland.
f. 163v. Salop.
f. 164v. Staffordshire.
Southampton.
f. 165v. Suffolk.
f. 166. Sussex.
f. 167. Surrey.
f. 168. Somerset.
f. 169v. Westmorland.
f. 170. Wiltshire.
f. 171. Worcestershire.
f. 172. Herefordshire.
f. 172v. Oxfordshire.
f. 173. Kent.
f. 174. Warwickshire.

f. 175. Writs to Sheriffs to summon 3 knights to York concerning Magna Carta and the Charter of the Forests, 27 March 1300.

f. 176. Writs de expensis to Sheriffs, 20 March 1300.

f. 179. Like to Bailiffs etc. 20 March 1300.

f. 180. Writ de expensis to Sheriffs, 30 January 1301.

f. 181. Like to Bailiffs etc. 30 January 1301.

f. 182. Truce between English and French, Scots included, 29 Edward I. Earl of Pembroke to Ambassadors. (See Prynne, *Records*, III, p. 874.)

f. 183. Truce between King of France and John Balliol, King of Scotland, 29 Edward I. (Ibid., p. 894.)

f. 184. Writ to observe Magna Carta and the Charter of the Forests, 16 February 1302. From Miscellanea in a certain box in the Tower of London.

f. 186. Writs of summons to Parliament to Sheriffs, 20 July 1302.

f. 188. Writs on prorogation of Parliament, 13 September 1302.

f. 189. Writs of summons to Parliament, 21 October 1302.

f. 191. Writ of supersedeas to Barons of Exchequer for Hugh Wake and Hugh Daudley, 21 October 1302. Collectors of 15th. (L.T.R. Mem. Roll, Comm., Rec., Trin. term, 31 Edward I.)

f. 192. Writ of supersedeas to same for Hugh Escotte, – October 1302. (Ibid., East. term, 31 Edward I.)

f. 193. Form of summons to Parliament at Westminster, 32 Edward I.

f. 194. Writs of summons to Edward, Prince of Wales etc. 12 November 1304. List.

f. 196. Writs of summons to Robert, Archbishop of Canterbury etc. 12 November 1304. Lists.

f. 199. Writ of summons to Roger le Brabazon etc. 12 November 1304. List.

f. 200. Writs of summons to Sheriffs, 12 November 1304.

f. 202. Writs de expensis to Sheriffs, 20 March 1305.

f. 204. Ordinance on receipt of petitions in Parliament (French). From Plac. Parl. (*Plac. Parl.*, pp. 240–1.)

f. 206. Writ on petitions received to Gilbert de Roubiry etc. 4 September 1305.

f. 207. Writ to come to treat on aid to knight Prince Edward, to Archbishop of York etc. 5 April 1306. List.

f. 209. Like writ to Henry de Lacy, Earl of Lincoln, etc. 5 April 1306. List.

f. 212. Writs on aid granted to knight Prince Edward (L.T.R. Mem. Roll, Comm., Brev., Trin. term, 34 Edward I), with notes from Patent Rolls, 34 Edward I and 35 Edward I.

f. 216. Letters Patent that grant of 30th should not prejudice, 30 May 1306.

f. 218. Writs of summons to Parliament, Carlisle, to Sheriffs, 3 November 1306.

f. 220. Writs de expensis, Parliament, Westminster, knights and burgesses, 30 May 1306.

f. 221. Writs to Sheriffs on aid for knighting Prince Edward, 5 April 1306.

f. 223. Writs on 20th. (L.T.R. Mem. Roll, Comm., Brev. Ret., Mich. term, 34 Edward I.)

f. 224. Parliament towards end of reign of Edward I. Assent to marriage between Prince Edward and daughter of King of France, from New Misc. Bundle, t. Henry III etc.

f. 229. Writs to Sheriffs on observance of Statute of Winchester, 22 July 1306.

f. 233. Mandate to Boniface de Saluciis on advowson of church of Bridgeford, 8 February 1307.

f. 234. Memorandum on Ordinance (French), 26 February 1307.

f. 236. Mandate to William Martin that conspirators not to be put on recognitions or assizes, 24 April 1307.

f. 238. On subsidies granted, 35 Edward I.

f. 239. Letters Patent on 30th and 20th granted, 1 December 1306.

f. 241. Like in liberties of Durham etc. 1 December 1306.

f. 243. Writs of summons to Parliament of Carlisle, 35 Edward I.

f. 244. Writ of summons from Placita Parliamentaria. (*Plac. Parl.*, pp. 318–20.)

f. 245. Certificates of Sheriffs on returns, from New Misc. Bundle, t. Henry III.

f. 253. Proclamation on dissolution of Parliament of Carlisle, 35 Edward I, from Plac. Parl. (*Plac. Parl.*, p. 289.)

f. 254. Writs de expensis to Sheriffs, knights, 20 January 1307.

f. 255. Like, 10 March 1307.

f. 256. Like to Mayors etc., burgesses, 20 January 1307.

f. 258. On death of Edward I at Burgh on Sands outside Carlisle, 35 Edward I, 7 July 1307. Memorandum on Fine Roll.

f. 260. The gathering of ships, 25 Edward I, is worth noting.

f. 261. Writs to Sheriffs etc. 27 April 1297. Lists.

f. 266. Mandates to Barons of Cinque Ports etc. that no man to leave realm without King's licence, 31 January 1297. List.

VOLUME 16

A volume of transcripts etc. from the Public Records and other sources, 1–8 Edward II. On flyleaf: 'Recorda ab anno lmo E. 2 ad annum 90. Vol. I tempore E. 2'. 257 ff.

f. 1. Letters Patent for John de Lent, 27 October 1307.

f. 3. The community of the realm to the King, 1 Edward II (French). From New Misc. Bundle, t. Henry III.

f. 5. Writ to Barons of Exchequer for burgesses of Great Yarmouth, 3 February 1308.

f. 7. On collection of 15th. To Vicar General of Bishop of Worcester. John, Bishop of Norwich, 8 Kal. February (25 January) 1300/1. (K.R. Mem. Roll, Comm., Hil. term, 1 Edward II.)

f. 9. Letters Patent to Roger le Brabazon etc. on matter of Bishop of Coventry and Lichfield, 24 November 1307.

f. 11. On the debts of Walter de Langton, Bishop of Coventry and Lichfield (French). (K.R. Mem. Roll, Mich. term, m. 21, 1 Edward II.)

f. 12v. Writ to Treasurer and Barons of Exchequer on above, 27 November 1307. (Ibid.)

f. 14. Letter to Constable of Bordeaux for Peter Gaveston, 1 December 1307.

f. 15. The Coronation Roll of Edward II (to f. 24v).

f. 25. The coronation of the King and his oath.

f. 26. Mandate (French).

f. 27. Form of oath of those of the King's Council (French).

f. 28. Writs to William Greenfield, Archbishop of York etc. to be present at the coronation, 18 January 1308. Lists.

f. 30v. After the return of the King from parts overseas. Writs to Robert Winchelsey, Archbishop of Canterbury etc. to be present at the coronation, 9 February 1308. Lists.

f. 33. Writs to Sheriffs to be present at the coronation, 18 January 1308.

f. 34. As f. 30v above.

f. 35. Oath at King's coronation, from Vespasian B. 7.

f. 36. Letters Patent on the King's coronation.

f. 37. As f. 26 above.

f. 38. Precept to cities, boroughs etc. on timber to Sheriffs. (K.R. Mem. Roll, Brev. Retorn., Hil. term, 1 Edward II.)

f. 39. The Reports of the Cases argued and adjudged in the time of Edward II, according to the ancient manuscripts in the hands of Sir John Maynard, Serjeant at Law to Charles II, Trin. term, 1 Edward II, on replevin. (French.)

f. 42. An Abridgment of several cases and resolutions of the Common Law, by Henry Rolle, Serjeant at Law. Vol. II, Title, prescription, 2 Edward II. (French.)

f. 43. Reports of cases argued and adjudged in the time of Edward II, Mich. term, 11 Edward II. On replevin. (French.)

f. 45. Writs of summons to Parliament, 26 August 1307. Lists.

f. 52. Charter for Peter Gaveston, 7 June 1308, with mandate thereon.

f. 56. Writ to Sheriff of Kent to be present at coronation, 18 January 1308.

f. 57. Letters Patent on the passage of Peter Gaveston from England (French), 18 May 1308.

f. 58. Petition to Council from Adam de Everingham, t. Edward II (French), from New Misc. Bundle, t. Henry III.

f. 56x. Writs de expensis, knights and burgesses, 13 May 1308.

f. 57x. Like, lists of Sheriffs and names of members, 13 May 1308.

f. 58xx. Proxy by Abbot of Reading, Sunday, Morrow of St. Mark, 2 Edward II (26 April 1308), appointing brother and chamberlain Brother Henry de Lynton. Given at Reading. From New Misc. Bundle, t. Henry III.

f. 59. Writ of summons to Parliament, 4 March 1308, from Bundle of Summons to Parliament, 2 Edward II.

f. 61. Writ de expensis to Sheriff of Kent, 10 January 1309, from Bundle of Brev. Reg., t. Edward II.

f. 62. Writs to William de Greenfield, Archbishop of York etc. on 15th, 30 November 1308. (K.R. Mem. Roll, Brev. Ret., Mich. term, 2 Edward II.)

f. 64. Inquisition ad quod damnum, Robert fitz Payn, on making town of Frampton a free borough, from Bundle of Inquisitions, 2 Edward II.

f. 65. Writ to Barons of Exchequer for John Danyel, 1 December 1308. (L.T.R. Mem. Roll, Brev. dir. Bar., Mich. term, 2 Edward II.)

f. 65v. Like for William Greenfield, Archbishop of York, 30 November 1308. (Ibid.)

f. 67. Letter from Edward II to Clement V, 16 June 1308.

f. 68v. Letter from Edward II to Philip, King of France.

f. 69v. Letter from Edward II to Clement V for Earl of Cornwall, 4 September 1308.

f. 71. Letters Patent for merchants of Portugal etc. 3 October 1308.

f. 72. Letters Patent to Roger le Brabazon etc. for Abbot of Westminster, 14 July 1308.

f. 73. Mandate to Robert de Kendale, for Abbot of Clive etc. 4 October 1308.

f. 74. Writs de expensis, knights and burgesses, 13 May 1309.

f. 76. Mandate for Bishops of Lincoln and London, collectors of triennial 10th, 10 December 1309.

f. 77. Letters Patent to magnates prohibiting them coming armed to Parliament. List. (French.) 7 February 1309.

f. 84. Writ (with endorsement), 16 December 1308, from New Misc. Bundle, t. Henry III.

f. 86. Writ of privy seal to John de Langton, Bishop of Chichester, Chancellor, sending articles (French), 14 August 1310 (ibid.), with reference to Fine Roll, 1 Edward II.

f. 88x. Petition of the prelates, earls and barons, 3 Edward II (French), from MS. Book, Laudes Brit. in Archives of city of London.

f. 89. Mandate to Sheriff of York etc. on removes, 18 December 1309.

f. 90. Charter for Peter Gaveston and Margaret, his wife, 5 August 1309.

f. 98. Letters Patent to be intendant to collectors of 25th, 30 May 1310.

f. 100. Letters Patent on the 10th, Ireland, delivered to Alexander Bicknor, 18 June 1310.

f. 101. On Council, York, under William Greenfield, Archbishop of York, 1311. (From Spelman, *Conc.*, II, p. 472.)

f. 102. Writs of summons to Parliament to Sheriffs, 16 June 1311.

f. 103. Mandate on goods and chattels etc. of Anthony, late Bishop of Durham, taken into King's hands, 3 March 1311.

f. 104. Letters Patent that subsidy granted for war against Scotland shall not prejudice, 26 February 1311, from Fine Roll.

f. 105. Writ to Treasurer and Barons of Exchequer on punishment of those acting against Statute of Carlisle, 16 December 1310.

f. 107. Writ to Barons of Exchequer on tallage on religious, 16 December 1310. (K.R. Mem. Rolls, Comm., Hil. term, 4 Edward II.)

f. 109. Letters Patent to Treasurer and Barons of Exchequer on attorney of Walter de Langton, Bishop of Coventry and Lichfield, 15 December 1310.

f. 110. Letter from Edward II to Pope, 4 May 1311.

f. 112. Writs of summons to Parliament for Robert Winchelsey, Archbishop of Canterbury etc. 16 June 1311.

f. 114. As f. 105 above.

f. 116. Writ to Treasurer and Barons of Exchequer on searching books and memoranda of Exchequer for manors and lands held of King in chief, 12 December 1310.

f. 117. Mandate to collectors of customs in Southampton for men of Island of Guernsey, 18 February 1311.

f. 118. Mandates to Bailiffs of Norwich etc. 18 December 1311.

f. 119. Writs de expensis to Sheriffs, 18 December 1311.

f. 120. Like to Sheriffs, 11 October 1311.

f. 121. Writs to Gilbert de Clare, Earl of Gloucester and Hertford etc. on coming to Parliament armed, 28 November 1311.

f. 122. Letters Patent to Hugh de Courtney and William Martin on search for Peter Gaveston at liberty in cos. Devon, Cornwall, Somerset and Dorset, 30 November 1311.

f. 123. Mandates to Sheriff of Cornwall etc. on castles of Peter Gaveston, 30 November 1311, from Fine Roll.

f. 124. Letters Patent for Walter Langton, Bishop of Coventry and Lichfield, 23 January 1312.

f. 125. Mandate to Sheriff of York etc. 24 February 1312.

f. 127. Document from Lib. de Antiq. Leg. in Archives of city of London, Monday after Assumption, 5 Edward II (16 August 1311). (French.)

f. 129. Mandate to Robert de Retford etc. 12 September 1311.

f. 130. Writs on prorogation of Parliament to Sheriffs, 20 January 1312.

f. 131. Writs of summons to Parliament to Sheriffs, 19 December 1311.

f. 132. Writ (with endorsement) to Mayor etc. of Lynne about mill of Lotheryn, 16 December 1311, from Bundle of Brev. Reg., 5 Edward II.

f. 134. Letter from Jurats of Bordeaux, Morrow of St. Thomas the Martyr, 5 Edward II (30 December 1311). (Ibid.)

f. 136. Writs of summons to Parliament to Roger Bigod, Earl of Norfolk, 1 November 1311, from MS. Register of Writs in possession of John Lapthorne.

f. 137. Writ to Barons of Exchequer for Ralph de Gorges, 16 July 1311. (L.T.R. Mem. Roll, Brev. dir. Bar., Trin. term, 5 Edward II.)

f. 139. Mandate to Walter le Keu etc. 20 July 1311.

f. 143. Certificate made to King concerning coming of certain Earls to Exchequer, 4 April 1312. (French.) (L.T.R. Mem. Roll, Comm., East. term, 5 Edward II.)

f. 145. Mandate to Robert fitz Payn to take into King's hands bailiffs and officers of forests South and North of Trent, 4 December 1311.

f. 146. Writs de expensis to Bailiffs of St. Albans etc. 11 October 1311, with translation.

f. 148. Writs to Sheriffs on continuation of Parliament, 11 October 1311.

f. 149. Writs of summons to Parliament to Robert Winchelsey, Archbishop of Canterbury etc. 19 December 1311.

f. 150. Writ de expensis to Sheriff of Wilts., 1 November 1311, from Bundle of Brev. Reg. 5 Edward II.

f. 152. Writ to Sheriff of Wilts. on liberties of Marlborough, 18 December 1311, with Inquisition, Clatford, Friday after Octave of St. Hilary, 5 Edward II (21 January 1312). (Ibid.)

f. 155. Writ to Sheriff of Hertford on writ de expensis to St. Albans, 20 January 1312. (Ibid.)

f. 161. Writs of summons to Parliament to Sheriffs, 13 February 1313.

f. 163. Writs of summons to Parliament to Sheriffs. Lists. 8 January 1313.

f. 165. Letters Patent to John de Bensted on correction of the Ordinances, 4 August 1312.

f. 167. Letters Patent for community of co. Notts., 15 April 1313.

f. 170. Writ de expensis to Sheriffs, 20 January 1313, from New Misc. Bundle, t. Henry III etc.

f. 172. Memorandum on adjournment of Parliament, 28 August 1312.

f. 173. Memorandum on birth of Edward, son of Edward II (13 November 1312).

f. 174. Writ of summons to Parliament to Sheriffs, 26 July 1313.

f. 176. Writs of summons to Parliament to Sheriffs, 26 November 1313.

f. 177. Writ de expensis to Sheriffs, 18 November 1313.

f. 178. Writ de expensis to Sheriff of Norf. and Suff., 25 July 1313.

f. 179. Book of 20th and 15th granted by laity to Edward II, at Westminster, 7 Edward II, at the Clerk of the Pipe. Account 1 December 1313, enrolled in K.R. Mem. Roll, Rec., Mich. term, 7 Edward I.

Writ to Barons of Exchequer for Nicholas de Audley, 1 July 1314. (Ibid., Brev. dir. Bar., Trin. term, 7 Edward II.)

f. 181. Writs to Walter Reynolds, Archbishop of Canterbury, on collection of 10th, 1 July 1314.

f. 182. Writ to Justices in Eyre, co. Kent, for Bartholomew de Badlesmere, 27 May 1314.

f. 183. Writs to Sheriffs for proclamation on loss of privy seal, 27 June 1314.

f. 184. Writs to Walter Reynolds, Archbishop of Canterbury, etc. on aid from clergy, 27 March 1314.

f. 186. Statute on bearing of arms, 7 Edward II. (French.)

f. 188. Letters Patent that no one to be imprisoned for death of Peter Gaveston, 6 November 1313. (French.)

f. 189. Like. (French.)

f. 191. Letters Patent for Thomas, Earl of Lancaster and his adherents, 5 November 1313.

f. 192. Letters Patent on collection and levying of 20th and 15th. List. 28 November 1313.

f. 195. Form of assessment of 20th and 15th. (French.)

f. 197v. Letters Patent to Barons of Cinque Ports, 10 May 1314.

f. 198. Letters Patent to John de Thornhill etc. 20 February 1314.

f. 200. Writ to Prior of Hospital of St. John of Jerusalem on wages of Templar, William de Langford, 10 May 1314, from Bundle of Writs, 7 Edward II.

f. 203. Mandate to Roger Mortimer, Justice of Wales, for Griffin de la Pole and Fulk Lestrange, 22 November 1313.

f. 205. As f. 197v above.

f. 206. Letters Patent to Sheriffs on molestation of Peter Gaveston, 16 October 1313. (French.)

f. 208. Letters Patent for community of co. Midd. etc. on 20th, 28 November 1313.

f. 210. Letter from Edward II to Clement V on issues of Duchy of Aquitaine, 28 October 1313. (*Gascon Rolls*, pp. 307–8.)

f. 211v. Letter from Edward II to Philip, King of France. (Ibid., pp. 308–9.)

f. 212v. Letter on customs etc. in Aquitaine assigned to Pope, 20 January 1314. (Ibid.)

f. 222. Mandate to Gilbert de Clare, Earl of Gloucester and Hertford on Bristol, 18 August 1313.

f. 224. Writs de expensis to Sheriffs, 24 October 1314.

f. 225. Writs of summons to Parliament to Sheriffs, 24 October 1314.

f. 227. Letters Patent to Walter Stapledon, Bishop of Exeter, etc. to open Parliament, 7 September 1314.

f. 228. Writ to Barons of Exchequer for men of Beverley, 11 June 1315. (L.T.R. Mem. Roll, Comm., Brev. dir. Bar., Trin. term, 8 Edward II.)

f. 230. Letters to Mayor etc. of Bordeaux, 12 June 1315. (*Gascon Rolls*, p. 394.)

f. 231. Letters Patent to William Inge etc. on making perambulations. List. 10 May 1315.

f. 233. Mandates to William Greenfield, Archbishop of York, and Walter Reynolds, Archbishop of Canterbury, on carrying Cross, 3 September 1314.

f. 234. Like to Dean and Chapter of St. Peter's, York, on same.

f. 235. Like to Sheriff of York on same.

f. 237. Mandate to Sheriff of York on extortions of religious houses, 11 June 1315.

f. 240. Petition of David, Earl of Athol (French). With answer, 8 Edward II.

f. 241. As f. 227 above.

f. 242. Concession to burgesses of St. Albans, translation only, from Parliament Roll, 8 Edward II.

f. 243. Names of Justices and others of King's Council summoned to Parliament, 8 Edward II, with reference to Dugdale, *Orig. Jur.*

f. 243v. Note that 'the whole Bundle of Writs of Summons and Returns to the Parliament held the next year, vizt. 9 E. 2, at Lincoln, is utterly lost; many more instances of the like nature might be given'.

f. 244. The texts of the documents translated (above, ff. 242, 243), from Parliament Roll, 8 Edward II, together with letters patent for the men etc. of St. Albans and the taking of the barony of the Abbot of St. Albans into the King's hands.

f. 246. Writs de expensis to Sheriffs, 9 March 1315.

f. 246v. Translation of part of f. 242 above.

f. 248. Translation of f. 246 above.

f. 249. As f. 240 above.

f. 250. Letters Patent to Sheriff of Staffs. and Salop on information received on hindrances made to the collectors of the 20th, 8 June 1315.

f. 252. As f. 250 above.

f. 254. Letter from John Ketton, Bishop of Ely, to the Treasurer and Barons of the Exchequer, 22 May 1315, from Bundle of Brev. Reg., 9 Edward II.

f. 255. Letters Patent for Master William de Bicton, 8 October 1314.

f. 257. Mandate to William de Ormesby etc. for men of cos. Norf. and Suff. at Lincoln at Parliament, 12 September 1314.

Like to Lambert de Trikingham etc. for assizes co. Lancs.

Like to John de Mitford etc. for Thomas Fillol and John de Grey, 13 September 1314.

VOLUME 17

A volume of transcripts etc. from the Public Records and other sources, 9–14 Edward II. On flyleaf: Recorda ab anno 9 Edw. 2 ad annum 15. Vol. 2. 230 ff.

f. 1. Letters Patent on musters against Scotland, 26 March 1316.

f. 5. Mandate to Sheriffs to cause to come before King's Council at Lincoln on perambulation, 25 June 1316.

f. 7. Writ to Keeper of Spiritualities of York, Parliament at Lincoln, 17 January 1316.

f. 7x. Like to Dean and Chapter of St. Peter's, York, on same.

f. 8. On various liberties granted to the clergy (extract only), from Statute Roll, 9 Edward II.

f. 9. Writ to William de Bereford to come to King, 27 December 1315.

f. 10. Writs of summons to Parliament, to Sheriffs, 17 October 1315.

f. 11. Writ of summons to Parliament to Walter Reynolds, Archbishop of Canterbury, 16 October 1315.

f. 12. Writ to Bailiffs of Salop on having counsel on the staple in France.

f. 13. Writs to Sheriffs on information on hundreds, cities, towns etc. 5 March 1316.

f. 14. As f. 9 above.

f. 15. As f. 7 above.

f. 16. Letters Patent on naturalization of Charles de Flisco, of the King's Council and household, 6 August 1315.

f. 17. Letters Patent for Roger le Brabazon, relief from office, 23 February 1316.

f. 19. Writ to Barons of Exchequer for King, 8 March 1316. (L.T.R. Mem. Roll, Brev. dir. Bar., Hil. term, 9 Edward II.)

f. 21. As f. 8 above.

f. 22. Form of grant of foot men from each vill for expedition in the Scottish war. (French.)

f. 24. Letters Patent for King on making of fealty in co. Westmorland etc. 17 December 1315, from Scottish Roll.

f. 25. Letters on the city of Vascati etc. 18 May 1316. (*Gascon Rolls*, p. 469.)

f. 28. Letters Patent on keeping and observing the perambulations, 16 February 1316.

f. 30. Letters for Almaric de Credonio concerning Bertrand de Gulo, 2 September 1316. (*Gascon Rolls*, p. 410.)

f. 33. Letters Patent for Margaret, Queen of England, 10 February 1316.

f. 35. As f. 13 above.

f. 36. Writ to Sheriff of Southampton, 25 June 1316. From Bundle of Writs to elect two knights to make perambulations of the forests, 9 Edward II.

f. 39. Mandate to knights etc. West Riding, co. Yorks. on 20th, 28 July 1315, from Fine Roll.

f. 40. Like to Mayors etc. of all cities etc. in West Riding on same.

f. 42. Mandate to Justices of Bench for Richard Lovel, 6 August 1315.

f. 43. Writs to Sheriffs on wines at a certain price, 10 July 1315.

f. 43v. Mandate to William Martin, Justice of West Wales, 6 August 1315.

f. 44. As f. 43 above.

f. 45. Mandate to Roger le Brabazon etc. on disputes of men of Yarmouth, 8 October 1315.

f. 46. As f. 42 above.

f. 47. Writ under secret seal to William Greenfield, Archbishop of York, etc. 16 July 1315 (French). From New Misc. Bundle, t. Henry III.

f. 49. Writs to William Greenfield, Archbishop of York, etc. on payment of 10th, 1 September 1315.

f. 53. Letters Patent for men of West and South Wales on observance of customs, 7 February 1316.

f. 55. Like for men of North Wales on same, 7 February 1316.

f. 57. Writs to Sheriffs to come before King's Council about perambulations, 28 June 1316.

f. 59. Writs to Sheriffs on information about perambulations, 20 February 1316.

f. 61. Like to Hugh le Despenser the elder on same.

f. 64. Writ to Roger le Brabazon, 8 March 1316.

f. 66. Writ to William de Bedford, Prior of Breamore, 26 June 1316. From select Bundle of Writs and Records, t. Edward II.

f. 67. Letters Patent for William de Bourne etc. 28 May 1316.

f. 69. Letters Patent for cathedral churches on loans, 21 March 1316.

f. 72. Mandate to Sheriffs to make proclamation on arms, 28 February 1316.

f. 73. Writs de expensis to Sheriffs, 8 August 1316.

f. 74. Letters Patent for William de Hibbaen etc., collectors of scutage, 7 September 1316.

f. 75. Letters Patent to Gilbert Pecche, kt., Seneschal of Gascony, 18 July 1316. (*Gascon Rolls*, p. 488.)

f. 78. Letters Patent for observing inviolably the Statute for the clergy, 24 November 1316.

f. 82. Writ to Walter Reynolds, Archbishop of Canterbury, on the subsidy of the clergy, 8 December 1316.

f. 84. Writ to the same etc. on levying and collecting the same, 15 February 1317.

f. 86. Writ to Abbot of St. Edmund's, 15 February 1317, from New Misc. Bundle, t. Henry III etc.

f. 87. Writ to William de Bourne on inquiry on taxors, 17 June 1317, from Fine Roll.

f. 89. Memorandum on Sheriffs and Coroners as Justices, 16 April 1317.

f. 100. Writ to Sheriffs on resistant officials, 20 February 1317.

f. 102. Letters Patent of safe conduct for Pope's messengers, 3 May 1317.

f. 103. Statute for clergy, 3 Edward I, from Statute Roll, 10 Edward II, 24 November 1316.

f. 106. Mandates to Sheriffs on proclamation on measures, 20 February 1317.

f. 109. Mandate for Prior of Bolton in Craven, 13 May 1317, from Fine Roll.

f. 110. Mandate for Friars Preachers to pray for King and Queen, 24 August 1316.

f. 111. Writ to Treasurer and Chamberlains of Exchequer on expenses of King's household, 1 October 1310.

f. 112. Memorandum on Keeper of Rolls, 19 August 1316.

f. 113. Letters Patent on aid, foot soldiers, 5 August 1316.

f. 115. Mandate to Robert de Kendale on taking money out, 6 August 1316.

f. 116. Writ to Barons of Exchequer for King, 22 November 1317, from L.T.R. Mem. Roll, Brev. dir. Bar., Mich. term, 11 Edward II.

f. 117. Writ for executor of Anthony, late Bishop of Durham, 8 July 1317. (Ibid.)

f. 118. Letters from Edward II to Pope, 25 August 1317.

f. 122. Writ to Sheriff of Devon for Walter, Bishop of Exeter, 10 May 1318, from Brev. Reg., 11 Edward II.

f. 124. Writs to Sheriffs on prorogation of Parliament, 3 March 1318.

f. 125. Writs of summons to Parliament to Sheriffs, 20 November 1317.

f. 126. Letters Patent to John Botetort etc. on inquiry on measures, 6 March 1318.

f. 127. Writs of summons to Parliament to Walter, Archbishop of Canterbury etc. 20 November 1317. List.

f. 128. Mandates to Sheriffs prohibiting taking victuals, 22 November 1317.

f. 130. Letters Patent to commissioners co. Kent etc. 14 March 1318. (French.) from Scottish Roll.

f. 132. Letters Patent to John, Bishop of Norwich etc. 20 March 1318.

f. 134. Mandates to Walter, Archbishop of Canterbury etc. on prohibition, 17 February 1318.

f. 135. Mandates to Sheriffs of Yorks. etc. on proclamation on Cardinals, 20 September 1317.

f. 136. Mandate to Sheriff of Lincs. on fair of Boston, 3 August 1317.

f. 138. Extract from manuscript of Abbey of St. James, Northampton, from Selden, *Titles of Honor*, p. 604.

f. 142. Writs of summons to Parliament to Sheriffs, 25 August 1318.

f. 143. Extract from Statute Roll, 12 Edward II.

f. 144. Letters Patent of pardon to Thomas, Earl of Lancaster, 22 October 1318.

f. 145. Writ to Treasurer and Barons of Exchequer for Ralph Basset of Drayton, 5 December 1318.

f. 146. Writs of summons to Parliament to Sheriffs, 29 March 1319.

f. 147. Letters Patent to Mayor etc. of London, 12 August 1318. List, from Scottish Roll.

f. 151. Letters Patent for Thomas de Hotton, 15 February 1319.

f. 153. Extract from Statute of York, from Statute Roll, 12 Edward II.

f. 154. Letters Patent to Bailiffs etc. of Great Yarmouth etc. on subsidy, ships, 16 April 1319.

f. 155. Letters Patent of pardon, 19 November 1318. List.

f. 157. As f. 151 above.

f. 161. Writ to Treasurer and Barons of Exchequer on counterfeit money, 2 February 1319.

f. 164. As f. 145 above.

f. 165. Writ to Treasurer and Barons of Exchequer for burgesses of Bamburgh, 26 November 1318.

f. 167. Writ to same on levying 18th, 30th May 1319.

f. 168. Writ on commissions, 18th and 12th, 6 June 1319.

f. 168v. Writ on fines for 12th, 8 June 1319.

f. 170. Letters Patent on assessing and levying of 10th, 30 May 1319. List.

f. 172v. Form directed to ecclesiastics in Province of Canterbury. (French.)

f. 179. Letters Patent to Sheriffs on 18th, 30 May 1319.

f. 179v. Letters Patent, commissions on same, 30 May 1319.

f. 181. Writ on contributions de expensis, co. Bedf., 16 January 1316.

f. 183. Mandates to William Inge etc. on estreats and rolls, 8 June 1318. List.

f. 186. Letters Patent for Jakinett de Mareguy, 26 November 1318.

f. 187. Mandate to Sheriff of Glouc. for John Giffard of Brimsfield, 18 January 1319.

f. 188. Letters Patent for Thomas de Grey, 17 May 1319.

f. 190. Mandates to Mayors etc. on loans, 20 July 1319. List.

f. 193. Mandate to Walter, Archbishop of Canterbury, on imperial notaries, 26 April 1320.

f. 193v. Mandate to Sheriff of London on same.

f. 195. Mandate to Richard Caleware for Hugh Daudley and Margaret, his wife, 1 July 1319, with reference to 20 July 1319.

f. 197. Memorandum, 4 June 1320, on King crossing overseas.

f. 199. Letters Patent to Sheriff of Notts. on men of ancient demesne and assizes, 21 January 1320.

f. 200. Mandate to William de Ayremyne on custody of lands late of Gerard Salvayn, 24 November 1320.

f. 201. Letters Patent to Henry Spigurnel etc., 27 November 1320.

f. 204. Letters Patent to Nicholas Kingston etc. on inquiry on salmon, 17 April 1321.

f. 205. Writ of supersedeas, subsidy, Archpriest of Dover etc., 18 July 1320.

f. 207. Letters Patent for William de Clyf, 6 November 1320.

f. 208. Letters Patent to Roger, Bishop of Salisbury, on goods of Abbot of Abingdon, 21 November 1320.

f. 209. Writ to Treasurer and Barons of Exchequer on sending measures to cos., 25 November 1320.

f. 210. Writ of privy seal to John, Bishop of Norwich, 26 October 1320. (French.) Bundle t. Henry III.

f. 211. Writ of privy seal to Keepers of Great Seal on treasure in Tower of London etc., 7 August 1320. (French.) (Ibid.)

f. 212. Letters Patent for Abbot of Cormeilles, 20 November 1320.

f. 214. Letters Patent to Thomas de Colvill etc. on Statute of York, 24 February 1321.

f. 216. Letters Patent to Henry Spigurnel etc. 18 December 1320.

f. 219. Petition by knights etc. on felonies. Appointments, 1 February 1321.

f. 221. Mandate to Abbot of Tintern on 10th granted, 10 Edward I, 28 December 1320. From Fine Roll.

f. 223. Mandate to Sheriff of London, summons to Eyre, 20 November 1320.

f. 226. As f. 201 above.

f. 229. Letters Patent. Memorandum on damages, men of Flanders.

VOLUME 18

A volume of transcripts etc. from the Public Records and other sources, 15–20 Edward II. On flyleaf: Recorda tempore Edwardi II, 15–21 [*sic*], 1321–1327. 185 ff.

f. 1. Mandate to Edmund, Earl of Arundel, Justice of Wales, on sending Welsh to Parliament, 18 April 1322.

f. 3. Process in Parliament against Hugh le Despenser, the elder and the younger, 15 Edward II. (French.)

f. 14. Letters Patent for Alesia, widow of Thomas, Earl of Lancaster, 27 June 1322. (French.)

f. 15. Mandate to Roger Beler and others on taking custodies and debts into King's hands, 1 May 1322.

f. 17. Mandate to Justice of Ireland, Abbots of Dore and Margam on Irish monasteries, 7 October 1321.

f. 19. Mandate to Bailiffs of York on articles of prises under form of charter, 14 April 1322. (French.)

f. 21. Letters Patent to community of realm that subsidy shall not prejudice, 20 May 1322.

f. 22. Mandate to Sheriffs etc. on victuals for Newcastle upon Tyne, 15 May 1322.

f. 24. Mandates to Bailiffs etc. on foot soldiers, 8 June 1322. List.

f. 31. On liberties to church in Magna Carta and Statutes. (French.)

f. 34. Note from Coram Rege Roll, Trin. term, 15 Edward I.

f. 35. Writ to Justices of Bench etc. on Statute, 15 Edward I, 20 May 1322. (French.)

f. 43. Revocation and annulment of process against Hugh le Despenser, the elder and the younger. (French.)

f. 46. Writ sending transcript of same to Justices of Bench, 10 May 1322.

f. 61. Mandate to John, Bishop of Norwich etc. for Hugh le Despenser, the elder and the younger, 24 January 1322.

f. 64. Letters Patent to Henry de Ribbeford, array, vills, co. Worcs., 10 June 1322.

f. 66. Mandate to Hervy de Staunton, fines on barons and bannerets not coming to King, 13 May 1322, from Fine Roll.

f. 70. Letters Patent to Ralph Savage etc. to pronounce Judgement on King's enemies, 23 March–28 April 1322.

f. 72. As f. 31 above (but extract only).

f. 73. Mandate to William de Herle etc. on fines taken from merchants against tenor of Statute of Staple, 22 February 1322.

f. 74. Mandates on temporalities of bishopric of Lincoln taken into King's hands, 13 June 1322.

f. 77. Writ to Treasurer and Barons of Exchequer on receiving subsidy granted, 3 June 1322.

f. 78. Mandate to Sheriff of Lincs. on men at arms in that co., 23 April 1322.

f. 79. Mandate to John de Birmingham, Earl of Louth, for men at arms from Ireland for Scottish war, 3 April 1322. Fines and payment.

f. 81. Mandate to Nicholas Dengayne etc. for levying in Wardrobe, 26 December 1321 etc.

f. 83. Mandate to Mayor etc. of Winchester for levying fines, 6 January 1322.

f. 84. Mandate to Mayor etc. of London not to permit suspects to enter the city during the Provincial Council, 30 November 1321.

f. 85. Mandate to Henry le Scrope etc. for Archdeacons etc. 3 November 1321.

f. 86. Mandate to Archbishop of Dublin, collector of 10th, 6 August 1321.

f. 87. As f. 31 above.

f. 90. Mandate to Sheriffs on proclamation 16th, 60th, 15 January 1322.

f. 92v. Mandate to Walter, Archbishop of Canterbury etc. on proclamation in churches on same.

f. 93. Letters Patent to commissioners on preservation of peace according to Statute of Winchester, 12 December 1321.

f. 95. Charter to Hugh le Despenser, the elder, granting him £70 from the issues of co. Southampton, the castle and manor of Brimsfield etc. 10 May 1322.

f. 97. Mandates, 16 May 1322. List.

f. 100. Letter to Charles, Count of Valois, on marriage of Prince Edward to his daughter, 12 June 1323.

f. 101. Mandate to Hugh de Courtney, Earl of Devon, etc. for ecclesiastics, 15 November 1322.

f. 102. Letters Patent for Bailiffs etc. of Kingston upon Thames, 16 July 1322.

f. 103. Mandate to Sheriff of London for John de Weston, 1 October 1322.

f. 104. Mandate to John de Henstede on victuallers of city of York, 10 November 1322.

f. 107. Writs of summons to Parliament to Sheriffs, 18 September 1322.

f. 109. Writs de expensis to Sheriffs, 29 November 1322.

f. 111. Letters Patent to Richard de Windsor etc. on peace according to Statute of Winchester, 22 January 1324.

f. 113. Memorandum on Great Seal, 23 January 1324.

f. 114. Letters Patent for John de Stonor etc. on inquiry on those who choose foot in various cos., 26 December 1323.

f. 116. Letters Patent to Mayor etc. of York on collection of 10th and 16th, 15 July 1324.

f. 116v. Form of collecting 10th and 16th. (French.)

f. 119. Letters Patent for men of Newborough, co. Anglesey, 27 April 1323.

f. 120. Mandate to Thomas de Leighton on levying scutage in co. Bucks., 28 May 1324.

f. 122. Letters Patent to Sheriffs on Roger Mortimer, 14 November 1323. (French.)

f. 124. The like, 24 March 1324.

f. 128. Letter of Stephen de Segrave, 1 June 1324. (French.)

f. 131. Letters Patent to John de Stonor etc. on inquiry, miracles, King's enemies, 2 October 1323.

f. 133. Letters Patent to Robert de Barton on Andrew de Harlca, 28 July 1323.

f. 134. Mandate to Roger Heron, Northumberland, for Henry de Lancaster, 29 March 1324.

f. 136. Case of quo warranto from *Les Reports des Cases Argue et Adjuge en le temps Edward II*, Trin. term, 18 Edward II.

f. 138. Writs of summons to Parliament to Sheriffs, 23 September 1324.

f. 139. The like, 24 September 1324.

f. 141. Writs de expensis to Sheriffs, 10 November 1324.

f. 142. Petition and answer to Archbishops etc. (French). From Bundle of Petitions to Parliament, 18 Edward II, with reference to *Plac. Parl.*, p. 619.

f. 143. Petition of John de Thorp (French), with answer. (Ibid.)

f. 145. Letters Patent for Roger Pridiaux and Elizabeth, his wife, etc. 22 September 1324.

f. 146. Mandate to Henry de Campo Arnulphi etc. on survey of measures, 3 November 1324.

f. 148. As f. 142 above.

f. 150. Letters Patent on array co. Chester, 24 January 1326.

f. 153. Letters Patent on keeping of peace co. Cumberland etc., 1 September 1325.

f. 155. Mandate to Walter, Archbishop of Canterbury, for William, Archbishop of York, 8 August 1325.

f. 157. Mandates to Walter, Archbishop of Canterbury etc. on Papal letters, 26 December 1325.

f. 159. Charter for burgesses of Lostwithiel and Penknek, 30 October 1325.

f. 161. Extract from Walsingham, 20 Edward II.

f. 164. Petition of community of realm, t. Edward II. (French.) From New Misc. Bundle, t. Henry III.

f. 166. Petition of monastery of York (French), with answer. From Bundle of Petitions to Parliament, t. Edward II.

f. 166v. Petition of commonalty cos. Norf. and Suff. (French), with answer. (Ibid.)

f. 168. Petition of John de Ver, Earl of Oxford (French), with answer. (Ibid.)

f. 170. Petition of Archbishop of Canterbury and prelates of Province of Canterbury (French), with answer.

f. 170v. Petition of Lewis, Bishop of Durham (French), with answer. (Ibid.)

f. 172. Petition of Geoffrey de Geynvill (French). (Ibid.)

f. 174. Letters Patent to William de Vesci on 15th, Ireland, 14 April 1326.

f. 175. Mandate to Mayor etc. of Sandwich etc. ships to Portsmouth, 12 August 1326.

f. 181. Mandate to Universities of Oxford and Cambridge to pray for King, 6 September 1326.

f. 182. Mandate to Walter, Archbishop of Canterbury, for King, 12 August 1326.

VOLUME 19

A volume of transcripts from the Public Records, mainly Summons to Parliament, 1–20 Edward II. On flyleaf: The Rights of the Commons in Parliament by Prescription. E 2.

305 ff.

f. 1. Writs of summons to Parliament, 26 August 1307. Lists.

f. 11. Extract from the Coronation Roll of Edward II, 1307.

f. 13. Forms of taxing and assessing the 20th and 15th granted in 1 Edward II, with the form of the oath of the taxors and lists of those appointed. (K.R. Mem. Roll, Comm., Hil. term, 1 Edward II.)

f. 24. Writs of summons to Parliament, 4 March 1308. With the writs de expensis, 13 May 1308.

f. 27. Writ de expensis for Bartholomew de Badlesmere and Fulk Payfour, Knights of the Shire, co. Kent, 10 January 1308. From Bundle of Brev. Reg. t. Edward II.

f. 29. Writs of summons to Parliament, 16 June 1311. Lists.

f. 33. Ordinances of 1311 (French). 41 Sections with note that they were revoked in the Parliament of York, 1322.

f. 57. The chapters or heads of the Ordinances of 1311 (45 heads). From Laudes Brit. in Archives of city of London.

f. 61. Writ which ordered publication of the Ordinances.

f. 62. Writs for the custody of castles etc. 20 January 1312.

f. 64. The 29th Ordinance of 1311 with translation (annual Parliaments).

f. 66. Writs for the King's peace, 26 January 1312.

f. 67. Writs of summons to Parliament, 19 December 1311.

f. 70. The like, 11 October 1311.

f. 71. The like, 12 September 1311.

f. 72. The like, 20 January 1312.

f. 74. The like, 8 July 1312.

f. 76. Writs de expensis, 16 December 1312.

f. 77. Memorandum on payment of knights, 28 August 1312.

f. 78. Writ of summons to Parliament, 23 May 1313.

f. 80. The like, 8 January 1313.

f. 81. The like, 26 November 1313.

f. 83. The like, 6 September 1313. List.

f. 84. Writ de expensis, 25 July 1313.

f. 87. Writs on no molestation for death of Peter Gaveston, 6 November 1313. (French.)

f. 90. Writs on proclamation of pardon for death of Peter Gaveston, 16 October 1313. (French.)

f. 92. Writs on no molestation for death of Peter Gaveston, 16 October 1313. (French.)

f. 95. Writs on bearing arms, 6 November 1313. (French.)

f. 97. Translation of the same from Rastell, *Stat.*

f. 97v. A note on inquiry on expenses.

f. 99. Writ to Roger Mortimer for Griffin and Fulk Lestrange, 22 November 1313.

f. 101. Writs of summons to Parliament, 24 October 1314.

f. 109. Writs on assessing tallage in the Cinque Ports, 4 November 1314.

f. 111. Writs to Gilbert de Ormesby and others, 12 October 1314.

f. 112. Writs of summons to Parliament, 29 July 1314.

f. 114. Writ to Sheriff of Wilts. on non payment of expenses, 1 November 1314. From Bundle of Brev. Reg., 8 Edward II.

f. 117. Writ for men of Beverley on attending Parliament, 11 June 1314. From L.T.R. Mem. Roll, Comm. Brev. dir. Bar., Trin. term, 8 Edward II.

f. 119. Writs to Henry Spigurnel and others on earls and barons at Parliament, 15 January 1315.

f. 122. Memoranda of Parliament of Lincoln made by William de Ayremyne, Clerk of Chancery, Lincoln, 1316. (French.)

f. 132. Writs to Sheriff to come before Council concerning perambulation, 25 June 1316.

f. 135. Writs of summons to Parliament, 16 October 1316.

f. 136. Writs to Sheriffs on perambulation, 27 June 1316.

f. 138. Extract from liberties granted to clergy, Lincoln, 1316.

f. 138v. Writs of summons to Justices to Parliament of Lincoln, nos. 1–33, with references to Liberate Roll, 9 Edward II.

f. 140. A note that the whole bundle of writs of summons for knights, citizens and burgesses to the Parliament of Lincoln, 1316, is lost.

f. 140v. A note on the articles of grievance of the church against the secular power, 1316

f. 141. Writs of summons to nobles to come to King, 28 January 1317. List.

f. 144. Writs of summons to Parliament, 20 November 1317.

f. 146. Writs on prorogation of Parliament, 4 January 1318.

f. 148. Writs on recall of Parliament, 8 June 1318.

f. 150. Writs on prorogation of Parliament, 3 March 1318.

f. 152. Writs on collection of Peter's Pence, 1 March 1318.

f. 152x. Letters Patent on Peter's Pence, 1 March 1318.

f. 152xx. Letters Patent of pardon for Thomas, Earl of Lancaster, 22 October 1318.

f. 153. Letters Patent of pardon for his adherents, 22 October 1318. List.

f. 154. Petition of Thomas de Westhill, 1318, with answer. (French.) From New Misc. Bundle, t. Henry III.

ff. 156, 300. The case of the Abbot of St. James, Northampton, concerning his discharge from coming to Parliament, 1318, because he nor his predecessors held anything from the King in capite, nor by barony, but only in pure and perpetual alms, with reference to Selden, *Titles of Honor*.

ff. 159, 301. A note in the margin, against the reference, to searching the Rolls of Chancery: 'The roll here mentioned, it seems was some Register of the names of such as ought to be summoned as Lords of Parliament, and a direction to the Clerks of the Petty Bag in making their writs, which is not now extant'.

f. 163. Petition of Matthew de Cauthorne, 1318, with answer. (French.) From Bundle of Writs, 12 Edward II, with reference to Prynne, *Animadversions; 4th Inst.*

f. 164. Writs de expensis. 20 May 1319, to Sheriff of Southampton, with answer. (Ibid.)

f. 165. Writ de expensis to Mayor etc. of Lincoln, 6 May 1319, with return. (Ibid.)

f. 167. Writ to Treasurer and Barons of Exchequer on levying 18th, 30 May 1319.

f. 168. Writ to same on commissions for levying 18th and 12th, 6 June 1319.

f. 168v. Writ to same on fines for 12th, 8 June 1319.

f. 171. Writs of summons to Parliament, 20 March 1319.

f. 172. Writs de expensis to Sheriffs, 25 May 1319.

f. 175. Writs of summons to Parliament, 25 August 1318.

f. 176. Writs de expensis to Sheriffs, 9 December 1318.

f. 180. Letters Patent of pardon to John de Gaunton and others by consent of Parliament, 17 March 1318.

f. 184. A declaration made in Parliament at York, 1318, that when the law was defective remedy ought to be provided in Parliament that full right might be done to the people (French). With translation from Rastell, *Stat.*, and writ to Chancellor of Ireland, 18 September 1318, and to Henry le Scrope and others, 1 December 1318.

f. 188. Extract from Chronicle of Adam de Murimuth in College of Arms, 1318.

f. 192. Writs concerning loans from clergy, 20 July 1319. Lists.

f. 196. Writs to Mayors and others concerning loans, 20 July 1319. List.

f. 203. Writs of summons to Parliament, 15 May 1321.

f. 204. Like, 5 August 1320.

f. 206. Writs de expensis to Sheriffs etc., 25, 26 October 1320.

f. 209. Provisions for keeping the peace and tranquillity of the people, 1321. (French.)

f. 213. That no one should be charged for felonies and trespasses done in the prosecution of the Despensers, 1321. (French.) From Tottel, *Stat.*

f. 217. Form of the charters of pardon for the prosecution of the Despensers. (French.) (Ibid.)

f. 219. Revocation and annulment of the process against the Despensers, 1322. (French.)

f. 222. On the state of the King's Household, 15 Edward II. From New Misc. Bundle, t. Henry III.

f. 226. Writs to Edmund, Earl of Arundel, Justice of Wales, and others, 18 April 1322.

f. 228. Writs of summons to Parliament, 14 May 1322.

f. 230. Like writ to Sheriff of Northants., 14 March 1322, with return. From Bundle of Summons to Parliament, 15 Edward II.

f. 232. Writs de expensis, 19 March 1322.

f. 234. Statute that matters should be treated of in Parliament as had been accustomed in times past, that is, by immemorial usage, and Coram Rege Roll, Trin. term, 17 Edward II, with writ, 19 May 1322.

f. 239. Writs on proclamation on King's wages against the Scots, 20 June 1322.

f. 241. Writ to Sheriff of Norf. and Suff. for villeins of John, Bishop of Norwich, 18 May 1322.

f. 242. Letter from Edward II to Pope, 14 May 1322.

f. 248. Letter to Charles, Count of Valois, on marriage of Prince Edward to his daughter, 6 June 1322.

f. 250. Writs of summons to Parliament, 18 September 1322.

f. 251. Writs de expensis, 29 November 1322.

f. 256. Writs to Sheriff of York etc. 30 October 1322

f. 257. Writs of summons to Council, 9 May 1324. List.

f. 260. Writs of summons to treat, 20 November 1323.

f. 262. Writs of summons to Parliament, 27 December 1323.

f. 264. Writs de expensis, 18 March 1324.

f. 266. Petition in Parliament by Archbishops etc. (French.) (*Plac. Parl.*, p. 619.)

f. 267. A note on the building of boats, 1377.

f. 268. Writ to Walter, Archbishop of Canterbury for Archbishop of York, 8 October 1324.

f. 270. Writ to Sheriff of Cornwall de expensis, 10 November 1324.

f. 271. Writs of summons to Parliament, 10 October 1325.

f. 274. Writs de expensis, 5 December 1325.

f. 275v. Petitions granted by King. (French.)

f. 279. Writs for prorogation of Parliament, 3 December 1326.

f. 287. Writs de expensis, 9 March 1327.

f. 289. The Apologia of Adam de Orleton, Bishop of Worcester, afterwards of Winchester, 1334. (French.) From end of *Decem Scriptores*.

f. 291. Writs on proclamation of peace, 24, 29 January 1327.

f. 293. On the Office of Lord High Steward of England (dangerous to be printed). From Vespasian B. 7.

VOLUME 20

A volume of transcripts from the Public Records, mainly from the Memoranda Rolls of the Exchequer 1–20 Edward II. On flyleaf: Several writs, records, commissions, summonses and transactions in Parliament and other Courts during the reign of Edward II. 491 ff.

f. 1. Writ to John Vernon on the Honor of Peverel etc. 9 October 1307. From K.R. Mem. Roll, Comm., Brev. Clausi, Mich. term, 1 Edward II. Writ appointing Ralph de Hengham and other Justices of the Bench. (Ibid.)

f. 1v. Writ appointing John Bacon Keeper of the Rolls and Writs of the Bench, 6 September 1307. (Ibid.)

Writ exempting John de Lentier, citizen of London, from being put on assizes etc., 20 October 1307. (Ibid.)

f. 2v. Writ under Exchequer seal to William de St. Georges and William Sanseton on state of castle of Cambridge. (Ibid., Comm.)

f. 3. Writ to Barons of Exchequer for Abbot of Revesby, 30 October 1307. (Ibid., Brev. dir. Bar.)

f. 3v. Writ to same for Elizabeth (blank), 12 June 1306. (Ibid.)

f. 4. Writ of Privy Seal to Treasurer and Chamberlains on Walter de Langton, Bishop of Chester, 27 November 1307. (French.) (Ibid.)

f. 5. Writ to Barons of Exchequer for Thomas, son and heir of William Luton, 28 February 1308.

f. 5v. Writ to same for Robert de Clifford, 1 March 1308. (Ibid.)

f. 6. Writ to same for executors of Richard Whelton, 22 May 1308. (Ibid., Trin. term.)

f. 6v. Writ to same for Andrew, son of Geoffrey de Brayborke, 14 May 1308.

f. 7. Writ to same for Robert, son of Payn, 16 June 1308. (Ibid.)

Writ of Privy Seal to same to be at Exchequer in vacation, 20 July 1308. (French.) (Ibid.)

f. 7v. Writ to same for William, son and heir of William de Hasting, 1 July 1308. (Ibid.)

f. 8. Certification touching Walter de Langton, Bishop of Chester. (Ibid., Rec., Mich. term.)

f. 8v. Letter from Treasurer and Barons of Exchequer to King for Earl of Lancaster. (Ibid.)

f. 9. Form of taxation of 20th and 15th. (French.) Mich. 1307. (Ibid.)

f. 11. Form of the oath of the taxors of the 20th and 15th. (French.) (Ibid.)

f. 11v. Names of those appointed to tax and collect the 20th and 15th in the counties, with the form of the letters patent sent, 28 November 1307. (Ibid.)

f. 14. On the collection of the clerical 15th. (Ibid., Hil. term.)

ff. 17, 19. Form of the oath of those of the King's Council, 1 Edward II.

f. 20. Plea in Common Bench, Trin. term, 1–2 Edward II, Norf. Robert de Hakebech as executor of will, summoned by Thomas de Hakebech.

f. 21. Writs under Exchequer Seal on proclamation of timber for King's works at Westminster. From K.R. Mem. Roll, Brev. Ret. Hil. term, 1 Edward II.

f. 23. Roll of debts of Walter de Langton, Bishop of Coventry and Lichfield, late Treasurer (French), with writ of Privy Seal thereon. 27 November 1307. (Ibid., Mich. term.)

f. 27. Letters Patent to Justice of Ireland concerning Peter Gaveston, 16 June 1308.

f. 27v. Letters Patent on assessment of 15th in city of London, 25 March 1308.

f. 28. Writs on the coronation, 18 January 1308. Lists.

f. 30v. The like to Robert, Archbishop of Canterbury, etc. on the same. List. 9 February 1308.

f. 35. Book of 20th and 15th granted to the King by the laity at Northampton, with the Clerk of the Pipe.

f. 37. Debts of Walter de Langton, Bishop of Coventry and Lichfield, in cos. Somerset, Cambridge, Wilts., Norf., Suff., Glouc. From K.R. Mem. Roll, Mich. term, 1 Edward II.

f. 44. Writ to Barons of Exchequer for Eleanor, widow of Robert de Stutvill, 30 September 1307. (Ibid., Brev. dir. Bar.)

f. 45. Debts of Walter de Langton, Bishop of Coventry and Lichfield, in cos. Norf. and Suff. (Ibid., Hil. term.)

f. 49. The like, cos. Midd. and Northants. (Ibid., Trin. term.)

f. 53. The like, cos. Devon, Bucks. (Ibid., Mich. term.)

f. 56. Writ of privy seal to Barons of Exchequer for William de Stixham, 20 June 1308. (French.) (Ibid., Trin. term.)

f. 56v. The like for Peter Gaveston, Earl of Cornwall, 20 June 1308. (French.) (Ibid.)

f. 57. Memorandum on Templars wages from L.T.R. Mem. Roll, Comm., Recorda, Hil. term, 1 Edward II.

Writ to Barons of Exchequer for Hugh de Courtney, 8 March 1308. (Ibid., Brev. dir. Bar., East. term.)

f. 57v. Petition of Walter de Maney. (French.) (Ibid., Rec.)

f. 59. Memorandum on bulls delivered to Master William de Halstede. (Ibid., Rec., Trin. term.)

f. 60. Commission under Exchequer seal to John de Lentier. (Ibid., Comm., Mich. term.)

f. 60v. Writ to Barons of Exchequer for Prior of Thurgarton, 6 October 1307. (Ibid., Brev. dir. Bar.)

f. 63. The like for John de Geminghill, 3 December 1308. (L.T.R. Mem. Roll, Brev. dir. Bar., Mich. term, 2 Edward II.)

f. 63v. The like for John Daniel, 1 December 1308. (Ibid.)

f. 64. Writs de expensis, knights and burgesses, 13 May 1309.

f. 65. Relief of Roger de Chandos, co. Heref. (L.T.R. Mem. Roll, Comm., Mich. term, 2 Edward II.)

f. 67. Writ to Barons of Exchequer for John de Erlegh, 16 May 1309. (Ibid., Brev. dir. Bar., Trin. term.)

f. 69. Writ under Exchequer seal to Isabella de Vescy, Keeper of castle of Bamburgh, 6 March 1309. (Ibid., Brev. Ret., Hil. term.)

f. 69v. Writs under Exchequer seal distraining various knights and sergeants to come to Exchequer, for the 20th, 24 August 1308. (Ibid., Trin. term.)

f. 71. Ordinance for the King's mines in Devon. (L.T.R. Mem. Roll., Rec., Mich. term.)

f. 72. Writs under Exchequer seal to Archbishop of York etc. 30 November 1308. (Ibid., Brev. Ret.)

f. 75. Writ of privy seal to Barons of Exchequer for Henry de Lacy, Earl of Lincoln, 4 November 1309. (French.) (Ibid., Brev. dir. Bar., Mich. term, 3 Edward II.)

f. 75v. The like writ to same for Henry, son of Hugh, 22 May 1310. (French.) (Ibid.)

Writ to same for mariners of Baddesey, 18 June 1310. (Ibid.)

f. 77v. Writ of Privy Seal to same for merchants of Society of Bellardi, 19 July 1310. (French.) (Ibid.)

f. 78. Writ to same for Abbot of Wardon, 6 July 1310. (Ibid.)

f. 78v. Writ under Exchequer seal to Council of Aquitaine, 21 November 1309. (Ibid., Brev. Irret., Mich. term.)

f. 79. Letters Patent of commission under the new Ordinances, 16 March 1310. From the MS. Stat. in poss. of John Peachey esq., of the Inner Temple.

f. 80. Writ to Treasurer and Barons of Exchequer on the punishment of those acting against the Statute of Carlisle, 16 December 1310.

f. 83. Case against Master William de Testa adjourned to Parliament, Mich. term, 4 Edward II. (L.T.R. Mem. Roll, Comm., Mich. term, 4 Edward II.)

f. 87. Writ to Barons of Exchequer for Roger de Bello Campo, 15 October 1310. (Ibid., Brev. dir. Bar.)

f. 87v. Writ to same for Bishop of Norwich, 12 November 1310. (Ibid.)

Writ to same for John de la Chaumbre of London, 26 August 1310. (Ibid., East. term.)

f. 89. Writ of Privy Seal to same for E. Passingham, 15 December 1310. (French.) (Ibid., Mich. term.)

Writ of same to same for Geoffrey de Hertepole, 27 December 1310. (French.) (Ibid.)

f. 91. Statute called Rageman on appointment of Justices, 4 Edward II. From MS. Statutes of John Peachey.

f. 93. Writ to Barons of Exchequer for Bishop and monks of Norwich, 8 May 1311. (L.T.R. Mem. Roll, Brev. dir. Bar., East. term, 4 Edward II.)

f. 93v. Writ to same for William, Archbishop of York, 20 May 1311. (Ibid.)

f. 95. Notes of certain matters touching the King's affairs in Gascony sent here by the King to be examined before his Council here. (Ibid., Rec., Mich. term.)

f. 102v. Writ to Barons of Exchequer for religious, 16 December 1310. (Ibid., Brev. dir. Bar., Hil. term.)

f. 103v. Form ordained by the Council for the selling of wines in London. (French.) Hil. term, 4 Edward II. (Ibid., Rec., Hil. term.)

f. 105. Writ of Privy Seal to Barons of Exchequer for John de Felton, 8 April 1311. (French.) (Ibid., Brev. dir. Bar., East. term.)

f. 105v. On the committal to prison of Jocelin Payn of Gascony. (Ibid., Rec.)

f. 106v. For Thomas de Ludlow committed to prison. (Ibid.)

f. 107v. On return of seal, Durham. Trin. term, 4 Edward II. (Ibid., Rec., Trin. term.)

f. 109. Mainprise of John de Berwick, Trin. term, 5 Edward II. (Ibid., Fines etc., Trin. term, 5 Edward II.)

Certification made to King of coming of certain Earls to the Exchequer. (Ibid., Rec., East. term.)

f. 111. Memorandum that John de Sandale not to concern himself as Treasurer, 23 October 1311. (Ibid., Mich. term.)

f. 113. Writ to Barons of Exchequer for Roger de Ughtred, 11 September 1311. (Ibid., Brev. dir. Bar.)

f. 113v. Writ to same for John de Stotvill, 12 November 1311. (Ibid.)

f. 114. Enrolment of charter to John de Clavering made 8 July 1199. (Ibid.)

f. 116. Writ to Barons of Exchequer for Ralph de Gorges, 16 July 1311. (Ibid., Trin. term.)

f. 117. Writs to Bishops of Carlisle, St. Asaph and Bangor on 15th. (Ibid., Mich. term.)

f. 117v. Writ to Sheriff of Cornwall, 11 October 1311.

f. 119. Writs to Sheriffs about Peter Gaveston, Earl of Cornwall, 28 January 1312.

Writs to Sheriffs on observance of peace, 26 January 1312.

f. 120. Writ to Barons of Exchequer for William Servat (incomplete). (L.T.R. Mem. Roll, Brev. dir. Bar., East. term, 5 Edward II.)

f. 121. Writ to Sheriff of Yorks, about Peter Gaveston. (French.) 18 January 1312.

f. 131. Writ to Barons of Exchequer for Laurence de Preston, 10 May 1313. (L.T.R. Mem. Roll, Trin. term, 6 Edward II.)

f. 133. Writ to same for Prior of Wallingford, 20 May 1313.

f. 135. Writs to Bishop of London and others, 23 May 1313.

f. 137. Writ to Barons of Exchequer for Bishop of Exeter, 28 October 1312. (L.T.R. Mem. Roll, Brev. dir. Bar., Mich. term, 6 Edward II.)

f. 137v. Writ to same for Thomas de Willoughby, 2 December 1312. (Ibid.)

f. 138. Charter of King John for Robert Warneford, 14 January 1201. (Ibid., East. term.)

f. 139. Writ for Richard Wake and John Wyke, 1 February 1313.

f. 141v. Writ to Barons of Exchequer for Simon, Bishop of Salisbury, 10 May 1313. (L.T.R. Mem. Roll, Brev. dir. Bar., 6 Edward II.)

f. 143. Letters Patent for Thomas Croxton and Thomas Vinter, office of coroner and attorney in Bench.

f. 145. Letters Patent on 20th and 10th, 18 November 1313. List.

f. 146. Statute on carrying arms. (French.)

f. 146v. That no one should be imprisoned for death of Peter Gaveston. (French.)

f. 149. Proceedings on Robert de Munceux charged with a rescue. (L.T.R. Mem. Roll, Rec., Trin. term, 7 Edward II.)

f. 151. Writ to Barons of Exchequer for William la Zouch, 24 September 1313. (Ibid., Brev. dir. Bar., Mich. term.)

f. 151v. Writ to same for burgesses of Kingston upon Hull, 20 November 1313. (Ibid.)

f. 152. That no one should be charged for death of Peter Gaveston. (Ibid., Rec.)

f. 152v. Writ to Barons of Exchequer for Nicholas de Audley, 1 July 1314. (L.T.R. Mem. Roll, Brev. dir. Bar., Mich. term.)

f. 153v. Returnable writ on taxation of 20th and 10th. (Ibid., Brev. Retorn, Trin. term.)

Writ to Barons of Exchequer for Prior of Hospital of Holy Cross, Reigate, 15 October 1313. (Ibid., Brev. dir. Bar., Mich. term.)

f. 155. Account of 20th on all moveables granted by clergy, 7 Edward II.

f. 157. Letters Patent that no one shall be imprisoned for death of Peter Gaveston, 6 November 1313. (French.)

f. 158. Like, 16 October 1313.

f. 159v. Writ to Barons of Exchequer for King, 16 February 1314. (L.T.R. Mem. Roll, Comm., East. term, 7 Edward II.)

Like for Alexander, King of Scotland. (7 Edward I.) (Ibid.)

f. 161. Statute that no one should be charged for return of Peter Gaveston. (French.) 7 November 1313. From MS. Statutes in possession of John Peachey of Inner Temple.

f. 163. Proceedings on complaint of magnates on exaction of scutage and the answer made by the King's Council. (L.T.R. Mem. Roll, Recorda, Hil. term, 8 Edward II.)

f. 165. Letters Patent concerning ecclesiastical persons, 3 November 1314.

f. 166. Letters Patent for Barons of Cinque Ports, 3 November 1314.

f. 166v. Letters Patent on enquiry on Gerard Salveyn, late Sheriff of Yorks., 8 October 1314.

f. 167v. Letters Patent on hindrance to collectors of 20th, 8 June 1315.

f. 168v. Letters Patent on enquiry on Hugh de Audley, late Sheriff of Salop and Staffs., 8 March 1315.

f. 170. Writ to Barons of Exchequer on gifts and grants by King, 2 April 1315. (L.T.R. Mem. Roll, Brev. dir. Bar., East. term, 8 Edward II.)

f. 171. Letters Patent for Master William de Buston, 8 October 1314.

f. 173. Writ of privy seal to Barons of Exchequer for Gerard Salveyn, 5 October 1314. (French.) (L.T.R. Mem. Roll, Brev. dir. Bar., Mich. term, 8 Edward II.)

f. 173v. Writ to Barons of Exchequer for Mayor etc. of Nottingham, 16 October 1314. (Ibid.)

Like on oppressions by Sheriffs, 10 October 1314. (Ibid.)

f. 174. Like for Prior of St. John of Jerusalem in England, 22 November 1314. (Ibid., Hil. term.)

f. 175. Like for Richard de Compton, 24 February 1315. (Ibid.)

f. 175v. Like for Ralph de Gorges and Peter Everey, 25 February 1315. (Ibid.)

f. 176. Like for John de Langley, 10 March 1315. (Ibid.)

f. 177v. Like for Arnald de St. Martin, 3 March 1315. (Ibid.)

Form of taxation and levying 10th. (French.) (Ibid., Rec.)

f. 179v. Commission to taxors of 20th. (Ibid.)

f. 180v. Letters Patent on information on hindrance of collectors of 20th, 4 June 1315.

f. 182. Writ to Barons of Exchequer for John, son of John de Hoyland, 15 March 1315. (L.T.R. Mem. Roll, Brev. dir., Bar., East. term, 8 Edward II.)

Like for Thomas de Wymtervill, 17 April 1315. (Ibid.)

f. 182v. Like for Prior and Convent of Westminster, 16 April 1315. (Ibid.)

f. 183. Like for Henry de Kydale, 25 April 1315. (Ibid.)

f. 184v. Like for John Dyne of Finchingfield, 17 April 1315. (Ibid.)

f. 185. Like for David, Earl of Atholl, 15 March 1315, followed by petition. (French.) (Ibid.)

f. 187. Like for Joan, widow of John le Botiler, 3 May 1315. (Ibid.)

f. 187v. Like for Joan de Bohun, 2 May 1315. (Ibid.)

f. 188. Like for William de Godyemton, 20 February 1315. (Ibid.)

f. 188v. Like for William Paynell, 3 May 1315. (Ibid.)

f. 189. Like for Henry, son of Hugh, 10 March 1315. (Ibid.)

f. 190. Like for William Touchet, 7 May 1314. (Ibid.)

f. 191. Like for John de Eglesfeld, 17 October 1314. (Ibid.)

f. 194. Account of 20th granted by laity, 8 Edward II.

f. 198. Writ to Barons of Exchequer for men of Beverley, 11 June 1315. (L.T.R. Mem. Roll, Brev. dir. Bar., Trin. term, 8 Edward II.)

f. 199. Letters Patent to William Bourne and others, 18 May 1315.

f. 200. Letters Patent on enquiry on Hugh le Despenser when Justice of Forest, 13 July 1315.

f. 203. Letters Patent on enquiry on salmon taken in co. Glouc. against Statute, 17 April 1321.

f. 204. Account of 16th of all moveables and 15th of boroughs etc. 9 Edward II.

f. 204v. Writ to Sheriff of Essex to come before King's Council on perambulation, 25 June 1316.

f. 206. Writ to Barons of Exchequer for Ingelram de Gynes and wife, 18 May 1316. (L.T.R. Mem. Roll, Brev. dir. Bar., East. term, 9 Edward II.)

f. 206v. Like for Richard de Sutton, 18 July 1315. (Ibid., Trin. term.)

f. 207v. Like for Nicholas Russel, 20 June 1316. (Ibid.)

f. 208. Like for Abbot of Woburn, 1 June 1316. (Ibid.)

f. 208v. Like for John le Mareschal, 16 May 1316. (Ibid.)

f. 209. Like for John de Stotvill, 13 July 1316. (Ibid.)

f. 209v. Proceedings for Agnes, widow of James de Sutton. (Ibid., Rec., Mich. term.)

f. 212. Writ to Barons of Exchequer for Gerard de Wachesham, 14 February 1316. (Ibid., Brev. dir. Bar., Mich. term.)

f. 214. Like for Simon, son of Ralph Perrot, 12 March 1316. (Ibid., Hil. term.)

f. 214v. Writ of pone, Walter le Fleming, 22 February 1316. From Brev. Reg., 9 Edward II.

f. 216. Writ to Keeper of Spiritualities of Archbishopric of York, 17 January 1316.

f. 216v. Writ to Dean and Chapter of St. Peter's, York, 17 January 1316.

f. 218. Writ to Barons of Exchequer for William, son of William de Monte Casino, 3 April 1316. (L.T.R. Mem. Roll, Brev. dir. Bar., East. term, 9 Edward II.)

f. 219. Writ to Roger Mortimer to be present at Parliament, 12 January 1316.

f. 220. Writ to Barons of Exchequer for Walter de Cokefeld, 18 September 1315. (L.T.R. Mem. Roll, Brev. dir. Bar., Mich. term, 9 Edward II.)

f. 220v. Like for men of Stamford of John de Warenne, Earl of Surrey, 2 October 1315. (Ibid.)

f. 221. Like for executors of Simon, Bishop of Salisbury, 3 October 1315. (Ibid.)

f. 221v. Like for John Picot, 21 September 1315. (Ibid.)

Like for Abbot of Tarrant, 16 October 1315. (Ibid.)

f. 222. Like for Joan, widow of Thomas de Ludlow, 13 October 1315. (Ibid.)

f. 223. Like for Thomas, son of Eustace, 10 August 1315. (Ibid.)

f. 223v. Like for William de Carburra, 1 November 1315. (Ibid.)

f. 224. Like for Prior of St. Mary's, Southwark, 6 November 1315. (Ibid.)

Like for Hugh de Cressy, 4 November 1315. (Ibid.)

f. 224v. Like for John Crispyn, 24 July 1315. (Ibid.)

f. 225. Like for Edmund le Botiler, 15 November 1315. (Ibid.)

f. 226. Like for Abbot of Stratford, 18 July 1315. (Ibid.)

f. 226v. Like for William de Staunton, 20 April 1316. (Ibid.)

f. 227. Like for Nigel Keneton, 8 May 1316. (Ibid.)

f. 227v. Like for Robert Crull, 12 May 1316. (Ibid.)

f. 228v. Like for William Botreaux, 9 May 1316. (Ibid.)

f. 229. Like for Henry, son of William de Campo Arnulphi, 8 May 1316. (Ibid.)

f. 230. Like for Thomas, Earl of Lancaster, 10 March 1316. (Ibid.)

f. 232. Like on ordinance concerning gifts, 26 April 1316. (Ibid.)

f. 232v. Like for Philip Hastang, 6 May 1316. (Ibid.)

f. 234. Writ that assizes not to be taken during Parliament, 14 January 1316.

Letters Patent on customs of men of North Wales, 7 February 1316.

f. 236. Writ to Barons of Exchequer on perambulation of forests, 8 March 1316. (L.T.R. Mem. Roll, Brev. dir. Bar., Hil. term, 9 Edward II.)

f. 238. Like for men of Causton, co. Norf., 4 October 1315. (Ibid., Mich. term.)

f. 240. Like for King to treat, 14 March 1317. (L.T.R. Mem. Roll, Brev. dir. Bar., East. term, 10 Edward II.)

f. 242. Letters Patent on election of coroners, 6 August 1316.

Letters Patent for John Giffard of Brimsfield, 30 December 1316.

f. 244. Letters Patent on assessment of 16th, co. Kent., 5 August 1316.

f. 245. Letters Patent on proclamation on measures, 20 February 1317.

f. 246. Letters Patent on form of taxation of 16th. (French.) 10 Edward II.

f. 250. Writ to Barons of Exchequer for men of vill of Aske, 20 September 1316. (L.T.R. Mem. Roll, Brev. dir. Bar., Mich. term, 10 Edward II.)

f. 250v. Like for Herbert, son of John, 4 September 1316. (Ibid.)

f. 251. Like for Richard de Furneux, 10 October 1316. (Ibid.)

f. 251v. Like for Prioress of St. Radegund, Cambridge, 14 October 1316. (Ibid.)

f. 252v. Like for Abbot of St. Mary's, York, 8 August 1316. (Ibid.)

f. 253. Like for Thomas de Roshale, 28 October 1316. (Ibid.)

f. 253v. Like for Roger de Felton, 4 September 1316. (Ibid.)

f. 254. Like for Loretta de Useflete, 4 September 1316. (Ibid.)

f. 254v. Like for Thomas de Ver and Agnes, his wife, 18 November 1316. (Ibid.)

f. 255. Like for Dean of St. Martin le Grand, London, 7 January 1317. (Ibid., Hil. term.)

f. 256. Like for Abbot of Croyland, 18 April 1317. (Ibid., East. term.)

f. 256v. Like for Robert de Meygnill, 1 May 1317. (Ibid.)

f. 257. Like for men of town of Lynn, 4 May 1317. (Ibid.)

f. 257v. Like for William, son and heir of William de Cantilupe, 13 May 1317. (Ibid.)

f. 258. Like for Abbot of Thornton, 15 June 1317. (Ibid.)

ff. 259, 262v. Letters Patent on assessment of 16th, 5 August 1317.

f. 260. Writs on clerical subsidy, 1 October 1316. List.

f. 262. Writs prohibiting Peter's Pence, 1 March 1317.

f. 264. Writ to Barons of Exchequer for John de Twyford, 17 September 1317. (L.T.R. Mem. Roll, Brev. dir. Bar., Mich. term, 11 Edward II.)

f. 264v. Like for John de Dyne, 16 October 1317. (Ibid.)

f. 265v. Like for Prior of Tonbridge, 25 October 1317. (Ibid.)

f. 266. Like for John, Bishop of Winchester, 25 October 1317. (Ibid.)

f. 266v. Like on Statute of Lincoln and Sheriffs, 17 November 1317. (Ibid.)

f. 267. Like on pleas in the Exchequer, 22 November 1317. (Ibid.)

Like for Prior of Barnwell, 3 December 1317. (Ibid.)

f. 267v. Like for Hospital of St. John's, London, 20 October 1317. (Ibid.)

f. 268v. Like for Robert de Lacy, 18 November 1317. (Ibid., Hil. term.)

f. 269. Like for Prioress of Aconbury, 12 January 1318. (Ibid.)

f. 269v. Writ of privy seal to Barons of Exchequer for Stephen Dabindon, 4 December 1317. (French.) (Ibid.)

f. 270. Writ to Barons of Exchequer for Robert de Eclugyham etc. 15 May 1318. (Ibid., East. term.)

f. 270v. Like for Master John de Wancogyn, Warden of Merton, Oxford, 24 June 1318. (Ibid.)

f. 271v. Like for executors of Anthony, Bishop of Durham, 15 July 1317. (Ibid.)

f. 272v. Acknowledgement by Walter, Archbishop of Canterbury etc. (Ibid., Recogn., Mich. term.)

f. 274. Writ to Barons of Exchequer for Sheriffs of London, 8 January 1317. (Ibid., Brev. dir. Bar., Mich. term.)

f. 275v. Like on ordinance on gifts, 9 June 1318. (Ibid., Trin. term.)

f. 278. Writs to Justices of Bench etc. to do justice notwithstanding writs of privy seal, 22 November 1317.

f. 284. Letters on arrears of payment of tax etc. 25 August 1318.

f. 286. Writs on levying 18th, 30 May 1319.

f. 286v. Writ to Chamberlain of Carnarvon for Roger Mortimer of Wigmore, 7 June 1319.

f. 287. Writ for Ralph Bassett of Drayton, 5 December 1318.

f. 287v. Writs on grant of clerical subsidy, 25 November 1318.

f. 288v. Writs of summons with horses and arms to Newcastle upon Tyne. List. 20 March 1319.

f. 292. Memorandum concerning Hugh de Audley (French). With answer to same.

f. 296. Proceedings concerning the Mayor and Aldermen of London. (L.T.R. Mem. Roll, Comm., Trin. term, 12 Edward II.)

f. 298. Proceedings concerning the Prior of Southwark. (Ibid.)

f. 299. Form of taxation of 18th. (French.) (Ibid.)

f. 304. Writ of privy seal to Treasurer for King, 2 January 1318. (French.) (L.T.R. Mem. Roll, Brev. dir. Bar., Hil. term, 12 Edward II.)

f. 304v. Writ to Sheriff of Southampton, 20 May 1318, with return on bailiffs of Bishop of Winchester. From Bundle of Writs, 12 Edward II.

f. 305. Writ to Mayor etc. of Lincoln, 6 May 1318, with return on dorse. (Ibid.)

f. 306. Writ to Barons of Exchequer for burgesses of Ipswich, 18 November 1317. (L.T.R. Mem. Roll, Brev. dir. Bar., Trin. term, 12 Edward II.)

f. 306v. Like for men and tenants of heirs of William Bassett, 3 September 1318. (Ibid., Mich. term.)

f. 307. Commission for levying 12th, co. Lincs.

f. 308. Proceedings concerning William Dumartin. co. Essex. (L.T.R. Mem. Roll, Communia, Trin. term, 12 Edward II.)

f. 310. Writ to Barons of Exchequer for Galvano de Twenge etc. 21 September 1318. (Ibid., Brev. dir. Bar., Mich. term.)

f. 310v. Like for Ankelin de Martival, 3 November 1318. (Ibid.)

f. 311v. Like for Abbot of Croyland, 8 November 1318. (Ibid.)

f. 312. Like for community of city of London. 20 (blank) 12 Edward II. (Ibid., Hil. term.)

f. 314. Account of 18th granted by laity at York.

f. 315. Writ to Barons of Exchequer for clergy of realm, 13 March 1319. (L.T.R. Mem. Roll, Brev. dir. Bar., East. term, 12 Edward II.)

f. 316. Petition of Matthew de Crauthorn (French). With answer on dorse. From Bundle of Petitions, 12 Edward II.

f. 317. Writ for Philip de Melton, 16 November 1318.

f. 318. Letters Patent on prises of goods of clergy, 24 November 1318. From MS. Statutes of John Peachey.

f. 320. Letters Patent of pardon for Earl of Lancaster, 22 October 1318.

f. 322. Writ to Barons of Exchequer on 18th, 6 June 1319. (L.T.R. Mem. Roll, Brev. dir. Bar., Trin. term, 12 Edward II.)

f. 322v. Like on provision of harness by citizens of London, 22 June 1319. (Ibid.)

f. 323v. Like for burgesses of Ilchester, 24 November 1318. (Ibid., Hil. term.)

f. 326. Like for city of London and co. Midd., 29 November 1318. (Ibid.)

f. 328. Like for Henry de Cobham, 1 December 1318. (Ibid.)

f. 334. Like for John de Hastings, 18 November 1318. (Ibid.)

f. 335. Like for men of co. Southampton, 30 May 1319. (Ibid., Trin. term.)

f. 336. Commissions under Exchequer seal on provision of victuals, 14 March 1319. (Ibid., Comm., Hil. term.)

f. 337. Commission to Abbot of Reading on loan to King's use, 14 March 1319. (Ibid.)

f. 338v. Declaration that Abbot of Croyland not a baron. (Ibid., Rec.)

f. 340. Calling of merchants for loan to King. (Ibid., East. term.)

ff. 342, 347v. Writ to Barons of Exchequer for Alan Castelayn, 8 April 1320. (L.T.R. Mem. Roll, Brev. dir. Bar., East. term, 13 Edward II.)

f. 344. Proceedings on Earl of Arundel's account. (Ibid., Rec.)

f. 345. Plea before the King's Council at Westminster, Trin. term, 13 Edward II. London. On certain men committed to prison in the Tower of London.

f. 347. Fines, rot 14, London.

f. 348. Writ to Barons of Exchequer for Bishop of Exeter, 30 November 1320. (K.R. Mem. Roll, Brev. dir. Bar., Mich. term, 14 Edward II.)

f. 350. Like for John Botetourt, 22 October 1320. (Ibid.)

f. 350v. Like for John de Bures and wife, 6 November 1320. (Ibid.)

ff. 351, 356v. Like for John de Harlegh, 8 November 1320. (Ibid.)

f. 352. On the seal deputed for the realm of England when the King was in France, 4 June 1321. (K.R. Mem. Roll, Rec., Trin. term, 14 Edward II.)

f. 354. Writ to Barons of Exchequer for Abbot of Croyland, 24 October 1320. (Ibid., Brev. dir. Bar., Mich. term.)

f. 355. Like for Robert de Haydon and others, 24 October 1320. (Ibid.)

f. 358. Letters Patent to John de Bousser on oppressions of Sheriffs, 8 May 1321.

f. 360v. Letters Patent to Henry Spigurnel etc. 18 December 1320.

f. 364. Letters Patent appointing Justices on disturbers of the peace, 27 November 1320.

f. 366. Proceedings concerning the Abbot of Croyland. (K.R. Mem. Roll, Rec. East. term, 14 Edward II.)

f. 370. Letters Patent to John de Ticheborn on array co. Southampton, 10 September 1326.

f. 374. Proceedings on allowance of liberties. Writ 17 February 1321. (L.T.R. Mem. Roll, Rec., East. term, 14 Edward II.)

f. 379. Proceedings concerning the Abbot of Pershore, co. Worcs. (Ibid., Trin. term.)

f. 381. Writs concerning the Despensers, the elder and the younger, 4 January 1322.

f. 383. Proceedings concerning the Bishop of Durham, 18 July 1322. (L.T.R. Mem. Roll, Rec., Hil. term, 15 Edward II.)

f. 385. Writs of summons of Welsh to Parliament of York, 18 April 1322.

f. 385v. Letters Patent on castle of Norham, 2 August 1326.

f. 387. Writ to Ingelram Berenger for Hugh Despenser, the elder, 7 May 1322.

f. 387v. Writ concerning a treaty at Doncaster, 12 November 1321.

f. 388v. Writs not to appear armed at treaty, 22 November 1321.

f. 390v. Writ for villeins of John, Bishop of Norwich, 26 May 1322.

f. 391v. Proceedings concerning Roger de Orfevre. (L.T.R. Mem. Roll, Rec., Hil. term, 15 Edward II.)

f. 393. Writs for Abbots of Dore and Margam, 17 October 1321.

f. 395. Proceedings on committal of Henry de Ayler to Fleet. (L.T.R. Mem. Roll, Rec., Mich. term, 15 Edward II.)

f. 396. Writ to Treasurer and Barons of Exchequer for King, 10 May 1322. (Ibid., Brev. dir. Bar., Trin. term.)

f. 397. Annulment of New Ordinances, from MS. Stat. of John Peachey.

f. 399. Writ to Treasurer and Barons of Exchequer, Dublin, under Exchequer seal, 4 June 1323. (L.T.R. Mem. Roll, Trin. term, 16 Edward II.)

f. 403. On the peace made with the Scots by Andrew de Harcla. (French.) (L.T.R. Mem. Roll, Rec., Hil. term, 16 Edward II.)

f. 407. Writs on the clerical subsidy, 27 November 1322.

f. 408v. Proclamation of treaty, York, 30 October 1322.

f. 409. Writs for restitution of lands to Hugh Mortimer, 20 December 1322.

f. 409v. Writ for Hugh Mortimer, kt., 16 August 1322.

Letters Patent on pronouncement of judgement on Andrew de Harcla, 27 February 1323.

f. 410v. Letters Patent for Earls etc. co. Chester, 15 July 1322.

f. 411. Form of taxation of 10th and 16th. (French.) (L.T.R. Mem. Roll, Rec., Mich. term, 16 Edward II.)

f. 415. Writ on committal to prison of Henry de Beaumont, 30 May 1323.

f. 416v. Writ under Exchequer seal on delivery of money to Roger Mortimer of Chirk in prison, 23 October 1322.

f. 417. Earls etc. co. Cornwall, 2 December 1322. (L.T.R. Mem. Roll, Rec., Mich. term, 16 Edward II.)

f. 419. Proceedings on attachment of John de Clavering. (Ibid., Mich. term, 17 Edward II.)

f. 423. Proceedings on attachment of men of Bridport. (Ibid.)

f. 424v. Proceedings on attachment of woman with false money. (Ibid.)

f. 426v. Proceedings on attachment of John de Crull for relief. (Ibid., Hil. term.)

f. 427v. Proceedings on attachment of William de Malebys for relief. (Ibid.)

f. 429. Proceedings on committal of Arnald Dispain to Fleet for false claim against city of London. (Ibid.)

f. 430v. Proceedings on exoneration of Richard de Playz for relief. (Ibid., Trin. term.)

f. 433. Letters Patent on Roger Mortimer of Wigmore, 24 March 1324. (French.)

f. 436. Writ to Sheriffs of London on burial of King's enemies hanged, 11 March 1324.

f. 437. Statute on capture and death of Peter Gaveston, 7 Edward II. From MS. Stat. of John Peachey.

f. 439. Ordinance for the state of the land of Ireland, 24 November 1323. (Ibid.)

f. 441. Writ to Chancellor of Ireland, 20 November 1323. From White Book of Exchequer of Ireland.

f. 441v. Letters Patent on 10th and 6th, co. Lancs., 20 January 1324.

f. 443. Form of article that those who took prises otherwise than they ought to be punished. (French.)

f. 445. Writ to Gilbert de Middleton, Archdeacon of Northampton, 1 January 1325.

f. 447. Writ to Barons of Exchequer for Walter Chesewyk, 16 June 1324. (K.R. Mem. Roll, Brev. dir. Bar., Mich. term, 18 Edward II.)

f. 447v. Writ to Treasurer and Barons for King. French war, 28 September 1324. (Ibid.)

f. 448v. Writ to Barons of Exchequer for men etc. of Thetford, 18 November 1324. (Ibid.)

f. 448xv. Writ of privy seal to Treasurer and Barons for King about victuals. (French.) (Ibid.)

f. 449. On prisoners delivered to the Tower of London from the Fleet Prison, 26 November 1324. (French.) (Ibid., East. term.)

f. 450. Writs to Sheriffs, 20 September 1324.

f. 450v. Like, 24 September 1324.

f. 452. Proceedings on Hugh de Nevill, 10 July 1323. (K.R. Mem. Roll, Rec., Trin. term, 18 Edward II.)

f. 454. Proceedings on William de Pinkney. (Ibid., Hil. term.)

f. 456. Writ to Barons of Exchequer for King on St. Peter's, York, 20 June 1325. (Ibid., Brev. dir. Bar., Trin. term.)

f. 456v. Writ of privy seal to Treasurer and Barons for King on usages of Exchequer, 10 August 1325. (French.) (Ibid.)

f. 459v. Ordinance of Barons of Exchequer on provision of victuals for Gascony, under Exchequer seal, 26 November 1324. (French.) (Ibid., Mich. term.)

f. 462. Writ under Exchequer seal for Roger Mortimer of Chirk and others, 2 October 1324. (Ibid., Brev. Ret., Mich. term.)

f. 464. Points handed by Council to William de Kirkby, clerk assigned for voyage to John Sturmy to the north, 16 February 1325. (French.) (Ibid., Comm. etc., Hil. term.)

f. 466. For men of Thetford, 18 November 1324. (Ibid., Rec., East. term.)

f. 468. On the 15th, 22 September 1324. (L.T.R. Mem. Roll, Rec., Mich. term, 18 Edward II.)

f. 468v. Form of assessment of 15th. (French.) (Ibid.)

f. 470. Oath of taxors of 15th. (French.) (Ibid).

f. 472. Writ to Barons of Exchequer for men of Cunham, 1 May 1326. (Ibid., Brev. dir. Bar., Trin. term, 19 Edward II.)

f. 473. Like for John de Bohun of Kilpeck, 8 July 1326. (Ibid.)

f. 473v. Like for King, war with King of France, 20 July 1326. (Ibid.)

ff. 476, 480. Proceedings concerning Thomas de Furnivall, the elder. (Ibid., Rec., Hil. term.)

f. 484. Statute of Arms. From MS. Stat. of John Peachey.

f. 486. Letters Patent to John de Cobham, 27 September 1326. (French.)

f. 488. That no one shall be charged with felonies or trespasses in prosecution of the Despensers. (Ibid.)

Inset at end of volume is the printed pamphlet 'The Pillars of Parliament' (see above, p. 392).

VOLUME 21

A volume of lists and excerpts from the Public Records, mainly of and from the Patent and Close Rolls, John to Edward II. On flyleaf: Quedam Memoranda ex Rotulis Patentium et Clausarum etc. Excerpta temporibus J. R., H. 3, E. 1, E. 2. This is followed by a table of contents of ff. 48–190. 203 ff.

ff. 1–8. List of letters patent, 3–17 John, entered with dates.

ff. 29–46v. Similar list of letters patent, 1–57 Henry III.

ff. 48–53. 20 Henry III, rot. 5, the title of which is in the Roll of the Aid granted to the King for the marriage of his sister to the Roman Emperor, with references to Pipe Rolls, Henry II–13 John.

ff. 126–33. Similar list of letters patent, 1–34 Edward I.

f. 134. References to Close Rolls, 24–34 Edward I, under title Parliament.

f. 134v. Like, 6–33 Edward I, under title Protection.

f. 136. Like, 26–9 Edward I, under title Attainder etc.

ff. 137–8. An alphabetical index to the above list of letters patent, Edward I.

ff. 190–99. Similar alphabetical index to Patent Rolls, 1–20 Edward II (without dates).

ff. 200–3. Similar entries from Close Rolls, Fine Rolls, Scottish Rolls, and Patent Rolls, 1–20 Edward II.

VOLUME 22

A volume of transcripts from the Public Records, 1–4 Edward III. On flyleaf: Recorda E. IIIti ab anno lo usque ad 5tum. Vol. I. 376 ff.

f. 1. Mandate to William Tatham etc. for execution of will of Thomas, late Earl of Lancaster, 26 May 1326.

f. 3. Mandate to Justice of Ireland for Roger Mortimer, 17 August 1327.

f. 5. Mandates to Sheriff of Glouc. etc. for William de Cardiff etc. on the dispute of Thomas, Earl of Lancaster, 17 February 1327. List.

f. 12. Letters Patent on the association made of Bishops, Earls and Barons according to the form of the Statute passed at Westminster, 16 July 1327.

f. 15. Mandates for William fitz Warin etc. on the dispute of Thomas, Earl of Lancaster, 22 February 1327. List.

f. 17. Letters Patent for John de Wylington, 18 February 1327.

f. 19. Letters Patent of pardon for the community of the city of London, 29 February 1327.

f. 21. Letters Patent for citizens of London, 6 March 1327.

f. 22. Mandate on perambulation of the chase of Knaresborough, 10 May 1327.

f. 24. Letters Patent for the Barons of the Cinque Ports, 25 February 1327.

f. 26. Mandates for Howel ap Howel etc. on the dispute of Thomas, Earl of Lancaster, 27 February 1327. List.

f. 28. Letters Patent for the orphans of the city of London, 3 March 1327. (French.)

f. 32. Extract from the Statute Roll, 1 Edward III.

f. 34. As f. 12 above.

f. 36. Mandate for Roger de Reigate, 23 May 1327.

f. 36v. Mandate for Richard de Mosele, 27 May 1327.

f. 38. Mandates for Richard de Stapleton, 7 February 1327 etc.

f. 42. Petitions for those who were of the dispute of Thomas, Earl of Lancaster, 3 February 1327. (French.)

f. 45. Letters Patent of pardon for Andrew de Selkford of London, 28 February 1327.

f. 47. Letters Patent on perambulation, 20 March 1327.

f. 49. Grant to Queen Isabella. 26 April 1327. From Roll of Extracts of Grants, 1 Edward III, with reference to Fine Roll.

f. 50. Letters Patent on preservation of peace in co. Cumberland, 8 March 1327. List.

f. 56. Mandate on mainprise of William de Aylemere, 20 August 1327.

f. 57. Letters Patent for Queen Isabella, 23 March 1327.

f. 59. As f. 22 above.

f. 61. Letters Patent for the community of co. Chester, 15 May 1327. From Scottish Roll.

f. 62. Mandate for the transference of the Exchequer with its rolls to York, 18 August 1327.

f. 63. Letters Patent appointing Edmund, Earl of Kent, as captain of the army, 6 June 1327. From Scottish Roll.

f. 64. Mandates on the magnates of Ireland, 14 February 1327. Lists.

f. 67. Like mandates, 16 July 1327. List.

f. 69. Mandates to Sheriffs on the new great seal, 3 October 1327.

f. 70v. Like on the seal of Ireland, 6 October 1327.

f. 71. Letter from Edward III to John XXII, 28 February 1327.

f. 74. Memorandum on coronation (partly French).

f. 78. As f. 21 above.

f. 80. Letters Patent for citizens of London on kiddles, 8 May 1327.

f. 83. Extract from Coram Rege Roll, Trin. term, 1 Edward III, on Richard de la Pole, Butler.

f. 88v. Writ of privy seal to Geoffrey le Scrope etc. on the Archbishop of York and the port of Hull. (French.)

f. 92. As f. 42 above.

f. 96. Extract from Coram Rege Roll, 1 Edward III. Citizens of London sought enrolment of charter of 6 March 1327.

f. 105. Mandate to late Prior of Bermondsey, 12 August 1327.

f. 107. As f. 74 above.

f. 109. As f. 32 above.

f. 110. As f. 19 above.

f. 111v. Letters Patent for Mayor etc. of London, 4 March 1327.

f. 113. Letters Patent on fines in Marshland, co. Norf., 13 March 1327.

f. 116. Memorandum on proclamation, 24 January 1327. (French.)

f. 118. Mandate to Sheriff of York for Prior of Hospital of St. John of Jerusalem in England 6 August 1327.

f. 120. Letters Patent for Barons of Cinque Ports, 25 February 1327.

f. 122. Mandate for John de Erlege, commission annulled, 6 March 1327.

f. 124. Mandate to Prior of Christ Church, Canterbury, 17 November 1327.

f. 126v. Mandate on those taken bearing letters prejudicial to the King etc. 12 December 1327.

f. 130v. Mandate on Elect of Worcester, 1 January 1328.

f. 132. Charter for Edmund, Earl of Kent, 27 February 1327.

f. 136. Letters Patent on preservation of peace in cos. Heref., Staffs., and Worcs., 8 June 1327.

f. 139. Charter for Geoffrey le Scrope, 20 December 1330.

f. 141. Letters Patent for Gaucelin, Cardinal, 10 March 1328.

f. 142. As f. 124 above.

f. 145. As f. 126v above.

f. 149v. As f. 130v above.

f. 151. Writs de expensis, knights, 31 October 1328.

f. 155v. Like, burgesses, 31 October 1328.

f. 156. Like, knights, 6 August 1328.

f. 156v. Like, burgesses, 6 August 1328.

f. 157. Like, knights, 14 May 1328.

f. 158. Like, burgesses, 13 May 1328.

f. 158v. Like, knights, 5 March 1328.

f. 159. Like, burgesses, 5 March 1328.

f. 160. As f. 157 above.

f. 161. Like, burgesses, 22 February 1328.

f. 162. Writs of summons to Great Council to William, Archbishop of York etc. 15 June 1328. Lists.

f. 167. Mandates to Sheriffs on prohibition of tournaments, 30 April 1328.

f. 169. Mandate to Robert de Barton for Archbishop of York, 8 August 1328.

f. 170. Mandate to Sheriff of Southampton to cause Bishop of Winchester to come, 11 November 1328, with note of mandate of 10 December 1330.

f. 171. Letters Patent on gathering at Kirkby Bellers, 18 May 1328.

f. 172. Letters Patent for Abbot of Egglestone on 10th, 6 August 1328.

f. 174. Letters Patent to William, Bishop of Norwich, on worsted, co. Norf., 19 May 1328.

f. 180. Mandate to Arnald Michol of Gascony, 28 June 1328.

f. 182. Petition of tenants of manor of Mansfield etc. (French), with answer, 2 Edward III. From New Misc. Bundle, t. Henry III.

f. 184. Mandates to Adam de Brome etc. 10 February 1328.

f. 185. Mandate for Edmund de Pinkney, 20 October 1328.

f. 187. Petition of men of Weardale (French) with answer. (*Plac. Parl.*, p. 636.)

f. 188v. Charter on Forest of Weardale, 27 March 1205.

f. 189. Letters Patent for Master Panci de Cintrovo, 11 May 1328.

f. 190. Letters Patent to William Marshall on proclamation, 7 March 1328. (French.)

f. 191. Mandate on fines etc. for life annulled, 28 June 1328.

f. 193. Mandate for Abbot of St. Nicholas, Anjou, 10 February 1328.

f. 195. Mandate to Sheriff of York on castles etc. of Henry, Earl of Lancaster, 16 January 1328. From Fine Roll.

f. 196. Mandate to Sheriff of York on congregations of armed men, 16 September 1328.

f. 197. Mandate for Dean and Chapter of York, 15 November 1328 etc.

f. 199. Letters Patent on delivery without verge of Parliament, 20 October 1328.

f. 200. Letters Patent for Bishop of Lincoln, 8 August 1328.

f. 202. Letters Patent of pardon for Gerard de Braybroc etc. 10 May 1328.

f. 205. Writ of liberate for Geoffrey le Scrope, 13 October 1328. From Liberate Roll.

f. 206. Charter for James le Boteler, Earl of Ormond, 2 November 1328.

f. 207. Letters Patent on possessions of Thomas, Earl of Lancaster, 3 March 1328.

f. 211. Letters Patent of inspeximus for prelates and clergy of England, 26 October 1328.

f. 219. Mandate on removal of Exchequer to Westminster, 20 October 1328.

f. 219v. Mandate on providing chests etc. for Exchequer and Bench, 20 October 1328.

f. 220v. Mandate on removal of Bench to Westminster, 20 October 1328.

f. 222. Mandate for collection of 20th in city of London, 8 June 1328.

f. 224. Mandate on delivery of castles to Master Henry de Clyff, 14 May 1328. (French.)

f. 225. Extract from Statute of Northampton from Statute Roll, 2 Edward III.

f. 227. Writs of summons to Parliament to William, Archbishop of York etc. 28 August 1328.

f. 229. Writs of summons to Parliament to Sheriffs, 5 March 1328.

f. 231. Writs of summons to Council, 15 June 1328.

f. 232. As f. 187 above.

f. 233v. As f. 188v above.

f. 234. Mandate on collection of 20th London, 10 May 1328.

f. 236. As f. 227 above.

f. 238. Mandate for Walter de Selby, 13 March 1329.

f. 239. Writs on continuation of Parliament, 8 February 1329.

f. 240. Letters Patent on collection of 20th in cos., 23 September 1329. (K.R. Mem. Roll, 3 Edward III.)

f. 242. Form of assessing and taxing in cos. (French.) (Ibid.)

f. 244. Letters Patent on collection of 20th in city of London, 23 September 1329. (Ibid.)

f. 245v. Letters Patent on collection of 20th in cities and boroughs, 23 September 1329. (Ibid.)

f. 248. Form of assessing and taxing in cities and boroughs. (French.) (Ibid.)

f. 251. Mandate on taking for King's castles etc. 22 May 1329. From Fine Roll.

f. 252. Letters Patent for Robert Fouke, 10 December 1329.

f. 254. Mandate on crosses in provinces of Canterbury and York, 14 June 1329.

f. 256. As f. 252 above.

f. 258. Letters Patent for Henry, Bishop of Lincoln etc. on association on the Statute, 3 November 1329.

f. 260. Letters Patent on enquiry on arms against the Statute of Northampton, 25 October 1329.

f. 262. Letters Patent on preservation of peace, 30 January 1329. List.

f. 265. Letters Patent to William de Ros etc. on walls and ditches, 3 September 1329.

f. 267. Letters Patent for Llewelyn ap Kenwrig, 20 June 1329.

f. 269. Letters Patent to Ralph le Boteler etc. 25 February 1329.

f. 271. Mandate to Simon, Archbishop of Canterbury, 14 June 1329.

f. 273. As f. 258 above.

f. 275. Letters Patent for Master Hugh de Camera, 3 March 1329.

f. 277. Extract from Coram Rege Roll, East. term, 3 Edward III, for John, Bishop of Winchester. (Cf. Coke, *4th Inst.*, ff. 15, 18.)

f. 281. Writ de supersedendo of gathering of co. Chester, 4 August 1329.

f. 283. Mandates for Archbishop of York etc. and Bishop of Durham, 28 October 1329.

f. 285. Letters Patent for Cardinals, 20 September 1329.

f. 286. Letters Patent for Edmund de Ramsbury, King's chaplain, 21 August, 16 September 1329.

f. 288. Letters Patent for burgesses of Richmond, 30 June 1329.

f. 289. Writs de expensis, knights, 22 February 1329.

f. 289v. Like, burgesses, 22 February 1329.

f. 291. Petition of men of Bristol (French), with answer. From Bundle of Petitions in Parliament, 4 Edward III.

f. 291v. Petition of Edmund, son of Edmund, Earl of Kent (French), with answer. (Ibid.)

f. 293. Extract from Pleas of the Crown in full Parliament at Westminster, Monday after St. Catherine the Virgin, 4 Edward III (26 November 1330) against Thomas de Berkeley.

f. 295v. Letters Patent for Thomas de Berkeley, 16 March 1337.

f. 297. Writs of summons to Parliament to Sheriffs, 23 October 1330.

f. 299. Writs to Sheriffs to come to Parliament, 3 November 1330.

f. 301. As f. 291v above.

f. 301v. As f. 291 above.

f. 302. Extract from Rolls of Parliament on money.

f. 304. Mandate to Bartholomew de Burghersh, Cinque Ports, Queen Phillipa, 27 February 1330.

f. 305. Mandate for men of Hexham, 28 November 1355.

f. 306. Judgement on Roger Mortimer, 4 Edward III (French).

f. 310v. Judgement on Simon de Bereford, 4 Edward III (French).

f. 311. Judgement on John Maltravers, 3 Edward III (French).

f. 312. Judgement on Bogo de Bayonne and John Deveryle, 4 Edward III (French).

Judgement on Thomas de Gournay and William de Ocle, 4 Edward III (French).

f. 312v. Agreement that no one shall be charged in consequence (French).

f. 313. For the Archbishop of York and other adherents of the Earl of Kent. (French.)

f. 314. Writ to Barons of Exchequer sending judgement on Roger Mortimer to enrol etc. 15 February 1331. (K.R. Mem. Roll, Brev. dir. Bar., Hil. term, 5 Edward III.)

The agreement translated out of French into English.

f. 316. Letters Patent for John Maltravers the elder, 5 August 1345.

f. 318. Like, 5 August 1345.

f. 322. Like, 8 February 1352.

f. 324. Mandate for Hugh de Northbury and Hugh, his son, 20 January 1331.

f. 327. Mandate for Thomas de Blaston, 17 January 1331.

f. 329. Mandate for executors of Walter de Langton, Bishop of Coventry and Lichfield, 11 January 1331.

f. 331. Mandate for Lambert de Trikingham, 20 December 1330.

f. 332. Letters Patent revoking presentation to Ottery St. Mary, 18 January 1331.

f. 333. Mandate for clergy of Durham superseding 10th, 25 October 1330.

f. 335. Charter for Ebul Lestrange and Alesia, his wife, 22 January 1331.

f. 337. Petition of Prior and Convent of Laund (French), with answer. From Bundle of Petitions to Parliament, 4 Edward III.

f. 338. Petition of clerks of Chancery on benefices (French), with answer. (Ibid.)

f. 339. Mandate to Sheriff of York on proclamation on money, 10 February 1330.

f. 340. Letters Patent for Queen Isabella, 20 January 1331.

f. 341. Extract from Statute Roll, 4 Edward III, on yearly Parliaments.

f. 342. Letters Patent for burgesses of Bristol, 26 December 1330.

f. 343. Letter from Edward III to Pope, 14 December 1330.

f. 345. Letter from Edward III to Peter, Cardinal, 14 December 1330.

f. 347. Mandate to Sheriff of London on those who came to Bedford, 14 December 1330.

f. 348. Letters Patent for John de Bedford, 12 December 1330.

f. 349. Mandate to Mayor etc. of London on burial of bones of Hugh le Despenser, 15 December 1330.

f. 350. Mandate to Sheriff of Berks. on bodies of traitors, 18 March 1330. List.

f. 352. Letters Patent for Hugh Daudley, 10 January 1331.

f. 353. Letters Patent for David, Earl of Athol, 2 January 1331.

f. 354. As f. 299 above.

f. 356. Letters Patent of pardon for homicides, 20 January 1331.

f. 358. Letters Patent on enquiry of goods of Edmund, Earl of Arundel, 24 August 1330.

f. 360. Charter for Henry, Earl of Lancaster, 20 December 1330.

f. 362. Charter for Edward de Bohun, 18 January 1331.

f. 365. Mandate for Richard de Arundel, 13 December 1330.

f. 367. Writ of summons to Parliament to Simon, Archbishop of Canterbury, 28 November 1330.

f. 369. Letters Patent for merchants of Bardi of Florence, 21 December 1330.

f. 370. Writ to Sheriff of York on confirmation of Magna Carta and the Charter of the Forests, 3 February 1331, from Statute Roll, 5 Edward III.

f. 371. Memorandum on great seal, 28 November 1330.

f. 372. Petition on order of Templars (French) with answer. From Bundle of Petitions in Parliament, 4 Edward III.

f. 374. Letters Patent for John de Crombwell and wife, 3 April 1330.

f. 376. Letters Patent of protection for Bishop of Lincoln, 10 January 1331.

VOLUME 23

A volume of transcripts etc. from the Public Records and other sources, 5–11 Edward III. On flyleaf: Recorda ab ao 5to Edw. 3 ad annum 12, Vol. II. 310 ff.

f. 1. Mandate prohibiting tournaments, 8 October 1331.

f. 2. Letters Patent for men of Chirk in North Wales, 24 March 1331.

f. 3. Petition by Bishop of Durham (French), with answer, 5 Edward III, followed by other documents in Latin and French, from New Misc. Bundle, t. Henry III etc.

f. 7. Mandate to Thomas, Earl of Norfolk and Marshal, etc. on Ireland, 15 October 1331. List.

f. 9. Writ to Sheriff of Yorks. on confirmation of Magna Carta and Charter of Forests, 15 October 1331, from Stat. Roll.

f. 15. Mandate to William Trussell, Escheator South of Trent, 24 February 1331.

f. 17. Like for Thomas Roselyn, 26 February 1331.

f. 18. Letters Patent for Mayor etc. of Bayonne, 3 February 1331, from Gascon Roll.

f. 20. Writs on revocation of Parliament, 23 March 1331.

f. 21. Letters Patent of oyer and terminer to William Trussell, 20 October 1331.

f. 23. Like for Silvester de Oldham, 1 October 1331.

f. 25. Mandate for Margaret, late wife of Earl of Kent, 1 March 1331.

f. 27. Writ to Barons of Exchequer on enrolment of judgement on Roger Mortimer, 15 February 1331, from K.R. Mem. Roll, Brev. dir. Bar., 5 Edward III, with note that it is enrolled in Red Book of Exchequer.

f. 28. Mandate on counterfeit money, 3 April 1331.

f. 29. Letters of Edward III to Pope on canonization of Thomas, Earl of Lancaster, 3 April 1331, from Roman Roll.

f. 30. Like to Peter, Cardinal etc. 3 April 1331, from same.

f. 32. As f. 20 above.

f. 34. Writs of summons to Parliament, 18 February 1331.

f. 35. Letters Patent to Abbot of Kirkstall for Countess of Kent, 5 October 1331.

f. 37. Like for Peter, Cardinal, 16 October 1331.
f. 38. Like for scholars of University of Oxford, 16 October 1331.
f. 39. Like for Lewis, Bishop of Durham, 2 November 1331.
f. 41. Mandate for community of co. Warw., 13 October 1331.
f. 43. Letters Patent for Vidall, Count of Podeux, 3 November 1331, from Gascon Roll.
f. 45. Like for jurats etc. of bastide of Hastings, 4 December 1331, from same.
f. 46. Like for Isard de Lamfar, lord of Lane, 23 November 1331, from same.
f. 49. Writ de expensis, knights, 12 September 1332.
f. 47. Mandate for Lewis, Bishop of Durham, 10 October 1332.
f. 51. Writs of summons to Parliament, 20 October 1332.
f. 52. Like, 27 January 1332.
f. 54. Letters for Master Thomas de Garton, 7 May 1332, from Roman Roll.
f. 55. Letters to Pope for John de Pulteney, Mayor of London, 26 July 1332, from same.
f. 56. Mandate on lands of Hugh Lorymer, 27 October 1332.
f. 57. Letters Patent for Thomas Creke, a Scot, 13 June 1480.
f. 58. Letters to Pope for Chapter of St. Mary's, Lincoln, 20 October 1332, from Roman Roll.
f. 60. Letters to Pope reserving bishopric of St. Andrews for King, 2 October 1332, from same.
f. 62. Letters Patent for Hugh, son of Hugh le Despenser the younger, 1 February 1332.
f. 64. Extract from Parl. Roll, no. 5, 6 Edward III.
f. 65. Mandate on victuals in Ireland, 6 February 1332.
f. 66. Letters Patent on enquiry on prises, 13 April 1334.
Like for Giles de Bello Campo, 1 April 1334.
f. 66v. Like exemplifying charter for Thomas, Earl of Norfolk, 1 March 1334.
f. 67. Like for Mayor etc. of Newcastle upon Tyne, 8 Edward III (incomplete).
f. 68. Extract from Coram Rege Roll, Mich. term, 27 Edward III, to enrol ordinances. (French.)
f. 69. Letters Patent for William de Monte Alto, 9 August 1333.
Like for enquiry into trespasses, town of Claworth, 8 July 1333.
f. 71. Like for Thomas Ughtred, 29 October 1339.
f. 73. Exchequer writ to Prior of Wymondham etc. on enquiry, from K.R. Mem. Roll, Comm., Hil., 4 Edward III.
f. 74. Form of ordinance by Council on selling wines in London (French), from K.R. Mem. Roll, Comm., Rec., Hil., 4 Edward III.
f. 77. Exchequer writ on goods of John Maltravers etc., 29 January 1331, from K.R. Mem. Roll, Brev. Retorn., Hil., 5 Edward III.
f. 78. Letters Patent on pronouncing judgement on contrariants, 14 July 1322.
f. 80. Proceedings on wife of Bartholomew de Burghersh, from L.T.R. Mem. Roll, Comm., Rec., Hil., 19 Edward II.
f. 81. Letters Patent for men of South Wales, 24 April 1332.
f. 83. Like for Henry, Earl of Lancaster, 1 February 1332.

f. 84. Like for John Scut of Carleton, 25 March 1332.

f. 86. Like, commissions on vagabonds etc. 21 March 1332.

f. 92. Writs on prorogation of Parliament to Simon, Archbishop of Canterbury etc. 11 December 1332.

f. 94. Letters Patent to Mayor etc. of London on 15th, 16 September 1332.

f. 95. Form of Taxation, 15th (French), 6 Edward III, from Patent Roll.

f. 98. Extract from Parl. Roll, nos. 5, 6, 7, 8, 6 Edward III.

f. 99. As f. 92 above.

102. Letters Patent on levying and collecting 10th and 15th, 16 September 1332.

f. 105. Extract from Parl. Roll, Remembrances of Parliament, York, 6 Edward III (French).

f. 108. Mandate superseding eyre in liberty of Durham, 11 November 1333, from Fine Roll.

f. 110. Writs of summons to Parliament, 2 January 1334.

f. 111. Mandate for Prior of Chapel of St. Saviour's, 12 February 1334.

f. 113. Like on plea, Bishop of Durham and Robert Clifford, 12 August 1334.

f. 115. As f. 69 above.

f. 118. Mandate to Sheriff of Lincs., on holding fairs beyond time, 25 May 1333.

f. 120. Form of taxation, 15th (French), from Patent Roll.

f. 123. Mandate on collectors of customs (French), 7 Edward III, from Fine Roll.

f. 125. Like to Sheriffs for Prior of Hospital of St. John of Jerusalem in England, 3 February 1333.

f. 127. Letters Patent on 15th and 10th, 12 December 1333.

f. 129. Petition of men of Oakham (French), from Bundle of Pet. in Parl., 7 Edward III.

f. 129v. Like on commissions of land, Sheriffs and conspiracies etc., with reply, from same.

f. 130v. Like by men of Northumberland (French), with answer, from same.

f. 131. Mandate to Sheriffs on ordinance on money (French), 6 June 1335, from Fine Roll.

f. 134. The oath of searchers of money (French), from same.

f. 134v. Note on money from Close Roll, 10 Edward III, Warden of money, exchange, London.

f. 135. Letter concerning concessions by King of Scotland, 1 March 1334 (French), from Scottish Roll.

f. 139. As f. 135 above.

f. 143. Petition by King of Scotland (French), from Bundle of Pet. in Parl., 21 Edward III.

f. 143v. As f. 135 above.

f. 146. Letters Patent on enquiry on prises, 13 April 1334.

f. 147. Like on sentences on maintainers of false complaints, 16 March 1334.

f. 149. Mandates on exactions by collectors of customs, 21 September 1334.

f. 150. Writs de expensis, knights, 23 September 1334.

f. 151. Like burgesses, 23 September 1334.

f. 152. Charter for Richard, Earl of Arundel, 22 September 1333.

f. 154. As f. 66 above.

f. 156. As f. 66v above.

f. 161. Writ to Sheriff of York, from MS. Book of Stat. entitled FF in poss. of William Petyt.

f. 164. Mandate for Abbot of Crowland, 5 July 1334.

f. 166. Writs of summons to Parliament, 24 July 1334.

f. 168. Note on Parliament of York and action on petition leading to Statute.

f. 169. Statute on alien merchants, 9 Edward III, from Stat. Roll.

f. 170. Translation of the same from Rastell, *Stat.*, with writ thereon, 30 June 1335.

f. 180. Letters Patent on assessment of 15th, 30 June 1335.

f. 182. Mandates to Sheriffs on proclamation of Stat. of West. I, cap. 34.

f. 184. Writs of summons to Parliament, 1 April 1335.

f. 185. Writ to Sheriff of Lincs., 9 Edward III, from MS. Book (as f. 161).

f. 187. Letters Patent on electing and sending men into liberties of Durham, 7 May 1335.

f. 189. Writ to Sheriff of Yorks., 9 Edward III, from MS. (as f. 161).

f. 193. Letters Patent for William de Monte Acuto, 1 May 1335.

f. 194. As f. 182 above.

f. 195. Letters Patent on preservation of peace, Stat. of Northampton, 26 July 1335.

f. 198. Mandates to Keepers of Exchanges on farthings, 6 July 1335.

f. 200. As f. 198 above.

f. 201. On the table of exchange and the whole manner of money ordained at Dover, 6 July 1335 (French), from Fine Roll.

f. 203. Note on Parliament of Nottingham, 10 Edward III, ordinance on outrageous viands, text from MS. (as f. 161 above), and translation.

f. 208. Letter from Treasurer and Barons of Exchequer on Letters Patent, 1 December 1337, from Small Bundle, t. Edward III.

f. 212. Mandate to Sheriff of London on proclamation on half pence and sterling, 18 April 1336.

f. 213. Writs of summons to Parliament, 14 January 1337.

f. 215. Mandate on levying 10th and 15th, 10 Edward III (incomplete), from Fine Roll.

f. 217. Like for Edmund de Beresford, 4 February 1336.

f. 219. Petition of prelates and earls on ancient laws and customs (French), from Bundle of Pet. t. Edward I etc.

f. 222. Reference to Close Roll, 10 Edward III, on Great Council, Nottingham and Parliament of York.

f. 223. Mandate for John de Monceux, 28 May 1336.

f. 225. Like for men of Ireland, 2 June 1336.

f. 226. Like for King, 10 Edward III.

f. 228. Letters Patent concerning meeting, with commission, to Duke of Albany, 30 May 1410, from Scottish Roll.

f. 229. Purveyors of King's Household etc., from Stat. Roll, 10 Edward III, writs to Sheriffs thereon, 1 April 1336.

f. 234. Statute on oppressions, murders, robberies etc., from Stat. Roll, 10 Edward III.

f. 236. Writs of summons to Council at Westminster, 2 September 1337, from Bundle of Summons to Council at West., 11 Edward III.

f. 239. Petition of prelates etc. on Church of Rome (French), with answer from a certain Box no. 10 in Tower of London.

f. 242. As f. 236 above.

f. 244. Writ to Sheriff of Southampton, with return, 3 March 1337, from New Misc. Bundle t. Henry III etc.

f. 245. Petition to Chancellor from Queen Isabella (French), from same.

f. 246. Mandate on grant to John de St. Pauls of Rolls of Chancery, 28 April 1337.

f. 247. Letters Patent making Henry de Lancaster, Earl of Derby, 18 March 1337, in schedule Memoranda of Letters returned to Chancery, 24 October 1339, from New Misc. Bundle t. Henry III etc.

f. 249. Mandate on supersession of publication of statute and ordinance, co. Chester, 8 June 1337.

f. 251. Letters Patent on prorogation of truce between Kings of England and France, 5 January 1338, from Gascon Rolls.

f. 253. Writs of summons to Parliament, 20 December 1337.

f. 254. Letters Patent to Thomas de la More on enquiry into felonies etc. 3 May 1337.

f. 257. Like on enquiries into trespasses against statute, 10 January 1338.

f. 260. Petition of John de Farendon, clerk (French), with answer, from Bundle of Pet. to Parl., 11 Edward III.

f. 263. Mandate to Sheriff of Salop on execution of writs, 30 March 1337.

f. 264. Like for William fitz Warin, 11 Edward III.

f. 265. Writs of summons to Council, 18 August 1337.

f. 267. Charter for William de Bohun, Earl of Northampton, 16 March 1337.

f. 269. Letters Patent for citizens of London, 26 March 1337.

f. 272. As f. 269 above.

f. 274. Note on making of barges from Close Roll, 1 Richard II.

f. 275. Letters Patent on taking of certain persons, 4 October 1337.

f. 277. Like for Thomas de Berkeley on death of Edward II, 16 March 1337.

f. 279. Charter for Henry de Lancaster, Earl of Derby, 16 March 1337.

f. 281. Mandate for William Page etc. 1 December 1337.

f. 284. Letter to Pope, 20 March 1337, from Roman Roll.

f. 286. Statute on foreign etc. merchants on export of wool, from Stat. Roll, 11 Edward III, writ to Sheriffs thereon, 28 March 1337.

f. 289. Mandate for Thomas de Swanlond, 4 January 1338.

f. 291. Letters to John, Duke of Brabant etc., 7 October 1337, from Almain Roll.

f. 295. Letters Patent of exemplification for heir of Roger Belers, 16 December 1337.

f. 297. Like on assent of Parliament of King's intention to treat of journey of magnates to Scotland with Earl of Warwick, 24 March 1337, from Scottish Roll.

f. 299. Mandate for Master Paul de Monte Florum, 5 March 1337.

f. 301. Like appointing new day against James de Stafford, kt., 3 June 1337.

f. 303. Mandates on levying 10th and 15th, 11 February 1337, from Fine Roll.

f. 305v. Form of taxation, 11 Edward III (extract only), from same.

f. 306. Mandate for Abbot of Stoneley, 18 October 1337.

f. 309. Like on liberties of Durham, 20 June 1337.

VOLUME 24

A volume of transcripts etc. from the Public Records and other sources, 12–15 Edward III. On flyleaf: Recorda E. III ab anno 12 usque as 16. Vol. III. 324 ff.

f. 1. Grant to Master and Hospital of Ospring, 26 February 1338, from Roll of Extracts of Gifts, 12 Edward III.

f. 2. Letters Patent for men of Kingston upon Hull, 4 March 1338.

f. 3. Like of pardon of 10th to men of Portsmouth, 12 June 1338.

f. 4. Grant to Abbot etc. of Colchester etc. 28 November 1338, from Roll of Ext. of Gifts, 12 Edward III.

f. 5. Like to Abbot of Waltham Holy Cross etc. 20 January 1338, same.

f. 6. Mandates for men of vills on 10th, 26 January 1338.

Like for William de Bohun, Earl of Northampton, 28 August 1338.

f. 11. Like to pay 10th and 15th to Robert de Wodehouse, Treasurer, 6 May 1338.

f. 12. Letters Patent on truce between England and France, 24 February 1338.

f. 16. As f. 1 above.

f. 16v. Mandates for men of Nottingham, Newark etc. 3 October 1338.

f. 20. Like for Thomas, Earl of Norfolk, 9 December 1338.

f. 22. Letters Patent on arrest of evildoers, 10 December 1338.

f. 24. Charter for William de Monte Acuto, Earl of Salisbury, 24 April 1338.

f. 30. Letters Patent for Edward, Duke of Cornwall, Keeper of England, 11 July 1338.

f. 30v. Letters to be intendant on Duke, 13 July 1338.

f. 31v. Note on commission to Duke of York, Protector etc., from Parl. Roll, 33 Henry VI.

f. 32. Letters Patent to Keepers of Peace, town of Stamford, 12 May 1338.

f. 34. Mandates on non-payment of 10th, 1 December 1338. List.

f. 36. Letters Patent on appointment of William de Falderley etc. 1 May 1338.

f. 37. Writs of summons to Council at Northampton of William, Archbishop of York, etc. 15 June 1338. List.

f. 41. As f. 37 above.

f. 42v. Notes from Almain Roll, 12 Edward III, on 10th and 15th, Patent Roll, 12 Edward III, on survey of arms.

f. 43. Mandate for Abbot of St. Albans, 8 October 1338.

f. 45. Letters Patent for Robert de Houel and Hugh de Berwick, Clerks of Market, 30 January 1339.

f. 46. Like of enquiry of those who sold against the Stat. of York etc. 15 January 1339.
f. 48. Like for Rhys ap Griffith, 9 June 1338.
f. 50. Mandate on superseding levy of scutage, 16 February 1338.
f. 52. Letters Patent on wool to Yarmouth, 24 June 1338, from Almain Roll.
f. 55. Mandates on wool levied by prelates, 6 October 1338. List, from Fine Roll.
f. 58. Letters to Duke of Brabant etc., 8 May 1338, from Almain Roll.
f. 61. Mandate to Abbot of Vale Royal, 12 March 1338.
f. 63. Like to Sheriffs on proclamation of King's new privy seal, 25 April 1338.
f. 64. Like for Bishop of Hereford on superseding wool levied, 20 November 1338.
f. 66. Letters to John, Archbishop of Canterbury, excusing King against his people, 28 March 1338, from Almain Roll.
f. 68. Truce with men of France, 24 February 1338, same, with reference to Patent Roll, 12 Edward III.
f. 72. Mandate for William de Bohun, Earl of Northampton, 20 November 1338.
f. 73. Like for Henry, Bishop of Lincoln, 1 May 1338.
f. 75. Like on keys of Treasury delivered to John de Horton, 3 February 1338.
f. 76. Like on collection of 2s. on each tun of wine, 16 February 1338.
f. 78. Like for Prior of Llanthony Prima in Wales, 27 February 1338.
f. 80. Like on continuation of plea between Henry, son of Hugh, and Roger Clifford, 16 February 1338.
f. 82. Like on continuation of assize against Henry, son of Hugh, 16 February 1338.
f. 84. Like for John de Bodenho, 12 February 1338.
f. 86. Like on plea on office of Usher of Exchequer, 10 February 1338.
f. 88. Commission, co. Devon, to dig for gold etc., 4 August 1338, from Fine Roll.
f. 91. Writs of summons to Council to William, Archbishop of York etc. 15 June 1338. List.
f. 97. Writs de expensis, knights, 2 August 1338. List.
f. 100. Like, burgesses, 2 August 1338. List.
f. 101. Letters on 10th and 15th, 2 years, at Exchequer, 4 August 1338, from Almain Roll.
f. 103. Mandate for men of Westminster, 10 November 1338.
f. 106. Like for John de Molyns, 5 March 1338.
f. 108. As f. 88 above.
f. 111. Writs to William, Archbishop of York, on arrays, 16 February 1339, from Almain Roll. Lists.
f. 115. Writ to Bailiff of Ospring, 4 June 1339, with return, from New Misc. Bundle, t. Henry III etc.
f. 117. Patents granted to men of England and Gascony, 13 Edward III; to Duke of Cornwall etc. 26 September 1339.
f. 119. The grant to the demand of the Magnates and Commons (French), from Parl. Roll, 13 Edward III. The answer of the Commons on the aid (French).
f. 120. Writs of summons to Parliament, 16 November 1339.
f. 122. Letters Patent prohibiting the sale of fees before the King's return, 6 May 1339.

f. 126. Mandate on collection of wool etc. in liberty of Durham, 3 July 1339.

f. 129. Writ to Coroners, co. Cambridge, 1 September 1339, with return, from New Misc. Bundle, t. Henry III etc.

f. 132. Mandate on molestation of taxors, 10th and 15th, co. Warw., 6 October 1339

f. 134. Letters Patent on beginning of Parliament, 19 January 1340.

f. 135. Remembrances of Parliament, Westminster, 13 Edward III, from Parl. Roll, with note from Coke, *4th Inst*.

Ad parliamentum tentum 9 Ed. 3 quando subsidium novi generis petitum fuit Comunes responderunt quod colloquium haberent cum suis Comitatibus et locis a quibus delegati erant antequam tractatum haberent de aliqua tali materia. Hoc allegatum est a Domino Coke in sua quarta parte Institutionum Regum Anglie pro quo ille citat Rot. Parl., 9 E. 3, no. 3 qui quidem Articulus necessario temporibus suis extitit cujus exemplar nullus dubito quin ille habuit At Eheu! tanta fuit aut malitia aut negligentia aliquorum hominum quamplurimis seculis ut hic ipse Rotulus Parliamentarius inter alios quamplurimos longe antiquiores ad irreparabile damnum omnium seculorum penitus depreditus et exisus est.

f. 140. Mandate to William, Archbishop of York, on subsidy from clergy of Province, 10 October 1339.

f. 142. Like to Adam, Bishop of Winchester, on delivery of wool to King, 12 June 1339.

f. 143. Stat. from Stat. Roll, 14 Edward III, 16 April 1340.

f. 145. On grant of 9th (French), from Parl. Roll, 14 Edward III.

f. 147. Mandates of supersedeas for Countess of Ulster and Henry de la Dale, 10 April 1340.

f. 148. Writ of Liberate for Geoffrey le Scrope, 15 May 1340.

f. 150. Mandate on levying 9th and 15th, 15 November 1340.

f. 151. Letters Patent to John, Archbishop of Canterbury etc. on surveying accounts, 2 July 1340.

f. 153. On petitions of Geoffrey de Staunton. A copy of the first petition with the answer made in Parliament (French). A copy of the writ under the great seal made on the petition and endorsement to Justices of Common Bench, 22 May 1340. A copy of letters under the privy seal to the same Justices to make judgement without further delay (French), 17 June 1340, from Parl. Roll.

f. 168. Writ of protection for the clergy founded on the Stat. 14 Edward III, from Reg. of Writs.

f. 171. Statutes on granting writs and plaints in Parliament on delays etc., from Stat. Roll, 14 Edward III.

f. 178. Mandate on continuation of assize, Ralph de Strubby, 18 July 1340.

f. 180. Like to Abbot of St. Edmund's on moving King's horses, 15 August 1340.

f. 182. As f. 143 above.

f. 184. Letter to ecclesiastics and laity of France, 8 February 1340 (French), from French Roll.

f. 187. As f. 184 above.

f. 190. Letters Patent on custody of the Marches, 16 July 1376, from Scottish Roll.

f. 192. Like on maintenance of King's right, 12 November 1340.

f. 195. Like on many men taken and arrested, 6 August 1340.

f. 197. Like for Giles de Bolunville, 15 October 1340.

f. 199. Like on observance of Stats. of Winchester and Northampton, 19 December 1340. List.

f. 201. Mandate to John, Archbishop of Canterbury on procurations of Cardinals, 20 September 1340.

f. 202. Writ to John de Stonor on suit of Geoffrey, son of William de Staunton, kt., and John de Staunton, 12 October 1340, from Select Bundle of Writs and Records, t. Edward III, with reference to Pleas, Mich. term, 13 Edward III, from Parl. Roll, 14 Edward III.

f. 213. Note on Stat. for Clergy, 14 Edward III, with Stat. from Stat. Roll, 16 April 1340.

f. 221. Note on creation of William, Marquis of Juliers, as Earl of Cambridge, and surrender of patent by his son. Charter to William, Marquis of Juliers, 7 May 1340, from Select Bundle of Writs and Records, t. Edward III. Memorandum on surrender by William, his son, on his death, 15 June 1366. Enrolment of writing of William, Duke of Juliers (French). Another writing, 15 June 1366, with memorandum of appearance in Chancery. Charter for William, Marquis of Juliers, Earl of Cambridge, 8 May 1340.

f. 241. Stat. 14 Edward III, from Stat. Roll, with translation from Rastell, *Stat.*

f. 244. Letter on subsidy in liberty of Durham etc., 25 August 1340, from Almain Roll.

f. 248. As f. 244 above.

f. 252. Mandate on receivers newly provided, 22 July 1340.

f. 254. Writs of summons to Parliament, 21 February 1340.

f. 255. Writs de expensis, burgesses, 10 May 1340.

f. 256. Like, knights, 10 May 1340.

f. 257. Letters Patent for Robert fitz Payn, illness, excused from coming to Parliament, 20 May 1341.

f. 258. Note on declaration of Parliament, 15 Edward III, on Magna Carta, Charter of Forests etc., from Stat. Roll, 15 Edward III.

f. 259. Petition of the clergy (French), with answer, from Parl. Roll, 15 Edward III.

f. 261. Mandate on expenses coming to Parliament, 1 March 1341.

f. 263. Writs to come to London to treat, 12 June 1341. List.

f. 265. Franchises of the church in Magna Carta, Charter of Forests etc. from Parl. Roll, 15 Edward III.

f. 266. Extracts from Parl. Roll, 15 Edward III. (French.)

f. 271. Mandate on ships, munitions and men, sent to Council, 12 February 1341. List.

f. 274. Like, on levying 9th in co. Lancs., 12 March 1341.

f. 276. Letters Patent for Robert Oseney, 20 October 1341.

f. 277. Stat., 15 Edward III, from Stat. Roll, with note it was revoked by King and note of revocation, from Parl. Roll, 15 Edward III.

f. 283. Extract from Parl. Roll, 15 Edward III.

f. 284. Mandate of prohibition to John, Archbishop of Canterbury, 1 October 1341.

f. 286. Letters Patent for Abbot of St. Augustine's, Bristol, on coming to Parliament, 2 May 1341.

f. 287. Extracts from Parliament Roll, 15 Edward III (French).

f. 289. As f. 261 above.

f. 300. As f. 277 above.

f. 305. Translation of Stat. 15 Edward III, from Rastell, *Stat.*

f. 309. As f. 287 above.

f. 311. Translation of Stat. 15 Edward III, from Rastell, *Stat.*

f. 313. As f. 284 above.

f. 315. Extract from Parl. Roll, 17 Edward III, reinstating certain parts of revoked Stat. (French.)

f. 317. Mandate of supersedeas for Richard de la Pole, 13 June 1341.

f. 318. Mandate to those who resist collection of 10th in co. Devon, 15 June 1341.

f. 320. As f. 283 above.

f. 322. As f. 284 above.

VOLUME 25

A volume of transcripts etc. from the Public Records and other sources, 16–39 Edward III. On flyleaf: Recorda E. 3 an ao. 16 usque ad 40. Vol. 4. 352 ff.

f. 1. Letters Patent on enquiry on sterling sent to parts overseas, 20 November 1342.

f. 3. Mandate on voyage of Robert Parning, Chancellor, 4 October 1342.

f. 4. Letter to Pope's Chaplains and Auditors, 28 July 1342, from Roman Roll.

f. 6. Letters Patent for men of Harwich, 12 August 1342.

f. 8. Letter from Parliament to Pope on provisions, 8 March 1343, in English, from Fox, *Acts.*

f. 11. Letters Patent on proclamation to take rebels etc. 4 November 1343.

f. 14. Prior of Coventry attached for trespass, from K.R. Mem. Roll, Comm., Rec., Hil., 17 Edward III.

f. 18. Writ for Thomas Musgrave, 1 December 1343, with endorsement and schedule, from New Misc. Bundle, t. Henry III etc.

f. 22. Note on case of burgesses of Barnstaple on petition to Parliament, 17 Edward III, from Patent Roll.

f. 24. Letter to Pope on provisions, 17 Edward III, from Roman Roll.

f. 27. Letter to Pope for Archbishop of Canterbury, 30 August 1343, same.

f. 29. As f. 8 above.

f. 33. As f. 27 above.

f. 35. As f. 14 above, with note on aid for marriage of King's daughter, from Account Roll of Aid.

f. 36. Letter to Pope for Master William de Norwich, 6 March 1344, from Roman Roll.

f. 38. Letters Patent concerning Tower of London, 8 April 1344 (French).

f. 40. Like on magnates appointed to hear complaints on petitions, 10 June 1344.

f. 42. Petition of Robert de Berners (French), with answer, from Bundle of Pet. to Parl., 18 Edward III.

f. 43. Petition of burgesses of Newcastle under Lyme (French), with answer, from same.

f. 44. Petition of clergy (French), with answer, 18 Edward III, from Parl. Roll, with note from Clement Maydestone's History of Master Richard Scrope, Archbishop of York, from *Anglia Sacra*.

f. 46. Ordinance, 18 Edward III, from Stat. Roll.

f. 48. Letter to Pope for Prior of Nostell, 11 July 1344.

f. 50. Writs of summons to Parliament, 20 April 1344.

f. 51. Ordinance, 8 July 1344, from Stat. Roll, 18 Edward III.

f. 55. Mandate on proclamation on provisors, 30 January 1344.

f. 63. Like to Sheriffs on provisors, 28 March 1344.

f. 67. Extract from Parl. Roll, 18 Edward III.

f. 73. As f. 40 above.

f. 75. As f. 42 above.

f. 76. Writ, 6 February 1344, from New Misc. Bundle, t. Henry III etc.

f. 78. Letter, Prince of Wales to France, 12 September 1345, from Close Roll.

f. 79. Letters Patent for John Maltravers, 5 August 1345.

f. 82. Like for John Maltravers, the elder, 5 August 1345.

f. 84. Like on the taking of Richard de Peshale, 20 November 1345.

f. 86. Like on collection of 10th in Scotland, 12 August 1346, from Scottish Roll.

f. 88. Petition of Hugh de Courtney (French), with answer, from New Misc. Bundle, t. Henry III etc.

f. 90. Mandate on 10th in city of York, 8 July 1346, from Fine Roll.

f. 92. Like on levying aid on knighting of King's eldest son, 1 November 1346, same.

f. 94. Letter by magnates to Lords of Parliament on knighting (French), from Parl. Roll, 20 Edward III.

f. 95. Mandates to Sheriffs on proclamation on rumours, 10 March 1346.

f. 96. Like on proclamation on importing Papal Bulls etc. 13 October 1346.

f. 97. Like for men of Creyke, 14 February 1346.

f. 99. Like on proclamation on course of money, 30 October 1346.

f. 101. Extract from Parl. Roll, 21 Edward III (French).

f. 102. Mandates on proclamation on gold, 27 June 1347. (French.)

f. 104. Judgement on Earls of Fife and Menteith, 22 February 1347 etc., from Scottish Roll.

f. 110. Mandate to John, Archbishop of Canterbury, prohibiting proclamation on Cardinals, 12 April 1347.

f. 114. Petition of Commons (French), with answer, from Parl. Roll, 21 Edward III.

f. 117. Petition of men of Broadway (French), with answer, from Bundle of Pet. to Parl., 21 Edward III.

f. 119. Mandate on levying 15th in city of London, 20 July 1348, from Fine Roll.

f. 121. Like on proclamation on money etc. 13 February 1348.

ff. 125, 127, 132, 133. Plea on assize of ancient demesne, from *Book of Assizes*, 22 Edward III, with note from Broke, *Grand. Abridg.*

f. 128. Part of Stat. of Provisors, 25 Edward III, from Stat. Roll.

f. 129. Writs of summons to Parliament, 14 February 1348.

f. 134. Letters for church of Dublin, 18 February 1348, from Roman Roll.

f. 136. Petition of Peter Maulever and John Vic (French), from Bundle of Pet. before King and Council, 23 Edward III.

f. 137. Mandate on levying 10th and 15th in city of London etc., 1 September 1349, from Fine Roll.

f. 139. On process against William de Thorp, 3 November, 19 November, 24 November 1350, from Patent Roll, continuing through process in Parl. Roll, 25 Edward III (French), and pardon, 10 March 1351.

f. 156. Mandate on lands of William Thorp, 15 November 1350, from Fine Roll.

ff. 157, 163. As f. 128 above.

ff. 159, 167. Ordinances for clergy made at Westminster, 25 Edward III, from Stat. Roll.

f. 165. Letters Patent on breaking down weirs, 12 May 1351.

ff. 171, 186. Stat. of Provisors, 25 Edward III, from Stat. Roll, see Stat. of Reservations and Provisions, from Parl. Roll.

f. 178. Letters Patent on survey of petitions by Archbishop of Canterbury etc. 1 September 1351.

f. 179. Writs on proclamation of Statutes made to Sheriffs, 6 March 1351, from Stat. Roll, 25 Edward III.

f. 180. Stat. cap. 2, from Stat. Roll, 25 Edward III.

f. 182. Inquisition on liberties of city of Carlisle, from Bundle of Escheats, 25 Edward III.

f. 185. Note on Stat. of Provisors.

f. 192. Taxors appointed in cos., 29 November 1351, from L.T.R. Mem. Roll, Comm., Rec., Mich., 25 Edward III.

f. 194. Letters Patent for Abbot of Gloucester not attending Parliament, 6 May 1352.

f. 195. Like that Abbot of Leicester is not bound to come to Parliament, 20 April 1353.

f. 198. Writs of summons to Council to Simon, Archbishop of Canterbury, etc. 15 July 1353. List.

f. 204. Statute of Frauds, from Stat. Roll, 27 Edward III. See Roll of Ordinances at Westminster, 23 September 1353, Stat. against the annulment of judgement of King's Court.

f. 205v. Statute of Staple, 27 Edward III, from *Book of Stat.* in French, extracts with notes from Parl. Roll, 27, 28 Edward III, Stat. Roll, 28 Edward III.

f. 208. Extract from Old MS. Book of Stat. in poss. of J. Lapthorn, 14 March 1353.

f. 215. Mandate on tolls etc. of John de Stonor to Roger Hilary, 22 February 1354.

f. 216. Like for Mayor etc. of city of York, 24 May 1354.

f. 217. Extract from Stat. Roll, 28 Edward III.

f. 218. Letter to Pope, 7 May 1301, from Close Roll.

f. 230. Extract from Parl. Roll, 27 Edward III.

f. 234. Mandate to Simon, Archbishop of Canterbury, etc. to pray for King, 10 October 1356.

f. 236. Plea (French), from *Book of Assizes*.

f. 238. Writ on service of Hatfield Peverel, 15 January 1356, with return and search in rolls and memoranda of Exchequer, from Bundle of Escheats, 30 Edward III.

f. 240. Extract from Stat. Roll, 31 Edward III, 1 August 1357.

f. 241. Mandate to Simon, Archbishop of Canterbury, etc. 22 February 1357.

f. 243. Letters Patent on enquiry on sale of salt fish, 12 July 1357.

f. 245. Like for Bishop of Durham, 10 March 1358.

f. 247. Letters of acquittance, 24 June 1358, from Scottish Roll.

f. 248. Letters to consuls etc. of barony of Briggerico, 12 April 1350, from Gascon Roll.

f. 250. Mandate to Constable of Bordeaux, 22 March 1358, from Fine Roll.

f. 253. Memorandum on delivery of great seal, 11 October 1359, from Close Roll.

f. 255. Mandate on convocation of clergy, Provinces of Canterbury and York, 18 November 1359.

f. 256. Like on proclamation on Irish, 20 July 1359.

f. 258. Letters on release of David Bruce, 31 October 1359, from French Roll.

f. 260. Mandate on lands unjustly seized, 20 June 1360.

f. 262. Letters Patent on enquiry on kiddles, 1 July 1361.

f. 264. Mandate to Sheriff of Surr., on abjuration of realm, 7 June 1361.

f. 266. Like on proclamation on killing animals in city of London, 25 February 1361.

f. 267. Like for Philip de Nevill, 6 February 1361.

f. 269. Letters Patent on enquiry on those who take money from both sides, 6 May 1361.

f. 271. Mandate (French), 26 February 1361.

ff. 273, 276. Extract from Stat. Roll, 36 Edward III.

f. 274. Writ on proclamation of Stat. to Sheriffs, 20 November 1362.

f. 278. Letters Patent for Peter de Grimsby, 3 November 1362.

f. 280. Like for Alexander de Mowbray, 12 November 1362, from Scottish Roll.

f. 282. On confirmation of Magna Carta and Charter of Forests, with references to Stat. Rolls, 36, 38 Edward III, 1, 5 Richard II, 11 Henry IV, 4 Henry V, 12 Edward IV.

f. 285. Charter for Ealbald, King, son of Adelbert, King, 618, from Charter Roll, 36 Edward III.

f. 287. Letters Patent for Prince of Aquitaine and Wales, 29 August 1362.

f. 288. Extracts from Parl. Roll, 36 Edward III, and Stat. Roll, 36 Edward III.

f. 290. Writs de expensis, knights, co. Lancs., 17 November 1362.

f. 292. Writ appointing John de Sheverston, Seneschal of Aquitaine, 8 June 1362, from Gascon Roll.

f. 294. Note on Stat. of Purveyors, 36 Edward III, with Stat. and mandate on proclamation, 20 November 1362, and translation from Rastell, *Stat.*

f. 306. Mandate, prohibition to Guy de Brian, 8 March 1362.

f. 308. Petition of Bishop of Durham (French), with answer, from Bundle of Pet. to Parl., 36 Edward III.

f. 310. Letters Patent on enquiry, lands of Cinque Ports outside liberty, 1 December 1363.

f. 312. Treaty with Spain, 1 March 1363, from Patent Roll.

f. 316. Letters Patent on temporalities of Deanery of York, 15 December 1364.

f. 320. Extract from Parl. Roll, 38 Edward III.

f. 322. Stat. of Provisors, 38 Edward III, from Stat. Roll.

f. 326. Mandates on search, export of money, 28 July 1365. List.

f. 331. Letters Patent on making of provisions, 3 November 1365 (French).

ff. 335, 336. Ordinance to observe Stat. of Provisors, 12 May 1365.

f. 339. Case on Stat. of Provisors, from Year Book, Mich. term, 39 Edward III.

f. 344. Mandate on Prior of Lewes not attending Parliament, 10 February 1365.

f. 351. Like to Sheriff of London that trespasses against Clerks of Chancery shall be pleaded before the Chancellor, 2 July 1365.

VOLUME 26

A volume of transcripts etc. from Public Records and other sources, 40–51 Edward III. On flyleaf: ab ao 40 Edw. 3 ad finem Regni sui. Vol. 5. 247 ff.

f. 1. Extract from Parl. Roll, 40 Edward III, on Universities of Oxford and Cambridge etc. (French.)

f. 4. Extract from same on marriage of Isabella (King's daughter) to Seigneur de Courcy etc.

f. 6. Like, Letters Patent, 13 April 1366.

f. 15. Mandate for William Septvans, 17 February 1369.

f. 17. Like, 21 February 1369.

f. 20. Extract from Parl. Roll, 40 Edward III, with reference to Close Roll, 40 Edward III, and note from Selden, *Ad Fletam*.

f. 22. Letters Patent for Duke of Aquitaine, 13 February 1366.

f. 23. Mandate to Sheriff of London for Clerks of King's Chancery, 24 July 1366.

f. 25. Like on state of Ireland, 10 November 1367.

f. 27. Extract from Parl. Roll, 42 Edward III.

f. 29. Letters Patent of protection for hostages of France, 5 February 1368.

f. 30. Like for William of Wykeham, Bishop of Winchester, 20 May 1368.

f. 32. Mandate on mainprise of Master John de Stretele, Dean of Lincoln, 13 November 1368.

f. 35. Like for Richard de Berkeley, kt., and wife, 15 May 1368.

f. 33. Extract from Parl. Roll, 42 Edward III.

f. 37. Mandate on adjournment of Courts, 22 May 1368 etc.

f. 39. Letters Patent of oyer and terminer on plaint of Robert de Staunton, kt., 30 November 1368.

f. 41. Like of restitution of temporalities to Archbishop of Canterbury, 5 January 1369.

f. 43. Extracts from Rolls of Parl., 43 Edward III.

f. 46. Mandate to William, Archbishop of Canterbury, on array of Clergy, 17 June 1369.

f. 48. Letters to Prince of Aquitaine on lands conquered in France, 19 June 1369 (French), from Gascon Roll.

f. 50. Mandate on grant, alien Priory of Minting, 6 October 1369, from Fine Rolls.
f. 52. Memorandum on France, 3 June 1369, from Close Roll.
ff. 54, 59. Extract from Parl. Roll, 43 Edward III, on time of general prescription.
f. 56. Petition of Commons (French), 51 Edward III, from Parl. Roll, with translation.
f. 60. Mandate to Sheriff of London on proclamation on French hostages, 26 April 1369.
f. 61. Letters Patent of confirmation of treaty with Flanders, 4 August 1370. (French.)
f. 63. Like to Sheriff of London on taking of heretics, 20 March 1370.
f. 64. Letters, 44 Edward III (French), from French Roll.
f. 65. Letters Patent on taking of John Hanle, 22 June 1370.
f. 71. Extracts from Parl. Roll, 45 Edward III.
f. 73. As f. 65 above.
f. 75. Mandate for men of Ireland on customs etc. 28 May 1372.
f. 77. Extract from Parl. Roll, 46 Edward III, on evidence.
f. 78. Mandates to William, Archbishop of Canterbury, etc. on praying for King, 11 August 1372.
f. 80. Extracts from Parl. Roll, 46 Edward III, on continuation of Parliament etc.
f. 86. Mandate for William Bardolf, 23 April 1372.
f. 88. Memorandum on Richard de Pembrugg, kt., Ireland, from Close Roll.
f. 90. Petition of Commons (French), 46 Edward III, from Parl. Roll.
f. 91. Extract from Parl. Roll, 46 Edward III.
f. 92. Mandate of proclamation, money, Scotland, 12 January 1373. List.
f. 96. Extracts from Selden, *Mare Clausum*, with references to Parl. Rolls, 46 Edward III, 8 Henry V.
f. 99. Mandates to Sheriffs to compel payment of subsidies, 4 August 1372.
f. 101. Like on removal of collectors, 10th, 22 January 1373.
f. 103. Like on subsidy, Ireland, 20 December 1373.
f. 104. Extracts from Parl. Roll, 47 Edward III.
f. 107. Ordinance on Parliament, 47 Edward III (French), from Close Roll.
f. 109. Mandate for Adam Wykemore on correction of process, 26 January 1374.
f. 111. Like on levying subsidy, Ireland, 6 March 1374.
f. 113. Letter to Pope, 11 March 1374, from Close Roll.
f. 115. Mandate on levying 10th and 15th, 14 November 1374, from Fine Roll.
f. 117. As f. 109 above.
f. 119. Letters on proclamation, money, Scotland, 24 July 1373, from Scottish Roll.
f. 121. Mandate of supersedeas for Prior of Hospital of Templebridge, 10 March 1374.
f. 123. Letters for John de Newenton, 14 March 1374, from Gascon Roll.
f. 123v. Letters on measuring cloth, 3 July 1374, same.
ff. 125, 127. Mandate on pardon for Roger Leget, 49 Edward III.
f. 129. Letters Patent on restitution of temporalities to Archbishop of Canterbury, 5 June 1375.

f. 131. Like on provision of victuals, 30 January 1375. (French.)

f. 134. Like for arrest of infringers of King's right, 20 May 1375.

f. 137. Like on arrest of William de Areston, 9 October 1375.

f. 138. Mandate to William de Windsor, Ireland, 13 February 1375.

f. 143. Like for Simon Bewyk, 26 October 1375.

f. 140. Like on proclamation, making of money, 13 February 1375.

f. 142. Ordinance on state of Ireland, 18 June 1375, from Patent Roll.

f. 146. Letters Patent confirming charter of Henry III to Roger Mortimer, 24 September 1376.

f. 148. Like of pardon for William, Lord Latimer, 8 October 1376.

f. 151. Like, 12 October 1376.

f. 153. Like for Gilbert de Almeryk, merchant of Lucca, 25 July 1376.

f. 154. Like of enquiry for Archbishop of Canterbury, 24 October 1376.

f. 156. Like appointing James Boteler, Earl of Ormond, Justice of Ireland, 24 July 1376.

f. 157. As f. 148 above.

f. 160. Mandate for citizens of Waterford, 18 September 1376.

f. 161. Like for burgesses of Calais, 15 October 1376, from Fine Roll.

f. 164. Like, 50 Edward III, same.

f. 165. Like on array, East Riding, co. Yorks., 11 July 1376.

f. 167. Letters Patent of oyer and terminer for Richard Lyons, 1 July 1376.

f. 169. Mandate on custody of ships under arrest, 10 June 1376.

f. 170. Letters Patent on enquiry, tannery, Penrith, 8 July 1376.

f. 172. Letters for burgesses of Blaye in Gascony, 3 July 1376, from Gascon Roll.

f. 173. Letter to Pope for John de Pultney, Mayor of London, 26 July 1332, from Roman Roll.

f. 174. Mandate on residence, canons of Exeter, 18 November 1376.

f. 176. Like on custody of sea, 20 March 1376, from French Roll. List.

f. 179. Like for men, co. Devon, 6 July 1376.

f. 181. Like for merchants of Staple of Calais, 15 December 1376, from Fine Roll.

f. 185. Like of proclamation of Ordinance of Staple, 16 December 1376, from same.

f. 187. Letters Patent on annual election of Aldermen, London, 2 November 1376.

f. 189. Like exemplifying petition of Dean and Chapter, 13 July 1376.

f. 191. Mandate for Prior of St. John of Jerusalem, Robert de Hales, Admiral, 24 November 1376, from Fine Roll.

f. 192. Letters Patent for residence, cathedral church of Exeter, 23 February 1377.

f. 195. Verdict of men of city of London, from New Misc. Bundle, t. Henry III etc.

f. 196. Petition of Commons on prescriptive right (French), 51 Edward III, from Parl. Roll.

f. 197v. Note on various liberties granted to clergy, 9 Edward III, from Stat. Roll.

f. 198. King renounces right, constitutions of clergy (French), 51 Edward III, from Parl. Roll.

f. 199. Letters Patent on palatinate for Duke of Lancaster, 28 February 1377.

f. 201. Extracts from Parl. Roll, 51 Edward III.

f. 213. Petition of Commons (French), 51 Edward III, same.

f. 214. As f. 201 above, with further extract from Parl. Roll.

f. 215v. Bill against Pope and Cardinals, 50 Edward III (French), same.

f. 216. Letters Patent for ecclesiastical persons, 15 February 1377.

f. 218. Like of pardon for Richard Lyons, 17 March 1377.

f. 221. Petition of Commons, 51 Edward III (French), from Parl. Roll.

f. 222. Letters Patent of pardon for John de Hawkwood, 2 March 1377.

f. 226. Like of pardon for Alice Perrers, 4 June 1377.

f. 227. On Official of Canterbury and Mayor and Sheriffs of London (French), from New Select Bundle, t. Edward III.

ff. 229, 232, 247. Petition of Commons, 51 Edward III (French), from Parl. Roll.

f. 231. Letters Patent for burgesses of Beverley, 14 February 1377.

f. 234. Mandate of supersedeas for Edmund, Earl of March, 16 February 1377.

f. 237. Letter on survey of musters, 28 April 1377, from Gascon Roll.

f. 239. Letters Patent to Robert de Boynton on custody of Berwick, 20 March 1377, from Scottish Roll.

f. 240. On form of enquiries in Marches, 10 June 1377, same.

f. 242. Letters Patent on delivery of writs and pleas to John, King of Castile, 13 April 1377.

f. 244. Like on restitution of temporalities to Bishop of Winchester, 18 June 1377.

f. 245. Protestation for Florentines, 31 October 1376, from French Roll.

f. 246. Letters on delivery of Florentines from prison, 3 February 1377, same.

f. 247. As f. 229 above.

VOLUME 27

A volume of transcripts etc. from the Public Records, 1–51 Edward III. On flyleaf: The Rights of the Commons in Parliament by Prescription. E. 3. 296 ff.

f. 1. Memorandum, 24 January 1327, on proclamation of peace in city of London, from Close Roll.

f. 1v. Mandates to Sheriffs on same, 29 January 1327.

f. 3. Memorandum on coronation, 1 Edward III, from Close Roll.

f. 5. Petition of those who were of the quarrel of Thomas, Earl of Lancaster (French), 7 March 1327, from Close Roll.

f. 9. Petition of Elizabeth de Burgo (French), from Bundle of Pet. to Parl., 1 Edward III, with reference to Cotton, *Posthuma*.

f. 10. Mandate to Richard de Ayremyn, Clerk of Privy Seal, 1 March 1327.

f. 13. Letters Patent for Elizabeth de Burgo, 26 February 1327.

f. 16. Like for Queen Isabella, 23 March 1327.

f. 18. Account of fines in Mershland, co. Norf., 13 March 1327, from Patent Roll.

f. 20. Note on Stat., 1 Edward III, with Stat. on Hugh le Despenser etc. from Stat. Roll, 1 Edward III.

f. 25. Annulment of process of 15 Edward II against Thomas, Earl of Lancaster, with Letters Patent of exemplification for Henry, Earl of Lancaster, 3 March 1327.

f. 40. Stat. from Stat. Roll, 1 Edward III.

f. 46. Mandates for Margaret, widow of Bartholomew de Badlesmare, 2 February 1327. List.

f. 49. Like to Walter, Archbishop of Canterbury etc. 3 July 1327.

f. 51. Writs of summons to Parliament, 7 August 1327.

f. 53. Writs de expensis, knights, 23 September 1327.

f. 54. Like, burgesses, 23 February 1327.

f. 55. Like, knights, 9 March 1327.

f. 56. Like burgesses, 23 September 1327.

f. 57. Writs of summons to Parliament, 10 December 1327.

f. 59. Like, 5 March 1328.

f. 61. Writs de expensis, knights, 14 May 1328.

f. 62. Like, burgesses, 13 May 1328.

f. 63. Writs of continuation of Parliament, 8 February 1329.

f. 64. Writs de expensis, knights, 22 February 1329.

f. 65. Like, burgesses, 22 February 1329.

f. 66. Writs of summons to Parliament, 28 August 1328.

f. 68. Writs de expensis, knights, 31 October 1328.

f. 69. Like, burgesses, 31 October 1328.

f. 70. Letters Patent deputing Henry, Bishop of Lincoln, Chancellor, etc. to open Parliament, 15 October 1328.

f. 71. Writs of summons to Council, 15 May 1328.

f. 73. Writs de expensis, knights, 6 August 1328.

f. 74. Like, knights, 5 March 1328.

f. 76. Letters Patent deputing Thomas, Bishop of Hereford, Treasurer, etc. to open Parliament, 9 February 1329.

f. 78. Writs of continuation of Parliament, 8 February 1329.

f. 79. Writs to Sheriffs to choose those wishing to come to Parliament (French), 3 November 1331.

f. 81. Writs of summons to Parliament, 25 June 1331.

f. 82. Writs de expensis, knights, 21 March 1330.

f. 83. Writs of summons to Parliament, 23 October 1330.

f. 84. Writs de expensis, knights, 9 December 1330.

f. 85. Like, burgesses, 9 December 1330.

f. 86. Writs of summons to Parliament, 16 July 1331.

f. 87. Writs de expensis, knights, 9 October 1331.

f. 88. Like, burgesses, 9 October 1331.

f. 89. Writs of summons to Parliament, 18 February 1331.

Writs revoking summons to Parliament, 23 March 1331.

f. 92. Writs of summons to Parliament, 27 January 1332.

f. 94. Like, 20 July 1332.

f. 95. Writs de expensis, knights, 12 September 1332.

f. 96. Like, burgesses, 12 September 1332.

f. 97. Writs of summons to Parliament, 20 October 1332.

f. 99. Writs to Simon, Archbishop of Canterbury, etc. proroguing Parliament, 11 December 1332.

f. 101. Writs de expensis, burgesses, 21 March 1332.

f. 102. Like, knights, 21 March 1332.

f. 103. Writs of summons to Parliament, 2 January 1334.

f. 105. Writs de expensis, knights, 26 January 1333.

f. 106. Like, burgesses, 26 January 1333.

f. 107. Writs of summons to Parliament, 24 July 1334.

f. 109. Writs de expensis, knights, 23 September 1334.

f. 110. Like, burgesses, 23 September 1334.

f. 111. Like, knights, 2 March 1334.

f. 112. Like, burgesses, 2 March 1334.

f. 113. Writs of summons to Parliament, 22 April 1335.

f. 114. Like, 1 April 1335.

f. 115. Writs de expensis, knights, 3 June 1335.

f. 115x. Like, burgesses, 3 June 1335.

f. 116. Writs of summons to Council, 24 April 1336.

f. 120. Writs de expensis, knights, to Council, 27 September 1336.

f. 121. Like, burgesses, 27 September 1336.

f. 122. Writs of summons to Parliament, 14 January 1337, with return, from Bundle of Writs of Summons to Parl., 10 Edward III, found in the White Tower by William Petyt Esq.

f. 126. Writ de expensis to Sheriff of Midd., 28 March 1336, with return and proceeding thereon in Chancery, from New Misc. Bundle, t. Henry III etc., with reference to Close Roll, 7 Edward III.

f. 130. Writs of summons to Parliament, 14 January 1337.

f. 132. Like, 29 November 1336.

f. 134. Writs de expensis, burgesses, 20 March 1336.

f. 133. Like, knights, 20 March 1336.

f. 135. Writs of summons to Parliament, 20 December 1337.

f. 137. Writs de expensis, knights, 20 March 1337.

f. 138. Like, burgesses, 20 March 1337.

f. 139. Writs on prorogation of Parliament, 3 March 1337.

f. 140. Writs of summons to Council to John, Archbishop of Canterbury, etc. 18 August 1337. Lists.

f. 147. Writs de expensis, knights, 4 October 1338. List.

f. 150. Like, burgesses, 4 October 1338. List.

f. 152. Like, knights, 14 September 1338.

f. 153. Like, burgesses, 14 September 1338, with memorandum.

f. 154. Writs of summons, certain persons to have conference, 18 August 1337. List.

f. 157. Writs de expensis, burgesses, 2 September 1337. List.

f. 160. Writs on convocation of Province of Canterbury, 5 August 1338

f. 163. Writs of summons to Parliament, 15 June 1338.

f. 165. Like, 16 November 1339.

f. 167. Writs de expensis, knights, 28 October 1339.

f. 168. Like, burgesses, 28 October 1339.

f. 169. Like, knights, 17 February 1339.

f. 170. Like, burgesses, 17 February 1339.

f. 171. Writs of summons to Parliament, 25 August 1339.

f. 173. Like, 30 May 1340.

f. 175. Writs de expensis, knights, 26 July 1340.

f. 176. Like, burgesses, 26 July 1340.

f. 177. Writs of summons to Parliament, 21 February 1340.

f. 179. Writs de expensis, knights, 19 February 1340.

f. 180. Like, burgesses, 15 September 1340.

f. 182. Like, burgesses, 19 February 1340.

f. 184. Writ to Justices to enquire on expenses, 1 March 1341.

f. 186. Writs of summons to Parliament, 3 March 1341.

f. 188. Writs de expensis, knights, 27 May 1341.

f. 189. Like, burgesses, 27 May 1341.

f. 190. Writs of summons to Parliament, 24 February 1343.

f. 192. Writs de expensis, knights, 20 May 1343.

f. 193. Like, burgesses, 20 May 1343.

f. 194. Petition of nobles and people. n.d. (French), from Bundle of Pet. t. Edward I, II & III of uncertain years.

f. 196. Writs of summons to Parliament, 24 February 1343.

f. 200. Letters Patent appointing magnates to hear plaints and petitions, 10 June 1344.

f. 203. Writs de expensis, knights, 28 June 1344.

f. 204. Like, burgesses, 28 June 1344.

f. 205. Writs of summons to William Scot etc. 30 July 1348. List. With reference to Liberate Roll, 20 Edward III.

f. 207. Writs of summons to Parliament, 30 July 1346.

f. 208. Writs de expensis, knights, 20 September 1346.

f. 209. Like, burgesses, 20 September 1346.

f. 210. Writs of summons to Parliament, 14 February 1348.

f. 213. Writ to King of Scotland to come to Parliament, 14 February 1348.

f. 214. Writs of summons to Parliament, 20 November 1348.

f. 215. Writs on prorogation of Parliament, 1 January 1349.

f. 218. Writs de expensis, knights, 12 February 1348.

f. 219. Like, burgesses, 12 February 1348.

f. 220. Writs on prorogation of Parliament, 10 March 1349.

f. 221. Writs of summons to Parliament, 25 November 1350.

f. 223. Like, 15 November 1351.

f. 225. Writs of summons to Parliament to Bailiffs etc. 20 July 1352.

f. 226. Like to Sheriffs, 20 July 1352.

f. 227. Writs of summons to Council to Simon, Archbishop of Canterbury, etc. 15 July 1353. List.

f. 234. Writs de expensis, knights, 12 October 1353.

f. 235. Like, burgesses, 12 October 1353.

f. 236. Writs of summons to Parliament, 15 March 1353.

f. 238. Like, 20 October 1355.

f. 239. Writs on prorogation of Parliament, 22 October 1355.

f. 241. Writs of summons to Parliament, 15 December 1357.

f. 243. Writs of summons to Council, 10 February 1360.

f. 246. Like, 26 February 1360.

f. 249. Writs of summons to Parliament, 3 April 1360.

f. 251. Like, 20 November 1360.

f. 254. Like, 14 August 1362.

f. 255. Writ, wages, knights, co. Lancs., 17 November 1362.

f. 256. Writs to Godfrey Foliant etc., Keepers of Peace, co. Lancs., 12 February 1363.

f. 257. Writs of summons to Parliament, 4 December 1364.

f. 258. Writ of summons to Parliament to Constable of Dover, 4 December 1364.

f. 259. Writs of summons to Parliament, 20 January 1367.

f. 261. Letters of alliance between King of England and King of Arragon, 10 January 1369, from Patent Roll.

f. 263. Letters of proxy thereon, 12 January 1369.

f. 268. Writs of summons to Parliament, 24 February 1368.

f. 269. Like, 6 April 1369.

f. 270. Like, 6 January 1371.

f. 272. Writs de expensis, burgesses, 17 June 1371.

f. 273. Like, knights, 17 June 1371.

f. 274. Writs of summons to Parliament, 1 September 1372.

f. 276. Writs on prorogation of Parliament, 6 October 1372.
f. 279. Writs of summons to Parliament, 4 October 1373.
f. 281. Like, 28 December 1375.
f. 286. Writs on prorogation of Parliament, 20 January 1376.
f. 288. Extract from Parl. Roll, 50 Edward III, on annual Parliaments. (French.)
f. 290. Writs of summons to Parliament, 1 December 1376.
f. 292. Writ of summons to Parliament to Abbot of Evesham, 16 January 1377.
f. 294. Writs de expensis, burgesses, Ireland (Cork), 27 August 1376.
f. 295. Writs de expensis, 2 March 1377, burgesses.
f. 296. Like, knights, 2 March 1377.

VOLUME 28

A volume of transcripts etc. from the Public Records and other sources, Henry III to Edward III. On flyleaf: Several writs, records, pardons, grants, patents, summonses and transactions in Parliament and elsewhere in the reigns of H. 3, E. 1, E. 2 & E. 3. 290 ff.

f. 1. Writ to Sheriff of Derby that outlawry on William de Gastincot reversed in Parliament, 16 February 1244.
f. 3. Letters Patent to Roger, Earl of Norfolk etc. that King agrees to sentence of excommunication at Westminster concerning Magna Carta and Charter of Forests, 13 May 1253.
f. 5. Letters Patent to Sheriff of Oxf. and Berks. on measure in England, 26 October 1273.
f. 7. Process against Llewelyn ap Gruffydd, Prince of Wales, 4 Edward I.
f. 13. Writs to Robert, Archbishop of Canterbury etc. on those who ought to serve King in army of Wales, 12 December 1276. List.
f. 13v. Letter to King from Mayor etc. of Bayonne, 8 October 1276.
f. 15. Letters Patent to communities of Salop and Staffs. etc. 6 February 1277.
f. 15v. Letters Patent to Nicholas de Stapleton on perambulation, 1 March 1277.
f. 17. Memorandum on homage of Alexander, King of Scotland, 6 Edward I.
f. 19. Letters Patent on inquisition on death of Roger de Drayton, 6 May 1292.
f. 21. Letters Patent to Roger de Monte Alto on 15th, 27 November 1293.
Letters Patent on enquiry, William de Vescy, Ireland, 10 December.
f. 22. Letters Patent, Thomas de Newton, co. Cumberland (incomplete).
f. 23. Writ to Henry de Lacy, Earl of Lincoln, 15 July 1295.
f. 24. Writ to Nicholas de Audley, 12 March 1295.
f. 25. Writ on mainprise of Gilbert de Umfravill. n.d.
f. 27. Letters Patent on enquiry on complaints of people in each co. (French.)
f. 29. Statute, 20 Edward I, from MS. of William Pierpoint, with reference to *Plac. Parl.*, p. 93; Rastell, *Stat.*
f. 31. Statute for Escheators, 29 Edward I, translation from Rastell, *Stat.*
f. 33. Extract on Parliament of Lincoln, 29 Edward I, from *Plac. Parl.*, p. 229.
f. 35. Ordinance on inquisitions returned into Chancery, 29 Edward I.

f. 35v. Writs of summons to conference at Lincoln to John de Metingham etc. 26 September 1300.

f. 36. Note from Liberate Roll, 28 Edward I etc.

f. 37. Form of Oath of Council (French), 35 Edward I.

f. 38. Form of Oath of Justices (French), 18 Edward I, from *Plac. Parl.*, p. 317.

f. 39. Letters Patent on aid for marriage of King's eldest daughter, 7 November 1302 etc.

f. 41. Writs on aid for knighting King's eldest son, 5 April 1306.

f. 42v. Mandates to Sheriffs on same, 5 April 1306. List.

f. 43. Mandates to Archbishop of York etc. on same, 5 April 1306.

f. 45. Memorandum on banishment of Peter Gaveston, 26 February 1307. (French.)

f. 94. Oath of King's Council (French), 1 Edward II.

f. 96. Mandate to Sheriff of York on Peter Gaveston, 20 January 1312.

f. 96v. Mandates to Sheriffs on same, 26 January 1312.

f. 98. Letters Patent that no one to be imprisoned for death of Peter Gaveston (French), 6 November 1313.

f. 100. Letters Patent to Sheriffs on Peter Gaveston (French), 15 October 1312.

f. 102. Letters Patent for Master William de Burston, 8 October 1314.

f. 104. Mandate to Roger Mortimer of Wigmore to be at Parliament, 17 January 1316.

f. 106. Letters Patent for William de Bourne etc. 28 May 1316.

f. 108. Memorandum on petition of Hugh Tansley etc., with answer, 12 Edward II.

f. 110. Mandate to Abbots of Dore and Margam, 7 October 1319.

f. 112. Mandate for Hugh le Despenser the elder, 7 May 1322.

f. 114. Process against Hugh le Despenser the elder and younger, 15 Edward II.

f. 118. Mandate for villeins of John, Bishop of Norwich, 26 May 1322.

f. 120. Mandate for Hugh le Despenser the elder and younger, 4 January 1322. List.

f. 122. Mandates on coming to York to treat, 31 May 1323. List.

f. 122v. Mandate for Hugh Mortimer, 20 December 1322.

f. 124. Mandate on proclamation coming to York to treat, 30 October 1322.

f. 126. Mandates on clerical subsidy, provinces of Canterbury and York, 7 November 1322

f. 128. Letters Patent to Sheriff of Kent on Roger Mortimer, 24 March 1324. (French.)

f. 132. Mandate for John de Lortye, 18 July 1324.

f. 134. Mandates to Sheriffs on gathering, 20 September 1324.

f. 134v. Like, 23 September 1324.

f. 136. Letters Patent to John de Cobham etc. (French), 27 September 1326.

f. 182. Letters Patent for Queen Isabella, 23 March 1327.

f. 184. Commission to Hugh le Despenser (French), incomplete.

f. 188. Letters Patent for Elizabeth de Burgo on petition to King and Council against a bond to King, 1 March 1327.

f. 200. Letters Patent for Elizabeth de Burgo, 26 February 1327.

f. 202. Letters Patent on annulment of process against Roger Mortimer, 24 July 1327.

f. 212. Letters Patent for Andrew de Settleford, pardon, 28 February 1327.

f. 213. Letters Patent to citizens of London, grant of Southwark, 6 March 1327.

f. 213v. Letters Patent of pardon for Robert de Mablethorp, 8 March 1327.

f. 216v. Statute against Hugh le Despenser the elder and the younger, from MS. Statutes in possession of William Petyt.

f. 220. Petition of those who were of quarrel of Thomas, Earl of Lancaster (French), 1 Edward III.

f. 230. Letters Patent of annulment of process against Thomas, Earl of Lancaster (French), 3 March 1328.

f. 232. Letters Patent of exemplification for Henry, Earl of Lancaster, on annulment of process against Thomas, Earl of Lancaster, 3 March 1328.

f. 233. Letters Patent of annulment of judgement against Bartholomew de Badlesmere, 30 March 1328, with exemplification of same for William de Ros and Margery, his wife, 19 November 1339.

f. 240. Extract from pleas Coram Rege at Worcester, Hereford, Gloucester and Westminster, Hil. term, 17 Edward II.

f. 246. Letters Patent of annulment of process against Adam, Bishop of Worcester and Hereford, 19 February 1329, with note under name of William Ryley that it agrees with the record. (Struck through.)

f. 256v. Commission to Thomas, Bishop of Hereford, Treasurer, to open Parliament, 19 February 1329.

f. 257. Mandate for Thomas, Bishop of Hereford, 16 February 1329.

f. 259. Parliament and error in King's Bench, Rastell, *Stat.*, p. 302.

f. 260. As f. 220 above.

f. 263. Mandate for William le Poer etc. (1329).

f. 264. Letters Patent for Master Hugh de Cavill, clerk, 3 March 1329.

Mandate for Thomas Roselyn, 26 February 1331.

f. 266. Mandate for Margaret, late wife of Bartholomew de Badlesmere, 1 July 1328.

Mandate for Matilda, late wife of William de Wyn, 7 May 1327.

f. 268. As f. 264 above.

Mandate for executors of William de March, 4 June 1327.

Mandate for Robert de Reigate, 25 May 1327.

f. 268v. Mandate for John de Hynkele, 23 April 1330.

f. 269. Mandate for William la Zouch of Mortimer, 5 April 1330.

f. 269v. Mandate for Edmund de Pinkney, 20 October 1328.

f. 270. Letters Patent for John de Crombwell and wife, 3 April 1330.

f. 271. Like, 4 March 1333.

Mandate for John de Lowther, 3 October 1333.

f. 271v. Letters Patent on Statute of Westminster I, 1 Edward III.

Letters Patent for John de Wilington, 18 February 1327.

f. 273. Mandate for Hugh de Northburgh and son, 20 January 1331.

f. 275. Memorandum on dower of Margaret, late wife of Bartholomew de Badlesmere, 5 Edward III.

f. 277. Letters Patent for Thomas Ughtred, 29 October 1339.

f. 279. Letters Patent for John Maltravers, 5 August 1345.

f. 281. Like for John Maltravers the elder, 5 August 1345.

f. 283. Like for John Maltravers, 8 February 1352.

f. 287. Letters Patent for Abbot of Gloucester on not attending Parliament, 16 March 1352.

f. 289. Letters Patent for Roger Mortimer, Earl of March, 30 March 1354.

f. 290. Like for same, 21 June 1354.

VOLUME 29

A volume of transcripts etc. from the Public Records and other sources, Edward III to Richard II etc. On flyleaf: Several writs, records, commissions, patents, summons and transactions in Parliament and elsewhere in the reigns of King John, H. 3, E. 3 and R. 2. On another flyleaf: Recorda temporibus Johannis, H. 3, Ed. 3 & R. 2. 535 ff.

f. 1. Extract from Book of 15th and 10th granted, 1 Edward III, with the Clerk of the Pipe.

f. 3. Letters Patent to Queen Isabella, 23 March 1327.

Commission on Hugh le Despenser the elder and younger (French).

f. 7v. Letters Patent for Elizabeth de Burgo on petition to King and Council against a bond to King, 1 Edward III.

f. 9v. Like for same, late wife of John de Burgo, 26 February 1327.

f. 11. Mandate on annulment of process against Roger Mortimer, 24 July 1327.

f. 19v. Letters Patent of pardon for Andrew de Hackford of London, 28 February 1327.

f. 20v. Like to citizens of London on grant of Southwark, 6 March 1327.

f. 21v. Like of pardon for Robert de Mablethorp, 8 March 1327.

f. 22. Stat. on Hugh le Despenser the elder and younger, 1 Edward III, from MS. Stat. in poss. of William Petyt.

f. 27. Petition for those of the quarrel of Thomas, Earl of Lancaster (French), from Close Roll.

f. 29. Letters Patent on Stat. of West. I, 1 Edward III.

Like for William de Wilington, 18 February 1327.

f. 31. Like for Matilda, late wife of William de Wyn, 7 May 1327.

Mandate for executors of William de March, 4 June 1327.

f. 31v. Like for Robert de Reigate, 23 May 1327.

f. 33. Like for Bishop of Hereford, 6 February 1327.

f. 35. Pleas coram Rege at York, Trin. term, 1 Edward III, and at Kingston upon Hull.

f. 41. Writ to Barons for Thomas Bardolf, 13 May 1327, from K.R. Mem. Roll, Brev. dir. Bar., Trin., 1 Edward III.

f. 43. Pleas coram Rege at York, Trin. term, 1 Edward III, and at city of London, 6 March 1327.

f. 49. Mandate for Sheriff of Yorks., 29 January 1327.

f. 51. Writs de expensis, knights, 14 May 1328, from Bundle of Writs, 2 Edward III.

f. 51v. Like, burgesses, 13 May 1328.

f. 53. Letters Patent of exemplification for Henry, Earl of Lancaster, of annulment of process on Thomas, Earl of Lancaster, 3 March 1328, with annulment of process, 3 March 1328.

f. 64v. Annulment of process against Bartholomew de Badlesmere, 19 November 1328, with exemplification of same for William de Ros and Margery, his wife, 26 March 1341.

f. 71. Mandates on annulment of fines and bonds for saving life, 28 June 1328.

f. 72. Like for William le Poer etc. 12 August 1328.

f. 73. Like for Edmund de Pinkney, 20 October 1328.

f. 75. Like for Margaret, late wife of Bartholomew de Badlesmere, 1 July 1328.

f. 77. Writs to Barons for John de Langton, 19 February 1328; to same on manor of Emeldon, 23 February 1328; for John de Wolverton, 18 May 1328; from K.R. Mem. Roll, Brev. dir. Bar., Hil., Trin., 2 Edward III.

f. 81. Mandates on bail for William Hert and John de Gosebroke, 14 January 1328 etc.

f. 83. Pleas coram Rege at Worcester, Hereford, Gloucester and Westminster, Hil. term, 17 Edward II.

f. 87. Letters Patent on annulment of record against Adam, Bishop of Worcester and formerly of Hereford, 6 February 1329.

f. 94v. Like to Thomas, Bishop of Hereford etc. to open Parliament, 19 February 1329.

f. 97. Writs to Barons for Abbot of Tilty, 12 May 1329; Simon de St. Omer, 6 February 1329; John de Dalton, 5 August 1329; John de Brandesby, 29 August 1329; Alexander de Ledes, 7 August 1329; divers Cardinals, 11 February 1329; Robert de Aston, 15 February 1329; Prior of Hospital of St. John of Jerusalem, 2 August 1328; Prior of Spalding, 4 July 1328; for transfer of Exchequer, 20 October 1328, from K.R. Mem. Rolls, Brev. dir. Bar., 2, 3 Edward III.

f. 107. Letters Patent for Hugh de Cavill, clerk, 3 March 1329.

f. 109. Stat. of Pardons, 3 Edward III, from MS. Stat. in poss. of John Peachey esq. of Inner Temple.

f. 111. Mandate on restoration of lands to Henry de Beaumont, 9 December 1330.

f. 113. Like for Hugh de Northburgh and Hugh, his son, 20 January 1331.

f. 115. Charter of Henry II of manor of Berkeley, from L.T.R. Mem. Roll, Comm., Rec., East., 4 Edward III.

f. 115v. Attachment of Thomas de Berkeley for relief, same.

f. 119. Mandate for William la Zouch of Mortimer, April 1330.

f. 121. As f. 113 above.

f. 123. Memorandum, Parliament, dower for Margaret, late wife of Bartholomew de Badlesmere, 5 Edward III, from Close Roll.

f. 125. On assignment of dower, 31 May 1331 (French), from K.R. Mem. Roll, Trin., 5 Edward III.

f. 125v. Indenture between King and Bardi (French), same. Lre. Pat & Script. Recog., Hil. 5 Edward III.

f. 127. Writs to Barons for Prior of Ware, 26 November 1330; David, Earl of Atholl, 2 January 1331; Isabella, Queen of England, 9 April 1331; William, son of Edmund Trussell, 29 April 1331; from K.R. Mem. Roll, Brev. dir. Bar., 5 Edward III.

f. 131. Writ to Roger Mortimer, Earl of March, Justice of Wales, 8 August 1330, from Brevia Regis, 5 Edward III.

f. 131v. Like, commission of North Wales by petition, 15 November 1330, same.

f. 133. Mandate for Thomas Rocelyn, 26 February 1331.

f. 135. Stephen Turpyn attached for relief, 5 Edward III; writ tested by Treasurer, 26 February 1331; from L.T.R. Mem. Roll, Comm., 5 Edward III.

f. 139. Writs to Barons for tenants of soke of Oswardbek, 12 June 1332; men of Edmund Boteler of manor of Compton, 18 April 1332; Mayor and Sheriffs of London on Ordinance of Staple, 16 December 1332; from K.R. Mem. Roll, Brev. dir. Bar., Trin., 6 Edward III.

f. 145. Mandate on ships arrested in Ireland, 25 July 1332.

f. 147. Sheriff of Northants. charged with false imprisonment of William Semor and Thomas, his brother, from L.T.R. Mem. Roll, Comm., Rec., Mich.

f. 149. Commission on silver mines, co. Devon, from K.R. Mem. Roll, Comm. & Lre. Pat., Mich., 7 Edward III.

f. 151. Letters Patent for John de Cromwell and wife, 4 March 1333.

Mandate for John de Lowther, 3 October 1333.

f. 153. Writs to Barons for Alexander, Archbishop of Dublin, 20 September 1333; for Abbot of St. Edmund's, 27 January 1333; from K.R. Mem. Roll, Brev. dir. Bar., 7 Edward III.

f. 157. Mandate for John de Gayton, 16 October 1333.

f. 159. Thomas de Cloune committed to Fleet, from L.T.R. Mem. Roll, Comm., Rec., East., 7 Edward III.

f. 161. Mandate for Alice, daughter of Adam Arundell, 5 July 1335.

f. 164. Proclamation on Stat. of West. I on rumours, 9 Edward III, from Close Roll.

f. 165. Commission of oyer and terminer for Edmund de Grymesby, 4 December 1335.

f. 165v. Mandate on retention of Guy, Count of Namiers, 26 August 1335.

f. 174. Like on making halfpence and farthings (French), 3 May 1336, from Fine Roll.

f. 176. Like on proclamation on halfpence and sterling, 18 April 1336.

f. 178. On relief of Norman Darcy, from K.R. Mem. Roll, East., 11 Edward III.

f. 180. Mandate on delivery of Richard Moneywood from prison, 19 March 1337.

f. 182. Mandate on having certain persons in Chancery, 3 May 1337.

f. 183. Writs to Barons for Abbot of Ramsey; Prioress of Appleton, 7 July 1347; from K.R. Mem. Roll, Brev. dir. Bar., Trin., 21 Edward III.

f. 188. Mandate for Sheriffs, 2 August 1338.

f. 190. Letters Patent for Thomas Ughtred, 29 October 1339.

f. 190xx. Mandate for men of Westminster, 25 August 1339.

f. 194. Letters Patent that no payment of fees should be made until King's return, 6 May 1339.

f. 196. On the prohibition made to Robert de Ver, kt., 12 October 1339; from L.T.R.

Mem. Roll, Comm., Rec., Mich., 13 Edward III, on John de Godefield; on relief of Henry de Filby; Letters Patent to hear account of William de la Pole, 1 July 1340.

f. 204. Stat. on sacks of wool, from MS. Stat. in poss. of John Peachey, 16 April 1340.

f. 206. Writ, 28 May 1341; writ to buyers and sellers of sheaves, cos. Norf. and Suff., 28 May 1341; from L.T.R. Mem. Roll, Brev. Retorn., Trin., 15 Edward III.

f. 210. Writs to Barons for John de Clifford, 8 September 1342; city of Carlisle, 28 April 1342; Warin de Basingbourne, 10 May 1343; Abbot of Beaulieu, 20 October 1342; from K.R. Mem. Roll, Brev. dir. Bar., 17 Edward III.

f. 216. Letters Patent for John Maltravers, 5 August 1345.

f. 217v. Like for John Maltravers the elder, 5 August 1345.

f. 220. Writ for Hospitals of Northgate and Harbledown, 20 November 1345; on Robert de Thelkeld etc.; on relief of Richard de Plies; writs to Barons for Abbot of Crowland, 1 May 1345; Abbot of Thornton, 4 April 1345; Master Robert de Cronque, Warden of Merton, Oxford, 12 April 1345, John de Musters, Sheriff of Notts. and Derby, 1 October 1345, from K.R. Mem. Roll, 19 Edward III.

f. 238. As f. 220 above.

f. 248. Ordinance on Justices at Westminster, 20 April 1346, from MS. Stat. in poss. of John Peachey.

f. 250v. Writ on exoneration of men at arms and keepers of sea coast by King's Justices, 1 May 1346, from French Roll.

f. 252. On certificate made for Bishop of Chester etc. 22 April 1347; writ for Geoffrey le Scrope, 20 February 1347; indenture between King and Thomas de Musgrave on custody of town of Berwick enrolled, 26 January 1347 (French); writ on 15th and 10th, 5 October 1346. List; from K.R. Mem. Roll, 21 Edward III.

f. 267. Letter to Pope, 20 July 1347, from Roman Roll.

f. 271. Like to College of Cardinals, 20 July 1347, same.

f. 275. Following Petitions from Petitions in Parliament, 21 Edward III:

Sir Nicholas Chastell, collector of aid for knighting King's eldest son, with answer.
Abbot of St. Albans, with answer.
John de Norwich, with answer.
John de Segrave and wife, with answer.
Robert de Barton and William, his brother, with answer.
John, son of John de Mowbray, and wife, with answer.
Isabel, late wife of William de Ros, with answer.
William Hereward, Archdeacon of Taunton, with answer.
Thomas Wake of Lydell, with answer.
Community of co. Kent, with answer.
On 'les niefs', with answer.
Richard Spynk and William, his brother, with answer.
Robert Bertram, with answer.
Joan, late wife of Adam de Peshale, with answer.
The same, with answer.
Mayor etc. of Staple, with answer.
Geoffrey Ridell, with answer.

f. 291. Letters Patent for Richard, Earl of Arundel etc., 3 November 1350; 9 November 1350; 3 November 1350; 3 November 1350; 19 November 1350.

f. 303. Record and process of judgement on William Thorp (French), 25 Edward III, from Parl. Roll.

f. 303v. Like for William de Thorp, 10 March 1351.

f. 309v. Letters Patent for John Maltravers, 8 February 1352.

f. 313. Writs to Barons for burgesses of Berwick, 1 May 1354; Robert de Warthcopp, 20 May 1353; from K.R. Mem. Roll, 27 Edward III.

f. 314v. Letters Patent for Roger Mortimer, Earl of March, 30 May 1354.

f. 318. Like for same, 21 June 1354.

f. 319. On relief of Humphrey de Bohun, Earl of Hereford, from K.R. Mem. Roll, 28 Edward III. Writ to Bishop of Carlisle, 20 November 1354.

f. 325. On relief of Roger Pedwardin, from same, 29 Edward III.

f. 335. Pleas coram Rege, Westminster, Mich. term, 33 Edward III.

Petition on dispute, Bishop of Ely, parsons in Tower (French), with answer (French).

f. 337. Writ to Barons for Thomas de Lucy, 3 May 1356, from K.R. Mem. Roll, Brev. dir. Bar., East., 33 Edward III.

f. 339. Writ for Master of church of Cornute, 22 November 1360; Acquittance of Robert de Marny enrolled; like writing of John Pecche, 9 February 1361; writ to Barons for John de Monte Alto, 5 May 1361; commission of Archbishop of Canterbury to collect 10th to Abbot of Faversham; writs on adjournment of all pleas of account and other business in the Exchequer touching thereon, 23 June 1361; from K.R. Mem. Roll, 35 Edward III.

f. 351. Writ to Barons for Mayor etc. of London, 27 June 1324, from K.R. Mem. Roll, Brev. dir. Bar., Trin., 17 Edward II.

f. 353. Like for Richard Ravenser, 1 October 1360, same, 35 Edward III.

f. 355. Acquittance of town of Montsegur annexed to crown of England, 5 May 1362, original, 35 Edward III, L.T.R.

f. 357. On relief William Placye, from L.T.R. Mem. Roll, Comm., Mich., 39 Edward III.

f. 367. Letters Patent for men of Chipping Norton, 3 June 1366.

f. 369. Mandate on arraying of clerks against the French, 6 July 1369.

f. 371. Like on same, 2 July 1369.

f. 375. Writ of privy seal to Barons for Walter Derby, 21 February 1373 (French); like for Thomas Fishame of Plymouth, 21 February 1373 (French); writ to Barons on vill of Malshale, co. Staffs., 20 June 1373; writ of privy seal to Barons for Roger Fulthorp, 25 June 1373 (French); on John de Rennesbury; day given to Chapter of Wyke, co. Devon; like, co. Wilts.; from K.R. Mem. Roll, 47 Edward III.

f. 395. Mandate to have Oliver Clayhin in Chancery, 6 October 1379.

f. 397. Stat. on Ireland, 4 Richard II, from MS. Stat. of J. Peachey.

f. 399. Mandate on fishery in Duchy of Lancaster, 5 Richard II.

f. 401. Record made at Westminster by Justices etc. 7 Richard II. Commission granted in Parliament to Robert Tresilian etc. against John Cavendish of London, fishmonger.

f. 403. Following Petitions from Petitions in Parliament, 8 Richard II:
Complaint of clergy (2).
Isabella de Wyndesore etc. (2).
Complaint of clergy.
Community of Realm.
Adam Corpandale of Beverley.
John Lumberd of Beverley.
Agnes, wife of William Lumberd of Beverley.

ff. 411–18. As ff. 403–9 above.

f. 419. Notes from Close Rolls, 8 Richard II to 7 Henry IV.

f. 421. Letters Patent for John Beauchamp, created Lord Beauchamp and Baron of Kidderminster, 10 October 1387, with reference to Selden, *Tit. of Hon.*

f. 423. Stat., 13 Richard II, 12 May 1390.

f. 425. Mandates committing William Briene and Robert Cocon to Tower, 1 December 1391.

Like summoning Percival Pensor before Council, 20 November 1391.

f. 425v. Like for Edward de Warreyn, 21 November 1391.

f. 427. Like to seize Lionel de Vinaldo of Genoa for not paying customs, 7 November 1392.

f. 429. Like to have Nicholas Lyllyng in Chancery, 27 February 1393.

f. 431. Like for John Drayton, 9 July 1393.

f. 433. Like to have John Mustenden and John Milton in Chancery, 10 July 1395.

Like to commit Howel ap Tudor etc. to Tower, 18 May 1394.

f. 433v. Like committing John Haket and Richard Laune to Tower, 21 April 1396.

f. 435. Like to deliver John Brightcock from prison, 6 July 1395.

f. 437. Letters Patent of pardon for Thomas Haxey, 27 May 1397.

f. 439. Mandate to make Lollards come coram Rege, 10 December 1396. Like to conduct Thomas Haxey before Archbishop of Canterbury, 5 February 1397.

f. 441. Like to deliver Thomas, Duke of Norfolk, 26 April 1398.

Like to deliver Laurence Bright from prison, 18 May 1398.

f. 441v. Like to receive Duchess of Hereford and Norfolk in Windsor Castle, 26 February 1398.

Like to receive John Seymor in Tower, 3 May 1398.

f. 442. Like to deliver John Cobham in Isle of Jersey, 3 February 1398.

f. 443. Like to arrest certain persons, 28 July 1397.

f. 445. Stat., 21 Richard II, from MS. Stat. in poss. of John Peachey.

f. 447. Mandate to have John Cobham in Parliament, 13 December 1397.

Like to have Richard Peryman and John Cavendish before Council, 1 December 1397.

f. 447v. Like to deliver body of Thomas, late Duke of Gloucester, 14, 18 October 1397.

f. 448. Like to have Duke of Gloucester at Portsmouth, 21 September 1397.

f. 453. Extracts from Knighton, death of King John and accession of Henry III.

f. 454. Extract from Matt. Paris, 1216, account of coronation.

f. 455x. Extract from Walsingham, Ypodigma Neustriae.

f. 455v. Letters Patent, 6 February 1217.

ff. 457–535. 'A Series of records abridged'. These are rather valueless translations, 1 Henry III to 21 Richard II etc. from Patent, Close, Memoranda, Coram Rege Rolls etc. and miscellaneous printed sources, with two extracts from Acts of Parliament, 4 and 7 James I.

Inset at end of volume the pamphlet *The Pillars of Parliament*, 1681, as above, p. 392.

On the title-page is written: This is imperfect as are all others I have seen in his Books. J(oshua) B(lew).

VOLUME 30

A volume of transcripts etc. from the Public Records and other sources, 1–10 Richard II. On flyleaf: Recorda from the 1st year of Rich. II to the 11th. On another flyleaf: Recorda R. II ab anno 1 usque 11. 243 ff.

f. 1. Memorandum on coronation, 1 Richard II.

f. 28. Petition of Commons (French), with answer, 1 Richard II.

f. 29. Writ of prohibition on Deanery of Lincoln, 8 December 1377.

f. 31. Mandate to Simon, Archbishop of Canterbury, to pray for King etc. 4 September 1377.

f. 33. Charter of Earldom of Buckingham, 16 July 1377.

f. 35. Mandate on proclamation on Alice Perrers, 19 November 1377.

f. 36. Mandates to Sheriffs on barges, 30 November 1377.

f. 40. Memorandum on delivery of Edward III's seal, 21 June 1377.

f. 42. Letters Patent of exemplification of pardon, Edward III etc. 20 July 1377.

f. 46. Letters Patent for burgesses of Beverley, 11 January 1378.

f. 47. Letters Patent for burgesses of Southampton, 1 December 1377.

f. 49. Letters Patent appointing King's Councillors, 20 July 1377.

f. 51. Statute, 1 Richard II, from Statute Roll, 1 Richard II.

f. 52. Letters Patent for Richard de Nevill, 10 December 1377.

f. 53. Letters Patent for burgesses of Calais, 16 November 1377.

f. 53v. Writ on proclamation on aliens, 20 December 1377.

f. 55. Writs of protection, 28 January 1378.

f. 57. Letters Patent of confirmation for Bishop, Prior and Convent of Ely of Edgar's charter.

f. 61. Letters Patent of confirmation, 19 March 1378. List.

f. 63. Petitions against Alice Perrers, Alice Pope of London. From Bundle of Petitions, 1 Richard II. (French).

f. 63v. Like by widow of John Toyolelaine.

f. 64. Like by John Birch, carpenter.

f. 64v. Like by Thomas Lapyn of Merston.

f. 65. Like by Robert Lucas and Margaret, his wife.

f. 66. Petitions on delays in court (French), with answer. From Rot. Parl.

f. 68. Petitions against Alice Perrers, of Prior and Convent of Holy Trinity, London (French). From Bundle of Petitions, 2 Richard II.

f. 69. Like by Robert Pikerell, citizen of London.

f. 70. Like by John Charnels.

f. 71. Like by William de Wyndsor and Alice, his wife

f. 72. Statute at Gloucester, 2 Richard II, 1378.

f. 76. Statute, 2 Richard II, cap. 7.

f. 80. Letters Patent for Bishop of Agen, 4 May 1380.

f. 82. Request of prelates on Abbot of Westminster (French), Rot. Parl.

f. 85. Like for Pope.

f. 87. Petition of knights of Kent (French), with answer. From Bundle of Petitions, 2 Richard II.

f. 88. Letters Patent for King of Castile and Leon and Duke of Lancaster, 10 November 1378.

f. 90. As f. 82 above.

f. 94. Petition of Abbot and Convent of Westminster (French). From Bundle of Petitions, 2 Richard II.

f. 97. As f. 82 above, with translation.

f. 106. Writ to Chief Justice of Bench on record and process of suit between William, Bishop of Winchester, and John Giffard, kt., 26 October 1379. From Bundle of scire facias, t. Richard II.

f. 107. Plea, Bench, before Robert Bealknap etc., Trin., 3 Richard II.

f. 134v. Letters Patent of exemplification of above, 21 November 1380.

f. 136. Statute, 3 Richard II, from Statute Roll.

f. 139. Writs de expensis, knights, 4 December 1380.

f. 140. Writ of supersedeas, Chester, 3 July 1380.

f. 142. Letters Patent of inspeximus, Malmesbury, 28 November 1381

f. 146. Statute, 5 Richard II, cap. 4, from Statute Roll.

f. 147. Writ of summons to Parliament, 24 March 1382.

f. 149. Letters Patent on Parliament summoned in Ireland, 29 March 1382.

f. 150. Extract from Statute, 5 Richard II.

f. 151. Letters Patent of pardon in Parliament for Thomas David, 2 February 1382.

f. 153. Writ of supersedeas, Chester, 12 March 1383.

f. 155. As f. 153 above.

f. 157. Writs to hasten payment of 10th and 15th, 6 December 1382.

f. 159. Letters Patent of exemplification, Tickford, 12 December 1382.

f. 161. Petition of Commons on preachers, 6 Richard II (French), from Rot. Parl.

f. 162. Writs on collection of subsidy of 3s. and 12d. in £, 13 November 1383.

f. 163. Letters Patent for Mayor etc. of London, 4 April 1384.

f. 165. Extract from Parliament Roll, 7 Richard II. (French.)

f. 172. Like, 7 Richard II.

f. 178. Treaty with enemies of Scots, 3 May 1385.

f. 180. Letters Patent appointing Justices of Assize, 21 January 1385. List.

f. 182. Letters Patent appointing Seneschal of Aquitaine, 1 March 1385.

f. 183. Letters Patent for burgesses of Kingston upon Hull, 22 October 1384.

f. 184. Extract, plea of avowry, from Fitzherbert, *Grand Abridg*.

f. 186. Proxy by Richard de Pyryton, Archdeacon of Colchester, under seal of Officiality of Colchester, 13 October 1385, with endorsement. From Bundle of Proxies of Clergy, 8 Richard II.

f. 188. Extract from Statute, 9 Richard II.

f. 189. Ordinance for various traitors, 9 Richard II. From Liber H.

f. 194. Charter of condemnation, John Northampton etc. 3 June 1386.

f. 199. Charter, John Northampton, 1 December 1391.

f. 201. Writ upon the above charter, 20 December 1391.

f. 203. Annulment of indictment and judgement against John Northampton, 18 Richard II. All from Liber H.

f. 206. Plea before King in Chancery, Oct. of Mich., 9 Richard II, from Bundle of Select Writs and Records, t. Richard II, Devon.

f. 208. On plea, Thomas Lovel and Archbishop of York, 4 December 1385.

f. 212. Extract from Parliament Roll, 9 Richard II.

f. 214. As f. 184 above.

f. 216. Writ on collection, 10th and 15th, Berks., 15 February 1386, with return; 12 January 1386, with return. From Bundle of Select Writs and Records, t. Richard II.

f. 219. Extract from Parliament Roll, 9 Richard II.

f. 221. Letters Patent of exemplification of petition of community of London, 4 December 1385. (French.)

f. 224. Letters Patent for University of Cambridge, 7 April 1386.

f. 226. Letters Patent for burgesses of Launceston, 16 October 1385.

f. 228. Extract from Statute Roll, 10 Richard II.

f. 228v. Letters Patent of exemplification of grants to community, 28 November 1386. (French and Latin.)

f. 238. Mandate for Walter Sibelle of London, 29 April 1387.

f. 241. Extract from Chron. H. Knighton, 10 Richard II.

VOLUME 31

A volume of transcripts etc. from the Public Records and other sources, 11–22 Richard II. On flyleaf: Records from the 11th Rich. 2 to the end of the reign. On another flyleaf: Recorda R. IIdi ab anno 11mo usque ad finem. 212 ff.

f. 1. Petition of Commons on limitation of Writs (French), with answer, from Bundle of Pet. to Parl., 11 Richard II.

f. 2. Extract from Statute Roll, 11 Richard II.

f. 4. Letters Patent for John Haddele and Nicholas Exton, 11 Richard II.

f. 6. Petition of Lords and Commons, extract only (French), from Bundle of Pet. to Parl., 11 Richard II.

f. 7. Petition of masters of ships and barges (French), with answer, from same.

f. 8. Memorandum on enrolments, 1 July 1389, from Close Roll.

f. 11. Extract from Knighton, Parl. Westminster, 11 Richard II.

f. 18. Mandate on taking of oaths, 15 March 1388. List.

f. 21. Like, to Sheriffs on making proclamation, 30 July 1387.

f. 23. Charter on Earldom of Rutland, 25 February 1388.

f. 26. Petition of John Cavendish, citizen of London (French), from Bundle of Pet. to Parl., 11 Richard II.

f. 27. Petition of prelates and clergy of Ireland (French), from same.

f. 29. Plea before King in Chancery, Oct. Trin., 21 Richard II.

Writ to Sheriff of Suff. with return, 30 April 1398, from Bundle of Writs of scire facias, 21 Richard II.

f. 34. Mandate to Sheriff of London on proclamation, 8 May 1389.

f. 36. Extract from Stat. Roll, 12 Richard II.

f. 37. Writ to Mayor etc. of Oxford, 2 August 1388, from Writs among records of city of Oxford.

f. 41. Extract from Knighton, 12 Richard II.

f. 43. Extract from Stat. Roll, 13 Richard II, 12 May 1390.

f. 51. Mandate on payment of 10th to Pope, 10 October 1389. List.

f. 54. As f. 51 above.

f. 58. 'There were different forms in penning petitions and answers thereto as appears in the Parliament of 17 Richard II'.

f. 59. Petition of Ralph Canon (French), with answer, from Bundle of Pet. to Parl., 17 Richard II.

f. 60. Petition of Alice, late wife of William de Windsor (French), with answer, from same.

f. 61v. Petition of John Harowe and Margaret, his wife (French), with answer, from same.

f. 63. Extract from Parl. Roll, 17 Richard II.

f. 64. Petition of Commons on provisions (French), with answer, from Parl. Roll.

f. 68v. Note on Statute, 13 Richard II, from Stat. Roll.

f. 70. Mandate to Sheriffs on proclamation, 3 May 1391.

f. 72. Letters Patent for William Sepyvans, kt., 2 December 1390.

f. 74. Extracts from Parl. Roll (French), 15 Richard II.

f. 76. Extract from Stat. Roll, 15 Richard II, caps. 5, 6.

f. 79. Protestation of William, formerly Archbishop of Canterbury (French), 16 Richard II, from Parl. Roll.

f. 82. Mandate on sessions of Justices of Assize at New Sarum, 1 November 1392.

f. 83. Statute of Provisors, 16 Richard II, cap. 5. Writ to Sheriffs, 1 May 1393, from Stat. Roll.

f. 89. Letters Patent appointing Mayor of Staple of Calais, 20 June 1393, from French Roll.

f. 91. Mandate to Sheriff of London on proclamation, 28 December 1392.

f. 93. Like on appointment of Sheriffs of London and Midd., 22 July 1392.

f. 94. Extract from Parl. Roll, 16 Richard II, touching provisors. (French.)

f. 95. As f. 82 above.

f. 96. As f. 83 above, with translation from Rastell, *Stat*.

f. 107. Statute, 17 Richard II, on money, from Stat. Roll, writ to Sheriffs, 1 June 1394, with translation from same.

f. 112. Mandate on half 10th and 15th levied, 12 October 1393, from Fine Roll.

f. 113. Letters Patent of pardon for William Chapman, 31 October 1393.

f. 114. Like on licence to prosecute execution of papal bulls, 4 March 1394.

f. 116. Like for array and repair of ships for King's passage to Ireland, 16 June 1394.

f. 120. Like for Philip Canon, 4 March 1394.

f. 122. Extract from Parl. Roll (French), 17 Richard II.

f. 123. Petition of John Dantry, kt., and wife (French), from Bundle of Pet. to Parl., 17 Richard II.

f. 125. Mandate on proceedings against Thomas, Earl of Warwick, 16 November 1394.

f. 133. Letters Patent for Thomas Mouselegh, clerk, 1 May 1395.

f. 135. Like for John, Duke of Lancaster, 10 September 1394, from Gascon Roll.

f. 140. Mandate for Duke of York, College of St. Botolph, 1 March 1395.

f. 142. Like to William, Archbishop of Canterbury etc. to pray for King, 16 October 1394. List.

f. 144. Like on proclamation for free elections against papal provisions, 8 February 1395.

f. 146. Letters Patent for John Chaundelour, 1 May 1395.

f. 148. Assent of Commons on provisions, from Parl. Roll, 20 Richard II.

f. 149. Letters Patent to men of ancient demesne, 6 June 1397.

f. 150. Like for William Hunt, 12 May 1397.

f. 151. Like on dispensation on illegitimacy of Beauforts, 9 February 1397.

f. 153. Oath of Mayor of London (French), 20 Richard II, from Close Roll.

f. 154. Mandate on proclamation on Queen's coronation, 4 December 1396.

f. 155. Letters Patent of pardon for Roger Scoyerton, 2 June 1397.

f. 157. Like for Earl of Oxford, 29 November 1397.

f. 158. Mandate to Sheriffs on proclamation on money, 19 November 1397.

f. 159. Like to Roger, Archbishop of Canterbury, on prayers for Thomas, late Duke of Gloucester, 6 October 1397.

f. 160. Oath (French), from Gascon Roll.

f. 162. Letters Patent for John, Duke of Lancaster, 6 July 1397, from Gascon Roll.

f. 165. Mandate on repair of bridge of New Temple, London, 24 March 1398.

f. 167. Letters Patent for Alexander de Besford, 12 May 1398.

f. 170. Mandate to Sheriff of Somerset for delivery of land to Robert Cary, 10 May 1398.

f. 174. Letters Patent of pardon for John Bussy, kt., etc. 1 May 1398.

f. 176. Like of exemplification for Mendicant Order, 20 March 1397.

f. 180. Extract from Stat. Roll, 5 Richard II.

f. 182. Writs of summons to Parliament, 24 March 1382.

f. 185. Extract on plea of avowry, from Fitzherbert, *Grand Abridg*.

f. 187. As f. 1. above.

f. 188. Charter for Duke of Gloucester, 16 February 1388.

f. 193. Writs of summons to Parliament, 17 December 1387.

f. 195. Like, 1 January 1387.

f. 197. Extract from Parl. Roll, 11 Richard II.

f. 199. 'Of the supreme and absolute power of an English Parliament together with the essential members thereof in and before Richard II's time'.

f. 200. Extract from Knighton, Life of Richard II.

f. 206. Record and process on Peter de Stapelton, clerk, 8 July 1380, from New Misc. Bundle, t. Richard II.

f. 207. Plea at Westminster before Robert Bealknap etc. Justices of Bench, East. term, 50 Edward III.

f. 209. Oath received of adversaries of Scots, 14 January 1399, from Scottish Roll.

f. 210. Letters Patent of pardon for Robert de Evere, Dean of St. Paul's, 15 January 1399.

f. 211. Like of licence of mortmain for Collegiate Church of Shottesbrook, co. Berks., 21 December 1398.

VOLUME 32

A volume of transcripts etc. from the Public Records and other sources, Richard II to Henry IV. On flyleaf: Recorda temp. Ric. II et Hen. IV. 323 ff.

ff. 1, 3. Writs of summons to Parliament, 4 August 1377.

f. 5. The end of Parliament (French), 1 Richard II, from Parl. Roll.

f. 6. Writs of summons to Parliament to Robert Bealknap etc. 22 September 1378. List.

f. 9. Writs de expensis, knights, 24 March 1382.

f. 7. Writ of supersedeas, co. Chester, 4 August 1379, from Close Roll.

f. 10. Writs of summons to Parliament, 24 March 1382.

f. 13. Letters Patent of summons to Parliament, Ireland, 29 March 1382.

f. 15. Writs of summons to Parliament to William, Archbishop of Canterbury, etc. 7 January 1383.

f. 21. Writ of summons to Parliament to Sheriff of London, 20 August 1383, from Liber H in Archives of city of London.

f. 23. Writs of summons to Parliament to William, Archbishop of Canterbury etc. 20 August 1383. List.

f. 31. Extract from Parl. Roll, 7 Richard II.

f. 41. Letters Patent excusing burgesses of Kingston upon Hull, 22 October 1384.

f. 43. Plea on avowry, Trin. term, 8 Richard II (French), from Fitzherbert, *Grand Abridg.*, with translation.

f. 47. Protestation of clergy (Latin), Richard II, from Parl. Roll, with translation.

f. 52. Writs of summons to Parliament, 17 December 1387.

f. 53. Like, 1 January 1388.

f. 54. Extract from Patent Roll, 1 Henry IV.

f. 56. Writs of summons to Parliament to William, Archbishop of Canterbury etc. 20 March 1388. List.

f. 57. Writs of summons to Parliament, 17 December 1387.

f. 59. Like, 20 November 1394.

f. 61. Writs of summons to Parliament to John, Duke of Aquitaine and Lancaster, etc. 5 November 1397. List.

f. 62. Dissolution of Parliament (French), 21 Richard II, from Parl. Roll.

f. 65. Mandate to Sheriffs on burning of writings, 30 November 1399.

f. 67. Letters Patent of confirmation of John de Scarborough as Under Clerk of Parliament, 11 November 1399.

f. 69. Charter creating Henry, Prince of Wales, 15 October 1399.

f. 70. General Prescription (Latin), 1 Henry IV, from Parl. Roll, with translation.

f. 75. As f. 69 above.

f. 77. Letters Patent of inspeximus of King's intention, 16 February 1390.

f. 82. Letter for William Clifford, 19 June 1400, from Rot. Viagii.

f. 84. Memorandum on seal in land of Ireland, 15 December 1399, from Close Roll.

f. 85. Like, for Earl of Northumberland, 19 October 1399.

f. 88. Letters on seisin of Duchy of Aquitaine in King's name, 10 May 1400, from Gascon Roll.

f. 91. Letters Patent for Duke of Suffolk, 15 November 1399.

f. 94. Like for Henry le Scrope, kt., 12 November 1399.

f. 97. Like of exemplification, pilgrim, 6 November 1399.

f. 98. Like of pardon for John Dere of Swavesey, 20 November 1399, from Pardon Roll.

f. 99. Like of restitution of temporalities to Thomas, Archbishop of Canterbury, 29 October 1399.

f. 100. Like, 21 October 1399.

f. 102. Like to John Holt and William Burgh, kts., 20 February 1400.

f. 104. Extract from Patent Roll on petitions in last Parliament, 1 Henry IV.

f. 106. Letters Patent to guard safely Richard, formerly King (French), from Parl. Roll, 1 Henry IV. List.

f. 107. Judgement on Richard II to prison (French), from same.

f. 107v. Commons party to judgement (French), from same.

f. 110. Statute, 1 Henry IV, from Stat. Roll.

f. 116. Extract from Parl. Roll, 1 Henry IV, translation, Rastell, *Stat.*

f. 118. Extracts from Stat. Roll, 1 Henry IV

f. 120. Oath taken by Richard II at coronation, from Parl. Roll, 1 Henry IV.

ff. 122, 124, 125. Declaration by Henry IV to guard the laws, from Parl. Roll, 1 Henry IV.

f. 128. Moderation of Statute of Provisors (French), 1 Henry IV, from same.

f. 129. Extract from Parl. Roll, 1 Henry IV.

f. 136. As f. 70 above.

f. 137. On the deposition of Richard II (French and English), from Judgement Roll, 1 Henry IV.

f. 155. Record of process of renunciation (Latin, French, and English), from Parl. Roll, 1 Henry IV.

ff. 181, 188, 196. Touching the Cistercian Order (French), from Parl. Roll, 2 Henry IV.

ff. 185, 186. Extract from Stat. Roll, 2 Henry IV.

f. 187. Extract from Parl. Roll, 2 Henry IV.

f. 191. The end of Parliament (French), from Parl. Roll, 2 Henry IV.

f. 193. Affirmation of moderation of Statute of Provisors (French), from Parl. Roll, 2 Henry IV.

f. 194. Letters Patent of exemplification, 12 March 1400.

f. 195. Extract from Parl. Roll (French), 2 Henry IV.

f. 200. Commons excused matters spoken in Parliament (French), from Parl. Roll, 2 Henry IV.

f. 201. Petition of Edmund Basset (French), with answer, from New Misc. Bundle, t. Richard II etc.

f. 203. Petition of Isabella, late wife of William Lescrope (French), with answer, from Bundle of Pet. in Parl., 3 Henry IV.

f. 208. Petition of Commons to King (English), from Bundle of Pet. in Parl., t. Henry IV etc.

f. 206. Petition of soldiers in March of Picardy (French), with answer, from Bundle of Pet. in Parl., t. Henry IV.

f. 209. Mandate on proclamation on grants, 15 August 1403. List.

f. 211. Like on proclamation against form of treaty with Flanders, 11 January 1403.

f. 212. Letters Patent granting John (son of King), Keeper of Berwick on Tweed, licence to grant safe conducts, 13 August 1403, from Scottish Roll.

f. 213. Extract from Stat. Roll, 4 Henry IV.

f. 214. Petition of Robert atte Mill of Guildford (French), with answer, from Bundle of Pet. to Parl., 4 Henry IV.

ff. 214v, 217. Petition of subjects, co. Pembroke (French), with answer, from same.

f. 215. Petition of burgesses of Lyme Regis, co. Dorset (French), with answer, from same.

f. 219. Letters Patent, commission cos. Northumberland, Cumberland and Newcastle upon Tyne, 20 November 1402.

f. 221. Apprentices, London, from Parl. Roll (French), 4 Henry IV.

f. 223. For Abbot of Newnham (French), from same.

f. 227. Affirmation of revocation of Provisors (French and English), 17 June 1402, from Parl. Roll, 4 Henry IV.

f. 229. Letters Patent giving Edward, Earl of Rutland, power to receive oaths, 28 August 1401, from Gascon Roll.

f. 230. Petition of community of city of London (French), from Bundle of Pet. in Parl., 4 Henry IV.

f. 231. Letters Patent of declaration of King's intention, 30 April 1405.

f. 233. Like for John Cornwall, kt., and wife, 4 May 1404.

f. 235. Mandate for Prince, manor of Mere, 15 July 1404.

f. 237. Extract from Stat. Roll, 5 Henry IV.

Petition of Commons (French) with answer, from Parl. Roll, 5 Henry IV.

f. 239. Mandate for collectors of great custom, 12 October 1403, from Fine Roll.

f. 240. Letters Patent for Arnald Savage, kt., 4 June 1403.

f. 241. Removal of confessors etc. (French), from Parl. Roll, 5 Henry IV.

f. 243. Removal of aliens from King's household etc. (French), from same.

f. 246. Letters Patent for Brother John Tyler, arrested, 7 March 1405.

f. 247. Like for Isabel, wife of William Lescrope, 12 November 1404.

f. 248. Like for Humphrey, son of King, 22 October 1404.

f. 249. Like for John, son of King, 25 January 1405, from Scottish Roll.

f. 250. Petition of Isabel, Dame Lescrope (French), with answer, from Pet. in Parl., 6 Henry IV.

f. 252. Mandates on castles seized for King, 6 March 1405. List.

f. 253. Extract from Stat. Roll, 7 Henry IV.

f. 255. Writ on privilege to Sheriff of London, 9 February 1406, from Liber I in Archives of city of London.

f. 259. Letters Patent of protection for executors of Edmund, Duke of York, 3 April 1406.

f. 260. Mandate on proclamation on aliens in benefices, 13 June 1406.

f. 261. Mandates to Sheriffs on execution of agreement, 16 August 1406.

f. 264. Writ, 7 June 1406 (French), from New Misc. Bundle, t. Richard II etc.

f. 270. Letters Patent for John, Earl of Somerset, 26 November 1406, with reference to Patent Roll, 11 Henry IV.

f. 272. Mandate for citizens of London, 5 June 1407.

f. 273. Like on levy of subsidy, 25 October 1406, from Fine Roll.

f. 275. Like on certain sums delivered to Treasurer, 22 December 1406.

f. 277. Like on subsidy of wool, co. Chester, 20 February 1407.

f. 278. Letters Patent for burgesses of Maldon, 26 November 1407.

f. 279. Like of pardon for Nicholas Tempest, 2 August 1408.

f. 280. Like on annexation of Brotelby to Duchy of Lancaster, 13 November 1408.

f. 283. Extract from Stat. Roll, 11 Henry IV.

f. 284. For Sir Walter Hungerford (French), from Parl. Roll, 11 Henry IV.

For Sir John Trebul, from same.

f. 288. Letters Patent of protection for Thomas Gerberg, kt. etc., 5 May 1410.

ff. 289, 292, 295. Pleas on replicare, avowry, gage deliverance (French), Mich. term, 11 Henry IV, from Fitzherbert, *Grand Abridg.*

f. 294. Letters Patent for Drogo Barentyn, 30 July 1410.

f. 298. Like for Richard de Hastings, 8 May 1410.

f. 300. Like for Treasurer of King's Household, 21 November 1409.

f. 301. Mandates to Sheriffs on proclamation, 40 librates of land and knighthood, 20 November 1410.

f. 302. Letters Patent on prorogation, men of King of Norway, 9 September 1411.

f. 306. Like of exemplification for Abbot of Furness, 1 February 1412.

f. 308. Petition of Abbot of Furness (French), with answer, from Parl. Roll, 13 Henry IV.

f. 310. Letters Patent appointing Lieutenant of Aquitaine, 11 July 1412, from Gascon Roll.

f. 310v. On power granted to the same (French).

f. 314. For Archbishop of Canterbury (French and Latin), from Parl. Roll, 13 Henry IV.

f. 321. Memorandum on John Pecbrigge, kt., 27 January 1413, from Close Roll.

f. 322. Letters under signet to Archbishop of Canterbury (French and English), 9 May (1413).

VOLUME 33

A volume of transcripts etc. from the Public Records and other sources, 1–10 Henry V. On flyleaf: Recorda tempore Henrici V, 1–10, 1413–1422. 184 ff.

f. 1. Letters Patent for Henry Lescrope, kt., 24 May 1413.

f. 2. Mandates for adjournment of Parliament from Westminster to Lincoln, 23 July 1413.

ff. 4, 9. Extract from Stat. Roll, 1 Henry V.

ff. 5, 18. Mandates for execution of King's will, 15 May 1413.

f. 7. Petition to levy expenses of knights etc. (French), with answer, from Parl. Roll, 1 Henry V.

f. 10. Letters Patent to receive homages in Aquitaine, 26 June 1413, from Gascon Roll.

f. 11. Like for Thomas, Earl of Dorset, 26 June 1413, from same.

f. 12. Like on estates in Bordeaux of Thomas, Duke of Clarence, 13 June 1413 (French), from same.

f. 16. Mandates on proclamation of King's peace, 21 March 1413.

f. 17. As f. 7 above.

f. 21. Letters Patent of exemplification respecting letters of Alphonso, King of Castille, 1 December 1414.

f. 23. Like of exemplification of articles of Statute, 42 Edward III, 24 January 1415.

f. 24. Charter for Bishop of Winchester, 26 September 1414.

f. 25. Extract on Ordinance on money (French), from Parl. Roll, 2 Henry V.

f. 27. No law to be made unless Commons gave their assent (French), from Parl. Roll, 2 Henry V, with reference to Selden, *Mare Clausum.*

f. 29. As f. 25 above, with translation and notes from Cotton, *Records*.

f. 33. Concerning knight's service in geldable lands (French), from Parl. Roll, 2 Henry V.

f. 34. Mandates on subsidies to John Bartelot etc., 12 January 1414.

f. 35. For John Salman (French and Latin), from Parl. Roll, 2 Henry V.

f. 38. As f. 25 above.

ff. 40, 49. As f. 27 above, with translation and note.

ff. 43, 52. Letters Patent appointing John, Duke of Bedford, Lieutenant of England, 25 July 1417.

f. 46. Approval of peace between England and France, 20 May 1421, from Parl. Roll, 9 Henry V.

f. 55. Extract from Stat. Roll, 2 Henry V, with reference to Rastell, *Stat.*

f. 56. Translation of extracts from Parl. Roll, 2 Henry V.

f. 57. Letters Patent to William, Bishop of Carlisle, for enquiry, 3 October 1414.

f. 59. Like of exemplification for burgesses of Southampton, 13 February 1415.

f. 62. As f. 23 above.

ff. 64, 80. Ordinance on elections during voidance of Papacy (French), from Parl. Roll, 3 Henry V.

f. 65. Letters Patent of exemplification for Henry Percy, 11 May 1415.

f. 69. Like for Thomas, Duke of Clarence, 15 May 1415.

f. 71. Mandate to Henry, Archbishop of Canterbury, etc., 28 May 1415.

f. 73. Like to Sheriff of Wilts. to compel soldiers to pay for victuals, 28 July 1415.

f. 74. Like for Roger Lansell etc., 20 October 1415.

f. 76. Like on mayoralty of King's Lynn, 19 October 1415.

f. 78. Petition on wages of knights in Parliament (French), with answer, from Parl. Roll, 3 Henry V.

f. 82. For Henry Barton (French), from same.

f. 83. Petition of Roger Lyneye of Newport, co. Salop (French), with answer, from Bundle of Pet. in Parl., 3 Henry V.

f. 84v. Petition of Henry Lakensnyder (French), with answer, from same.

f. 85v. Petition of John Sampson of Dartmouth (French), with answer, from same.

f. 86v. Petition of John Atwood etc. (French), with answer, from same.

f. 88. Petition of men of Sandwich (French), with answer, from same.

f. 90. Mandate for Constance, late wife of Thomas, Lord Despenser, 8 December 1415.

f. 93. For men of Sandwich (French), from Parl. Roll, 3 Henry V.

f. 95. For David Howell of Pembroke (French), with answer, from Parl. Roll, 4 Henry V.

f. 97. Letters Patent on revocation for St. John of Beverley, 6 June 1416.

f. 100. For Abbey of Fountains (French), from Parl. Roll, 4 Henry V.

f. 102. Confirmation of alliance King and King of Romans (French and Latin), 15 August 1416, from Parl. Roll, 4 Henry V.

f. 113. Extract from Stat. Roll, 4 Henry V.

f. 115. Another extract from same.

f. 116. Mandates to collectors of subsidy on wool, 26 November 1417, from Fine Roll.

f. 117. Like on proclamation to Chancellor of Duchy of Lancaster on manor of Walton, 28 November 1417.

f. 119. Letters Patent of safe conduct for Archbishop of Rheims, 10 November 1417, from Norman Roll.

f. 120. Mandates to Sheriffs on proclamation on status of nobles of Burgundy, 5 April 1417.

f. 121. For Duke of Exeter (French), from Parl. Roll, 5 Henry V.

f. 123. Letters Patent to Henry, Archbishop of Canterbury, for array of clergy, 6 July 1418. List.

f. 125. Like of safe conduct for Laurence Pranasyn etc., 11 February 1419.

f. 126. Mandates on proclamation on Britanny, 8 February 1419.

f. 127. Letters Patent of pardon for Nicholas Stokes, 1 March 1419.

f. 128. Like for Sir John Ratclif, kt., 16 May 1419, from Gascon Roll.

f. 129. Like for John, Duke of Bedford, on treaty, 9 January 1420.

f. 130. Like appointing John, Duke of Bedford, Lieutenant in England, 30 December 1419.

f. 132. Mandate for Prior of Tortington, 10 March 1420.

f. 136. On Kingdoms of England and France (French), from Parl. Roll, 8 Henry V.

ff. 138–40. Extract from Stat. Roll, 8 Henry V.

f. 142. Approval of peace between England and France, 21 May 1421, from Parl. Roll, 9 Henry V.

f. 145. 'An Act of Parliament made 9 H. 5 concerning the practitioners of physic and surgery worthy of observation'.

f. 146, 155. Petition (English), with answer, among Pet. in Parl., 9 Henry V.

f. 147v. Ordinance on French matters, from Parl. Roll, 9 Henry V.

f. 159. Petition of Alice, late wife of Richard de Arundell, kt., etc. (French), with answer, from Bundle of Pet. to Parl., 9 Henry V.

f. 162. Security to King's creditors (French), from Parl. Roll, 9 Henry V.

f. 163. Extract from Stat. Roll, 9 Henry V, cap. 11.

f. 165. Letters Patent of exemplification of peace, 2 May last, 1 June 1421, from French Roll.

f. 168. For Griffith Donne (French), from Parl. Roll, 9 Henry V.

f. 170. Letters Patent of safe conduct of Ambassador of Britanny, 17 July 1422.

f. 172. Mandates on subsidy of 3s. on the tun and 12d. on the lb., 21 May 1422, from Fine Roll.

f. 174. Like on adjournment of assizes, co. Devon, 16 July 1422.

f. 176. Like on delivery of John Mortimer, kt., 27 May 1422. Like to receive same.

f. 176v. Like on custody of same.

f. 177. Petition of Margery Boys etc. (English), with answer, from New Misc. Bundle, t. Henry IV etc.

f. 180. Memorandum of Petition to Parliament held 16 October 1419, by commonalty of realm, for Margery Boys etc. (Latin).

VOLUME 34

A volume of transcripts etc. from the Public Records and other sources, 1–20 Henry VI. On flyleaf: Recorda tempore Henrici VI, 1422–1442. On another flyleaf: Records from the 1st year of Henry VIth to the 21st. 408 ff.

f. 1. Memorandum on delivery of great seal to Chancellor, 31 August 1422, from Close Roll

f. 3. On style on King's seal (French), from Parl. Roll, 1 Henry VI.

f. 5. Confirmation of liberties, annuities and offices, from same.

f. 7. Letters Patent on enquiry into age of Theobald Gorges, 20 February 1423.

f. 9. Mandate on allowance to Keeper of Hanaper, 8 December 1422.

f. 10. Letters Patent of confirmation to town of Salop (abstract), 1 Henry VI.

Like for Prior of St. John of Jerusalem in England (abstract), same.

f. 11. Mandate to Sheriff of London on burning of heretics, 1 March 1423.

f. 13. Like to Sheriffs on proclamation of peace, 1 October 1422.

f. 14. Like to Sheriffs on proclamation of 10th and 15th, 26 November 1422.

f. 16. Pronouncement on Parliament, 6 November 1422, from Parl. Roll, 1 Henry VI.

f. 21. As f. 14 above.

f. 23. Mandate on delivery of prisoners out of Fleet, 16 June 1423.

f. 24. Letters Patent of exemplification for Robert Darcy, 20 January 1423.

f. 26. Like for Katherine, Queen of England, 6 November 1422.

f. 28. Like for Poncio, Lord of Castillon, 28 April 1423, from Gascon Roll.

f. 29. Like for John Ratclif, kt., 13 June 1423, from same.

f. 29v. Like for Lord de Durar, 18 May 1423, from same.

f. 30. Like for Bernard Angevin, 7 July 1423, from same.

f. 31. Like for John Ratclif to receive the King's grace, from same.

f. 32. Like appointing Richard, Archbishop of Dublin, Chancellor of Ireland, 19 May 1423.

f. 33. Like appointing Humphrey, Duke of Gloucester, Chamberlain of England, 30 November 1422.

f. 34. Like to same on Parliament begun at Westminster, 6 November 1422.

f. 35. Like to Henry de Bromley, Sergeant at Arms, on Flemish goods, 26 January 1423.

f. 36. Like on execution of will of Henry V, 18 December 1422.

f. 39. Like of confirmation to John, Duke of Bedford, 20 May 1423.

f. 41. Like of confirmation for burgesses of Shaftesbury, 24 June 1423.

f. 44. Like appointing Thomas, Bishop of Durham, Chancellor of England, 16 November 1422.

f. 45. Like appointing John, Duke of Bedford, Protector and Defender of Realm, 5 December 1422.

f. 47. Like for Anne, wife of Duke of Bedford, 20 October 1423.

f. 50. Like of confirmation for Prior of St. Bartholomew's of charter of Henry I, 1133, 2 Henry VI.

f. 54. Like for Joan, Queen of England (abstract), 2 Henry VI.

Like of confirmation of Edington to Bishop of Winchester (abstract), same.

f. 54v. Like for Bishop of Chester and Prior and Convent of Rochester (abstracts), same.

f. 55. Like of pardon for William Yerd, 20 October 1423.

f. 57. Like for Katherine, Queen of England, 20 October 1423.

f. 59. Mandate to receive Robert Giresme, Elect of Melun in France, 8 February 1423.

f. 60. Letters Patent for Humphrey, Duke of Gloucester, to hold Parliament, 19 October 1423.

f. 62. Like of pardon for Thomas Seintcler, 8 February 1423.

f. 63. Like for Henry Benet, 6 June 1423.

f. 64. Mandate for Anne Courtney, Countess of Devon, on co. Chester, 24 November 1423.

f. 65. Letters Patent granting treasurership of town of Calais, 21 December 1423, from French Roll.

f. 65v. Like for Nicholas Horton, 5 March 1423, from same.

f. 66. Like for John Lescrope, kt., 15 February 1423.

f. 68. As f. 65 above.

f. 69. Extract from Stat. Roll, 2 Henry VI.

f. 70. On John Mortimer of Bishop's Hatfield, co. Hertf., from Parl. Roll, 2 Henry VI.

f. 74. Petition of Margery, late wife of Henry Dey (French), with answer, from New Misc. Bundle, t. Richard II etc.

f. 76. For Duchess of Gloucester (French), from Parl. Roll, 2 Henry VI.

f. 78. Appointment of Humphrey, Duke of Gloucester, as Lieutenant of Ireland (French), from Ordinance Roll for King's Council, 1–3 Henry VI.

f. 80. On payment of tallies (French), from Parl. Roll, 2 Henry VI.

f. 81. Letters Patent of confirmation for burgesses of Grampound, 17 February 1424.

f. 82. For Earl of Huntingdon (French), from Parl. Roll, 2 Henry VI.

f. 84. Writ to Constable of Dover, 1 September 1423, with return, from New Misc. Bundle, t. Richard II etc.

f. 86. Letter to Henry VI from William, Bishop of Coventry and Lichfield, appointing proctors, 22 October 1423, from same.

f. 87. Like from Thomas, Abbot of Malmesbury, 1 October 1423, from same.

f. 88. Like from Abbot of Hyde, 15 October 1423, from same.

f. 90. Like from Geoffrey, Abbot of Bardney, 6 October 1423, from same.

f. 92. Like from Robert, Bishop of St. Asaph, 10 October 1423, from same.

f. 95. Like from Henry, Archbishop of York, 29 September 1423, from same.

f. 97. Like from John, Bishop of Ely, 10 October 1423, from same.

f. 99. Like from John, Bishop of Salisbury, 12 October 1423, from same.

f. 101. Mandate for Thomas de Forges, 30 April 1425.

f. 105. Letters Patent appointing Richard, Earl of Warwick, Lieutenant of Calais, 1 March 1425, from French Roll.

f. 106. Like appointing same Captain of Calais, 3 March 1425, from same.

f. 107. Like to Thomas Bankes etc. to enquire, 12 February 1425.

f. 109. Writs of summons to Parliament, 24 February 1425.

f. 111. 'On the case John, Earl Marshal, and Richard, Earl of Warwick. The arguments are entered at large in English in Rot. Parl. 3 H. 6, the first precedent of that kind I ever yet saw in all my searches and enquiries'.

f. 113. Extracts from Parl. Roll, 3 Henry VI.

f. 141. Letters Patent of confirmation on stannaries, 8 May 1425.

f. 143. Like of confirmation for Eleanor Welles, 30 April 1425.

f. 144. Memorandum on petition of John Lescrop, 30 April 1426, from Close Roll.

f. 148. Letters Patent for Prior of Holy Trinity, York, 18 March 1426.

f. 150. Like for John Talbot, 29 January 1426.

f. 151v. Like appointing John Fray, Third Baron of Exchequer, 26 May 1426.

f. 152. Mandates to Sheriffs on proclamation on Flanders, 30 July 1426.

f. 153. Letters Patent for merchants of the Hanse in Germany, 18 February 1426.

f. 155. Extracts from Stat. Roll, 4 Henry VI.

f. 156. Letters Patent for citizens of Waterford (abstract), 5 Henry VI.

Like for citizens of Dublin (abstract), same.

f. 158. Letters Patent of confirmation for burgesses of Tintagel, 19 November 1426.

f. 160. Mandate on tenants of ancient demesne quit of toll, Godmanchester, 27 January 1427.

f. 161. Letters Patent of confirmation for Archbishop of Canterbury, 14 March 1427.

f. 165. For John Sutton, kt., from Parl. Roll, 6 Henry VI.

f. 166. Letters Patent on aid to construct Tower of Ravenspur, 28 November 1427.

f. 168. Like on King's education, 1 June 1428.

f. 170. Mandate for John, Prior of Charterhouse, London, 14 February 1428.

f. 172. Letters Patent for Earl of Huntingdon, 1 March 1428.

f. 174. Like for Ralph, Earl of Westmorland, 4 December 1427.

f. 176. Like appointing William Westbury etc. Justices, 3 May 1428.

f. 177. Like to William Rider, 8 July 1428.

f. 178. Like for Peter Durant, 24 June 1428, from Gascon Roll.

f. 179. Like for John Bastard kt. (Bastard of Thomas Duke of Clarence), 11 July 1428.

f. 180. Mandate on proclamation of security of peace for John de Kingsley, 1 December 1427.

f. 182. Letters Patent for Thomas, Lord Roos, 13 October 1427.

f. 184. Petition on election of knights (French), with answer, from Parl. Roll, 6 Henry VI.

f. 186. Letters Patent of safe conduct for James, King of Scotland, 1 December 1428, from Scottish Roll.

f. 187. Like for Bishop of Hereford, 18 June 1429.

f. 187v. Mandate for Humphrey, Earl of Stafford, grant of marriage, 15 June 1429.

f. 188. Letters Patent for Henry, Cardinal of England, 18 June 1429, from French Roll.

f. 190. Like for freemen of Company of Grocers, London, 16 February 1429.

f. 192. Mandates to Sheriffs on shortening Parliament, 3 August 1429.

f. 194. Writ on Ireland, 17 June 1429, with return, from New Misc. Bundle, t. Richard II etc.

f. 200. Extract from among the Petitions to Parliament by the Commons, with the answers, from Parl. Roll, 8 Henry VI.

f. 201. Mandates to Sheriffs on proclamation of grants by King's ancestors, 1 February 1430.

f. 202. Petition, William Lark (French), with answer, from Parl. Roll, 8 Henry VI.

f. 205. Petition, London (French), with answer, from same.

f. 208. Petition, Calais (French), with answer, from same.

f. 210. Extract from Stat. Roll, 8 Henry VI, cap. 1, with translation from Rastell, *Stat.*

f. 214. Letters Patent on coming with King of Scotland, 20 November 1429, from Scottish Roll.

f. 215. Like on treating with same, 15 November 1429, from same.

f. 217. Like for John Raynwell, Mayor of Staple of Calais, 23 February 1430, from French Roll.

f. 218. Mandates to Sheriffs on proclamation on Frenchmen's lands, 21 October 1429.

f. 219. Letters Patent on enquiry on election of knights, 10 July 1430.

f. 221. Like on markets, Brabant, 19 July 1430.

f. 222. Like to Richard Arnall of ratification of prebend, 27 November 1429.

f. 222v. Like granting Richard, Duke of York, 200 marks fee, 25 November 1429.

f. 223. Like appointing Richard, Duke of York, Constable of England, 20 January 1430.

f. 224. Like granting licence for Irish to stay in England, 26 May 1430.

f. 226. Like for John Hamsterley, 19 August 1430.

f. 227v. Like appointing Master Walter Colles Constable of Bordeaux, 28 June 1431, from Gascon Roll.

f. 228. Writs of summons to Parliament, 27 November 1430.

f. 231. For John Pope (French), from Parl. Roll, 9 Henry VI.

f. 232. Letters Patent of naturalization for Gilbert Groote, 23 November 1430.

f. 233. For co. Cambridge (French), from Parl. Roll, 9 Henry VI.

f. 236. Letters Patent for Richard Laundrey, University of Cambridge, 2 July 1431.

f. 237. Like prohibiting association with the Cardinal (Henry Beaufort), 7 November 1430.

f. 238. Like on exemplification for John, Lord Tiptoft, 23 April 1431.

f. 241. Like to Cardinal of England, licence, wool, 18 April 1431.

f. 241v. Like to William Gyllyng of ratification on church of Wolvesley, 7 May 1431.

f. 242. Like for Lewis Gollen, esq., 12 January 1431.

f. 244. Like for Cardinal of England, 10 Henry VI.

f. 246. Like of naturalization for John Erthe, 28 November 1431.

f. 248. Like for William Brown, 20 June 1432.

f. 249. Like of protection for Robert Holme, 16 July 1432, with reference to Patent Roll, 9 Henry VI.

f. 251. Like for Master John Fusiler, 28 September 1431, from French Roll.

f. 252. Mandate to allow Pope's ambassador to cross with gold etc. 12 July 1432.

f. 253. Like for Godfrey Shorthose, esq., 28 June 1433.

f. 254. Like not to take corn outside, Keepers Passage of Plymouth etc. 12 August 1433.

f. 255. Letters Patent of naturalization for Master John Rynel, 8 July 1433.

f. 256. Like for Andrew Ogart, 8 July 1433.

f. 257. Letters Patent for John, Earl of Huntingdon, 15 November 1432.

f. 257v. Like for Cardinal of England, 16 February 1433.

f. 259. Like of licence in mortmain for Prioress of St. Nicholas, Middlemore, co. Oxf., 8 July 1433.

f. 261. Like for men of Kingston upon Hull, 8 July 1433.

f. 263. For John, Earl of Arundel etc. (Latin, English, and French), from Parl. Roll, 11 & 12 Henry VI.

f. 272. Letters Patent for Humphrey, Duke of Gloucester, and wife, 8 July 1433.

f. 274. Like for John, Duke of Bedford, 8 July 1433.

f. 275. Mandates on proclamation on weights and measures, 4 January 1434.

f. 276. Like for men of ancient demesne, quit of tolls, 12 July 1434.

f. 277. Like mandates, 8 May, 12 July 1434.

f. 279. Letters Patent for Bishop of London, 8 May 1434.

f. 280. Like for Abbot of Glastonbury, 13 May 1434.

f. 280v. Like on walls of Alnwick, 1 June 1434.

f. 283. Like for William, Bishop of Lincoln, etc. to receive oaths, 1 May 1434. List.

f. 290. Names of persons delivered in Chancery to take oaths, 20 January 1434, from Close Rolls.

f. 291. Writ of summons to Parliament to Thomas, Bishop of Hereford, etc. 1 November 1433. List.

f. 293. Mandates on collection of subsidy on wool, 10 November 1433, from Fine Roll.

f. 294. Letters Patent for Earl of Oxford, 5 February 1435.

f. 295. Like for Bishop of Exeter, 13 February 1435.

f. 296. Like of naturalization for John Mundet, 4 November 1434.

f. 297. Like for Reymund Wacher, 16 May 1435.

f. 298. Letters Patent for John Ratclif, kt., 22 June 1435.

f. 299. Like for Edmund, Earl of Mortain, 9 December 1435.

f. 300. Like to Thomas, Bishop of Exeter etc. on loans to King, 24 February 1436. List.

f. 301. Like for Jaquitta de Luxenbergh, 6 February 1436.

f. 302. Like appointing John Juyn, Chief Justice of Common Bench, 9 February 1436.

Like of John Fray as Chief Baron of Exchequer, 9 February 1436.
f. 303. Mandates on proclamation under Stat. of West. I on false rumours, 14 Henry VI.
f. 305. Letters Patent for Richard, Earl of Warwick, 19 May 1436.
f. 306. Like for Richard, Duke of York, 26 January 1436.
f. 307. Like for Mayor etc. of Bristol, 15 December 1435.
f. 308. Like for Humphrey, Duke of Gloucester, 1 November 1435.
f. 309. Like for soldiers of town of Calais, 5 March 1436.
f. 310. Like of naturalization for Thomas Franc, LL.D., 26 July 1436.
f. 311v. Letters Patent for John Pate of Deanery of Tamworth, 26 August 1436.
f. 312. Like of naturalization for Rhys ap Madog of Wales, 14 January 1436.
f. 313. Mandate for tenants of ancient demesne to be quit of tolls, Mutford, 29 November 1435.
f. 314. Letters Patent for Bishop of Ely, 28 May 1436.
f. 316. Like for Bishop of Durham, 28 February 1437.
f. 319. Like for John, Duke of Norfolk, 18 March 1437, from Scottish Roll.
f. 320. Like of oyer and terminer for Robert Umfravill, kt., etc. in East March, 15 October 1436, from same.
f. 320v. Like of safe conduct for William Iver, kt., etc. 4 March 1437.
f. 321. Like for Clays Hughson of Wykedeppe See in Holland, 18 October 1437, from French Roll.
f. 322. Like giving powers to Earl of Warwick, 16 July 1437, from same.
f. 324. Like appointing John Willes to custody of city of Norwich, 15 July 1437.
f. 325. Like of naturalization for Clement Vincent, 7 October 1438.
f. 326. Mandate of restitution of possessions to Queen, 1 February 1436.
f. 327. For Isabel, late wife of John Boteler of Beausey, kt. (English and French), from Parl. Roll, 15 Henry VI.
f. 329. Letters Patent for Humphrey, Duke of Gloucester, and wife, 6 March 1437.
f. 331. Like for Mayor etc. of Norwich, 29 November 1437.
f. 333. Like for Geoffrey Chirch, 20 May 1438.
f. 334. Like appointing John Molyner etc. Auditors, 16 July 1438, from Gascon Roll.
f. 334v. Like for Mayor etc. of Bordeaux, 16 July 1438, from same.
f. 336. Like to Ralph Garneys to enquire, 24 May 1438.
f. 338. Like for Friars Preachers, London, 13 May 1438.
f. 339. Like for Maurice Bruyn, kt., 30 May 1439.
f. 340. Like of safe conduct for William Small etc., 28 March 1439, from Scottish Roll.
f. 341. Like for John Matheson etc., 17 August 1439, from same.
f. 342. Letters Patent for Rhys ap Thomas, 12 February 1439.
f. 344. Like for Richard, Earl of Salisbury, giving power to grant safe conducts, 9 December 1438, from Scottish Roll.
f. 346. Like of safe conduct for Alexander Seton etc., 20 October 1438, from same.

f. 345. Letters Patent for Henry Percy, 14 July 1439, from same.

f. 347. Letters Patent for Ralph Rochfort, 6 January 1439.

f. 348. Mandate to George de Latimer, kt., to appear Coram Rege, 28 December 1438.

f. 349. Letters Patent of safe conduct for Henry de Colvigne, 10 March 1439, from French Roll.

f. 350. Like of naturalization for Nicholas Morlart, 4 January 1439.

f. 351. Letters Patent for Cardinal of England, 21 May 1439, from French Roll.

f. 352. Like giving Cardinal power to grant safe conducts, 23 May 1439, from same.

f. 354. For collectors of 10th and 15th (French and English), from Parl. Roll, 18 Henry VI.

f. 356. Letters Patent for city of Norwich, 13 December 1439.

f. 357. Like for Garter King at Arms, 21 October 1439.

f. 358. Writs to Sheriffs notifying place of Parliament, 22 October 1439.

f. 359. Letters Patent of safe conduct for B. de Beaurain, 9 February 1440, from French Roll.

f. 360. Like for Master John de Fuselier, from same.

Like for Huet de Seint Mars etc., from same.

f. 361. Against aliens selling spices (English and French), from Parl. Roll, 18 Henry VI.

f. 362. On Staple of Calais (English and French), from same.

f. 364. For John Carpenter, Letters Patent, 3 December 1439.

f. 367. Like for citizens of Norwich, 13 December 1439.

f. 369. Like of naturalization for Margaret Warner, 1 December 1439.

f. 370. Like for Master Macdon etc. 5 March 1440.

f. 371. Like for Peter Heripin, 18 December 1439.

f. 372. Letters Patent excusing Bishop of Coventry and Lichfield for not coming to Parliament, 12 December 1439.

f. 374. Like for Hertory van Clux, 11 May 1440, from French Roll.

f. 375. Like to enquire, 3 June 1440. List.

f. 378. Like of pardon for John Cressy, 20 January 1440.

f. 381. Like of naturalization for John Gerard, 26 June 1441.

f. 382. Like for John Martell, 28 November 1440.

f. 383. Like for Master Genase de Vulre, 21 January 1441.

f. 385. Letters Patent for same, 22 October 1440.

f. 387. Like for Prioress of St. Mary de Pratis, St. Albans, 17 September 1440.

f. 391. Mandate for men of manor of Gertley, 8 May 1441.

f. 392. Letters Patent of exemplificaton of petition in Parliament, community of Yorks, etc., 15 April 1441.

f. 396. Like appointing Robert Mansfield purveyor, 7 February 1442.

f. 397. Like to John Mounshill to arrest and take, 5 December 1441.

f. 398. Mandate to receive Roger Bultbroke etc. from Tower, 16 November 1441.

f. 399. Letters Patent giving power to William, Bishop of Rochester, etc., 3 November 1441, from French Roll.

f. 401. Like for William, Bishop of Lincoln, 24 April 1442.

f. 404. Like of exemption for Henry Vavasour, 22 March 1442.

f. 406. Like to Justices of Assize, co. Yorks, to enquire, 20 July 1442.

f. 408. Mandate for William, Earl of Suffolk, 1 November 1441.

VOLUME 35

A volume of transcripts etc. from the Public Records and other sources, 21–49 Henry VI. On flyleaf: Recorda ab anno 21 Hen. 6 ad finem Regni sui. On another flyleaf: Records from the 21st year of Henry VI to the end of his reign. 265 ff.

f. 1. Letters Patent for William Gwilym ap Gruffyd, 24 January 1443.

f. 3. Like for Richard Waterton, 27 June 1443.

f. 5. Like of naturalization for Prior of Deerhurst, 24 February 1443.

f. 7. Like for Michael Belwell, 7 February 1443.

f. 8. Mandate to Nicholas Aysshton, Serjeant at Law, etc. 14 February 1443.

f. 9. Letters Patent of naturalization for James Trothe, 20 February 1443.

f. 11. Like for Thomas Montach, 23 November 1442.

f. 12. Like for Dederic Fille, 28 January 1443.

f. 14. Letters Patent to Robert Hunt, Sheriff of Camb. & Hunts., 27 February 1443.

f. 16. Like for Bishop of Salisbury, 11 July 1443.

f. 17. Like for Richard Riche, citizen and mercer, 21 Henry VI.

f. 21. Like for Hamo Sutton, 26 November 1442.

f. 23. Like for Robert Cobbe, philosopher, 6 July 1443.

f. 24. Like for Thomas Thurlawe, 3 February 1443.

f. 25. Statute for wages of knights of shire in Parliament, 23 Henry VI, from MS. Stat. in poss. of William Petyt. 'The roll is missing. Cap. 11'. With translation from Rastell, *Stat.*

f. 32. Another Statute who should be knights of the shire etc., with manner of election etc., 23 Henry VI, cap. 15. From same, with translation from Rastell, *Stat.*

f. 44. Extract on co. Northumberland from Parl. Roll, 23 Henry VI.

f. 45. Letters Patent of safe conduct for Andromicus Effomato etc., 25 January 1445, from French Roll.

f. 47. Letters Patent for Adam Moleyns, Dean of Salisbury, Ambassador, 11 August 1445.

f. 49. Like to John, Archbishop of York etc. 20 July 1445.

f. 51. Like on repayment of loans, 16 October 1444. List.

f. 53. Statute, 23 Henry VI, cap. 15 (see f. 32 above), from the MS. Book of Stat. in French etc.

f. 58. As f. 25 above.

f. 61. Statute, 23 Henry VI, on Sheriffs, cap. 8, from MS. Stat., with translation from Rastell, *Stat.*

f. 69. Letters Patent for Richard, Duke of York, on John Pauncefot, kt., 11 March 1445.

f. 71. Mandate for men of Bromsgrove, quit of toll etc. 3 February 1446.

f. 72. Letters Patent for Bernard Guares, 18 September 1445.

f. 73. Like for John de Foix, Viscount de Castillon, 16 January 1446.

f. 76. Mandate to Justices of Bench etc. on adjournment of Courts, 30 January 1447.

f. 78. Letters Patent on Treaty with Duke of Burgundy, 14 December 1446, from French Roll.

f. 79. Like on treaty with Charles, King of France, 14 December 1446, from same.

f. 82. Like for John de Foix, Viscount de Castillon, 18 November 1446, from Gascon Roll.

f. 83. Mandate to Escheator, co. Hertf., for Queen of England etc. 8 June 1448.

f. 84. Letters Patent of pardon for William Strete, monk, 24 February 1449.

f. 85. Like for George Longville, 3 March 1449.

f. 86. Like to Justices of Peace on enquiry on aliens, 26 July 1449.

f. 89. Like for Thomas Walsingham, 16 November 1448.

f. 91. Like for William Somerby, 6 February 1449.

f. 93. Like for Archbishop of Canterbury, etc. 20 January 1450.

f. 96. Mandate to Sheriff of London, proclamation on arms in city, 20 February 1450.

f. 97. Like to Sheriffs on proclamation of peace, 11 March 1450. List.

f. 99. Extract from Parl. Roll, 28 Henry VI, on murders. (English.)

f. 102. Stat., 28 Henry VI, cap. 3.

f. 104. Letters Patent of pardon, Robert Winter etc., 1 December 1449.

f. 106. Like granting prebend of Langford to John Faulkes, Clerk of Parliament, 11 December 1449.

f. 107. Like to Robert, Bishop of Durham etc., 23 October 1449, from Scottish Roll.

f. 109. Copy of petition by inhabitants of County Palatine of Chester to Henry VI, from Daniel King, *The Vale Royal of England*.

f. 115. Letters Patent to William, Earl of Arundel, etc. on enquiry, 4 May 1451.

f. 117. Mandate to Sheriff and Escheator, co. Yorks., on usurpation, 2 August 1451.

f. 121. Letters Patent to Justices of Peace on levy of subsidy, 14 July 1451.

f. 124. Grant of subsidy, 29 Henry VI (English), from Roll for Merchants of Newcastle upon Tyne.

f. 127. Stat., 29 Henry VI, cap. 3.

f. 129. As f. 109 above.

f. 133. Letters Patent on revocation, Ralph Leigh, 20 May 1452.

f. 137. Like for John Cheyne etc., 17 February 1452.

f. 139. Like to arrest Leon de Walleys etc. 26 February 1452.

f. 140. Like to Sheriffs on conference, 26 February 1452. List.

f. 143. Like for Earl of Shrewsbury, 27 June 1452, from French Roll.

f. 145. Like to William de Bonvill etc. to punish, 14 February 1452.

f. 147. Like to arrest James Styward, kt., etc. 13 April 1452, from Pardon Roll.

f. 148. Like appointing Clement proctor, 7 November 1454.

f. 149. Like for Richard, Earl of Warwick etc. to take muster, 19 August 1453.

f. 150. Stat., 31 Henry VI, cap. 11.

f. 155. Letters Patent appointing John, Earl of Shrewsbury, Lieutenant in Aquitaine, 1 September 1452, from Gascon Roll.

f. 156. Like for Viscount Lisle, 7 March 1453, from same.

f. 157. Like for Richard, Earl of Salisbury, to treat, 14 May 1453, from Scottish Roll.

f. 159. 'The famous case of Thomas Thorpe, who being Speaker of the House of Commons, t. H. VI, was in the time of prorogation taken in execution at suit of Richard, Duke of York'.

f. 160. Request by Commons for delivery of their proctor (French), from Parl. Roll, 31 & 32 Henry VI.

f. 160v. Declaration by Richard, Duke of York, against delivery (English), from same.

f. 164. Letters Patent for Thomas Thorpe, 24 March 1455.

f. 166. Mandate on enrolment of writing for Richard, Duke of York, 2 February 1456.

f. 169. An Act for Roger Thorpe (son and heir of Thomas Thorpe), from Parl. Roll, 1 Henry VII.

f. 175. Letters Patent of exemplification for Robert Chamberleyn, 15 May 1454.

f. 178. Like appointing Walter Moyle, Justice of Bench, 9 July 1454.

f. 180. Like of exemplification for Richard, Duke of York, 6 December 1453.

f. 182. Like, James, King of Scotland, vassal, 26 July 1454.

f. 184. Like on prorogation and adjournment of Parliament, 6 November 1453.

f. 185. Like of safe conduct for Thomas Jehan etc., 15 March 1454, from French Roll.

f. 187. Like for Richard, Duke of York, Captain of Calais, 18 July 1454, from same.

f. 188. Like for Earls of Warwick and Salisbury, 10 February 1455, from Scottish Roll.

f. 189. Writs of summons to Parliament, 26 May 1455.

f. 191. Letters Patent for Richard, Duke of York, 20 May 1455, from French Roll.

f. 192. Like, 4 November 1454, from same.

f. 193. Like for Brian Rouclyf, 20 May 1455.

f. 195. Mandate for Duke of Somerset, 5 February 1455.

f. 196. Letters Patent for Edmund, Duke of Somerset, 31 March 1455.

f. 198. Memorandum, 5 February 1455, from Close Roll.

f. 199. Letters Patent for William Boughchier of Fitzwarin, kt., 2 December 1455, from Gascon Roll.

f. 200. Extract from Rastell, *Entries*, on error, against Lords of Parliament, with note from Roll, Mich. term, 31 Henry VI.

f. 204. Extract from Year Book, East. term, 33 Henry VI.

f. 210. Letters Patent for Mayor etc. of Carlisle, 24 November 1455.

f. 212. Petition to surcease process, Abbot of Bury (English and Latin), from Bundle of Pet. to Parl., 33 Henry VI.

f. 213. Memorandum for Bishop of Durham, 33 Henry VI, from Close Roll.

f. 215. Writ of privy seal to Calixtus III, December 1455, from Cleopatra E. 3. List.

f. 218. Writ to Thomas Stanley to come to Parliament, 15 January 1456.

f. 219. Letters Patent for Bishop of St. David's, 15 February 1457.

f. 221. Like for Queen of England, 3 March 1457.

f. 223. Mandate for tenants of ancient demesne, Churchtown, 11 June 1459.

f. 224. Letters Patent for Maurice de Berkeley, 16 December 1458.

f. 226. Extract from Parl. Roll, 38 Henry VI, on Sheriffs.

f. 228. 'A Packed Parliament summoned to Coventry, 38 H. 6, which was repealed at another Parliament held at Westminster, 39 H. 6'.

f. 229. Stat. 39 Henry VI, cap. 2, with translation from Rastell, *Stat.*

f. 234. Extract from Parl. Roll, 39 Henry VI, for Walter Clark, burgess present Parliament (English).

f. 236. Stat. 39 Henry VI.

f. 238. Letters Patent of pardon for Abbot of Evesham etc. 18 December 1470.

f. 244. Like appointing John Langstrother, Prior of Hospital of St. John of Jerusalem in England, Treasurer, 20 October 1470.

f. 244v. Like appointing Richard Illingworth, kt., Chief Baron of Exchequer, also Barons of Exchequer.

f. 245. Like appointing Thomas Billyng, Chief Justice of King's Bench, also Justices of King's Bench.

f. 245v. Like appointing Robert Danby, kt., Chief Justice of Common Bench also Justices of Common Bench.

f. 246. Petition of Agnes Chirche (English), from Misc. Bundle, t. Henry VI.

f. 248. Writs of summons to Parliament to Thomas, Archbishop of Canterbury etc. 15 October 1470. Lists.

f. 257. As f. 248 above.

VOLUME 36

A volume of brief extracts or summaries, mainly from the Patent Rolls 1 Edward III to 22 Edward IV. On flyleaf: Quedam Memoranda ex Rotulis Patentium et Clausarum etc. Excerpta temporibus E. 3, H. 4, H. 5, H. 6 et E. 4ti.: Several writs, records, confirmations, patents, pardons, summonses and transactions in Parliament and elsewhere in the reigns of E. 3, H. 4, H. 5, H. 6 and E. 4. 162 ff.

ff. 1–16. Brief entries on summaries of certain entries in Patent Rolls, 2–50 Edward III.

ff. 17–18v. A few similar entries in Close Rolls, 1–15 Edward IV.

ff. 19–36v. Petitions and their answers, 1 Edward III.

ff. 37–43. Similar entries of Petitions, 3 & 4 Edward III.

f. 43. A few brief entries in Close and Patent Rolls, 1 Edward III, Close Roll, 2 Edward III, Scottish Roll, 14, 20–6 Edward III, and Gascon Roll, 46 Edward III.

ff. 62–8v. Brief entries or summaries of certain entries on Patent Rolls, 1–21 Richard II.

ff. 88–95. Like, 1–14 Henry IV.

ff. 109–11v. Like, 1–9 Henry V.

ff. 123–33. Like, 1–39 Henry VI.

ff. 153–62. Like, 1–23 Edward IV.

VOLUME 37

A volume of transcripts and extracts from chronicles and other printed and manuscript sources etc. with a few from the Public Records. On flyleaf: De electione et Coronatione Regum Will. 2, Hen. 1, Stephani, Hen. 2 et Ric. 1. 315 ff.

f. 1. On the election and coronation of William II, from Eadmer, Hoveden (with reference to Ann. of Waverley) and the Saxon Chronicle.

f. 5. Plea against Anselm, 7 William II, from Eadmer with note from Alan de Insulis' *Prophet. Merlini.*

f. 25. Evidence against Ranulf Flambard, the judge of William II and the exactor of the whole realm, from Malmesbury, Ordericus Vitalis, and Matt. Paris.

f. 33. On the death and character of William II, from the Saxon Chronicle and Alan de Insulis.

f. 40. On the election and coronation of Henry I, from the Abbreviatio Compensiosa Chronicorum Anglie, 1000–39 Henry III in Claudius D. 6. 'Scripta ut putatur a Matt. Paris proprique manu'; the Saxon Chronicle, Eadmer, and Florence of Worcester.

f. 44. The order of the coronation of Henry I, with the oath, and the coronation of the Queen, from Ordo Coronationis, from Claudius A. 3.

f. 66. The relation by Eadmer of the marriage contracted between Henry I and Matilda, the daughter of Malcolm, King of Scots.

f. 71. Extract from Dr. Brady's *Compleat Hist. of Engl.*, with 'my answer to Dr. Brady's account touching the marriage of Henry I and Maud, the daughter of Malcolm, King of Scots', with extracts from Symeon of Durham, Brompton, Florence of Worcester, and Hoveden.

f. 76. The Great Charter of Henry I, from Lambard, *De Prisc.*, with notes from the Red Book of the Exchequer, Matt. Paris, Selden, *Titles of Honor*, and Rudburn (from *Anglia Sacra*).

f. 83. An old transcript of the Great Charter of Henry I, from the ancient transcript in possession of Peter le Neve, Rouge Croix (French), with a note from Eadmer.

f. 88. The solemn promise which Henry I made in the celebration of Whitsun at London, from Eadmer and Matt. Paris.

f. 92. Extract from Spelman, *Conc.*, 3 Henry I.

f. 94. Extract from Brompton, 3 Henry I.

f. 97. The gathering of the whole English kingdom, 14 Henry I, in which Ralph, Bishop of Rochester, was elected Archbishop of Canterbury, from Eadmer, with note from Florence of Worcester and Dr. Heylin, *Stumbling Block.*

f. 103. The Parliament summoned at Salisbury, 16 Henry I, in which William, the King's son, was declared heir to the Kingdom and all did homage and swore fealty, from Eadmer, Malmesbury, Gervase of Canterbury, Symeon of Durham, Florence of Worcester, Matt. Paris, Brompton, and Polydore Vergil and additional note from Huntingdon and the Chron. of Melrose.

f. 110. Purification, 1121. Council of the whole realm called at Windsor; the marriage of Henry I to Adelina, daughter of the Duke of Lorraine, from Hoveden, Gervase of Canterbury, Symeon of Durham, Brompton, *Antiquitates Brit.*, and Hemingford.

f. 116. 26 Henry I. The Synod of London from the Continuation of Florence of Worcester, with note from Spelman, *Conc.*, and Brompton.

f. 124. 28 Henry I. General Council at London. The Empress Matilda as heir, from the Annals of Waverley, Malmesbury, Gervase of Canterbury, William of Newburgh, Thomas Wykes, the Chron. of the Monk of Coggeshall in Vespasian D. 10.

f. 131. 28 Henry I. Papal Legate called General Council, from Spelman, *Conc.*, Continuation of Florence of Worcester, Walter of Coventry, from Vitellius E. 13.

f. 136. On the great plea held at Northampton, 30 Henry I or 31 Henry I, in which it was discussed whether Matilda, the King's daughter, should be sent to the Duke of Anjou, her husband, or not, from Henry of Huntingdon and du Fresne, *Gloss.*

f. 137. On another plea at London, 32 Henry I, from Ann. of Waverley.

f. 139. On the election and inauguration of King Stephen, from the Cartulary of Monastery of Ely, in Vespasian A. 19, with notes from Malmesbury, Hist. Norman. Script. Antiq., Richard of Hexham, John of Hexham, Hoveden, Matt. Paris, and Galba A. 2.

f. 144. Confirmation of the liberties of the Church of England by Stephen after his coronation, in a Common Council called at Oxford, 1 Stephen, from an old Register of various charters relating to the church of Salisbury, in the possession of William Petyt (cf. above 511, Volume 18); Patent Roll, 29 Edward III with notes from Hemingford and Vitellius E. 13.

f. 147. The Great Charter of Stephen, from the MS. in the Archives of the city of London, De Laud. Brit.

f. 148. A transcript of the same from the ancient transcript in possession of Peter le Neve, Rouge Croix (French).

f. 149. Bull of Innocent II to Stephen, from Richard of Hexham.

f. 152. The Universal Council at Westminster, 3 Stephen, 1138. Privileges of sanctuary to Westminster, from the charter of Stephen in the Westminster cartulary, Faustina A. 3, with notes from *Anglia Sacra*, the Continuation of Hist. Eliens., Gesta Stephani.

f. 161. Stephen in anno 5 was summoned by the Legate to the Ecclesiastical Council at Winchester, from Malmesbury.

f. 164. The declaration of Stephen, from Galba A. 2.

f. 171. The exchange of Stephen and the Earl of Gloucester, from Malmesbury.

f. 179. Another Ecclesiastical Council called at Winchester, 7 or 8 Stephen, from Malmesbury.

f. 181. General Council, London, 17 Stephen, from Gervase of Canterbury and John of Hexham.

f. 182. Public gathering called in city of Winchester, 1153, 18 Stephen, from Saxon Chronicle, Gervase of Canterbury, Brompton.

f. 184. Charter of Stephen confirmed at Westminster after the gathering at Westminster, from Brompton.

f. 190. The Gesta Stephani of uncertain authorship and contemporary.

f. 198. An example of a charter of Stephen, the exchange of the manor of Sudton and the manor of Morden with the church of Winchester, from the collection of Robert Glover, Somerset, in poss. of Peter le Neve, Rouge Croix.

f. 203. Coronation of Henry II (and his son Henry), from William of Newburgh, Thomas Wykes, Ralph de Diceto, Birchington.

f. 207. The Great Charter of Henry II, from De Laud. Brit.

f. 209. General Council, London, 1 Henry II, from Domitian A. 2, with note from Ralph de Diceto.

f. 211. General Gathering, London, 2 Henry II, from Gervase of Canterbury.

f. 212. Like, London, 4 Henry II, from the same.

f. 214. 8 Henry II. End of the dispute between the church of Lincoln and the Abbey of St. Albans, from Matt. Paris, Vita Henrici II, and Additamenta.

f. 223. Charter of Henry II agreeing to the above, from old Cotton MS. (Vespasian E. XVI). (Reference to Mon. III, f. 268.)

f. 226. General Council or Full Parliament, Clarendon, from Quadrilogus, with notes from Gervase of Canterbury, Hoveden, Matt. Paris, Ralph de Diceto, Fitzstephen, Vita T. Archiep. Cantuar. in Julius A. 11, Matt. of Westminster, *Antiq. Brit.*, Godwin, *De Presul.*, Spelman, *Conc.*, Roger Twysden, *Historical Vindication of Church of England*, Selden, *Titles of Honor*, Spelman, *Gloss.*

f. 233. Assize of Forest, from MS. book of Peter le Neve, Rouge Croix.

f. 238. On the coronation of Henry, son of Henry II, 1170, at Westminster, from Gervase of Canterbury, Benedict Abbas in Julius A. 11, Hoveden.

f. 241. 21 Henry II, Great Council at Windsor, from Benedict Abbas.

f. 243. 22 Henry II, General Council, London, from Hoveden, Benedict Abbas, Ralph de Diceto.

f. 246. 22 Henry II, General Council, Nottingham, from Hoveden.

f. 248v. Assize of Clarendon renewed at Northampton.

f. 252. 1166. General Council, Windsor, from Benedict Abbas, Hoveden, Ralph de Diceto.

f. 255. General Council, Oxford, 23 Henry II, creating John, King of Ireland, from Hoveden.

f. 259. Battle between Henry II and his son, Henry, 1173, from Chronicle of Melrose.

f. 260. 26 Henry II, Henry II and his son, Henry, from Ralph de Diceto.

f. 262. 31 Henry II, Great Council, London, on crown of Jerusalem, from Matt. Paris.

f. 267. Peace and concord, Henry II and his sons, Henry, Richard, and Geoffrey, 1174, from Benedict Abbas.

f. 272. Letters of Henry II to his magnates at Westminster, from Ralph de Diceto, Thomas Wykes.

f. 274. 35 Henry II, Great Council at Geddington, from Chron. of Melrose, Hoveden, Walter of Coventry, with notes from Ann. of Waverley, Gervase of Canterbury, William of Newburgh, Brompton, Thomas Wykes.

f. 278. Mandate and list from Close Roll, 14 John.

Letters Patent for man going to land of Jerusalem, from Patent Roll, 18 John, 18 May 1216.

f. 278v. Letters Patent prohibiting export of corn, from Patent Roll, 44 Henry III.

f. 280. 1189. General Council, London, 1 Richard I, Coronation and Oath, from Hoveden, Ralph de Diceto, with notes from Matt. Paris and Vitellius D. 5.

f. 288. On election, hereditary right and coronation, Richard I.

f. 290. The Panbritannic Council, Abbey of Pipewell, 1 Richard I, from Spelman, *Conc.*, Hoveden, Ralph de Diceto, Brompton, Chron. of Priory of Dunstaple, Tiberius A. 10.

f. 297. Peace between Bishop of Ely, Papal Legate and Chancellor, and John, Count of Mortain, 2 Richard I, from Hoveden.

f. 298. Richard I, Common Council, London, John disseised, from Hoveden.

f. 300. 2 Richard I, Common Council, city of London, Bishop of Ely deposed, Archbishop of Rouen instituted, from Hoveden.

f. 301. Second Coronation of Richard I, from Hoveden, with reference to Gervase of Canterbury.

f. 305. 5 Richard I, Great Council, Nottingham, from Hoveden, with notes from W. Thorne, William of Newburgh.

f. 303. 4 or 5 Richard I, letter on aid for ransom, from Hoveden, Ralph de Diceto, with reference to Ann. of Waverley.

f. 311. Petition to Richard I by Hubert, Archbishop of Canterbury, 9 Richard I, from Hoveden.

f. 312. Sudden death of Richard I in Aquitaine and will to John, from Hoveden, Walsingham's Ypodigma Neustria.

f. 314. Testimonium, Henry de Bracton, De Legibus et Consuetudinibus Anglie.

VOLUME 38

A volume of transcripts and extracts mainly from the Public Records, t. John, with some from printed and manuscript sources. On flyleaf: Monumenta Parliamentaria tempore Regis Johannis. 184 ff.

f. 1. Testimonium Henrici de Bracton De Legibus et Consuetudinibus Anglie with appointment as Justice from Close Roll, 29 Henry III.

f. 2. Dialogue on the foundations of the law of England and on equity, by Christopher de St. German (editions from 1523).

f. 3. Charter moderating fees of great seal, 7 June 1199, from an Old Reg. in Archives of Archbishop of Canterbury.

f. 6. On the election and coronation of John, Count of Mortain, as King of England, from Matt. Paris, Hoveden, Brompton, William of Hemingford.

f. 11. Solemn coronation of Isabella, wife of John, as Queen, 5 May 1204, from Charter Roll, with note from same, 17 John.

f. 16. 6 John. Common Council in which Assize of Money made, 26 January 1205, from Patent Roll, with notes from Mirr. of Justice, Coke, *2nd Inst.*, Hoveden, Matt. Paris, Close Roll, 23 Edward I, MS. Stat. in poss. of William Petyt, Pynson, Antiq. Stat., Vespasian B. 7, Close Roll, 27 Edward I, Parl. Roll, 5 Edward III, Fine Roll, 9 Edward III, Patent Roll, 16 Edward III, Stat. Roll, 25 Edward III, Parl. Roll, 2 Henry V, Davys, *Reports*.

f. 23. Great Council or Parliament, London, 14 John, on relaxation of interdict, 15 June 1212, from Close Roll, with translation from Dr. Brady's Introduction.

f. 28. Letters Patent on subsidy for relaxation of interdict, 8 March 1214. List. With translation.

f. 31. Writ to Barons of Exchequer for men of town of Coventry, 18 October 1306, from L.T.R. Mem. Roll, Brev. dir. Bar. Mich., 34 Edward I, with translation.

f. 35. Resignation of crown to Pope. Bull of Innocent III, 12 November 1213, from Cleopatra E. 1.

f. 42. Mandate on arrears of payment, 19 January 1275.

f. 44. Extract from Parl. Roll, 40 Edward III, on process for homage and tribute of 1,000 marks.

f. 46. King John's letter to King of Morocco, from Matt. Paris.

f. 53. Extract, 16 John, from Daniel, *Hist. of Engl.*

f. 57. Letters Patent on taking and desseising, 10 May 1214.

f. 58. Letter sent from Rome by John Mauclerc to John, 1214, in Tower. (Prynne, *Records*, III.)

f. 63. Chapters of Articles sought by Barons, granted by King. Agrees with the original charter under the great seal of John in possession of Gilbert, Bishop of Salisbury, 21 May 1689, by Joseph Washington and Fr. Milles.

f. 73. Agreement between King and Robert, son of Walter Marshal etc., 17 John, from Close Roll.

f. 75. Grant and confirmation of Magna Carta, 17 John, with references to Close Roll, 28 Henry III, Matt. of West., Roger of Wendover, Close Roll, 17 John, Magna Carta in Augustus A. 2, 15 June 1215, with note from Roger of Wendover, Vitellius E. 13.

f. 97. Charter of John for security of peace and liberties, from Matt. Paris,

f. 102. Extract from Matt. Paris.

f. 107. Writs to proclaim and observe Magna Carta, from Patent Roll.

f. 109. Letters Patent on proclamation, 9 June 1215.

f. 111. Like to Sheriffs, 27 June 1215.

f. 112. Mandate to Sheriff of Southampton, 28 June 1215.

f. 113. Letter to Pope, King and Crusade, 29 May 1215, from Close Roll.

f. 118. Choice of Louis, son of King of France, from Matt. Paris, Roger of Wendover.

f. 121. Two papal bulls on Magna Carta and excommunication, Innocent III, 24 August 1215, Innocent III, 23 August 1215, from Close Roll.

f. 130. Letters Patent for Richard, Earl of Clare etc. 9 November 1215.

f. 131. Rejection of John and election of Louis, from Walter of Coventry, from MS. Reg.

f. 131v. The deeds of Philip Augustus, King of France, from French printed sources.

f. 133. More of the deposition of John and election of Louis, from W. Thorne.

f. 140. Dr. Brady's explication of certain articles of Magna Carta concerning granting of aids to crown, from *Compl. Hist. of Engl.*

f. 143. Mandate to Sheriffs on election and coming of Louis, 14 April 1216.

f. 144. Fines with King, William, son of Hamo, John de Nevill, Walter de Percy, citizens of York, men of Beverley, Gilbert, son of Reinfrid, from Rot. Fin., 17 John.

Letters Patent giving power to Peter, Bishop of Winchester, 16 June 1216.

f. 146. Like to Peter de Mauley, 28 September 1216.

Fine with King, Simon, son of Walter, like Simon Irybym, from Fine Roll.

f. 149. Proclamations which John sent to cos. and Cinque Ports from Patent Rolls.

f. 154. Brief collection of fines and oblations which cities, towns etc. gave to John for confirmation of liberties etc.: Kingston, Beverley, Scarborough, Shrewsbury, Gloucester, York, Appleby, London, Oxford, Preston, Norwich, Southampton, Dunwich, Helston, Grimsby, Launceston, Prior of Tywardraeth, Dean and Chapter of Bath, Templars, Iorwerth, Ithel, knights of Stafford, Acelin de Watervill, Hervey Bagot, Ivo de Heric, William, son of Walkelin, Bishop of Exeter, Prior of Lancaster.

f. 164. Bull of Innocent III to Abbot of Abingdon, 15 December 1216, from Matt. Paris.

f. 166. Perjury and tyranny of John on subjects, from Matt. Paris, Old Reg. in Archives of Archbishop of Canterbury, Chron. of Melrose, Ann. of Waverley, Matt. of West. (28 articles.)

f. 183. Letters Patent of inspeximus of Athelstan's charter to Abbey of Malmesbury, 28 November 1381.